C000256155

Daniel Sperber

THE JEWISH LIFE CYCLE
Custom, Lore and Iconography

Jewish Customs from the Cradle to the Grave

Daniel Sperber

The Jewish Life Cycle

Custom, Lore and Iconography

Jewish Customs from the Cradle to the Grave

Bar-Ilan University Press, Ramat Gan

OXFORD
UNIVERSITY PRESS

Translated from the Hebrew by Ed Levin

Published with the assistance of:
Stiftung Irene Bollag-Herzheimer, Basel
The Milan Roven Chair for Talmudic Studies, Bar-Ilan University
The Rector's Fund for the Support of Publications, Bar-Ilan University
The Naftal Yoffe Center for the Study and Dissemination of Oral Law, Bar-Ilan University

Bar-Ilan University Press publishes the fruits of scholarly research
in Jewish Studies, the Humanities and the Social Sciences.

Oxford University Press, Inc., publishes works that further
Oxford University's objective of excellence in research, scholarship, and education.

Oxford   New York
Auckland   Cape Town   Dar es Salaam   Hong Kong   Karachi   Kuala Lumpur
Madrid   Melbourne   Mexico City   Nairobi   New Delhi   Shanghai   Taipei   Toronto
With offices in
Argentina   Austria   Brazil   Chile   Czech Republic   France   Greece
Guatemala   Hungary   Italy   Japan Poland   Portugal   Singapore
South Korea   Switzerland   Thailand   Turkey   Ukraine   Vietnam

Oxford is a registered trademark of Oxford University Press

ISBN 978 965 226 334 6

©
Copyright Bar-Ilan University
All rights reserved, including those of translation. No part of this book
may be reproduced or utilized in any form or by any means, electronic or mechanical
including photocopying and recording, or by any information storage and retrieval system,
without permission in writing from Bar-Ilan University and Oxford University Press.
Printed in Israel on acid free paper — 2008
by Graphit Press Ltd., Jerusalem

Bar-Ilan University Press
Ramat Gan 52900, Israel
www.biupress.co.il

Oxford University Press, Inc.
198 Madison Avenue, New York, New York 10016
www.oup.com
ISBN-13: 978-0-1-9530759-7 (cloth:alk. paper)
ISBN-10: 0-19-530759-3 (cloth:alk.paper)

Library of Congress Cataloging-in-Publication Data is Available

Dedicated to Blanca Roven Wintner
a great lady and a dear friend

CONTENTS

Introduction   7

Part 1

LIFE

1. Some North African Fertility and Pregnancy Customs   13
2. Protective Charms for the Pregnant Woman   19
3. New Mother Impurity   36
4. Circumcision only while Standing?   50
5. Circumcision over Earth or over Water   71
6. Circumcision as a Form of Sacrifice   78
7. Who Drinks the Circumcision Wine and the Place of Women in
   Society   84
8. Women *Mohalot*   94
9. The Two Wine Cups of Circumcision   101
10. One and Twelve Candles at the Circumcision   107
11. *Tahanun* on the Day of the Circumcision   112
12. The Third Day after the Circumcision   114
13. Aspects of the Redemption of the Firstborn   119
14. On the "Reasons" for Customs: The *Halakah*   126
15. The Wimpel   143
16. The Breaking of Plates during the *Tena'im* Ceremony   151
17. Betrothal Rings   158
18. Some Wedding Preparations   166

19. Wedding Dates   171

20. Fasting on the Wedding Day   183

21. The *"Huppah"* — The Wedding Canopy / Ceremony   194

    Appendix: The Nature of the *Huppah*   250

22. The Wedding Ring in the Cup of Wine   265

23. Throwing a Shoe at a Wedding   281

24. "Confetti": The Throwing of Wheat Kernels at Weddings   287

25. "How they Dance before the Bride"   294

26. The Bride's Entry into the Bridal Suite   315

27. The Lighting of Candles after the Wedding   319

28. The Morning After   323

29. The *Regel Redufin* of Caucasus Jewry   327

30. The *Halitzah* Ceremony   332

31. On Divorce   353

Part 2
DEATH

1. Omens of Approaching Death   359

2. The Manner of Sitting while Visiting the Sick   423

3. The Moment of Death   433

4. Asking Posthumous Pardon of the Dead   446

5. The Custom of the Deceased's Wife Passing under the Bier   451

6. The Firstborn of an Animal in the Cemetery   453

7. Opening the Coffin before Burial   465

8. The Construction of the Coffin in the Cemetery   494

9. The Table for the Coffin   497

10. The Rolling and Overturning of the Coffin   502

11. How the Deceased is Laid in his Grave   506

12. A Separate Row of Graves for Women who Died during
    Childbirth   514

13. The Direction of Graves   518

14. The Seven Evil Spirits and the Seven Funeral Stations   524

15. Casting Seven Coins next to the Deceased   531

16. The Plucking of Grass when Leaving the Cemetery   538

17. The Candles, Spices, and Flutes of the Deceased   542

18. *Kohanim* Walking on the Graves of the Righteous   546

19. A Kerchief around the Neck of the Mourner, and the Practice of Covering the Head   550

20. The Meaning of the *Kaddish*: "May His Great Name"   555

21. The Memorial Candle   567

22. The Eastern Mourning Practices   588

23. Mourning for the Firstborn   591

24. "The Death of a *Nasi*" and the Mourning for Moses   603

Bibliography   611

General Index   657

INTRODUCTION

This volume has had a long period of gestation. It began almost forty
years ago, when I started to give ten-minute talks on Friday nights in the
synagogue service where I served as Rabbi. The subject I chose was Jewish
customs, and I tried to relate them to the weekly portion of the Law. I
was very conscious of the fact that people practiced all sorts of customs
without having any notion as to their meaning or origin. I would spend
much of my Thursday nights, well into the early hours of the morning,
preparing these ten-minute talks, in which I sought to trace the history and
diffusion of commonly held Jewish practices. My audience-congregation
was extremely distinguished, including many prominent academic Torah
scholars, who would comment on my talks, add to them, and at times
correct my suggestions. But what was more troubling was the fact that
they would remember them so well so that even after two or three decades
I dared not repeat myself. Some of these brief concentrated talks formed
the basis of courses of lectures at the University on the History of Jewish
Customs, and were later worked up into several articles that were published
in a variety of scholarly journals. After a while, these articles began to
pile up, and I decided to collect them together in a single volume, which
became the first volume of *Minhagei Yisrael* (Jerusalem, 1989). Initially,
it never occurred to me to have follow-up volumes, and, hence, there was
no indication on the cover that this was "Volume One." However, much to
my surprise, and indeed to the surprise of the publishers — Mossad Harav
Kook — the volume was such a success that it rapidly went into several
impressions. This encouraged me to dip into my numerous single-page notes
prepared for the talks, and continue to develop them into full-length, fully
annotated chapters. This process eventually led to the eight-volume series
of "green books," called *Minhagei Yisrael* (*Customs of Israel*), which is
found in so many Jewish homes. As the volumes appeared one by one, I
received a flood of comments, corrections and additions from a surprisingly

broad spectrum of readers — heads of rabbinic academies in Bnei Brak, scholars from Europe and the USA, academics from a variety of scholarly institutions, and even nostalgic notes from housewives and children who wished to record their memories and insights. Many of these, after careful examination, were edited and included in subsequent volumes. But this meant that a single topic might be discussed in several different volumes, a phenomenon that triggered constant complaints from my readers. This source of inconvenience has been partially rectified by the cumulative index that appears at the end of the eighth volume. Nonetheless, this situation often requires one to sit with a whole series of volumes in order fully and correctly to understand a single topic.

Out of this vast, rather unmanageable mass/mess of material appearing in these many volumes, I chose several chapters relating to the Calendrical Cycle, which were translated into English and published by Ktav Publishing in 1999, under the title "Why Jews Do what they Do."

This volume is in a sense a follow-up, in that it encompasses the life cycle. Here the material was far more copious and complex, and had not only to be translated, but also to be put into a reasonable order, corrected, edited, updated, with all references checked, etc. Thus, in effect, it is an almost totally new composition. In this volume I have sought to explain the evolution of many customs relating to the major Jewish "rites of passage" — birth, circumcision, marriage, divorce, death and mourning, etc. I have not discussed those areas where I felt I had little new to contribute. Here, we will not find a history of the Bar Mitzvah ceremony, which was amply covered many years ago.[1] So too, regarding the more modern phenomenon of the Bat Mitzvah, which has recently merited a number of fine studies.[2] Nor does this volume seek to be a comprehensive encyclopedia of life-cycle customs.[3] Such would require a multivolume series. However, those topics that are discussed,

1   See Isaac Rivkind, *Le-Or u-le-Zikaron: Toldot "Bar-Mitzvah" ve-Hitpatchutah be-Haggei ha-Am ve ha-Tarbut* (*Bar-Mitzvah: A Study in Jewish Cultural History with an Annotated Bibliography*) (New York, 1942).
2   E.g., *Traditions and Celebrations for the Bat Mitzvah*, ed. Ora Wiskind Elper (Jerusalem-New York, 2003).
3   See, for example, J.D. Eisenstein, *Otzar ha-Dinim ve Minhagim — A Digest of Jewish Law and Custom* (New York, 1912); Yom-Tov Lewinsky, *Entzsiklopedia shel Havai u-Masorot ba.Yahadut* (*Encyclopedia of Folklore, Customs and Traditions in Judaism*) (Tel Aviv, 1975); and, most recently, Shalom Sabar, *Maagal ha-Hayyim* (*The Life Cycle*) (Jerusalem, 2006).

are treated in considerable breadth, depth and detail, with much comparative material from the fields of ethnography and folklore. Furthermore, plentiful use has been made of pictorial evidence, both Jewish and non-Jewish, which constitutes yet another hitherto largely unexploited source for the study of Jewish customs.

The work entailed in the preparation of the volume was, as indicated above, very considerable. The translator, Ed Levin, who also checked the bibliographic references, etc., was presented with a Herculean challenge — the manuscript I gave him was really messy — and he handled it with commendable success, and to him my heartfelt thanks. Ed's wife Michal also became a partner in this very considerable project. For it was she who produced the bibliography and the indices for which every reader should be thankful.

The research that forms the basis of this volume, as of the original chapters in *Minhagei Yisrael*, has benefited from the thoughtful comments and corrections of numerous friends and colleagues: fellow workers and the Department of Talmud at Bar-Ilan University, members of my congregation, and knowledgeable and insightful readers from around the world. They are too numerous to be listed by name, but I should single out certain individuals with whom I have had constant ongoing discussions on the subjects discussed: the late Prof. Israel Ta-Shema, my former neighbor, a world expert in the field of Ashkenazic custom, with whom I met almost daily at morning services, etc., and with whom I had a continuous dialogue; my dear friend, Dr. Meir Rafeld, whose chapters in *Minhagei Yisrael* greatly enriched our knowledge of a number of medieval issues; and two *talmidei hachamim*, rabbinic scholars from Monsey, whom I have never actually met, but who showered me with their illuminating comments, evidence of their vast knowledge and learning, Rabbis Mordechai Menachem Honig and Yitzhak Tessler. Several chapters, dealing with various aspects of marriage customs, the *huppah*, dancing at the wedding, etc., were written jointly with my son. To them all I am deeply grateful. Ed Levin, translator and editor, also contributed material relating to Buddhism and Eastern esotericism, which I gratefully acknowledge.

Incidentally, it should be noted that these volumes of *Minhagei Yisrael* opened up a new field of research, namely the systematic scientific analysis of the sources, historical development and geographic diffusion of Jewish customs. An ever-growing library of invaluable studies has emerged in the wake of these volumes, several of them written by friends and colleagues whom I greatly encouraged to publish their findings.[4]

The cost of producing such a volume is considerable, and we were fortunate to benefit from the generosity of several benefactors, such as Mr. Ilan Kaufthal, and Mr. Isaac Pollack. Others who wished to remain anonymous also contributed generously to defray the expenses. May they all be rewarded for their help and for their *matan be-seter* (anonymous gifts). And, of course, special mention must be made of Mrs. Blanca Roven Wintner, to whom this volume is dedicated, for her unending support of my researches over the many years. A true lady, veritably she merits my enduring respect and thanks.

It is my deep regret that my dear parents did not live to see the publication of this project. My father was my greatest teacher, and it is from him that I learned and gained most; my mother was, for me, a source of infinite love and unremitting encouragement.

An undertaking of this scope could not have been undertaken without a conducive and supportive family framework. I refer to my ten children, my wonderful, ever-helpful parents-in-law, Nana and Papa Magnus, and, over and above all else, my incredible wife, Chana, without whom none of all this could ever have happened.

And last, but certainly not least, I thank the Almighty for having blessed me with what I have, for it is from his beneficence that all flows.

---

4   See in greater detail the introduction to the eighth volume (Jerusalem, 2007), pp. 7–9.

PART 1
LIFE

1

SOME NORTH AFRICAN FERTILITY
AND PREGNANCY CUSTOMS

In any examination of the nature and origin of customs, especially those related to beliefs, charms, and the like, consideration must also be given to the local popular culture and its influences, just as we have shown[1] how the Christian European popular culture of the medieval period left its mark on some of the practices of Jewish Europe, and how motifs that had their beginnings in antiquity influenced the customs of the Jewish communities in the Land of Israel and in Babylonia. Attention must therefore also be devoted to the world of popular Islamic culture in the East and in the Maghreb.[2] An investigation into the local cultural background will cast light on several phenomena in the customs of the various Eastern Jewish communities. We shall illustrate this principle with a few examples from the customs common among Moroccan Jewry.

A recent collection of the practices of this community, *Noheg be-Hokhmah* by Rabbi Yossef Ben Naim of Fez,[3] with alphabetically arranged entries that

---

1   *Minhagei Yisrael*, Vol. 1, pp. 15–18 and n. 14.
2   See H.Z. Hirschberg, *A History of the Jews in North Africa* (Leiden, 1974), pp. 163–73; N. Wieder, *Islamic Influences on Jewish Worship* (Oxford, 1947), p. 73 (Hebrew; = idem, *The Formation of Jewish Liturgy in the East and the West* [Jerusalem, 1994]); E. Brauer, *The Jews of Kurdistan*, ed. R. Patai (Jerusalem, 1947), pp. 90 ff. (Hebrew); *Teshuvot ha-Rambam (Responsa of Maimonides)*, ed. J. Blau (Jerusalem, 1960), Vol. 2, para. 320 (= ed. A.H. Freimann [Jerusalem, 1934], para. 99), p. 589; see also I. Ben-Ami, *Le Judaisme Marocain: Etudes Ethno-Culturelles* (Jerusalem, 1975), pp. 153–68 (Hebrew).
3   Rabbi Yossef Ben Naim, *Noheg be-Hokhmah*, ed. M. Amar (Israel, 1986).

provide clear and accessible information, proclaims on its title page that it is a "treasure trove of customs, for all four sections of the *Shulhan Arukh*, that were practiced in all Jewish communities in the East and in the West [= Maghreb]." A perusal of the book yields some examples of local non-Jewish influences on practices observed within this community;[4] the following two practices come from the realm of pregnancy.

> From the entry on *"Segulah* [Charm]":[5]
> The Maghreb women's practice of swallowing the foreskin of males that is excised during the circumcision in order to give birth to males would seem to be prohibited. According to *Tosefot*, however, this is permitted: Rabbi Solomon ben *ha-Rashbatz* [Rabbi Simeon bar Zemah Duran], *Rashbash*, para. 518; R. Mordecai Banet, para. 79: *Zokhor le-Avraham*, *Yoreh Deah*, para. 20 [should be: 40]. See the commentary of Rabbenu Hananel, 79:6, who cited *Likkutei le-Yitzhak* 218, *Yoreh Deah*, "Water," para. 1. See also *Hikrei Lev*, para. 37; what he wrote on this topic here he [also] cited in *Yishrei Lev*, see there; with a reference to Rabbi Solomon son of R. Simeon ben Zemah Duran at the end of para. 518. He was cited by R. Mordecai Banet, para. 79, *Yoreh Deah*; see *Kol Eliyahu*, Vol. 2, *Ba-Mahaneh Yisrael*, para. 84, with a reference to his father, of blessed memory, in the above-mentioned [passage from] *Hikrei Lev*.

The custom of eating the foreskin is reported by Westermarck:[6]

> Among the Ait Warain it often happens that the boy's mother, immediately after the operation, swallows the foreskin with some water; they believe that if she does so her son will never be found out if he commits theft, adultery with another man's wife, or any other crime.

Ben Naim further writes:[7]

> It is the custom that when the *mohel* [circumciser] excises the foreskin, a small bowl stands ready before him, full of sand, in which he places the foreskin.[8] It is said that the reason for this is derived from "and

4 *Minhagei Yisrael*, Vol. 1, pp. 222–32; Vol. 2, pp. 291–99.
5 Para. 5, pp. 135–36.
6 E. Westermarck, *Ritual and Belief in Morocco* (London, 1926), Vol. 2, p. 427.
7 S.v. *"Milah* [Circumcision]," para. 7, p. 114.
8 See below, chap. 5, "Circumcision over Earth or over Water."

the serpent's food shall be earth" [Isa. 65:25]. Afterwards, the infant's mother takes the foreskin, wraps it in a piece of cloth, and places it under the pillow on which the infant sleeps, [leaving the foreskin there] until it decomposes. When I was a *haver* [an official] of the city of Larache, I saw that he [the circumciser] preserves all the foreskins that he excises in a sort of red dirt called in Arabic *azarkin*, and he puts them away for safekeeping. I saw that he has a small box full of thousands of foreskins, and he told me that they should be buried with him, to show in the world of recompense [i.e. Heaven] how many instances of the commandment of circumcision he had performed. I did not know the reason for this, for [the reasons for] several positive commandments were caused by Heaven to be forgotten. On the contrary, it seems to me that it is not good to bury them with him, for this [the foreskin] is part of the impurity of the serpent, as is known to those privy to esoteric knowledge.[9]

This bears comparison with the report by Westermarck (loc. cit.):

The foreskins are among the Ait Sadden, also, preserved by the barber [= the circumciser], who would thereby be able to prove that he is a professional, should any of the boys circumcised by him die and he be accused of having caused his death. [...] Among the Ait Yusi, again, the foreskin of the circumcised boy is taken by his mother. [...] She then suspends it from the *ahammar*, or ridge-pole, of the tent, and leaves it there for seven days, after which she throws it away. As the foreskin dries up, so will also the wound dry up.[10]

The material collected by Raphael Patai[11] is of special relevance here:

Among several peoples that practice circumcision, the foreskin is thought to be capable of curing infertile women. The eating of the foreskin for the sake of [entering] pregnancy is common among the Eastern Jewish communities. In Safed and in Jerusalem, barren Sephardic Jewish women ate the foreskin as a charm for pregnancy. In most instances, the circumcisers were ordered, in advance, by the

9 See also below, chap. 6.
10 Cf. also pp. 419, 421–22, 425.
11 R. Patai, "Folk Customs and Charms Relating to Birth," *Talpioth* 6, 1–2 (1953), pp. 246–47 (Hebrew).

husbands of infertile women to save the foreskins for the latter, for which they [the circumcisers] also were paid. Among the simple masses of Egyptian Jewry, the barren woman would swallow the foreskin so that she would be capable of becoming pregnant. This same practice was also prevalent among the Jewish and Muslim women in Tripoli, in Northern Africa. The Jews of Yemen keep the foreskin as a charm for infertile women. Among Turkish Jewry, if a woman bore a child once and then ceased to give birth, she would eat a foreskin in order to become pregnant once again.

Traces of this popular practice are to be found in several books of charms: "So that a barren woman will become pregnant, she should swallow the foreskin of an infant who was circumcised" (*Mareh Yeladim[, in Which Are Collected Several Remedies, Cures, Charms and Portents from Several Manuscripts from East and West ... and Also from Printed Books]*, by Rabbi Rephel Ohana [Jerusalem, 1908], fol. 78b), or: "Take the circumcision of a youth, smear it with honey, and swallow it" (*Mareh Yeladim*, loc. cit.; fol. 35b).

Another version of this method of inducing fertility was common among Yemenite Jews. They were accustomed to place a vessel [with water] under the Chair of Elijah, and a bride would later drink from what had collected in the vessel. This practice was also prevalent among Sephardic women in the Land of Israel, where both barren women and those who no longer entered pregnancy would drink the [now bloody] water, that was called "the water of Elijah" (E. Ha-Reuveni, ["Aromatic Plants in the Religious Customs of Our Different Communities in Palestine and Abroad,"] [*Me'asaf*] *Zion* [4] [1930], p. 102 [n. 31]).

This custom was somewhat more refined in Europe: "A woman who cannot become pregnant should gaze upon the knife of circumcision after a circumcision" (Rabbi Nahman of Bratslav, *Sefer Hanhagot Yesharot* [Lvov, 1840], s.v. "*Herayon* [Pregnancy]," "*Mohel* [Circumciser]"; [A. I. Sperling,] *Sefer Ta'amei ha-Minhagim u-Mekorei ha-Dinim* [Lvov, 1906–07], Vol. 2, fol. 42a, and more) and in the vicinity of Warsaw: "The childless [...] scrupulously drink from the cup [over which] the circumcision blessing [is recited]" ([Rabbi Yehuda Elzet,] *Reshumot*, Vol. 1, p. 363).

The swallowing of the foreskin is also efficacious for the birth of a son, specifically: "When the foreskin is excised, women swallow [it], as a charm in order to give birth to males" (*Sefer Refuah ve-Hayyim*, by Rabbi Hayyim Palache [Palaggi], [Izmir, 1875; Jerusalem, 1908], para. 12, fol. 35b).

This consumption of foreskins also raised a question regarding the halakhic permissibility of the custom: "One view permits: *Mahazik Berakhah, Yoreh Deah*, para. 79; see the end of the book *Yad Ne'eman*; and what he further cited, that this should not be done in Israel" (ibid.). This practice was the subject of a discussion by Torah scholars that extended over several generations, and was summarized by the Sephardic Chief Rabbi of Tel Aviv-Jaffa, Rabbi Jacob Moses Toledano, in his book *Yam ha-Gadol* ([Cairo, 1931], p. 81, para. 53): "I saw fit to examine whether the law [prohibiting the consumption] of human flesh is from the Torah, whether this falls under the category of [the Noahide prohibition of the consumption of] a limb from a living creature and [the parallel prohibition of consuming] meat from a living creature, and the halakhic distinction regarding the consumption by women of the foreskin of an infant as a charm for pregnancy, and the like."

A similar belief and practice was recorded among the women of the Salonikan community:[12]

Another means that was considered to be extremely effective against infertility was to have a barren women swallow the foreskin of an infant close to his circumcision.[13]

Finally, pregnant Muslim women in Morocco were wary of sleeping by moonlight. As Westermarck writes:[14]

A woman who is with child should be particularly careful not to sleep under the moon.

12 See also M. Molho, "Birth and Childhood among the Jews of Salonica," *Edoth* (*Communities*) 2, 3–4 (1947), p. 257 (Hebrew).

13 See also R. Patai, "Folk Customs and Charms Relating to Birth," *Talpioth* 9, 1–2 (1964), p. 242 (Hebrew). A related remedy for epilepsy is prescribed by Rabbi J.J. Rubinstein, *Zikhron Yaakov Yosef* (Jerusalem, 1930?), fol. 57b: "Take the menstrual blood of a girl who has seen this [i.e. had her period] for the first time, put it in wine, and give to the [epileptic] youth to drink" (this book received writs of approval from, among others, Rabbi Joseph Hayyim Sonnenfeld!). For the medicinal uses of blood, see *Minhagei Yisrael*, Vol. 2, pp. 59–65, esp. p. 61 n. 28; p. 308.

14 Westermarck, *Ritual and Belief in Morocco*, Vol. 1, pp. 127–28.

Rabbi Yossef Ben Naim writes in a similar vein:[15]

> It is customary for women not to take nursing children outside at night, not even within the courtyard, from one house to another. If they [nevertheless] take them out, they cover them well, and they do not move them under the open air, nor **under the moon** when it shines.

Westermarck adds the following details regarding deleterious lunar influences:[16]

> It is considered bad to point at the moon: when you speak of it you may look at it — that is all. To sleep in a place where the moon is shining is as bad as to sleep in the sun; if you sleep out-of-doors on a moonlit night you should lie in the shade of something. Otherwise you will become ill; the moon may strike your shoulder or make you crooked for ever (Ait Warain) or give you a headache. Some people even maintain that he who is struck by the moon can never be cured (Aglu). At Demnat I was assured that if the moon shines on a person who is lying, or even sitting, it consumes the same quantity of his blood as the quantity of barley eaten by a horse.

In light of all these superstitions and fears, we can easily understand why people were reluctant to expose an infant to the moonlight, and would carefully wrap the child if they had to take him outside at night.[17]

15 Ben Naim, *Noheg be-Hokhmah*, p. 20.
16 Westermarck, *Ritual and Belief in Morocco*, Vol. 1, pp. 127–28.
17 D. Ovadia, *The Community of Sefrou* (Jerusalem, 1985), Vol. 3, p. 80 (Hebrew).

2

PROTECTIVE CHARMS FOR
THE PREGNANT WOMAN

1. THE OPENING OF THE TORAH ARK

This symbolic act frequently serves as a protective charm. The first of the following few examples that are related to birth and the safeguarding of the pregnant woman is from *Minhagei ha-Hida*:[1]

> The custom is for the person whose wife has entered the ninth month of her pregnancy to take care to perform in that month the commandment of **opening the Ark**, which is a fine practice, and has a basis in the esoteric teachings.

This practice also appears in a halakhic responsum[2] concerning "the sale of the commandments of the Torah scroll [i.e. the honor of being called up to the reading from the Torah], the opening of the doors, the bringing out of the Torah scroll and its rolling [...], and the *Haftarah* [the supplemental reading from the Prophets that follows the Torah reading on Sabbaths and Festivals]." A question was raised because someone "wanted to buy the opening of the Ark, for it is said that [the performance of] this commandment is a charm capable of easing the suffering of [giving] birth."[3]

---

1   R. Amar, *Minhagei ha-Hida* (Customs of the *Hida*) (Jerusalem, 1990), Vol. 2, p. 196, following Azulai's works: *Moreh ba-Etzba* (Leghorn, 1782) 3:4, *Le-David Emet* (Leghorn, 1786); cited by *Kaf ha-Hayyim* 134:12, and more.
2   Rabbi Hayyim David Azulai, *She'eilot u-Teshuvot Yosif Ometz* (Leghorn, 1798), para. 57.
3   Cf. *idem*, *She'eilot u-Teshuvot Hayyim Sho'al* (Leghorn, 1795) 1:2; also cited

We see, therefore, that the opening of the Ark is efficacious for the easy opening of the woman's womb.

in *idem*, *Sefer Refuah ve-Hayyim* (*The Book of Healing and Life*) (Izmir, 1875; Jerusalem, 1908), fol. 27b–28a; Rabbi Abraham Hamawi, *Abiyah Hidot* (Leghorn, 1879), fol. 68b and the sources listed there. Cf. Rabbi Yehuda Elzet (= Avida, Zlotnik), *Reshumot* (Odessa, 1918), Vol. 1, p. 362, para. 59. R. Patai, "*Masekhet Segulot* [The Tractate of Charms]," *Sefer ha-Shanah li-Yehudei Amerika* (*Yearbook of American Jews*) 10–11 (1949), p. 485 (Hebrew), is of the opinion that this custom is a development of the original practice, in which a Torah scroll was brought to a woman experiencing a difficult childbirth: the scroll was brought into her room, where it was placed on a table or given into her hand, or even placed on her bosom. This routine aroused the opposition of Torah sages, who regarded it as debasing the Torah scroll. However, due to the difficulty of uprooting a custom that is firmly established in popular practice, they permitted the opening of the Ark and praying there on behalf of the woman (cf. Elzet, para. 60). Such an interpretation of the altered practice, however, is not obligatory, since the symbolism of the opening of the Ark is self-understood, and apparently suffices to alleviate the opening of the womb. This custom of opening doors, locks, and the like, to facilitate childbirth and open the womb, is observed in numerous cultures. See the abundance of material collected by J.G. Frazer, *Taboo and the Perils of the Spirit* (part of the third edition of *The Golden Bough* [London, 1911]; first edition: London, 1891), pp. 296–97; and again in *Aftermath: A Supplement to the Golden Bough*[3] (London, 1936), p. 17. Additionally, in Bodenschatz's illustration of a birth (Johann Bodenschatz, *Kirchliche Verfassung der heutigen Juden, sonderlich derer in Deutschland* [Ellangen, 1748], opposite p. 60), a Torah scroll stands on the table (cf. Bodenschatz, Vol. 2, opposite p. 32 [Fig. 1]), apparently as a charm to overcome the difficulties in childbirth that the woman encountered. The birth scenes in Kirchner's *Judisches Ceremoniel* also contain a Torah scroll in the room of the woman giving birth (Fig. 2), reflective of a practice that is mentioned by *poskim*. See, e.g., Rabbi Issachar Baer Eylenburg, *Be'er Sheva* (Frankfurt, 1709), novellae on Sanhedrin, chap. 10, fol. 101, s.v. "*Amar R. Yohanan*": "It appears to me that from this we find support and endorsement **for the practice of the world**, to place a Torah scroll on a woman experiencing a difficult birth, or to read verses for her, for this [difficulties in childbirth] entails great danger to life." (See *Shulhan Arukh, Yoreh Deah* 179:9; *Pithei Teshuvah* 179). See, however, the objections to this practice raised by Rabbi Solomon Kluger, *She'eilot u-Teshuvot Tuv Ta'am ve-Da'at* (Podgorze, 1900), Vol. 2, para. 47. See also J. Trachtenberg, *Jewish Magic and Superstition: A Study in Folk Religion* (Philadelphia, 1961), pp. 105–106, 292 n. 1; also, p. 169. The protective incantations "*Sanvai Sansanvai Sanamgolf* [should read: *Semanglof*]" appearing in Kirchner (Fig. 2) and "*Hutz Lilit Adam ve-Havah* [Out Lilith, [leaving] Adam and Eve]" in the illustration in Bodenschatz, *Kirchliche Verfassung der heutigen Juden* (Fig. 1), are very well known; see Trachtenberg, p. 169; G.B. Sarfatti, "Latin

2. THE USE OF KEYS FOR PREGNANT WOMEN

A key is also effective for a woman experiencing a difficult childbirth, as we find in various books of charms, such as *Segulot Yisrael*,[4] which prescribes "suspending on her neck a cemetery key."[5]

in Hebrew Script in the Plastic Arts," *Leshonenu la-Am* 47,1 (1996), pp. 124–25 (Hebrew). For the *"Sanvai ..."* formula, see the fascinating, but questionable, article by M. Gaster, "Two Thousand Years of a Charm against the Child-Stealing Witch," *Studies and Texts in Folklore, Magic, Mediaeval Romance, Hebrew Apocrypha, and Samaritan Archaeology* (London, 1925–28 [photocopy edn.: New York, 1971]), pp. 1005–38. Note should also be paid to the sword that is suspended behind the expectant mother's bed (see below, the section on the sword).

Especially appropriate in this context is the following passage from E. and M.A. Radford, *Encyclopaedia of Superstitions* (New York, 1949), pp. vii–viii:

> Take, as an example, childbirth. To ensure easy labour for a woman it was the custom in northwest Argyllshire, Scotland, to open every lock in the house. Regard this in the light of the Roman custom of presenting women in labour with a key as a charm for easy delivery. The Argyllshire custom could be stretched into a corruption of the Roman key by reason of the occupation of these islands by the Romans, and the consequent copying of custom and beliefs; but what can be said in explanation of the beliefs of the natives of the Island of Salsette, near Bombay, and of parts of Java, or Chittagong in the East Indies where, from the earliest times, all doors were opened to ease a mother in her labour?

4   Rabbi Shabbetai ben Jacob Isaac Lipschutz, *Segulot Yisrael* (Munkacs, 1905; with additions: 1944), fol. 69a, para. 99:11, based on Rabbi Hayyim Palache (Palaggi), *Sefer Refuah ve-Hayyim (The Book of Healing and Life)* (Izmir, 1875), chap. 9. Cf. Trachtenberg, *Jewish Magic and Superstition*, p. 169, who describes a similar custom, that of placing a synagogue key in this woman's hand, taken from Joseph Yuspa Hahn, *Yosif Ometz* (Frankfurt, 1928 [photocopy edition: Jerusalem, 1965]), p. 351 (reference in Trachtenberg, p. 300 n. 28); I have not succeeded in confirming this reference. Trachtenberg further refers to J.J. Schudt, *Judischer Merckwurdigkeiten* (Frankfurt and Leipzig, 1714), Vol. 4, chap. 2, p. 223. See also H. Schauss (Shoys), *The Lifetime of a Jew throughout the Ages of Jewish History* (Cincinnati, 1950), p. 67.

Incidentally, *Segulot Yisrael*, op. cit., subsection 19, prescribes: "Give her [the woman having a difficult childbirth] to drink her husband's urine from his shoe, in the measure of one cup." Cf. Westermarck, *Ritual and Belief in Morocco*, Vol. 2, p. 370 n. 2: "In Syria a parturient woman whose delivery is difficult drinks water from her husband's shoe (Eijub Abela, 'Beitrage zur Kenntnisse aberglaubischer Gebrauche in Syrien', in *Zeitschrift des Deutschen Palastina-Vereins*, vii [Leipzig 1884], p. 89)."

In Kurdistan, as well, the woman experiencing difficult labor would drink water from

A key is also useful in opening the womb of a barren woman, as is demonstrated by the following passage:[6]

> her husband's shoe (see E. Brauer, "Birth Customs of the Jews of Kurdistan," *Edoth* 1 [1945–46], p. 69 [Hebrew]); and in Serbia and Bosnia (see P. Bartels-Reitzenstein, *Das Weib* [1927], Vol. II, pp. 461 sqq., cited by Brauer, p. 65). In a comparable practice, in Amadiya and Zakho the wife drank water in which her husband's foot had been washed (Brauer, loc. cit.). See also Patai, *Masekhet Segulot*, p. 481 n. 55. For the use of urine for magical-medical ends, see Y. Deviri, *The Light in Dicta and Adages of the Sages* (Holon, 1976), pp. 128–39 (Hebrew). Deviri concludes this passage:
>
>> Modern gynaeological medicine has recently made surprising achievements in doing away with barrenness. Urine serves as an effective means, thanks to its hormonal influence, in overcoming even prolonged barrenness: "At present we use the urine of postmenopausal women from which a hormone called HMG is extracted. This hormone is capable of activating the ovaries in women lacking this hormone, and to cause ovulation, and consequent pregnancy. These women could not possibly conceive without this treatment. We were the first in Israel to treat cases of barrenness with this method. Thanks to this treatment, we count to our credit more than 300 pregnancies, which is to be regarded as a major success." (Stated by Prof. Rabo, the former head of the gynaecological department of Tel Hashomer [hospital], in 1927.)
>
> As we have seen, the doctors of Tel Hashomer were not the first to employ this method.

5   Rabbi Rephel Ohana, *Mareh ha-Yeladim, in Which Are Collected Several Remedies, Cures, Charms, and Spells from Several Manuscripts from East and West ... and Also from Printed Books* (Jerusalem, 1908), fol. 70a (Hebrew); *Sefer Refuah ve-Hayyim*, fol. 28a; *Abiyah Hidot*, fol. 68b; Rabbi Nahman of Bratslav, *Sefer ha-Middot, o Hanhagot Yisrael* (Jerusalem, 1986), s.v. "*Leidah* [Birth]," no. 23 [= no. 133], p. 36. See Patai, "Folk Customs and Charms Relating to Birth," *Talpioth* 6, 1, p. 250; *idem*, "*Masekhet Segulot*," p. 481. We should also mention an incident from the Geonic period involving a sorceress that is related by S. Abramson, "On R. Baruch ben מלך," *Tarbiz* 19 (1948), pp. 42–44 (Hebrew):

> Yohani *bat* [daughter of] Ratibi was a sorceress, and she would cast a spell on every woman so that she would not give birth. She would place the charm between two vessels, and as long as the two vessels were not opened, the woman's womb would not be opened. She would pretend to pray on behalf of the expectant mothers, and when she prostrated herself to [seemingly] engage in supplications, she would open those two vessels, the sorcery would be negated, and the woman's womb would be opened. Once two Torah scholars came to her, to pray for a woman who was experiencing difficulty in childbirth, and they found the two vessels [in which was] the sorcery. They unintentionally opened the vessels, the woman's womb was opened, and she gave birth, without their intent. Then they realized that she was engaged in sorcery.

Write these on seven iron keys, write all these [divine] names on each one. Afterwards, wash those keys in seven springs or wells, and pour this water on her head after her washing, and this is what you shall write [...].[7]

Just as a key is capable of opening the womb, it can also close it, so that the woman will not deliver her fetus prematurely. As a Moroccan woman in Jerusalem attests:[8] "It was customary among the Jews in Morocco to choose a bachelor to tie a belt around the stomach of a pregnant woman, and to close the belt with a little lock. As long as the lock remained closed, the woman's womb also would remain closed, and she would not deliver her fetus. When the months of [full] pregnancy passed, the young man would open the lock, and the woman was then ready to give birth." The nineteenth-century author Moses Reischer similarly teaches:[9] "Pregnant women [...] hang a closed lock on their necks, and they throw away the key." According to a rabbinic tradition, however, the "key of barrenness,"[10] or the "key of the womb,"[11]

Cf. the version in R. Nissim ben Jacob, *Yafeh me-ha-Yeshu'ah*, cited in B.M. Lewin, *Otzar ha-Geonim*, Vol. 11 (Jerusalem, 1942), *Sotah*, pp. 241–42; and in the edition by H.Z. Hirschberg, *Rabbenu Nissim b. R. Jacob of Kairouan: Hibbur Yafeh me-ha-Yeshu'ah* (Jerusalem, 1970), pp. 35–36. M. Bar-Ilan, *Some Jewish Women in Antiquity* (Atlanta, 1998), p. 124 n. 31, writes that this is an example of sympathetic magic for the **opening** of the womb by the **opening** of the vessels.

6 See Patai, "Folk Customs and Charms Relating to Birth," p. 257.

7 Cf. Westermarck, *Ritual and Belief in Morocco*, Vol. 2, p. 189; Vol. 1, pp. 89–90, 158, 327. This should be compared with the method for removing and canceling the Moroccan *taqaf*, as described by Ben-Ami, *Le Judaisme Marocain*, p. 159: "Another version, that [...] is meant to break the *takaf*, is performed as follows: water that was drawn from seven wells is taken, and seven heated keys are immersed in it. The one under a spell is washed with this water, at the same time that ammoniac glue is burned.

8 Patai, "Folk Customs and Charms Relating to Birth," p. 250. A similar procedure, which he terms "homoeopathic magic," is cited by Frazer, *Taboo and the Perils of the Spirit*, p. 296.

9 M. Reischer, *Sha'arei Yerushalayim* (Warsaw, 1879), p. 91; cited in Patai, "Folk Customs and Charms Relating to Birth."

10 *Tanhuma*, Genesis, Vayetze 16, ed. Buber (Lvov, 1885), p. 155.

11 Gen. Rabbah 73:4, ed. Theodor-Albeck, p. 848. This motif is quite common in world folklore and magic, and could easily be the subject of a broader discussion. We shall merely refer to W.M. Brashear and A. Bulow-Jacobsen, *Magica Varia* (Brussels, 1991), p. 78 and their extensive bibliography.

is one of the keys held by the Holy One, blessed be He, Himself, that were not entrusted to an emissary.[12] R. Hayyim Palache formulated his prayer for a pregnant woman in accordance with this tradition:[13]

> In Your hand, our God and the God of our fathers, is **the key of birth**, that was not entrusted to any angel. Therefore, recall Your mercy, O Lord, and Your compassion [...].

Notwithstanding this, the human use of this key may sometimes be efficacious as a charm to open or close the womb, as needed.[14] The act of **throwing away a key** also ensures the continued closure of the womb until the proper time for its opening.[15]

This is the place to discuss a Libyan custom mentioned by the traveler-scholar Dr. Nahum Slouschz,[16] who relates that the night of *Rosh Hodesh* Nisan is called "the night of *el-Basisah*" or "*Basisat el-Marqumah*" (the meaning of these terms is quite vague). The name *basisah* is especially

12 BT Taanit 2a (with the wording: "the key of a *hayah* [woman in childbirth]"); *Midrash Tehillim* 78:5. Cf. BT Sanhedrin 113a, and the other parallels listed by Buber.

13 Rabbi Hayyim Palache (Palaggi), *Yimtza Hayyim* (Izmir, 1831), para. 13, fol. 9a.

14 See *Midrash Tehillim*, loc. cit., that "when the Holy One, blessed be He, so desired, He gave the righteous [the key] of the barren woman"; and likewise, in *Tanhuma*, loc. cit. See R. Patai, *Man and Earth in Hebrew Custom, Belief and Legend: A Study in Comparative Religion* (Jerusalem, 1942), pp. 204–205 (Hebrew).

15 See also Patai, *Man and Earth*, p. 263 n. 9, for the closing of a door in Serbia and Bosnia to close a woman's womb. See also ibid., p. 265 n. 23, for the use in Serbia of locks for this purpose. See also F. Grunberg-Guggenheim, "A Lock in a Grave as Means to Stop a Pestilence," *Yeda-'Am* 5, 1–2 (1959), p. 8, for the burial of the dead together with a lock, the key to which is then cast away, to lock the deceased against destructive agents and as a prophylactic measure against plagues. Grunberg-Guggenheim also refers to A. Rappaport, *Schlussel und Schloss* (Vienna, 1937), and to A. Wuttke, *Der deutsche Volksaberglaube der Gegenwart* (Berlin, 1900), para. 744. See also *Semahot* 8:6 (*Treatise Semahot*, ed. M. Higger [New York, 1937], p. 152): "He said to him: We hang the key and writing tablet of the deceased because of the sadness of the soul. When Samuel the Small died, they hung his key and his writing-tablet in his coffin, **because he had no son**" (see Part 2, chap. 7 ["Opening the Coffin before Burial"], n. 7).

16 Cited in Y.L. Baruch, *Sefer ha-Moadim* (Tel Aviv, 1956), Vol. 2: *The Three Festivals: Pesah*, p. 400 (Hebrew); also mentioned by A. Elmaleh, "From the Life of the Jews in Tripolitania," *Mizrah Oumaarav (Orient et Occident)* 3,7 (1929), p. 52, but with the omission of the holding of the key.

applied to the porridge that is consumed as a dip on this evening. At that time, all the members of the family gather at the house of the father or the family elder, who places oil in a cup that will be used as a lamp on this night, into which gold coins — a sign of abundance — are thrown; some say that this is an atonement for the sin of the Golden Calf. In other communities, coins are thrown in all four corners of the room, and the head of the household lights the "lamp" in commemoration of the destruction of the Temple, **while he holds a key in his hand**, and recites a blessing (in Arabic) over the *basisah* bowl:

> You open with no key,
> The One who gives, who is not of flesh and blood,
> Give us our needs from Your hand alone,
> And may it be His will that the next year shall be better than this one.

This, then, is a symbolic act accompanied by a symbolic statement, with a "key" serving as the symbolic object.

3. THE *KAPARAH* AS A PROTECTIVE CHARM

While still on the topic of protective measures for women undergoing difficult childbirth, mention should be made of the *kaparah* practice in Kurdistan, by which an animal is slaughtered and symbolically effects atonement. A rooster (or a sheep, by the rich) is slaughtered, and its blood is sprinkled on the location where the birth is to take place, or even on the woman in labor herself (thus in Amadiya). In Zakho, a rooster and a hen — the rooster for the hoped-for son, and the hen for the expectant mother — would be waved above the latter's head. The fowl would then be slaughtered, and their meat would be distributed among the poor.[17] This is an obvious variation of the *kaparot* that are slaughtered on the eve of Yom Kippur that have been discussed at length elsewhere.[18] The exchange of a person (or the infant) by an animal that is "sacrificed" in his stead, with the slaughter effecting atonement, is a symbolic act by means of which a person's fate, if negative, is transferred to the "sacrifice."[19]

17 Brauer, *The Jews of Kurdistan*, p. 130; *idem*, "Birth Customs of the Jews of Kurdistan," p. 68; Patai, "*Masekhet Segulot*," p. 479.
18 *Minhagei Yisrael*, Vol. 1, pp. 33–34; Vol. 2, pp. 84–85 n. 18.
19 This is naturally an element of any sacrifice, but the intent of the individual offering

4. THE SWORD HELPING TO PRESERVE LIFE

We will continue our discussion of protective measures by describing one of the ways in which the newborn is rescued from the cruel clutches of Lilith,[20] as was practiced by German Jewry in the eighteenth century. A sword was placed under the new mother's head, and once on each of the thirty-one nights following the birth, the woman would arise from her bed, take the sword, and brandish it as if she were cutting the four corners of the room, and also over the floor — all in order to banish Lilith, as can be seen in the illustrations in Kirchner and Bodenschatz.[21] And, from the seventeenth century, we read in the *Wormser Minhagbuch*:[22]

the sacrifice is of cardinal importance, while, in the popular *kaparot*, the very act is of primary significance. Consequently, this act assumes a nature close to the magical.

20 For Lilith and all her traits, see R. Margaliot, *Malakhei Elyon: That Are Mentioned in the Babylonian and Palestinian Talmuds, in All the Midrashim, Zohar and Tikkunim, Targumim, and Yalkutim ... of the Holy Books of the Kabbalah* (Jerusalem, 1945), pp. 238–41; Trachtenberg, *Jewish Magic and Superstition*, pp. 36–37; 277–78 nn. 32, 33; 280–81 n. 51, and more. See now S. Sabar's remarks in his article: "Childbirth and Magic: Jewish Folklore and Material Culture," in *Cultures of the Jews: A New History*, ed. D. Biale (New York, 2002), pp. 695–98.

21 Patai, "Folk Customs and Charms Relating to Birth," p. 260. Cf. ibid., pp. 250–51, for the circumcisor's knife as a means of protecting the infant. The well-known book by Paul Christian Kirchner (an apostate Jew), *Judisches Ceremoniel, das ist: Allerhand Judisch Gebrauche* (published in Frankfurt in 1720, together with J. Meelfuhrer, *Synopsis Institutionum Hebraicarum*), which contains illustrations of various aspects of Jewish life, includes an engraving of a woman giving birth, with a prominently displayed sword suspended next to her bed(!). See S. Seligmann, *Der Bose Blick und Verwandtes: ein Beitrag zur Geschichte des Aberglaubens aller Zeiten und Volker* (Berlin, 1910); G. Finamore, *Tradizioni popolari abruzzesi* (Palermo, 1890), p. 69. We learn from these sources that the practice of placing a metal object next to the bed of a pregnant woman was observed in Germany and in Italy. See also T.H. Gaster, *The Holy and the Profane* (New York, 1955), pp. 10–11, and his notes, pp. 226–27. Gaster observes (p. 11) that the sword was such a common prophylactic means against demons that charms for this purpose were also called "sword." Thus the Greek Coptic source: the *Sword of Dardanos*, a name also appearing in Harba de-Moshe, an early Jewish magical source, published by M.H. Gaster (T.H. Gaster's father) as *The Sword of Moses: An Ancient Book of Magic* (London, 1896) (see also J.G. Gager, *Moses in Greco-Roman Paganism* [Nashville and New York, 1972], pp. 135, 160). See T. Schrire, *Hebrew Amulets: Their Decipherment and Interpretation* (London, 1966), p. 152, for fig. 22: a silver knife-shaped charm that is meant to protect the new mother from demons, and

> A woman who stands next to [the new mother] to attend to her takes an outstretched sword, encompasses the new mother a number of times, and utters some incantations, as are known to women; and she acts thusly every night for four weeks after the birth.

This was a well-known Germanic-Slavonic practice,[23] which also was observed in Afghanistan.[24] This symbolic act of expelling Lilith with a sword is reminiscent of the token meaning of the shaking of the *lulav* (one of the Four Species taken on Sukkot; here, the three species that are bound together), as specified by the Talmud:[25]

> R. Aha ben Jacob would wave [the *lulav*] to and fro, saying "This is an arrow in the eye of Satan."[26]

especially from Lilith, since this knife mentions the three angels who protect against the queen of demons: "*Sanvai Sansanvai Semanglof*" (cf. p. 118). In a similar ceremony in Morocco, the father waves a sword and strikes the walls of the new mother's room in order to banish the demons; this action is repeated each night until the circumcision. See Ben-Ami, *Le Judaisme Marocain*, p. 163.

22 R. Jousep (Juspa) Schammes, *Wormser Minhagbuch*, ed. B.S. Hamburger and E. Zimmer, Vol. 2 (Jerusalem, 1992), p. 158 (Hebrew).

23 F. Nork, *Die Sitten und Gebrauch der Deutschen und ihrer Nachbarvolker ... Mythen und Volkssagen* (Stuttgart, 1849), p. 555 (see J.G. Frazer, *The New Golden Bough*, ed. T.H. Gaster [New York, 1959 (New York, 1972)], p. 269, para. 171).

24 See the recent book: B.Z. Yehoshua, *From the Lost Tribes in Afghanistan to the Mashhad Jewish Converts of Iran* (Jerusalem, 1992), pp. 357, 367, 389 (Hebrew).

25 BT Sukkah 38a.

26 See Rashi ad loc. For an understanding of this topic, see E.R. Goodenough, *Jewish Symbols in the Greco-Roman Period*, Vol. 2 (New York, 1953), pp. 238–41, for his discussion of "The Much-Suffering Eye"; considerable additional research is required. The motif of taking out the eye of Satan (or that of the Angel of Death) appears in Islamic legend in the struggle of Moses with the Angel of Death. The latter seeks to take the soul of Moses, who puts up a fight and takes out the angel's eye. The Angel of Death complains about this to Allah, who restores his sight. Thus in the *Tzahifa* of Wahb ibn Munabbih (636–719), one of the early versions of the *hadith*. And, according to another tradition (of Abu Harira, in the name of Abd al-Sha'arani, 1493–1565), Moses received permission from the Creator to do so. See H. Schwarzbaum, *Biblical and Extra-Biblical Legends in Islamic Folk-Literature* (Waldorf-Hessen, 1982), pp. 31, 139 n. 77. This lends itself to an intriguing comparison with the practice of the Jews of Afghanistan to sprinkle on the "*hesht*" (a "small offering" for magical purposes, consisting of onion peel, salt, pepper, pomegranate peel, a broken piece of glass, cotton wool, a coin, and grains

And so, the shaking of the *lulav* serves the same end as the movements of a person fighting against Satan and the forces of evil.[27]

of *espang* — little grains that explode when they come into contact with fire and exude a fragrant smell) drops of water that have the appearance of two eyes, and then to pierce these two drops with the point of a knife, "for if the evil eye was cast upon a sick person, his illness will be canceled by the piercing of the eyes" (Yehoshua, *From the Lost Tribes of Afghanistan*, p. 369).

It is also fascinating to find this motif in a different context, that of the blowing of the *shofar* (ram's horn), which is considered to be a sort of "arrow in the eye." See Kalonymus ben Kalonymus (1286–1328), *Even Bohen*, ed. A.M. Habermann (Tel Aviv, 1956), p. 26.

The Talmud continues: "This is not proper, because [Satan] might be provoked," to which Rashi comments: "It is not proper to speak thusly, [because] Satan, who is the evil inclination, will provoke him, and lead him to err against his Creator, and act in a [forbidden] manner."

Of course, the main form of protection for women in childbirth was the famous amulet found in *Sefer Raziel ha-Malakh* (Amsterdam, 1701) (Fig. 3), in which the three angels mentioned above ("*Sanvai Sansanvai Semanglof*") banish Lilith. See the illustration by Bodenschatz (Fig. 1), in which these names appear on the wall. See also my *Magic and Folklore in Rabbinic Literature* (Ramat Gan, 1994), p. 80. There is, as yet, no really satisfying explanation for these angel names. Gaster, "Two Thousand Years of a Charm against the Child-Stealing Witch," made a brave attempt to connect *Sansanvai* with the Slavonic St. Sysnie and *Sanvai* with Syno-doros, and *Samglof* presumably with Gylo, all found in Slavonic and Romanian versions of the complete version of Sisiu and the Evil Spirit, which he published in full (pp. 1019–24; cf. pp. 1015–18 for another version). Gaster based his English translation on two Greek texts found in Leone Allaci, *Leo Allatius De Templic Graecorium* (Cologne, 1645), pp. 126–29, 133–35 and E. Legrand, *Bibliothèque grecque vulgaire*, Vol. 2 (Paris, 1881), p. vxiii. However attractive his suggestions might be, they remain highly conjectural. As to the forms of these creatures, they seem to have evolved from Horus-Harpocrates types frequently found in Egyptian and Hellenistic-Roman cameo amulets, as cock- or falcon-headed creatures with two legs that curve upwards like serpents. See, e.g., C. Bonner, *Studies in Magical Amulets, Chiefly Graeco-Egyptian* (Ann Arbor and London, 1950), Pl. VII–IX; *Magic and Folklore in Rabbinic Literature*, p. 93; E.A.W. Budge, *Amulets and Talismans*[2] (New York, 1961), pp. 208–209 (Gnostic amulets); Goodenough, *Jewish Symbols in the Greco-Roman Period*, Vol. 3, nos. 1062, 1082–1083, 1094–1095 (the source of our Fig. 4). For other sorts of protective amulets for women and children, see H. Matras, "Amulets for Childbirth and the Child in Jerusalem Today," *Rimonim* 5 (1997), pp. 15–27 (Hebrew).

27 The taking of protective measures against demons by actions involving utterance (written or oral charms) is an extremely broad topic, and has been extensively

Corroborating this conception, we see a sword suspended behind the bed in the illustration reproduced by Kirchner.[28]

The use of a sword as a protective agent for a woman in childbirth was not limited to the Germanic-Slavonic area. It was also found much further to the east, among Kurdish Jews, as Sabar has demonstrated. We can do no better than to quote him:[29]

> The strong belief in the power of the sword in the context of childbirth is best demonstrated by a popular custom of the Iraqi Kurdish Jews, who used a miniature symbolic sword for an extended period in the life of the child. This object is known in the special neo-Aramaic dialect of Kurdish Jews as a *seipa* (cf. the Hebrew term *sa'yif*, "sword") [Fig. 5].[30] In order to resist the evil eye in every way possible, the material for the *seipa* was customarily acquired from three silversmiths: a Jew, a Muslim, and a Christian. The silver obtained from these sources was then melted down and reworked by a Jewish silversmith who prepared a small sword with one, two, or three holes at the ends. The *hakham* would inscribe on it the protective formulas, such as Psalm 121, *shemoth*, protective angels with meaningful names (e.g. Azriel, Shamriel), and the three angels who combat Lilith. The crowded and lengthy inscription significantly ends with the words: "a barrier and fence to the bearer of this amulet." The sword was sewn to the cap of the child, who wore it everywhere for several years. In some cases the lad would wear the cap with the *seipa* until he started to don *tefillin* (perhaps as a sort of replacement for the protection provided by the sword).[31]

researched. Trachtenberg, *Jewish Magic and Superstition*, has encompassed the entire issue, and it has also been discussed by many other scholars, including Max Grunwald (e.g. "Aus Hausapotheke und Hexenkuche III," *Jahrbuch fur Judische Volkskunde* [1925], 178–226), Zlotnik, Patai, and others. Nevertheless, a renewed and exhaustive discussion is still needed, and I hope to return to this at another time.

28 Above, section 3.

29 Sabar, "Childbirth and Magic," pp. 697–98.

30 Cf. Brauer, *The Jews of Kurdistan*, pp. 173–74.

31 The *tefillin*, and especially the head *tefillin*, were considered to be protective agents, because the letter *shin* on its box, the *dalet* in the main knot of the straps, and the additional *yod* in the knot comprise the sacred name *Shaddai*, which is a powerful means of protection (and also appears on the *mezuzah*). (See M.M. Kasher, "Regarding the Incision Made in the *Tefillin* to Insert the '*Yod*,'" *Noam* 7 [1964],

Sabar continues:

> In Kurdistan the symbolic and psychological function of the sword
> dominated, but the battle waged against Lilith in other communities
> was more fierce. In Morocco and Ashkenaz, for example, a much larger
> sword was used, preferably one that had shed blood — as if an actual
> fight were under way. Known as *sif* ("sword") *d'tahdid*, the Moroccan
> sword was thought to be the best weapon against the enemies of the
> newborn. The *tahdid* is a ceremony conducted every evening between
> childbirth and circumcision. Before the ceremony begins, a real, large,
> iron sword, preferably one that has "proved itself" in the past, is
> placed under the pillow of the woman in childbed.[32] A celebration is
> then held at home, with relatives and other guests present. The festive
> meal is accompanied by the reading of selections from various sources,
> with special emphasis on the *Zohar*, which to Moroccan Jews is an

pp. 10–28 [Hebrew]; *idem, Divrei Menahem: Clarifications of Various Halakhot
in Shulhan Arukh, Orah Hayyim, with Added Responsa*, Vol. 1 [Jerusalem, 1957],
pp. 56–67 [Hebrew], on the *yod* in the knot.) This aspect is clearly indicated in
the following passage from a thirteenth-century source (Rabbi Abraham ben Azriel,
Arugat Habosem, ed. E.E. Urbach, Vol. 2 [Jerusalem, 1947], pp. 88–89):

> R. Simeon ben Yohai taught: "And all [the peoples of the earth] shall see [that
> the Lord's name is proclaimed over you]" [Deut. 28:10] — even four spirits,
> even demons [following PT Berakhot 5:1]. R. Eleazar [of Worms], of blessed
> memory, wrote: in the knot of the head *tefillin* [the letter] *dalet* is like a [final]
> *mem*. This, together with [the letter] *shin* in the boxes [of the *tefillin*] forms [the
> word] *shem* [the Name], [the three letters *shin*, *dalet*, and *yod* now forming the
> component of the Divine Name-combination] *El Shaddai* [meaning] "God of
> faith." This Name has the purpose of protecting against demons [*shedim*] and
> robbers [*shodedim* — all formed from these same letters], in *Sefer ha-Kavod*.
> [...] The two *shins* on the two sides of the *tefillin*, on the right and on the left,
> are four Names, so that the Holy One, blessed be He, shall guard you all around,
> so that your feet shall not swerve [see, e.g., Ps. 44:19]. This is the meaning of
> what is said: "For you shall spread out to the right and the left" [Isa. 54:3] —
> the Lord is to your right and to your left.

The form of the *dalet* that is doubled, so that it has the appearance of a final *mem*
(in accordance with *Zohar, Pinhas* 258), has been the subject of much discussion,
to which we hope to relate elsewhere.

32 For an example from Marrakech (95 cm. in length), see the reproduction in the
Israel Museum exhibition catalogue: A. Muller-Lancet (ed.), *La vie Juive au Maroc*
(Jerusalem, 1986), p. 97.

extremely sacred and protective text.[33] At midnight the windows and doors are closed and the sword is removed from under the pillow. The master of the house brandishes the weapon in all directions, as if he is dispelling Lilith and the other demons, while he and all the others loudly recite protective verses.[34]

We see, then, two distinct forms of the imagery of the sword as a protective agent: the one, as an amulet, which is inscribed with protective formulas; and the other, which requires a symbolic act of battle against the forces of evil.[35]

---

33 See H.E. Goldberg, "The Zohar in Southern Morocco: A Study in the Ethnography of Texts," *History of Religions* 29, 3 (1989–90), pp. 233–58.

34 See R.J. Bensimon, *Le Judaisme marocain (Life and Tradition in the Life Cycle)* (Lod, 1994), pp. 55–58 (Hebrew).

35 See *Minhagei Yisrael*, Vol. 3, pp. 113–34, for the use of symbolic actions; see above, chap. 2.

1. Bodenschatz, Erlang 1748

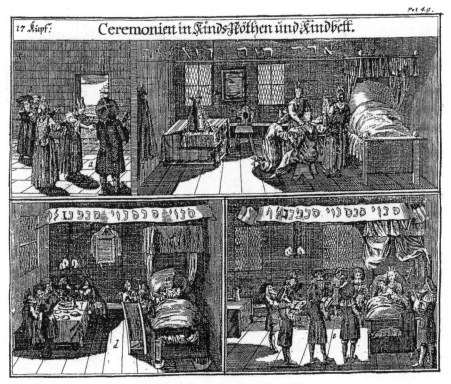

2. Kirchner, Nuremberg 1724

3. *Sefer Raziel ha-Malach*

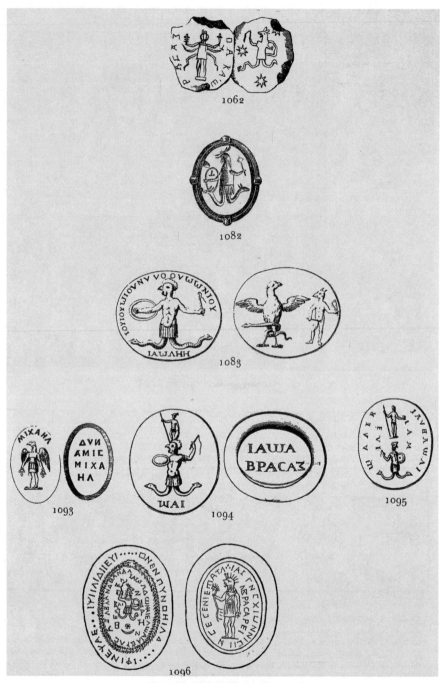

4. Gnostic Amulets, Goodenough

5. **Seipa (sword) amulet, Iraqi Kurdistan,
early 20th century. Engraved silver
(Gross Family collection, Tel Aviv)**

3

NEW MOTHER IMPURITY

An extremely fine, and quite vague, line separates a practice sanctioned by Jewish law from one that is not.[1] On the one hand, the leading *poskim* felt dutybound to justify practices that we would regard as transgressions, such as the consumption of *stam yeinam* (nonkosher wine),[2] the consumption of blood,[3] and the like. On the other hand, we have already presented[4] a wealth of material from the *Rishonim* and *Ahronim* (medieval and later authorities), showing that they took a vigorous stance against customs that they viewed as invalid and erroneous. The question arises, how do we distinguish between a justified practice that is to be maintained, and one that is to be abrogated?

MAIMONIDES' RULING REGARDING THE "DAYS OF PURITY" OF A NEW MOTHER AND KARAITISM

At times the polemical tone of the rabbinic criticism of "erroneous" customs reveals the background of the attack by the rabbinical authorities. Thus, for example, Maimonides states definitively:[5]

---

1 See also *Minhagei Yisrael*, Vol. 1, pp. 31–38; and the instructive treatment, replete with sources: M. Benayahu, *Studies in Memory of the Rishon Le-Zion R. Yitzhak Nissim* (Jerusalem, 1985), chap. 12 ("Erroneous Custom"), pp. 285–95 (Hebrew). See also *Minhagei Yisrael*, Vol. 2, pp. 49–52 n. 23.

2 *She'eilot u-Teshuvot Rema* (Jerusalem, 1971), para. 124, pp. 484–88.

3 Rabbi Jacob Reischer, *She'eilot u-Teshuvot Shevut Yaakov* (Lvov, 1861), Vol. 2, para. 70, pp. 59–65.

4 *Minhagei Yisrael*, Vol. 1, pp. 32–38.

5 Maimonides, *Mishneh Torah, Hil. Isurei Biyah* (*Laws of Forbidden Sexual Relationships*) 11:14.

In some places the menstruant woman remains for seven days in her [status of] menstruation, even if she saw [her flow] only a single day, and after this seven she continues through the seven days of cleanness.[6] **This custom is an error**, from the authority who so ruled, and no attention need be paid to it.

6   Which is the practice of the island of Djerba. See Rabbi Moses ha-Kohen, *Berit Kehunah ha-Shalem*[4] (Bnei Brak, 1990), "*Kunteres Torat ha-Minhagim* [The Regulations of Customs]," para. 31, pp. 567–68. See BT Shabbat 13a-b:

> [It is taught in] *Tanna de-Vei Eliyahu*: It once happened that a certain scholar who had studied much [Mishnah], read much [Bible], and had served scholars greatly [nevertheless] died in middle age. His wife took his *tefillin* and carried them about in synagogues and study halls, and she complained to them: It is written in the Torah: "For thereby you shall have life and shall long endure" [Deut. 30:20] — my husband studied much [Mishnah], read much [Bible], and served scholars greatly, why did he die in middle age? No one could answer her. One time I [i.e. Elijah] was a guest in her home, she told me the entire tale, and I said to her: "My daughter, how was he to you during your menstrual periods?" She replied, "Heaven forfend! He did not touch me, not even with his little finger." "And how was he to you during your time of white [garments]?" "He ate with me, and drank with me, and slept together with me in bodily contact, and it did not occur to him to do otherwise." I replied to her, "Blessed be the Omnipresent for killing him, that He was not partial on account of the Torah, for the Torah said: 'Do not come near a woman during her period of uncleanness' [Lev. 18:19]."

Cf. *Seder Eliyahu Rabbah*, chap. 15 (16), ed. M. Ish Shalom (M. Freidmann) (Vienna, 1901 [photocopy edn.: Jerusalem, 1960]), p. 76; see the preceding passage, and the editor's gloss (para. 24). See also *Avot de-Rabbi Nathan*, version A, chap. 1, ed. S. Schechter (Vienna, 1887 [photocopy edn.: New York, 1945]), pp. 8–9; Maimonides, *Mishneh Torah, Hil. Isurei Biyah* (*Laws of Forbidden Sexual Relationships*) 11:18:

> A man may not come into close contact with his wife during these seven days of cleanness, even though she be clothed, and he be clothed. He may not draw near to her nor touch her, not even with his little finger, nor may he eat with her from the same bowl. The general rule is: he is to behave towards her as he does during the time of her menstrual period, for he still is subject to [the punishment of] *karet* [for engaging in sexual relations with a menstruant woman] until she immerses, as we have explained.

See the analysis by S. Ben-David, "The Prohibitions Relating to Keeping Apart during the *Niddah* Period," *Granot* 3 (2003), pp. 202–206 (Hebrew).

This question, however, is not so straightforward, for Y. Dinari, "The Impurity Customs of the Menstruate Woman — Sources and Development," *Tarbiz* 49 (1979–80), pp. 310 ff. (Hebrew), has shown the substantial difference between the perception of the seven days of white garments by the Babylonian rabbis and that

And, in *halakhah* 15:

> Similarly, there are some places, and responsa by some Geonim,
> in which the woman who gives birth to a son is not to engage in

of their counterparts in the Land of Israel. The Babylonian Geonim, headed by
Rav Sherira Gaon, unanimously rejected the drawing of any distinction between the
seven days of the menstrual period (*niddah*) and the seven days of white garments:
"just as [all manner of relationships] are to be prohibited during the first [period], so
are [they] to be prohibited during the later [period]" (L. Ginzberg, *Geonica* [New
York, 1909], Vol. 2, p. 206; see Ginzberg's explanation, pp. 203–204). The rabbis
of the Land of Israel, in contrast, saw fit to distinguish between these two time
periods, and, according to Dinari, maintained that the actual menstrual period was a
perilous time for others, and, therefore, that they should keep their distance from the
menstruant woman. The prohibition applying to the days of wearing white garments,
however, was instituted solely as an additional preventive measure to keep people
from sinning; this period is one of lesser severity, and includes only the specific
prohibitions mentioned in the Babylonian Talmud (Ketubot 61a; Shabbat 13b: the
pouring of a cup, the making of a bed, joint eating and drinking from a single
vessel, and the like). We read in a responsum by R. Isaac Alfasi (*Shaare Teshubah:
Responsa of the Geonim*, ed. W. Leiter [New York, 1946]; *She'eilot u-Teshuvot
Rabbenu Yitzhak Alfasi*, ed. W. [Z.] Leiter [Pittsburgh, 1954], para. 297):

> Query: Concerning a menstruant woman who bathed after the time of her
> menstrual period in drawn water [i.e. not in a ritual bath], and she observes the
> seven days of cleanness, is she [included in the prohibitions of a man sitting on
> a surface on which the woman has] lain or sat, or not?
>
> Response: If you are asking concerning the basic Torah law, as long as the
> menstruant woman does not immerse in the water of the ritual bath, she is as all
> other menstruant women [...] and she is [included in the prohibitions of] lying
> or sitting. At the present time, however, people distance themselves from [the
> surface on which such an impure woman has] lain or sat, only so that the law
> of purity shall not be forgotten in Israel. Since she has cleansed herself of her
> menstruation and has bathed in drawn water, they need not distance themselves
> from [the surface on which such an impure woman has] lain or sat. All this is
> the popular practice in this generation.

See Zimmer, *Society and Its Customs*, "The Seven Days of *Niddah*," pp. 240–59,
who delineates the development of the custom of bathing after the seven days of
menstruation and before the seven days of white garments. Zimmer cites *Mahzor
Vitri* (from the school of Rashi), p. 608: "After the menstruation ceased, they
would bathe and wear fine clothing, since it was difficult for them to be so greatly
unattractive. [...] The women would serve their husbands during those days, but it
is forbidden to do so. [...] Praiseworthy is the woman who does not dress in white,
does not bathe, and is always repulsive to her husband until the immersion." In other

intercourse until forty days have passed, and in the case of a woman who gives birth to a female, until eighty [days] have passed, even though she saw blood only within the [first] seven [days]. **This custom**

words, some women made light of the seven clean days after they bathed; Rashi and those of his school struggled against this conception. Zimmer quotes R. Shemaiah, a pupil of Rashi, who asserts: "She is forbidden to draw near to her husband as long as she has not immersed; thus I saw R.[Rashi?] behave, and even when giving over a key or any object from his hand to her he would desist [from coming into any contact]" (*Mahzor Vitri*, loc. cit.; Zimmer, p. 243). He shows that in the time of Rabbeinu Tam this bathing had metamorphosed into immersion in a ritual bath, so that there would be a "double immersion" following menstruation. Rabbeinu Tam wrote (*Sefer ha-Yashar*, ed. S.F. Rosenthal [Berlin, 1898], para. 59; *Sefer ha-Yashar, Helek ha-Hiddushim* ["Novellae"], ed. S.S. Schlesinger [Jerusalem, 1959], p. 126): "In Rome, however, they sent [a reply] that they were not stringent concerning the white garments. They possessed such a tradition, without explanation, and I do not regard this to be proper." All the above teaches that some people drew a complete distinction between the *niddah* period and that of the days of white garments, and regarded the latter period (regardless of the number of days that this constituted) with much greater leniency.

This question was further investigated by I.M. Ta-Shma, *Ritual, Custom and Reality in Franco-Germany, 1000–1350* (Jerusalem, 1996), in the chapter "The Practices of Women Distanced on Account of *Niddah* in Early Franco-Germany — Life and Literature," pp. 280–88 (Hebrew), who showed that "only the sages of Franco-Germany, and only them, following the tradition of those in the Land of Israel, ascribe halakhic weight to these stringencies" (p. 282). Ta-Shma further demonstrated, based on *Ha-Pardes* (from the school of Rashi), *Hil. Niddah* (*Laws of* Niddah), "that after the interim bathing within the seven days of uncleanness, those women were in total proximity to their husbands; with the exception of sexual relations, they cast off all harsh decrees, including those of Talmudic origin, and they regarded distancing themselves as a sinful practice" (p. 283), to the displeasure of the rabbinical authorities. The laws of *niddah* in *Sefer ha-Pardes*, according to Ta-Shma, originated in early Land of Israel laws that came to the Franco-German center and were reformulated by Rashi; a full discussion of this complex issue would exceed the purview of this work. We therefore may state that if a woman bathed or immersed in a ritual bath following the seven days of *niddah*, there is a basis for leniency during the days of white garments. If, however, she neither bathed nor immersed, such leniency is unwarranted.

To the best of our knowledge, the "double immersion" was not practiced during the time of R. Moses Isserles, and therefore this leniency was not in force. This leniency is merely a remnant of the earlier procedure depicted above, as we definitely see from the fact that *Bah* (R. Joel Sirkes), *Taz* (R. David ha-Levi, author of *Turei*

is [the result of] **an error in those responsa. It is the manner of heresy** [that is prevalent] **in those localities, and it was learned from the Sadducees**.

In this passage Maimonides reveals the object of his attack, which is directed against the Karaites, who follow "the manner of heresy [...] from the Sadducees." The Karaite interpretation of the verses (Lev. 12: 4–5) that speak of the "period [literally, days] of purification"[7] was known to

Zahav), and *Shelah* (R. Isaiah ben Abraham Horowitz, author of *Shenei Luhot ha-Berit*) expressed their wonder at the practice of the *Rema*, writing that it was a foolish practice, and completely prohibited (*Bah* on *Tur*, *Yoreh Deah*, para. 195, s.v. "*Hayav*"; *Turei Zahav*, *Yoreh Deah* 195:9; *Shenei Luhot ha-Berit*, "*Sha'ar ha-Otiyot*" [Josefov, 1878], p. 67; Dinari, "The Impurity Customs of the Menstruate Woman," p. 323). *Maharshal* (Rabbi Solomon ben Jehiel Luria) attests that "all the communities assembled and placed a ban on this" (*Be'er ha-Golah*, *Yoreh Deah* 195:9). This is expressed even more strongly by Isserles himself, in his gloss on *Yoreh Deah* 195:14 (commenting on the ruling by R. Joseph Caro: "All these distancings [between husband and wife] are to be observed, whether during the time of her menstrual flow, or whether during the time of her wearing white garments, that [together] comprise all the days of her count; and there is no distinction in all these [regulations] between actually seeing [menstrual flow] and finding a stain"): "According to one opinion, stringency should not be observed during the time of her wearing white garments regarding the prohibition of eating together with her from the same dish (gloss, *Mordekhai*, in the name of *Ravyah*), and they are lenient in this matter, **but stringency is to be observed**" (emphasis added — D. S.). Isserles emphatically opposed this leniency, and saw no reason to distinguish between the period of menstruation and that in which white garments are worn. This puzzling custom could possibly be explained by the practice presented above, of engaging in two immersions, the first of which was in drawn water (i.e. not in a formal ritual bath) after the seven days of menstruation, as we see in many German illustrations of such an immersion in a sort of tub, as in Kirchner, *Judisches Ceremoniel* (Fig. 1); Aaron Wolf Herlingen, *Berakhot le-Nashim* (Vienna, 1739) (Fig. 2); the *Grace after Meals* executed by Meshullam of Polna in 1751, MS. Budapest 64.626 (Fig. 3), and more (in contrast to Fig. 4 in Bodenschatz, *Kirchliche Verfassung der heutigen Juden*). All these perhaps depict the first immersion, or possibly the woman bathing before immersing in the ritual bath; this question has yet to be resolved.

7 See Rabbi Aaron ben Elijah of Nicomedia, *Keter Torah* (Ramleh, 1972), on Lev. loc. cit., pp. 62–63; idem, *Gan Eden* (Eupatoria, 1866), "*Inyan Tumah ve-Taharah* (Ritual Purity)," chap. 8, fol. 114a–115a; Rabbi Elijah Bashyazi, *Aderet Eliyahu* (Israel, 1966), pp. 245–47, and more. See the discussion of the seven and additional seven days of the *niddah* (menstrual impurity) period in the Karaite Halakhah: S. Allony, *Studies in Medieval Philology and Literature*, Vol. 3 (Jerusalem, 1989),

Rabbinite scholars, who vigorously opposed it.[8] Following Maimonides, R. Israel Isserlein (fifteenth century) ruled:

p. 172 (Hebrew). See also A. Geiger, *Kevutzat Ma'amarim (Collected Articles)*, ed. A.A. Poznanski (Warsaw, 1910), pp. 89–91; B. Revel, *The Karaite Halakah and its Relation to Sadducean, Samaritan, and Philonean Halakah* (Philadelphia, 1913), p. 42. This was recently discussed in terms of the Samaritan Halakhah: I.R.M.M. Boid, *Principles of Samaritan Halachah* (Leiden and New York, 1989), pp. 318 ff. See also H.J. Zimmels, *Ashkenazim and Sephardim: Their Relations, Differences, and Problems as Reflected in Rabbinical Responsa* (London, 1958), p. 229. See S. Abramson, *Inyanut be-Sifrut ha-Geonim (A Direct Examination of the Geonic Literature)* (Jerusalem, 1974), p. 85.

8 Ibn Ezra apparently expressed his opposition to the Karaite view in his commentary on Lev. 12:5, s.v. *"Bi-Demei Toharah"*: "that is the blood of purification, that is in contrast with the blood of *niddah*, and that does not confer impurity [...] **this is already clear and proven**." See I. Twersky, *Introduction to the Code of Maimonides (Mishneh Torah)* (New Haven, 1980), p. 344, and more, for the anti-Karaite polemic in Maimonides' *Mishneh Torah*. See the instructive article on these writings by Maimonides by Rabbi Ovadiah Yosef, *She'eilot u-Teshuvot Yabi'a Omer*[2] (Jerusalem, 1986), Vol. 3, *Yoreh Deah* 11, pp. 143–44; Vol. 4, *Yoreh Deah* 11, pp. 250–51, 254; see also *She'eilot u-Teshuvot ve-Piskei Ma-ha-Rik he-Hadashim (Responsae and Decisions of Rabbi Joseph Colon)*, ed. E. Pines (Jerusalem, 1984), para. 143; Rabbi Benjamin Ze'ev ben Mattityahu, *She'eilot u-Teshuvot Binyamin Ze'ev* (Jerusalem, 1959), para. 144; see the important work by Y.A. Dinari, *The Rabbis of Germany and Austria at the Close of the Middle Ages: Their Conceptions and Halacha-Writings* (Jerusalem, 1984), pp. 218–19 (Hebrew), on *Terumat ha-Deshen*, para. 245; *Ha-Agudah* on Pesahim 166, para. 96; *Sefer ha-Pardes le-Rabbenu Shlomo Yitzhaki (Rashi), Zikhrono Li-Vrakhah*, ed. H.J. Ehrenreich (Budapest, 1924), p. 11. See also the comment by S. Spitzer, "The Practice of Austrian Jewry: Its Source and Development in the Medieval Period," *Sinai* 87 (1980), p. 62 (Hebrew); *Noda bi-Yehudah, Moed Katan*, para. 54; Rabbi Jonathan Eybeschuetz, *Kreiti u-Peleiti* (Altona, 1763), *Yoreh Deah*, para. 192; Zimmels, pp. 197–98; and the more recent book by I.J. Yuval, *Scholars in Their Time* (Jerusalem, 1989), pp. 70–71 (Hebrew). This practice continued until the present day in certain Jewish communities; see the extensive discussion: Yosef, *She'eilot u-Teshuvot Yabi'a Omer*, Vol. 4, *Yoreh Deah*, para. 11, fol. 250b ff.; see also the editor's gloss, ha-Kohen, *Berit Kehunah ha-Shalem*, end of section 1, n. 13, for the practice on the island of Djerba. This was also the custom of the Bene Israel in India; see H.S. Kehimkar, *The History of the Bene Israel of India* (Tel Aviv, 1937), p. 28; and also of many additional communities. See R. Bonfil, *The Rabbinate in Renaissance Italy* (Jerusalem, 1979), p. 281 n. 61 (Hebrew), from a responsum by R. Aaron ben Israel Finzi of Reggio, for an explanation of the Italian custom. For the longevity of customs, even those that were rejected, see PT

It is the practice of the women of Austria to wait 7 days. [...] my teacher expounded that they are not to be prevented from doing so, since this [ruling] was issued by the Geonim, even though it is written by Maimonides that this is the way of the heretics. Those, however, who wait 80 days to immerse after [the birth of] a female **are to be prevented from doing so,** for Maimonides also wrote regarding this that it is the way of the heretics, and he was more stringent regarding this than regarding the above case.[9]

Maimonides' prohibition of this widespread[10] practice was a consequence of his adamant view that this was a form of heresy.[11]

Pesahim 5:1, 30(c-d): "Women who are accustomed not to work upon the departure of the Sabbath: this **does not** constitute a custom, until the study hall lets out." We nonetheless find in *Tashbetz (Katan)*, para. 88: "Women may perform labor after the conclusion of the Sabbath after *Havdalah* [the ceremony formally concluding the Sabbath]. Women did, indeed, conduct themselves accordingly, as is taught in the Palestinian Talmud." And in the glosses on *Tashbetz* by Rabbeinu Peretz (*ot* 1): "It is the universal practice not to perform work on Saturday night." See J.Z. Lauterbach, "The Origin and Development of Two Sabbath Ceremonies," *HUCA* 15 (1940), p. 380 n. 24. For the survival of another ancient practice, see Y. Dinari, "Custom and Law in the Responsa of Ashkenazic Rabbis in the 15th Century," in *Benjamin De Vries Memorial Volume*, ed. E.Z. Melamed (Jerusalem, 1968), p. 182 n. 101 (Hebrew), that some communities in Kurdistan allocated special houses for menstruant women, any form of contact with whom was avoided by all (in contrast with normative Jewish law, which places such a total ban on contact only on the menstruant woman's husband), following M Niddah 7:4: "בית הטמאות [the place of unclean women]" (and not "בית הטומאות [the place of uncleannesses]," as in the printed editions). See J.J. Rivlin, *Shirat Yehudei ha-Targum* (*The Poetry of the Jews of the Targum: Narratives and Heroic Episodes by the Jews of Kurdistan*) (Jerusalem, 1959), p. 53, para. 15. See *Minhagei Yisrael*, Vol. 2, chap. 8 ("The Survival and Disappearance of Customs"), pp. 227–39.

9 R. Joseph (Joselein) ben Moses (ca. 1460), *Leket Yosher*, ed. J. Freimann (Berlin, 1903 [photocopy edn.: Jerusalem, 1964]), Vol. 2, p. 22.

10 See *Ha-Agudah* on BT Pesahim 166, para. 96; *Sefer ha-Pardes*, ed. Ehrenreich, on Pesahim 166, para. 96, "*Pardes*," p. 11.

11 See Dinari, "Custom and Law in the Responsa of Ashkenazic Rabbis in the 15th Century," pp. 193–94. As regards the second law (in *Mishneh Torah, Hil. Isurei Biyah* 11:14) that Maimonides categorized as "heresy" (that of women counting seven clean days only after the conclusion of the seven days from their first witnessing the beginning of menstruation), which was also practiced by "the women of Austria": R. Isserlein explains: "It presumably would seem that the practice of

Despite Maimonides' objection to the forty-day waiting period followed by the new mother's immersion, this practice was maintained among different Jewish communities, and even gave birth to additional rites and customs. We hear[12] of the "celebration of the forty [days]" among Libyan Jewry, that was observed as follows:

> When the child is forty days old, his mother conducts for him a small celebration, that consists of the lighting of candles in the home, and the cooking of beans or *hametz* [leavened matter], which she distributes to the neighbors. This night is called the "Night of the Forty."
>
> These are two seeming explanations for this practice, and the notion on which it is based:
>
> (1) this number of forty is analogous to the forty days required [according to the Talmudic notion] for the fetus to acquire [human] form; just as the mother-to-be counts forty days from the time of conception until she knows that she is carrying a fetus in her womb, she correspondingly counts forty days after its birth.[13]

the women of Austria comes from those places of the pupils of those authorities, and they therefore would always customarily wait seven days" (*Terumat ha-Deshen*, para. 245). *Maharil* also writes: "I heard from my master, of blessed memory [possibly R. Shalom of Vienna], that some act in this manner in the bloody land [= Austria] and the neighboring communities. This was not regarded as heresy; in these lands [i.e. Germany], however, all act in accordance with the rulings of Maimonides" (*She'eilot u-Teshuvot ha-Maharil*, ed. Y. Sats [Jerusalem, 1979], pp. 236–37; see Dinari, loc. cit; Zimmels, loc. cit.). In this same responsum Moellin provides an explanation for this procedure: "Those who wait 40 days for a male [birth] and 80 for a female: for it is written in *Ha-Agudah* [Pesahim, para. 96], we learn from [the chapter] *Arvei Pesahim* [chap. 10 of tractate Pesahim], that since her flow is presumed to continue [she therefore continues to be impure]. I explained this to R. Hayyim Sarfati of Augsburg (see *She'eilot u-Teshuvot ha-Maharil he-Hadashot* [*New Responsa of Rabbi Yaacov Molin-Maharil*] [ed. Y. Sats (Jerusalem, 1977), pp. 95–96], para. 93:3; see there), whom, I have heard, resides near you."

12 *Yahadut Lub*, p. 390.

13 A comparison with early Greek ritual practice is of interest in this context. We shall quote from R. Parker, *Miasma: Pollution and Purification in Early Greek Religion*[2] (Oxford, 1996), p. 48:

> We turn now from death to birth. According to Censorinus, probably echoing Varro, "in Greece they treat fortieth days as important. For the pregnant woman does not go out to a shrine before the fortieth day..." (from the moment that she becomes aware that she is pregnant?) (*De die natali* 11.7). A ritual exclusion

(2) Jewish law prescribes the immersion of a new mother forty days after giving birth, after which she is permitted to engage in marital relations. The conclusion of this period of conjugal abstinence is a natural occasion for a family celebration, the true reason for which is concealed. Modest Jewish women accordingly accredited this joyous occasion to the new infant, while in reality, it was the happy time of the parents.

This latter hypothesis finds additional support in the fact that the celebration following the birth of a daughter is held eighty days following the birth [corresponding to the purification period for a female delivery], and not after forty days.

Morgenstern[14] devotes part of a chapter to the fortieth-day celebration among various Bedouin tribes and other communities (pp. 27–28):

Among the Bedouin of the Arabian Desert a woman is regarded as unclean for forty days immediately following childbirth. Among the Fuqara Bedouin the customary sacrifice is offered and the name is given to the child upon the fortieth day after birth. Similarly among the Hamaideh and the Beni Saher Bedouin women remain for the first forty days after childbirth without washing, because the water of the country is **maskouneh**, "inhabited by a spirit," and therefore could harm them. In Jerusalem mother and child are conducted to the

of forty days sounds more Semitic than Greek, but in Greek medical texts the forty-day period is of particular importance precisely in relation to pregnancy and birth; during the first forty days after conception, for instance, menstruation continues, and miscarriage is a constant danger, while by the end of this period the embryo is formed and the male child begins to move. See W.H. Roscher, "Die Tesserakontaden und Tesserakontadenlehre der Griechen und anderer Volker," *Ber. Sachs. Ges. Wiss.* 61.2 (1909), 28–34, 40, 85–101; see esp. Censorinus, loc. cit., Arist. *Hist. An.* 7.3. 583a27–583b15. On wide diffusion of gynaecological forties cf. G. Eichinger Ferro-Luzzi, *Anthropos* 69 (1974), 148–52. Views on the timing of these matters were however very varied in Greece, cf. E. Nardi, *Procurato Aborto nel mondo greco romano*, Milan, 1971, 93–115, 123–32. The dangerous transitional period therefore lasts forty days, and during this period, if Censorinus is right, the mother is excluded from communal life.

There is also a "fortieth-day festival" after birth. See Parker, p. 52. On the impurity of a woman after childbirth, see ibid., pp. 49–50.

14 J. Morgenstern, *Rites of Birth, Marriage, Death and Kindred Occasions among the Semites* (Cincinnati, 1966 [photocopy edn.: New York, 1973]), pp. 27–30, 204–205.

bath upon the fortieth day after birth. [...] In Upper Egypt too [...] And among the Moslem Albanians the mother may not under any condition leave the house during this period. [...] Maronite women also [...] Among the Shiite Moslems of Persia when a child is born to a bride, they stick needles in her clothes, and let them remain there for forty days, so that no demons may approach her or touch her. [...] In northern Africa, the newborn child frequently goes by the general name **mahqub** (literally, "the protected one") during the first forty days after birth. [...] In Morocco the first hair of the child is frequently cut upon its fortieth day.

To this we should add a Sephardic custom recorded by Raphael Patai:[15]

Until the last generation, the Sephardic Jews in Safed observed the "custom that new mothers would not enter the house of a bride all forty days (following the birth) because it would be detrimental for her, [namely] that she would not conceive. If she [nevertheless] were to enter, the bride would take a piece of cloth from the clothing of the new mother, which she would soak in water; after her immersion, she would pour this water over her body, as a charm for fertility."

The conclusion that Patai draws from the numerous testimonies cited in his article is that the infant is in constant danger during the first forty days of his life, and various methods and means are employed to protect him from the all too abundant demons and other destructive agents. This period is concluded by the redemption ceremonies that finally release him from this peril. The mother, too, is endangered, and she, as well, must undergo the forty-day perilous period (literally, the "time of the anger" of the demonic spirits). The verses in Leviticus 12 are unquestionably the primary source of the forty- and eighty-day celebrations of Libyan Jewry. The immediate influence for these festivities, however, seems to have come from the local Islamic culture (that initially also drew upon Jewish sources, with additional local elements). The reason for celebrating, therefore, is the mother and child's successfully passing through this time of danger, and having emerged from the darkness of fear to the joy of security and life.[16]

15 "Folk Customs and Charms Relating to Birth," *Talpioth* 6, p. 224.
16 See Morgenstern, *Rites of Birth*, pp. 81–82, for the immersion practices of various Christian sects, on the fortieth day after the birth of a son and eighty days after that of a daughter. The Jewish, or even the biblical, influence here is patent.

The subject of the forty-day period of impurity incurred by the new mother after having given birth and her subsequent leaving the house in order to immerse herself was discussed in detail by Morgenstern,[17] who provides a wealth of reports from various tribes in the Middle East, North Africa, and the like.[18] An interesting parallel appears in one of the Armenian Adam books,[19] according to which Adam and Eve were created on the sixth day, at the third hour, and forty days later were transferred to the Garden of Eden. Both, unfortunately, sinned two days later during this same third hour of Friday; the symbolic connection is obvious.[20]

The direction of such cross-cultural influences cannot always be easily determined. Thus, e.g., Westermarck, *Ritual and Belief in Morocco*, Vol. 1, p. 141; Vol. 2, pp. 448, 458, 527, 528, attests that the Muslims in Morocco feared even numbers, and therefore would not place an even number of stones on a grave, nor would they wrap the corpse in an even number of shrouds. See the entire discussion that BT Pesahim 110a devotes to this question of whether even numbers should be avoided; for an expanded discussion, see Part 2, chap. 7 ("Opening the Coffin before Burial"), n. 22. See also J. Blau, *Das altjudische Zauberwesen* (Budapest, 1898), p. 77; R.C. Thompson, *Semitic Magic: Its Origins and Development* (London, 1908), pp. xxxi–xxxii.

17 Morgenstern, *Rites of Birth*, pp. 27–30, 81–82.

18 It should also be noted that this practice spread beyond these geographical areas. See, e.g., A.B. Ellis, *The Ewe-Speaking Peoples of the Slave Coast of West Africa* (1890 [photocopy edn.: Amsterdam, 1970]), p. 153, the Tshi-speaking peoples of the Ivory Coast: "The mother and child [after birth] are considered unclean, and it is not until forty days have elapsed that the former may return to her usual avocations, though she is usually purified with lustral water seven days after the birth." This issue should be the subject of a comparative study.

19 As noted by M.A. Stone, "Discoveries Relating to the Armenian Adam Books," *Journal for the Study of Pseudoepigrapha* 5 (1989), p. 106.

20 Cf. M.D. Johnson, "The Life of Adam and Eve," in J.H. Charlesworth, *The Old Testament Pseudepigrapha*, Vol. 2 (Garden City, N.Y., 1983), pp. 258, 260; cf. W. Dittenberger, *Sylloge Inscriptionum Graecarum*³ (Leipzig, 1920), Vol. 2, p. 112, para. 983 (Lindos): (second century CE), the prohibition of entering the temple for forty days after a miscarriage; see A.D. Nock, *Early Gentile Christianity and Its Hellenistic Background* (New York, 1964), pp. 17–18.

1. Kirchner, *Judisches Ceremoniel*

הַגָּדוֹל :
בָּרוּךְ אַתָּה יְיָ אֱלֹהֵינוּ מֶלֶךְ הָעוֹלָם ·
אֲשֶׁר קִדְּשָׁנוּ בְּמִצְוֹתָיו · ו
וְצִוָּנוּ עַל מִצְוַת חַלָּה :
סֵדֶר לְהַנָּדָה ·

הֲרֵינִי מוּכָן וּמְזוּמָן לְקַיֵּם הַמִּצְוָה ·
לְטַהֵר אוֹתִי לְבַעֲלִי · כְּמוֹ שֶׁצִּוָּה לָנוּ

**2. Aaron Wolf Herlingen. Israel
Museum, Jerusalem, 1739**

**3. Meshullam of Polna, 1751
Jewish Museum, Budapest**

Fig. VII. ~ *Von der Reinigung der Kindbetterinen* ~ *p. ch. 79.*

4. Bodenschatz, *Kirchliche Verfassung der heutigen Juden,* **Erlang 1748**

4

CIRCUMCISION ONLY WHILE STANDING?

The prominent Jerusalem *mohel* Rabbi Joseph Weisberg explains in his compendium on circumcision:[1]

> According to one view, the *mohel* [circumciser] is not fit to be the *sandak* [the person who holds the infant on his knees during the circumcision; commonly translated as "godfather"], while according to another opinion, he may fill this role.

In a note,[2] Weisberg cites *Peri Megadim*,[3] that the reason why the *mohel* should not also be the *sandak* is because the blessing for circumcision must be recited while standing,[4] and the *Ahronim* (later halakhic authorities) accordingly ruled that the *mohel* must stand while performing the circumcision; if the *mohel* is also the *sandak*, he cannot stand.[5] In another note,[6] Weisberg cites the opinion of R. Elijah ben Moses Zevi Posek, the author of *Koret ha-Berit*:

---

1 Rabbi Yosef David Weisberg, *Otzar Habrith: Encyclopedia of Brith Milah*, Vol. 1 (Jerusalem, 1986), p. 136, para. 14 (Hebrew).

2 Weisberg, loc. cit., n. 29.

3 *Peri Megadim, Mishbetzot Zahav*, para. 1, on *Shulhan Arukh, Orah Hayyim* 585.

4 Based on the "Palestinian Talmud" that is cited in *Beit Yosef* on *Tur, Orah Hayyim* 18 (and that is not in the extant editions of the PT), that all the blessings are to be recited while standing. See R. Joel Sirkes, *Bah* on *Orah Hayyim* 585:8; see also *Minhagei Yisrael*, Vol. 2, p. 82, that this is the Land of Israel practice, based on *Soferim* 13:8; 18:3; 21:5.

5 See Rabbi Elijah ben Moses Zevi Posek, *Koret ha-Berit* (Lvov, 1893).

6 Weisberg, loc. cit., n. 30.

We should not think that circumcision must be [performed while] standing, since in a case in which there is an obligation [to be performed] while sitting, such as this instance, in which he has been appointed *sandak*, it was not said that he must perform the circumcision while standing.[7]

This implies that the *mohel* is fundamentally required to stand while performing the circumcision.

Support for this obligation is apparently provided by the ruling by R. Abraham Klausner (died ca. 1408),[8] who states that "when an infant is circumcised, the law is [for the circumciser] to be standing," and brings as a proof-text: "And all of the people entered into [*va-ya'amod*, literally, "stood"] the covenant" (II Kings 23:3). Klausner's ruling is based on *Tashbetz* (first edn.: Cremona [1557]), by R. Samson ben Zadok (fourteenth century):[9]

One stands while circumcising the infant, and he brings a proof from "the people entered into [*va-ya'amod*, as above] the covenant"; and from the Talmud, for it is said in the chapter of "Rabbi Eliezer of circumcision" (BT Shabbat 137b): "The one performing the circumcision recites the blessing: 'Blessed are You, O Lord our God, King of the universe, who has sanctified us with His commandments, and has commanded us concerning circumcision,' and those **standing** there proclaim: 'Just as he has entered the covenant, so, too, may he enter into the Torah, the wedding canopy, and good deeds.'"

The requirement of standing is based on testimony (in the Prague edition of his responsa) concerning the practice of R. Meir of Rothenburg:[10]

He [R. Meir] would customarily stand during the reading of the Torah and [when] an infant was circumcised, and he brought a proof from the Bible: "the people entered into [*va-ya'amod*, as above] the covenant"; and a proof from "R[abbi] E[liezer] of circumcision": "The one performing the circumcision recites: 'Blessed [...] who has sanctified

---

7 See the complete discussion, Weisberg, loc. cit.

8 Rabbi Abraham Klausner, *Sefer Minhagim*, ed. Y.Y. Dissen (Jerusalem, 1978), para. 147, *Hagahah* (gloss) 3.

9 Rabbi Samson ben Zadok, *Tashbetz*, para. 396.

10 Rabbi Meir of Rothenburg, *She'eilot u-Teshuvot ma-ha-Ram mi-Rutenburg*, ed. M. Bloch (Budapest, 1898 [photocopy edition: Tel Aviv, 1969]), para. 504.

us with His commandments, and has commanded us,' and those **standing** there [proclaim]: 'Just as he has entered the covenant.'"[11]

R. Meir's proof, however, is based on a close reading of the wording "and those standing there proclaim," but this refers to the **congregation**, and not to the *mohel*, which also is implicit from the first part of this passage, that "he would customarily stand [...] and [when] an infant was circumcised" — not when he himself was the *mohel*, but when he was among the participants at the circumcision ceremony. This is also stated explicitly by R. Aaron ha-Kohen of Lunel (fourteenth century):[12]

From this [the wording of the *baraita* in BT Shabbat], R[abbi] M[eir], may he rest in peace, brought a proof that **the entire congregation** is to stand when the infant is circumcised [...] and he was accustomed to stand on his feet.[13]

Maharil (R. Jacob ben Moses Moellin) similarly mandates:[14] "When the infant is circumcised, the law is for **the public to stand**, as it is written, "And all the people entered into [*va-ya'amod*, as above] the covenant."[15]

11 Cited in R. Meir ben Baruch (*Maharam* of Rothenburg), *Teshuvot Pesakim ve-Minhagim ... me'et Yitzhak Ze'ev Kahana*, Vol. 2 (Jerusalem, 1960), pp. 260–61, para. 28, with a reference in the notes to *Mordekhai*, Shabbath 602, with additions in *Shiltei ha-Gibborim*, subsection 1, who brings a proof from PT Bikkurim 3:3, and concludes: "This is a proof that a person must **stand** before those engaged in the performance of a commandment." The statement of R. Meir of Rothenburg also appears in *Sefer Minhagim de-ve Maharam ... me-Rotenberg* (*Sefer Minhagim of the School of Rabbi Meir ben Baruch of Rothenburg*), ed. I. Elfenbein (New York, 1938), p. 80, and in the following sources. See S. Alpert, "Practices and Customs of His Honored Holiness, Our Master, the [author of] *Penei Menahem* of Gur, May the Memory of the Righteous and the Holy be for a Blessing, regarding Circumcision," *Ohr Torah* 3, 3 (11) (Nisan 1998), p. 143, para. 4, and n. 4 (Hebrew), for the practice of R. Pinhas Menahem Alter of Gur (the author of *Penei Menahem*), to immediately stand up when he saw the infant being brought in.
12 Rabbi Aaron ha-Kohen of Lunel, *Orhot Hayyim*, Vol. 2 (Berlin, 1902), *Hil. Milah* (*Laws of Circumcision*), para. 7, p. 8.
13 Cf. *Kol Bo* (Naples [1490]), para. 73, p. 42.
14 *Sefer Maharil* (*The Book of Maharil*), ed. S.J. Spitzer (Jerusalem, 1989), p. 479.
15 This also appears from a close reading of R. David Abudarham, *Abudarham ha-Shalem*, ed. S.A. Wertheimer (Jerusalem, 1963), *Hil. Berakhot* (*Laws of Blessings*), Sha'ar 9, p. 351: "They respond and stand there."

R. Jeruham[16] cites R. Meir of Rothenburg,[17] and then writes: "And it appears to be that this [standing] is not limited to the reading [of the Torah], for it is the way of the Talmud to say 'standing there,' even though people were sitting." Y.Z. Kahana[18] comments on the passage in *Tashbetz* 182:

> *Maharam* [R. Meir of Rothenburg], of blessed memory, would stand during the reading of the Torah, and cited the Book of Nehemiah (8:5): "as he opened it, all the people stood up"; according to the simple meaning, he actually stood.

Kahana observes[19] that the gloss by R. Peretz on *Tashbetz* states:

> The Talmud, however, interprets in Sotah [39a]: "stood up" — the intent is to silence; but sitting is permitted. This can also be understood from the Palestinian Talmud [Megillah 4:1], just as that one who was leaning during [his] reading [of the Torah]: "He said to him, It is forbidden for you [to lean]. As was its giving, so, too, is its reading: just as it was given in awe and while standing,[20] so, too, its reading

16 Rabbi Jeroham ben Meshullam, *Toledot Adam ve-Havvah* (Constantinople, 1516), *Netiv* 1, end of section 2, fol. 14c.

17 This should read ר"מ (= Rabbeinu Meir), and not רמ"ה (= R. Moses Isserles), as in the printed editions.

18 *Teshuvot Pesakim ve-Minhagim ... me'et Yitzhak Ze'ev Kahana*, Vol. 1 (Jerusalem, 1957), p. 161, para. 109.

19 Ibid., n. 2.

20 PT Megillah 4:1 teaches: "Just as it was given in awe and fear, so, too, we are required to relate to it with awe and fear," with no mention of any requirement to stand. The PT similarly asserts that this refers to "someone standing **and serving as translator**, leaning on a column"; see the note by Kahana ad loc. Rabbi Baer Ratner, *Ahavat Tziyyon ve-Yerushalayim* (*Ahawath Zion we-Jeruscholaim*) (Vilna, 1912), pp. 80–81, brings accounts by *Rishonim* (albeit mostly paraphrases, and not direct quotations) that this refers to the **reading of the Torah**. Rabbi I. Tamar, *Alei Tamar, Moed*, Vol. 3 (Alon Shevut, 1995), p. 151 (Hebrew): "Even according to our version, the law [that one must stand] is to be learned from the law of the translator; how much more so [as regarding circumcision]." Tamar also cites Rabbi Jacob of Vienna, *Peshatim u-Perushim* (Mainz, 1888), *Vaethanan*: "It is preferable to be careful than to find support from the reading of the Torah; and similarly, it is written, regarding prayer: 'Phinehas stood up and prayed' (Ps. 106:30), and in PT: Just as its giving was while standing, as it is written: 'And all of the people entered into [*va-ya'amod*, literally, "stood"].'" R. Tamar observed that this passage from the PT is not extant.

is in awe and while standing."[21] This means specifically that the one reading from the Torah must stand, while the others are permitted to sit, as was his [i.e. R. Meir's] custom.

Tur[22] rules: "One must **bless while standing**, as we learn from [the analogous wording] "*lakhem* [you] — *lakhem* [you]," which *Perishah* explains:

> For it is written, regarding circumcision, "every male among you [*lakhem*] shall be circumcised" [Gen. 17:10]; regarding the *Omer* [sheaves], it is written, "And you [*lakhem*] shall count off seven weeks" [Lev. 23:15]; and there [regarding the *Omer*] it is written, "when the sickle is first put to the standing grain [*ba-kamah*]" [Deut. 16:9] — do not read *ba-kamah* [to the standing grain], but *ba-komah* [while standing].

The glosses and notes on *Tur*[23] give *Pesikta Zutarta* by R. Tobias[24] as the source of this exposition, but R. Moses Isserles[25] formulates this as follows: "The father and the *mohel*, when blessing, must stand (*Tur* and *Beit Yosef*, in the name of the author of *Ha-Ittur*)." It is known that Isserles himself

As to whether the *Targum* is to be rendered while standing or sitting, see what Tamar, loc. cit., writes, based on *Seder R. Saadiah Gaon* (Jerusalem, 1941), p. 360: "Neither the reader nor the one rendering the *Targum* may lean against a wall or a column," based on this passage from the PT. Yemenite Jews, however, render the *Targum* while sitting, as Kahana, loc. cit., writes. Rabbi Y. Kafih, *Jewish Life in Sana* (Jerusalem, 1963), p. 68 (Hebrew), does not mention this practice, but attests, to the contrary: "a youth **stands** [...] and recites *Targum Onkelos* after the [Torah] reading"; and, similarly, in J. Saphir, *Masa Teman* (*Yemen Journey*), ed. A. Ya'ari (Jerusalem, 1945), p. 10.

21 For standing during the reading of the Torah, see *Minhagei Yisrael*, Vol. 1, p. 89; Vol. 2, pp. 83, 113, 262–63, 309.

22 *Tur, Yoreh Deah* 265.

23 *Tur*, ed. Machon Yerushalayim (Jerusalem, 1993), p. 101 n. 19. We should add the recent comprehensive discussion in E.Y. Gur-Aryeh, *Chikrai Minhagim: Sources, Reasons, and Studies in Habad Practice* (Kfar Habad, 1999), pp. 62–71 (Hebrew).

24 R. Tobias ben Eliezer, *Pesikta Zutarta* (first edn.: Vilna, 1880), end of *Lekh Lekha* (end of the laws of circumcision); *Emor* (end of the para. "*Ad mi-Maharat* [the day after]"); end of *Shelah*. Also attributed to *Pesikta Zutarta* in *Ha-Ittur, Hil. Tzitzit*, fol. 76d; and in *Shibbolei ha-Leket, Hil. Milah* (*Laws of Circumcision*), para. 4. See also the introduction to *Pesikta de-Rav Kahana*, ed. Buber (Vilna, 1925), pp. 4–7; see *Tur, Yoreh Deah* 265.

25 *Rema* on *Shulhan Arukh, Yoreh Deah* 265:1.

did not provide any references, and these were added by one of the many individuals engaged in the publication of Isserles's glosses.[26] *Tur* relates to the blessing by the **father** that must be recited while standing, for he writes (loc. cit.): "The father of the son recites the blessing [...] and he must recite the blessing while standing." *Beit Yosef* gives *Ha-Ittur* as the source,[27] but the latter speaks of the blessing by the *mohel*.[28] At any rate, by combining the rulings in *Tur* and *Beit Yosef*, we learn that those reciting the blessing during the circumcision ceremony must stand while doing so.

Tur then cites R. Meir of Rothenburg (as related in *Mordekhai*[29]), who speaks of the practice of the entire congregation. Based on the latter, R. Moses Isserles writes: "According to one opinion, all in attendance at the circumcision stand, as it is said, 'And [all of] the people entered into [*va-ya'amod*, literally, "stood"] the covenant'; this is the practice, with the exception of the person holding the infant, who sits." The Vilna Gaon wrote on this:[30] "'According to one opinion....' And as it is written in the Talmud, they stand there.... **All this is merely a stringency**!" In other words, we have not found any early source that explicitly requires the *mohel* to stand **while performing the circumcision**, that is not necessarily time-congruent with the recitation of the blessing that the *mohel* recites **immediately preceding** the performance of the commandment of circumcision.[31]

26 This is absent from the first edition of the *Shulhan Arukh* with the glosses of *Rema* (Cracow, 1578–80); see *Minhagei Yisrael*, Vol. 2, p. 283, and the references there. See also the recent *Shulhan Arukh, Orah Hayyim*, ed. Machon Yerushalayim, Vol. 1 (Jerusalem, 1994), Introduction, pp. 35–36, which states that the references first appear in the Cracow 1608–09 edition.

27 *Ha-Ittur, Hil. Milah* (*Laws of Circumcision*), Part 4, fol. 54d; *Hil. Tzitzit, Sha'ar* 3, Part 2, fol. 76d.

28 See the glosses and notes in *Tur, Yoreh Deah* 265:18.

29 *Mordekhai*, Shabbat, chap. 19, para. 882.

30 In his commentary on *Yoreh Deah* 265, para. 5.

31 See the rules of circumcision of his father Jacob, committed to writing by Rabbi Gershom ben Jacob ha-Gozer, *Zikhron Berit le-Rishonim*, ed. Rabbi Jacob Glassberg (Cracow, 1892), p. 79: "The blessing must be recited prior to the cutting of the foreskin [based on BT Pesahim 7b]." P. 80 n. 1 cites *Rif* (R. Isaac Alfasi), *Hil. Tzitzit*, fol. 87b: "The blessing for a commandment whose implementation is upon the conclusion of the action must be recited at the beginning of the action, such as circumcision." The editor adds: "This requires further study, and perhaps we should say: If he did not recite the blessing beforehand, he may do so during the entire act." The difficulty that Glassberg finds here is puzzling. Weisberg, *Otzar Habrith*,

R. Akiva Eiger (1761–1837) writes in his novellae on *Yoreh Deah*:[32]

> One must stand when reciting a blessing, **and circumcision itself must be performed while standing**; see *Bah* (*Orah Hayyim* 8): When the infant is brought to be circumcised, they are required to stand before

Vol. 1, p. 146, cites Rabbi Abraham Danzig, *Hokhmat Adam*, para. 149, who wrote that the *mohel* does not begin the circumcision until he has completed the recitation of the blessing, unlike the *mohalim* who exhibit their alacrity by cutting as soon as they begin the blessing, which is an act based in ignorance. And, likewise, in Rabbi Zevi Elimelech Schapira of Dynow, *Derekh Pikudekha* (Lvov, 1851), cited in *Otzar Habrith*, loc. cit., n. 42, who explains that the blessing is to be recited after the cutting, immediately preceding the *peri'ah* (the uncovering of the corona), because the cutting is not the completion of the commandment. R. Simeon ben Zemah Duran, *She'eilot u-Teshuvot ha-Tashbetz* (first edn.: Amsterdam, 1638), Vol. 2, para. 277: "since he performed the circumcision [i.e. cut] but did not perform *peri'ah*, it is as if he has not performed the circumcision, and he recites the blessing [after the cutting] before the *peri'ah*, and this is [considered to be the fulfillment of the rule that a blessing for a certain act must be recited] 'immediately prior to their performance'" (i.e. of this commandment); also cited in Rabbi Jehiel Michal Epstein, *Arukh ha-Shulhan, Yoreh Deah* 265:10. Epstein further notes, after having written that the blessing apparently is to be recited prior to the circumcision, that there is no complaint against those *mohalim* who recite the blessing while cutting (in contrast with the view of *Hokhmat Adam*); on the contrary, they act well, firstly since **they conclude the blessing at the completion of the cutting**, which is immediately prior to the performance of the act, as with the "*Ha-Motzi*" ("... Who has brought forth bread ...") blessing, which is concluded upon the completion of cutting the bread, as is said in BT Berakhot 39a: "The bread with the conclusion of the blessing," implying that the cut is to be made with the conclusion of the blessing. This is confirmed by Bodenschatz, *Kirchliche Verfassung der heutigen Juden, sonderlich derer in Deutschland*, Vol. 4, p. 63, para. 19: "Indem er de letzen Worte sagt, so schneidet er zugleich die Vorhaut." In other words, Bodenschatz knew that the practice was to make the cut while reciting the last word of the blessing (unlike the view of J. Buxtorf, *Synagoga Judaica*[3] [Basel, 1712; first edition in German, entitled *Juden Schul*, 1603], p. 97, who maintains that the cut is made following the blessing). If so, then the *mohel* had to stand while performing the circumcision, since this was also the time of the blessing (see below). Note should also be taken of the disagreement among the *Rishonim* (medieval authorities) as to when the father of the infant recites his blessing: following the recitation of the blessing by the *mohel*, or does the father recite his blessing first, then to be followed by the *mohel*? If the former, does the father's blessing follow the circumcision or precede it? This issue is the subject of a lengthy and thorough discussion by Rabbi Jacob Werdiger, *Edut le-Yisrael*[2] (Bnei Brak, 1965), pp. 123–24.

32 R. Akiva Eiger, in his novellae on the *Shulhan Arukh, Yoreh Deah* 265.

them; [R. Obadiah] Bertinoro (Bikkurim 3:3); see *Turei Zahav* below (368:2).

An examination of the passage in *Bah*, however, reveals that his ruling relates to standing **at the time of the blessing**; moreover, the mishnah in Bikkurim to which Eiger refers:[33] "And all the craftsmen in Jerusalem stand before them [those bringing the first fruits], and greet them" refers solely to the congregation that stands before those engaged in the performance of a commandment, and not to those performing it themselves.[34]

All the above sources indicate that there is no early source that clearly mandates that, after reciting the blessing, the *mohel* must stand while performing the circumcision itself. We shall discuss a number of issues relating to circumcision,[35] and we have reproduced a number of illustrations that depict the circumcision ceremony:[36] in some of these depictions, the *mohel* is standing while performing his task (such as Figs. 1–4),[37] while in the others, the *mohel* performs the act of circumcision on bended knees (as in Figs. 5–10).[38] The latter kneeling position is also assumed by the *mohel* in an early illuminated manuscript from the thirteenth century (Fig. 11),[39] and in an additional manuscript that portrays a circumcision (Fig. 12).[40] The

33 And the passage from the PT mentioned above (n. 11).

34 Those bringing the first fruits apparently walked (and, therefore, were standing upright) when they entered Jerusalem, as we might possibly understand from a close reading of PT Bikkurim 3:2: "On the way they would proclaim: 'I rejoiced when they said to me, "We are going [*nelekh*, i.e. walking] to the house of the Lord"' [Ps. 122:1]. [Once] inside Jerusalem, they would declare, 'Our feet stood inside your gates, O Jerusalem' [ibid., v. 2]." Those participating in the pilgrimage festivals, however, would also enter the city riding on beasts or in carriages. See the definitive treatment by S. Safrai, *Pilgrimage at the Time of the Second Temple* (Jerusalem, 1985), pp. 113–14, 120 (Hebrew).

35 See below, chaps. 8, 9, and 11.

36 Ibid.

37 Fig. 1, from *Sefer ha-Mohalim* (*The Book of* Mohalim) (Vienna, 1728); Fig. 2, from MS. Naples (fifteenth century); Figs. 3–4, from *Amsterdam Minhagim Book* (1662), *Amsterdam Minhagim Book* (1708).

38 Fig. 5, by Romeyn de Hooghe (Holland, 1665); Fig. 6, by Bernard Picart (Amsterdam, 1722); Fig. 7, from Bodenschatz, *Kirchliche Verfassung der heutigen Juden* (1748); Figs. 7–8, from Paul Christian Kirchner, *Judisches Ceremoniel* (Nuremberg, 1724); Fig. 9, from Leusden, *Philologus Hebraeo-Mixtus*[2] (Utrecht, 1682); Fig. 10, MS. Budapest (Germany, fifteenth century).

39 From a thirteenth-century German manuscript (MS. Budapest).

mohel is also sitting in Christian depictions of the circumcision of Jesus, which undoubtedly were influenced by Jewish practice (Figs. 13–15).[41]

The chair on which the *sandak* sits as he holds the infant in his arms[42] seems to be of regular height, and so it was more comfortable for the *mohel* to kneel during the circumcision, as we see in the above illustrations. *Mohelim* who preferred to stand also had to bend their knees while actually engaged in the circumcision (see Fig. 16),[43] possibly because they did not want to kneel, which was a non-Jewish posture.[44] The later procedure, which was formulated

40 MS. Fermo, Biblioteca Palatina 3596, fol. 267r; appearing in T. and M. Metzger, *Jewish Life in the Middle Ages: Illuminated Hebrew Manuscripts of the Thirteenth to the Sixteenth Centuries* (New York, 1982), p. 223, no. 332. Many more such examples could be mentioned, such as the title page of *Seder Berakhot* (Amsterdam, 1687), in which the *mohel* is kneeling on one bended knee (see Fig. 13). This illustration is reproduced in R. Porter and S. Harel-Hoshen (eds.), *Odyssey of the Exiles: The Sephardi Jews 1492–1992* (Tel Aviv, 1992), no. 56.

41 Fig. 14, by Hans Leonhard Schaufelein (ca. 1480–1538/40), based on Fig. 15, by Albrecht Dürer, ca. 1505. See W. Kurth (ed.), *The Complete Woodcuts of Albrecht Dürer* (New York, 1963), p. 184. This is not to say that the artist personally witnessed a Jewish circumcision, but that he had indirect knowledge of the ceremony. For the knowledge of Jewish customs possessed by Christians, see below, chap. 26, n. 66. Interestingly, they knew that the circumcision was performed over a certain vessel, but they seemingly were unaware of the contents of this vessel: water, earth (or perhaps it was empty); they apparently thought that the sole purpose of this vessel was to collect the blood. Bodenschatz, Vol. 4, the illustration facing p. 69; p. 62, subsection 9; p. 64, subsection 12, speaks of the "Sand schussel." See below, chap. 4.

42 We should note here the evidence that some communities, in addition to the Chair of Elijah, also had a special chair for the *sandak*. The source for this custom is in the *Zohar, Lekh Lekha* (1:932): "And for this we have learned that a person is required to prepare **another** chair for his honor." See also *Mahzor Vitri*, Vol. 2, p. 625, which prescribes: "One prepares two chairs, and covers them with a cloak or any kind of ornamental covering, one for the use of Elijah, who comes to sit and watch the carrying out of the commandment." This was also the practice in Tunisia. See Rabbi David Settbon, *Kunteres Alei Hadas: Collection of Halakhic Practices of the Jewish Community of Tunis* (Jerusalem, 2003), chap. 18, para. 2, p. 163 (Hebrew). See also R. Jacoby, "The Relation between the Elijah's Chair and Sandak's (Godfather's) Chair," *Rimonim* 5 (1997), pp. 43–53 (Hebrew); *idem*, "The Small Elijah Chair," *Jewish Art* 18 (1992), pp. 70–77. See also Y. Leben, "Customs Pertaining to the Elijah's Chair in the Jewish Communities of Southern Tunisia," *Rimonim* 5 (1997), pp. 54–55 (Hebrew).

43 See above, n. 37.

44 This issue was discussed at length in the excellent work by E. Zimmer, *Society and*

under the influence of *poskim* among the *Ahronim*, such as R. Akiva Eiger and others, called for the mohel to stand during the circumcision. This might possibly be related to the practice, as we have seen, for the cut to be made at the conclusion of the blessing; since the blessing is recited while standing, the act of the circumcision itself must also be performed in this stance.[45] To facilitate the labor of the circumcision for the *mohel*, a special high chair was fashioned for the *sandak*, who had a pillow placed on his lap to further elevate the infant,[46] thus enabling the *mohel* to comfortably and safely perform the circumcision, even while fully erect.[47]

The fashion of standing during the circumcision spread throughout most Jewish communities, from Iraq in the east to Morocco in the west. Among Yemenite Jewry, which meticulously preserves early practices, the *mohel* would sit on the ground with his legs folded under him, with the *sandak* sitting before him on a thick cushion.[48]

> *Its Customs* (Jerusalem, 1996), pp. 88–97; see esp. pp. 96–97 and n. 141 (Hebrew). Possibly in the period when kneeling was not stringently prohibited, the *mohel* would perform his task in this position for his own comfort, thus obviating the need for a high chair, pillows, etc. Conversely, in localities and in periods in which kneeling was frowned upon (and in accordance with the practice of R. Isaac Luria, who would not kneel; see Zimmer, op. cit., p. 97 n. 145), the *mohel* stood and the chair was elevated; this, however, remains in the realm of conjecture.

45 See above, n. 31.

46 See, e.g., R.D. Barnett, *Catalogue of the Permanent and Loan Collections of the Jewish Museum* (London, 1974), Ill. no. 503: a double chair at a height of 50 inches; *Manumenta Judaica Katalog* (Cologne, 1964), fig. 29, no. E.111: a double chair 153 cm. high (eighteenth century); see also L. Bialer and E. Fink, *Jewish Life in Art and Tradition: from the Collection of the Sir Isaac and Lady Edith Wolfson Museum, Hechal Shlomo, Jerusalem*[2] (Jerusalem, 1980), p. 75 (Fig. 17): the eighteenth-century chair in the Wolfson Museum in Hechal Shlomo, Jerusalem, with the inscription: *"Hevrat ba'alei berit Avraham* [the society of the members of the covenant of Abraham]"; the *sandak* sits in an elevated position, with his feet resting on a sort of small shelf.

47 See, e.g., the paintings by R. Uri Phoebus (Fig. 18).

48 See, e.g., A. Ben-Jacob, *Minhagei Yehudei Bavel ba-Dorot ha-Ahronim (Customs of Iraqi Jewry in Recent Generations)*, Vol. 1 (Jerusalem, 1993), p. 39, based on *Sefer Tzorkhei Huppah ve-Milah (The Book of Wedding Ceremony and Circumcision Needs)* (Baghdad, 1892), p. 7. For the practice in Morocco, see Ben Naim, *Noheg be-Hokhmah*, p. 116, para. 12. Incidental to the discussion of circumcision, note should be paid to the conception (below, chap. 6, "Circumcision as a Form of Sacrifice") that this ceremony is a form of sacrifice.

1. *Sefer ha-Mohalim*, Vienna 1728, Ms. Prague 243

2. Circumcision, Ms. from Naples, end of 15th century, Carné Art Bibliothèque, Nîmes, Ms. 13, fol. 181v

3. Circumcision
Sefer ha-Minhagim, Amsterdam 1682

4. Circumcision
Sefer ha-Minhagim, Frankfurt 1708

5. Circumcision, Romayn de Hooghe, Rijksmuseum, Amsterdam 1665

6. Circumcision, Picard, Amsterdam 1722

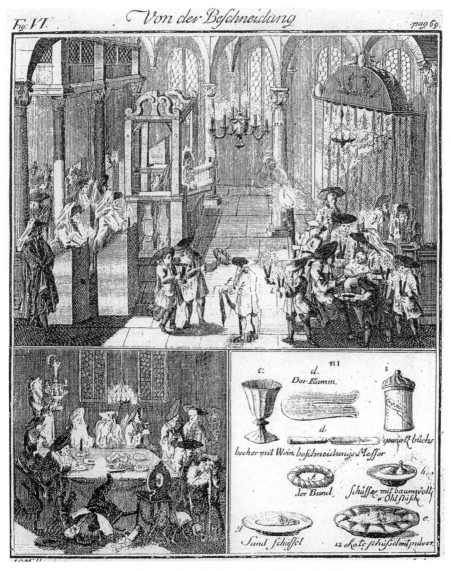

7. Circumcision, Bodenschatz, Erlang 1748

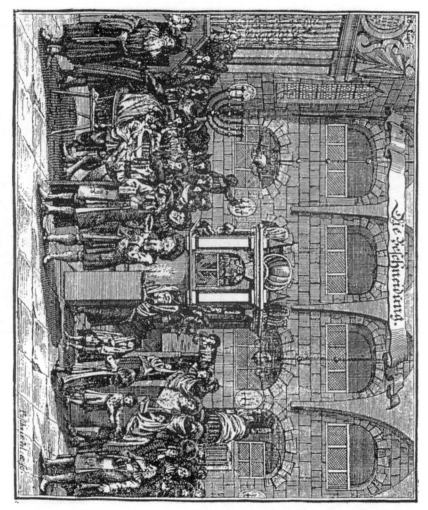

8. Circumcision, Kirchner, Nuremberg 1724

9. Circumcision, Leusden, Utrecht 1682

**10. Circumcision, Germany, early 15th century
Budapest, Hungarian Academy of Sciences,
Ms. A 383f. 40v**

11. Circumcision, 13th century

12. Circumcision, Ms. Parma Bibl. Palatina 3596, c. 267r Ministry for Cultural Assets and Activities

13. *Seder Berachot* **Amsterdam 1678**

14. Circumcision, Hans Leonard Schauflein ca. 1550

15. Circumcision, Dürer 1505

16. Circumcision
Sefer ha-Mohalim,
Vienna 1728

17. Circumcision Chair,
18th century

18. Circumcision, Uri Feibusch 1741

5

CIRCUMCISION OVER EARTH OR OVER WATER

In the preceding chapter we saw how halakhic authorities, the parties to disagreements, rejected the practices of the opposing authority. This rivalry between competing views and practices is brought into clear focus in the diatribe by Pirkoi ben Baboi, a pupil of Rav Yehudai Gaon (who was the Gaon in Sura, 760–64 CE), who sought to persuade the Jews of the Land of Israel to abandon their custom, the "custom of apostasy" (which was a result of their inability to study properly, due to anti-Jewish persecutions), and adopt in its place the practice observed in Babylonia, even in matters of mere custom, and not points of actual law. An example of these differences between the two centers relates to the manner of performing circumcision: those in the Land of Israel did so over earth, while the Babylonians were accustomed to performing circumcisions over water.[1] R. Yehudai Gaon

---

1   See L. Ginzberg, *Genizah Studies in Memory of Doctor Solomon Schechter*, Vol. 2 (New York, 1929), pp. 563–64, and Ginzberg's explanation, pp. 541–42 (Hebrew). See *Ha-Hillukim she-bein Anshei ha-Mizrah u-Benei Eretz Israel* (*The Differences between the People of the East and Those of the Land of Israel*), ed. M. Margoliouth (Margulies), (Jerusalem, 1938), para. 17, pp. 80–81, and the clarification by Margoliouth, pp. 125–26. See also, most recently, S. Elizur's critical edition: *The Liturgical Poems of Rabbi Pinhas Ha-Kohen* (Jerusalem, 2004), p. 222, where she notes that he writes in his "Grace after Meals for the Sabbath and Circumcision" (p. 737, no. 134, l. 8): "Sand for the Sabbath is prepared for the child," meaning that sand for the circumcision is prepared in advance, before the Sabbath. Cf. *Tur* and *Beit Yosef, Yoreh Deah* 265, for the need to prepare the earth in advance. For the question of whether earth or sand should be used, see Elizur, p. 222 n. 3, and the sources she cites.

writes in a responsum regarding this difference, that it is immaterial and has no source in either of the Talmuds:[2]

> As to your query, of [whether to] circumcise a newborn over sand or over water, and to bring the infant to the synagogue: this is inconsequential, and neither [custom] entails a prohibition, that [would require] us to order them to alter their practice.

His zealous pupil Pirkoi ben Baboi, on the other hand, found five severe transgressions(!) in the Land of Israel practice:

> And whoever does not do so [i.e. follow the Babylonian custom] commits five transgressions: one, because [the Land of Israel custom entails] danger, because hot water is not placed over the male while he is being circumcised; the second, that he demeans the blood of circumcision; the third, that he presses against the wall [i.e. he places the foreskin into the earth, and then presses it into a crack in the wall] on the Sabbath; and these are archetypes of work [prohibited on the Sabbath] for [the commission of which] one is liable to be stoned.[3]

Our wonder at the sharp words expressed by Pirkoi ben Baboi is somewhat lessened by the discovery of the Torah scholar and researcher Dov Revel,[4] who showed that the early Land of Israel practice of circumcising over earth, which is mentioned in *Pirkei de-Rabbi Eliezer*,[5] was based on the

2 *Teshuvot ha-Geonim: Sha'arei Tzedek* (Jerusalem, 1966), Vol. 3, *Sha'ar* 5, p. 51, paras. 10–11. See *Ha-Hillukim she-bein Anshei ha-Mizrah u-Benei Eretz Israel*, p. 126.

3 Ginzberg, *Genizah Studies*, loc. cit.; *Ha-Hillukim she-bein Anshei ha-Mizrah u-Benei Eretz Israel*, p. 126 n. 7. For the following subject in *Genizah Studies*, pp. 564–66, concerning the fast days of the Ten Days of Repentance, to which Pirkoi ben Baboi was vehemently opposed, see Y. Gartner, "Fasting on Rosh Hashanah," *Hadorom* 36 (1973), pp. 125–62 (Hebrew); *idem*, "The Jewish Precedent for the Islamic Fast of Ramadan," *Sinai* 103 (1989), pp. 261–72 (Hebrew).

4 D. Revel, "The Renewal of Ordination Four Hundred Years Ago," *Horeb* 6 (1942), pp. 9–11 (Hebrew).

5 *Pirkei de-Rabbi Eliezer*, chap. 29, ed. Rabbi David Luzzatto, fol. 66a: "Hence the Sages instituted that the foreskin and the blood should be covered with the dust of the earth. [...] When Balaam came, he said, 'Who can count the dust of Jacob' [Num. 23:10]. Moreover, [Israel] is compared to dust, as it is said, 'Your descendants shall be as the dust of the earth' [Gen. 28:14]." Cf. *Targum Yerushalmi* to Num. 23:10: "And when Balaam saw that [even] the wicked ones of the House of Israel were

idea that circumcision is as important as the offering of a sacrifice; the blood of circumcision is equated with the blood of sacrifices, and circumcision is performed over earth, in place of the earthen altar. This concept is also to be found in *Pirkei de-Rabbi Eliezer*:[6]

> "The sailors [correct reading: men] feared the Lord greatly; they offered a sacrifice to the Lord" [Jonah 1:16] — did they offer a sacrifice? For a sacrifice from idolaters is not accepted! Rather, this refers to **the blood of circumcision, that is like the blood of a sacrifice**."

And, again:[7]

> When Isaac was born, when he was eight days old, [Abraham] brought him for circumcision, as it is said: "And when his son Isaac was eight days old, Abraham circumcised him" [Gen. 21:4], and he brought him for an offering on the altar.

This concept also is expressed in *Tanya Rabbati*:[8]

> Whoever presents his son for circumcision is as the *kohen*, who presents an offering on the altar.[9]

And, again, in *Pirkei de-Rabbi Eliezer*:[10]

> And on the day when Israel went forth from Egypt all the people were circumcised. [...] They would take the blood of circumcision and the blood of the Paschal lamb, and they would put it on the lintel of their houses. When the Holy One, blessed be He, passed over to smite the Egyptians, and He saw the blood of circumcision and the blood of the Paschal lamb, He was filled with compassion for Israel, as it is said, "When I passed by you and saw you wallowing in your blood, I said

cutting off the foreskins and burying them in the sand of the desert" (he realized how blameless Israel was, in fact).

6 *Pirkei de-Rabbi Eliezer*, chap. 10, ed. Luzzatto, fol. 26b.
7 Chap. 29, ed. Luzzatto, fol. 65a.
8 *Tanya Rabbati* (first edn.: Cremona, 1565), end of para. 96 (in the name of "*Baraita de-Rabbi Eliezer*").
9 Cf. *Shibbolei ha-Leket, Hil. Milah* (*Laws of Circumcision*), para. 9, p. 377. See the gloss by Luzzatto, para. 41.
10 Chap. 29, ed. Luzzatto, fol. 65a.

to you: 'Live in spite of your blood.' Yea, I said to you: 'Live in spite of your blood'" [Ezek. 16:6].[11]

This same concept is reiterated, in slightly altered form, in a different passage in *Pirkei de-Rabbi Eliezer*:[12]

> And in the same place where Abraham underwent circumcision and his blood remained, there the altar was built. Accordingly, it is said: "and all the rest of its blood he shall pour out at the base of the altar" [Lev. 4:30, 34].

The dashing of the blood of circumcision against the lintel of the house is also mentioned by *Targum Jonathan* to Ex. 12:13:

> And the blood of the Paschal lamb, and [the blood from] the cutting of the foreskin are mingled, to make the sign on the houses which you inhabit, and I will see the merit of the blood, and I will spare you.

This idea was adopted by Anan, the founder of the Karaite sect, who equated the circumcision of a minor with the sacrifice of a small beast (i.e. a sheep or goat), and the circumcision of an adult with the sacrifice of a large animal (i.e. an ox), and the child is to be set aside for two days, as is the *tamid* offering;[13] the utensil used to perform the circumcision is like the service vessels in the Temple, and can be fashioned only by an Israelite;[14] and the foreskin must be salted and coated with oil, as for an animal sacrifice and a meal-offering.[15] When Pirkoi ben Baboi spoke of the foreskin being "pressed

---

11 Just as the blood, and later the *mezuzah*, were protective measures, so, too, the cross on the lintel fulfilled a similar function in Christian society. See J.C. Lawson, *Modern Greek Folklore and Ancient Greek Religion: A Study in Survivals*[2] (New York, 1965), p. 140: "The means by which women most commonly protect themselves on these occasions are the wearing of amulets; the fastening of a bunch of garlic over the house-door; the painting of a cross in black upon the lintel (this custom may be a Christianized form of the ancient practice, mentioned by Photius, of smearing houses with pitch on the birth of children as a means of driving away powers of evil). ..." This would appear to be based on the Judaic (biblical) tradition, rather than the Greek one.

12 *Pirkei de-Rabbi Eliezer*, chap. 29, ed. Luzzatto, fol. 62a.

13 J.N. Epstein, "New Fragments of *Sefer ha-Mizwot* of Anan," *Tarbiz* 7 (1936), pp. 285–86 (Hebrew).

14 *Sefer ha-Mitzvot le-Anan*, pub. A. Harkavy (St. Petersburg, 1903), pp. 75–76, 78, 83.

15 Ibid., p. 84.

against the wall," he probably was referring to the dashing of the blood of circumcision also on the doorpost. This Land of Israel practice could possibly have been influenced by the Karaite teaching that regarded circumcision as a sort of sacrifice (the Paschal lamb). Although this custom has its origins in early Land of Israel teachings, its adoption by the Karaites led to strange practices. The Geonim of Babylonia, who were apprehensive that the Land of Israel practice would be influenced by this Karaite philosophy, sought to completely cancel the practice of conducting circumcision over earth, as well as the dashing of the blood of circumcision, to distance the Jews of the Land of Israel from any possible Karaite inclination.[16]

Despite these disapproving statements by the Geonim, the Land of Israel tradition proved more durable than the rulings of the Babylonian Pirkoi ben Baboi. *Maharshal* (Rabbi Solomon ben Jehiel Luria) already questioned this:[17]

> And another question: We follow the Babylonians, both in leniencies and in severities; why should we not follow their practice? It is difficult, however, to overturn the practice of placing it [the foreskin] in the sand.

The practice of covering the foreskin in sand was accepted in several lands.[18] Some authorities attempted to establish a compromise that drew upon both customs:[19]

> Now sand is taken, **in accordance with both views**, for sand is called [both] earth and water.[20]

This was formulated even more plainly in *Sefer Mitzvot Katan* (Zurich):[21]

16 See ibid., p. 85: "When we circumcise him, we wash the blood with water." This, however, refers to the washing of the penis.
17 *Yam shel Shlomo*, Yevamot, end of 8:7.
18 *Or Zarua*, Vol. 2, *Hil. Milah* (*Laws of Circumcision*), para. 107; *Mahzor Vitri*, p. 626; Abudarham, ed. Wertheimer, *Hil. Birkat Milah* (*Laws of the Circumcision Blessing*), and more.
19 See *Minhagei Yisrael*, Vol. 2, chap. 2 ("Compromise in Custom"), pp. 23–75.
20 R. Eliezer ben Samuel of Metz, *Sefer Yere'im* (Vilna, 1892), para. 402, fol. 222a; *Hagahot Maimoniyot*, end of *Hil. Milah* (*Laws of Circumcision*); Rabbi Menahem ben Benjamin Recanati, *Piskei Recanati* (Bologna, 1538), para. 599.
21 *Semak mi-Zurikh*, ed. Y.Y. Har-Shoshanim-Rosenberg, Vol. 2 (Jerusalem, 1977), Commandment 154, p. 46.

It is stated in *Pirkei de-Rabbi Eliezer* (chapter twenty-nine) that "who can count the dust of Jacob" [Num. 23:10]. He saw that the entire wilderness was filled with the foreskins of Israel, and therefore it is the practice of the world [i.e. universal Jewish practice] to perform circumcision in [i.e. over] sand. And, additionally, because those in the East disagreed with those in the West: the Easterners say [to perform circumcision] in [above] earth, and the Westerners say, with water. **Consequently, it is the practice of the world to perform it over mud, in accordance with both views**.

Esoteric allusions to this are also to be found by employing numerology.[22] As R. Jacob ben Asher, the author of the *Turim*, writes on Num. 23:10:

The numerical value of עפר (earth) is the same as ערלה בחול (foreskin in sand). Why? Because the foreskin is placed in the sand.[23]

This is given as the law in the *Shulhan Arukh*:

The foreskin is placed in sand and earth.[24]

Over the course of time, different reasons have been offered for this practice. See, e.g., *Levush on Yoreh Deah* 265:10:

It is customary to place the foreskin in sand and earth as a [symbolic] sign, for it is written: "I will make your offspring as the sands of the sea" [Gen. 32:13]; and [regarding] earth, for it is written: "I will make your offspring as the dust of the earth" [Gen. 13:16]. I heard [an additional] reason, because it is written: "If your enemy is hungry, give him bread to eat" [Prov. 25:21], it is written, regarding the serpent: "and the serpent's food shall be earth" [Isa. 65:25], and sand is also earth; and you already know, by the esoteric knowledge of the Kabbalah, that the foreskin is from the element of the serpent. Consequently, it is placed in the earth, to give it bread and to shut its

---

22 See *Minhagei Yisrael*, Vol. 2, chap. 8 ("Numerology as a Factor in the Determination of the Liturgical Text and the Formation of Customs"), pp. 157–98.

23 The Jews of Salonika would perform circumcision over a box filled with earth; see Molho, "Birth and Childhood among the Jews of Salonica," p. 261.

24 *Shulhan Arukh, Yoreh Deah* 265:10; see *Ha-Hillukim she-bein Anshei ha-Mizrah u-Benei Eretz Israel*, pp. 126–27.

mouth from raising accusations [i.e. against Israel], in the manner of the mysterium of Azazel; understand this.

An additional reason for having the foreskin fall into earth is given in *Olelot Efrayim*:[25]

> For, according to the nature of all Creation, every element of man will return to its origin [i.e. "dust to dust"], for the material came from the earth, and to it it shall return. Thus His wisdom, may He be blessed, decreed, that every element shall return to its root. Consequently, by this placing a covenant is made with all bodies, that they shall return to be dust. Accordingly, the body of the righteous one is not, Heaven forbid, superior to that of the wicked.

Incidentally, R. Yehudai Gaon writes in his responsum:

> But we are accustomed to boiled water containing myrtles and spices from which a very fine aroma exudes. The infant is circumcised over the water, so that the blood of circumcision will fall into the water, that is used to wash all those *na'arim* [youths; should be *noadim* — those present], this is the blood of the covenant between the Omnipresent and the Patriarch Abraham, may he rest in peace.[26]

And in the rules of rules of circumcision by Rabbi Gershom ben Jacob ha-Gozer:[27]

> I found in *Ma'asei ha-Geonim* that the ancient ones would cast the foreskin and the blood into a vessel containing water and spices, and the congregation leaving the synagogue would wash their hands and their faces, to show their affection for the commandment.

---

25 R. Ephraim of Luntshits, *Olelot Ephrayim* (Amsterdam, 1710), fol. 92a (Vol. 3, para. 439).

26 And, likewise, in R. Abraham ben Nathan of Lunel, *Sefer Ha-Manhig*, ed. Y. Raphael (Jerusalem, 1978), *Hil. Milah* (*Laws of Circumcision*), para. 123, pp. 980–81; cf. *Ha-Ittur, Hil. Milah*, and more. See the references by Raphael, p. 580, on l. 42; see also B.M. Lewin, *Otzar ha-Gaonim*, Vol. 2 (Haifa, 1930), Shabbath, Responsa, para. 383, pp. 123–24. Vestiges of this custom have survived in various Jewish communities. See, e.g., Ben Naim, *Noheg be-Hokhmah*, s.v. "*Milah* [Circumcision]," pp. 116–18.

27 *Zikhron Berit le-Rishonim*, ed. Glassberg, pp. 18–19.

6

CIRCUMCISION AS A FORM OF SACRIFICE

We saw in the preceding chapter that one view regards circumcision as a sort of sacrifice, and "Whoever presents his son for circumcision is as the *kohen*, who presents an offering on the altar."[1] This notion is also expressed by Rabbeinu Bahya:[2]

> In homiletical fashion, the commandment of circumcision is as a sort of sacrifice; and just as the blood of the sacrifice is for atonement on the altar, so, too, the blood of circumcision atones. Accordingly, it is commanded to be performed on the eighth day, for the sacrifice is not fit until the eighth day, as it is said: "and from the eighth day on it shall be acceptable" [Lev. 22:27]. And just as it is written, regarding a sacrifice: "these things shall be eaten only by those for whom expiation was made with them" [Ex. 29:33], [i.e.] that the eating of the sacrifice is for the purpose of atonement, so, too, Israel holds a banquet on the circumcision day.[3]

According to some of the sources, this, then, is the reason for the festive meal that accompanies the circumcision.[4] This may possibly also explain why the women, in some communities, swallow the foreskin.[5]

1 *Tanya Rabbati*, end of para. 96.
2 In his commentary on *Lekh Lekha* (ed. C.B. Chavel [Jerusalem, 1966]), Vol. 1, pp. 161–62.
3 The same thought is also expressed in the *Zohar* (*Shelah*, fol. 164a): "[...] circumcision, which is actually a sacrifice"; see Chavel's gloss on R. Bahya, ad loc. See also Rabbi M.M. Kasher, *Torah Shelemah, Tzav*, Vol. 27 (Jerusalem, 1975), p. 111, para. 213, who brings additional sources for this concept. See also Rabbi Gershom ben Jacob ha-Gozer's rules of circumcision, in *Zikhron Berit le-Rishonim*, ed. Glassberg, vol. 1, p. 5.
4 See Werdiger, *Edut le-Yisrael*, p. 147.

This idea is also set forth in *Sefer ha-Ittur*,[6] explaining that the father of the infant stands next to the circumciser during the performance of this rite because circumcision is as a sacrifice; the circumciser is the father's agent; and as the rabbis rhetorically asked:[7] "How can a person's sacrifice be offered, and he is not standing beside it?"[8] Rabbi David Taharani of Beitar Ilit sent me the following important observation on this point:

> Support for his [i.e. your] assertion is to be found in the responsum by R. Hayyim Palache [Palaggi] in his book *Nishmat Kol Hai* (Vol. 1 [Salonika, 1832], *Yoreh Deah* 62), who discusses at length the prohibition of engaging in labor by the child's father on the day of the circumcision, either before or after the circumcision, since the day that a person offers a sacrifice is his holiday, and circumcision is like a sacrifice. The partners, however, of the child's father may engage in labor in their commonly owned shop. The *mohel* and the *sandak* are similarly permitted to engage in labor on the day of the circumcision, since the *mohel* is simply as the *kohen* [one of the priestly class] who offers the sacrifice, and the *kohen* is not forbidden to engage in labor when he offers the sacrifice of others. The *gaon* Rabbi Mordecai [ben Abraham] Carmi, *Maamar Mordekhai* [Leghorn, 1786] (*Orah Hayyim* 468:1) wrote that labor should be prohibited for [these] three engaged in the circumcision. It is understood from their statements that they regarded circumcision as a sacrifice in all respects — not merely conceptually, but in practice.

Allusions to this thought are also to be found in sources from the world of art, in the circumcision bowls embellished with a depiction of the Binding of Isaac.[9]

Additionally, there are circumcision bowls with a portrayal of the *Akedah* (the Binding of Isaac), that obviously symbolizes, and exemplifies, a sacrifice. Mention should also be made of a circumcision cup from Bohemia (1852?) with a drawing of the Binding of Isaac in the Feuchtwanger

5   See above, chap. 1, "Some North African Fertility and Pregnancy Customs," pp. 13–18.
6   *Ha-Ittur*, Vol. 2, *Sha'ar* 3 (the Gate of Circumcision), part 4 (fol. 53a).
7   BT Taanit 27a.
8   See *Shulhan Arukh, Yoreh Deah* 265:9.
9   See, e.g., *Synagoga* (Cologne, 1961), c267; *Judaica* (Warsaw, 1993), p. 183. See also above, chap. 4 ("Circumcision Only While Standing?"), n. 47.

Collection.[10] It would seem, however, that the iconographic elements in this illustration originate in Christian iconography, since the trees above the altar are in a cruciform arrangement, as appears in Christian art.[11]

The Stieglitz Collection of the Israel Museum also includes a seventeenth-century(?) circumcision knife from Italy, with an engraved wooden handle with a depiction of the Binding of Isaac: Abraham is standing, with the knife in his right hand, while his left holds the head of the kneeling Isaac (see Fig. 2).[12] It is noteworthy that this depiction is somewhat reminiscent of the Binding of Isaac in the southern gate of the cathedral of Jara, Spain (ca. 1100), in which, as well, a standing Abraham holds a knife in his right hand, and the head of Isaac in his left (Fig. 3); this issue is worthy of further inquiry.

For an example of the numerous circumcision bowls, see the bowl from nineteenth-century Poland in the Wolfson collection in Hechal Shlomo;[13] some of the literature, however, describes these bowls as intended for the *pidyon ha-ben* (redemption of the firstborn) ceremony. As I. Shachar writes:[14]

> Salver for Redemption of Firstborn: [...] This plate was probably used by the father for presenting the money during the Redemption of the Firstborn: "I was meticulous when I had the fortune to redeem my firstborn son ... to give the Priest ... and I even presented him with a *silver plate* full of gold and silver coins, as is the custom here..." (*Sepher Yoseph Omes*, Frankfurt, 1928, p. 346; Hebrew). "At first the father placed the equivalent of one and a quarter Rhenish in a *silver vessel* and asked the rabbi concerning the sum of coins, and one of the lads replied: But the *vessel* is worth more than five *sela'im* of the redemption fee!..." (*Sepher Mahryl*, Amsterdam, 1730, fol. 68r; Hebrew) [= ed. Spitzer, p. 489].

10 See I. Shachar, *Jewish Tradition in Art: the Feuchtwanger Collection of Judaica*, trans. and ed. R. Grafman (Jerusalem, 1981), pp. 22, 24, no. 10 (Fig. 1).

11 See A. Henry, *Biblia Pauperum: A Facsimile and Edition* (Ithaca, NY, 1987), in his explanation on p. 99 of the Binding of Isaac depiction on p. 96. A thorough examination of this question would exceed the scope of the current discussion. See my article, "Isaac of Prostitz's Akedahs," in *Eshkolot: Essays in Memory of Rabbi Ronald Lubofsky*, ed. A.R. Blay (Melbourne, 2002), pp. 213–15.

12 See the catalogue: Ch. Benjamin, *The Stieglitz Collection* (Jerusalem, 1987), no. 206, pp. 310–11.

13 Bialer and Fink, *Jewish Life in Art and Tradition*, p. 78 (Fig. 4).

14 *Jewish Tradition in Art*, p. 34, no. 52.

Although some communities did use a bowl for the *pidyon ha-ben* ceremony, as portrayed above, a special bowl was also employed during circumcisions (see below, chap. 6), as can be learned from the illustrations in the current chapter. And, similarly, in Bodenschatz;[15] and in Picart. See also the bowl in the Cluny Museum: a seventeenth-century Italian bowl from Padua, with a relief of a circumcision, around which is the engraved verse: "And when his son Isaac was eight days old, Abraham circumcised him, as God had commanded him" (Gen. 21:4) (incidentally, the *mohel* is sitting).[16] In my opinion, the motif of the Binding of Isaac is more suitable to the circumcision ceremony than to that of *pidyon ha-ben*, as can be seen from a circumcision knife in the Cluny Museum[17] from 1698 in Holland, with a crystal handle that is engraved on all four sides. Two sides portray the Binding of Isaac and the circumcision ceremony, and the two other sides contain the "verse" apparently from Gen. 21:4: "And Abraham circumcised his son Isaac" (thereby denoting the Hebrew year that corresponds to the numerical value of the Hebrew letters in this verse).[18] I have recently discovered that in the Greek community of Ioannina, circumcision songs, the most popular of which was "*I Thysia tou Isaac* [the Binding of Isaac]," were chanted at the banquet held on the night preceding the circumcision (called *Salamatia*, possibly from the Greek *s'alla matia* = in the presence of all).[19]

In this context, mention should also be made of a generally unknown custom that is based on the perception of circumcision as a sacrifice:[20]

> Since earth was efficacious for this, earth merited to be [an element] in the circumcision, in which the foreskin would be deposited. He [R. Avigdor] also ruled that a bit of salt is to be mixed in the earth, to fulfill that which is said (Lev. 2:13): "with all your offerings you must offer salt," which is the current practice of all the sages.[21]

15 *Kirchliche Verfassung der heutigen Juden*, Vol. 4, p. 69 (Fig. 5).
16 See V. Klagsbald, *Catalogue raisonné de la collection juive du Musée de Cluny* (Paris, 1981), p. 27 (Fig. 6).
17 Klagsbald, op. cit., p. 28, no. 12.
18 See the instructive comment by Klagsbald, ad loc.
19 See R. Dalven, *The Jews of Ioannina* (Philadelphia, 1990), p. 79.
20 *Perushim u-Pesakim le-Rabbi Avigdor* (as yet unpublished), fol. 18.
21 See A. Lipshitz, *Studies on R. Bahya ben Asher ibn Halawa's Commentary on the Torah* (Jerusalem, 2000), pp. 60–61 (Hebrew).

**1. Circumcision cup
Bohemia 1852(?),
Feuchtwanger Collection**

**2. Circumcision knife
Italy, 17th century (?)**

**3. Binding of Isaac
Spain, ca. 1100**

**4. Binding of Isaac,
Circumcision plate (?)
Poland, 19th century**

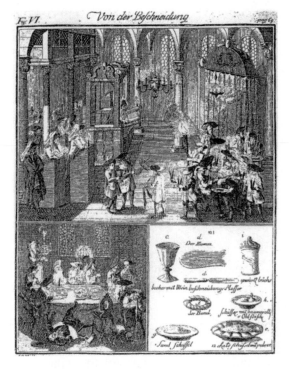

5. Circumcision, Bodenschatz, Erlang 1748

6. Circumcision plate, Padua, 17th century

7

WHO DRINKS THE CIRCUMCISION WINE AND
THE PLACE OF WOMEN IN SOCIETY

The actual act of circumcision is followed by the recitation of a blessing over the wine, the recitation of a second blessing (which concludes with "... who establishes the covenant"), and an additional supplicatory prayer ("preserve this child for his father and mother"). When, during this prayer, the congregation recites "Live in spite of your blood" (Ezek. 16:6), the newly circumcised infant is given a taste of the wine. Until this became the universal Jewish practice, however, different views were voiced and disparate practices were in effect.

According to the *Shulhan Arukh*,[1]

> The father of the infant, the circumciser, or one of those present recites the "who creates the fruit of the vine" blessing over the cup [of wine] [...] when [the congregation] comes to "Live in spite of your blood," he puts wine, from his finger, into the infant's mouth.

R. Joseph Caro did not specify who drinks the major portion of the cup.[2] R. Moses Isserles[3] writes:

> According to one opinion [that even without fasting] the obligation [i.e. the act of drinking of the wine, that must follow the recitation of the blessing over the wine] is fulfilled [by having the infant taste the

---

1   *Shulhan Arukh, Yoreh Deah* 265:1.
2   See his discussion in *Beit Yosef* on *Tur, Orah Hayyim* 559.
3   Gloss on *Shulhan Arukh, Yoreh Deah* 265:4.

wine] [*Kol Bo*, end of para. 73], but this is not the practice. Rather, the *sandak*[4] drinks [when he is not fasting], while *Shakh* [R. Shabbetai ben Meir ha-Kohen], loc. cit. [subsection 14] writes: "And in all the places where I was, this is not the practice, rather, small children are given to drink.

Pithei Teshuvah[5], however, writes on this:

It is written in the book *Hamudei Daniel* [manuscript]: "It seems that this should not be done, for the children do not hear the blessing, and it is preferable that the one who recites the blessing drinks."

The Vilna Gaon writes:[6] "That is, the one who recites the blessing." *Hokhmat Adam* specifies:[7]

It is proper, however, that the *sandak* or the beadle drink all of it or a mouthful,[8] as is the law regarding every matter for which a cup [of wine] is required.

The very fact that the *poskim* suggest different candidates for the drinking of the wine — the *sandak*, the one who recites the blessing, the beadle, and children — is extremely puzzling. Although we are unable to resolve this enigma, we nevertheless can reconstruct the development and source of the current practice.

A survey of the *Rishonim* presents a different picture of this practice. *Kol Bo* (para. 73) writes:

It was customary to put some wine in the mouth of the little circumcized one when they come to "Live in spite of your blood." And this suffices [as the drinking following the blessing] so that the circumciser will not

4 See R. Shemtob Gaguin, *Keter Shem Tov* (Kedainiai, 1934), para. 637, p. 555; R. Joseph ben Hayyim Jabetz, in his prayerbook: "And following the conclusion of the other blessings that are recited over it [the cup], it was the popular practice to give the *sandak* to drink from it." See Werdiger, *Edut le-Yisrael*, pp. 126 ff., who cites additional sources.

5 On *Shulhan Arukh, Yoreh Deah* 265, subsection 8.

6 *Beur ha-Gra*, on *Shulhan Arukh, Yoreh Deah* 265, subsection 29.

7 *Hokhmat Adam, Hil. Milah* (Laws of Circumcision) 149:26.

8 For the required quantity that must be imbibed, see the discussion in *Beit Yosef* on *Tur, Yoreh Deah*, 265; and in Rabbi Gershom ben Jacob ha-Gozer's rules of circumcision, in *Zikhron Berit le-Rishonim*, ed. Glassberg, pp. 72–73, 128 ff.

drink from the same wine that they give [the infant] to taste. Rather,
it is sent to his mother. [...]

And if the day of the circumcision is a fast day[9] [...] some of the
Geonim, of blessed memory, wrote: No blessing is recited over the
cup following the circumcision; the wine is left until the night, and
the infant's mother drinks it.

Kol Bo, however, rejects this latter custom, based on the opinion of
Ha-Ittur,[10] and ends by stating: "some are of the opinion that the obligation
is to be fulfilled by the circumciser's drinking."[11] In other words, the basic
law (when, according to all views, the circumcision is not performed on a
fast day) calls for the mother of the infant to drink from the wine, and not
the *sandak*, the one reciting the blessing, or any of the other candidates
proposed above by the various authorities.

Maharil[12] rules:

It is customary to dribble drops of wine into the infant's mouth, and
the mother is also given to drink from the cup over which the blessing
is recited.

The midrash *Sekhel Tov* similarly mandates:[13]

[The one reciting the blessing] drinks from the cup of the blessing,
and the rest is sent to the mother of the infant.

This view was also held by the Geonim and the *Rishonim*, who did not
disclose the reasoning behind the practice. Rabbi Gershom ben Jacob
ha-Gozer asks:[14]

Why is a blessing recited over the wine on the day of the circumcision?
Wine is not mentioned in the Talmud,[15] but only by the Geonim:

---

9 See ha-Gozer, op. cit., p. 72, in the name of a responsum by R. Isaac bar Judah to
   R. Menahem ben Makir.
10 *Ha-Ittur, Hil. Milah* (*Laws of Circumcision*), fol. 53b.
11 This opinion was cited by R. Moses Isserles in his glosses (see above).
12 *Sefer Maharil, Hil. Milah* (*Laws of Circumcision*), p. 478.
13 *Midrash Sekhel Tov*, ed. Buber (Berlin, 1900), Vol. 1, p. 19.
14 In his rules of circumcision, in *Zikhron Berit le-Rishonim*, p. 88.
15 Cf. also R. Simeon bar Zemah, *Tashbetz (ha-Gadol)*, Vol. 3, para. 65: "Mention is
   not made in any place in the Talmud of a cup of wine [...] at the circumcision"; and
   likewise in *Beit Yosef* on *Tur, Yoreh Deah* 265, s.v. "*Ve-Katav ha-Rav Abudarham*":

R. Yehudai, Rav Sherira, and other Geonim enacted this, similar to the seven blessings for the groom's cup. And in *Ma'aseh ha-Geonim*,[16] I found: Rabbi Zadok Gaon, of blessed memory, said [...]: And the cup of circumcision is sent to the mother of the infant, since a song of praise [i.e. a blessing] was recited over it [the cup].[17] And whoever recites the "[...] who creates the fruit of the vine" blessing without drinking has uttered the divine Name for no purpose.

Hemdah Genuzah[18] offers an additional explanation for giving the infant a taste of the wine (in the name of R. Zemah Gaon?):

And why his mother? Because a song of praise was recited over it [the cup], and the congregation prayed for the infant and for his mother, as it is customary to recite: "Just as You have entered him into the covenant, so, too, enter him to Torah, the wedding canopy, and send healing," [because] his mother is sick and requires [divine] mercy and healing. Consequently, his mother drinks [from the wine]. It is impossible, however, to pour it out and waste it, since the "[...] who

"The same person who initially recited 'who creates the fruit of the vine' recites the blessing over the cup. I did not find this explained in the Talmud, nor in the commentaries by R. Isaac Alfasi or Maimonides, rather, based on the commentators and the Geonim, I will write in this paragraph that it seems to be universally acknowledged [practice] to recite this blessing over the cup. And it appears from the statement by *Mordekhai* in the tractate of Yoma that the reason is because of what was said [Berakhot 35a] that songs of praise are recited only over wine." See also Werdiger, *Edut le-Yisrael*, p. 108; the responsum by a Gaon, in Lewin, *Otzar ha-Gaonim*, Vol. 3 (Jerusalem, 1931), Eruvin, p. 32, para. 86.

16 Cf. also *Ma'aseh ha-Geonim*, ed. A. Epstein and J. Freimann (Berlin, 1909), p. 59, para. 64 ("The Subject of Circumcision"): "This question was asked of our master, R. Isaac bar Judah [...] if the day of the circumcision fell on a fast day [...] is a blessing recited over the wine, and is it imbibed by the one who recites the blessing, or by (the mother of) the infant." Parallels appear in *Ha-Pardes*, ed. Ehrenreich, para. 282, p. 76; *Mahzor Vitri*, para. 503, ed. S. Hurwitz (Nuremberg, 1923 [Jerusalem, 1988]), p. 624, in the name of "R. Menahem ben Makir [who asked] his cousin, R. Isaac ben Judah." Cf. the additional sources listed by the editors: Ehrenreich (n. 9); Hurwitz (n. 100). I did not, however, find the statement by ha-Gozer in *Ma'aseh ha-Geonim*.

17 Following BT Berakhot 35a (see above, n. 15); Erakhin 11a; see ha-Gozer's rules of circumcision, op. cit., pp. 97–98.

18 *Teshuvot Geonim Hemdah Genuzah* (Jerusalem, 1963), para. 118.

creates the fruit of the vine" blessing has been recited over it; it may not be wasted, and it must be imbibed.

This is stated explicitly in the earlier Geonic source, *Seder Rav Amram Gaon*:[19]

> The cup is sent to the mother of the infant. And why to the mother of the infant? Because a song of praise was recited over it, and the congregation prayed for the infant and for his mother [...] therefore the mother of the infant drinks it.

These Geonic teachings were based on an early Land of Israel source that they refer to as *"Yerushalmi."* Thus we find in *Or Zarua*:[20]

> It is customary to dribble with a finger from the wine in the cup into the mouth of the infant. Rabbenu Samuel bar Natronai, of blessed memory, explained **the reason, because it is said in the** *Yerushalmi* that the one [i.e. the father or the circumciser] who would pray over the cup would chant "and send healing"[21] [...] and because of the custom to pray over the cup, it was the practice to give the infant and the mother to drink from the cup.

This source is also mentioned by Rabbi Eliezer ben Joel ha-Levi of Bonn:[22]

> As is shown in *Yerushalmi,* **in** *Perek R. Eliezer [de-Milah]*,[23] the entire blessing, until "may the one who bore you rejoice, send a remedy of health and mercy from the Lord of Heaven to cure this child, who needs healing."[24] It accordingly was customary to dip a finger in the wine in

---

19 *Seder Rav Amram Gaon*, ed. D. Goldschmidt (Jerusalem, 1971), Vol. 2, para. 145.

20 *Or Zarua*, Vol. 2, *Hil. Milah* (*Laws of Circumcision*), para. 107.

21 And similarly in *Maharil*, ed. Spitzer, *Hil. Milah* (*Laws of Circumcision*); *Hiddushei Anshei Shem* on *Mordekhai*, end of Yoma, para. 1, from the "*Yerushalmi*," in the name of R. Jacob ben Samson.

22 Rabbi Eliezer ben Joel ha-Levi of Bonn (*Ravyah*), *Ravyah*, ed. V. Aptowitzer (Jerusalem, 1938 [Jerusalem, 1964]), para. 383 (Vol. 1, p. 413).

23 I.e., chap. 19 of Shabbat.

24 There are various versions of this supplicatory prayer, as that in *Maharil*, p. 478: "Send a remedy of life and mercy from before the Lord of Heaven to cure this child, who needs healing, and cure him as You healed the plague that afflicted Miriam when she became leprous, and the plague of Jericho by Elisha; so, too, cure this young child, speedily and in our time, and say, Amen." And similarly in *Siddur R. Saadia Gaon*, eds. I. Davidson, I. Joel, and S. Assaf (Jerusalem, 1941), p. 99; and in

the cup to put it in the mouth of the infant, and what remained in the cup was sent to the mother to drink, as a remedy, and this is the practice throughout the kingdom of Lombardy.[25]

The editor of *Ravyah*, Aptowitzer, comments:[26]

I am convinced that the "*Yerushalmi*" in which our master [= *Ravyah*] and R. Samuel bar Natronai found this prayer is "*Sefer Yerushalmi*,"[27] that was added to the Palestinian Talmud from *Seder Rav Amram Gaon* or the prayerbook of [R.] Saadiah [Gaon].[28]

In actuality, two prayers were recited, as is specified in *Or Zarua*:

"Send healing of life and mercy from the Lord to cure this child, who is in need of a remedy" [...] and, additionally, "Send healing of life and mercy **to the mother of this boy**, for she is in need of a remedy."[29]

an analogous version in *Midrash Sekhel Tov*, Vol. 1, p. 19, but with the variant: "[...] thus cure this boy from all grave maladies [...]." Cf. also *Seder Rav Amram Gaon*, Vol. 2, para. 145, p. 179. See additionally the detailed discussion in Werdiger, *Edut le-Yisrael*, pp. 131–33; see also Gaguin, *Keter Shem Tov*, p. 568, para. 651.

25 Cf. also para. 289, Vol. 1, p. 360; para. 891, Vol. 3, p. 680.
26 *Ravyah*, p. 360 n. 12.
27 See V. Aptowitzer, *Mavo le-Sefer Rabiyah* (*Introductio ad Sefer Rabiyah*) (Jerusalem, 1938), pp. 275–77 (see also I. Davidson, *Thesaurus of Mediaeval Hebrew Poetry* [New York, 1925–33], Vol. 3, p. 543), who maintains that this is a Land of Israel *piyyut* (liturgical poem) (see *MGWJ* 25 [1876], pp. 419–25), a view that is shared by S. Buber ("Rebuilt Jerusalem," in A.M. Luncz [ed.], *Jerusalem* 7 [Jerusalem, 1906 (photocopy edn.: Tel Aviv, 1972)], p. 209) and B. Ratner, *Ahavat Tziyon ve-Yerushalayim* (*Ahawath Zion we-Jeruscholaim; Varianten und Erganzungen des Textes des Jerusalemitschen Talmuds*) (Vilna, 1901–12), Berakhot, p. 209. L. Ginzberg (*Al Halakhah ve-Aggadah* [*On Law and Legend*] [Tel Aviv, 1960], p. 272 n. 30), however, argued that the use of the word *ravya* (literally, "boy") to denote the infant who is circumcised points to the Babylonian nature of this *piyyut*, even though it is quoted as if coming from a Land of Israel source. Ginzberg further commented that this word is absent from the version of R. Saadiah Gaon (*Siddur R. Saadiah Gaon*, p. 99). See also the remarks by Y.-T. Lewinski, "River and Sea Staunch Blood," *Yeda-'Am* 2,1 (September 1953), pp. 9–10 (Hebrew).
28 The supplicatory prayer also appears in *Seder Rav Amram Gaon*, Vol. 2, para. 145, p. 179; and according to the testimony of Abudarham (139:4), also in the prayerbook of R. Saadiah Gaon (p. 99) (*MGWJ*, loc. cit.).
29 The two supplicatory prayers are from *Maharil*, loc. cit. and *Sekhel Tov*, loc. cit, and they already appear in *Seder Rav Amram Gaon*, p. 180, and especially in *Siddur*

In other words, the two participants who are need of a cure, the infant and his mother, imbibe of the wine, and are mentioned in the prayer for divine mercy and healing.

The testimony by the Geonim and *Rishonim* that originated in the passage in the "*Yerushalmi*," teaches that the mother of the infant would drink from the wine after her newly circumcised son had been given a taste, since the congregation had offered a special prayer for her health.[30] The question then arises, how was the practice of giving the mother to drink abrogated, beginning from the time of the *Shulhan Arukh*, to be replaced by having many other estimable individuals imbibe of the wine, with the mother no longer deemed worthy to do so?

The answer to this question is most probably to be found in the ruling by R. Meir of Rothenburg, as cited by his pupils. As is attested by R. Jacob ben Moses Moellin *(Maharil)*:[31]

> *R. Saadia Gaon* (p. 99 n. 3). L. Ginzberg (*Geonica*, Vol. 1: *The Geonim and Their Halakic Writings* [New York, 1909], p. 143), however, writes that the supplicatory prayer for the mother is a later addition, as he demonstrated in *ZHB*, Vol. 9 (1905), p. 106, since the Geonic sources speak of a supplicatory prayer only on behalf of the child, and not the mother. Goldschmidt (*Seder Rav Amran Gaon*, gloss on l. 13, pp. 179–80) challenges Aptowitzer: "On the other hand, it is cited in the name of *Yerushalmi* [...] in *Ravyah*, para. 289 (p. 360), and in *Maharil, Hil. Milah*, fol. 66b, and is mentioned in the book *Hemdah Genuzah*, para. 118, and was copied in the midrash *Sekhel Tov*, p. 19, from a Geonic source; its style resembles the prayer that preceded it. Consequently, it seems that it belongs to this composition (i.e. *Seder Rav Amram Gaon*). (It is not explicitly mentioned in *Hemdah Genuzah*, but only incidentally, in the following language: "The congregation prayed for the infant and his mother [...].")

30 This would appear to be at complete variance with the halakhah as presented in *She'iltot, Aharei, She'ilta* 96 (ed. S.K. Mirsky [Jerusalem, 1966], Vol. 4, *She'ilta* 113, p. 184), which reads: "Some say, a menstruant woman does not drink from the cup of the blessing." This law (which is not in accordance with the accepted halakhah; see *Shulhan Arukh, Yoreh Deah* 195:4, gloss, based on the view of *Rabad* [R. Abraham ben David of Posquières], *Baalei ha-Nefesh*, ed. J. Kapih [Jerusalem, 1965], "*Sha'ar h-Perishah*," p. 20; *Ha-Eshkol*, ed. Auerbach et al. [Halberstadt, 1867], *Hil. Niddah [Laws of Menstruation]*, p. 97; cf. p. 117; Meiri on Ketubot 4b, p. 24; see Rabbi Naphtali Zevi Berlin, *Ha-Emek She'elah* [Jerusalem, 1967], p. 185, para. 24; Mirsky's notes in his edition of *She'iltot*) is special, and applies solely to menstruant women (and possibly also to brides, see *Masekhtot Kallah*, ed. M. Higger [New York, 1936], p. 127).

31 *Maharil*, end of *Hil. Milah (Laws of Circumcision)*; in R. Meir ben Baruch, *Teshuvot*

The *Maharil* said, that *Maharam* [R. Meir of Rothenburg] wrote: The woman who is *baalat ha-berit*, [the woman designated] to take the child from the new mother in order to bring him to the synagogue for circumcision, brings him to the entrance of the synagogue. She shall not, however, enter [the synagogue] to also be the *sandak* so that the child will be circumcised on her knees; [this is in order] to prevent licentiousness, [consisting of] a woman going among men. Thus wrote *Maharam* in a responsum cited by *Tashbetz* [R. Simeon ben Zemah] [para. 397, and some of his pupils]:[32] It does not seem to me to be proper, as is customary in most places, for the woman to sit[33] in the synagogue with men, with the infant resting on her bosom, even if her husband [is the] circumciser, or her father, or her son, for it is not the way [of the world] for an adorned woman to enter among men and before the Divine Presence. [...] Whoever is capable of protesting [against this custom] must do so, and anyone who is stringent shall be blessed and enjoy peace. Meir ben Baruch, may his memory be for the life of the World to Come.[34]

Pesakim ve-Minhagim ... me'et Yitzhak Ze'ev Kahana, Vol. 2, p. 262, para. 211. My thanks to Prof. I.M. Ta-Shma for drawing my attention to this teaching by R. Meir of Rothenburg.

32 *Sefer Minhagim de-ve Maharam ... me-Rotenberg*, ed. Elfenbein, p. 80; Rabbi Jacob ben Judah Weil, *She'eilot u-Teshuvot Mahari Weil* (first edn.: Venice, 1523, and many additional editions), para. 32 (in brief); see *Teshuvot Pesakim ve-Minhagim*, ed. Kahana, p. 149, para. 155.

33 יושבת; variant reading: נכנסת (enter into). See *Teshuvot Pesakim ve-Minhagim*, Addenda and Corrigenda, p. 279.

34 See also *Teshuvot Pesakim ve-Minhagim*, para. 156. Although R. Meir of Rothenburg's formulation presumably implies the impropriety of the woman, with her infant, sitting together with men in a synagogue, this may be an additional, and unstated, element to his ruling. For it is well known that a woman is impure for a certain period of time after giving birth (see above, chap. 3, "New Mother Impurity"), and is certainly so on the eighth day after the birth. And it was especially accepted in medieval Europe that a woman in a state of impurity should not enter a synagogue (see Nahmanides, commentary on Gen. 31:35; Rabbi Jacob Landau [fifteenth century], *Ha-Agur*, ed. M. Hershler [Jerusalem, 1942], p. 230, and more). I have discussed this issue at some length in my article: "Three Puzzling Practices, and the Place of Women in the Synagogue," in *To Be a Jewish Woman*, ed. M. Shilo, Vol. 2 (Jerusalem, 2001), pp. 30–33 (Hebrew), and have further elaborated on the topic in my forthcoming Vol. 8 of *Minhagei Yisrael*; I therefore do not wish to duplicate the material here. Cf. above, n. 30.

The view of R. Meir of Rothenburg, that "it is not the way [of the world] for an adorned woman to enter among people and before the Divine Presence," was accepted as the definitive halakhah,[35] as R. Moses Isserles rules:[36]

> A woman may not be the *sandak* for an infant when it is possible for a man [to fill this role], for this is like licentiousness.[37] At any rate, she [may] help her husband and bring the infant **until the synagogue**, when a man takes [the infant] from her and he becomes the *sandak*.

We learn from this legal discussion that, until the time of R. Meir of Rothenburg (d. 1293), it was perfectly correct for a woman to be the *baalat-berit* or *sandak*, and the infant's mother was also present within the confines of the synagogue and heard the blessing, for if she had not heard it, "her drinking from it certainly does not absolve him [the one reciting the blessing] from [the transgression] of reciting a blessing for naught."[38] This maternal presence in the synagogue also enables us to understand the early practice of having both the infant and his mother taste of the wine. The ruling by R. Meir of Rothenburg, however, which banished the mother from the synagogue,[39] also put an end to the early custom of giving the infant's

35 This is also most probably the reason for the removal of the second mention of the mother's health, which is already absent from the procedure of this ceremony as specified by the *Ahronim* (see, e.g., Werdiger, *Edut le-Yisrael*, pp. 113, 131–33).

36 *Darkei Moshe*, on *Tur, Yoreh Deah* 265:11; glosses on *Shulhan Arukh, Yoreh Deah* 265:11.

37 Mention should be made here of an anecdote cited by I. Elfenbein, "Year-Round Customs from Ashkenaz of Rabbenu Isaac of Dura [= Dueren]," *Horeb* 10 (1948), pp. 133–34 (Hebrew): "I heard from my father and teacher, R. Isaac, may he live long, that when he learned Torah from my master, the rabbi, R. Tobias in France, R. Jehiel of Paris came there, and he saw that many important students were sitting with him, and a wet nurse sat opposite the light with the son of the rabbi, R. Tobias." Admittedly, this was in a private house, and not in a synagogue; nor is it certain that the wet nurse was in the same room. A simple reading of this narrative, however, would seem to indicate that this was the case.

38 *Beit Yosef* on *Tur, Yoreh Deah* 265:11.

39 This entire question should be viewed within the broader context of the status of women at the time, and the contemporary laws governing modesty. See, e.g., *Sefer Hasidim*, ed. Margaliot, para. 168: "Boys and girls should not mingle, lest they be led into temptation"; and the "bad act" of a woman who was unfaithful to her husband, "and [her father] came [...] to take counsel with his son, to guide him

mother to drink from the wine of the blessing; she was now replaced by the one reciting the blessing, the *sandak*, the beadle, young lads, and others.

whether it was permitted to kill his daughter by drowning her in the river and [thus] removing her from the world"; this solution, however, was not sanctioned (*She'eilot u-Teshuvot Maharam mi-Rothenburg*, ed. R.N.N. Rabbinovicz [Lvov, 1860], para. 310; *Mordekhai*, Yevamot, chap. 2; and concisely: *Hagahot Mordekhai*, Yevamot, chap. 2, para. 121; *Hagahot Maimoniyot*, "Responsa Belonging to the Book of *Nashim*," para. 25: a responsum by R. Meir of Rothenburg). See M. Guedemann, *Ha-Torah ve-ha-Hayyim be-Artzot ha-Maarav bi-Yemei ha-Beinayim* (= *Geschichte des Erziehungswesens un der Cultur der abend-landischen Juden wahrend des Mittelaters*), Vol. 1 (Warsaw, 1897), pp. 192–93. Notwithstanding this, some women were quite involved in the public and commercial life of the period. See the instructive article by Z. Falk, "The Standing of Women in the Communities of Germany and France in the Medieval Period," *Sinai* 48 (1961), pp. 361–67, and bibliography. The question of the place of women in the synagogue is worthy of a separate discussion. For this entire issue, see now A. Grossman, *Pious and Rebellious: Jewish Women in Europe in the Middle Ages* (Jerusalem, 2001), esp. pp. 312–26 (Hebrew). The issue of circumcision performed by a woman will be discussed in the next chapter.

8

WOMEN *MOHALOT*

The question of a woman's fitness to perform circumcisions is the subject of controversy in the Talmud,[1] and among the *Rishonim* and *Ahronim*. R. Joseph Caro writes:[2] "All are fit to circumcise, even a slave, **a woman**, and a minor," on which R. Moses Isserles adds the reservation: "Some say that a woman should not circumcise (*Sefer Mitzvot Katan* and *Hagahot Mordekhai*). It is also customary to look for a man." R. Joseph Caro's opinion follows that of R. Johanan in BT Avodah Zarah loc. cit., and the conclusion of the Talmud that "a woman should be considered as being among the 'circumcised' [and therefore is fit to circumcise]."[3] *Tosafot*,[4] in contrast, states:

> We must rule in accordance with Rav, and a woman is not fit to circumcise. [...] Even though in a disagreement between Rav and R. Johanan, the law follows R. Johanan, in this case the law follows Rav.

---

1 See BT Avodah Zarah 27a.
2 *Shulhan Arukh, Yoreh Deah* 264:1.
3 This is also the ruling of *Bahag*; *She'iltot*, beginning of *Shemot*, ed. Mirsky, Vol. 3 (Jerusalem, 1964), *She'ilta* 39, p. 3; *Lekah Tov* on Ex. 4:25; R. Isaac Alfasi; Maimonides (*Mishneh Torah, Hil. Milah* [*Laws of Circumcision*], beginning of chap. 2; see *Hagahot Maimoniyot* ad loc., note 1); and similarly, in *Midrash he-Hefetz* (MS) (Rabbi M.M. Kasher, *Torah Shelemah*, Vol. 8 [New York, 1944], p. 200, para. 151, on Ex. 4:25) (and in *Midrash ha-Hefets*, ed. M. Havatselet [Jerusalem, 1990], p. 287); *Sefer Mitzvot ha-Gadol; Mordekhai* (Shabbat, para. 468); Rabbi Gershom ben Jacob ha-Gozer's rules of circumcision, in *Zikhron Berit le-Rishonim*, p. 58; *Sefer Yere'im*; Recanati, para. 595, and other authorities.
4 Avodah Zarah 27a, s.v. "*Isha Lav Bat Milah Hi.*"

The leading Ashkenazic authorities[5] ruled in accordance with this view, despite the Torah's stating (Ex. 4:25) "So Zipporah took a flint and cut off her son's foreskin," and despite the question posed by the Talmud:[6] "Does anyone maintain that a woman may not [perform circumcision]?" (see, however, the continuation of the discussion in the Talmud).[7]

The following sources should cast additional light on this longstanding question. *II Maccabees* relates:[8]

> For two women were brought in **for circumcising their children**, and they led them publicly about the city with their babies hanging at their breasts, and then threw them down from the top of the wall.

This passage implies that the women themselves performed the act of circumcision, and therefore were given a "punishment that fit the crime," with the fruits of their "criminal act" being hung from their necks. Saul Lieberman[9] relates to the mention of a similar "tit for tat" punishment in *Sifrei*:[10]

> They hung the unripe figs from her neck, and the herald [marched] before her proclaiming: "For these unripe fruits she is being punished."

Tanhuma explains:[11] "This is similar to a thief who is caught: the stolen [item] is hung around his neck."[12]

5 *Sefer Mitzvot Katan* (Commandment 157; and in *Sefer Mitzvot Katan* of Zurich, ed. Har-Shoshanim-Rosenberg, Vol. 2, Commandment 154, p. 42), *Hagahot Mordekhai*, R. Moses Isserles.

6 BT Avodah Zarah loc. cit.

7 For the statement by Isserles, "It is also customary to look for a man," see the question raised by *Siftei Kohan* and *Be'ur ha-Gra* (on *Shulhan Arukh, Yoreh Deah* 265). See also Isserles, *Darkei Moshe (He-Arokh)* on *Shulhan Arukh, Yoreh Deah*, who also cites the ruling by *Kol Bo* (para. 73, fol. 42a), in the name of R. Isaac, forbidding circumcision by a woman, but nevertheless writes that this might be permissible, from the outset.

8 *II Maccabees* 6:10, in E.J. Goodspeed (trans.), *The Apocrypha: An American Translation* (New York, 1959), p. 461.

9 S. Lieberman, *Greek in Jewish Palestine* (New York, 1965), p. 162.

10 *Sifrei*, Numbers, para. 137, ed. Horovitz, p. 183.

11 *Tanhuma*, Cod. Di Rossi (cited in the introduction to *Tanhuma*, ed. S. Buber, p. 157).

12 See the appendix to this chapter, which is an expansion of what I wrote in my book: *Magic, Folklore and History in Rabbinic Literature* (Ramat Gan, 1994), pp. 134–36.

The parallel in *I Maccabees*, however, seems to indicate a different reality:[13]

> The women **who had circumcised their children** they put to death under the decree, hanging their babies around their necks, and destroying their families **and the men who had circumcised them**.

This depiction seems to indicate that the women did not circumcise their children with their own hands, but rather ordered others to perform this act.[14]

The passages from *Maccabees* bear comparison with the version in *Megillat Antiochus*:[15]

> Also, a certain Jewish woman gave birth to a son after the death of her husband, and she circumcised him on the eighth day. She ascended the wall of the city [Jerusalem], with the child that she had circumcised in her hand. She began to speak: "[...] The covenant of our fathers shall not cease, [neither] from me, nor from the sons of our sons!" She cast her son under the wall, fell after him, and both died.

The author of this (relatively late) version understood, based on *II Maccabees*, that the mother herself circumcised her son, possibly leading him to add that she was a widow, and therefore the obligation to circumcise her child was incumbent upon her.

Abraham Epstein's comment concerning Beta Israel (Falasha) practice is relevant in this context:[16]

> Immediately following the birth, cold water is poured over the infant,

---

13 *I Maccabees* 1:60–61 (trans. Goodspeed, p. 378).

14 See the gloss in the Hebrew edition: A. Kahana (ed.), *Ha-Sefarim ha-Hitzonim* (*The Apocrypha*)[2] (Tel Aviv, 1956), p. 150, gloss on 1:60. The verse itself is grammatically rather difficult, and it is not altogether clear who conducted the circumcision. See U. Rappaport, *The First Book of Maccabees: Introduction, Hebrew Translation, and Commentary* (Jerusalem, 2004), p. 121, gloss to v. 61. What he writes, however, in his gloss to v. 60, namely, that "one cannot assume that the mothers themselves circumcised their children, for this is against the Jewish law," is inaccurate, and requires correction.

15 M.Z. Kadari, "The Aramaic Megillat Antiochus (I)," *Bar-Ilan* 1 (1963), p. 94 (Aramaic text); rendered into English from the Hebrew translation (p. 103).

16 *Kitvei Avraham Epstein* (*Collected Writings of Abraham Epstein*), ed. A.M. Habermann (Jerusalem, 1950), pp. 169–70 (Hebrew).

and he is blessed in the name of the God of Israel. This procedure, that they call *ardit*, was apparently learned from the Christians [see *Orient* 1848, col. 262]. On the eighth day the infant is circumcised by women.

Aaron Zeev Aescoly writes[17] that the Beta Israel infant is circumcised when seven days old, and goes on to note (p. 40) that this follows their version of the Torah, and show that earlier researchers (Faitlowich, Rathjens, and others) erred on this point. He also mentions that the Beta Israel circumcise their daughters, as well, as is standard practice in Ethiopia as a whole, but makes no mention of women as the circumcisers. A student of mine, Yossi Ziv, who is researching Ethiopian Jewish customs, has, in an as yet unpublished paper, solved this apparent contradiction. He has conclusively demonstrated that Ethiopian Jews would not carry out the circumcision ceremony on the eighth day if that day fell on a Sabbath; in such an event, they would circumcise on the seventh day. In all other cases, the circumcision would take place on the eighth day, in accordance with the simple understanding of the biblical text (Gen. 17:12; Lev. 12:3). This, of course, is contrary to rabbinic law that mandates circumcision on the eighth day, even if it falls on the Sabbath.[18] Ziv also indicates how this "non-rabbinic" conclusion was reached.

Yaakov S. Spiegel[19] takes note of three different halakhic views among European Jews on this question. The sages of France and Germany maintained that, *ab initio*, a woman is ritually fit to circumcise, just like a man. A few Spanish authorities, some German sages, and most of the authorities of Provence mandated that a woman is permitted to perform a circumcision only in the absence of a qualified male. R. Joseph Caro, following R. Isaac Alfasi, Maimonides, and Rabbenu Asher, codified this latter view in the *Shulhan Arukh*. Some Ashkenazic authorities set forth a third opinion, which disqualified women from performing circumcision at all.

Thus, while the Sephardic authorities all held the same opinion, we find three different views among the Ashkenazim of Europe. This may reflect a developing tendency among the latter to issue increasingly stringent rulings,

---

17 A.Z. Aescoly, *Sefer ha-Falashim* (*The Book of the Falashas: The Culture and Traditions of the Jews of Ethiopia*) (Jerusalem, 1943), p. 39 (Hebrew).

18 BT Shabbat 135b; see Kasher, *Torah Shelemah*, Vol. 3 (Jerusalem, 1931), p. 707.

19 Y.S. Spiegel, "Woman as Ritual Circumciser — the *Halakhah* and Its Development," *Sidra* 5 (1989), pp. 149–57 (Hebrew).

while an additional social factor may also have been at work here, giving additional incentive to some of the Ashkenazic authorities to adopt the stringent view that totally forbade circumcision by a woman.[20]

APPENDIX: *PAGGEI SHEVI'IT* AND THE INNOCENT VICTIM

The full text in *Sifrei*[21] reads as follows:

> To what may this be likened? To two women who were sentenced in court. One was sentenced for adultery, and the other because she stole[22] *paggei shevi'it* [unripe figs of the Sabbatical year]. The latter woman says: "I beg of you, publicize my sinfulness, so that those who witness [my execution] may not think that, just as one was adulterous, so, too, was this one." They hung the unripe figs from her neck, and the herald [marched] before her proclaiming: "For these unripe fruits she is being punished."

The difficulties in the parable are immediately obvious, and most strange is the juxtaposition of the two crimes: adultery, on the one hand, and stealing unripe fruit of the Sabbatical year, on the other. Saul Lieberman (cited above) discussed this passage, proving conclusively that the rabbis used the phrase *paggei shevi'it* metaphorically, alluding to an unmarried woman having relations with a man, or a betrothed woman with her bridegroom. He goes on to explain that some of the variants of our parable tell that the woman was of "exalted birth," so that her unseemly behavior was a stain on the reputation of the whole family.[23]

---

20 See n. 39 in the preceding chapter.

21 *Sifrei*, Numbers, para. 137, ed. Horovitz, p. 183. Cf. Num. Rabbah 19:2; BT Yoma 86b. There are some additional parallels, such as *Sifrei*, Deuteronomy, para. 26, ed. Finkelstein, pp. 36–37; Lev. Rabbah 31:4, ed. Margulies, p. 719; Deut. Rabbah 2:6, ed. Lieberman, p. 50. In the latter versions, the form of the parable has been somewhat altered, so that it is no more than a late addition to other texts. This was first noted by Finkelstein, *Sifrei*, p. 36 note to l. 2, and accepted by Lieberman, *Greek in Jewish Palestine*, p. 162 n. 7.

22 See Lieberman, p. 162 n. 5: "שגבבה?," meaning she gathered, collected, instead of שגנבה, she stole.

23 See Lev. Rabbah 31:4, and parallels, See Lieberman, *Greek in Jewish Palestine*, p. 125; *idem, Hilkhot ha-Yerushalmi (The Laws of the Palestinian Talmud) of Rabbi Moses ben Maimon* (New York, 1948), pp. 46–47, para. 9 (Hebrew).

Now, whereas Lieberman was undoubtedly correct in his interpretation of the wording *paggei shevi'it*, our passage still remains puzzling. If, indeed, her actions constituted a blot on the family's public image, why should she want her sins to be publicly proclaimed? Why did she want the world to know that her misdeed was not identical with that of her unhappy fellow condemned prisoner?

Before we attempt to suggest a solution to this problem, we should note that Lieberman also demonstrated that it was standard practice for a criminal to be paraded before the execution of his sentence, bearing objects that indicated his crime, Thus, we find in a manuscript version of *Tanhuma*: "It is like a thief who was caught; they hang the stolen goods across his shoulders."[24] Similarly, argues Lieberman, the unripe figs of the Sabbatical year denote lustful activities before the rightfully permitted time.[25]

We know, however, of situations in which a woman was led to public execution bearing a wreath of unripe figs around her neck, even though she was completely innocent of any crime. This took place in ancient Greece, most especially in Athens, where there were special people, usually of a lowly status, supported by the state, who would be sacrificed as a scapegoat in time of crisis — plague, famine, war, or the like. A male served for the men, and usually a woman for the women. The man would have a black cord wound round his neck, while the woman wore a wreath of unripe figs around hers. They were led down the main streets of the city with pomp and taken to a place outside the city, where they were stoned to death.[26] This barbaric

---

24 *Tanhuma*, ed. Buber, Introduction, p. 157.

25 Lieberman, *Greek in Jewish Palestine*, p. 125; see also *idem*, "Roman Legal Institutions in Early Rabbinics and in the *Acta Martyrum*," *JQR* 35 (1944), p. 35. See further I. Ziegler, *Die Konigsleichnisse das Midrasch beleuchtet durch die romische Kaiserkeit* (Breslau, 1908), p. 121. The practice still survives in certain Islamic countries. See Y. Ratzaby, *Bem'agloth Teman (Yemen Paths): Selected Studies in Yemenite Culture* (Tel Aviv, 1988), p. 42 (Hebrew); Kafah, *Jewish Life in Sana* (Jerusalem, 1969)[3], p. 288.

26 See Helladius (fifth century BCE), cited by Photius (ninth century CE), *Bibliotheca*, ed. Bekker (Berlin, 1924), p. 534; Scholiast to Aristophanes, *Frogs* 734; and to *Knights* 1136; Hesychius (fifth century CE), *Lexicon*, s.v. "φάρμακον". See Frazer, *The Golden Bough*, Part VI: *The Scapegoat*[3] (1913), pp. 253–54, with relevant bibliography. To this we should add the basic study of "Pharmakos" by Jane Ellen Harrison, in her classic *Prolegomena to the Study of Greek Religion* (New York, 1955 [first edn.: Cambridge, 1903]), pp. 95–106, esp. pp. 97–100; and her additional remarks in her *Themis: A Study of the Social Origins of Greek Religion* (Cambridge,

practice apparently made a deep impression on the spectators, and the custom was not forgotten by later generations, so much so that it is mentioned in Roman and even Byzantine sources.[27] Perhaps, then, some hazy recollection of this practice filtered down into second- and third-century Roman Palestine. The rabbis of that time (the period of the authorship of *Sifrei*) knew of the possibility of two women being led to execution, one guilty of the serious sin of adultery, the other wholly innocent of any crime. The innocent one wore a wreath of unripe figs around her neck. The rabbis interpreted this scene in terms of their own contemporary understanding, turning the unripe figs into unripe fruit of the Sabbatical year, with the special idiomatic allusion taken from this special year. The woman begged to be adorned with this wreath, which would proclaim her innocence. In accordance with their own understanding (or, perhaps, more correctly: misunderstanding) of the scene, they supplemented the theme with their own additional elements, such as her being of noble descent.

Admittedly, our suggestion is somewhat hypothetical. Nonetheless, it does serve to reconstruct a background *Sitz in Leben* for the original source (what we have called "the scene"), from which the rabbis of the midrash drew. Their partial understanding of the true meaning of the scene led them to interpret it in their own way, using it for their own homiletic purposes and elaborating upon it to their own ends.

1912), p. 416. Also, L.R. Farnell, *The Cults of the Greek States*, Vol. 4[2] (New York, 1977), pp. 271, 275–82, 416–19, has an extended discussion on certain aspects of this ritual. Further insights into the complexity of the pharmakos ritual have been offered by Lawson, *Modern Greek Folklore and Ancient Greek Religion*, pp. 355–60. E. Rohde, in his *Psyche: The Cult of Souls and Belief in Immortality among the Greeks*, trans. H.B. Hills from the eighth (1920) edition (New York, 1972), pp. 216, 321 n. 87, 590, also discussed the pharmakos ritual, noting that figs have a cathartic purpose. For figs as a means of purification, see A.B. Cook, *Zeus: A Study in Ancient Religion*, Vol. 2: *Zeus, God of the Dark Sky (Thunder and Lightning)*, Part 2 (Cambridge, 1925 [New York, 1965]), p. 1103 n. 4, with bibliography. See also F. Goldmann, "La Figue en Palestine à l'époque de la Mischna," *REJ* 62 (1911), pp. 216–35; ibid., 64 (1912), pp. 185–209.

27 See the previous note, Harpocration, loc. cit.; Hesychius, loc. cit. For the latter, see my *A Dictionary of Greek and Latin Legal Terms in Rabbinic Literature* (Ramat Gan, 1984), pp. 94–104.

9

THE TWO WINE CUPS OF CIRCUMCISION

We know of the double cups bearing the inscription "the cup of *metzitzah* [the sucking of blood by the circumciser]," "the cup of blessing," or in their Hebrew initials: כ.ש.ב כ.ש.מ, which obviously were used during the circumcision ceremony, as is mentioned by R. Jousep (Juspa) Schammes:[1]

> And two silver goblets containing wine for blessing and for *metzitzah*, are held [prior to the circumcision, as a synagogue honor] by the one who purchased everything necessary for circumcision on Simhat Torah, for the entire year. These two goblets are in readiness for every circumcision, donated for this purpose from the charitable deeds fund.[2]

Schammes further writes (p. 72):

> The circumciser immediately commences, and recites the blessing "[...] Who creates the fruit of the vine" **over the second cup**, excluding the cup of *metzitzah* [from the blessing].

Schammes adds, in his own notes to the *Wormser Minhagbuch*:

> That he did not drink from it at the time of the *metzitzah*, nor did he disgorge into it after the *metzitzah*.

The editors explain in a gloss (n. 93) that

> circumcisers in Germany would customarily take a little wine into their mouth, before the *metzitzah*, from a cup designated for that [...]

---

1   Schammes, *Wormser Minhagbuch*, Vol. 2, p. 69.
2   See *idem*, n. 66; cf. p. 65.

for the sucking of the blood, and afterwards to expectorate it into the cup of *metzitzah*.[3]

This bears comparison with the alternative practice depicted by Rabbi Juda Loew Kirchheim[4] that "afterwards the *metzitzah*-wine is then poured out before the Torah Ark." And likewise in *Wormser Minhagbuch*:[5] "The cup of *metzitzah* is poured out on the steps before the Torah Ark, and the remaining wine is for the beadle."

This can also be compared with the testimony of Rabbi Jacob ben Moses Moellin (*Maharil*):[6]

> *Mahari Segal [= Maharil]* said: It is customary in Austria to spit the *metzitzah* from his mouth on the earth, as the foreskin. This is not the case in the Rhineland, where he uses his mouth to return the *metzitzah* to the wine from which he took to perform the *metzitzah*, and only the foreskin is cast onto the earth. The wine cup of *metzitzah* is customarily poured under the Torah Ark in the synagogue.[7]

The reason for the pouring out of the wine before (or under) the Torah Ark seems to be the perception in the religious literature of the word מילה (*milah*, circumcision) as an acronym composed of the initial letters of the words *malakh yoshev lifnei ha-aron* ("an angel sits before the Ark"), or in accordance with the explanation given by Rabbi Solomon ben Adret (*Rashba*):[8]

> The practice of performing circumcisions in the synagogues is based on what is written: "And [the two of them] entered into a pact [*berit* — the same word meaning "circumcision"] before the Lord" [I Sam. 23:18], and *berit* means only circumcision.[9]

---

3 See the sources listed in the gloss.
4 Rabbi Juda Loew Kirchheim, *The Customs of Worms Jewry*, ed. I.M. Peles (Jerusalem, 1987), pp. 84–85 (Hebrew).
5 Vol. 2, p. 72.
6 *Maharil*, ed. Spitzer, p. 482.
7 See *Maharil*, n. 3. Cf. also Rabbi Gershom ben Jacob ha-Gozer's rules of circumcision, in *Zikhron Berit le-Rishonim*, p. 21. For the circumcision of an infant over earth or water, see above, chap. 5 ("Circumcision over Earth or over Water"). See also Weisberg, *Otzar Habrith*, Vol. 2, pp. 296–97.
8 *She'eilot u-Teshuvot ha-Rashba, Part 7: Responsa Attributed to Nahmanides* (ed. Machon Yerushalayim), (Jerusalem, 2001), para. 536.
9 See Weisberg, *Otzar Habrith*, Vol. 2, p. 270.

This is confirmed by the illustration in Bodenschatz[10] (Fig. 1), which portrays a circumcision that is being conducted in front of the Torah Ark.[11]

This enables us to understand an illustration from a Napolitean prayerbook from the late fifteenth century,[12] in which we see, on the left side, the circumcision ceremony; the circumciser stands to the right, holding two cups in his hands. One cup, which is probably the cup of *metzitzah*, seems to hold more wine than the other (see Fig. 2).[13] This could possibly indicate a tendency to equate the cup/cups of circumcision with the cup/cups of the wedding ceremony.[14]

And also in *Sefer ha-Minhagim* (Amsterdam, 1662) we see the father of the son(?) holding in his hands what appears to be two cups, and so too in the Frankfurt edn. of 1708 (Figs. 3, 4). A similar scene, albeit in reverse, appears in a Grace after Meals booklet published in Wilhermsdorf in 1687.[15]

---

10 Bodenschatz, *Kirchliche Verfassung der heutigen Juden*, Vol. 4, p. 69.

11 Prof. Shalom Sabar informed me that during this period circumcisions in Germany were indeed performed in the synagogue. Proof of this is provided by many illustrations in addition to that in Bodenschatz's book, such as the one in the Hebrew manuscript by Aaron Benjamin Zeev of Jevico (or Gewitsch), from Vienna 1728, "The Laws of the Prayers Connected with Circumcision" (collection of the Jewish Museum in Prague, MS. 243), where we see the performance of a circumcision facing the Ark. See D. Altshuler (ed.), *The Precious Legacy: Judaic Treasures from Czechoslovak State Collections* (New York, 1983), p. 197. (See our Fig. 1.)

12 Carré Art Bibliothèque Municipale, Nimes, MS. 13, fol. 181v, reproduced in N. Berger, *Jews and Medicine: Religion, Culture, Science* (Tel Aviv, 1995), p. 17; and in Metzger, *Jewish Life in the Middle Ages*, p. 222, no. 333. Cf. p. 220, the description accompanying no. 333; p. 226. Sabar told me that since this manuscript comes from Naples, a Spanish area, the question therefore arises, whether kindred cups were also used in Spain. If so, then the paintings by Bernard Picart and by Romeyn de Hooghe (see below) do not confirm the Ashkenazic practice, but rather teach of such a procedure among the Portuguese Jews in Amsterdam. Sabar also shared with me his uncertainty as to whether the figure holding the two cups is really the circumciser, due to the difference between his garb and that of the circumciser to the right.

13 For the shape of these cups, see below, chap. 21 ("The '*Huppah*' — the Wedding Canopy/Ceremony"), p. 194.

14 See the sources cited by Werdiger, *Edut le-Yisrael*, pp. 126–27.

15 *Seder Birkat Hamazon* (*Bendicion Despues de Comer*), ed. M. Hovav (Jerusalem, 1981), p. 64. The illustration in the *Frankfurt Minhagim Book* (Frankfurt, 1708) also follows this model. The illustration in the Venice *Minhagim* book (1601), however, differs totally, both in style and composition, and the cup of wine is absent from the tableau it depicts.

Continuing in this vein, a close look at the etching by Romeyn de Hooghe from 1665 (*Circumcision*) reveals a person standing behind the *sandak*[16] holding a cup in his hand; another man stands a little to the left, similarly holding a second cup. The same scene unfolds in the engraving by Bernard Picart from 1721 (Fig. 5), where two people, one on each side of the Chair of Elijah, hold cups in their hands.[17]

16 For the various uses of the terms *sandak* and *kwater*, see H. Pollack, *Jewish Folkways in Germanic Lands (1648–1806): Studies in Aspects of Daily Life* (Cambridge, MA, 1971), pp. 23–24; the rules of circumcision of Jacob ha-Gozer, *Zikhron Berit le-Rishonim*, "Addenda," pp. 236–41.
17 This engraving by Picart was also used to embellish boxes containing the circumciser's equipment, such as that in the Christies auction catalogue (Amsterdam, June 20, 1990), p. 118, no. 261 (possibly from the United States, twentieth century).

1. Bodenschatz, Erlang 1748

2. Circumcision, Italy, 15th century

3. Circumcision
Sefer ha-Minhagim
Amsterdam 1662

4. Circumcision
Sefer ha-Minhagim
Frankfurt 1708

5. Circumcision
Picard
Amsterdam 1727

10

ONE AND TWELVE CANDLES AT
THE CIRCUMCISION

R. Jousep (Juspa) Schammes tells of an interesting practice related to circumcision:[1]

> The father of the child dresses in his holiday finery, and he brings with him to the synagogue a large wax candle, that is called *Judische kerze*,[2] and twelve small wax candles.[3]

1   *Wormser Minhagbuch*, Vol. 2, pp. 64–65.
2   *Judische kerze*, the "candle of circumcision." "*Judischen*" in Western Yiddish means "to Judaize," i.e. to circumcise. See Schammes, op. cit., p. 61 n. 2. Cf. *Pinkas Kehillot Shnaittakh (Acta communitatis Judaeorum Schnaittach)*, ed. M. Hildesheimer (Jerusalem, 1992), p. 363; *Minhagei K[ehilah] K[edoshah] Fuerth (Practices of the Fuerth Community)* (Fuerth, 1767), para. 9. See Pollack, *Jewish Folkways in Germanic Lands (1648–1806)*, pp. 18–19, 213 nn. 28–32, who argues that the *Judische kerze* custom was limited to southern Germany, in the area between the Rhine valley and the vicinity of Fuerth, with a reference to M.L. Bamberger, "Aus meiner Minhagimsammelmappe," *JJV* 1 (1923), p. 327, para. 6, n. 3.
3   The continuation in *Wormser Minhagbuch* reads:
    Also a jar with wine for [giving the infant] to suck. The *Judische kerze* is placed on the stand before the Reader, and is lit immediately. It is left to burn until the third day after the circumcision [see below, chap. 13], when it is extinguished, and it is put in its place in the synagogue. It is [then] lit together with the other prayer candles for [the morning and evening prayers of] *Shaharit* and *Aravit*, until it is completely burnt. Also, the two chairs of the circumcision remain in the place where they were set up until after the third day after the circumcision [see below, chap. 13], when they are returned to the place where they regularly stand in the synagogue the entire year. [As regards] the twelve small candles, the

This use of candles is also mentioned by Rabbi Juda Loew Kirchheim,[4] who adds that these twelve candles correspond to the twelve tribes.[5] The practice is likewise attested in the Fuerth community:[6]

> Three days before the circumcision, the beadle proclaims in the streets of the city (*zur Judische kerze*) [for the *Judische kerze*], and the women who are close [to the new mother] gather at the new mother's house and make a waxen candle that will burn until the third day after the circumcision, and also twelve braided candles, that are called [tribes].

The source for this custom is to be found in *Sefer Maharil*:[7]

> It once happened in Mainz that twins had to be circumcised, and

one rewarded with the task of lighting takes them and lights them before *Barkhu* ["Bless"]; four of the candles are placed on the candelabrum on the right side of the [Reader's] stand, four on the candelabrum on the left side of the stand — these are the lamps on which the *yahr zeit kerzen* [death date anniversary memorial candles] are placed the entire year; and the remaining four are placed on the four corners of the *bimah* [raised platform for Torah reading].

The editor observes (n. 21) that "in many communities the circumcision chairs were kept within the synagogue, and were used as seats." See his references ad loc., and in the rules of circumcision of Jacob ha-Gozer, *Zikhron Berit le-Rishonim*, "Addenda," p. 231. See above, chap. 5 ("Circumcision Only While Standing?"). Bodenschatz, *Kirchliche Verfassung der heutigen Juden* (above chap. 9, Fig. 1), however, portrays only a single chair; see below, n. 14.

4 Kirchheim, *The Customs of Worms Jewry*, p. 82.
5 See the editor's gloss, no. 4. For the number of candles, see also Werdiger, *Edut le-Yisrael*, p. 139, and Werdiger's discussion of the source of the custom. See also the rules of circumcision of Jacob ha-Gozer, *Zikhron Berit le-Rishonim*, "Addenda," para. 8, pp. 230–31; see also Pollack, *Jewish Folkways in Germanic Lands (1648–1806)*, loc. cit.; *Maharil*, ed. Spitzer, p. 483 n. 1; *Otzar Habrith*, Vol. 1, pp. 140–41 n. 10. Dr. Shalom Sabar informed me that Eastern Jewish communities and Sephardic Jews of the *Yishuv ha-Yashan* (pre-Zionist Jewish community in the Land of Israel) in Jerusalem used candelabra with many candles, albeit not of fixed number. This custom is also current among Jews of Syrian descent in Mexico.
6 Rabbis Israel and Koppel, the sons of Gumpel, *Sefer Minhagim de-Kehillatenu be-Fiurde* (*The Book of Customs of Our Community in Fuerth*) (Fuerth, 1767 [photocopy edn.: Williamsburg, 1991]), para. 9.
7 *Maharil*, ed. Spitzer, p. 483.

Mahari Segal [= R. Jacob ben Moses Moellin [*Maharil*)] ordered that, as was his custom, a double quantity of candles be prepared, for it is usual to kindle twelve small candles, corresponding to the twelve tribes,[8] and a longlasting candle that will burn for three days,[9] and they prepared twenty-four small and two large [candles].

In an engraving of a circumcision ceremony that is presented by Bodenschatz[10] (above chap. 9, Fig. 1), we see this ceremony conducted in a synagogue[11] in the presence of a quorum.[12] Around those directly engaged in the circumcision ceremony, three other individuals hold four candles each, two in each hand, for a total of the twelve "small candles,"[13] while another person holds a much larger candle (that is to burn for three days). In other

8 See above, n. 3.

9 See below.

10 Bodenschatz, *Kirchliche Verfassung der heutigen Juden, sonderlich derer in Deutschland*, Vol. 4, facing p. 68.

11 The synagogue in Bodenschatz's depiction is apparently based on the one in Fuerth. See below, chap. 22 ("The *Huppah* — the Wedding Canopy/Ceremony"), n. 53, and Figs. 24–25; see also Fig. 3 in that chapter. Cf. above, end of n. 2, that the *Judische kerze* custom is from the same region.

12 Cf. *Maharil*, ed. Spitzer, p. 476: from Rabbi Abraham Klausner, *Sefer Minhagim le-R. Avraham Klausner* (para. 147, n. 6, ed. Y.Y. Dissen [Jerusalem, 1978], p. 135): "The simple custom is that a quorum of ten is to be sought for the circumcision." See Rabbi Isaac Or Zarua, *Or Zarua* (Zhitomer, 1862), Vol. 2, p. 107; and similarly in *Tur, Yoreh Deah*, para. 265, in the name of R. Zemah Gaon; *Shulhan Arukh, Yoreh Deah* 265:6.

13 Kirchner (*Judisches Ceremoniel*, p. 157), as well, states that twelve wax candles are used, corresponding to the twelve tribes, while the depiction from his book (our Fig. 1) seems to indicate that a person is standing in the synagogue and holding a *menorah* (candelabrum) with seven candles. The details in this woodcut, however, are apparently plagued by inaccuracy, for we also see a large *menorah* with **seven** branches (see *Minhagei Yisrael*, Vol. 6, pp. 183–91). The synagogue in Kirchner's books is that in Fuerth (see above, n. 12). No candles appear in the illustration in Leusden, *Philologus Hebraeo-Mixtus*, next to p. 354 (our Fig. 2). Candles were used during the circumcision ceremony in other communities as well. Thus, we find in M. Yosefov, *Ha-Yehudim ha-Harariyim ba-Kavkaz uve-Yisrael* (*The Mountain Jews in the Caucasus and in Israel*) (Jerusalem, 1991), p. 175, a description of a circumcision accompanied by candlebearers.

words, this woodcut precisely matches the practices of *Maharil* and the Worms community.[14]

14 The scene in the center of the woodcut, the presentation of the *bund* or *wimpel* (the cloth used during the circumcision), is described in detail by Schammes, *Wormser Minhagbuch*, Vol. 2, p. 61, paras. 237–238 and nn. 4–8. Incidentally, only a single cup appears in the illustration in the book by Bodenschatz.

Also worthy of study are the shapes of the Chair/Chairs (the double chair) of Elijah in the sources and visual depictions, and minor details such as the small footstool under the feet of the *sandak* (rules of circumcision of ha-Gozer, *Zikhron Berit le-Rishonim*, "Addenda," p. 228); cf. the illustration reproduced in Metzger, *Jewish Life in the Middle Ages*, p. 226, no. 340: Budapest, Hungarian Academy of Sciences, MS A 383, fol. 40r (Germany, first half of the fifteenth century; above chap. 4, Fig. 10); the chair appearing in Bialer and Fink, *Jewish Life in Art and Tradition*, p. 75; cf. Schammes, *Wormser Minhagbuch*, Vol. 2, pp. 64 n. 6. I was recently informed by Rabbi Zalman Friedman of Lakewood, New Jersey, that when the young child is first introduced to the letters of the Jewish alphabet, it is the practice of some to light a candle with thirteen wicks, one that had been lit at his circumcision, and that is kept to be lit once again as he is brought to the wedding canopy. This practice, which was previously unknown to me, undoubtedly originated in the Ashkenazic custom described above, together with the rule that "since one commandment has been performed with it, let another commandment be performed with it," that was discussed in detail in *Minhagei Yisrael*, Part 2, chap. 6 ("Since One Commandment Was Performed with It, We Perform Another with It"), pp. 193–202.

1. Circumcision, Kirchner, Nuremberg 1724

**2. Circumcision, Leusden,
Utrecht 1682**

11

TAHANUN ON THE DAY OF THE CIRCUMCISION

On occasion, social conditions influence the development of customs, a fine example of which is the question of whether the *Tahanun* supplicatory prayer is to be recited on the day of a circumcision. R. Joseph Caro writes:[1]

> It is customary not to fall on one's face [the posture of entreaty assumed while reciting the beginning of the *Tahanun* prayer, and, by extension, the recitation of the prayer as a whole] [...] in the synagogue on the day of a circumcision.

R. Moses Isserles adds:

> Specifically when the circumcision [...] is [performed] in the same synagogue. If, however, the circumcision is not in the synagogue, even though it is [performed] in another synagogue, *Tahanun* is recited ([R. Israel Isserlein,] *Piskei Mahari*, para. 81).

Magen Avraham (subsection 11), in the name of *Ha-Knesset ha-Gedolah*, in contrast, maintains that *Tahanun* is not to be recited in the synagogue, even if the circumcision was held elsewhere, provided that the father of the infant prays there. *Sha'arei Teshuvah* (subsections 11–12) writes that if most of the people in the city pray in the synagogue in which the circumcision is performed, then *Tahanun* is not recited in the other prayer venues, as well. This tradition is based on *Minhagim* by R. Isaac of Dueren:[2]

---

1 *Shulhan Arukh, Orah Hayyim* 121:4.
2 Rabbi Isaac ben Meir of Dueren, *Minhagim Yeshanim mi-Dura*, ed. I. Elfenbein (New York, 1948 [photocopy edn.: Jerusalem, 1969]), p. 152.

But on a day in which there is a circumcision, people do not fall [on their faces] for supplications throughout the entire city, even if there are two synagogues in the city. Elijah comes to the city, all are happy, and this is a holiday for all.[3]

Nimukei Hayyim develops this line of reasoning further:[4]

In large cities (such as Warsaw and the like) that have such large populations so that it is impossible that they would not have at least one circumcision every day, and consequently *Tahanun* would never be recited, it is not possible to behave in such a manner.[5]

Accordingly, the size of the Jewish population in a large city was the decisive factor in the recitation of *Tahanun* under these circumstances.[6]

3   Cited in R. Isaac Tyrnau, *Sefer ha-Minhagim (Rulings and Customs)*, ed. S.J. Spitzer (Jerusalem, 1979), p. 149, para. 40; *Sefer Minhagim de-ve Maharam ... me-Rotenberg*, ed. Elfenbein, p. 78.
4   Rabbi Hayyim Eleazar Schapira of Munkacs, *Nimukei Orah Hayyim* (Tyrnau, 1930 [photocopy edn.: Jerusalem-Brooklyn, 1968]), p. 72.
5   Rabbi J. Lewy, *Minhag Yisrael Torah*[2] (Israel, 1994), Vol. 1, on *Orah Hayyim* 131, p. 167.
6   See also *Shulhan Arukh, Yoreh Deah* 343: "**In a small village**, greetings are not exchanged when there is a corpse in the settlement." See also *Minhagei Yisrael*, Vol. 3, p. 76 n. 16.

12

THE THIRD DAY AFTER THE CIRCUMCISION

In a number of sources we read of the custom of lighting a large candle, which will burn for three days, after the circumcision ceremony. The reason for this practice[1] is clarified by a comparison with a practice described in the *Wormser Minhagbuch*:[2]

> The practice of the third [day after the] circumcision: In the morning, after people leave the synagogue, the women, led by the rabbi's wife, come and bathe the infant. In the afternoon the father of the infant conducts a banquet, which is called "*shelish ha-milah* [the third of the circumcision]."

We further read in the rules of circumcision by Rabbi Gershom ben Jacob ha-Gozer (thirteenth century):[3]

> The chairs[4] remain standing in the synagogue, set out in the room, all three days. And why was this *tikkun* [corrective measure] done? So that the congregation shall see this continuously, and pray for the infant

---

1 See above, chap. 11 ("One and Twelve Candles at the Circumcision").
2 Schammes, *Wormser Minhagbuch*, Vol. 2, para. 243, p. 79.
3 In *Zikhron Berit le-Rishonim*, ed. Glassberg, p. 60.
4 Two chairs were usually used; in some localities, only a single chair was employed (see below, the citation from *Matteh Moshe*; above, chap. 11, n. 14). Two chairs are also mentioned in the book by Herman Wallich, *Die Mayerische Synagoga in Greiffswalde* (Greiffswalde, 1690), p. 3 (cited by J. Kalir, "The Jewish Service in the Eyes of Christian and Baptized Jews in the 17th and 18th Centuries," *JQR* 56 [1965/6], p. 55).

and for his mother.[5] And why three days? Because the lad is weak for three days, as it is said, "On the third day, when they were in pain" [Gen. 34:25].[6]

Matteh Moshe,[7] as well, wrote:

It is customary to leave the chair[8] for three days following the circumcision, as was formulated by the *paytan* [composer of liturgical poems] in the *shalmonit*[9] for circumcision: "For the Gileadite is moved by his zeal for You,[10] [...] a chair [Elijah's] is readied as a testimony for the future; chairs are set[11] for three days."

5 Cf. above, chap. 8 ("Who Drinks the Circumcision Wine and the Place of Women in Society").
6 See also Pollack, *Jewish Folkways in Germanic Lands (1648–1806)*, p. 216 n. 60.
7 R. Moses of Przemysl, *Matteh Moshe*, ed. M. Knoblowicz (London, 1958), p. 382.
8 Cf. above, n. 4.
9 A *shalmonit* is a liturgical poem or supplicatory prayer, following the model established by R. Solomon ben Judah ha-Bavli. This *piyyut* is recited during a circumcision that is performed on a day on which *Selihot* (penitential prayers) are recited, possibly during the Ten Days of Repentance. It begins with the plea, "Do not violate Your covenant with us," and was composed by *Ravyah* (Rabbi Eliezer ben Joel ha-Levi of Bonn, ca. 1140–1225). See A. Aptowitzer, *Introduction to Sefer Ravya* (Jerusalem, 1938), pp. 134–35; Davidson, *Thesaurus of Mediaeval Hebrew Poetry*, Vol. 1, p. 193, para. 4202; see also the comments by Aptowitzer, op. cit., p. 138 nos. 45, 46, with a reference to the rules of circumcision by Rabbi ha-Gozer, *Zikhron Berit le-Rishonim*, pp. 59, 61. In regard to the first three days, ha-Gozer cites a verse from Hosea (6:2): "In two days He will make us whole again; on the third day He will raise us up," on which he writes: "Consequently, the chairs are arranged for three days, so that they [the congregants] will pray for them [the mother and child]." This custom appears earlier, in the *Yotzer* [blessing preceding the *Shema*] for a circumcision conducted on the Sabbath composed by *Raban* (Rabbi Eliezer ben Nathan, twelfth century). This liturgical hymn, which was customarily recited in the Bohemian rite, attests (following *Minhag K[ehilah] K[edoshah] Posnen u-Ketzat Agafe[ha]* [Dyhernfurth, 1796], fol. 7a): "Indeed, two chairs are accordingly used, for the father of the son to sit and watch, before the testimony [of the covenant] for an everlasting sign, **to be healed on the third [day]**, for which a chair is prepared. **This is an allusion that on the third day you shall arise and be healed**, in 'Lo, I will send [the prophet Elijah] to you' [Mal. 3:23]." (See Davidson, pp. 323–24, para. 7144.) This source clearly teaches that the healing is on the third day (with thanks to Prof. Jonah Fraenkel, who clarified these *piyyutim* for me).
10 See I Kings 19: 9–10.
11 See above, nn. 4, 8.

The washing of the infant on the third day after his circumcision is already mentioned in the Mishnah:

> R. Eleazar ben Azariah says: The child may be washed on the third day [even] if this falls on a Sabbath, as it is said, "On the third day, when they were in pain" [Gen. 34:25].[12]

And similarly:

> From where do we learn that the circumcised [infant] may be washed on the third day that falls on the Sabbath? As it is said, "On the third day, when they were in pain."[13]

The importance of the third day was emphasized by R. Solomon Luria (*Maharshal*), as we see from the following report:[14]

> My master, our master and teacher, the rabbi, R. Solomon, said that the *seudah shel mitzvah* [meal related to a religious observance] of the third day following circumcision is greater than [that of] the day of the circumcision itself,[15] for the third day of circumcision is mentioned in relation to the banquet explicitly [*le-hedya*], concerning Abraham,[16] while [the banquet of] the day of the circumcision itself is derived only concerning the weaning of Isaac;[17] so also he heard from his father-in-law, R. Kalonymus.

---

12 M Shabbat 19:3.

13 Ibid. 9:3.

14 *Hanhagat Maharshal*, ed. Y. Raphael (Jerusalem, 1961), para. 50, p. 29.

15 Cf. *Shulhan Arukh, Yoreh Deah* 265:12. C.A. Schwab, *Diplomatische Geschichte der Juden Mainz und dessen Unsgehang ...* (Weisbaden, 1969), p. 339, relates that women were permitted to be frivolous in the house of the new mother only ten days after the birth, that is, on the third day of the child's being circumcised; Ben Naim, *Noheg be-Hokhmah*, pp. 115–16, states that the practice of placing a chair in the house of the circumcised infant three days after the circumcision was also observed in Tunis, as was the custom of holding a banquet on the third day. Ben Naim maintains that "this practice originated in the words of the holy [Eleazar ben] Kallir; see there."

16 In actuality, this is not stated explicitly in the biblical text. See Gen. 18:11, and the exposition in BT Bava Metzia 86b: "This was the third day from Abraham's circumcision."

17 See Gen. 21:8; cf. *Pirkei de-Rabbi Eliezer*, chap. 29.

This last source indicates that the banquet is one of thanksgiving, for the circumcised newborn being out of danger. The fact that the large *Judische kerze* candle must burn for only three days teaches that only these three days are fraught with danger; and since a part of the day is considered to be as the day in its entirety, the afternoon of this third day is the time to offer thanks. According, however, to the above mishnayot from the tractate of Shabbat, it would seem that the infant is still in danger for the entire third day. R. Abraham Ibn Ezra goes even further, and asserts:[18]

> "On the third day" — the third is always difficult, since it is half of the [week, which is one] quarter [of the month].[19]

This sentiment is already echoed in *Pirkei de-Rabbi Eliezer*:[20]

> R. Hanina ben Dosa says: All the circumcised are in pain on the third day, for it is said, "On the third day, when they were in pain."[21]

The commentary of the *Tur* on the Torah, in contrast, writes:[22]

> "When they were in pain" — Rashi explained that every wound is **more** [emphasis added — D. S.] painful on the third day. *Perek R. Eliezer de-Milah*, however, does not indicate this, for it says: "The child is bathed **even** on the third day that falls on the Sabbath, and certainly on the first day [after the circumcision, that falls on the Sabbath].[23]

And, with a similar understanding, in *Minhah Belulah*:[24]

---

18 Ibn Ezra on Gen. 34:25.

19 See Ibn Ezra's explanation of the verse.

20 *Pirkei de-Rabbi Eliezer*, ed. D. Luria (Warsaw, 1852), fol. 64a-b.

21 This appears in Rabbi Solomon Adeni, *Melekhet Shlomo* (pub. in the Vilna edition of the Mishnah), Shabbat 19:43. See Kasher, *Torah Shelemah*, Vol. 8 (*Shemot*), p. 1328, para. 51. See Luria, *Pirkei de-Rabbi Eliezer*, n. 12, that this is the view held by Maimonides, *Mishneh Torah, Hil. Milah* (*Laws of Circumcision*) 2:8, and by Rabbeinu Nissim (*Perek R. Eliezer de-Milah*), that the sick usually become stronger on the third day.

22 The commentary by the author of the *Turim* on Gen. 34:25.

23 Cited by Kasher, *Torah Shelemah*, op. cit., para. 50, who questions this assertion, which does not appear in Rashi or in the Talmud, and states that further study is required.

24 Rabbi Abraham Menahem ben Jacob Rapoport, *Minhah Belulah* (Vienna, 1594).

[...] or shall we say, "when they were in pain," for they were in pain and regretted the circumcision?[25] This is correct, because the Rabbis, of blessed memory, said in *Perek R. Eliezer de-Milah*: "The child is bathed **even** on the third day that falls on the Sabbath," **for the wound is insignificant for him, and is close to being healed.**[26]

This view is also held by R. Menahem Meiri, who wrote:[27]

R. Eleazar ben Azariah differs, saying that even the third day is dangerous and washing is permitted, and this is the law, and certainly on the second day, since "On the third day, when they were in pain" was stated [to mean] only that **they still were in pain**, and if it were later than this, they would be healed.

So too is the view of R. Yom Tov Ishbili (*Ritba*):[28]

In this case, that specified the third day, the intent is to the third day **as well**, for the first two days undoubtedly entail greater danger.[29]

On this point *Ritba* followed his teacher, R. Solomon ben Adret (*Rashba*).[30] This tradition accordingly regarded the third day as the **end** of the dangerous period, and therefore was an appropriate time to hold a thanksgiving banquet, "*shelish ha-milah*."

---

25 Cf. *Torah Shelemah*, op. cit., para. 52.
26 This, too, is cited in *Torah Shelemah*, op. cit., para. 50.
27 As is noted by Luria, *Pirkei de-Rabbi Eliezer*, fol. 64a-b, n. 12.
28 To Shabbat 134b, ed. M. Goldstein (Jerusalem, 1990), p. 878.
29 In the editor's gloss 31: "And likewise Maimonides (in the name of '*yesh omrim*' — one opinion)"; *Rashba* [...]; Rabbenu Nissim, *Shitah le-Ran*; and Rabbeinu Nissim to Nedarim (31b, s.v. "*Di-Khtiv*"), and similarly, Rashi above, 86a, s.v. "*Minayin*." See the continuation of *Ritba*'s commentary ad loc.
30 See also Luria, loc. cit., with references to additional sources.

13

ASPECTS OF THE REDEMPTION OF THE FIRSTBORN

The obligation of redeeming the firstborn, of both humans and livestock, is established by several verses from the Torah. Ex. 13:2 mandates: "Consecrate to Me every firstborn; man and beast, the first issue of every womb among the Israelites is Mine"; Deut. 15:19 specifies: "You shall consecrate to the Lord your God all male firstlings that are born in your herd and in your flock"; and the inclusive prescription in Num. 18:15 reads: "The first issue of the womb of every being, man or beast, that is offered to the Lord, shall be yours; but you shall have the firstborn of man redeemed, and you shall also have the firstling of unclean animals redeemed." *Mekhilta* expounds:[1]

> "Is Mine" [Ex. 13:2] — why was this stated? Because it says "You shall consecrate to the Lord your God all male" [Deut. 15:9]; [you might think:] Consecrate it to receive reward; or [you might think:] if you consecrated it, then it is hallowed, but if you did not consecrate it, then it is not hallowed. Scripture teaches: "is Mine" — under any circumstances. Then what does Scripture teach by stating "You shall consecrate"? Consecrate it in order to receive reward.

And, similarly, in the Talmud:[2]

> If a person did not consecrate it, would it not be hallowed? It is

---

1   *Mechilta d'Rabbi Ismael*, ed. H.S. Horovitz and I.A. Rabin (Jerusalem, 1998), p. 58. See Y. Gelis, *Tosafot ha-Shalem*, Vol. 7 (Jerusalem, 1988), p. 148: "'קדש לי כל בכור [consecrate to Me every firstborn]' has the numerical value of זהו לקבל בשכרך [this means, to receive your reward]."

2   BT Arakhin 29a, on "You shall consecrate ... male" (Deut. 15:19).

sacred from the womb. Since, therefore, it is sacred even if it were not [specifically] sanctified, there is no need to sanctify it.

This should be compared with the following passage, also from the Babylonian Talmud:[3]

Whence do we know that one is obligated to sanctify the firstling that is born in one's house? As it is said, "You shall consecrate ... male." [...] If he does not consecrate it, is it not holy?

The rabbis understood from these verses that the (animal) firstling is sacred from the womb, even if no act of sanctification is performed. This conception was unquestionably transferred to the human firstborn as well, for the midrash relates:[4]

The Holy One, blessed be He, said to Israel: My sons, I demand nothing of you, save when a firstborn **son** is born to you, sanctify him for My name; this is the meaning of what is written, "Consecrate to Me every firstborn."[5]

We have shown[6] that the *perushim* enacted this in accordance with Scripture, but the firstborn was "sanctified" (i.e. designated) for a life of Torah study. Even without this act of setting aside, however, the firstborn would still possess this sacred standing. As this is expressed by *Seforno*:[7]

They were all obligated for redemption, as all other holy objects, so that they would be permitted for mundane labors; for without the redemption, **they would be forbidden for the performance of any mundane labor**. [...] The redemption [value] for them is the value for a one month old that is specified in the portion of *arakhin* [valuations; Lev. 27:6], since that is the time of its redemption. For it is said: "Take as their redemption price, from the age of one month up" [Num. 18:16].

And on v. 15 in the same chapter:

---

3   BT Nedarim 13a.
4   Cant. Rabbah 7:2.
5   Cf. Eccl. Rabbah 3:9.
6   Part 2, chap. 23, "Mourning for the Firstborn."
7   On Ex. 13:2, s.v. "*Kadesh Li Kol Bekhor.*"

And the firstborn of Israel were deserving to be smitten together with them [the Egyptians] [...] but they were saved by their being consecrated to Him, in such a way that the firstborn of man in Israel would be as Nazirites, or those specially designated for the service of the Lord, may He be blessed, and prohibited from engaging in mundane labor. [...] And [the provision of] "You must redeem every firstborn among your sons" [Ex. 34:20] [was given] so that they would be permitted to engage in mundane labor.[8]

People could therefore erroneously think that the firstborn is sanctified to the Lord from the womb. This notion is reinforced by the Land of Israel redemption of the firstborn ceremony published by Margalioth, which reads as follows:[9]

This son is a firstborn, and the holy Torah said to redeem him, as it is said, "The Lord spoke further to Moses, saying: Consecrate to Me every firstborn ..." [Ex. 13:1–2]. This is followed by the declaration of the *kohen*: "[...] **when you were in your mother's stomach, you belonged to your Father in Heaven; now that you have emerged from the stomach of your pregnant mother, you belong to your Father in Heaven and to me** [for I am a *kohen*], and to my brother *kohanim*. Your father and your mother wish to redeem you from me for five silver *sela'im*.

The main passage published by Margalioth (p. 30), entitled "*Afrukta de-Bekhora* [The Redeeming of the Firstborn]," states:

They say to the father: That one [your son] is sacred to the All-Merciful and to [the *kohen*]. Release him.

These sources clearly teach of a singular conception that the firstborn belongs to Heaven, while still in his mother's womb,[10] and upon his birth he falls under the authority of the *kohanim*, from whom the child's father

---

8 See Kasher, *Torah Shelemah* (New York, 1948), Vol. 12, *Bo*, p. 94, para. 28.

9 M. Margoliouth [Margulies], *Hilkhot Eretz Yisrael min ha-Genizah* (*Land of Israel Halakhot from the Genizah*) (Jerusalem, 1972), p. 16, Genizah fragment T-S J 3/23.

10 See the versions of the blessing in S.E. Stern, "The Order of the Redemption of the Firstborn Ceremony according to Our Masters the Geonim and the *Rishonim*," *Kovetz Torani Zekhor le-Avraham* (Heshvan 1992), pp. 16, 18 (Hebrew).

must redeem him. This (popular) understanding was expressed in a query directed to R. Israel Isserlein:[11]

> As regards what you wrote, that if [the father] would give the son to the *kohen*, he would fulfill his obligation [...] this is a mistake. [...] For in any case, redemption is required.

The individual who addressed his query to R. Isserlein thought that the father of the firstborn could simply give the *kohen* what belongs to the latter, thereby evading the need to redeem his son. The author of *Terumat ha-Deshen* takes the trouble to reject this suggestion, and continues:

> And even if this is legally effective in that case [regarding the redemption of the firstling ass], this is because the body of the ass is consecrated, even for obtaining benefit [from it], prior to its redemption, which is not the case regarding the firstborn son, for we clearly learn that **he is totally nonconsecrated**. As what is he to be given to the *kohen*? Not as a slave, because a freeman does not become a slave. Not as a son, because he [the boy] is not his [the *kohen*'s] offspring!

Indeed, there was good reason to think that the newborn belonged to the *kohen*, and that the parents were not obligated to redeem him. Such a notion, mistaken though it might be, is reflected in a number of procedures in different Jewish communities, as we learn from Michele Klein's collection of practices related to birth:[12]

> Jews from some Sephardic and Syrian communities recall that a first-time mother dressed in her bridal gown; in Persian communities, she wore the veil from her wedding.[13] The new mother formally begged the *cohen* to return her baby. He would refuse, and she would persist in her pleas until the *cohen* reluctantly consented. The happy outcome was celebrated. In Salonika in the early twentieth century, the mother pretended to yearn for the return of her baby while the father avowed that he would prefer to sleep undisturbed at night, and guests teased

---

11 *Terumat ha-Deshen, Rulings*, para. 235.
12 M. Klein, *A Time to Be Born: Customs and Folklore of Jewish Birth* (Philadelphia, 1998), p. 188.
13 H.C. Dobrinsky, *A Treasury of Sephardic Laws and Customs: The Ritual Practices of Syrian, Moroccan, Judeo-Spanish, and Spanish and Portuguese Jews of North America* (New York, 1986), p. 8.

and joked. A wealthy father offered a valuable gold or silver bracelet instead of the five biblical shekels; a poor father offered a new item of clothing.[14] Iraqi Jews report that when it was performed, the ceremony was a dramatic game between the *cohen* and the baby's father, using a kiddush cup instead of jewelry, and eventually ending when the father gave the *cohen* a symbolic sum of money.[15]

An echo of the notion that until his redemption the firstborn belonged to the *kohanim* is to be found in the practice that was observed in some Jewish communities, of hanging around the neck of an unredeemed child a medallion bearing the inscription *"ben kohen* [literally, son of (or, more broadly, belonging to) a *kohen*]," and the Hebrew letter *heh*, whose numerical value of 5 refers to the five shekels that the parents pay for the redemption of their son.[16] Interestingly, R. Moses Isserles, in his gloss on *Yoreh Deah*, changed the text of what he wrote in *Darkei Moshe*, where he wrote: "And he writes on it *'ben bekhor* ["firstborn son"; it probably should read: *ben kohen*].'"[17] In his gloss, in contrast, Isserles wrote: "They write on a gold tablet[!] **that he is not redeemed.**"[18] Interestingly, in recent generations the meaning of this plate was no longer understood, and people thought it to be a sort of

14 Molho, "Birth and Childhood among the Jews of Salonica," pp. 255–69 (Hebrew).

15 E. Morad, *Childhood Scenes from Father's House: Poems* (Tel Aviv, 1985), p. 198 (Hebrew); Aslan and Nissim, *From the Customs and Way of Life of Iraqi Jewry*, p. 198; E. Brauer, *The Jews of Kurdistan* (Detroit, 1993), pp. 164–66, etc.

16 See J. Gutmann, *The Jewish Life Cycle (Iconography of Religions* 23 [Leiden, 1987]), p. 9; cf. Patai, "Folk Customs and Charms Relating to Birth," *Talpioth* 9, p. 251; cf. also *Shulhan Arukh, Yoreh Deah* 305:15, gloss by *Rema* (R. Moses Isserles), in the name of *Maharil* (= *Maharil*, ed. Spitzer, p. 492, in the name of "our master, R. Nathan" = R. Nathan of Igra; see Spitzer's nn. 4–5); *Yosif Ometz*, p. 347 (based on *Maharil*).

17 As is taught in *Maharil*, from whom he brought this practice. The version *"ben bekhor"* also appears in *Yosif Ometz*, p. 237.

18 See also *Be'er Hetev*, ad loc., that it is preferable for the rabbinical court to immediately redeem the child, because the plate will be lost. For the court's obligation regarding circumcision, see Kasher, *Torah Shelemah*, Vol. 3 (Jerusalem, 1938), *Lekh Lekha*, pp. 703–704, para. 66. See also Paolo Medici, *Riti e Costume degli Ebrei Confutati*[5] (Venice, 1757), p. 19: "Si muore il Padre, e la Madre non puo riscattarlo, ella si presenta al Sacerdote, affinche egli resti certificato, che quello e primogenito. S'attacca allora uno polizza al collo del bambino, dove si asserisce, che non e riscattato, accioche si riscatti da se, giungendo alla puberta, che secundo gli Ebrei e di tredici anni, e sei mei, Bagarut e da essi addimandata."

charm for the child's protection. Proof of this misunderstanding is provided by such a plate bearing the inscription "הק"ה" (an apparent representation of the divine Name), above which is "*Shaddai*" (the Almighty), that is undoubtedly a thaumaturgic inscription. We also know of charms with the names of angels, written around a large letter *heh*.[19] All these sources clearly teach that the inscription "הק"ה" was understood as the name of God. This, however, is not the end of the story, since the formulation *heh-kuf-heh* was also understood in a different manner. *Hida* (R. Hayyim Joseph David Azulai) writes:[20]

> It therefore is customary to be saved from the Evil Eye by fashioning a silver *heh*. [...] People also habitually recite "*hamishah* [five]" to be saved from the Evil Eye.

This "*heh*," then, is the "*hamishah*" (= 5) mentioned above, that we have discussed elsewhere;[21] it also is the open, five-fingered hand (*hamsah*) that is very commonly used as a charm against the Evil Eye. As *Yalkut Reuveni* prescribes:[22]

> The letter *heh* is efficacious against the Evil Eye. Fashion a letter *heh* of silver or other metals, and suspend it from the infant's neck.[23]

Proof of what we wrote above can be found in dedicatory plaques from Ioannina, Greece, in which the letter *heh* in the date הכת"ר (1860) is larger than the other letters, and those that bear the inscription: "For a remembrance and sign that this son, Elijah son of Isaac, may the Lord preserve him and

---

19 See Gutmann, *The Jewish Life Cycle*, p. 9, Table 17, fig. 2. See Shachar, *Jewish Tradition in Art*, nos. 934, 935, 959–966: amulets with holy names and characters encompassing a large letter *heh*; ibid., nos. 781–782: charms written on parchment with formulas containing a large *heh*. See also Schrire, *Hebrew Amulets*, fig. 19, and the discussion, p. 151.

20 *Petah Einayim* (Leghorn, 1790), on Berakhot 20a, s.v. "*Ve-Derekh.*"

21 *Minhagei Yisrael*, Vol. 1, p. 227.

22 Rabbi Reuben Hoeshke ben Hoeshke Katz, *Yalkut Reuveni* (Wilmersdorf, 1681), *Vayehi*, on "Joseph is a wild ass" (Gen. 49:22), citing Rabbi Isaac Onkeneira, *Ayumah ke-Nigdalot* (Constantinople, 1577 [Berlin, 1601]).

23 See *Noheg be-Hokhmah*, p. 154; and, recently, Isaac Pahah, *Ulei Ayin* (Jerusalem, 1990), p. 187, paras. 32–33; opposite p. 24: a charm with both a hand-*hamsah* and a large *heh*. See also Shachar, *Jewish Tradition in Art*, no. 986 (opposite p. 290): a *hamsah* with a *heh*.

keep him alive, is the firstborn and was not redeemed. With God's help, when he grows up, he will be obligated to redeem himself; born on the eleventh day of the month of Tishrei, Sunday, in the year הכת"ר, according to the full [i.e. written out] date." The word "redeemed" is inscribed next to the date (see Fig. 1).[24]

1. Redemption of firstborn medallion, Ioannina (Greece) 1859

24 Dr. Bracha Yaniv drew my attention to the Ioannina plaque.

14

ON THE "REASONS" FOR CUSTOMS:
THE *HALAKAH*

1. INTRODUCTION

Over half a century ago, Rabbi Chaim Williamowsky[1] wrote a short article on "Jewish Custom and Its Importance," which deserves to be cited at length:[2]

> It is known that our ancient forefathers ascribed great importance to the practice of the Jewish people, to such an extent that they said: "Practice overrides halakhah" [PT Bava Metzia, beginning of chap. 7]. "If Elijah were to come and proclaim: *Halitzah* [see below, Chap. 30] is not to be performed with a sandal, he would not be heeded, for the people have already adopted the practice of [using] a sandal [for this purpose]" (Yevamot 102[a]). "If [a question of] the law is weak in court and it does not know how to decide, let it see how the public acts, and it shall decide [accordingly], for this is the essence of the halakhah" (PT Peah 7:6).
>
> The Rabbis had a saying: "Go and see what is the practice of the people" (Berakhot 45[b; Eruvin 14b; Menahot 32b]); and when the law escaped the memory of Hillel the Elder, he would rule in accordance with the practice of the people (Pesahim 66[a]). As regards [the

---

1 "*Rabbinic Registry 1965* (*Reshimat Hevrei Histadrut ha-Rabbanim de-America, 5725*) (provided by S. Lieman) offers the following details: "Rabbi Chaim Williamowsky, 6500 — 9th Avenue, Hyattsville, Maryland, Chaplain, St. Elizabeth's and Mt. Alto US Soldiers' Home Hospital."

2 *Ha-Yehudi* 1, 11–12 (1936), pp. 217–19 (Hebrew).

imposition of] fines, the Rabbis did not distinguish between custom and halakhah: "Just as a fine is imposed for [the violation of] halakhah, so, too, is it imposed for the [the violation of] custom" (PT Pesahim 4:3).

Not all practices are on the same level as regards their nature, their reason, or their source.[...]

We must examine the source and reason of each custom, and determine if the practice is homegrown, and originates in the soul of the [Jewish] people, or whether it is a foundling, that we have adopted from another people.

For example, the practice of covering the bride's face — for bashfulness and modesty — is, as is known, not unique to we Jews, but is rather to be found among most peoples;[3] this is the veil of brides. The custom of breaking a glass cup during the wedding ceremony[4] is mentioned in all the medieval [Jewish] *minhagim* books, based on what is taught (Berakhot 31[a]) that Mar the son of Ravina broke a precious cup of crystal at a marriage feast for his son, as did R. Ashi; and *Tosafot* wrote [s.v. "*Aitiy*"]: "The practice of breaking a glass cup at weddings [is derived] from this." According to one opinion, this breaking signifies the groom's presumptive ownership [i.e. of his wife], for it was the law in Germany to ratify a legal ruling by the breaking of a staff. In the famous painting *Marriage of the Virgin* by Raphael, we see how one of the guests standing to the right of the groom breaks a staff over his knee.[5] The Bulgarians smash vessels after the bride is found to be a virgin.[...] It is the custom of those in the Caucasus and Byelorussia to smash vessels on joyous occasions.[6]

3 See, e.g., *Medieval Folklore: A Dictionary of Myths, Legends, Tales, Beliefs, and Customs*, ed. C. Lindahl, J. McNamara, and J. Lindow (Santa Barbara, Denver, and Oxford, 2000), Vol. 2, p. 631; the monumental work by E. Westermarck, *The History of Human Marriage*[5] (New York, 1922), Vol. 2, pp. 277, 527–28.

4 See below, chap. 21, "The '*Huppah*' — The Wedding Canopy/Ceremony"; J.S. Lauterbach, "The Ceremony of Breaking a Glass at Weddings," *HUCA* 2 (1925), pp. 351–80; Westermarck, op. cit., pp. 457–64, with a wealth of examples from diverse cultures.

5 This is probably not the correct understanding of Raphael's painting. See below, chap. 21 ("The '*Huppah*' — The Wedding Canopy/Ceremony"), n. 14. For the breaking of the staff, see Westermarck, pp. 463–64.

6 See Westermarck, pp. 459–61, who describes (p. 461) the intriguing Slavic custom

We learn from this matter that many practices entered the ranks of our people since it was situated in proximity to the people whose customs it adopted.[7] We must carefully examine, when was the time of this contact

of the bride encircling the groom three times; for more on such rounds, see Westermarck, pp. 512–16.

7   Examples of this phenomenon abound in the seven volumes of *Minhagei Yisrael* to the present. See, e.g., Vol. 1, pp. 16–17; pp. 217–27; Vol. 4, p. 86 n. 12; p. 90 n. 17 (cf. Westermarck, op. cit., pp. 529–30); p. 91 n. 20 (the latter three are also in the English edition: below, chap. 21, nn. 18, 28); Vol. 6, p. 104 n. 35 (English edition: Part 2, chap. 7, n. 22), and many more.

An additional instance of this phenomenon appears in Zinner, *Nitei Gavriel, Marriage Law*, Vol. 1 (Jerusalem, 1998), 36:7, p. 217: "It is the practice of some that immediately following the wedding ceremony the groom places his right leg on the bride's left leg." Zinner ad loc., n. 14, provides copious sources for this practice, such as *Midrash Talpiyyot* (by Rabbi Elijah ha-Kohen ha-Itamari), "*Anaf Hatan ve-Kallah*" [*Bride and Groom*]; *Hesed le-Avraham* (by R. Abraham Azulai); *Ma'amar* [Essay] *Ma'ayan* 4, *Nahar* 48; *Keter Shem Tov*, p. 625, and more. *Midrash Talpiyyot*, loc. cit., explains, in the name of *Hesed le-Avraham*: "There is a great reason inherent in this, that if the groom is careful to place his right foot on the bride's left foot during the Seven Blessings, this display of force empowers him, that he shall rule her all his life, and she shall be subjugated and heed him in all." A similar practice is observed by the Jews of Tunis. See Settbon, *Kunteres Alei Hadas*, p. 183; also mentioned in J. Chetrit et al. (eds.), *The Jewish Traditional Marriage: Interpretative and Documentary Chapters* (Haifa, 2003), p. 505 (Hebrew): "And if the bride is careful to place her left leg on the right leg of the groom, she shall rule him all her life." See the continuation of the lengthy discussion in *Midrash Talpiyyot* based on the Kabbalah. See Westermarck, *The History of Human Marriage*, Vol. 2, pp. 491–95: the various methods by which the groom seeks to dominate his bride, or vice versa. And here, we find in *Medieval Folklore*, Vol. 2, p. 631: "In thirteenth-century German villages [...] Once the vows were declared the groom took possession of his wife by stepping on her foot, the same gesture used in Germany to seal business deals." This parallels the custom in Cochin: following the betrothal ceremony, the groom would grab hold of the *tzitzit* (ritual fringes) of the *talit* (prayer shawl) of the rabbi, to effect a sort of acquisition (see M. Klein, *Wedding Traditions of the Various Jewish Communities* [Tel Aviv, 1994], p. 61 [Hebrew]). This act was also performed by the members of the Shar'ab community in Yemen (see below, chap. 20, "Wedding Rings," where we demonstrate that this form of acquisition has its origins in the Geonic literature, is also mentioned in the Karaite literature, and was maintained in several communities until recently. I am not convinced, however, that this is the root of the custom; it is rather, as was set forth above, a manner of imposing the husband's control over his wife. As Brauer writes in his *The Jews of Kurdistan*, p. 111: "So that the groom shall dominate the bride, he places his right leg

and taking, and we must also clarify if the reason, as well, was taken along with the custom from the foreign people, or whether it was

on the left leg of the bride, who stands next to him, and he would stand in this manner during the Seven Blessings." And similarly in Afghanistan: "At the conclusion of the dancing, before the groom and bride enter their house, the groom steps on the bride's foot. This symbolizes his superiority in the home" (Klein, *Wedding Traditions*, p. 97). This was also the practice among Bukharan Jewry. See B. Moshavi, "Customs and Folklore of the Nineteenth Century Bukharian Jews in Central Asia: Birth, Engagement, Marriage, Mourning and Others," Ph.D. diss., Yale University, 1974, pp. 156, 163–66 (Hebrew). This was also observed by the Uzbeks, as Moshavi notes, with a reference to (N.P. Lobacheva), "Wedding Rites in the Uzbek SSR," *Central Asian Review* 15, 4 (1967), p. 296; and (p. 165) an additional reference to the explanation by R. David Azulai (*Hesed le-Avraham* [Lvov, 1863], *Ma'ayan* 4, *Ein Yaakov, Nahar* 45) that the placing of the right leg on the bride's left one affords the groom mastery over her for his entire life. These communities were undoubtedly unaware of the European acquisition methods. Westermarck, op. cit., Vol. 2, p. 493, also records a similar practice meant to ensure mastery of one spouse over the other: "[...] in the Swedish-speaking communities in Finland she, for the same purpose [dominion over her husband], tries to place her foot before his during the nuptial ceremony. In Pellinge, in Finland, the bride's mother, on the same occasion, used to throw her daughter's skirt over the heels of the bridegroom, if she wanted her to rule over him." These are merely a selection of the diverse range of customs that different cultures believe give the husband mastery over his wife, or the opposite (see Westermarck, pp. 491–94). See also *idem, Marriage Ceremonies in Morocco* (London, 1914 [photocopy edn.: London and Dublin, 1972]), pp. 355–57; see also T.H. Gaster, *Myth, Legend, and Custom in the Old Testament* (Gloucester, MA, 1981), Vol. 2, p. 449, para. 123 (iii), who shows that stepping on someone as a mark of control over the latter already appears in the Bible, such as in Ps. 8:7: "You have made him master over Your handiwork, laying the world at his feet," and also in Ugaritic, Phoenician, and Egyptian sources (loc. cit., and p. 540). See also Y.M. Sokolov, *Russian Folklore*, trans. C.R. Smith (Detroit, 1971), p. 207, that the removal of the husband's shoes by the bride signified her submission to him. Cf., however, below, chap. 23, "Throwing a Shoe at a Wedding," n. 16. This motif, of the performance of a certain action at the wedding to ensure the husband's mastery over his wife, is present in several Jewish customs. For example, the practice advocated by R. Jacob ben Moses Moellin (*Sefer Maharil*, ed. Spitzer, p. 467): "Immediately [after the wedding ceremony], the groom, in a joyful manner, is hastened to enter the bridal chamber **before** the bride." And, in a different formulation (ibid., "Variants," n. 13): "To thereby fulfill — to say that he shall be master in his house and rule it — regarding this I saw a practice by *Mahari Segal* [= Moellin] of Mainz; in another place: 'Go and see what is the practice of the people.'" We will end this discussion with the conclusion by Zinner in *Nitei Gavriel*: "According to one opinion, it is given a new rationale and spiritual content, since it is very common, especially in our people already from ancient times, to take over various practices from other people and "clothe them in [priestly] robes"[8] — to impart to them a meaning that is wholly pure.

We must act very carefully and with great comprehension in this matter — the investigation of the place in which each custom was born and formulated. [...] It is extremely essential and worthwhile that our Orthodox scholars and writers will devote themselves, in complete seriousness, to this important and so highly valuable labor. Methodical and orderly work will unquestionably succeed in restoring the honor of Israel, and also infuse the breath of life in the customs of our forefathers.

An inquiry into the roots and antiquity of the custom of the *Halakah* will serve as a fine example of the mission that Rabbi Williamowsky has set for us.

2. THE ANTECEDENTS OF THE *HALAKAH*

In 1990 R. Yosef Serebryanski published a book entitled *Yalkut ha-Tisporet*,[9] in which he sought to explore the custom of giving a child his first haircut at the age of three years. Serebryanski begins his work with the admission that "it is not clear when the [practice] originated of first cutting the child's hair when he reaches the age of three years" (p. 9). He finds an allusion to this in the Palestinian Talmud,[10] which connects the cutting of a young child's hair with the laws pertaining to the harvesting of a field.[11] He concludes from

preferable not to do so, regarding which it is said: 'You must be wholehearted with the Lord your God' [Deut. 18:13]," based on *Keter Shem Tov*, loc. cit.; R. Saul Schapira, *She'eilot u-Teshuvot Hemdat Shaul* (Odessa, 1903), para. 43.

8　Following Zech. 3:4.

9　R. Yosef Yitzchok Serebryanski, *Yalkut ha-Tisporet: Likkut Nifla ba-Inyanei ha-Tisporet ha-Rishonah* (*The Haircut Collection: A Marvelous Collection on Aspects of the First Haircut*) (Beverly, NJ, 1990).

10　PT Peah 1:4.

11　See Serebryanski, p. 12. The Palestinian Talmud comments on M Peah 1:5: "Among trees, the sumac [...] is liable the law of *peah* [one of the gifts for the poor; left from the corners of one's field]" that "There are those who wish to deduce this from here [...] and it is written, 'When you beat down the fruit of your olive trees, do not go over them again' [Deut. 24:20] [this is an explicit prohibition of the application

this and additional allusions[12] that "it therefore may be stated that **there are already indicators in the earliest times** of this practice of haircutting in the midrash, and in statements by *Radbaz* [Rabbi David ben Zimra] [each in its own context], until we find it in its [final] form by the *Ari* [R. Isaac Luria], of blessed memory.[13] Since then, the custom has spread throughout all Israel."[14]

of *peah* to fruit trees]. How did you hear [a prohibition of *peah* from fruit trees] here? R. Jonah said: This accords with what is said: 'You shall not round off the side-growth [*pe'at*] on your head' [Lev. 19:27]." This passage from the PT was therefore seen as already connecting the cutting of hair with the laws governing the reaping of the field.

12 Proof is usually brought from *Tanhuma, Kedoshim* 4: "'And plant [...] you shall regard as forbidden' [Lev. 19:23] — Scripture speaks of a young child. 'Three years it shall be forbidden for you' [ibid.], [meaning] that it cannot speak or talk, 'in the fourth year all its fruit shall be set aside' [v. 24] — [meaning] that his father sets him aside for Torah study."

13 For the sources relating that R. Isaac Luria cut his son's hair in Meron, see A. Yaari, "History of the Pilgrimage to Meron," *Tarbiz* 31 (1962), pp. 85–90 (Hebrew); see also M. Benayahu, *Sefer Toledot ha-Ari* (*The Toledoth ha-Ari and Luria's "Manner of Life"* [*Hanhagoth*]) (Jerusalem, 1967), p. 314 (Hebrew); and the glosses by R. Bezalel Landau to R. Menahem Mendel Rabin, *Masa Meron*[3] (*Meron Journey*) (Jerusalem, 1983), p. 133, based on R. Hayyim Vital, *Sha'ar ha-Kavanot*, and what he cited from "an ancient manuscript, that has come to us from the time of the disciples of R. Isaac Luria [...] and prayer is fine when the youths' hair is cut." For somewhat of an objection to the thesis of Yaari, see M. Benayahu, "Devotion Practices of the Kabbalists of Safed in Meron," pp. 29–30 (who also mentions the above "fine prayer").

14 See Landau, *Masa Meron*, pp. 131–37; *idem*, "The Education of Children by Means of the 'Halakhah' Haircut," *Zekhor le-Avraham: Kovetz Torani* 1993, pp. 502–510 (Hebrew). Several studies on the *Halakah* custom have recently been published, the most important of which are the following: the booklet *"Kuntres Pe'at ha-Rosh ..."* (*The* Peah *of the Head Booklet, Containing All the Aspects of the Laws and Customs of the Halakah, the First Shearing of the Little One, and* Lag be-Omer *Songs*), edited by M.M. Hoffman, was published in Jerusalem in 1993; three years later the book *Nitei Gavriel, Laws and Practices of the Festival of Pesah*, Vol. 3, by R. Gabriel Zinner appeared (Brooklyn, 1996), with the laws and customs of the shearing of children's hair, pp. 300 ff.; 2002 saw the publication of R. Shimon Guttman, *Tiglahat Mitzvah ve-Inyanei Lag be-Omer* (*The Religiously-Mandated Cutting of the Hair and Matters Relating to* Lag be-Omer) (Bnei Brak, 2002); and in 2003 R. David Steinberg published *Sefer Pe'ot ke-Halakhah* (*The Book of Proper Sidelocks*) (New York, 2003), that contained "*Kuntres Tiglahat Mitzvah* [Booklet of the Obligatory Haircut]," pp. 345–55. None of these works, however, attempts to

Although we shall not examine the entire development of this practice,[15] its sources and roots undoubtedly are to be found, as Serebryanski puts it,

study the history of the custom, since any such study would be out of place in these books, that focus on the practical *halakah* and *minhag* (i.e. binding practice). See also B. Naor, "The Practice of Cutting the Son's Hair ("*Opsherenish*"), *Ohr Yisroel* 5, 4 (20) (2000), p. 146 (Hebrew); see also the response by the editors, *Ohr Yisroel* 6, 1 (21) (2000), p. 251 (Hebrew).

15 It is noteworthy that R. Joseph (Joselein) ben Moses (ca. 1460), *Leket Yosher, Orah Hayyim*, p. 97, states, in the name of the author of *Terumat ha-Deshen* (R. Israel Isserlein, 1390–1460), that "he would permit shearing the head of the young child who was 13 weeks old, on the eighteenth day of the *Omer*" (with references in Guttman, *Tiglahat Mitzvah ve-Inyanei Lag be-Omer*, p. 16; Serebryanski, *Yalkut ha-Tisporet*, p. 23; but see the latter's comment, p. 24 n. 3). The basis for this permission is unclear, but we propose the following hypothesis to explain the specified age of thirteen weeks: the rabbis assert that pregnancy lasts for a period of 271–273 days (see BT Niddah 38a-b; according to PT Yevamot 4:1, PT Niddah 1:3, the full term is 271–274 days; see A. Steinberg, *Encyclopedia of Jewish Medical Ethics*, Vol. 2 [Jerusalem, 1991], pp. 173–74 n. 18 [Hebrew]). In other words, pregnancy extends for some 39 weeks, and 13 weeks is the time when the fetus has reached one-third of term. The fetus is recognizable after three months of pregnancy (BT loc. cit. and PT loc. cit.; see Steinberg, op. cit., p. 96 n. 256; cf. pp. 177–78 n. 49). This means that the thirteenth week, which is about one-third of its term, is also the time when it becomes noticeable. This number might possibly have led R. Isserlein to determine that the infant will be sufficiently strong 13 weeks **after the birth** so that he would not be harmed in some fashion or other by the cutting of his hair; this still is quite doubtful. At any rate, in medieval Germany, some parents took care not to cut their child's hair until a relatively advanced age, that is, not before he reached the age of seven years. Thus in Wetterau, in A. Wuttke, *Der deutsche Volksaberglaube der Gegenwart* (Hamburg, 1860), p. 202 (with a reference in B. Bonnerjea, *A Dictionary of Superstition and Mythology* [London, 1927?], p. 117); and Wuttke, third edition, ed. E.H. Meyer (Berlin, 1900), para. 607, p. 395; see the Index, p. 506b, s.v. "haare." These different and diverse sources indicate that hair was perceived as signifying strength, and the cutting of the hair could weaken the body, especially that of an infant. See Gaster, *Myth, Legend, and Custom in the Old Testament*, Vol. 2, pp. 436, 536 n. 18, with a wealth of sources (based on J.G. Frazer, *Folk-Lore in the Old Testament: Studies in Comparative Religion, Legend and Law* [London, 1918], Vol. 2, pp. 484–86). To show how widespread this notion was, see M.M. Hyatt, *Folk-Lore from Adams County, Illinois* (New York, 1935), nos. 2897 ff., p. 141. And, likewise, V. Newall, *An Egg at Easter: A Folklore Study* (London, 1971), p. 135, which portrays a fascinating Gypsy custom from southern Hungary, based on E.O. Winsted, "Forms and Ceremonies," *Journal of the Gypsy Lore Society* 2 (Edinburgh, July 1908–April 1909), p. 341: "The south Hungarian

in "the earliest times";[16] a nineteenth-century scholar, W. Robertson Smith,[17] writes, concerning "Offerings of Hair":[18]

> Among the Hebrews and the Arabs, and indeed among many other peoples both ancient and modern [...] [there was] the practice of shaving the head or cutting off part of the hair and depositing it in the tomb or on the funeral pyre [pp. 323–24].
>
> [...] Now among the Semites and other ancient people the hair-offering is common, not only in mourning but in the worship of the gods [p. 325].
>
> [...] At Delphi, where Greek Ephebi were wont to offer the long hair of their childhood, this peculiar cut [a tonsure] was called θησηίς, for Theseus was said to have shorn only his front locks at the temple [loc. cit., n. 2].[19]

tent gypsies observe a curious ritual when a child first has his hair cut. Three eggs laid by a black hen are mixed with salt water and massaged into the scalp. In many races hair-cutting is an important occasion, for it was once supposed that a person's strength lay partly in his hair. Eggs were perhaps to counteract this loss and also to guard the child against malignant influence, which he would be specially prone to on the first occasion."

16 This was touched upon by Gaster, *The Holy and the Profane*, pp. 106–107.

17 W. Robertson Smith, *Lectures on the Religion of the Semites: First Series: The Fundamental Institutions*, second, expanded edition (London, 1894), pp. 323 ff. In an introduction written in 1963 the renowned psychologist Theodore Reik states in *Pagan Rites in Judaism: from Sex Initiation, Magic, Moon-Cult, Tattooing, Mutilation, and Other Primitive Rituals to Family Loyalty and Solidarity* (New York, 1964), p. 46: "I refer to the *Lectures on the Religion of the Semites* by W. Robertson Smith — a book whose essential findings are, after more than seventy years, still not outdated."

18 Morgenstern, *Rites of Birth, Marriage, Death and Kindred Occasions among the Semites*, pp. 36–47, discusses Robertson Smith's conception in "Offerings of Hair"; see the expansion, pp. 84–106, esp. p. 88. See Westermarck, *Ritual and Belief in Morocco*, Vol. 2, p. 407: "According to the Muhammadan traditions the child should have its head shaved on the seventh day after its birth, when it is named and a sacrifice is made." See also pp. 413–16, for Westermarck's reservations concerning the explanations by Robertson Smith.

19 See J.E. Harrison, *Themis: A Study of the Social Origins of Greek Legislation* (Cleveland, 1962), pp. 441–42, who cites Plutarch (ca. 50–120 CE) (Vit Thes. V), that this was the practice of those passing from childhood to adulthood, to go to Delphi and bring the first fruits of their hair to the god. Cf. pp. 337 n. 1, 379, 498. Additional relevant sources from the Greek literature are to be found

[...] Among Lucian's Syrians [*Dea Syria* VI], on the other hand, the hair of boys and girls was allowed to grow unshorn as a consecrated

in J. Marquardt, *Das Privatleben der Romer*, Vol. 2 (Leipzig, 1866 [photocopy edn.: Darmstadt, 1964]) (= *Handbuch der romischen Alterthumer*, 7), pp. 599–600 nn. 7–8. Thus, e.g., we read in *Anthologia Graeca*, Vol. 6, p. 279 (*LCL* edition: *The Greek Anthology*, Vol. 1 [London, 1916], p. 449), in the name of Euphorion (third century BCE) (trans. Paton): "When Eudoxus first shore his beautiful hair, he gave to Pheobus the glory of his boyhood; and now vouchsafe, O Far-shooter, that instead of these tresses the ivy of Acharnae may ever rest on his head as he grows." "The ivy of Acharnae" refers to the garland of ivy that came from Acharnae (near Athens) that was placed on his head as a prize in a musical competition. Additionally, *Anthologia Graeca*, Vol. 6, p. 278, by Rhianus (ca. 200 CE) (ed. *LCL*, Vol. 1, p. 449): "Gorgus, son of Asclepiades, dedicates to Phoebus the fair this fair lock, a gift from his lovely head. But, Delphinian Phoebus, be gracious to the boy, and establish him to good fortune till his hair be grey"; ibid., Vol. 6, p. 173 (by Rhianus); p. 156 (by Theodoridas, third century BCE), and more. We learn from these and additional epigrammatic testimonies of a literary genre related to these donations-offerings. For the connection between Phoebus (= Apollo, who is identified with the sun-god Helios, especially in the Roman period; see W. Smith [ed.], *Dictionary of Greek and Roman Biography and Mythology* [London, 1848], Vol. 2, p. 375b); see I. Goldziher, *Mythology among the Hebrews and Its Historical Development*, trans. R. Martineau (London, 1877 [photocopy edn.: New York, 1967]), p. 137, who observes that the rays of the sun are called "*Crines Phoebi*" (see also *Thesaurus Linguae Latinae*, Vol. 10 [Leipzig, 1904–09], p. 1205 l. 6, s.v. "crinis"). For Apollo-Phoebus, see also L. Preller, *Theogonie und Goetter*[4] (= Vol. 1 of his *Griechische Mythologie*) (Berlin, 1894), pp. 231–32; *Paulys Realenzyclopaedie der classischen Altertumswissenschaft*, Vol. 39 (Stuttgart, 1941), p. 348; and in Plutarch, *Moralia*, "The E at Delphi," paras. 384F, 393C (ed. *LCL*: trans. F. Babbit [1936], Vol. 5, pp. 293, 247). Goldziher further writes (p. 138): "The Beaming Apollo, moreover, is called the Unshaven; and Minos cannot conquer the solar hero Nisos, till the latter loses his golden hair." He refers (n. 5) to F.L.W. Schwartz, *Der Ursprung der Mythologie, dargelegt an griechischer und deutscher Sage* (Berlin, 1860), p. 144. Cf. J. Grimm, *Teutonic Mythology*[4], ed. J.S. Stallybrass (Berlin, 1875–78 [New York, 1966]), Vol. 2, p. 738. (Also of interest, albeit not directly relating to the matter at hand, is the continuation of his note: "Bernhard Schmidt (Das Volksleben der Neugriechen [Leipzig, 1871], 1, p. 206) says, 'In Zante I encountered the idea that the entire power of the ancient Greeks lay in three hairs on the breast, and vanished if these were cut off, but returned when the hairs grew again.'" This is reminiscent of the midrash in Gen. Rabbah 3:6 [ed. Theodor-Albeck, pp. 1156–57]: "R. Hanan said: When his [the biblical Judah's] ire was aroused, the hairs of his chest would rend his clothing and emerge"; and in *Tanhuma, Vayigash* 3: "R. Yuden said: When Judah's ire was

thing from birth to adolescence, and was cut off and dedicated at the sanctuary as a necessary preliminary to marriage.[20] In other words, the hair-offering of youths and maidens was a ceremony of religious initiation, through which they had to pass before they were admitted to the status of social maturity. [p. 329]

As time passed, however, among the Arabs and other tribes, what had initially been a ceremony of initiation into manhood now became a ceremony conducted while the child was still in infancy;[21] as an example, Smith

aroused, two hairs would emerge from his bosom and rend his garments." See the parallels cited by Albeck ad loc., who observed that this legend was known to Arab and Syrian authors, as well, with a reference to I. Schapiro, *Die haggadischen Elemente im erzahlenden Teil des Korans* [Leipzig, 1907], Vol. 1, p. 66.) See also W.A. Becker, *Charicles: or Illustrations of the Private Life of the Ancient Greeks*, trans. F. Metcalfe (London, 1866³), p. 454, who discusses this practice and indicates its currency over a lengthy period; indeed, it continued to exist in the Roman period, as well, albeit with changes. See *idem, Gallus: or Roman Scenes of the Time of Augustus*, trans. Metcalfe, new edn. (London, 1907), p. 428: the first shaving off of the beard was observed as a holiday. Thus, e.g., Dio Cassius (second-third centuries CE), *Romaika*, 48:34 (ed. *LCL: Dio's Roman History*, trans. E. Cary, Vol. 5, p. 291): "For example, when Caesar now for the first time shaved off his beard, he held a magnificent entertainment himself besides granting all the other citizens a festival at public expense." For additional sources, see Cook, *Zeus*, Vol. 3: *Zeus God of the Dark Sky (Earthquakes, Clouds, Wind, Dew, Rain, Meteorites)* (Cambridge, 1914), pp. 23–25, 593, 859–60: "hair-cutting rite dedication to Zeus, always by men"; ibid., Vol. 3, Part 2 (Cambridge, 1940), p. 1066. For additional bibliography, see W.H.D. Rouse, *Greek Votive Offerings* (Cambridge, 1902), pp. 240–45; L. Sommer, *Das Haar in Religion und Aberglauben der Griechen* (Muenster, 1912), pp. 1–86; H. Bachtold-Staubli, *Handworterbuch des deutschen Aberglaubens* (Berlin-Leipzig, 1930–31), Vol. 3, pp. 1288–39, s.v. "Haar"; Farnell, *The Cults of the Greek States*, Vol. 5, p. 422 n. 72.

20 The Greeks regarded the cutting of young women's hair prior to their marriage to be a sacrifice (known as "προτέλεια"). See *Pollux* 3:38: "ἡ δέ πρό γάμου θυσία προτέλεια." See W. Burkert, *Homo Necans: The Anthropology of Ancient Greek Sacrificial Ritual and Myth*, trans. P. Bing (Berkeley, Los Angeles, London, 1972), pp. 62–63, and the references in n. 20.

21 Ibid., p. 330. At this juncture it would be appropriate to cite Edward W. Lane, the outstanding Arabist and author of *An Arabic-English Lexicon* (1863–93), in his well-known work, *An Account of the Manners and Customs of the Modern Egyptians* (first published in England in 1836; London 1966 edition, based on the 1860 edition), p. 55: "When a boy is two or three years old, or often earlier, his head

mentions that in Sidon it was forbidden to cut an infant's hair before he reached the age of one year.[22]

> The "hair-offering" was also related to pilgrimage ceremonies; as Smith expresses this: the hair-offering formed part of the ritual in every Arabian pilgrimage [p. 331].

He then explains (loc. cit.) that, in this manner,

is shaven; a tuft of hair only being left on the crown, and another over the forehead"; and ad loc., n. 1, he elaborates: "It is customary among the peasants throughout a great part of Egypt, on the first occasion of shaving a child's head, to slay a victim, generally a goat, at the tomb of some saint in or near their village, and to make a feast with the meat, of which their friends, and any other persons who please, partake. This is most common in Upper Egypt, and among the tribes not very long established on the banks of the Nile. Their Pagan ancestors in Arabia observed this custom, and usually gave, as alms to the poor, the weight of the hair in silver or gold. (This custom may perhaps throw some light on the statement in 2 Sam. xiv. 26, respecting Absalom's weighing the hair of his head 'when he polled it.') The victim is called 'akeekah', and is offered as a ransom for the child from hell. The custom of shaving one part of a child's head and leaving another was forbidden by the Prophet"; and similarly, in his *Arabian Society in the Middle Ages: Studies from The Thousand and One Nights* (London, 1883), p. 191. For the "akeekah," see Westermarck, *Ritual and Belief in Morocco*, Vol. 2, p. 408: "It is also prescribed that the father of the child should give in alms to the poor the weight of the hair in silver or gold." See also ibid., pp. 413–14; Lane, *Arabian Society in the Middle Ages*, loc. cit; F. Legey, *The Folklore of Morocco*, trans. L. Hotz (London, 1935), pp. 148–49. It is noteworthy that among the Jews of India, "when a child reaches the age of four or five years, a day of feasting and celebration would be held. The boy would be taken to the synagogue in a magnificent and joyous procession, his entire head would be closely cut with scissors, **all of his hair would be weighed in silver or gold**, each according to his means, and the money of its value was given to the synagogue fund, or would be distributed to the poor" (J. Saphir, *Even Sappir*, Vol. 2 [Mainz, 1874], p. 47; also cited in the glosses by R. Bezalel Landau to *Masa Meron*, p. 137). Cf. Serebryanski, *Yalkut ha-Tisporet*, pp. 70–72, who offers additional sources for this practice. See also Guttman, *Tiglahat Mitzvah* 1:12, p. 13. The source is given as *Radbaz* (Rabbi David ben Zimra), *She'eilot u-Teshuvot ha-Radbaz*, section 2, para. 608, who writes, concerning prostrating oneself at the tomb of Samuel the prophet: "They were accustomed to bring vows and freewill offerings, and they gave the weight of the hair for the needs of the place, to light wax and oil in its [the hair's] place, and its other needs."

22 Ibid., p. 329, end of n. 1, based on M. Gruenbaum, "Einige Parallelen zu dem Aufsatze-Beitrage ...," *ZDPV* 8 (1885), p. 85.

the worshipper [...] desired to attach himself as firmly as possible to a deity and a shrine with which he could not hope to keep up frequent and regular connection.[23]

This chapter did not set out to paint a complete and comprehensive picture of the development of juvenile haircutting,[24] among other reasons, because

23 Cf. Smith, *Lectures on the Religion of the Semites*, pp. 483–84. J.G. Frazer, *Taboo and the Perils of the Soul*, cited varied customs related to the cutting of children's hair (p. 263), and again in his later book *Folk-Lore in the Old Testament*, Vol. 3, pp. 188–89. Surprisingly, Frazer, who was paramountly erudite in the scholarly literature of folklore, seemingly made no use of Robertson Smith's work that had appeared some two decades earlier. Frazer had, however, begun to investigate this subject in his translation and commentary of Pausanias: *Pausanias's Description of Greece* (London, 1898; second edn.: London, 1913), Vol. 3, p. 279, only four years after the publication of Robertson Smith's book, and in his other works, he mainly cited his own studies. The scope of the comparative material is too vast for us to encompass in the present context.

24 To this we should add what was written in E. Burnett Tylor's classic *Religion in Primitive Culture* (New York, 1959; first published as *Primitive Culture* in 1871), Vol. 2, p. 487: "Thus there is some ground for interpreting the consecration of the boy's cut hair in Europe as a representative sacrifice." In his introduction to the 1957 edition, Paul Radin writes (p. IX): "Taylor's major theses [...] essentially stand today despite the many criticisms to which they have been subjected." William Graham Sumner adds, in his classic study *Folkways* (New Haven, 1906 [New York, 1959]), p. 556 (reprint): "The connection between child sacrifice and the temple consecration of girls is in the substitution of the latter for the former as a ransom. [...] In later times (second century A.D.) we find the sacrifice of a woman's hair as a substitute for herself (Lucian, *De Syria Dea*, 6)." This, too, is the view of Erwin Rohde, *Psyche: The Cult of Souls and Belief in Immortality among the Greeks* (London, 1925), p. 45 n. 14. And so, also, apparently, is the opinion held by E.F. Bruck, *Totenteil und Seelgerat im griechischen Recht*[2] (Munich, 1926), p. 31; cf. R. Garland, *The Greek Way of Death*[2] (Ithaca, NY, 2001), p. 35.
A similar picture emerges from the depiction by Lane (above, n. 20); further support is gathered from a comparison with the material brought by Saul Lieberman, *Hellenism in Jewish Palestine* (New York, 1962), p. 151: "**Consecration by way of cutting some of the victim's hair and offering it to the gods**. R. Johanan's opinion, which is conclusive, is that 'the consecration takes effect when the animal is shorn and an act of worship is performed with it.' It was the regular practice of the Greeks to cut some hair of the victim immediately before slaughtering and offer it to the gods. The rabbis correctly took the offering of the hair as the actual *consecratio* of the victim. R. Johanan defined the *consecratio* according to the *graecus ritus* which was followed by many heathens in Palestine, Syria and Egypt." See Lieberman

of the large chronological gaps between the sources, which thus preclude a continuity of testimonies that would enable us to provide a detailed portrayal of the development of the custom.[25] Nonetheless, these quotations suffice to delineate the path taken by these milestones on the way to the *Halakah*.

3. "CLOTHE THEM IN ROBES"

We opened our discussion with Rabbi Williamowsky's description of the "naturalization" process by which customs of non-Jewish origin are adopted by the Jewish people, where they receive "a new rationale and spiritual content" and are enwrapped in "'robes' — to impart to them a meaning that is wholly pure." We have seen this in practice, regarding the first haircut of children. Since we do not presume to possess any esoteric understanding, we will cite the following passage from the book by Rabbi Serebryanski:[26]

> A passage from a manuscript [from *bukh* (ledger) MS. 94, in the library of the holy crown, *Admor*, *shelita* (honorific titles for a Hasidic rabbi) of Lubavich (...)]:[27]
> As regards the understanding of the matter of the cutting of the child's hair when he is three years old, that is not mentioned in the *Shulhan*

ad loc., nn. 35–36, for the sources on which this is based, including P. Stengel, *Opferbrauche der Griechen* (Teubner, 1910), pp. 40–47. An intriguing comparison is afforded by the description by Westermarck, *Ritual and Belief in Morocco*, Vol. 1, p. 357, of the offering of the goat's hair together with its fat, making balls of the mixture (this, however, would seem to have no bearing upon the current discussion).

25 We have already presented several examples of the survival for centuries of ancient customs, apparently by oral transmission, such as the slaughter of a hen that crowed like a rooster (see Part 2, chap. 1, "Omens of Approaching Death," p. 359); the use of iron as a means of protection (*Minhagei Yisrael*, Vol. 1, pp. 16, 233); sprinkling salt over newborn babies (*Minhagei Yisrael*, Vol. 1, p. 224 n. 1). See also my book, *Magic and Folklore in Rabbinic Literature*, p. 97 n. 29; cf. above, n. 19, the reference to Becker, *Charicles*.

26 Serebryanski, *Yalkut ha-Tisporet*, pp. 94–95.

27 "By the holy crown, *Admor*, *shelita* [apparently R. Shneur Zalman of Kapust], the day after Yom Kippur [5]690 [= 1889], on the haircutting of his grandson, his followers requested a Torah discourse. He asked his grandson if he should deliver a Torah discourse, and he answered in the affirmative. The holy crown, *Admor*, *shelita*, said jokingly, What does he care if he were to say [...]. Afterwards, he delivered this teaching."

Arukh, nor any [other] place; and similarly, the prayerbook of R. J[acob] Emden, of blessed memory, who accounts man's conduct with his son from the day of the latter's birth, did not account the practice of cutting the hair of the three-year-old son; it is explained in the writings of the *Ari* [R. Isaac Luria], of blessed memory, that this is a great matter, for R. Jacob Saruk attested to R. Hayyim Vital, of blessed memory [in *Peri Etz Hayyim*, "*Sefirat ha-Omer*," para. 7], that the *Ari*, of blessed memory, went with his son to the village of Meron, at the tomb of R. Simeon bar Yohai and his son R. Eleazar, to cut his hair[28] [this implies that (the son) was three years old]. His wife was there, as well, and he spent three days there at a feast. Accordingly, since this is a great matter, it is surprising why this is not to be found anywhere. This matter, of the writing of the Tetragrammaton *E-l* [God; see Ex. 34:6], as is explained in the writings of the *Ari*, of blessed memory, the beginning of the Thirteen Attributes of [Divine] mercy, is from the *tikkun* [mystical remedial measure] of the word *E-l*, that is the first *tikkun* [of the thirteen such *tikkunim*], which is not the case for the two mentions of the Tetragrammaton, that are on a higher level than the thirteen *tikkunim*. These are called the *pe'ot* [sidelocks] of the head, and from the place where the *pe'ot* end, begin the Thirteen Attributes of [Divine] mercy, that are called the *zakan* [beard]. This is the place where the beard begins to expand: this is a small place, from the cheekbone under the ear, that is the conclusion and end of the sidelocks. From here begins the beard, that is the Thirteen Attributes of [Divine] mercy. Therefore, the *Ari*, of blessed memory, when he trimmed his sidelocks (for his sidelocks were short), would leave enough so that the beard would connect with the sidelocks, etc. This is the meaning of [from the liturgy] "And so [*u-ve-khen*] may Your Name be sanctified," etc. The numerical value of *u-ve-khen* is 78, which is also the numerical value of *mazla* [fortune]. The Thirteen Attributes of [Divine] mercy effect Divine revelation, from the aspect of *Malkhut En-Suf* of the aspect of "Your name," of the aspect of "[the Tetragrammaton] *E-lokenu*," *Hokhmah* ["Wisdom"], and *Binah* ["Intelligence"]. This is the meaning of "They crowned Him as God" [from the liturgy]. [...] Based on this, we can understand why the

---

28   See above, n. 13.

[first] haircut was not mentioned in the *Shulhan Arukh*, or in any other place [in the revealed sources]: because from this aspect [...] the two sidelocks [that are formed during the haircut] whose root is in the two Tetragrammatons, that are above the Thirteen Attributes of [Divine] mercy.[29]

29 See also Serebryanski, op. cit., pp. 92–93, for the teaching he cites in the name of R. Isaac Duber, the son of the *Admor* R. Hayyim Schneur Zalman, the son of the *Tzemah Tzedek*. Other, nonesoteric reasons are listed in Guttman, *Tiglahat Mitzvah ve-Inyanei Lag be-Omer*, pp. 1 ff.; e.g. para. 1: "Of especial importance is the first haircut given to a young child that is called *Halake* [n. 1 ad loc.: "from the language of the verse]: 'and I am smooth-skinned [*halak*]' (Gen. 27:11), adding that *Keter Shem Tov* (p. 591) wrote that this is an Arabic word], because it constitutes the beginning of the boy's education in the observance of the commandments, as the father educates him regarding the observance of this prohibition, as it is written: 'You shall not round off the side-growth on your head' [Lev. 19:27]. In this he shall be different from all the [non-Jewish] peoples, so that he will not be assimilated and absorbed within them; and it is a sort of protection against idolatry."

In a related vein, an instructive example of the giving of "reasons" (that originate in a completely different realm) for a certain practice is to be found in the question of the shape of *matzah*. In earlier times, all *matzot* were round, as can be seen in illuminations of medieval *Haggadot*. The reason is that this was the easiest way to make these unleavened wafers, as pittah bread is prepared to the present. When machines for *matzah* production were introduced toward the middle of the nineteenth century, these *matzot* were initially round, in the traditional shape. In 1858 a group of rabbis headed by R. Solomon Kluger, the head of the Brody rabbinical court, which a passionate attack against machine-made *matzot*, which included seven reasons for their prohibition. See the booklet edited by Kluger, with the views of the rabbis prohibiting machine-made *matzot: Moda'ah le-Beit Yisrael* (Breslau, 1859; the new [Jerusalem, 1993] edition includes *Bittul Moda'ah* by R. Joseph Saul Nathanson, the head of the Lemberg rabbinical court, which contains the opinions of the rabbis who took a permissive view). One of the reasons given for the prohibition is that when round *matzot* are machine-produced, the problem of "*obfal*" (the remaining dough, after the circles are cut out) arises: dough is reused, even more than once, and the dough might be from a mixture prepared more than eighteen minutes previously (and therefore meeting the halakhic definition of leaven). This objection was answered by R. Jacob Jacob Ettlinger of Altona (fol. 14a): "Even though there is no fear of a prohibition if the *matzot* are not round, nonetheless, this would be something new for the masses who are accustomed to round matzot, and it would not be correct to do so. I therefore enacted that they be cut round, quickly. From what remains, [...] square or five-sided ones are to be made. This is also the view of R. Jacob Wirtzburger [fol. 36a]." As time passed, however, machine-made *matzot* were accepted by the majority of Jews, and they are usually square in shape, for the reason cited above. (See G. Lichtman, "Why Is Matza Square?", *In Jerusalem*, pre-Passover edition 1998, p. 6, based on a lecture I delivered at the Yakar Educational and Cultural Center.) And yet, there are some who sanctify the rounded shape of *matzot*, by understanding "unleavened cakes [*ugot matzah*]" (Ex. 12:39) as mandating round *matzot*. R. Mordekhai Meir Shtemer recently wrote an entire article in the *Zanz* journal (Nisan 5703 [2003]) entitled (in a paraphrase of the language of the *Haggadah*) "Why Is This *Matzah* Round?", in which he brings a lengthy list of presumed "reasons," both those following the rules of regular halakhic reasoning and those with esoteric roots, why *matzot* are round. For example, he cites a responsum by R. Judah Azsod, *She'eilot u-Teshuvot Yehudah Ya'aleh, Orah Hayyim*, para. 157. The passage from the article by Shtemer reads as follows: "An additional reason for round *matzot*: from a close reading [of the responsum], he cites the midrash [Lam. Rabbah 3:15]: "'He has filled me with bitterness [*ba-mrorim*]' [Lam. 3:15] — this refers to the first day of Pesah, regarding which it is written, 'with unleavened bread and bitter herbs [*u-merorim*]' [Num. 9:11]. 'He has sated me with wormwood' [Lam. op. cit.] — with what He filled me on the first night of Pesah, He sated me on the night of the Ninth of Av." This is implicit in *Tur* [*Orah Hayyim* 428], from the *At-bash* system for determining the day [of the week] on which holy days will fall. [...] [The day of the week] on which the first day of Pesah falls is always [the day of the week] on which the Ninth of Av will fall, as is symbolized by 'They shall eat it with unleavened bread and bitter herbs [i.e. alluding to the fast day]. For this reason *Rema* [R. Moses Isserles] wrote: 'It is customary in some places to eat eggs at the meal, as a sign of mourning; it seems to me that the reason is because the night of the Ninth of Av is set as the [first] night of Pesah." Rashi comments (on Gen. 25:30) on the passage 'Give me some of that red stuff to gulp down': 'Red lentils. That was the day that Abraham died, and Jacob cooked the lentils as the first food given to a mourner. Why lentils? Because they are round as a wheel, for mourning [comes] around in cyclic fashion; furthermore, just as lentils have no mouth, so, too, the mourner has no mouth, for he may not speak [i.e. he may not greet others].' Consequently, it is customary to give the mourner eggs at the beginning of his meal, for they are round and have no mouth, just as the mourner has no mouth." Or, to explain this in an alternative fashion (p. 40): "On another occasion (during the recitation of the *Haggadah* at the *Seder* night, on the second night of Pesah 5742 [1982], published in *Divrei Torah*, no. 688), the holy crown, our master, the *Admor* [of Zanz], may his merit protect us, spoke in his holiness on such matters, on the one hand, as an advocate for the Israelites who were in the Egyptian exile at that time, that when they were about to go forth from within the exile, each one completely repented out of love. This is as Jonathan ben Uzziel explained in his *targum* on the verse (Ex. 2:25): "'God looked upon the Israelites, and God took notice of them" — the affliction of the slavery of the Israelites was revealed before the Lord, and the repentance that they had undertaken in secret, so that one person did not know about the other, was revealed before Him,' which may be why no person was attuned to his fellow, because one did not know that the other had repented, but rather thought that the other was immersed within the 49 gates of impurity [of Egypt], and that it was forbidden to speak with the latter, as is shown from this (from [BT] Yoma 9b): I am willing to engage in a transaction without witnesses with someone who accompanies Resh Lakish in the marketplace. Consequently, continues the holy crown, the *Admor*, may his merit protect us, it is our practice to make round *matzot*, for the square *matzot* can be joined together to appear as one, that is not the case for the round ones, that teach of this matter, that each one actually repented, but none of the others knew that he, too, had repented." The homiletical reasons were brought to strengthen the standing of the round handmade *matzot*, in comparison with the machine-made ones, and establish, in some measure, the "custom" of round *matzot*. As fine as these "reasons" may be, they have no bearing upon the source of the practice.

15

THE WIMPEL

After an object has served one ritual purpose in a certain context, rather than being discarded immediately after its use, Jewish custom frequently employs this object for some additional religious end. Thus, according to some views, the leftover oil from the Hanukkah lamps should be used for burning *hametz* (leaven) before Passover. Similarly the *aravot* (willow branches), one of the Four Species used during the Sukkot festival, were often thrown into the oven used for baking the Passover *matzot*; and the *hadassim* (myrtle) from the Four Species were used as the spices required by the *Havdalah* ceremony marking the conclusion of the Sabbath, and so forth.[1]

We find a similar development in Germany regarding the "wimpel":[2]

---

1 See *Minhagei Yisrael*, Vol. 2, chap. 6 ("Since One Commandment Was Performed with It, We Perform Another with It"), pp. 193–202. See also Rabbi Elyakum Dvorkes, *Bi-Shvilei ha-Halakhah, Shabbat u-Mo'adim* (Jerusalem, 1996), Vol. 2, pp. 139–51.

2 The source of the word is "wimpel," "wimpal" (in High German), "wimple" in English: a type of garment in which the head is enwrapped (see *Shorter Oxford English Dictionary*, p. 2430a, s.v. "wimple"), and not as Spitzer writes (*Sefer Maharil*, p. 668); see the recent objection by D.Z. Hillman, "Separating Challa from One Kind on Another; Foreign Words in Maharil's Works," *Tzfunot* 3,1 (9) (1990), p. 54 n. 19 (Hebrew). "Wimpel" in German does indeed have the meaning of "flag": according to the dictionary of G. Wahrig, *Deutches Worterbuch* (1982), p. 4188b, the wimpel is "a small triangular flag, a signal flag," thus in modern German. In Middle-High German, however, it denoted "a cloth band with which hair was bound, and that protected the head." A thorough discussion of the wimpel was recently written by Rabbi B.S. Hamburger, *Shorshei Minhag Ashkenaz (The Roots*

When the child is brought to the synagogue for the first time [or perhaps for his Bar Mitzvah — D. S.], he brings with him his present to the synagogue, his "flag" ("wimpel"), which consists of a wide band on which the child's name, his birth date, and blessings, are written in [different] colors, or embroidered, and decorated in various ways. [...] This flag is used to bind the Torah scroll before being placed in its mantle. [...] The material from which the "flag" [is made] is comprised of the cloths that were worn by the child during his circumcision and were saved since then for this purpose.[3]

This custom apparently originated in an incident related in *Sefer Maharil*:[4]

Once *Mahari Segal* [Rabbi Jacob ben Moses Moellin] was a *sandak*, and no cloth was available for wrapping the infant's legs after the circumcision, so that the circumcision would not be harmed. The rabbi, may the memory of the righteous be for a blessing, ordered that a cloth in which the Torah scroll was enclosed be taken out and used to wrap the child's legs. He declared that even a sheet of parchment from a Torah scroll could be used to wrap the body [of the infant] in the synagogue, because this was a matter of life and death. He also said that the sanctity of the cloth was not thereby harmed; rather, it should later be cleansed of the blood and returned to the Torah scroll; something should be given to charity, so that benefit would not be derived from this sanctified object for nothing.

From the time of *Maharil* (R. Jacob ben Moses Moellin), or possibly even

---

of Ashkenazic Custom) (Bnei Brak, 2000) (Hebrew), Vol. 2, pp. 322–604, with many illustrations of wimpels. He concludes from this (pp. 353–55) that "it is with this meaning that we understand the word wimpel, in Jewish custom as well: a band or cloth for **binding** the Torah scroll and **protecting** it." Hamburger also brings a proof from BT Megillah 26b for the utilization of wornout Torah binders for another important purpose: "Mar Zutra said: Binders of scrolls that are worn out may be used for shrouds for a *met mitzvah* [a corpse of unknown identity, whose burial is incumbent upon all], and this constitutes their 'storing away.'" Maimonides cites this Talmudic teaching as binding halakhah (*Mishneh Torah, Hil. Tefilin, u-Mezuzah, ve-Sefer Torah* [*Laws of* Tefillin, Mezuzah, *and Torah Scroll*] 10:3). For illustration of wimpel see below chap. 21, Figs. 31–33.

3 A. Ona, "Ashkenazic Customs," in A. Wasserteil (ed.), *Yalkut Minhagim* (Jerusalem, 1980), pp. 35–36 (Hebrew).

4 *Sefer Maharil*, ed. Spitzer, *Hil. Milah* (*Laws of Circumcision*), pp. 488–89.

earlier, this practice has been observed in Germany and the neighboring lands.[5]

5 Cf. *Maharil, Hil. Purim* (*Laws of Purim*), p. 427, which describes this incident (with minor variations); also cited by R. Moses Isserles in *Darkei Moshe, Yoreh Deah* 265:11. Cf. also *Maharil*, p. 452; *Darkei Moshe, Orah Hayyim*, end of 147. See *She'eilot u-Teshuvot ha-Maharil*, ed. Sats, para. 121, p. 211: "Even though it is the universal practice to make a Torah ark curtain from old cloths, this is not a part of the Talmud to which Rabina is a signatory [here, meaning that this is not authoritative], and when asked, he replied to purchase new ones" (see the editor's gloss 14). *Maharil* relied on *Ha-Agudah*, which prohibited in the chapter "*Ha-Kometz ha-Gadol*" (BT Menahot 22a) the purchase of cloaks used by laymen (i.e. people other than *kohanim*) ("Just as the altar has not been used by a layman, so, too, the wood [...]"). Y. Dinari wrote ("Custom and Law in the Responsa of Ashkenazic Rabbis in the 15th Century," p. 193 n. 196): "We have seen that in much more severe instances, in which *minhagim* [customs] clash with halakhah, the sages of the fifteenth century did not refrain from defending the *minhag*. It would seem that the reason for the opposition in our case is not the opinion of *Sefer ha-Agudah*, but the very practice itself, which makes light of the sanctity of the synagogue, and which the *Maharil* did not find fit to adopt. Since *Ha-Agudah* also wrote similarly [to purchase new cloths], he [*Maharil*] obviously brought support for his own view from this book."

These cloths were embellished with popular embroidered decorations. To Rahav's bibliography we should add: S.S. Kayser and G. Schoenberger (eds.), *Jewish Ceremonial Art: A Guide to the Appreciation of the Art Objects ... Principally from the Collections of the Jewish Museum ...* (Philadelphia, 1955), p. 33; L.S. Freehof and B. King, *Embroideries and Fabrics for Synagogue and Home: 5000 Years of Ornamental Needlework* (New York, 1966), p. 79; B. Kirshenblatt-Gimblett, *Fabric of Jewish Life: Textiles from the Jewish Museum Collection* (New York, 1977), pp. 18–19, 46–48, 96–100. Mention should also be made of the writings on this subject by Joseph Gutmann. In his book *The Jewish Life Cycle*, pp. 6–8, in which he asserts that the practice began in Catholic Bavaria, in southern Germany, ca. 1500, possibly under the influence of a German Catholic custom; and his articles: "Jewish Medieval Marriage Customs in Art: Creativity and Adaptation," in D. Kraemer (ed.), *The Jewish Family: Metaphor and Memory* (Oxford, 1989), pp. 47–50; "Die Mappe Schuletragen — An Unusual Judeo-German Custom," *Rimonim* 5 (1997), p. 56–59 (Hebrew) (and in English translation: "Die Mappe Schuletragen — An Unusual Judeo-German Custom," *Visible Religion* 2 [Leiden, 1983], pp. 167–73); and the booklet: *Wimpel-Cloth for a Torah Scroll, A Memento from the Bar Mitzvah of Yair Agamnon, Jerusalem, 19 Tammuz 5760 [July 2000]*.

See also G. Korman, "On the Practice of Enrapping a Torah Scroll in a 'Wimpel,'" in *Jubilee Volume of the Ahavat Torah Congregation in Haifa* (Haifa, 1990), pp. 82–84 (Hebrew); Schammes, *Wormser Minhagbuch*, Vol. 2, pp. 157–58 and

I received the following valuable testimony from R. Yehoshua Neuwirt:

> We observed the bringing of the wimpel to the synagogue, when the child was about three years old, basing this on the verse "Three years it shall be uncircumcised for you" [Lev. 19:23], that as long as he had not reached this age, [he is] uncircumcised. When, however, he reached this age, and "it will be set aside for jubilation" [based on the following verse], he is brought to the synagogue with a wimpel, and he begins to learn the [Hebrew] alphabet.

It should be added that this practice is based on an exposition in *Tanhuma*:[6]

> "And plant [...] you shall regard as forbidden" [Lev. 19:23] — Scripture speaks of a young child. "Three years it shall be forbidden for you" [ibid.] — [meaning] that it cannot speak or talk, "in the fourth year all its fruit shall be set aside" [v. 24] — [meaning] that his father sets him aside for Torah study.

This is the source for the practice of giving the child his first haircut at the age of three,[7] in a ceremony that was also the child's first educational experience in the synagogue.[8]

Attention should likewise be paid to the account by Raphael Patai of a charm used by Jerusalem Jews in the nineteenth century against miscarriages:[9]

---

nn. 5–8 contains much instructive material on this subject. See the fine article by M. Kaniel, "The Wimpel: Binding the Family to the Torah," *Jewish Action* 53 (1993), pp. 41–44. Gutmann writes ("Die Mappe Schuletragen," *Rimonim*, p. 57 n. 7): "The attempt to link this custom with the *Maharil*, [...] who lived in the fifteenth century in Mainz-Worms, is not convincing. The reason that compelled the *Maharil* in that description to request the Torah scroll binder to enwrap the infant was the lack of a handy cloth with which to wrap the legs of the infant following the circumcision."

6 *Kedoshim* 14; for the text, see above, chap. 14 ("On the 'Reasons' for Customs: The *Halakah*"), p. 126.

7 See the responsa by my grandfather Rabbi David Sperber, *Afarkasta de-Aniya*[3] (Brooklyn, 2002), Vol. 1, para. 161, p. 380.

8 I.G. Marcus, *Rituals of Childhood: Jewish Acculturation in Medieval Europe* (New Haven and London, 1996), chap. 2, "The Initiation Rite," pp. 18–34, 124–25. See also above, chap. 14.

9 *Talpioth* 1, 1–2 (1953), p. 258.

[...] or he takes the cloth of the Torah scroll, and he ties it around her stomach, so that she shall not lose the blessing of the womb.[10]

In other words, the wimpel that was donated to the synagogue — I assume that this is what Patai means when he speaks of "the cloth of the Torah scroll" — to commemorate the child's birth is also effective to ensure the successful birth of another infant.[11]

Finally, we should call attention to the observation by Ivan G. Marcus:[12]

> The similarity between the child being wrapped and carried from home to synagogue in the initiation ceremony and customs about carrying a Torah scroll from ark to ark is but one of several similarities in Jewish culture between the treatment of small children and Torah scrolls.[13]

He continues by connecting the covering of Torah scrolls with the wimpel, and concludes (ibid.):

> In Ashkenaz a tradition developed further linking circumcision, a small boy's first rite of passage, and the Torah. Attested only beginning in the fourteenth century but reflecting the earlier association of Torah and children, the *wimpel*, or cloth in which the baby was held during circumcision, was set aside and later embroidered with the baby's name and possibly this statement from the circumcision ceremony: "as he has entered the covenant (*brit*) so may he enter the Torah, the marriage chamber, and (a life of) good deeds." This wimpel would later be used as a Torah binder during the child's public bar mitzvah ceremony, a rite of passage that developed only in late medieval Ashkenaz.

The actual ceremony of bringing the child to the synagogue and the

---

10 Reischer, *Sha'arei Yerushalayim*, p. 91; Rabbi Jekuthiel Judah Teitelbaum, *Avnei Zedek* (Lemberg, 1885), para. 13.

11 Intriguingly, a somewhat similar practice is observed by the Jews of Afghanistan, where Torah scrolls are enwrapped in one or more mantles that were donated to the synagogue by the wives or other relatives of the donors of the Torah scrolls themselves, or by their mothers or children. See Brauer, *The Jews of Kurdistan*, p. 213.

12 Marcus, *Rituals of Childhood*, p. 77.

13 On p. 150 n. 15, Marcus refers to H.E. Goldberg's article, "Torah and Children: Symbolic Aspects of the Reproduction of Jews and Judaism," in *idem* (ed.), *Judaism Viewed from Within and Without: Anthropological Studies* (Albany, 1987), pp. 107–30.

presentation of the wimpel, known as *"Die Mappe Shuletragen,"* was memorialized in a famous picture from 1869 by Moritz Daniel Oppenheim as part of his *Bibler aus dem altjudischen Familienleben* series (see Fig. 1).[14] The text accompanying the picture[15] relates that:

> when the child reaches the age of one year old, he is brought, in accordance with an ancient Jewish custom, on the Sabbath to the synagogue for the Shaharit service — and after the Torah reading the father brings his son in from the synagogue lobby to the *bimah* [Reader's stand], and there at the end of tying the Torah scroll (*gelilah*) the child touches the [wooden] silvered handles of the Torah (*etzei hayyim*), in order to express the idea of "She is a tree of life to those that lay hold upon her" (Proverbs 3:18).

Oppenheim's picture shows two wimpels — one on the *bimah*, bearing the Hebrew inscription "[May he grow to] good deeds. Amen. *Selah*," and the other rolled around the Torah, showing the Hebrew name of the artist: "Moshe ben Gedalia Oppenheim."[16]

Oppenheim's illustrations were copied, with slight changes, by the non-Jewish German painter Hermann (Phillip Ludwig Friedrich) Junker in a series of postcards produced in the late nineteenth or early twentieth centuries. His version of the wimpel, entitled *Schule-Tragen* (Fig. 2),[17] depicts a

14 Moritz Daniel Oppenheim, *Pictures of Traditional Jewish Life*, ed. A. Werner (New York, 1976), p. 273; E. Cohen, "Moritz Daniel Oppenheim," *Bulletin des Leo Baeck Instituts* 16–17 (1977–78), p. 71; *Chronicle of Jewish Traditions: A Sentimental Journey: Yeshivah University Museum, March 8, 1992* (New York, 1992), p. 5; R. Drose-Gisermann, M. Kingreen, and A. Merk, *Der Zyklus "Bilder aus dem altjudischen Familienleben" un sein Maker Moritz Daniel Oppenheim* (Hanau, 1996), pp. 58–59; G. Heuberger, A. Merk (eds.), *Moritz Daniel Oppenheim: die Entdeckung der Judischen Selbstbewusstsein in der Kunst* (= *Jewish Identity in 19th Century Art*, catalogue of an exhibition held at the Judisches Museum, Frankfurt am Main, December 16, 1999–April 2, 2000) (Cologne, 1999), p. 201; Gutmann, "Die Mappe Schuletragen," *Rimonim*, p. 56; Hamburger, *Shorshei Minhag Ashkenaz*, Vol. 2, pp. 507–508. The picture is in the Jewish Museum, New York.

15 In the Frankfurt a.M. edition (1886), chap. 2.

16 See S. Sabar, "In the Footsteps of Moritz Oppenheim: Hermann Junker's Postcard Series of *Scenes from Traditional Jewish Family Life*," in the Judisches Museum catalogue, p. 262.

17 Sabar, "In the Footsteps," pp. 260–63 (Junker was born in Frankfurt am Main in 1838, and died in 1899 [p. 259 nn. 3, 4]).

nearly identical scene set in a similar interior. Sabar notes,[18] however, that:

> the significant difference which Junker introduces here concerns the "Wimpel" lying on the Bimah. Its partially open section reveals the following curious word in Hebrew letters: "Junker." Obviously the name does not appear in the right place of the binder, as the unrolled section is near the end of the "Wimpel" and not at the beginning. [...] But despite this mistake, the insertion of his name on the Jewish object demonstrates how well Junker understood the custom and attempted to emulate it. To this one should add the fact that the artist made an effort to spell his non-Jewish name correctly according to the Judeo-German spelling and pronunciation.

Lion Wolff provides us with a detailed description of this rite:[19]

> When the child reaches the age of one year, he brings to the synagogue the binder [on which, as an infant, he had been placed during his circumcision], and he holds the *etz hayyim* at the time of the *gelilah* of the Torah scroll. While the child holds the *etz hayyim*, his father recites the following prayer: "'I praise the Lord with all my heart in the assembled congregation of the upright.' 'It was this boy I prayed for; and the Lord has granted me what I asked of Him' [Ps. 111:1]. I Sam. 1:2]. 'But I, through Your abundant love, enter Your house' [Ps. 5:8]. The child with whom You have favored Your servant has been weaned from milk, removed from the breast — may he be supported, blessed, and held by the Tree of Life [*etz hayyim*]. May his pure heart be blessed twofold with a spirit of compassion. Draw him near to Your Torah, teach him Your commandments, guide him in Your way, train him to love and fear Your Name. Train the lad in Your way; he will not swerve from it even in old age.[20] 'The living, only the living can give thanks to You as I do this day. Father, relate to children Your acts of grace' [Isa. 38:19]. Blessed is the One who has kept us alive, sustained us, and brought us to this season."[21]

---

18 Sabar, "In the Footsteps," pp. 262–63; Hamburger, *Shorshei Minhag Ashkenaz*, Vol. 2, p. 510.

19 L. Wolff, *Universal-Agende für judische Kultursbeamts: Handbuch für den Gebrauch in Synagoge, Schule und Haus*[2] (Berlin, 1891), p. 40.

20 Cf. Prov. 22:6.

21 Gutmann, *Rimonim*, "Die Mappe Schuletragen," pp. 56–57.

1. M. Oppenheim, 1869

**2. Herman Junkers,
late 19th century**

16

THE BREAKING OF PLATES DURING THE
TENA'IM CEREMONY

The practice of breaking a plate at the writing of the *tena'im* (the "[pre]-conditions of the marriage"; also known as *shidukhin* — not to be confused with the modern term *shidukhim*, marital matches proposed by matchmakers),[1] or at the conclusion of the reading of this document,[2] is mentioned in *Eliyahu Rabbah*,[3] in the name of *Malbushei Yom Tov* by R. Yom Tov Lipmann Heller (1579–1654). R. Jousep (Juspa) Schammes similarly attests:[4]

> In most instances, the *Kynoss* [= the marital agreement ceremony][5] is deposited in the house of the rabbi,[6] and immediately following **the breaking of a plate** at the *Kynoss*, those in attendance there proceed to the house of the groom and say to him: "*Mazal tov!*"

Schammes thus provides us with testimony that in sixteenth-century Ashkenaz (i.e. central Europe) (at the latest) a plate would be broken during the *tena'im* ceremony.

1   In reference to what R. Moses Isserles writes in his gloss on *Shulhan Arukh, Orah Hayyim* 560:2: "It is customary in some localities to break the glass during the wedding ceremony," a well-known practice that is in memory of the destruction of the Temple.
2   Thus in R. Herman (Isaac Zevi) Lebovics, *Shulhan ha-Ezer* (Dec. 1929), Vol. 1, fol. 52; see B. Adler, *Nisu'in ke-Hilkhatam*[2] (*All the Laws and Customs of Proper Marriage*) (Jerusalem, 1985), Vol. 1, p. 103 (Hebrew).
3   R. Elijah ben Benjamin Wolf Shapira, *Eliyahu Rabbah* (Prague, 1660–1712), on *Orah Hayyim* 560:7.
4   *Wormser Minhagbuch*, Vol. 2, p. 1.
5   See *She'eilot u-Teshuvot Rabbeinu Moshe Mintz*, ed. Y.S. Domb (Jerusalem, 1991), para. 31; the gloss by Hamburger, *Wormser Minhagbuch*, loc. cit.
6   See the gloss by Hamburger ad loc., nn. 2, 34.

Variants of this practice developed in different communities. According to one view, the mothers of the bride and the groom break the vessel,[7] while another maintains that the fathers perform this act.[8] Some shattered a pottery vessel[9] that was already broken,[10] while others smashed a whole vessel, "a bowl that is called *Teller*, and not a pot, and so I have seen [practiced by] the great ones of the generation."[11]

7 *Shulhan ha-Ezer*, loc. cit.; Adler, *Nisu'in ke-Hilkhatam*, loc. cit.

8 Adler, *Nisu'in ke-Hilkhatam*, Vol. 1, p. 183 n. 135, provides a reference to R. Isaac of Shedlitz (Siedlce), *Matamim* (Warsaw, 1889), s.v. "*Hatan ve-Kallah* [Bride and Groom]," Letter ח (perhaps should read: ה״ר), fol. 14b. See G. Silvain, *Images et traditions Juives: un Millier de Cartes Postales (1897–1917)* ... (Paris, 1980), p. 406, a picture postcard from the end of the nineteenth century (1894) in Germany, that shows a man, apparently the father of the groom or of the bride, smashing a plate (*Teller*; see below, near n. 11), and two children looking on in amazement. A sort of Star of David bearing the inscription "*Mazal tov*" hangs on the wall. The picture is entitled "Das Knas legen" (Fig. 1).

9 *Eliyah Rabbah* reads "*kaderah* [pot]"; and in *Wormser Minhagbuch*, as above. See *Peri Megadim, Mishbetzot Zahav* on *Orah Hayyim* 560:4; *Matamim*, para. 6: "A pottery vessel, specifically, is broken, while under the bridal canopy a glass vessel is smashed, as it is said, a pottery vessel that is broken cannot be mended, a broken glass vessel may be mended, to be made from anew. It is taught in books that it is preferable to sever the marital bond by a writ of divorce than to sever the *tena'im* bond, and there is a reason for this. *Sha'arei Shamayim* [by the Vilna Gaon, Vilna, 1871, in the name of R. Hayyim of Volozhin]." See Adler, *Nisu'in ke-Hilkhatam*, Vol. 1, p. 183 nn. 133, 136, who cites additional sources. See also R. Hayyim Hezekiah Medini, *Sedeh Hemed ha-Shalem* (Bnei Brak, 1963), "*Asifat Dinim* [Collection of Laws]," *Ma'arekhet* 7, para. 12 (Vol. 7, p. 396), who cites R. Hayyim Palache (Palaggi), *Moed le-Kol Hai* (Izmir, 1861), para. י, section 96.

10 *Peri Megadim*, loc. cit. (so that this would not violate the prohibition of needless destruction); cf. what I wrote in *Minhagei Yisrael*, Vol. 7 (Jerusalem, 2003), chap. 12, pp. 167–77, where I showed, on the basis of illustrations in fifteenth-century Haggadot, that the searching out of *hametz* (*bedikat hametz*) was performed with a broken platter, based on the ruling that if no morsel of *hametz* is found, the platter, at least, should be burned, so that the custom of burning *hametz* before Pesah would not be forgotten. A broken platter was used, so as not to destroy a whole vessel and thereby cause monetary loss. Later, however, the practice was accepted of laying out (ten) morsels of *hametz* before the search began, so that the burning of the platter was no longer relevant. See, however, *Sedeh Hemed ha-Shalem*, loc. cit., who opposes this custom.

11 Rabbi Israel Hayyim Friedman, *Likkutei Maharih* (Sighet-Satmar, 1911 [photocopy edn.: New York, 1965]), Vol. 3, fol. 129a.

A detailed description of this practice is provided by the apostate Gamaliel ben Pedahzur (born as Abraham Meer),[12] who writes that following the signing of the *Kynoss*,

> the Priest(s) then takes a Glass of Wine in his hand, and pronounces some Prayer, and after that takes a new Pipkin, and flings it down on the Floor, before the Feet of the Bridegroom, with a Force that breaks it into many Pieces; which done, the Priest wishes him Joy first, and all the Company with him Joy next; and than [sic] they are treated with Wine, Drams, Coffee, Tea, Chocolate, Sweet-Meats, Cakes, &c. Every Bridegroom treats according to his Circumstances, which is the End of this Ceremony. Excepting that the Bachelors generally strive to carry off a Bit of the broken Pipkin believing it likely to promote their being married soon after.

According to Pedahzur, it is the rabbi who breaks a single vessel, and the bachelors who attempt to take pieces of it for themselves, as a charm for their own expeditious matches.

This custom is depicted in two illustrations from the eighteenth century, one in the book by Kirchner[13] (Fig. 2), and the other in that by Bodenschatz[14] (Fig. 3). In both pictures we see in the background a table, at which people are signing a document; these are probably the witnesses affixing their signatures to the *tena'im* document. Bodenschatz's picture has two individuals (apparently the witnesses) sitting at the table, while Kirchner depicts three people, one sitting and writing, and two standing; one of

12 Gamaliel ben Pedahzur, *The Book of Religion, Ceremonies, and Prayers of the Jews* (London, 1738), p. 20.

13 Paul Christian Kirchner, *Judisches Ceremoniel* (Nuremberg, 1724). Kirchner was a Jew who converted to Christianity in the early eighteenth century, and who published a booklet depicting the circumstances of his conversion (1815). Soon after his apostasy, he began to publish short descriptions directed to Christians of Jewish customs and ceremonies (1717–20), which formed the basis for his comprehensive work *Judisches Ceremoniel*, the 1724 edition of which contains etchings and engravings on paper. See R.I. Cohen, "The Visual Image of the Jew and Judaism in Early Modern Europe: From Symbolism to Realism," *Zion* 57 (1992), p. 332 (Hebrew).

14 Johann Bodenschatz, *Kirchliche Verfassung der heutigen Juden, sonderlich derer in Deutschland.*

these three is most likely the rabbi who is supervising the writing of this document.[15]

As regards the act of smashing: in both, the vessel — that is a **jug**, and not a bowl (or *Teller*) — is in the hands of the men, and not the women. Most intriguingly, however, the individuals in the picture in Bodenschatz's book are breaking a **number** of jugs: one vessel lies broken on the floor, and two others are lifted up in people's hands, and are about to be thrown down. The depiction in Bodenschatz's book, therefore, offers us something new, to which later sources albeit allude, for *Sedeh Hemed*[16] writes that this practice originated with the Ashkenazim, "who are accustomed to break **pots** during the writing of the *tena'im*."[17] I have not yet found this practice

15 See the editor's gloss, Schammes, *Wormser Minhagbuch*, Vol. 2, p. 1 n. 2, for the importance of the presence of the rabbi, or the rabbinical judge, during the writing of the *tena'im*, with a plethora of references.

16 The practice is fundamentally Ashkenazic, although it was adopted by a number of Eastern Jewish communities. See *Sedeh Hemed ha-Shalem*: "And when I came to these localities, I saw that the people of this city, the Krimchaks, may the Lord protect them, customarily smash a cup when they make a match, as well. It would seem that they took this practice from the Ashkenazim, may the Lord protect them, who usually **break plates** during the writing of the *tena'im*, as the rabbi [the author of] *Peri Megadim* wrote in para. 560, in *Mishbetzot* [*Zahav*], subsection 4, that is, in order to agitate, so that the rejoicing would not be complete and in memory of the Destruction; see *Sha'arei Teshuvah*. And now, after many unlettered people have followed this practice, it has changed for them from grief to joy, for at **the breaking of the cup**, their mouths are filled with laughter and derision, and the rafters shake from the sound of their uproarious laughter. They did not know that, in place of gladness, there should be trembling in memory of the destruction of our Temple — what has this to do with rejoicing? If I had the strength, I would cancel this, for the absence of good is better than the presence of what is not good," This source therefore indicates the breaking of **plates**; such rejoicing and revelry is apparent in the illustration of Bodenschatz.

17 Lauterbach, "The Ceremony of Breaking a Glass at Weddings," describes this custom (p. 375), and, in n. 36, he suggests that the reason for the practice was to drive away the demons who lay in wait for the newlyweds. Lauterbach compares this to the *Polterabend*, the German ceremony on the night preceding the wedding, in which plates were smashed, with a reference to E. Samter, *Geburt, Hochzeit und Tod: Beitrage zur vergleichenden Volkskunde* (Leipzig and Berlin, 1911), p. 60. As additional comparative material, see Radford, *Encyclopaedia of Superstitions*, p. 253; I.A. Opie and M. Tatem, *A Dictionary of Superstitions* (Oxford and New York, 1992), p. 435; Westermarck, *The History of Human Marriage*, pp. 457–64. (Westermarck, in contrast, regards the diverse range of breaking customs that he

described in the literature from the eighteenth century, but this examination is not yet completed.

The upper left hand corner of the illustration in Kirchner's book shows a later phase of the ceremony, namely, the *Knas mahl* (*Knas* [= *Kynoss*] — banquet) that marks the final formulation of the betrothal agreement, with the young couple standing by the table and exchanging gifts.[18] Schammes[19] expands on this:

> Immediately following the smashing of the pot during the *Kynoss* [ceremony], those present go to the house of the groom, and call out to him: "*Mazal tov* [Congratulations]!" If they so wish, they also proceed to the house of the bride, to wish her "*Mazal tov.*" [...] On the *Kynoss* day, the groom conducts a banquet, that is known as the "*Knas mahl.*"[20]

brings from different cultures as a sign of the "breaking" of the wife's virginity; his collection of customs might, however, be merely a hodgepodge of different matters that resemble one another only partially and superficially.) See also Pollack, *Jewish Folkways in Germanic Lands (1648–1806)*, pp. 29–30; J. Guttmann (ed.), *Beauty in Holiness: Studies in Jewish Customs and Ceremonial Art* (New York, 1970), p. 316.

18 See Cohen, "The Visual Image of the Jew and Judaism in Early Modern Europe," p. 332.

19 See Schammes, *Wormser Minhagbuch*, Vol. 2, para. 227, pp. 1–2.

20 See the editor's gloss, n. 8, for the different spellings and pronunciations of this term.

1. *"Tena'im,"* postcard, 1908

2. *"Tena'im,"* Kirchner, Nuremberg 1724

3. *"Tena'im,"* **Bodenschatz, Erlang 1748**

17

BETROTHAL RINGS

Elsewhere we observed that "there are customs that have hardly been mentioned in the Jewish *Minhagim* books, but testimonies to their existence are to be found in manuscript illuminations."[1] In addition to these illustrations, such testimonies are also to be found in other types of religious objects. An intriguing example of this is provided by the singular betrothal rings (popularly called "engagement rings") that were in use in Europe, and especially in Italy, from the fourteenth century on. These rings, of gold or silver, or with different platings, at times had inlaid onyx stones, and/or the ring was topped by a small synagogue-shaped "house," with the engraved inscription "*Mazal Tov*," and on occasion the date[2] (see Fig. 1).[3] Patently, these rings were not intended to effect the actual betrothal, because the halakhah requires a ring without any stone, engraving, name, or plating.[4]

1   *Minhagei Yisrael*, Vol. 4, p. 143.
2   See Abrahams, *Jewish Life in the Middle Ages*, pp. 196–200. See the examples in the Feuchtwanger Collection: Shachar, *Jewish Tradition in Art*, nos. 74–76, pp. 42–43; Barnett, *Catalogue of the Permanent and Loan Collections of the Jewish Museum*, nos. 454–465, pp. 84–85; Kayser and Schoenberger, *Jewish Ceremonial Art*, nos. 163–68, pp. 152–53; see also F. Landsberger, "Jewish Artists before the Emancipation," *HUCA* 16 (1941), p. 374: these (Italian) rings were apparently crafted by Jewish artisans.
3   Based on Kayser and Schoenberger, loc. cit.; A. Wolf, s.v. "Rings," *Jewish Encyclopedia* (New York, 1905), Vol. 10, p. 428; J. Weinstein, *A Collector's Guide to Judaica* (London, 1985), p. 195.
4   *Shulhan Arukh, Even ha-Ezer* 31. See Adler, *Nisu'in ke-Hilkhatam*, Vol. 1, paras. 6–13, pp. 213–15, and more. This law is also cited by Bodenschatz, *Kirchliche Verfassung der heutigen Juden, sonderlich derer in Deutschland*, p. 125. An allusion to this law was found in the verse: [הזה] את בתי נתת לאיש ("I gave this man my

Kayser and Schoenberger write (p. 152):

> While the wedding ring which the bridegroom gave to his bride to keep, as symbol of the legality of their marriage, was to be a simple circlet, it need not necessarily have been used in the wedding ceremony itself. The rings on display here were used in the ceremonies. In many cases they were not owned by individuals, but remained the property of the congregation. They were worn by the newly-wed women during the week following the marriage ceremony. Sometimes these rings are crowned by a small synagogue building.

J. Gutmann already noted the problematic nature of these rings.[5]

The question remains: what purpose did these rings serve? Didn't Jewish religious authorities fear that people would use them to betroth women, despite their unfitness for the purpose? The following suggestion might answer these questions. The *Shulhan Arukh*[6] prescribes:

> Ashes are to be placed on the groom's head, where the *tefillin* are placed [i.e. the forehead], in mourning for Jerusalem, as it is written: "To provide for the mourners in Zion — to give them a turban instead of ashes" [Isa. 61:3].

And in the Talmudic source:[7]

> A woman may wear all her ornaments, but leave out something. What should this be? Rav said: The depilation of the [upper and lower] temple,[8]

daughter"; Deut. 22:16), with the highlighted letters spelling out the words אבן לא יש — there is no stone (J. Leusden, *Philologus Hebraeo-Mixtus*[2] [Utrecht 1682], p. 174; I have not yet found his source). See also A. ha-Levi Langbank, "Concerning the Practice of Betrothing with a Ring," *Bikkurim* 1 (1864 [photocopy edn.: Jerusalem, 1978]), pp. 114–15. See the catalogue by S. Pappenheim, *The Jewish Wedding* (New York, 1977), pp. 45–51, which devotes a short discussion to halakhic and other aspects of these rings, with references to *Shulhan Arukh, Even ha-Ezer* 28, and the gloss by R. Moses Isserles ad loc., from which we learn that a borrowed ring may be used for this purpose, if its temporary use is equivalent in value to a *perutah* (the minimum value required to effect betrothal).

5 See the introduction to *The Jewish Life Cycle*, p. 15; see also A. Kanof, *Jewish Ceremonial Art and Religious Observance* (New York, n. d.), p. 198.

6 *Shulhan Arukh, Even ha-Ezer* 65:3.

7 BT Bava Batra 60b.

8 See *Midrash Tehillim* 127b, p. 524; Tosefta, end of Sotah, ed. S. Lieberman, p. 244

as it is said: "If I forget you, O Jerusalem, let my right hand forget its cunning; let my tongue stick to my palate [if I cease to think of you, if I do not keep Jerusalem in memory even at my happiest hour]" [Ps. 137:5–6]. What is "even at my happiest hour"? R. Isaac replied: This is the ashes from the hearth that [are placed on] the head of grooms. R. Papa asked Abbaye: Where are they placed? On the place of the *tefillin*, as it is said: "To provide for the mourners in Zion — to give them a turban instead of ashes" [Isa. 61:3].

The applying of ashes to the groom's forehead is also set forth by Maimonides[9] and R. Joseph Caro,[10] and in greater detail by R. Jacob ben Moses Moellin:[11]

He would place burnt ashes under the turban on his head, where the *tefillin* are placed, in memory of the Destruction.

This continues the description of the mourning headwear described by the *Maharil* on the preceding page (p. 464):

His turban is tucked in around his neck, as is the practice in the Rhineland, in commemoration of the Destruction, to keep Jerusalem in memory, in his heart, even at his happiest hour.[12]

R. Moses Isserles mentions nuptial mourning practices:[13]

In some localities it is customary to break a cup during the wedding ceremony[14] or to place a black cloth[15] or some other sign of mourning on the groom's head.[16]

l. 130; cf. S. Lieberman, *Tosefta ki-Fshutah*, Vol. 3: *Order Mo'ed* (New York, 1962), Shabbat, p. 120.

9 Maimonides, *Mishneh Torah, Hil. Ta'anit* (*Laws of Fastdays*) 5:13.

10 *Shulhan Arukh, Orah Hayyim* 560:2.

11 *Maharil, Hil. Nisu'in* (*Laws of Marriage*), ed. Spitzer, p. 465.

12 In a clear allusion to the verse from Psalms cited as a proof-text by Rav in Bava Batra (above). For an understanding of this headwear, see A. Rubens, *A History of Jewish Costume* (London, 1967), pp. 102–103, nos. 140–141: Germany, mid-sixteenth century. For more on this verse, see below, chap. 21 ("The *Huppah*"), p. 195.

13 Gloss on *Shulhan Arukh, Orah Hayyim* 560:2.

14 For the breaking of the cup, see Lauterbach, "The Ceremony of Breaking a Glass at Weddings," pp. 351–80.

15 See Part 2, chap. 19 ("A Kerchief around the Neck of the Mourner"); *Minhagei Yisrael*, Vol. 3, p. 151.

16 See Werdiger, *Edut le-Yisrael*, p. 57. Jerusalem is also mentioned in *ketubot* (mainly

R. David ben Samuel ha-Levi attests:[17]

> I saw in some communities that the beadle recites this verse [i.e. "If
> I forget you, O Jerusalem ..."] and the groom repeats after him, word
> by word, and this is correct.

This is indeed the current practice in most Jewish communities. The
verses "If I forget you, O Jerusalem ..." are recited, and symbolic acts
are performed[18] for the groom that connect him with the second verse: "if
I do not keep Jerusalem in memory ...," namely, the placing of ashes on
the groom's forehead, and/or the draping of a black cloth over his head.
Additionally, it is the groom who smashes the glass.

There is, however, no mention of Jerusalem in connection with the **bride**,
nor is there any symbolic act to connect her with the first verse ("If I forget
you, O Jerusalem ..."). This may possibly explain the placing of this special
ring on the finger of the **bride**, since it is put on her **right hand**.[19]

Scholarly research has already noted that these rings were embellished
with a small building that symbolized the Temple in Jerusalem. As Abrahams
puts it (p. 198): "The ornamental building worked on the ring always

Italian ones) in illustrations of the city and the Temple, with inscriptions such
as "I will keep Jerusalem in memory even at my happiest hour" (based on Ps.
137:6); "Jerusalem, hills enfold it" (Ps. 125:2), and similar passages. See I. Fishof,
"'Jerusalem Above My Chief Joy': Depictions of Jerusalem in Italian Ketubot,"
Journal of Jewish Art 9 (1982), pp. 61–75. Note should also be taken of the report
by Z. Falk, *Jewish Matrimonial Law in the Middle Ages* (Oxford, 1966), p. 67: in
the fourth century Gregory of Nazianzus (Cappadocia) quoted a form of (wedding)
blessing modeled on Ps. 128: "The Lord shall bless thee out of Zion — and bring
about this union — and thou shalt see thy children's children" (*Epistle to Eusebius*
231 [Migne, *Patrologia Graeca*, Vol. 37, p. 373]).

17 *Turei Zahav, Orah Hayyim* 560:4.

18 See *Minhagei Yisrael*, Vol. 3, chap. 3 ("The Place of the Symbol in the World of the
Custom").

19 See below, chap. 21 ("The *Huppah*"), p. 195. Abrahams, *Jewish Life in the Middle
Ages*, pp. 197–98, in contrast, argues that these rings were not actually worn,
because this would have been extremely painful. This, however, does not seem to
be the case, at least not for the majority of such rings that I examined. At any
rate, in symbolic fashion, these rings certainly associatively recalled the right hand.
Additionally, the time when the rings were placed on the woman's hand — either
at the betrothal, or during the marriage ceremony — has not been determined (see
below).

represents the Temple of Jerusalem or one of its more modern counterparts — a synagogue."[20] These rings are described in greater detail by Alfred Wolf:[21]

> A large number of such wedding-rings have been preserved [...], although only a very few are older than the sixteenth century, and not one can be assigned to a date earlier than the thirteenth century.[22] In the earliest examples the hoop is frequently formed of two cherubim and is crowned by a model of the Temple at Jerusalem. [...] In other cases this representation assumes rather the shape of a synagogue with a small tower [...], on which sometimes is perched a weathercock.[23]

20 V. Mann, in her article in *Artibus et Historiae, an Art Anthology ... in Honour of Rachel Wischnitzer, IRSA* 17 IX (Vienna, 1988), p. 23 n. 9, questions the identification of this structure as a representation of the Temple, and correctly notes that Abrahams brought no proof for his hypothesis. Nonetheless, Abrahams seems to be accurate. See Pappenheim, *The Jewish Wedding*, p. 48.

21 Wolf, "Rings," *Jewish Encyclopedia*, pp. 428–30.

22 The earliest ring whose date is known to us dates from the beginning of the fourteenth century; see M. Sauerlandt, "Ein Schmuckfund aus Weissenfels vom Anfang des 14. Jahrhunderts," *Cicerone* 9 (1919), p. 520. To this we should add the observation by Therese and Mendel Metzger that in the upper right-hand corner of a *ketubah* from the late fourteenth century we see the groom presenting a ring to the bride, who is facing him, in the upper left-hand corner, bedecked in a crown. The large ring has a precious stone set in it, thus leading the Metzgers to conclude that this was a special ring, for use only in the ceremony. The *ketubah* is from Vienna, Cod. Hebr. 28, Osterreichische National Bibliothek. See Metzger, *Jewish Life in the Middle Ages*, p. 228, fig. no. 342. (For the crown ornamentation on the bride's head, see N. Feuchtwanger, "The Coronation of the Virgin and of the Bride," *Jewish Art* 12–13 [1986/87], pp. 213–24; see also below, beginning of chap. 22, "The Wedding Ring in the Cup of Wine.") Additional information is provided by the following sources: J.M. Fritz, *Goldschmiedekunst der Gotik im Mitteleuropa* (Munich, 1982), no. 318; *Monumenta Judaica: 2000 Jahre Geschichte und Kultur der Juden am Rhein* (catalogue of the exhibition in the Cologne Stadtmuseum, October 15, 1963–March 15, 1964), no. E 162; Y. Hackenbroch, *Renaissance Jewellery* (Munich, 1979), p. 50 (inventory of the Munich Kunstkammer of 1593); Historisches Museum Frankfurt am Main, *Synagoga: Judische Altertumer, Handschriften und Kulturgerate*, exhibition catalogue (1961), fig. 166. See the article by Mann, pp. 13–14, and nn. To these we should add W. Hausler, *Judaica: Die Sammlung Berger: Kult und Kultur des Europaischen Judenthums* (Vienna and Munich, 1979), Table 17.

23 G. Seidmann, "Marriage Rings Jewish Style," *Connoisseur* 206 (1981), p. 50, saw

Others, again, display only a hoop more or less richly decorated with rosettes, lion-heads, and the like [...] occasionally, however, bearing a small shield at the top. [...] The rings bear, almost without exception, an inscription [...] reading בטוב גדא [...] on the earliest specimens, but on later ones מזל טוב or מ"ט, an expression of felicitation which did not come into use until the fifteenth century. [...] Most of these rings were made at Venice [...] and hence were probably produced by Jews.[24]

It therefore would appear that these rings initially symbolically commemorated the Temple on the bride's right hand on the day of her rejoicing, serving as an additional tangible expression of the metaphor in the above verse from Psalms. As time passed, however, this aspect of the ring was forgotten in some localities, and the Temple-synagogue structure vanished from the crown of the rings, which then took on other meanings that we as yet insufficiently understand.[25]

Or, alternatively, these were **betrothal** rings. Rabbi Isaac Lampronti (Ferrara, 1675–1756) attests:[26]

It once happened that a *kohen*, who was **betrothed** to an orphan girl, **sent her a ring, as was the local custom**. A long time passed, by fault of the matchmaker, and she accepted betrothal from another, without the annulment of the *nisu'in* [i.e. betrothal] before the court, as is the custom.[27]

these "houses" as symbols of the woman, basing this conjecture on the Talmudic expression "a person's wife is as his house" (usually meaning a man's wife is the linchpin of the house), but this is far from the mark.

24 Non-Jewish practices may have been at work here. See, e.g., M.L. Ricciardi, "Lorenzo Lotto Il *Gentiluomo* della Galleria Borghese," *Artibus et Historiae* 19 (1989), pp. 98–106, for the use of wedding rings in sixteenth-century Italy, albeit ones that are not similar to the rings under discussion. For Jewish wedding rings, see the article by Gertrude Seidman, in the catalogue: *International Silver and Jewelry Fair & Jewish Marriage Rings Seminar, 22–25 April 1989*, pp. 29–34.

25 See below, chap. 27 ("Candle Lighting after the Wedding"), n. 12: rings with the inscription: "to light the Sabbath lamp."

26 *Pahad Yitzhak* (Lyck, 1864), fol. 3a.

27 See *Pahad Yitzhak*, fol. 3b. See also Jacob ben David Tam Ibn Yahya, *Tummat Yesharim (Oholei Tam)*, ed. Rabbi Abraham Motal (Venice, 1620), where he published *Ohalei Tam* by Rabbi Tam Yihye, Responsum 100: "In a city where presents of betrothal are sent, which is followed by the [formal] request, they have

In this instance, our ring has become a betrothal ring.[28] These rings may possibly have been so ornately decorated in order to emphasize the fact that they were used as an instrument of betrothal, and not of marriage.[29]

an agreement between them, that close to the wedding, the future groom sends a ring to his future bride, to publicize the matter. This is called the 'first marriage'; and after this he sends them additional presents, that are called *sivlonot*. It was their practice that if the woman candidate was not desirous of her proposed mate, she shall take these *nisu'im* [i.e. the presents] and she casts them before the Court, and she is free to [marry] whomever she wishes."

28 This is also indicated by what H. Pollack wrote in *Jewish Folkways in Germanic Lands (1648–1806)*, p. 35; p. 222 n. 112, with a reference to the article by Salfeld in *JJLG* 23, p. 73, and more. According to Pollack, the gifts received by the bride prior to the wedding ceremony as *sivlonot* included a ring; and similarly in Schammes, *Wormser Minhagbuch*, Vol. 2, p. 30; see the erudite n. 51 by the editor, with a reference to *She'eilot u-Teshuvot R[abbi] Y[edidyah] T[ayah] Weill, Even ha-Ezer*, para. 65: "the rings that he gave in honor of the bride"; *Responsa of Rabbi Yaacov Molin — Maharil*, ed. Y. Satz (Jerusalem, 1979), para. 61; *Maharil*, ed. Spitzer, gloss: "The bride is adorned, and she is given rings." See *Maharil*, ed. Spitzer, pp. 463–65. And, further, in Schammes, *Wormser Minhagbuch*, Vol. 2, p. 43: "the groom is honored with a gift, that is called '*drash fingerlein*,' which means a ring" (n. 139).

29 It has been suggested that the "houses" on the rings symbolize the new "faithful house" (i.e. proper Jewish home) that the couple are to establish. See M. Grunwald, s.v. "Marriage Ceremonies," *Jewish Encyclopedia*, Vol. 8 (New York, 1904), p. 340b. Additionally, N. Feuchtwanger(-Sarig), "Interrelations between the Jewish and Christian Wedding in Medieval Ashkenaz" (see below, chap. 21 ["*Huppah*"] for full details), p. 34, mentions the presence of a Star of David on one of the walls of the "house" on a German ring from the seventeenth or eighteenth century, that she connects with the "wedding stone" (see below, chap. 21, p. 195). On the marriage ring, and especially its manufacture, see the recent work by Rabbi Elyakum Dvorkes, *Bi-Shevilei ha-Minhag: Sources and Explanations of Jewish Customs*, Vol. 1 (Jerusalem, 1994), pp. 100–101 (Hebrew). Prof. Shalom Sabar also wrote me: "Your interpretation for the possible significance of the structure on the ring is extremely interesting. This might possibly be related to what Yaakov Meshorer wrote concerning the Byzantine ring discovered in the Temple Mount excavations in Jerusalem." He suggests that the structure on this ring is that of the Church of the Holy Sepulchre that was commemorated by Christian pilgrims. These rings made their way back to Europe, where they may have been seen by Jews, who, in contrast to the Christian depiction, portrayed on their own rings the Temple (that Christian theology required to be in ruins). See also the recent article: J. Gutmann, "'With This Ring I Thee Wed': Unusual Jewish Wedding Rings," in *idem* (ed.), *For Every Thing a Season: Proceedings of the Symposium on Jewish Ritual Art* (Cleveland, 2002), pp. 133–44, who questions the dating of these rings.

Or, possibly, both explanations are correct, and these rings at first served as a reminder of the destruction of the Temple, and later were designated as betrothal rings.

1. Types of engagement (?) rings

18

SOME WEDDING PREPARATIONS

Elsewhere[1] we have indicated the similarities between many Jewish customs in Morocco and local Muslim practices in that region. In this chapter, we shall discuss two such customs relating to the period shortly before the wedding.

One of these is described by R. Yossef Ben Naim:[2]

> It is customary that, a few days before the wedding, the female relatives of the groom, his neighbors, and their close friends come to the bride's house raucously, and they plait the bride's hair. Seven days after the wedding, small schoolchildren come and release her hair. [...] That day is called in Arabic *leilay ukhta*, that is, the night for releasing the knots. I found a basis for this practice in the book *Otzar Minhagei Yeshurun*, para. 16:5, that the reason is that: it is known that there was a decree in the Land of Israel that a Jewish woman was required to first engage in sexual relations with a *tapsar* [high official], as it is written (BT and PT Ketubot). Two things were done to be saved from that harsh decree: when the bride was brought to the groom's house, her face was covered, so that it would not be seen [from] her face that she was a virgin; and her hair would be loosened, so that she would be revolting at that time. The *tapsar*'s underlings who would see her would [therefore] say that this was a *sotah* [married woman suspected of infidelity] who was brought publicly before the *kohen*

---

1   *Minhagei Yisrael*, Vol. 1, pp. 222–37; Vol. 2, pp. 291–99; see above, chap. 1, "Some North African Fertility and Pregnancy Customs."
2   *Noheg be-Hokhmah*, p. 73, para. 16.

for judgment as a *sotah*. Even though this decree was annulled, the custom remained, either in remembrance or out of fear.

The forced nature of this explanation is self-evident. The practice of plaiting the bride's hair is known from various tribes in Morocco, but in that land it is usually the groom who braids and later loosens her hair.[3] Moroccan Jews call the ceremony of loosening the bride's plaited hair *a'fssai n'ihf*.[4] There were some differences in this act, as it was performed by members of the two faiths. The Muslims plaited only the hair on the right side of the bride's head, and her hair was loosened by her new husband. The first plaiting of the Jewish bride's hair, before her wedding, obviously could not be performed by her husband to be, and her hair was freed at the end of the seven days of marital rejoicing by children; notwithstanding these differences, these ceremonies share the same symbolism. The reasons for the other variations in practice are deserving of further study.

This ceremonial hairdressing was also performed in additional Jewish communities, such as Yemenite Jewry. R. Joseph Kapih attests:[5]

> In the house of the bride, in the late afternoon, after all the women have finished eating, the bride is taken out to the inner courtyard of the house, "*alhigreh*." Dozens of women encircle her, now they uncover her head and undo her hair. They cover her face with her hair, and comb it before all the women. The *majniyah* plays music and sings to a fast beat, to excite the women dancers [...]. At this time no male may be seen in the courtyard, whether adult or child, so as not to commit the sin of gazing upon a woman's hair. When they finish, the bride is brought in to the hall, while wearing special jewelry, and they continue the music and song until the evening [i.e. Wednesday night, the evening of the betrothal, that is called "*Lelat al-Qiddush*"].

The following discussion by Joshua Trachtenberg is instructive in this context:[6]

---

3   Westermarck, *Marriage Ceremonies in Morocco*, pp. 237, 247, 248, 252, 261, 305.
4   Westermarck, p. 252: "[...] the ceremony called *dfssai n-ihf*, the loosening of the hair (lit. "head"), that is, her hair, which has been tied up with a knot behind, is now loosened, combed, smeared with henna, and arranged in the fashion of married women."
5   *Jewish Life in Sana*, p. 134.
6   Trachtenberg, *Jewish Magic and Superstition*, p. 127.

The belief that anything that binds or in any way implies a binding may have a restrictive or harmful effect is widespread in ancient and modern superstition. It has found its way into Jewish folklore in such precautions as to loosen the bride's hair before the marriage, to untie all the knots in the clothing of bride and groom, and to be careful that no knots are found in a shroud. These precautions were based not only on the general superstitious dread of knots, but equally on the fear that such knots might have been the subject of a sorcerer's interest. For binding knots was a common homeopathic device, and even served as a description of magic, which, in the Talmud, was said to consist of "binding and loosing." In the book of Daniel (5:12, 16) the ability "to loose knots" is listed as one of the magician's accomplishments. Talmudic literature contains several examples of this knot-magic, and the commentaries on the well-known reference in the Koran (Sura 113) to the magical use of knots relate that a Jewish magician bewitched Mohammed by tying knots, so that he became weak, refused food and neglected his wives. Nor was the physical act of tying a knot required; the magician could produce the same effect by word of mouth. The idea of binding is the constantly recurring refrain of a post-Talmudic Aramaic incantation: "bound, bound, bound" may be all the spirits and the demons and the magicians; and another Geonic spell summons the "evil spirit who sits in the cemetery and takes away healing from man" to "go and place a knot in N N's head, in his eyes, in his mouth, in his tongue, in his throat, in his windpipe...."[7]

This practice is also related to an additional custom recorded by Ben Naim:[8]

It is customary that seven days before the wedding, the women bring from the bride's house a fine silken girdle and they tie it to the groom, over his stomach. The belt remains on him the entire week until the time of the wedding ceremony, when the bride unties it with her own hand.

Ben Naim also provides the reason for this custom:

7   For more on the magical qualities and various functions of knots, see the index volume of Frazer, *The Golden Bough* (Vol. 8), p. 336, s.v. "Knots."
8   *Noheg be-Hokhmah*, p. 72, para. 12.

I found that there already were allusions to this in books; in the book *Hoshev Mahashavot* by Rabbi Ashkenazi, some reasons for customs are written at the end of the book, and it is written there as follows: "The reason why it is customary to untie any knot in the groom's clothing and for them to take from him every object or money that he has when he enters under the wedding canopy, is to allude to him that he shall have no other tie save that with which he has bound himself to his wife, and that he shall have no love for any precious object save his loving his wife. I heard that the women act in the same manner with the bride.

The same author likewise suggests a different reason for this custom:[9]

It is customary that a sort of girdle that the bride gives the groom, from her own belongings, is tied over the flesh of his stomach. When the bride comes to his house, she unties the knot of the girdle with her own hands. The reason for this is the fear of sorcery, lest he be the victim of some spell that prevents him from engaging in coupling, from their being attracted to each other. See what is written in the book *Nishmat Kol Hai* by our master and rabbi, the rabbi M[...] ben Israel, of blessed memory, *Ma'amar* 3, para. 18, who cited Jonathan ben Uzziel's rendition of the verse "A handmill or an upper millstone shall not be taken in pawn" [Deut. 24:6].

Westermarck describes the parallel custom in Moroccan society:

The bridegroom now passes a while with the bride. Before they part she gives him two cotton kerchiefs (*drer*, sing. *derra*) embroidered with silk, one of which he ties round his waist as a belt, using the other as a handkerchief, and a *tsekka*, or cord for keeping up the trousers, with embroidered and fringed ends to hang down in front; and it is the custom that the bride herself should thread this cord through the trousers.[10]

Afterwards, however, he removes the belt and goes about without it,[11] because "tangles or knots are looked upon as magical impediments and are

9 *Idem*, p. 105, para. 2.
10 Westermarck, *Marriage Ceremonies in Morocco*, pp. 226–27.
11 See *idem*, pp. 225, 264, 281, 293, 324, 350.

therefore not infrequently avoided at childbirths and weddings" (p. 264). Once again, the distinctions between the Jewish and Muslim customs are clearly defined; nonetheless, their shared elements are striking.[12]

12 For an additional example of cultural crossover from North African customs, from another sort of wedding custom, see Rabbi Shushan ha-Kohen, *Kunteres Geulei Kehunah*, appended to *Berit Kehunah ha-Shalem*, p. 581, "*Huppah*" for the practice on the island of Djerba, in which the relatives of the groom and the bride arrange silver or gold coins next to the bride, as a propitious sign. For various reasons, this custom was abandoned in recent generations. Cf. Westermarck, *Marriage Ceremonies in Morocco*, pp. 146, 148.

19

WEDDING DATES

1. THE WEDDING ON WEDNESDAY OR THURSDAY IN ASHKENAZIC CUSTOM

The Mishnah prescribes, at the beginning of the tractate of Ketubot:

> A virgin should be married on a Wednesday, and a widow on a Thursday, for [rabbinical] courts sit in towns twice in the week, on Mondays and on Thursdays; so that if he [the husband] would lodge a suit against [his bride's lack of] virginity, he may go early in the morning [i.e. immediately] to the court.[1]

The post-rabbinic Halakhah, however, as determined by the *Tur*,[2] states:

> At the present time, when there is no fixed time for the sessions of the court, a person may marry on any weekday that he so desires, provided that he has prepared the requirements of the banquet. If he does not have this prepared, then he may not marry before Wednesday.

Beit Yosef finds the source for this distinction in the Talmud:[3]

> R. Samuel the son of R. Isaac said: This [law] was taught only beginning from the enactment of Ezra, that courts are in session

1 M Ketubot 1:1; see the recent article by Y. Brandes, "The Marriage Date: A Rejected Halakhah and Its Significance," *Akdamot* 13 (2003), pp. 57–76 (Hebrew). For suitable times for weddings in general, see J. Bergman, *Jewish Folklore*[2] (Jerusalem, 1961), pp. 32–33, 245 nn. 1–3.
2 *Tur, Even ha-Ezer* 64.
3 BT Ketubot 3a.

exclusively on Mondays and Thursdays. In a location, however, where the courts are in session every day, a woman may be married every day..., provided that he [the bridegroom] is occupied [with the preparations].[4]

The issue of permissible marriage days was well summarized by Rabbi Benjamin Adler:[5]

In the region of Central Europe, it was the practice to always marry a virgin on Wednesday,[6] as had been customary in the time of the Talmud.

4   The wording of the Talmud (Ketubot 3a-b) is as follows: "If there are courts that are in session nowadays as before the enactment of Ezra, then a woman may be married any day [of the week]. What, then, regarding [the requirement] [2a] that 'they [the grooms] were diligent' [concerning the preparations for the wedding]? [This refers to a case] in which he had [already] troubled himself. What is [the source of] 'they were diligent'? For it has been taught in a *baraita*: Why was it stated that a virgin is married on a Wednesday? For if he [the groom] would lodge a suit against [his bride's lack of] virginity, he may go early in the morning to the court. But, then, let her be married on a Sunday, and if he would lodge a suit against [his bride's lack of] virginity, he could go early in the morning [i.e. on the immediately following Monday] to the court? The Rabbis were diligent on behalf of the daughters of Israel, so that a person would be occupied with [the preparation of] the banquet for three days, on Sunday, Monday, and Tuesday, and then marry her on the fourth day." See B.M. Lewin, *Otzar ha-Gaonim*, Vol. 8 (Jerusalem, 1938), Ketubot, Commentaries, p. 6: "This is logical, regarding a virgin, that is, that she be married on a Wednesday, for if he [the groom] says that he was occupied, he is believed. If, however, a person comes to marry the other weekdays, if we see he was occupied, then we permit this, otherwise, not. Rav Ahai, of blessed memory (R. Aaron ha-Levi, cited in *Shitah Mekubetzet*, but not in our version of *She'iltot*)." For the enactment by Ezra, see I. Schepansky, *The Takkanot of Israel* (Jerusalem, 1991), Vol. 1, pp. 192–94; for the determination of the wedding date, see Vol. 2, pp. 193–205 (Hebrew). Note that Bergman, pp. 32–33, claims that in medieval Germany weddings were also conducted on Tuesdays, because this was considered a propitious day, "one in which the word 'good' is twice mentioned" (Gen. 1:10, 12).
5   Adler, *Nisu'in ke-Hilkhatam*, Vol. 1, p. 167. See *Minhagei Yisrael*, Vol. 3, p. 107, end of n. 99, that the practice in Yemen and Aden, as well, was to conduct weddings on Thursdays.
6   R. Samuel ben David ha-Levi (Poland, 1624–81), *Nahalat Shivah* (Amsterdam, 1667; Warsaw, 1887, and others), para. 12: "For the custom of the Talmud remains in force, even though the reason no longer exists. Another reason: so that those who are invited to the wedding from distant locations will be able to return home before the Sabbath. See the [Babylonian] Talmud, Ketubot 5a, which states, regarding the

One of the *poskim* [decisors of Jewish law] wrote that it is proper to be meticulous, and conduct weddings on Thursdays, because this [in itself] is somewhat auspicious.

The "one of the *poskim*" is R. Jacob Joshua ben Zevi Hirsch Falk, the author of *Penei Yehoshua*,[7] who wrote that, according to *Haggahot Asheri* (on *Rosh* [Rabbeinu Asher], Ketubot 1:10), since this (marriage on Thursday) was permitted by the Talmud for the marriage of a widow, this day (Thursday) is also preferable for a virgin. It was not said, he continues, that a virgin should marry on a Wednesday because it, too, is somewhat propitious,[8] but rather for another reason (the possibility of coming to the court the following day); however, in our times, when the second reason no longer exists, it is still preferable for her (the virgin) to be married on a Thursday.[9]

The source that Falk cites, *Haggahot Asheri*, was written by R. Israel of Krems (in Austria), a fourteenth-century scholar, whose teachings are those of the sages of the Franco-German center, such as R. Isaac Or Zarua, R. Isaac of Vienna, some of the Tosafists, and the like.[10] His approach to custom was extremely conservative, and he therefore writes in his gloss on Bava Batra (1:5), regarding what had been cited in the name of Rabbeinu Tam, "that there are customs that are not to be regarded as authoritative, even where it is taught 'all [should act] as the local practice'":

> We do not know which custom should not be regarded as authoritative, it rather seems to me that even a [practice] of lesser [standing] than this is a [valid] custom.[11]

subject of marriage on a Wednesday, that this [in itself] is somewhat of a blessing" (ad loc., n. 30).

7 *Penei Yehoshua*, Ketubot, "*Kuntres Aharon*" (Appendix), para. 1, on BT Ketubot 5a.
8 Ketubot 5a: "Come and hear: Bar Kappara taught: A virgin is to be married on a Wednesday, and intercourse is to be performed on the fifth day [i.e. Wednesday night], because on it [the fifth day of Creation] the blessing for fish was delivered. A widow is to be married on a Thursday, with intercourse to be performed on the sixth day [i.e. Thursday night], because on it [the sixth day] the blessing for man was delivered. [...] If so, then intercourse should also to be performed with a widow [following her wedding] on the fifth day [= Wednesday night], since on it the blessing for fish was delivered? The blessing of man is preferable for him." On the connection between fish and marriage, see below, chap. 22, "Dancing at the Wedding," n. 28).
9 Cited in *Pithei Teshuvah, Even ha-Ezer* 64:6.
10 See E.E. Urbach, *The Tosafists*[4] (Jerusalem, 1980), p. 443 (Hebrew).
11 The intent there is to civil law (i.e. monetary issues), but this also holds true for

To return to the assertion in *Nahalat Shivah*, that the practice of Ashkenaz is always to conduct a wedding on Wednesday, as the Talmud prescribes: this is, indeed, the early practice in Ashkenaz, as we learn from *Ma'aseh ha-Geonim*:[12]

> It is the practice of the Rhine River [communities] to lead the bride on a Wednesday to the house of the groom, or to another house in which the groom is residing, where the wedding blessings [i.e. the blessings of the wedding ceremony] are recited.

This is also implicit in *She'eilot u-Teshuvot ma-ha-Ram mi-Rutenburg*,[13] which states that "an incident came before the rabbi, that four wedding ceremonies had been conducted on a Wednesday." This practice continued for generations, since R. Jousep (Juspa) Schammes attests in *Wormser Minhagbuch* (ca. 1648):[14] "Most weddings between a young man and a virgin are conducted on a Wednesday. If so, it is puzzling why R. Israel of Krems, who takes such great care to preserve the tradition of Ashkenaz practice, would digress from local custom in this matter."

Furthermore, during most of the period of the *Rishonim* (apparently in the wake of the Crusader massacres in 1296)[15] the practice of permitting

other customs. See Dinari, *The Rabbis of Germany and Austria at the Close of the Middle Ages*, p. 195, with the summation: "The tendency that is sensed at times in the writings of the *Rishonim* [medieval authorities] [such as *She'eilot u-Teshuvot ha-Rosh* 58:10], to limit the custom to some degree, was voided in the period under discussion"; see also the continuation of Dinari's discussion.

12 *Ma'aseh ha-Geonim*, p. 55.

13 *She'eilot u-Teshuvot ma-ha-Ram mi-Rotenburg* (ed. R.N.N. Rabbinovicz [Lvov, 1860], para. 23, p. 16 = *Teshuvot Maharam me-Rotenberg* [ed. M.A. Bloch, Budapest, 1895], para. 17, fol. 3a = *Mordekhai* on Megillah, 3:808).

14 Schammes, *Wormser Minhagbuch*, Vol. 2, para. 229, p. 9. See the assessment by Hamburger that this accords with the Land of Israel practice, as recorded in *Ha-Hillukim she-bein Anshei ha-Mizrah u-Benei Eretz Israel*, p. 86, para. 38; see the extended discussion, p. 158. Margalioth demonstrated that the conclusion of the PT (Ketubot 1:1) that even in a place where the court is in session every day, she still may be married only on Wednesday, "so as not to move the time from Wednesday," is opposed to the explanation in BT Ketubot (3a), that "if, at the present time, there are courts that are in session as they were prior to the enactment of Ezra [that courts are in session only on Mondays and Thursdays], a woman may be married on any day."

15 The preference in Ashkenazic communities of conducting weddings on Friday is well-known; see Rabbi Eleazar ben Judah of Worms, *Roke'ah*, ed. B.S. Schneersohn

weddings on the eve of the Sabbath was renewed in Ashkenaz, most likely to reduce the expenses of the wedding. As this is formulated by the author

(Jerusalem, 1967), para. 353, p. 139; *Mordekhai* on Betzah, para. 5; *Ravyah* (Rabbi Eliezer ben Joel ha-Levi of Bonn), cited in *Hagahot Maimoniyot, Hil. Ishut* (*Laws of Marriage*), chap. 10, para. 40; *She'eilot u-Teshuvot ma-ha-Ram mi-Rutenburg*, ed. Rabbinovicz, para. 151; *Kol Bo, Hil. Ishut* (fol. 44c); *Maharil* (Rabbi Jacob ben Moses Moellin), *Hil. Nisu'in* (*Laws of Marriage*), para. 2, ed. Spitzer, p. 464; *Levush, Even ha-Ezer* 63:3, and more. See also I. Abrahams, *Jewish Life in the Middle Ages*[2] (London, 1932), p. 202; S. Steiman, *Custom and Survival: A Study of the Life and Work of Rabbi Jacob Molin (Moelln) Known as the Maharil ...* (New York, 1963), p. 47. According to the law as formulated in the Talmud, however, the conducting of a wedding on Friday is forbidden, "because of the honor of the Sabbath" (PT Ketubot 11, 24[d]; cf. BT Ketubot 5a; see Lieberman, *Tosefta ki-Fshutah*, Vol. 6: *Order Nashim*, Ketubot [New York, 1967], pp. 185–86). Nonetheless, it was customary in the medieval period to conduct weddings on Friday in Ashkenaz (and also in Spain); the reasons given for this choice of day were either "it is propitious, for then Venus [the goddess of love] is in the ascendant" (*Roke'ah*, p. 239) or "because of the regulation instituted on behalf of the poor" (*Ravyah*, in *Hagahot Maimoniyot*, loc. cit.). See also Bergman, *Jewish Folklore*, p. 33, who also suggests that the goddess Freya was a factor in this choice. Venus and Freya are also interrelated in some popular religions. On the relationship between Freya, the Teutonic goddess, and Friday and Venus, see Grimm, *Teutonic Mythology*, Vol. 1, p. 128, citing Matthew of Westminster (Flores ed. [1601], p. 82): "Post illum colimus deam inter ceteras potentissimam, vocabulo **Fream**, cujus vocabulo **Friday** appelamus. Fream ut volunt quidam idem est quod **Venus**, et dicutur Frea, quasi Froa a frodos [A-frod-ite — from froth?] quod est spuma maris, de qua nata est Venus secundum fabulas, unde idem dies appelatur **dies Veneris**," on which Grimm remarks: "Anglo-Saxon legend then, unconcerned at the jumbling of foreign and homespun fable, has no doubt at all about the high antiquity of the names among its people." And on pp. 299–311 he discusses the relationship between two different names-personalities: Freya, or more correctly, Freyja and Frigg, or Frouwa and Frikka. Frigg is the wife of Odin, and Freya the sister of Freyr, and because of their similar names were often confused. After discussing in detail the philological and etymological complexity of the differences between the Old High German Friatar, "which ought clearly to be Friggjardagr in Old Norse, and the Old Norse **Freyjudagr** [which] should be Frouwuntac in Old High German," he explains that "even the meanings of the two names border closely on one another. **Freyja** means the gladsome, gladdening, sweet gracious goddess, **Frigg** the free, beautiful, loveable; to the former attaches the general notion of frau [mistress], to the latter that of fri [woman]" (p. 302). And on p. 301 he writes: "In so far as such comparisons are allowable, **Frigg** would stand on a line with Here or Juno, especially the pronuba, Jupiter's spouse; and **Freyja** with Venus" (see also his n. 1).

of *Ma'aseh ha-Geonim*: "Why was it the practice to begin the wedding

The regulation prohibiting the conducting of weddings on Fridays was still in force in Spain, and was brought as the law by Maimonides, *Mishneh Torah, Hil. Ishut* 10:14, who writes: "Women are not married on Friday, nor on Sunday; this is a regulation that was enacted, lest one come to desecrate the Sabbath in the preparation of the banquet, for the groom is occupied with the banquet." This view was also accepted by *Maggid Mishneh* (ad loc.), and by *Ran* (R. Nissim ben Reuben Gerondi, on *Rif* [R. Isaac Alfasi], Ketubot 5a [2a in the pagination of Alfasi]), who states, in the name of Nahmanides, that "this is a custom of the ignorant, but it was not prohibited." The prohibition against conducting weddings on Friday is therefore not related to this being the prayer day of Muslims (as is posited by Bergman), but rather is to be viewed as the natural continuation of the Talmudic halakhah that forbade weddings on this day of the week. To the contrary, it is the custom in Ashkenaz that is surprising, since it deviates from the Talmudic ruling. Zimmels, *Ashkenazim and Sephardim*, p. 177, raises the possibility that the practice of conducting weddings on Friday might have spread as a reaction to the Karaite prohibition against marrying on this day (see Aaron ben Elijah, *Gan Eden*, fol. 151c: "It is not proper to perform a wedding on Friday, because of the prohibition of sexual relations on the Sabbath"; cf. Bashyazi, *Aderet Eliyahu, Seder Nashim* 7, fol. 157a; Zimmels, ad loc., n. 10). This reason seems somewhat forced, because this practice first spread in twelfth-century Ashkenaz (Zimmels, loc. cit.), which did not have a pronounced Karaite presence. Furthermore, according to the findings of M.A. Friedman, in his monumental work *Jewish Marriage in Palestine: A Cairo Geniza Study*, Vol. 1 (Tel Aviv and New York, 1980), pp. 99–100, only one of twenty-three Land of Israel *ketubot* teaches of a Friday wedding (see Friedman's discussion, n. 6). The practice of conducting weddings on Friday was also known in France and in Italy. See A.H. Freimann, *Seder Kiddushin ve-Nissu'in Aharei Hatimat ha-Talmud* (*Marriage Law after the Conclusion of the Talmud*) (Jerusalem, 1945), pp. 41, 43, 46, and more. See also L.I. Rabinowitz, *The Social Life of the Jews of Northern France in the XII–XIV Centuries, as Reflected in the Rabbinical Literature of the Period* (London, 1938), p. 145; Abrahams, *Jewish Life in the Middle Ages*, p. 186. For the instance in which R. Moses Isserles performed a wedding on a Friday, see *She'eilot u-Teshuvot ha-Rema*, para. 125. Isserles' colleagues protested that he had acted improperly, and the rabbinical authorities in Cracow enacted a regulation prohibiting Friday weddings; if it nevertheless was necessary to perform such a ceremony on this day of the week, it should be done outside the confines of the city. See Rabbi Hayyim Nathan Dembitzer, *Kelilat Yofi* (Cracow, 1881), p. 17 (see also *She'eilot u-Teshuvot ha-Rema*, ed. A. Ziv [Jerusalem, 1970], p. 489 n. 4). We may further note that, probably quite unrelatedly, in Muslim Egypt, Friday was a preferred day for the bridegroom to receive his bride. See Lane, *An Account of the Manners and Customs of the Modern Egyptians* (1966 edn.), pp. 166–67.

banquet on the Sabbath? Perhaps because of the great poverty suffered by the majority of the community."[16]

16 Hamburger adds a lengthy and detailed footnote at this juncture (*Wormser Minhagbuch*, loc. cit.), a portion of which I will cite. Hamburger first listed the sources for conducting weddings on Fridays: see *Raban* (Rabbi Eliezer ben Nathan of Mainz), beginning of Ketubot; *Rokeah* (Rabbi Eleazar ben Judah of Worms), paras. 352, 353; *Sefer Minhagim Maharam me-Rotenberg*, p. 83; *Hagahot Maimoniyot, Hil. Shabbat* (*Laws of the Sabbath*) 3:2; *Rosh*, Ketubot 1:3; *Maharil, Hil. Nisu'in; Hilkhot u-Minhagei Rabbeinu Shalom me-Neustadt*[2] (*Decisions and Customs of R. Shalom of Neustadt*), ed. S.J. Spitzer (Jerusalem, 1977), para. 470; *Terumat ha-Deshen, Pesakim u-Khetavim*, para. 80; *She'eilot u-Teshuvot ve-Piskei Ma-ha-Rik he-Hadashim*, p. 215; *She'eilot u-Teshuvot Rabbeinu Moshe Mintz*, ed. Domb, para. 109. "Indeed, some *poskim* prohibit weddings on the eve of the Sabbath"; see *Shulhan Arukh, Even ha-Ezer* 64:3. Whatever the reason, the ancient practice of conducting most virgin weddings on Wednesdays was reestablished in Ashkenaz, while, in other European lands, weddings were still conducted on Fridays. *Kitzur Shelah* (a citation from *Nahalat Shivah*), para. 100, similarly states: "In the main, weddings are conducted in the land of Ashkenaz in the middle of the week [...] and in the land of Poland, weddings are conducted on Sabbath eves." *Penei Yehoshua*, last booklet of tractate Ketubot, para. 1, writes that it is fitting for a virgin to be married on a Wednesday because of the blessing of that day, as is taught in the Talmud, and he finishes: "It seems to me that anyone desirous of fulfilling the dicta of the Rabbis should first be sensible of the reason for the blessings, and he shall be the recipient of blessings. And it seems to me that such was the practice in several holy [i.e. Jewish] communities, and this is the ancient practice." For the Polish custom to conduct marriages on the eve of the Sabbath, see also *Rama* (R. Moses Isserles), 339:4, 550:3; *She'eilot u-Teshuvot Rama*, para. 125; *She'eilot u-Teshuvot ha-Bah he-Hadashot*, para. 55; *Shenei Luhot ha-Berit, "Ot Kedushah"*, ed. Josefov, Vol. 1, p. 132; *Magen Avraham* 546:4; *Mekor Hayyim* (Bachrach) 132:2; *She'eilot u-Teshuvot Hatam Sofer, Yoreh Deah* 189.

In the communities of Ashkenaz, during the time of R. Schammes, the practice of conducting weddings on Sabbath eves was almost abrogated; and when in the year 1701 one of the worthies of Frankfurt a.M. thought to be wed in a ceremony held on the eve of the Sabbath, with the wedding celebration on the Sabbath [...] the order of this wedding was published by itself, with the following prefatory remarks; "After some forty years have already passed ... in which there were no wedding celebrations here in our community, and there truly is no memory of [the practices of] our predecessors regarding such a celebration."

It should be noted that, according to Westermarck, *The History of Human Marriage*, Vol. 2, p. 569, in certain parts of Germany Friday was considered to be lucky, and auspicious for conducting weddings. See ad loc., n. 3, with numerous sources. It should also be noted that *She'eilot u-Teshuvot Rama*, para. 125, asserts

Marriage on Thursday was, indeed, the practice in Babylonia, as we learn from *Ha-Hillukim she-bein Anshei ha-Mizrah u-Benei Eretz Israel*:[17] "The people of the East conduct the marriage ceremony on Thursdays, and those in the Land of Israel, on Wednesdays."[18] It should also be recalled that man was blessed on the fifth day of Creation (BT Ketubot 5a);[19] nonetheless, the ruling by R. Israel of Krems for a marriage to take place on Thursday is contrary to the early practices of the Franco-German center, as we have shown above.

Possibly the practice of the author of *Haggahot Asheri* was somewhat influenced by the habits of his contemporary non-Jewish surroundings. It is known that the Teutonic peoples considered Tuesdays and Thursdays to be most propitious for conducting wedding ceremonies,[20] a notion that exists to the present. Since Tuesday is unsuitable, because of the "they are diligent" factor,[21] the author of *Haggahot Asheri* is compelled to designate Thursday as the day for weddings.

that weddings are not to be conducted on Sundays, because this is a non-Jewish practice (see Adler, *Nisu'in ke-Hilkhatam*, p. 166, with a citation of R. Moses Isserles' statement in *Pithei Teshuvah* 64:4). Westermarck provides Germanic and Scandinavian sources that reveal that Friday became the preferred day of the week for weddings.

17 Loc. cit.

18 We would have expected an Ashkenazic authority such as R. Meir of Rothenburg to follow the Land of Israel practice, since the customs of Ashkenaz were closely bound to those of the Land of Israel, as I showed in *Minhagei Yisrael*, Vol. 1, p. 196; Vol. 4, pp. 250–53.

19 See above, n. 8.

20 See Westermarck, op. cit., p. 569, who cites the observation by E.H. Meyer in the latter's *Deutsche Volkskunde* ([Strassburg, 1898], p. 174), that these days were preferable because they had been dedicated to the gods of marriage Tio or Zio and Donar; the latter is Thorr, to whom Thursday is dedicated: Thorrsday; for Thorr, see Grimm, *Teutonic Mythology*, Vol. 1, pp. 166–92; Vol. 4, pp. 1388–89. For Tio-Zio, see ibid., Vol. 1, pp. 193–208; Vol. 4, pp. 1349–53. Westermarck cites additional sources that indicate Thursdays' preferred status for the conducting of weddings: P. Sartori, *Sitte und Brauch*, Vol. 1 (Leipzig, 1910), pp. 60 ff.; Wuttke, *Der deutsche Volksaberglaube der Gegenwart*³, pp. 60–61, 368; K. Simrock, *Handbuch der deutsche Mythologie mit Einschluss der nordischen* (Bonn, 1887), p. 600; J. Sepp, *Volkerbrauch bei Hochzeit, Geburt und Tod* (Munich, 1891), p. 56, and more.

21 See above, n. 4. And in *Perishah* (on *Tur, Even ha-Ezer* 64): "Since most people do not have the requirements of the banquet prepared, they instituted this enactment, to conduct weddings only on a Wednesday."

2. MARRYING WHEN THE MOON IS FULL

R. Joseph Caro writes in the *Shulhan Arukh*:[22] "Women are to be married only during the fullness of the moon," following which R. Moses Isserles writes in a gloss:[23] "It is the practice to marry women only at the beginning of the month, when the moon is full [i.e. approaching its fullness] (*Ran* [R. Nissim ben Reuben Gerondi], end of the chapter "Four Deaths" [= BT Sanhedrin, chap. 7])."[24] The source for this practice appears in *Nimukei Yosef*:[25]

> [...] rather, this is merely symbolic, and therefore it is permitted, as it is customary to marry women during the fullness of the moon, as a propitious sign.

This same notion recurs in a responsum by *Rashba* (Rabbi Solomon ben Abraham Adret):[26]

> The practice in some lands of not marrying women until the moon is full does not constitute divination; rather, just as kings are anointed at a spring so that their reign may endure,[27] so, too, this is done in fullness, and not in deficiency. This is an auspicious sign, analogous to the drawing of wine through pipes before grooms, and this does not constitute Amorite practices.[28]

From this we learn that the custom originated in the Iberian peninsula,[29] before it went to R. Moses Isserles in Ashkenazic Europe.

There is no hint of this practice in the rabbinic literature, nor in that of the

22 *Shulhan Arukh, Yoreh Deah* 179:2.
23 *Hagahot, Shulhan Arukh, Even ha-Ezer* 64:3.
24 I did not find this in *Ran*, end of chap. 7 of Sanhedrin; see *Sanhedri Gedolah*, Sanhedrin, Vol. 7: *Hiddushei ha-Ran*, ed. Y. Zaks (Jerusalem, 2001), pp. 260–61.
25 *Nimukei Yosef* on Sanhedrin, end of chap. 7 (fol. 16b, in the pagination of R. Isaac Alfasi).
26 *She'eilot u-Teshuvot ha-Rashba*, Part 7: *Responsa Attributed to Nahmanides*, p. 233; also cited in *Orhot Hayyim*, Vol. 2, p. 620.
27 See BT Horayot 12a.
28 T Shabbat 7(8):16 (ed. Lieberman, pp. 27–28). Cf. BT Berakhot 50b; *Semahot* 8:4 (*Treatise Semahot*, ed. M. Higger [New York, 1937], p. 150). See S. Lieberman, *Tosefta ki-Fshutah*, Vol. 3 (New York, 1962), pp. 99–100.
29 In his commentary on *Yoreh Deah* 179:2, the Vilna Gaon gave *Tikkunei Zohar*, fol. 104b, as the source; I have not yet found this.

Geonim; moreover, the wording of *Rashba* clearly indicates his indecision as regards this custom, which is foreign to us as well, and which could be suspected of constituting divination and an idolatrous practice, had he not found a way to validate it. It therefore is not surprising that many halakhic authorities did not view this practice as mandatory, and were not particular regarding its observance.[30]

Numerous parallels to this practice are to be found among European peoples,[31] and even in cultures more distant in time and place.[32] We are grateful to Frazer[33] for providing a plethora of sources that show the widespread nature in various cultures of the belief that any action performed when the moon is waxing will be successful. When this celestial orb is full, it brings everything to perfection, while the period of its waning does not bode well. Thus, for example, Tacitus (first century CE) relates that the German tribes regarded the period of the full moon as the most advantageous for business,[34] and Julius

30 Rabbi Judah Aszod, *She'eilot u-Teshuvot Yehudah Ya'aleh* (Lvov-St. Petersburg, 1873–80), Vol. 2, para. 24; *Arukh ha-Shulhan, Yoreh Deah* 64:13, and more. See the many sources listed by Adler, *Nisu'in ke-Hilkhatam*, pp. 181–82 n. 150; on pp. 182–83 Adler discusses the approaches of those taking a stringent view. See also Y.Y. Lerner, *Shmiras Haguf Vihanefesh* (*Guarding the Body and the Soul*) (Jerusalem, 1988), Vol. 2, para. 160, pp. 466–71, for the detailed treatment of this practice in its entirety, the particulars of which would exceed the present discussion.

31 See Westermarck, *The History of Human Marriage*, p. 561, who provides many sources for this from Europe as well, mainly from the Teutonic sphere and the Scandinavian lands, such as: Wuttke, *Der deutsche Volksaberglaube der Gegenwart*, p. 268; Sartori, *Sitte und Brauch*, Vol. 1, p. 60 n. 4; Simrock, *Handbuch der deutschen Mythologie mit Einschluss der nordischen*, p. 600, and more.

32 E.g., ancient Greece: see W.A. Becker, *Charikles, Bilder altgriechischer Sitte*, ed. H. Goell (Berlin, 1877–78), Vol. 3, p. 360; India: *The Grihya-sutras: Rules of Vedic Domestic Ceremonies*, trans. H. Oldenberg (Oxford, 1886), Vol. 1, pp. 164, 277; R.B. Bainbridge, "The Saorias of the Rajmahal Hills," *Memoirs of the Asiatic Society of Bengal*, Vol. 2: 1907–10 (Calcutta, 1911), p. 50; the Katchins in Burma: P.Ch. Gilnodes, "Marriage et Condition de la Femme chez les Katchins (Birmanie)," *Anthropos* 7 (Vienna, 1913), p. 367; mentioned (without detail) in Abbé J.A. Dubois, *Hindu Manners, Customs and Ceremonies*,[3] trans. H.K. Beauchamp (Delhi-New York-Oxford, 1906), p. 214.

33 J.G. Frazer, *Adonis, Attis, Osiris: Studies in the History of Oriental Religion*, Vol. 2 (= *The Golden Bough*[3], Part IV [New York, 1935]), chaps. 8–9, pp. 129–50. See also *idem, Folk-Lore in the Old Testament: Studies in Comparative Religion, Legend and Law* (London, 1918), Vol. 1, pp. 52–53.

34 *Germania* 11 (Frazer, op. cit., p. 141).

Caesar (also of the first century CE) maintains that certain tribes despaired of emerging victorious from any battle conducted before the appearance of the new moon.[35] Frazer describes many additional instances of this notion.[36]

This general idea was also absorbed in various circles within Jewish society, both in the Iberian peninsula and in the Franco-German center. Thus we find in the *Zohar*:[37] "The waning of the moon is a cursed time"; and similarly:[38] "the waning of the moon [...] what effect does it have? Because [Samael = the powers of evil] comes and sucks away strength for his retinue from the left side of the moon to strengthen himself."[39]

Similarly, we read in *Sefer Hasidim*:[40]

> Those people who have a commandment to perform, such as beginning to teach small children, or the commencement of another commandment, say [to themselves]: Let us wait until *Rosh Hodesh* [the beginning of the month, i.e. the new moon]."[41]

This conception is already implied in the blessing for *Kiddush Levanah* (the "sanctification of the [new] moon"): "To the moon He said to renew itself as a diadem of splendor for those who have been carried from the womb, who shall renew themselves like it, and to glorify their Maker for the name of His glorious kingship."[42]

With this widespread notion in the background, we can readily understand the inclination of some religious authorities to insist that weddings be

---

35 *De Bello Gallico* 1:50 (Frazer, loc. cit.).

36 See also Aulus Gellius (early second century CE), *Noctes Atticae* 20:8. See Harrison, *Themis: A Study of the Social Origins of Greek Legislation*, p. 192; P. Sebillot, *Croyances, mythes et légendes des pays de France* (Paris, 2002), pp. 33–38; E. Burnett Taylor, *The Origins of Culture* (= *Primitive Culture* [1871], Vol. 1) (New York, 1958), p. 30, and more.

37 *Vayakhel*, 2:205a.

38 *Pinhas*, 3:248b (*Raya Mehemna*).

39 See H. Pedayah, "Sabbath, Saturn, and the Deficiency of the Moon — The Holy Connection: Letter and Depiction," in *idem* (ed.), *Eshel Beer-Sheva* 4: *Myth in Judaism* (Beersheva, 1996), pp. 143–91, esp. 157–58, 182–84 (Hebrew).

40 *Sefer Hasidim*, ed. R. Margaliot (Margulies) (Jerusalem, 1957), para. 59, p. 120.

41 Cf. *Shitah Mekubetzet*, para. 135; Hahn, *Yosif Ometz*, fol. 151b, and the editor's gloss, para. 7; see Trachtenberg, *Jewish Magic and Superstition*, pp. 186, 255–56.

42 See BT Sanhedrin 42a; *Soferim* 19:1 (ed. M. Higger [New York, 1937], pp. 338–40); Maimonides, *Hil. Berakhot* (*Laws of Blessings*) 10:16, and more.

performed specifically at the time when the chances for success are optimal. They ascribed such importance to this factor that they maintained that it did not violate the prohibition of divination, but was merely "a propitious sign." Since, as was shown above, this belief was current among Spanish scholarly circles, it was accepted by R. Joseph Caro, who codified it in *Shulhan Arukh, Yoreh Deah*. Similarly, since broad sectors among Ashkenazic Jewry also subscribed to this idea, R. Moses Isserles could copy it in his glosses on *Orah Hayyim*. Conversely, in those regions in which this belief was most likely not endorsed, the halakhic authorities were cool to the corresponding practice; they counseled against adherence to it, and even opposed revealing such a custom to those about to be wed.

20

FASTING ON THE WEDDING DAY

The bride and groom, especially in Ashkenazic communities, usually fast on their wedding day, until the drinking of the wine during the marriage ceremony. This custom is specified by R. Moses Isserles:[1] "It is customary for the groom and the bride to fast on the day of their wedding; see *Orah Hayyim 573*."

The passage in *Orah Hayyim* to which Isserles refers reads as follows:

> If a person is to be wed on Hanukkah, he does not fast. If, however, he is to be wed in the month of Nisan, even on *Rosh Hodesh* Nisan, he is to fast on his wedding day, because this is one of the days on which fasting is permitted, as taught below, end of para. 580[2] ([R. Shalom of Neustadt], *Hagahot, Minhagim, ve-Likkutei Maharash*).

R. Benjamin Adler adds:[3] "The source [of this law] is in *She'eilot u-Teshuvot Maharam Mintz*, para. 109, and more." In his lengthy and detailed responsum,[4] which discusses the laws and customs of marriage,[5] R. Moses

---

1 *Hagahot, Shulhan Arukh, Orah Hayyim* 61:1.
2 The intent is to "the days on which one is to fast" of which this paragraph teaches. Section 2 states: "On the first of Nisan the sons of Aaron died." This date, and the entire section, is based on *Megillat Taanit Zuta* (or *Batra*), which I discussed in detail in *Minhagei Yisrael*, Vol. 1, pp. 182–91.
3 Adler, *Nisu'in ke-Hilkhatam*, p. 196 n. 47. See also Rabbi Hayyim Meir Zoldan, *Motza Tov: Marriage Laws and Customs* (Jerusalem, 1999), pp. 62–63 (Hebrew), with references to the sources of the practice.
4 *She'eilot u-Teshuvot Rabbeinu Moshe Mintz*, ed. Domb, pp. 523–52.
5 In his wording (p. 540): "And here, I recorded some of the prevalent customs that I saw."

Mintz (*Maharam Mintz*) writes: "It is customary for the groom and the bride to fast on the wedding day, until after the blessing [i.e. the wedding ceremony]," and gives two reasons for this practice (see below).

Mintz was born ca. 1415 in northern Italy, possibly in Lucca,[6] and studied primarily in Germany, in the yeshivot of Nuremberg and Erfurt, and also with R. Israel Isserlein (the author of *Terumat ha-Deshen*). Mintz served as a rabbi and rabbinical judge in Mainz until the expulsion of the Jews from the city in 1443, going from there to Posen (Poznan) in Poland, where, apparently, he died ca. 1480.[7] Thus, his teachings and practices are based on the tradition of the Ashkenazic Torah scholars.

The source of the gloss by the Rema precedes the period of Mintz's ruling, as is specified in *Tziyunei ha-Rema*.[8] This practice already appears in *Sefer Minhagim de-ve Maharam ... me-Rotenberg*:[9] "it is customary that on the day of the blessing [i.e. the wedding ceremony] the groom and the bride do not eat until after the blessing." The author of this collection has not been determined,[10] but we may conclude that he lived in the early fourteenth century,[11] and "the greatest by far portion [of *Sefer ha-Minhagim*] consists of a collection of rulings and practices from the school of Rabbeinu Meir ben Baruch."[12]

This practice can be dated even earlier, to the twelfth-thirteenth centuries, since it is mentioned by Rabbi Eleazar ben Judah of Worms (1140–1225), who writes:[13]

> I found in the *aggadah* that [the custom] of grooms [*hatanim*] is to fast until after the blessing because the commandment is beloved of them, as was the custom of the early pietists, who would fast for a beloved

---

6 See the introduction by Domb, Vol. 1, pp. 12, 19–22.

7 Ibid., pp. 15–16.

8 On *Shulhan Arukh, Orah Hayyim*, loc. cit. These references were not written by Isserles; see *Minhagei Yisrael*, Vol. 2, p. 283. I have not yet found the reference to "*Likkutei Maharash*" in *Hilkhot ve-Minhagei Rabbeinu Shalom me-Neustadt* (Rabbenu Shalom of Neustadt, died 1413).

9 *Sefer Minhagim de-ve Maharam ... me-Rotenberg*, ed. Elfenbein, p. 82.

10 See the introduction by Elfenbein, pp. vi–xi.

11 Ibid., p. xi.

12 Ibid., p. ix. The manuscript itself was most likely written between 1450 and 1480 (ibid., p. iii), that is, congruous to the period of *Maharam Mintz*.

13 Rabbi Eleazar ben Judah of Worms, *Rokeah*, para. 353, pp. 239–40.

commandment, such as *lulav* [one of the Four Species used on Sukkot; by extension, the entire commandment of the Four Species] and other matters.[14]

14 See the editor's comment at the end of the book (p. 30 in notes): "It is written in *Gilyonot ha-Shas*, Pesahim 108, that the simple intent is apparently to those who would fast on the eve of Sukkot, while on the Festival [itself] it is forbidden to fast (end of quotation). Further study is required, as to the nature of this belovedness, for the fasting on the eve of Sukkot for the commandment of *lulav*, that will be observed only the following day; for you must say that the fast is terminated by the Festival meal; if so, the fast bears no relation to the observance of the commandment. Moreover, we should say that the fast on the eve of the Festival is for the commandment of sitting in the *sukkah*, that is observed in the evening. It would appear, however, that the intent is that they fasted on the Festival until after the fulfillment of the commandment; this does not entail the prohibition of fasting on a Festival, since this [the fast] is maintained only until after the fulfillment of the commandment. As regards tracing this to the early pietists: even though the law, as explained in Sukkah 38 and delivered as a ruling in *Shulhan Arukh [Orah Hayyim]* 652:2, is that it is forbidden to eat before taking the *lulav* (see there), we should say that perhaps, by strict law, only eating [i.e. a meal] is forbidden, but tasting is permitted, as is explained in *Shulhan Arukh*, loc. cit, and they [the early pietists] were stringent with themselves, to fast and not even to taste. It appears from the statement by our master [Rabbi Eleazar ben Judah] that only the grooms fast, for they are the ones who perform the commandment [see the beginning of chap. 2 of Kiddushin and Rabbenu Nissim ad loc.]; it is our practice, however, for the bride, as well, to fast, since there are additional reasons to fast [see R. Moses Isserles, *Even ha-Ezer* 61; the commentaries on the *Shulhan Arukh*, loc. cit.]."

Rabbi Eleazar ben Judah may possibly be referring to *Hol ha-Moed* (the intermediary days of the Festival), instead of the eve of Sukkot. More plausible, however, is that his primary intent was to the "other matters," and *lulav* was mentioned only incidentally. The wording "I found in the *aggadah*" is most puzzling, and I have yet to fathom his intent. As regards the close reading by the editor, that it is only the groom, and not the bride, who fasts, see Adler, *Nisu'in ke-Hilkhatam*, pp. 198–99, para. 32, and esp. n. 60, that "*Maharil*, beginning of Laws of Marriage, as well, indicates that the bride does not fast on the day of her wedding." An examination of *Sefer Maharil*, ed. Spitzer, p. 468 n. 10, revealed that the editor wrote: "Our master [*Maharil*] did not mention here that the groom and the bride fast on their wedding day, even though this custom is mentioned in Rokeah, loc. cit., and in *[Sefer] Minhagim de-ve Maharam*." And in ibid., "Variant Readings": "Consequently, also in MS. *Shin*: I copied from a very ancient *Minhagim* and it is customary that the **groom and the bride** do not eat until after the blessing." ("'MS. *Shin*' is MS. Schechter Rabbin 532 [JNUL MS. 39222] written in Italy in 1473" — from the editor's introduction, p. 12). Possibly *Maharil* did not mention

The language and style of Rabbi Eleazar ben Judah clearly show that this practice originated in the teachings of the circle of the German *hasidim* (pietists), who are termed "early pietists" in the literature of their period,[15] and who are known for their many fasts and excessive asceticism.[16] It is said of R. Judah he-Hasid that he would fast every day, including Sabbaths, as is attested by the *Shulhan Arukh*.[17] This custom of fasting on the wedding

this practice, because, according to his custom (*Sefer Maharil*, p. 468): "In Mainz the [wedding] blessing is recited immediately after the morning prayer." (And in "Variant Readings": "when they leave the synagogue"; and ibid., "Addenda": "And there are localities where the blessing is conducted in the afternoon, in the wedding room.") As regards what is written in *Sefer Maharil* at the beginning of the Laws of Marriage (p. 463), that "the wedding feast is conducted after the *Minhah* [prayer; i.e. in the afternoon]," this refers to the *siblonot* (betrothal presents) banquet (see *Sefer Maharil*, ad loc., n. 3). Schammes, *Wormser Minhagbuch* (ca. 1648), p. 25, writes: "It is the practice for the groom and the bride, whether he is a *bahur* [i.e. previously unmarried], or whether a widower who is marrying a widow, to fast on the day of the marriage ceremony, even if this is on *Rosh Hodesh* on which the *Tahanun* [prayer] is not recited [i.e. the day has a semiholiday status]"; see the glosses by Hamburger, pp. 40–42. See also below, regarding the widower and widow (n. 20).

15 See, e.g., *Arugat ha-Bosem*, ed. Urbach, Vol. 4 (Introduction and Indexes) (Jerusalem, 1963), p. 83: "The early pietists concealed the esoteric knowledge until the advent of our holy master, R. Judah he-Hasid." See *Minhagei Yisrael*, Vol. 2, p. 271.

16 See *Minhagei Yisrael*, Vol. 2, pp. 106–107 and the bibliography listed ad loc., n. 60, (to which many more sources could be added); *Minhagei Yisrael*, Vol. 2, pp. 128–30. For the *hasidim* of Ashkenaz, see the instructive article by H. Soloveitchik, "Three Themes in the *Sefer Hasidim*," *AJS Review* 1 (1976), pp. 311–57; I.G. Marcus, *Piety and Society: The Jewish Pietists of Medieval Germany* (Leiden, 1981); the important collection: I.G. Marcus (ed.), *Religion and Society in the Teachings of the Hasidim of Ashkenaz* (Jerusalem, 1987) (Hebrew). See also Zimmels, *Ashkenazim and Sephardim*, pp. 194–95, 238–43.

17 *Shulhan Arukh, Orah Hayyim* 288:3. Even though R. Judah he-Hasid wrote in *Sefer ha-Hasidim*, para. 52: "This category includes those who constantly engage in fasts, which is not a good path; likewise, it was said [Taanit 11a, 22b; this is a paraphrase]: 'Whoever fasts for the sake of self-affliction is called a sinner, lest he come to need the help of his fellow men.'" See what R. Margaliot (Margulies) wrote in his edition of *Sefer Hasidim* (Jerusalem, 1970), p. 112, para. 7: "Although our master, [R. Judah] he-Hasid fasted every day, and even on the Sabbath [...] this was a case of his body rejecting food, by his adhering to his Torah and his prayer, and he did not sense the affliction of the fast; this is the way of a man who is exalted above the people, who has set himself apart from all affairs of this world, save that which is necessary to maintain the body for the service of the Lord." *Sefer Hasidim* was not composed by a single author, but rather consists of a number of *kuntresim* (separately authored

day by the groom and the bride, and even by their relatives (!), is recorded by R. Ephraim ben Jacob of Bonn (1132–97/8), a contemporary of R. Judah he-Hasid who was also in contact with the latter.[18] He writes in his commentary on wedding *piyyutim* (liturgical poems):[19]

> It seems to me that the reason why the groom, the bride, **and their relatives** fast on the wedding day is so that there will be complete joy [at the time of] the wedding ceremony.[20]

The "reason" that he mentions is presented in detail in a preceding passage, when he explains the custom of throwing the cup and smashing it:[21]

> "In the place where there is rejoicing there should [also] be trembling,"[22] in accordance with the verse "rejoice with trembling" [Ps. 2:11] [...] and certainly after the destruction in which all joy was annihilated and banished,[23] so that it not be complete, in order that we will remember the destruction above our highest joy.[24]

It is quite reasonable that the "destruction" is not limited to the ruin of the Temple in Jerusalem, but also encompasses the decimation of the Rhine communities during the First Crusade (1096), and on the background of the anti-Jewish persecutions that preceded this catastrophe "already from

compositions) and expositions that were collected from the literary product of several generations of the families of these pietists. See the article by J.F. Baer, "The Religious-Social Tendency of 'Sepher Hassidim,'" *Zion* 3,1 (1938), p. 6 (Hebrew); J. Reifmann, *Ma'amar Arba'ah ha-Rashim* (Prague, 1860), pp. 6–20; I.G. Marcus, "The Recensions and Structure of *Sefer Hasidim*," *PAAJR* 45 (1978), pp. 131–53; and the recent article by H. Soloveitchik, "Piety, Pietism and German Pietism: 'Sefer Hasidim 1' and the Influence of 'Hasidei Ashkenaz,'" *JQR* 92, 3–4 (2002), pp. 456–93. According to Soloveitchik, paras. 1–152 of *Sefer Hasidim* comprise a single composition, which he labels "SH1" (this assessment is opposed to the view of the majority of the German pietists themselves); consequently, para. 52 does not contradict the tradition in the *Shulhan Arukh* regarding R. Judah he-Hasid.

18 See *Arugat ha-Bosem*, ed. Urbach, Vol. 4, p. 40.
19 Ibid., p. 44.
20 And, in the continuation, he writes: "If a widower marries a widow, it is not customary for them to fast, for their joy is not so complete." See above, n. 14.
21 See above, chap. 19, p. 171.
22 BT Berakhot 30b.
23 Following Isa. 24:11.
24 Following Ps. 137:6.

previous times in Ashkenaz."[25] R. Ephraim ben Jacob of Bonn is also the author of *Sefer Zekhirah* (*The Book of Remembrance*) that depicts these horrendous events,[26] and he, to the best of our knowledge, was the first to mention the *Av ha-Rahamim* prayer that was instituted in the wake of the massacres of the First Crusade.[27] It therefore would appear that this practice, no mention of which exists prior to this period, was a product of its time and of the inclination to asceticism and fasting by the German pietists.

This custom spread in Central Europe as indicated by the above sources, to which we may add a responsum by R. Israel Bruna[28] and a passage in *Matteh Moshe*.[29] The reason cited above, however, was forgotten over the course of time, and other rationales were offered for the custom. Thus, R. Samson ben Zadok (fourteenth century) writes:[30]

> Just as Israel fasted on it [the day of the Giving of the Torah], so, too, the groom [only!] fasts; and at the Giving of the Torah they [i.e. Israel] were married, as it is written, "your love as a bride" [Jer. 2:2]. Ten times Israel is called a bride before the Omnipresent, seven times in the Song of Songs and three times in other books, corresponding to the Ten Commandments, and also corresponding to the ten who assemble for the wedding ceremony, as it is said, "Then [Boaz] took ten elders" [Ruth 4:2],[31] and as it is said, "He inscribed them on two tablets of stone, which He gave to me" [Deut. 5:19]. Thus the groom signs the *ketubah* (marriage contract) and hands it over. And just as Israel were in Egypt for twelve months from the time that it was said

---

25 *Arugat ha-Bosem*, ed. Urbach, Vol. 4, pp. 46–47.

26 See A.M. Habermann, *Gezerot Ashkenaz ve-Tzarefat* (*Persecutions in Germany and France*) (Jerusalem, 1971), pp. 115–16; see also the singular work by S. Spiegel, *The Last Trial* (New York, 1969).

27 Urbach (*Arugat ha-Bosem*, op. cit., p. 49 and n. 51) concludes that "the prayer was established during the First Crusade."

28 *She'eilot u-Teshuvot R. Yisrael Bruna*, ed. M. Hershler (Jerusalem, 1973), para. 93, p. 70. R. Israel Bruna was born ca. 1400, and lived most of his life in Regensburg; he was quite close to R. Israel Isserlein (see the introduction by Hershler).

29 R. Moses of Przemysl, *Matteh Moshe*, ed. Knoblowicz, "*Hil. Hakhnasat Kallah*," para. 2, p. 344. The author lived between 1540–1606.

30 *Tashbetz* 336, para. 445.

31 See Adler, *Nisu'in ke-Hilkhatam*, chap. 10, para. 44, p. 271; *Shulhan Arukh, Even ha-Ezer* 34:4; 64:4.

"Each woman will borrow from her neighbor" [Ex. 3:22], so, too, the woman is given twelve months to provide for herself with jewelry.[32]

This passage weaves a splendid tapestry of numerical symbols, with fine associative connections,[33] but it is highly questionable if they were the reason for the formulation of this practice.

Other reasons were set forth by various sages, such as those in the above responsum by R. Moses Mintz:

> According to one view, the reason is because this is a day of forgiveness, since it is known that their sins are pardoned,[34] as the exposition[35] of the verse, "He took the knife" [Gen. 22:6]. According to another opinion, the reason why fasting is necessary is for fear lest they become intoxicated, and they will not be of sober mind during the marriage ceremony. And, according to the latter reason, if a father marries off his minor daughter, who cannot contract the marriage, rather it is her father who contracts the marriage, then the father is required to fast, lest he be inebriated at the time of the marriage ceremony.

32 See M Ketubot 5:2; see what I wrote in *Resh Kallah u-Mai Huppah* (Jerusalem, 2002), pp. 9 ff. (Hebrew).

33 For numerology as an element in the fashioning of customs, see *Minhagei Yisrael*, Vol. 2, chap. 5, "Numerology as a Factor in the Establishment of the Version of the Prayers and the Fashioning of Custom," pp. 137–92; cf. *Minhagei Yisrael*, Vol. 1, pp. 121–24 (for an English version: D. Sperber, *Why Jews Do What They Do: The History of Jewish Customs throughout the Cycle of the Jewish Year*, trans. Y. Elman [Hoboken, NJ, 1999], chap. 13, pp. 141–49). The entire passage in *Tashbetz* is in the spirit, and apparently under the influence, of the German pietists. A fine example of this pattern appears in the book *Sodot ha-Tefilah*, passages from which are cited by J. Dan in his article "On the Historical Personality of R. Judah Hasid," in *Culture and Society in Medieval Jewry: Studies Dedicated to the Memory of Haim Hillel Ben-Sasson*, ed., M. Ben-Sasson, R. Bonfil, and J.R. Hacker (Jerusalem, 1989), pp. 393–94 (Hebrew). Dan writes (p. 392): "It can hardly be doubted that the work was composed by one of the disciples of R. Judah he-Hasid."

34 The editor comments in a gloss (p. 540, n. 165): "It is written in the Palestinian Talmud that we possess that the groom is forgiven his sins, while nothing is said regarding the bride. See [Rabbi Ovadiah Yosef,] *She'eilot u-Teshuvot Yabi'a Omer*, 3, *Even ha-Ezer*, para. 9."

35 PT Bikkurim 3:3; Gen. Rabbah 67:13, ed. Theodor-Albeck, p. 768; *Midrash Samuel* 17. PT Bikkurim loc. cit.: "And was her name Mahalath? Why, her name was Basemeth! Rather, he was pardoned [*nimhal*] for all his transgressions." See Rabbi M.M. Kasher, *Torah Shelemah, Toledot*, Vol. 4 (Jerusalem, 1934), p. 1116, para. 26.

R. Israel Bruna comments on this reason, in his above responsum:

> I answered, the custom has already spread throughout all Israel not to
> **eat** until one emerges from under the wedding canopy [i.e. until the
> conclusion of the wedding ceremony]. I heard the reason, so as not to
> become intoxicated, or so that it would not be said that one had been
> in this state at the time of the marriage ceremony, and that this was
> a marriage contracted in error, or [subject to] several types of fears
> and deceptions that are common at the time of their wedding;[36] and
> so that he will see whom he is marrying, for it is obligatory to see her
> prior to the wedding, as is taught in the second chapter of Kiddushin
> [41a]. I heard that it is written in *Hiddushei Moreinu ve-Rabbeinu,*
> *ha-Rav Shalom me-Neustadt* [*Novellae of R. Shalom of Neustadt*] that
> he ate on his wedding day, which fell on Hanukkah. Perhaps it [the
> wedding ceremony] extended until the night, and it is forbidden to fast
> on Hanukkah, as is taught in *Megillat Taanit.* [...] And in my youth
> I stated the reason for the groom's fasting, because of what is said
> in the Palestinian Talmud, Rosh Hashanah 1:3, that a king is judged
> every day, and a groom is comparable to a king. Since it is the day
> of judgment for him, then he must fast as on Yom Kippur. [...] The
> above reason is not [valid], for if so, then he should fast until *tzet*
> *ha-kokhavim* [the appearance of the stars]. I further heard, according
> to what is stated in the Talmud [PT Berakhot 3:3], that the sins of
> the one who fasts are forgiven.[37] Since he attains this elevated status,
> he may fall prey to sin, and [his greatness] would be canceled; he must
> therefore repent and inflict some discomfort [upon himself] until after
> his wedding ceremony, when he may eat. I further said in the time of
> my youth, that it is said [BT Shabbat 130a]: "There is no *ketubah* in
> which discord in not sown," for every commandment that Israel did
> not accept joyfully.... Accordingly, it seems to me that in this case,
> when the wedding ceremony fell on 14 Adar I [which would be the

36 Possibly alluding to actions mentioned in Freimann, *Seder Kiddushin ve-Nissu'in*
   Aharei Hatimat ha-Talmud, pp. 39–40, 60–66, 93–94, and in my *Resh Kallah u-Mai*
   Huppah, p. 12 n. 21.
37 For fasting as an element of repentance, see the editor's introduction to Rabbi
   Eliezer ben Judah of Worms, *Sefer Rokeah: Hilkhot Teshuvah he-Shalem*, ed. E.
   Rosenfeld (Brooklyn, 2000), pp. 12 ff.

date of Purim in a nonleap year], and certainly on Hanukkah, Purim, and *Rosh Hodesh*, when the wedding ceremony was conducted in the morning, one may not eat until after this wedding ceremony. Israel of Bruna.

We therefore see how the sages of Ashkenaz struggled mightily throughout the ages to find a reason for this practice, with all its variations;[38] they sought explanations, at times quite forced,[39] with consequent legal distinctions.[40]

This practice was accepted mainly in Germany and Poland, as is attested by Rabbi Hayyim Joseph David Azulai (*Hida*):[41] "Those in Ashkenaz and Poland, myriads of thousands of Israel, and several towns, along with the districts that follow in their ways," thus confirming our assumption of the origins of the custom in twelfth–thirteenth-century Germany.[42]

Although it seems that this practice arose in the wake of the massacres of Ashkenazic Jewry in the eleventh century, and found fertile ground among the German pietists, this is also a longstanding custom within non-Jewish European cultures. As Westermarck puts it:[43]

There are taboos prohibiting bride and bridegroom from eating or

---

38 The subject is excellently summarized by Adler, *Nisu'in ke-Hilkhatam*, pp. 197–98, who presents five reasons.

39 See the extreme formulation by J. Trachtenberg, *Jewish Magic and Superstition: A Study in Folk Religion* (Philadelphia, 1961), p. 172: "A variety of far-fetched explanations were offered for this custom; one, which attained the height of absurdity, was that the groom might not be suspected of inebriety during the ceremony."

40 See the differing opinions: Adler, *Nisu'in ke-Hilkhatam*, p. 199.

41 Rabbi Hayyim Joseph David Azulai, *Birkei Yosef* (Leghorn, 1774), *Orah Hayyim* 470:2.

42 Adler, *Nisu'in ke-Hilkhatam*, p. 198 n. 55, brings additional sources for this determination. The custom entered only a few of the Spanish parallels (Adler, loc. cit.). (See Chetrit et al., *The Jewish Traditional Marriage: Interpretive and Documentary Chapters*, p. 372.) See Settbon, *Kunteres Alei Hadas*, p. 174, para. 3. See Yosef, *She'eilot u-Teshuvot Yabi'a Omer*, Vol. 3, *Even ha-Ezer*, para. 9; *idem*, *She'eilot u-Teshuvot Yehaveh Da'at*, Vol. 4 (Jerusalem, 1981), para. 61, pp. 300–301; see Rabbi Jacob Hayyim Sofer, *Kaf ha-Hayyim* (first edn.: Jerusalem, 1910–26), *Orah Hayyim* 583:14; Rabbi Shabbetai ben Abraham Ventura, *Nahar Shalom* (Amsterdam, 1774), *Orah Hayyim* 583:2. See also Zimmels, *Ashkenazim and Sephardim*, p. 176; *idem*, "Nachtalmudische Fasttage," *Jewish Studies in Memory of G.A. Kohut* (New York, 1935), p. 605.

43 Westermarck, *The History of Human Marriage*, Vol. 2, pp. 544–45.

drinking in public, from eating much, from eating certain victuals, or from eating anything at all — evidently with the object of preventing evil influences from entering the system by means of food.[44] Such taboos are found in Europe,[45] Morocco,[46] and elsewhere. The old custom in Russia is for the betrothed pair to eat nothing on the day of their marriage until after the ceremony.[47]

These testimonies attest to the widespread distribution of this custom among different peoples and lands, including early Germany, and this fasting is related to deeply entrenched beliefs prevalent in ancient times.[48] It therefore appears these were the origin of this, and many other Jewish customs,[49]

---

44 A.E. Crawley, *The Mystic Rose* (London, 1902), p. 343.

45 F.X. von Schoenwerth, *Aus der Oberpfalz, Sitten und Sagen*, Vol. 1 (Augsburg, 1957), p. 97; Sartori, *Sitte und Brauch*, Vol. 1, p. 194 (Germany); J.W. Boecler and F.R. Kreutzwald, *Die Ehsten aberglaubliche Gebrauche: Weisen und Gewohnheiten* (St. Petersburg, 1851), p. 35; J. Piprek, *Slawische Brautwerbungs- und Hochzeitsgebrauche* (Stuttgart, 1914), pp. 87, 95, 106, 128; K. Rajacic, *Das Leben, die Sitten und Gebrauche, der in Kaiserthume Oesterreich lebenden Sydslaven* (Vienna, 1873), pp. 157–61, 181.

46 Westermarck, *Marriage Ceremonies in Morocco*, pp. 341–42.

47 H.C. Romanoff, *Sketches of the Rites and Customs of the Greco-Russian Church* (London, Oxford, and Cambridge, 1869), p. 192; to which we should add: Sokolov, *Russian Folklore*, p. 205.

48 H. Pollack writes as follows of some of these beliefs in his fine book: *Jewish Folkways in Germanic Lands (1648–1806): Studies in Aspects of Daily Life*, p. 224 n. 125: Cf. A. Wuttke, *Der deutsche Volksaberglaube der Gegenwart*[2], Berlin 1869, p. 206, # 312; pp. 206–7, # 31; p. 346, #558; *Handworterbuch des deutschen Aberglaubens* [=HDA], IV (1931–32), p. 153, # 2:

> It was the belief of the German folk that a joyous occasion, such as a wedding, was threatened with tragedy. The apprehension of death was apparent at marriage festivities, for special precautions would be taken not to permit the joyous event from being disrupted either by arousing the anger of the "evil spirits" or by negligence in exercising control over them. See HDA, IV, 148, # 1; 153, #2; 154, #2, for some general practices in warding off any threat of death during the marriage celebration. The bride and groom, for instance, visited the graves of their relatives before their wedding. See p. 188, n. 213. No marriage ceremony would be held while there was an opened grave in the cemetery. During the wedding every available chair was occupied, so that Death could not take a seat and bring harm to the couple.

49 See the many examples in Part 2.

and this abstention from food and drink was adopted by the Ashkenazic communities, where it took root,[50] for the reasons listed above, with various other reasons being advanced in explanation of the practice over the course of time.

50 See Baer, "The Religious-Social Tendency of 'Sepher Hassidim,'" pp. 7–10, 26–29, that "in their severe asceticism and self-abasement (humilitas), these pietists were influenced by the Christians" (p. 10). See M. Beer, "On Penances of Penitents in the Literature of *Hazal*," *Zion* 46, 3 (1981), pp. 159–81 (Hebrew). For the great influence of the latter's article on Baer, see Marcus, *Religion and Society in the Teachings of the Hasidim of Ashkenaz*, p. 19. It is noteworthy that the Sephardic *Hida* wrote in *Birkei Yosef, Orah Hayyim* 61, para. 1, that this was not customary in the Land of Israel. In other words, this custom did not spread among the inhabitants of the Land of Israel, while it later was accepted there, as well. See Rabbi Eliyahu Biton, *Ir ha-Tzevi: The Customs of the Holy City of Safed, from Eretz ha-Hayyim by R. Haim Sitehon* (Safed, 1996), p. 126 (Hebrew).

21

THE *"HUPPAH"* —
THE WEDDING CANOPY/CEREMONY

Elsewhere I wrote[1]: "Another extremely fascinating question is the reflection of customs in Jewish art, in illuminations of manuscripts, and the like." Some practices have left hardly any trace in the *minhagim* literature, but are the subject of testimonies in manuscript illuminations.[2] Naomi Feuchtwanger writes, in an excellent article on bridal coronets:[3]

> Therefore, Jewish literary sources alone cannot provide sufficient evidence to show an uninterrupted continuity of this custom from biblical times throughout the Middle Ages to the dawn of the Modern Era.

This phenomenon is plainly exemplified by the multiplicity of customs and composite practices relating to the wedding canopy, and indeed, to the term *huppah* itself, which can be interpreted in a number of ways (such as: the physical wedding canopy, or the formal wedding ceremony as a whole), and whose place in the sequence of the elements of the wedding ceremony is unclear, but which nevertheless seems to be a formal requirement of this rite of passage. We have indicated the questions that have been raised

1 *Minhagei Yisrael*, Vol. 1, end of the Introduction (p. 19).
2 Regarding the bride's coronets (or garlands) of which she speaks, see Falk, *Jewish Matrimonial Law in the Middle Ages*, pp. 65, 72. It should be noted that such coronets were already worn by the bride and the groom in ancient Greece. See, e.g., Becker, *Charicles*, p. 487; Lawson, *Modern Greek Folklore and Ancient Greek Religion*, pp. 558–59, 560.
3 Feuchtwanger, "The Coronation of the Virgin and of the Bride," pp. 213–24, esp. 220.

concerning the essential nature of the *huppah* that were expressed by R. Moses Isserles in his glosses.[4] These uncertainties gave birth to many diverse understandings of this concept, and even to the combining of different views "in order to fulfill one's [halakhic] obligation, according to all opinions."[5] It appears that not all of these possibilities are expressed in the halakhic literature, but are to be found in manuscript illuminations and in illustrations in printed books. The following is the result of a study of the hidden treasures that are to be found in Jewish art, and their interpretation in accordance with the halakhic sources.

In earlier times, when an Israelite man wanted to take a wife, he would first betroth her (i.e. effect *kiddushin* — betrothal; also known as *erusin*) before witnesses, with money or with a writ, thereby making her his *arusah* (a woman who is betrothed; not to be confused with the modern Hebrew meaning of this word, "fiancee"), and leave her in her father's house. When the day of the wedding (*nisu'in*) arrived, he would "take her under the *huppah*" and bring her to his house.

Beginning in the period of the *Rishonim*,[6] it was customary to conduct the *kiddushin* and *nisu'in* together, in the formal wedding ceremony. The former is effected with a ring. As regards the *huppah*, which is already mentioned in the Talmud, the *Rishonim* disagree regarding its nature and when it occupies center stage. At any rate, beginning in a certain period, the *huppah* became the central component of the wedding ceremony, and its standing is expressed in the betrothal blessing that concludes with the words "by the *huppah* and *kiddushin*."[7] Until the woman "stands under the wedding canopy" (i.e. participates in the formal wedding ceremony), she

---

4   On *Shulhan Arukh, Even ha-Ezer* 51:1; see *Minhagei Yisrael*, Vol. 1, p. 45 end of n. 18; Vol. 2, p. 257; Vol. 3, p. 172 n. 152.

5   Cf. *Minhagei Yisrael*, Vol. 2, chap. 2 ("Compromise in Custom"), pp. 23–75.

6   Apparently beginning in the time of Rashi; see Freimann, *Seder Kiddushin ve-Nissu'in Aharei Hatimat ha-Talmud*, pp. 28–29; see also J. Werdiger, *Edut le-Yisrael*[2] (Bnei Brak, 1965), p. 32, citing R. Menahem Meiri, who writes that *erusin*-betrothal had already been appended to the *nisu'in* ceremony in the Geonic period. See Falk, *Jewish Matrimonial Law*, chap. 2 (pp. 35–85), who discusses this issue at length. See also what I wrote in *Resh Kallah u-Mai Huppah*, pp. 9–11.

7   BT Ketubot 7b. For the formula of the blessing, see *Enziklopedia Talmudit* (*Talmudic Encyclopedia*), Vol. 4 (Jerusalem, 1984), cols. 420 ff., s.v. "*Birkat Erusin*" ("Betrothal Blessing"); S.Y. Friedmann, "*Huppah* and *Kiddushin* in the Betrothal Blessing, [in] the Printed Editions of *Sefer Abudarham*," *Sinai* 76 (1975), pp. 260–64 (Hebrew).

remains under the authority of her father;[8] from then on, she is permitted (if her husband is a *kohen*, i.e. a member of the priestly class) to eat of *terumah* (the heave-offerings, that may be eaten only by one of the priestly class), and this right is not even abrogated by any rabbinic strictures.[9]

Many depictions of the wedding ceremony have been rendered throughout the Jewish world, whether as illuminations of the *ketubah* (marriage contract), as part of ornaments for the bride, or in oil paintings.[10] When we examine these artistic representations, we find practices that are unfamiliar, or that even seem strange, to the contemporary observer: is this how the marriage ceremony appeared? On the other hand, the artist obviously presented the reality of his time, or that to which he was accustomed, and these details were not foreign to those of his time and place. An examination of the sources reveals that each illustration reflects a custom or certain view that was current, and a study of these depictions will enable us to determine the location and distribution of the custom, the distinctions between varying practices, and the combination of others.[11]

8 BT Ketubot 48b.

9 BT Ketubot 27b; see Maimonides, *Mishneh Torah, Hil. Terumot* (*Laws of the Heave-Offering*) 7:3; 8:7.

10 And also on wimpels (Torah binders); see above, chap. 16, "The Wimpel"; Kaniel, "The Wimpel," pp. 41–42, 44; P.J. Abbink Van der Zwan, "Ornamentation on Eighteenth-Century Torah Binders," *The Israel Museum News* 1978, pp. 64–73 (with bibliography, p. 73), esp. p. 71, with a discussion of the depiction of the wedding canopy in the wimpels. As was noted above (chap. 16), when a child is first brought to the synagogue (or possibly at his Bar Mitzvah), he brings with him a present of a wimpel. The art sources clearly show that this is a representation of a small child being brought to the synagogue for the first time. This is discernible in the painting by Moritz Oppenheim (in *Pictures of Traditional Jewish Life*, p. 26), which shows the ceremony of bringing a one- (or three-) year-old child to the synagogue. The father, who is holding the young child, helps his son, and guides the child's hand to touch the *etzei hayyim* (wooden handles) of the Torah scroll. A wimpel rests next to the person holding the Torah scroll; I have heard that this is still practiced to the present.

11 It is fitting here to cite the finely formulated and important general statement by Rabbi Abraham Isaac ha-Kohen Kook on art: "Literature, painting, and sculpture are meant to realize all the spiritual concepts inherent in the depths of the human soul. As long as a single depiction that is concealed within the human soul has not been actualized, the artistic endeavor is obligated to so realize it" (*Olat Re'iyah Prayerbook* [Jerusalem, 1962], Vol. 2, p. 2, where Rabbi Kook refers to "literature, and its painting, and its sculpture." This follows the original version published in

Fig. 1 portrays a Jewish wedding in eighteenth-century Venice (attributed to Pietro Longhi):[12] the couple are sitting on chairs, with no hint of a wedding canopy, as is the case in Fig. 2, which depicts a wedding of Tunisian Jews.[13] Is a Jewish marriage possible without the *huppah*, which is the obligatory

the *Ha-Mizrachi* journal [Cracow, 1903], which appears in Z. Yaron, *The Philosophy of Rabbi Kook* [Jerusalem, 1974], p. 178). Yaron comments (ad loc., n. 23): "In this article, as he wrote it, Rabbi Kook unquestionably referred to the three forms of art: literature, painting, and sculpture [*hituv*, literally, carving]"; see also ibid., n. 21. For art in the thought of Rabbi Kook, see A.Y. Zuckerman, "On Art in Rabbi Kook's Teachings," in *Yuval Orot* (*A Jubilee of* Orot), ed. B. Ish Shalom, S. Rosenberg (Jerusalem, 1988), pp. 153–57 (Hebrew); Y. Gelman, "'Esthetics' in Rav Kook's Writings," in *Yuval Orot*, pp. 159–68.

It would also appear from this teaching by Rabbi Kook that from these graphic representations we can also learn the details of halakhot and various integrated practices. Just as many topics in the rabbinic literature cannot be understood without being cognizant of the contemporaneous reality, from archeological finds and the like, it is similarly essential to have knowledge of paintings that describe halakhot that are the subject of our inquiry. Such illustrations are capable of teaching things that are not to be found in the written sources; for example, practices that combine different views and customs, in order to fulfill one's obligation by any possible view. Such combinations are not written in books, but we know of their observance from the paintings before us. Similarly, much of Talmudic literature can be properly understood only by reference to visual evidence found in archeological artifacts, as I demonstrated in my book, *Material Culture in Eretz-Israel during the Talmudic Period* (Jerusalem, 1993), pp. 14–15, and throughout the volume (Hebrew).

12 See G. Fiocco, "Una pittura di Pietro Longhi," *Arte Veneta* 10 (1956), pp. 206–207, with a reference to Fiocco in S. Sabar, "The Use and Meaning of Christian Motifs in Illustrations of Jewish Marriage Contracts in Italy," *Journal of Jewish Art* 10 (1984), p. 62 n. 67.

13 This painting is on a postcard, which I estimate to be from the beginning of the twentieth century (I have not yet found its source), and which depicts a Tunisian wedding, as is clearly indicated by the clothing worn by the participants. See Rubens, *A History of Jewish Costume*, pp. 62–67, and no. 79. The reverse side of the postcard reads: "Judische Hochzeit — Jewish Wedding — Noce juive," and bears the printer's mark: "R 107. R & JD." See the recent article: Y. Lavan, "The Embroidered *Talitot* from the City of Tunis," *Mahut* 12 (1994), p. 45, Fig. 2 (Hebrew). See K.R. Stow, "Marriages Are Made in Heaven: Marriage and the Individual in the Roman Jewish Ghetto," *Renaissance Quarterly* 48 (1955), p. 449, who writes of a painting from ca. 1455/6 of a wedding scene that apparently indicates that the painter was a Christian. In light of our explanation, this is not at all a convincing proof. The entire article (pp. 449–91) is of interest, but is in need of correction (my thanks to my colleague Dr. Jeffrey Wolf for drawing my attention to this article.)

conclusion of the marriage ceremony? (The giving of the ring is solely *kiddushin*, and does not create the final marital bond.) Then where is the *huppah* in this wedding? A close examination of the painting reveals the answer: the bride's face is covered by a transparent cloth. R. Moses Isserles wrote, concerning such a veil:[14] "According to one opinion, the *huppah* [i.e.

14 Gloss on *Shulhan Arukh, Even ha-Ezer* 55. The "one opinion" to which Isserles refers is that of *Tosefot*, Yoma 13b, s.v. "*Ve-la-Hada*," that is cited by *Beit Yosef, Even ha-Ezer*, para. 61, s.v. "*U-Mai Shena*; see below, n. 24. For non-Jewish parallels of the wedding veil, see Westermarck, *The History of Human Marriage*, Vol. 2, pp. 527–28, with bibliography (n. 9); E. Samter, *Familienfeste der Griechen und Romer* (Berlin, 1901), pp. 47 ff.; Sartori, *Sitte und Brauch*, p. 79; Edwin Hall, *The Arnolfini Betrothal: Medieval Marriage and the Enigma of Van Eyck's Double Portrait* (Berkeley, Los Angeles, London, 1994), p. 39, for the veil among Christians. Schammes, *Wormser Minhagbuch*, Vol. 2, p. 24 (and again on pp. 25, 31) mentions "the *ma'aleh* [i.e. bench] that is prepared for the groom and bride to sit upon." Cf. S.G. Cusin and U. Nahon, *Art in the Jewish Tradition* (Milan, 1963), p. 17, the reconstruction of a wedding canopy from Mantua in the eighteenth century, in which we see a sort of raised platform with two steps (and also with chairs under the wedding canopy; see below, nn. 64–65), as is also visible in this painting. See also Rabbi Saadiah Hozeh, *Sefer Toledot ha-Rav Shalom Shabazi u-Minhagei Yahadut Sharab be-Teiman (The History of R. Shalom Sharabi and the Customs of Yemenite Jewry)* (Jerusalem, 1973), p. 91; Ovadia, *The Community of Sefrou*, Vol. 2, p. 79; *Noheg be-Hokhmah*, p. 110; see J. Werdiger, *Avodat Yisrael* (Bnei Brak, 1965), pp. 56–58. For a general discussion of the veil in the rabbinic period, see R. Bonfil, "Un Antico Uso Nuziale Ebraico," *Annuario di Studi Ebraici* (1964–65), pp. 1–20 (my thanks to Prof. Bonfil for providing me with this article). Also of relevance is the article by J. Riefmann, *Moadei Arev* 1 (Vilna, 1863), p. 31, in which he writes: "The practice in ancient times for the bride to go forth 'in a veil, with her head uncovered' (M Ketubot 2:1), that are the signs of mourning, as is written in the Palestinian Talmud (Ketubot 2:1), was established during that time of persecution (when the military governor possessed the right of *jus primae noctis*) (PT Ketubot 5:5). Clear proof of this is provided by the statement in the Babylonian Talmud (Ketubot 17b), in the name of a *baraita*, that the practice of a virgin bride going forth in a veil and with uncovered head was observed only in the land of Judea, because this decree was in effect there." In this painting, as in Fig. 3, we see people holding candles (or torches), a practice that is mentioned in *She'eilot u-Teshuvot Rabbeinu Moshe Mintz*, ed. Domb, para. 109, p. 534; *Maharil, Hil. Nisu'in (Laws of Marriage)*, ed. Spitzer, p. 464. See *Tashbetz (Katan)*, para. 465. This has its source in BT Gittin 89a; Sanhedrin 32b. See *Magen Avraham* 298:16. The practice of accompanying the bride with torches is already mentioned in *He-Arukh*, s.v. "לפד" (*Arukh ha-Shulhan* 5, p. 51). The leading of the groom with torches is mentioned in

the conclusion of the marriage ceremony] of a virgin is effected from when she goes forth in a veil."

Maharil, Hil. Nisu'in; see also Adler, *Nisu'in ke-Hilkhatam*, Vol. 1, p. 371. In the painting by Oppenheim (Fig. 13), several of those present hold poles with clothes tied to their tops, a feature also to be seen in the painting by Bernard Picart from 1721 (Fig. 9). I have not as yet found this in the *minhagim* literature; it possibly is related to the use of candles/torches. An intriguing comparison presents itself in the work by Picart, two people hold such poles (the artists writes that two children precede the groom and the bride with these "adorned sticks," in his language), while Oppenheim portrays four such individuals. A parallel exists for candles: *Matteh Moshe*, beginning of *Hil. Hakhnasat Kallah*, p. 344, writes that only two *shushvinim* carry a candle in their hand, for a total of two candles, thus paralleling the two poles in Picart's painting. *Orhot Hayyim, Hil. Kiddushin* (*Laws of Marriage*), p. 67, writes that four candles are to be lit, which corresponds to the four poles in the painting by Moritz Oppenheim.

It is also noteworthy that the caption of Picart's illustration specifies that (two) children carry the poles, and various sources state that the wedding canopy itself is supported by children (four, in this case). See, e.g., Buxtorf, *Synagoga Judaica*, p. 631: "quatuor pueri conopaeum quatuor perticus alligatum"; and then Bodenschatz, *Kirchliche Verfassung der heutigen Juden* (1748), Vol. 4, p. 123: "Auf allen 4 ecken gehet eine Stange herunter. Damit deiser himmel von 4 Buben getragen [...] werden kan." (For the use of the term "himmel," see below, n. 28); and similarly, Leusden, p. 173: "sed quatuor vire sive pueri tenent conopaeum" — once again, the emphasis on the part played by children in the wedding ceremony (see Fig. 11). Not to be outdone, *He-Arukh*, s.v. "לפד" speaks of ten torches. The matter of the candles or torches in the bridal procession has an interesting parallel (source?) in the Roman wedding ceremony: see W. Smith, W. Wayte, and G. E. Marindin, *Dictionary of Greek and Roman Antiquities*[3] (London, 1890), Vol. 1, p. 830, s.v. "Fax": "The use of torches after sunset, and the practice of celebrating marriages at that time, probably led to the consideration of the torch as one of the necessary accompaniments and symbols of marriage. Among the Romans the *fax nuptialis* [Cic. *pro Cluent*. 6], having been lighted at the parental hearth, was carried before the bride by a boy whose parents were alive [Plaut. *Cas.* i. 30; Ovid. *Epist.* xi. 101; Servius, *in Virg. Ecl.* viii. 29; Plin. *H. N.* xvi. 18; Festus, s.v. *Patrimi*.]"

Furthermore, it is interesting to note that just as ten participants were required in a Jewish wedding (see *Shulhan Arukh, Even ha-Ezer* 62:4, based on BT Ketubot 8b, a statement by R. Johanan, a Land of Israel authority of the third quarter of the third century CE; see further Adler, *Nisu'in ke-Hilkhatam*, Vol. 1, pp. 271–73), and, according to some views, also at a betrothal ceremony (*Shulhan Arukh, Even ha-Ezer* 34:4; see *Tur, Beit Yosef*, ad loc.), so, too, at a Roman wedding of the *confarreatio* type, ten witnesses and the high priest were required (see Gaius 1:112; Ulpianus 9:1). (See Smith, Wayte, and Marindin, *Dictionary of Greek and Roman*

Thus, in the painting, the obligation of *huppah* (by means of veiling) was already fulfilled, and all that remained was to betroth her with a ring. In

Antiquities, Vol. 2, p. 1406, s.v. "*Matrimonium*"; A. Berger, *Encyclopedic Dictionary of Roman Law* [*TAPS* NS 43/2], [Philadelphia, 1953], p. 406a, s.v. "*Confarreatio*," with bibliography.)

The very comparison between these sticks and the torches, however, is questionable, and far from convincing. I now believe that I have discovered the source of these sticks. The Protoevangelium (= James 8:2 — 9:1; see M.R. James, *The Apocryphal New Testament* [Oxford, 1966], p. 42) relates that when Mary, the mother of Jesus, came of age, the High Priest Zechariah, following the command of the angel of the Lord, ordered all the widowers in the land to assemble, each with his rod, and the one to whom the Lord would show a sign would marry Mary. The heralds went forth to announce this throughout Judea, and all the widowers gathered together before the High Priest, but no divine sign was given. Joseph also cast down his rod and came to the High Priest. The latter took all the rods, but he saw no sign upon them. Joseph, however, received the last rod, and behold, a dove came forth from the rod and flew upon Joseph's head. The High Priest then declared that he would be Mary's husband. However, in a variant of this legend that appears in medieval Christian illustrations, undoubtedly influenced by Num. 17: 17–27, the sign consisted of the blossoming of Joseph's rod. This legend was quite popular during the medieval period and the Renaissance (see B. Kleinschmidt, *Die heilige Anna: ihre Verherung in Geschichte, Kunst und Volkstum* [Dusseldorf, 1930]; C. Cecchelli, *Mater Christi*, four vols. [Rome, 1946–54], cited by E. Hennecke, *New Testament Apocrypha*, ed. W. Schneelmelcher, trans. R.M. Wilson et al., Vol. 1 [Philadelphia, 1963], p. 368). This motif was quite well-known from the painting of Raphael, *La Sposalizio* from 1504 (Breira Museum, Milan, Fig. 34), which was based in no small measure on the painting with the same name by Perugino, on the same subject and from almost the same time (currently in Caen). In Raphael's work we see on the right-hand side (in contrast with the painting by Perugino, in which this element is on the left), four "suitors" who stand with poles in their hands; another suitor, in the front of the picture, is bending down and breaking his stick on his knee, while the stick of Joseph budded. It therefore seems that the sticks in the hands of the youths in the painting by Picart somewhat combine the traditional Jewish torches and the sticks of this Christian tradition. The ornamentation topping these adorned sticks is reminiscent of the budding at the top of Joseph's stick, and symbolizes the correct choice and even fertility — symbols that are quite appropriate for the wedding ceremony. I have yet to find these in the *minhagim* sources, or in Buxtorf (*Synagoga Judaica*), Leusden, Bodenschatz (*Kirchliche Verfassung der heutigen Juden*), or similar works. See also BT Gittin 57a: "Betar was destroyed through the shaft of a litter. It was customary when a boy was born to plant a cedar tree, and a pine tree when a girl was born; when they married, the tree was cut down, and a canopy was made of the branches." All these may be connected.

this vein, R. Joel Sirkes (*Bah*) wrote that it was customary, already on the morning of the wedding day, to cover the bride's head with a kerchief.[15] A woodcut from 1705 in Germany (Fig. 3)[16] shows the bride covered with a veil, even before her wedding; the groom is not beside her, and apparently is being brought to stand under the wedding canopy. In an even more extreme case, we find a wedding with no trace of a wedding canopy, in which the groom merely places the ring on his bride's finger (Figs. 4, 5, 6).[17] This could be understood in accordance with the view of the *Rishonim*, headed by Maimonides,[18] that the

15 *Tur*, para. 61, s.v. "*Ve-Nireh; She'eilot u-Teshuvot Rabbeinu Moshe Mintz*," para. 109 (see below). The early covering of the bride's head is also mentioned by R. Eliezer of Bonn, and is cited by Rabbi S.E. Stern, *The Order of Betrothal and Marriage According to Our Early Masters* (Bnei Brak, 1990), p. 56 (Hebrew). Stern writes that according to one opinion, the veil constitutes the *huppah* (i.e. the concluding element of the wedding ceremony), while, according to another view, it follows Rebekah's "she took her veil" (Gen. 24:65). See Stern, p. 55; *Minhagei Yisrael*, Vol. 2, p. 297; *Derishah* on *Tur*, loc. cit. Some explain the wording of the blessing: "by the *huppah* and *kiddushin*" — *huppah* precedes *kiddushin*, corresponding to the reality: first, the *huppah*, by the spreading of the veil, and only afterwards is the *kiddushin* effected. See *Enziklopedia Talmudit*, Vol. 16, col. 420; and my discussion in *Resh Kallah u-Mai Huppah*, pp. 17–21. For the version of this blessing, see ibid., n. 5, as in the ruling by *Derishah, Yoreh Deah* 342:1. It is universally agreed that the veil does not constitute the *huppah*, and another reason was given for it; see, e.g., *Shulhan ha-Ezer*, Vol. 2, fol. 25–26; Rabbi Isaac Lipets of Siedlce, *Matamim he-Hadash* (Warsaw, 1894), "*Hatan ve-Kallah* [Groom and Bride]," para. 3. R. David Horowitz, *Imrei David* (Bilgoraj, 1934) wrote that if the veil constitutes the *Huppah*, the bride and groom must have the corresponding intent when the veil is spread. As to whether the groom is required to spread the veil, see the different views on this question in *Otzar ha-Poskim*, Vol. 16 (Jerusalem, 1986), p. 82. See Friedmann, "*Huppah* and *Kiddushin* in the Betrothal Blessing."

16 Reproduced in *Jewish Encyclopedia* (New York, 1903), Vol. 5, p. 536. The synagogue in the background is in Furth. See below, n. 53.

17 Fig. 4: from the manuscript of *Berakhot* by R. Meir of Rothenburg, Italy 1477. See B. Narkiss, *Hebrew Illuminated Manuscripts* (New York, 1974), p. 159; Fig. 5: from MS. Rothschild 24, Italy ca. 1470, in M. Hakohen, *Hayyei Adam: Kelulot* (*Jewish Life Cycle: Marriage*) (Jerusalem, 1986), p. 63 (Hebrew); Fig. 6: from an Italian *mahzor* (holiday prayerbook), Pesaro 1481, in the Hungarian Academy of Sciences, Budapest, MS. 380/II, fol. 230, reproduced in Gutmann, "Jewish Medieval Marriage Customs in Art," p. 54.

18 Maimonides, *Mishneh Torah, Hil. Ishut* (*Laws of Marriage*) 10:1; *Tosefot R. Yitzhak ha-Zaken*, Kiddushin 10b; *Rashba* (Rabbi Solomon ben Abraham Adret), Ketubot 4a; *Tur, Even ha-Ezer* 61; Rabbi Menahem ben Aaron ben Zerah, *Tzeidah la-Derekh*

huppah (i.e. the conclusion of the wedding ceremony) consists of the *yihud* (the bride and groom being together alone) after the wedding ceremony. This

(Ferrara, 1554), *Ma'amar* 3, *Kelal* 2, para. 1. *Ran* (R. Nissim ben Reuben Gerondi), beginning of Ketubot, s.v. *"O she-Persah"*; *Ha-Ittur*; and *Orhot Hayyim* (cited in MS. *Even ha-Ezer* 61) maintain the same view, but negate the need for *yihud*; rather, his bringing her to his house constitutes *huppah*. This is analogous to what was cited by a student of *Rashba* (quoted in Stern, op. cit., p. 30): "Others have understood the *huppah* [i.e. the formal wedding ceremony] as consisting of *yihud*, that is to say, they are left by themselves in one house for marital relations and the like." *Beit Yosef* added to this view that there must be something new in this designated house, such as embroidered sheets (this actually constitutes a separate opinion; see below). See also *Mordekhai*, beginning of Ketubot, who maintains, in a view also consistent with this painting, that the *huppah* consists of what the father gives the groom on the morning of the wedding.

Incidentally, we see in the lower right-hand side of this painting (Fig. 4) a small dog, watching from the side. This dog symbolizes the faithfulness between husband and wife, and is a well-known motif in Christian art. See the comprehensive work by E. Panofsky, *Early Netherlandish Painting: Its Origins and Character* (New York, 1971), p. 203. A small dog also makes his appearance in the bottom left of Fig. 11 in Bodenschatz, *Kirchliche Verfassung der heutigen Juden* (our Fig. 25). A dog signifying loyalty also is to be found in a *ketubah* from Pisa (1760), sitting on the lap of a woman (upper right). See S. Sabar, *Ketubbah: Hebrew Marriage Contracts of the Hebrew Union College Skirball Museum and Klau Library* (Philadelphia-New York, 1990), no. 66, p. 134. Sabar identifies this symbol, and draws our attention to *Venus of Urbino* by Titian (1538), in which Venus lies nude on her bed, with a small dog curled up next to her. T. Reff, "The Meaning of Titian's Venus of Urbino," *Pantheon* 21 (1963), pp. 359–66, contends that this dog "in such scenes is a symbol of faithfulness and loyalty in marriage." This symbolic canine also appears in Andrea Alciati's famous work, *Emblematum liber* (1531 et al., and in the 1621 Padua edition that Sabar used [p. 812]), where we see a man (on the right side) holding with his right hand the right hand of a woman (to the left), both sitting. A small dog, at the feet of the man, is barking(?). Sabar further refers to C. Ripa, *Iconologia* (Padua, 1611; *Garden Series* 21 [New York, 1976], pp. 17, 164–65), in which a small dog appears as a symbol of love, fraternity, loyalty, and sincerity (Sabar, pp. 136–37). Cf. also Sabar, "The Use and Meaning of Christian Motifs," pp. 55–56, who provides yet another painting that depicts *matrimonium* (marriage), with a short Latin poem. In this picture a man and woman hold each other's right hand ("Ecce puella, viro qua dextra iungitur") and a small dog is at their feet ("Haec fidei est species"). The subtitle reads: "In fidem uxoriam" (p. 56). See also Hall, *The Arnolfini Betrothal*, pp. 114–15, 164 n. 36. For the book by Alciati, see H. Green, *Andrea Alciati and His Books of Emblems: A Biographical and Bibliographical Study* (London, 1872), who offers a list of no less than 179

is established as law by the *Shulhan Arukh*,[19] and therefore, according to this opinion, in the marriage ceremony there is no need for the canopy.

editions of this work and subsequent books (Sabar ad loc., n. 38). For iconology in general, see E.H. Gombrich, "Icones Symbolicae," in *idem, Gombrich on the Renaissance*[3], Vol. 2 (London, 1985), pp. 123–91; for Ripa, ibid., pp. 139–45. See also N. Berger (ed.), *Where Cultures Meet: The Story of the Jews of Czechoslovakia* (Tel Aviv, 1990), p. 85: a picture of a wedding from Bohemia, ca. 1750, with a small dog. Attention should also be paid to the circle on the shoulder in this painting (and in that by Leusden, 1682 [Fig. 11]). This was a badge that European Jews were required to wear on their clothing, in accordance with regulations issued in the thirteenth century (in England: in 1218, Castile: from 1219, Provence: from 1234, and in the Papal States: from 1257). By the fifteenth century these regulations had come into force throughout Europe, albeit without strenuous enforcement by all the local authorities. This distinctive marking was usually round, like a ring, and thus was known as the "rouelle." In most places it was yellow, and was worn on the breast. See Rubens, *A History of Jewish Costume*, pp. 110–18; p. 102, no. 139 (Germany, 1530); no. 140 (Germany, 1588); p. 104, no. 143 (Italy, beginning of the fifteenth century), and more. See also the major article by G. Kisch, "The Yellow Badge in History," *Historia Judaica* 19 (1957), pp. 89–142. This badge disappeared in France after 1789, in Italy after 1798, and in Prussia after 1812 (Kisch, p. 122).

An additional depiction of a wedding without a canopy, on a Torah binder (Germany, 1792), is reproduced in Shachar, *Jewish Tradition in Art: The Feuchtwanger Collection of Judaica*, p. 31. For more pictures of weddings lacking a canopy, see Gutmann, "Jewish Medieval Marriage Customs in Art," pp. 54, 57. See also Gutmann's explanation of the Christian origins of the breaking of the cup, the wedding canopy on poles, and the *talit* held over the bride and groom; cf. Falk, *Jewish Matrimonial Law*, pp. 65, 75, and more. See also Metzger, *Jewish Life in the Middle Ages*, p. 135, no. 187, which clearly depicts the practice of the rabbi holding the hands of the groom and the bride; cf. Leusden, p. 174; Figs. 5, 6; see the above article by Gutmann. This custom appears mainly in Italian paintings from the seventeenth century; and also in Buxtorf, *Synagoga Judaica*, p. 632: "Rabbinus, qui utriusque manus jungit, extremitate cilicii Talles appellant sponsi collo circumjecti, caput sponsae tegit." Interestingly, the paintings and captions from Holland show only a portion of this custom, namely, the shaking of hands.

The holding of hands in the *dextrarum iunctio* ceremony mentioned above was an ancient Roman custom, and we find it in a third-century Roman sarcophagus in San Lorenza fuori le Mura. See U.E. Paoli, *Das Leben im Alten Rom* (Bern, 1948), Table LV, right-hand illustration, p. 217, no. 7 (Fig. 36). This motif appears in early Christian art, such as a mosaic in the Santa Maria Maggiore church in Rome. See Feuchtwanger, "The Coronation of the Virgin and of the Bride," p. 217, no. 7; and even earlier: a bowl from Cyprus (ca. 610–30) with an engraved depiction of the wedding of King David and Michal. This bowl has been the subject of extensive

We have already mentioned the veil, with which we are familiar from modern-day weddings, but what of the sheet in which the groom is enwrapped in the two central figures in Fig. 7 (engraving from Germany,

discussion; see S.H. Wander, "The Cyprus Plates: The Story of David and Goliath," *Metropolitan Museum Journal* 8 (1973), p. 90; cf. p. 102, no. 18: this motif on a medallion on a wedding girdle. This motif continued to appear in Italy; see M. Weiss, *Painting in Florence and Siena after the Black Death: The Arts, Religion, and Society in the Mid-Fourteenth Century* (New York, 1964), p. 109, nos. 101–102, 105–106 (and it also was present in fifteenth-century Germany; see Feuchtwanger, p. 215, no. 4, by the painter known as Anonymous Constance). For this motif, see E. Panofsky, "Jan Van Eyck's Arnolfini Portrait Re-examined," *Burlington Magazine* 44 (1934), pp. 117–27; and some objections to Panofsky: P. H. Schabacher, "*De Matrimonio ad Morganaticam Contracto*: Jan Van Eyck's 'Arnolfini' Portrait Reconsidered," *Art Quarterly* 35 (1972), pp. 375–98; and a justification of Panofsky, by L. Freeman Sandler, "The Handclasp in the *Arnolfini Wedding*: A Manuscript Precedent," *Art Bulletin* 66 (1984), pp. 491–588; p. 490, no. 3, shows a priest holding the hands of the couple (in a fourteenth-century painting, in accordance with canon law). See Falk, *Jewish Matrimonial Law*, pp. 65, 75. Incidentally, this is an example of a custom that, to the present, is unknown in the literature, and is known mainly from artistic sources; see, above, our introductory remarks to this chapter. Cf. also Judah Hadassi, *Eshkol ha-Kofer* (Goslow [Eupatoria], 1836), fol. 146a. See also Metzger, *Jewish Life in the Middle Ages*, p. 224, nos. 335–336, the pictures of a cloth wedding canopy over the heads of the groom and bride (see below, nn. 24, 28).

19 *Shulhan Arukh, Even ha-Ezer* 55:1; the reference in *Rema, Even ha-Ezer* 61:1, is to 54:1, the intent being to 55:1. This disparity is due to the fact that in the Cracow 1578 edition (the first edition of the *Shulhan Arukh* with the glosses of R. Moses Isserles) para. 60 is our para. 61, and para. 54 = our para. 55. This is because para. 52 in the Cracow edition has four subsections, and para. 53, a single subsection, while in our editions para. 52 contains a single subsection, and para. 53, three subsections; the end of para. 52 (Cracow) = the end of para. 53 (our editions). The printers of the editions that succeeded the Cracow edition apparently forgot to correct the internal reference in Isserles so that it would correspond to the new numeration. The numeration in the Cracow and succeeding editions is uniform beginning with para. 67, because the former, for some reason, skipped para. 66 in its count (similar to the omission of the number for para. 169 of *Yoreh Deah* in the early editions). This was noted by R. Margaliot, "The First Printed Editions of the *Shulhan Arukh*," in *Rabbi Yosef Caro: Studies and Researches in the Teachings of Maran, the Author of the Shulhan Arukh*, ed. Y. Raphael (Jerusalem, 1969), pp. 94–95 (Hebrew). See *Tur he-Hadash, Even ha-Ezer*, Vol. 1 (Jerusalem, 1993), p. 436, glosses and notes on para. 52:1.

1705)?[20] In some traditions, this sheet is used for the *huppah*, when the groom spreads it over the bride, in an action that is reminiscent of Ruth's words when she asked Boaz to marry her: "Spread your robe over your handmaid,"[21] and as is portrayed in Fig. 8.[22] In this painting the bride does not wear a veil, since the cloth canopy spread over her effects the marriage; while in Fig. 9, by Bernard Picart (Amsterdam, 1721),[23] we find both the spreading of a sheet and a veil, a combination that we shall presently discuss.[24]

20 Reproduced in Hakohen, *Hayyei Adam: Kelulot*, p. 73.

21 Ruth 3:9.

22 Title page (bottom) of the Latin translation of the Mishnah by Guilielmus Surenhusius, published by Gerardus & Jacobus Borstius (Amsterdam, 1700), Vol. 3, *Nashim*.

23 See J.F. Bernard, *Cérémonies et coutumes religieuses de tous les peuples du monde* (Amsterdam, 1721); this work was translated into English, and the illustrations were reproduced in other books, such as: A. Banier and J.B. le Mascrier, *Histoire générale des cérémonies, moeurs, et coutumes religieuses de tous les peuples du monde, representées in 243 figures dessinées de la main de ..., Bernard Picard(!)*, Paris (1741).

24 See *Ha-Ittur*, "*Birkat ha-Hatanim* (The Wedding Blessing Ceremony)," section 2; *Orhot Hayyim, Hil. Kiddushin (Laws of Betrothal)*, cited in *Rema, Even ha-Ezer* 52:1; *Tashbetz (Katan)*, para. 461; Meiri, Ketubot 7b. And likewise, R. Isaiah the Younger, *Piskei Hariaz*, ed. A. Liss (Jerusalem, 1973), Ketubot 1:11; Abudarham, *Seder Birkat Erusin (Order of the Betrothal Blessing Ceremony)*; Maharil, *Hil. Nisu'in (Laws of Marriage)*; *Ha-Manhig*, para. 109; R. Eliezer of Bonn, in Freimann, *Seder Kiddushin*, p. 56; a pupil of *Maharsha*, p. 66; R. Moses of Marseilles, p. 73; Schammes, *Wormser Minhagbuch*, Vol. 2, p. 33, and additional sources in n. 72. There were several views regarding this procedure of spreading. Some would unfurl a portion of the groom's clothing; e.g.: "According to one opinion, a strip of the groom's *mitron* is the *huppah*" (*Maharam Mintz*); others spread out a *talit*; and yet others used a plain piece of cloth. For this use of a *talit*, see Rabbi Abraham Halfon, *Hayyei Avraham* (Leghorn, 1861), fol. 51b, para. 347: "The reason why the groom wears a *talit* during the *huppah* was written by *Roke'ah* [R. Eliezer ben Judah of Worms], following what is said: 'You shall make tassels [on the four corners of the garment with which you cover yourself]' [Deut. 22:12], and in close proximity, 'A man marries a woman' [v. 13]." See *Minhagei Yisrael*, Vol. 2, pp. 304–305. Since the groom was already wearing his *talit*, it was then used for spreading the *huppah*. See also Falk, *Jewish Matrimonial Law*, p. 65; see also Schammes, p. 33 n. 72. This procedure was rejected by *Beit Yosef, Even ha-Ezer*, para. 61, who writes: "If one says that the *huppah* consists of a cloth that covers their heads, this view is incorrect." See M.A. Pinari, *Beit Hatanim* (Jerusalem, 1982), p. 31, and n. 1. See also *Knesset ha-Gedolah*, para. 61, glosses

Interestingly, the *poskim* tend to deliver rulings that comply with all the

on *Beit Yosef*, 1; *Beit Oved* prayerbook (first edition: Leghorn, 1843), p. 198, writes that the bride is covered by the *talit* only during the marriage blessing (within the wedding ceremony), which might possibly enable us to understand an engraving in which, at the time the ring that effects betrothal is given, the heads of the bride and the groom are covered by different cloths. It would seem that only after the betrothal portion of the ceremony were the cloths unfurled as the *huppah*, which followed the betrothal. See the engraving by Jan Luyken in Leone Modena, *Kerk-zeeden en de gewoonten: die huiden ingebruik zyn onder de jooden* (trans. A. Godart, Amsterdam, 1683), in S. Sabar, *Mazal Tov: Illuminated Jewish Marriage Contracts from the Israel Museum Collection* (Jerusalem, 1993), p. 112. But see R. Abdullah Somekh, *Zivhei Tzedek* (Baghdad, 1904), end of Vol. 2, who implies that the cloth is unfurled during the giving of the instrument of betrothal. See also R. Hayyim Vital, *Even ha-Shoham: Shulhan he-Arukh mi-Kitvei ha-Ari, Zal* (Jerusalem, 1989), *Even ha-Ezer*, pp. 103–104, who cites *Zohar ha-Rakiya, Mishpatim*, fol. 97, gloss, who wrote: "It is our practice for the groom and the bride to enwrap themselves at the time of the betrothal." Vital writes ad loc.: "Implicit from his language, that this is before the betrothal." Vital further explains that the spreading of the cloth has only an esoteric reason, and not one that can be derived by rational thought; see also *Yahadut Lub*, p. 393; R. Jousep Juspa Kaschmann, *Noheg ka-Tzon Yosef* (Frankfurt a.M., 1718 [Tel Aviv, 1969]), in the name of *Bahag*, para. 22; R. Raphael Meldola, *Huppat Hatanim* (Leghorn, 1797), "*Dinei Birkat Erusin* (Laws of the Betrothal Blessing Ceremony)"; R. Elijah ben Joseph Gaj, *Zeh ha-Shulhan* (Algier, 1889), Vol. 3, "*Minhagei Algeria* (Algerian Customs)," para. 104; R. Hayyim Palache, *Ginzei Hayyim* (Izmir, 1871), 8:17, writes that this is the Izmir custom; R. Rahamim Isaac Palache, *Yafeh la-Lev* (Izmir, 1846), Vol. 4, 55:2; R. Joseph Hayyim ben Elijah Al-Hakam, *Ben Ish Hai* (first edition: Jerusalem, 1892), Vol. 1, *Shoftim*, para. 12, wrote that the Sephardic Jews in Jerusalem followed this procedure. Rabbi Sinai Shiffer, *Sitri u-Magini* (Tirnoi, 1932–33), para. 43 wrote that this was the practice in central Europe. R. David Pipano, *Avnei ha-Efod* (Sofia, 1913–14), *Even ha-Ezer* 45:1 states that this was the procedure followed in Arta (Greece) and Constantinople. *She'eilot u-Teshuvot Nahalat Shivah* 12:40 attests that the *huppah* in Poland consisted of a cloth on poles, while in central Europe a *talit* was spread forth. See also above, the end of n. 18, and below, n. 28, with references to additional such depictions. In Fig. 9 the rabbi is holding a branch in his left hand; the explanation for this could possibly be found in PT Sotah, the end of chap. 11, that people would dance before the bride with myrtle twigs. See also BT Ketubot 17a; PT Avodah Zarah 3:3; Peah 1:16b; Gen. Rabbah 59:4; BT Shabbat 110a; Berakhot 56b; Sotah 49b; for myrtles also being held under the canopy, see Eruvin 40a and Rashi. This branch, however, might be from an olive tree, which symbolized fertility and blessing for the Romans (H. Weiss, *Kostumkunde: Geschichte der Tracht und des Gerathes im Mittelalter von 4ten bis zum 14ten Jahrhundert* [Stuttgart, 1964], Vol.

different opinions.[25] In Fig. 10 (A. Calmet, Leiden, 1725),[26] we see a practice

1, p. 1109 n. 4; *He-Atid* 1923, p. 100). The Jewish sources mention that it was placed on the head, as a garland (PT Sotah, end of chap. 11). Alternatively, the branch might have been used for the blessing over spices that was recited under the *huppah*, as is stated in *Halakhot Pesukot, o Hilkhot Re'u*, ed. A.L. Schlossberg and S.Z.H. Halberstam (Versailles, 1886), p. 84: "What is the 'blessing of the grooms' [that is mentioned in Ketubot 8b]? One first recites '[...] who has created the fruit of the vine and spice trees.'" The last proposal seems most plausible.

25 A Jewish wedding in Italy (copper etching by Augustin Calmet), taken from the Leiden 1725 edition of *Byvogzel tot het Algemeen Groot Historisch Oordeelkundig, Chronologisch, Geographisch, en Letterlyk Naam-en Woord-Boek van den Ganschen H. Bybel...*, opposite s.v. "Bruitloft," p. 54. See Sabar, "The Use and Meaning of Christian Motifs in Illustrations of Jewish Marriage Contracts in Italy," p. 62 n. 59, who writes that according to A. Rubens, *A Jewish Iconography* (London, 1954), p. 5, the copper etchings in Calmet's book "seem to have been designed and engraved in Amsterdam." Sabar adds that, according to Edward Maeder, Curator of Textiles at the Los Angeles County Museum of Art and an expert on eighteenth-century European garb, the items of clothing in this print "look late 17th — early 18th century Italian and definitely are not Dutch."

In this engraving we see how the *ketubah* is displayed during the wedding. This motif (or possibly the reading of the *ketubah*) also appears in Bodenschatz, *Kirchliche Verfassung der heutigen Juden* (see below, n. 32). See a picture reproduced in Rubens, op. cit., p. 9, no. 1091, from Amsterdam, 1683. See S. Sabar, "The Beginnings of *Kettubah* Decoration in Italy: Venice in the Late Sixteenth to the Early Seventeenth Centuries," *Jewish Art* 12–13 (1986/87), p. 99. The *ketubah* was publicly read during the wedding ceremony in order to separate the two elements of the wedding ceremony: *erusin* (betrothal) and *nisu'in* (marriage); this is first mentioned in the twelfth century, in a responsum by R. Meshullam, *Sefer ha-Yashar* of Rabbeinu Tam (ed. S.F. Rosenthal [Berlin, 1898], p. 92). See Freimann, *Seder Kiddushin ve-Nissu'in Aharei Hatimat ha-Talmud*, p. 41, with a reference (n. 2) to the booklet *Teshuvah ba-Inyan Kri'at ha-Ketubah bein Birkat Erusin la-Birkat Nisu'in* (*A Responsum Regarding the Reading of the* Ketubah *between the Betrothal Blessing and the Wedding Blessing*) by R. Nehemiah of Bialystok (Vienna, 1859). This became the universal Jewish practice (see Sabar, pp. 99–100). See also Falk, *Jewish Matrimonial Law*, pp. 83–85. It should be added at this point that the wedding canopy in this engraving has two poles, in contrast to the more common four. Such a *huppah* supported by only two poles may also appear in a wimpel from Germany (1751) reproduced in *In the Spirit of Tradition: B'nei B'rith Klutznick Museum*, ed. I. Altshuler (Washington, 1988), p. 25, no. 42; cf. p. 72; and possibly also in the German wimpel from 1776 in M. Kaniel, *A Guide to Jewish Art* (New York, 1989), pp. 74–75. According to Pappenheim, *The Jewish Wedding*, pp. 38–39, no. 119, an additional engraving in Buxtorf, *Synagoga Judaica* (ed. Rotterdam, 1681) portrays a round wedding canopy on four poles.

that is common to the present day, which combines the above procedure (a sheet held over the bride and groom), with another, which also is observed at present, and that is mentioned by R. Moses Isserles:[27] "The plain practice now is to conduct the wedding where a simple cloth is spread over poles, the groom and bride are brought under it before the public, and he betroths her there."[28] The *Ahronim* already observed that they combined the different practices.[29]

26 See *Minhagei Yisrael*, Vol. 1, chap. 3; Vol. 2, chap. 2, esp, p. 10.

27 *Shulhan Arukh, Even ha-Ezer* 55:1.

28 R. Benjamin Aaron Slonik, *Mas'at Binyamin* (Cracow, 1632), para. 90, should be quoted at this juncture: "This is somewhat implicit from the statement by my teacher, our master, the rabbi, R. Moses Isserles, of blessed memory, in his gloss, para. 55, who wrote that after the *huppah* they are led to their house, where they eat together in a secluded place. The reason is because the Rabbis, of blessed memory, have doubts concerning our *huppah*, in which a *talit* is spread over four rods, and the groom and bride are married there, and it is said that whoever does so is in error, for this does not constitute *huppah*, and this *huppah* does not effect acquisition, [neither] to be as his wife, nor for anything in the world." See *Beit Yosef, Even ha-Ezer*, para. 61, in the name of *Ha-Ittur*. See also Rabbi Samuel ben Joseph Joshua, *Nahalat Yosef* (Jerusalem, 1907), p. 27. Y. Avishur writes in *The Jewish Wedding in Baghdad and Its Filiations* (Haifa, 1990), p. 110 (Hebrew), that it was customary in Baghdad to have a curtain before the bride (cf. Fig. 2), and in other places a *tzitzit* [i.e. a *talit*] was extended over the heads of the bride and groom (see above, n. 24), which they considered to be a *huppah*. Ninety years ago, Avishur continues, the practice was instituted of holding a canopy on poles, while some people reverted to the earlier custom. See above, the end of n. 18. For a similar Christian custom, which possibly influenced the Jewish practice, see Westermarck, *The History of Human Marriage*, Vol. 2, pp. 529–30: a "himmel" (i.e. "sky") would be held (cf. Bodenschatz, *Kirchliche Verfassung der heutigen Juden*, cited above, n. 14; below, n. 51) above the bride, in the open. See Falk, *Jewish Matrimonial Law*, p. 76.

29 As R. Joel Sirkes (*Bah*) writes, on *Shulhan Arukh, Even ha-Ezer* 61:1, s.v. "*Ha-Ish*"; and also, *She'eilot u-Teshuvot Nahalat Shivah* 18:8. See also Fig. 9: a different combination of practices, namely, the cloth canopy and the veil. Regarding the placing of a cloth on poles, as R. Moses Isserles describes, see also *Imrei David*, para. 29, that the poles must stand on the earth, and not be held in the air, for otherwise, this would be a movable (literally, thrown) tent, that is not considered to be a tent. A.I. Sperling, *Sefer Ta'amei ha-Minhagim u-Mekorei ha-Dinim* (*The Book of the Reasons for Customs and the Sources of Laws*) (Jerusalem, 1982), para. 963, writes, in the name of Rabbi Meir Ibn Gabbai, *Tola'at Yaakov* (Constantinople, 1560), that it must be constructed of costly fabrics. And, indeed, an illumination of a *huppah* on a *ketubah* shows an extremely luxurious *huppah*, within which are

(The wedding portrayed in Fig. 11, by J. Leusden,[30] follows the view of R. Isserles, which resembles the generally-accepted current practice.)

This same compound practice is portrayed in a painting by Moritz Oppenheim (*Die Trauung* [*The Wedding*], Fig. 14) from 1882. Oppenheim also drew an additional painting (by the same name) of a wedding (Fig. 13), only with a cloth veil, and not a canopy supported by four poles, from which we learn that the painter witnessed both procedures.[31] The former[32]

fine and magnificent lights (see Sabar, *Mazal Tov*, p. 190). See also Werdiger, *Edut le-Yisrael*, pp. 25–26 (see also below, n. 53).

30 In *Philologus Hebraeo-Mixtus*[2] (Utrecht, 1682), opposite p. 172.

31 Actually, Fig. 13, which was executed in color, is earlier, and was painted in 1861. It is held by the Israel Museum (M1149–3.56). Fig. 12 is Oppenheim's last painting, and was completed shortly before his death in 1882. See E. Cohen, "Moritz Oppenheim, 'The First Jewish Painter,'" *Israel Museum News* 1978, p. 92. For a more extensive general treatment of Oppenheim, see Cohen's article, "Moritz Daniel Oppenheim," *Bulletin of the Leo Baeck Institute* 53/54 (1977–78), pp. 42–74; the catalogue of the 1983 exhibition held in the Israel Museum: *Moritz Oppenheim, the First Jewish Painter*, ed. E. Cohen (Jerusalem, 1983) (Hebrew and English), esp. the enlightening article by I. Schorsch, "Art as Social History: Oppenheim and the German Jewish Vision of Emancipation," pp. 46, 51 (English section), on *The Wedding* and the ideological and social background of the painting.

32 This painting was reproduced on a nineteenth-century marriage plate from Germany; see R.D. Barnett, *Catalogue of the Permanent and Loan Collections of the Jewish Museum, London* (Greenwich, CT, 1974), no. 465; see also no. 21b (see Fig. 35). The painting was based on the work by Picart. This apparently belonged to a series of platters for the Jewish festivals with reproductions of works by various artists. Oppenheim's painting possibly reflects the custom of the "bridal girdle" under the wedding canopy (see Fig. 12). This practice apparently originated in the Roman world, as the girding of the cingulum. See Marquardt, *Das Privatleben der Romer*, Vol. 1, p. 45. For the Byzantine period, see E.H. Kanterowicz, *On the Golden Marriage Belt and the Marriage Rings of the Dumbarton Oaks Collection*, *Dumbarton Oaks Papers* 14 (1960), pp. 3–16; Feuchtwanger, "The Coronation of the Virgin and of the Bride," p. 217 n. 26. See also Rabbi Isaac Lampronti, *Pahad Yitzhak*, Vol. 3 (Venice, 1798), "*Taba'at Sha'ulah* [A Borrowed Ring]," para. 72, fol. 67a, for someone who effected betrothal with a golden belt; special note should be taken of Rabbi Shalom Moses ben Hayyim Gaguine, *Yismah Lev* (Jerusalem, 1878–88), para. 14, fol. 34d, for someone who betrothed with a *shora*, which is a sort of decorative belt embroidered with gold-coated silver threads; Rabbi Hayyim Nissim Raphael Mutsiri, *Be'er Mayim Hayyim* (Salonika, 1794), end of para. 13, discusses the same issue (also cited in *Otzar ha-Poskim*, on *Even ha-Ezer* 31:2, Vol. 11, fol. 148a, subsection 10). For the continuation of this practice in the medieval

(Fig. 14) has a number of noteworthy elements: first, it clearly shows the bride extending her index finger to the groom, as in most of the illustrations

period, see Rubens, *A History of Jewish Costume*, p. 124; for an example from France in 1454, see the article by R. Girard in *Speculum* 28 (1953), p. 490: a wedding belt of gold cloth; also mentioned by Bodenschatz, *Kirchliche Verfassung der heutigen Juden*, Vol. 4, p. 122, who cites Buxtorf, *Synagoga Judaica*, p. 627. Cf. also above, chap. 18, "Some Wedding Preparations," pp. 166–170. For this belt, see also Schammes, *Wormser Minhagbuch*, Vol. 2, p. 12 n. 13; p. 19; *Noheg be-Hokhmah*, p. 72; Ovadia, *The Community of Sefrou*, Vol. 4, p. 77; Freimann, *Seder Kiddushin ve-Nissu'in*, p. 93, and more.

The Central European custom is as drawn by Oppenheim: the rabbi conducting the ceremony reads the *ketubah* (see above, n. 25). See a responsum from 1499: *She'eilot u-Teshuvot Maharam Mintz*, ed. Domb, Vol. 2, para. 109, p. 531; R. Benjamin Wolf Hamburg, *Sha'ar ha-Zekenim* (Sulzbach, 1830), Vol. 2, fol. 148b; Rabbi S[alomon] Carlebach, *Pele Yoets: Ratgeber fur das judische Haus: ein Fuhrer fur Verlobung, Hochzeit und Eheleben* (Berlin, 1918), p. 74; Rabbi Menahem Gottlieb, *Darkei Noam* (Hanover, 1896–98), chap. 304, *Dibbur* 10; M.J. Perath, "Jewish Institutions, Customs and Lore in Amsterdam," in *Studies on the History of Dutch Jewry*, ed. J. Michman, Vol. 1, p. 313 ("A Jewish Wedding in Amsterdam, Thirty Years Ago") (Hebrew); also mentioned by Schammes, *Wormser Minhagbuch*, Vol. 2, p. 32 n. 96. See also Werdiger, *Edut le-Yisrael*, p. 15; Falk, *Jewish Matrimonial Law*, pp. 36, 47–48, 65–66. For weddings conducted in the synagogue courtyard, see Schammes, Vol. 2, p. 32 n. 66; *Edut le-Yisrael*, pp. 26–28. This venue for the ceremony is also evident in many illustrations. Cf. Falk, p. 76, for a Christian wedding next to the church entrance. A violinist and a *badhan* (for this term, see below, chap. 22) stand behind the wedding canopy, for it is meritorious to bring joy to the groom and bride, as is taught in BT Berakhot 6b; *Shulhan Arukh, Even ha-Ezer* 65:1; *Tur, Even ha-Ezer* 65. This requirement is a positive rabbinic enactment, as is explained by Maimonides, *Mishneh Torah, Hil. Avel* (*Laws of Mourning*) 14:1. See also Rabbi Abraham David Wahrman, *Ezer mi-Kodesh* (Bilgoraj, 1933), para. 65; Rabbi Moshe Neusbaum, *Divrei Torah* (Warsaw, 1849), para. 8, attests that Rabbi Issachar Baer Bloch (the author of *Benei Yissakhar*), would customarily give the groom a *rvi'it* (a measure of volume, i.e. a cup) of wine, to cause him to rejoice. See also R. Mordecai Leib Winkler, *Levushei Mordekhai*, second edn. (Budapest, 1917–24), para. 56. For a general discussion, see Adler, *Nisu'in ke-Hilkhatam*, Vol. 2, pp. 397–98. See also the illustrations of a *badhan* amusing the bride, Hakohen, *Hayyei Adam: Kelulot*, pp. 24, 90; and Klein, *Wedding Traditions of the Various Jewish Communities*, p. 48. The Romans were already known to engage such jesters; see G. Williams, "Some Aspects of Roman Marriage Ceremonies and Ideals," *Journal of Roman Studies* 48 (1958), p. 16. See also E. Tietze-Conrat, *Dwarfs and Jesters in Art*, trans. E. Osborn (London, 1957). For *badhanim* and *kleizmerim*, see I. Ganuz, "The Wedding in the *Shtetl* — Life and Customs That Are No More: Their Reflection

in which this element could be identified. This practice is also specified in *Sefer Asufot*:[33] "and the ring must be placed on the finger of her right hand next to the thumb." In Fig. 15, however, we see that the bride wears the ring on her middle finger, and not as prescribed above. This detail, as well, is the subject of a disagreement, since *Keter Shem* Tov (p. 612) states, in the name of R. Moses Zacuto,[34] that the Land of Israel custom called for the groom to place the ring of betrothal on the middle finger. He further wrote that, in his time, it was accepted in the Land of Israel, as well, to place the ring on the index finger, in an apparent change from the earlier practice.[35] *Nahalat*

in the Idyll *Ha-Hatunah shel Elka* by Saul Tchernichowsky," *Mahut* 17 (1996), pp. 78–82, 92 (Hebrew), with references to J. Stutschewsky, '*Klezmorim' (Jewish Folk Musicians): History, Folklore, Compositions* (Jerusalem, 1959) (Hebrew) and I. Rivkind, *Jewish Folk Music: A Study in Cultural History* (New York, 1960) (Hebrew).

It is also noteworthy that the rabbi in Oppenheim's paintings is enwrapped in a *talit*, as was the practice of R. Jacob ben Moses Moellin (*Maharil*, p. 465); see Schammes, *Wormser Minhagbuch*, Vol. 2, pp. 34–35: the editor (p. 35 n. 76) surmises that the rabbi in Oppenheim's painting was "probably Rabbi Zevi Hirsch [ben Phinehas ha-Levi] Horowitz, the author of *Mahaneh Levi*" (Offenbach, 1801; Lvov, 1861). For a general discussion of the place of the rabbi in the wedding ceremony, and in relation to the Christian rite, see Freimann, *Seder Kiddushin ve-Nissu'in*, p. 94; E. Cohen and E. Horowitz, "In Search of the Sacred: Jews, Christians, and Rituals of Marriage in the Later Middle Ages," *Journal of Medieval and Renaissance Studies* 20 (1990), pp. 229–36.

33 *Sefer Asufot* (manuscript); cited in Stern, *The Order of Betrothal and Marriage according to Our Early Masters*, p. 56; also in *Rokeah*, para. 351; *Rif*, and *Maharam Mintz* (cited in *Be'er Hetev* on *Shulhan Arukh, Even ha-Ezer* 27:1). See also *Knesset ha-Gedolah*, para. 27, *Hagahot* 2; Friedman, *Likkutei Maharih*, "*Seder Nisu'in* (Marriage)," Vol. 3, fol. 125a.

34 In his glosses to *Tikkunei Zohar, Tikkun* 10, n. 1.

35 See *Be'er Hetev* on *Shulhan Arukh, Even ha-Ezer* 27:1, in the name of *Maharam Mintz*, that the ring is to be placed on the index finger, because that is where people usually wear rings. Even though, in contemporary (i.e. in his time) practice, people normally wear rings on the little finger, the ring of betrothal is still placed on the index finger, because the early wedding practice remains in force. See *Rokeah*, para. 351; *Maharil, Hil. Nisu'in. Nahalat Shivah*, para. 2, *Mehudashim* (Addenda), section 2, writes that the ring is to be placed on the index finger, because it is more visible there than on any other finger. *Likkutei Maharih*, "*Seder Nisu'in*," brings an allusion to this from the *Zohar*. See *Huppat Hatanim*, "The Laws of the Wedding Ceremony"; *Ben Ish Hai, Shoftim*, para. 9; Rabbi Ben-Zion Mordecai Hazan, *Rav Pealim* (Jerusalem, 1913), Vol. 2, "*Besod Yesharim*," para. 1, writes that there is an

Shivah, in the name of R. Moses Mintz, asserts that "the groom must effect betrothal with his right hand, and also with the right hand of the bride; he is to place the ring on the finger next to the thumb, and not on the thumb [itself]." By specifying "and not on the thumb" he thereby attacked the seemingly prevalent custom of his time to indeed use the thumb for this purpose, as is confirmed by Fig. 16, which clearly shows the ring on the bride's thumb.[36]

A second question that arises is that of the positioning of the bride and groom. In many depictions the bride stands to the right of the groom, in accordance with the view of the *poskim*. Oppenheim (Figs. 13, 14), however, has the bride standing to the left of the groom (see also Figs. 1, 2, 5, 6, 10, 25[37]). A few religious authorities wrote that this (Kabbalistic) practice should not be abrogated where it was customarily observed.[38]

esoteric reason to place the ring on the middle finger, but since *Knesset ha-Gedolah* attested to the practice of using the index finger, this custom should be followed. See R. Hayyim Palache (Palaggi), *Hayyim ve-Shalom* (Izmir, 1857), Vol. 1, para. 19. See also *Otzar ha-Poskim*, Vol. 10, p. 40. Schammes, *Wormser Minhagbuch*, Vol. 2, p. 16, specifies that "the groom shall place the ring on the finger next to the bride's thumb, on her right hand." See also *Pahad Yitzhak*, "Betrothal on the Fourth Finger," p. 71; Falk, *Jewish Matrimonial Law*, p. 75. See also Hall, *The Arnolfini Betrothal*, pp. 33–35, 127, that the Christians (in Italy) placed the wedding ring on the first (i.e. index) finger. And see Lucas van Leyden's *The Fiancés*, ca. 1519, where the ring is on the index finger (Fig. 37) (Strasburg Fine Arts Museum).

36 A majolica bowl from Gubbio, Italy, ca. 1530 (Florence). See G. Liverani, *Five Centuries of Italian Majolica* (New York, 1960), plate 68; Sabar, "The Use and Meaning of Christian Motifs in Illustrations of Jewish Marriage Contracts in Italy," p. 59. Sabar (p. 58) explains that in sixteenth-century Italy such bowls were ordered "as a commemorative item (of their own wedding)." Sabar maintains that this is a clearly Christian bowl.

37 The last picture appears in Bodenschatz, *Kirchliche Verfassung*.

38 For the sources, see Adler, *Nisu'in ke-Hilkhatam*, Vol. 1, pp. 374–75 and notes; see also *Yafeh la-Lev*, Vol. 4, para. 8; Rabbi Jacob Lauberbaum, *Derekh ha-Hayyim* prayerbook (Berlin, 1860 [Vilna, 1871]), the wedding ceremony; Rabbi Solomon Ganzfried, *Kitzur Shulhan Arukh* 147:2; Rabbi Israel Hayyim Friedman, *Likkutei Maharih* (who described his local [i.e. Hungarian] practice); *Shulhan ha-Ezer*, Vol. 2, fol. 32b; *Otzar ha-Poskim*, Vol. 16, p. 88; see also *Knesset ha-Gedolah*, who writes that this positioning is based on the verse "the consort stands at your right hand" (Ps. 45:10); *Rokeah*, para. 351, and *Knesset ha-Gedolah* write that in Tirya the groom customarily stood to the right of the bride, "and I stopped this practice, and I instituted that the bride stands to the right of the groom." See also Rabbi Aaron

A third issue: our painting shows a lad holding a platter with two small bottles. But no one is holding the cups, so how shall the wine be imbibed? directly from the bottle? In Fig. 1,[39] we do see a child with two glasses.[40] This

Alfandari, *Yad Aharon* (Izmir, 1756), *Even ha-Ezer* 71:4; *Edut le-Yisrael*, p. 63, cites *Zohar, Pinhas* 230b: "The groom to the right, and the bride to the left"; see *Sedeh Hemed*, "Bride and Groom," para. 30: "It is obvious that if *Knesset ha-Gedolah* had seen the passage by R. Isaac Luria, he would have upheld the practice of Tirya, and would not have negated it." See also *Hesed le-Avraham, Ma'ayan* 4, *Ein Yaakov, Nahar* 58; see also Buxtorf, *Synagoga Judaica*, p. 631: "Sponsa stat a latere sponsi dextero."

39 A *ketubah* from Rotterdam, Holland (1648), in the holdings of the Israel Museum. A picture of it appears in *Encyclopaedia Judaica* (Jerusalem, 1971), Vol. 10, opposite col. 939.

40 See Silvain, *Images et traditions Juives*, p. 406: a postcard, probably from the beginning of the twentieth century, with a picture of a European wedding with a wedding canopy in a synagogue(?), with a *talit* over the heads of the bride and groom, and a scarf over the head of the bride (although her face is uncovered); the rabbi holds in his hand a cup over which he recites a blessing; a second cup rests on the table that is between the couple, under the wedding canopy. I have yet to find the original of this painting. See also the painting *The Wedding* (1861) in the holdings of the Israel Museum (Sabar, *Mazal Tov*, p. 86), in which the lad holds only a single jar of wine. A picture in Gutmann, *Beauty in Holiness*, p. 329, plainly presents only a single glass. The silence of the sources is not to be taken as unequivocal proof of the use of only a single vessel, since in the book *Sefer Tefilot u-Minhagim* from Germany (1590), the groom has only one cup, but the accompanying text notes that an additional bottle is subsequently brought. See also *She'eilot u-Teshuvot Rabbenu Moshe Mintz*, para. 109.

One of the two cups is for the wedding blessing; see *Shulhan Arukh, Even ha-Ezer* 34; Schammes, *Wormser Minhagbuch*, Vol. 2, p. 32, and the other, for the blessing "... who creates the fruit of the vine," that precedes the Seven Blessings (Schammes, Vol. 2, p. 39); *Shulhan Arukh, Even ha-Ezer* 62:9; see also *Sefer Maharil*, ed. Spitzer, p. 466; the French *Mahzor Vitri*, p. 589. All this follows *Tosafot*, BT Pesahim 102b, s.v. *"She-Ein Omrim,"* and *Mordekhai*, Ketubot, beginning of chap. 3. See also above, the end of n. 14.

On the question of why two cups are required, why a single one is not sufficient, and when this custom came into being, see the detailed discussion in Werdiger, *Edut le-Yisrael*, pp. 28–38. R. Moses Mintz writes in his responsa, para. 109: "In our lands only a single cup is used, and it is first filled for the betrothal blessing; after they have drunk from it, it is filled a second time for the marriage blessing." This is also implicit in *Mahzor Vitri*, para. 475, p. 592: "The remainder is to be poured out, and the cup is to be refilled, so that the marriage blessing would not be recited on the same cup, for commandments are not fulfilled bound together." If another, is also mentioned by Schammes:[41] "And two *tzintzenot* filled with wine."

second cup were in use, then there seemingly would be no need to spill out the wine from the betrothal blessing. R. Moses Isserles on *Shulhan Arukh, Even ha-Ezer* 65:3, however, teaches of the use of two cups. The practice of using two cups is in accordance with Rabbenu Tam in *Sefer ha-Yashar*, ed. Rosenthal, Responsa, 45:5, p. 82: "Another one. There are some who have become accustomed to perform the betrothal and marriage blessings over a single cup. This is puzzling, since the marriage blessing has been established [to be recited] in the wedding hall, and the betrothal blessing in the engagement chamber. Since they were established for two different places, they cannot be included together. We [therefore] are forced to say, that if they were enacted [to be recited] over a cup, then this refers to two cups. But if they were not enacted [to be recited] over a cup, the one who comes to recite them over two cups is to do so corresponding to the establishment of the two places, and not to conduct the two sanctities [i.e. blessings] over a single cup."

This issue is discussed in greater detail in the query addressed by R. Meshullam to Rabbenu Tam, and in the latter's response to R. Meshullam (*Sefer ha-Yashar* 46:7, pp. 92–93; 48:8, p. 100). A portion of this exchange follows:

(from the query:) "As regards the betrothal and marriage blessing [recited] over a single cup, I stated before Rabbenu Elijah that the practice in our land [Provence] is to use only a single cup, and I discussed this before them and before all the sages of Paris. [...] Logically, the essential obligation requires performing them with a single cup, since this is all a single matter. If you insist upon the custom of two cups, do as you wish. Certainly, if you were to follow the practice of Rabbenu Solomon [= Rashi], to stop and move away, and to engage in another matter and read the *ketubah*, and afterwards [perform] the marriage blessing, this is the best [practice], but [to recite them] consequently, to recite the blessing and drink, and then bless, is completely incorrect. [...]"

(from the responsum by Rabbenu Tam:) "As regards what you wrote, that you discussed before the great ones of Paris concerning the betrothal and marriage blessing, and they accepted your view: they did not act correctly, not even according to your view. For you admit that the practice of our master Solomon, who enacted somewhat of an intermission, is the best [practice]. They, his disciples, should certainly act in accordance with him, and set aside your [view]." This responsum therefore teaches of a disagreement between the Provençal and French authorities: the former were accustomed to performing the entire wedding ceremony over a single cup, while the French rabbis required two. This difference is also indicated by R. Menahem Meiri, *Magen Avot*, ed. Y. Cohen (Jerusalem, 1989), para. 8, pp. 65–70: "We [in Provence] are always accustomed to perform the betrothal and wedding together, to recite the betrothal and wedding blessing[s] over a single cup. They, however, protest, and require that the betrothal blessing be recited over one cup, and the wedding blessing over a second one" (p. 66). See his lengthy dispute with the "great ones of France" (p. 68; the intent is to Rabbenu Tam, n. 30) and also

The editor notes[42] that the *tzintzenet* is a glass cup.[43] If so, then why are there only two bottles in this illustration?

The answer to this is provided by R. Jacob ben Moses Moellin:[44]

> For a virgin, a narrow-mouthed jar is used [for drinking the wine], to [symbolically] say that she is still a virgin.[45]

This, then, is the practice that was witnessed by the artist, that of using "a narrow-mouthed jar." The Talmud already mentions special practices that were observed during the wedding of a virgin, so that all would know that the bride was unsullied. A cup of wine from *terumah* would be passed before a virgin bride, and R. Adda ben Ahavah remarked: "A closed [cask] is passed before her if she is a virgin, and an open one if she had already engaged in intercourse."[46] All this was for the benefit of the witnesses to the ceremony, so that they would know and recall that this was the wedding of an untainted woman. The practice involving the narrow-mouthed jar was therefore a means employed, in accordance with the procedure set forth in the Talmud, to show those in attendance that this was the wedding of a virgin bride.[47]

with the Spanish authorities (see the illuminating notes by the editor, p. 66 n. 2; p. 68 n. 29, and more, with a lengthy list of relevant sources). As we have seen, this controversy gave birth to two customs regarding the cup in the wedding ceremony. See Adler, *Nisu'in ke-Hilkhatam*, Vol. 1, pp. 32–33, and more.

41 *Wormser Minhagbuch*, Vol. 1, p. 34.

42 Ibid., n. 77.

43 See *Ravyah*, ed. Aptowitzer, para. 92 and n. 10.

44 *Maharil, Hil. Nisu'in*, ed. Spitzer, p. 466.

45 See Buxtorf, *Synagoga Judaica*, p. 633: "Si sponsa virgo fuerit, angustum (vitreum bombylium vel baucalium) cyathum vulgo capiunt."

46 BT Ketubot 16b.

47 As was concluded by Hakohen, *Hayyei Adam: Kelulot*, p. 152. See Kanof, *Jewish Ceremonial Art and Religious Observance*, p. 198: "Among objects of interest created for the wedding ceremony is a barrel-shaped double-cup, from which two ceremonial sips of wine are drunk." See *Encyclopaedia Judaica*, Vol. 11, opposite col. 1068: such a double cup from Germany (eighteenth century). This double cup is a development of the two cups mentioned above (n. 40). I initially thought that the shape of the cask is related to the above passage in Ketubot 16b (see Fig. 18), but additional study disproves such a conjecture, since we know of several cups identical in shape to these, bearing the inscriptions "the cup of *metzizah* [suction]" or "the cup of blessing," or with the respective initials: .ב.ש.כ ,.מ.ש.כ. These, obviously, are circumcision cups. See Shachar, *Jewish Tradition in Art: The Feuchtwanger*

Another fascinating detail in this painting is the *"huppah* stone" with a
Star of David carved in it, that is affixed in the wall of the synagogue, and
against which the cup is thrown and broken (Fig. 17[48]). (Current practice
calls for smashing the cup underfoot; see the broken cup in Fig. 11.) There
are different types of *huppah* stones, with a star and various verses (see
the examples in Figs. 20, 21, 22, 23).[49] This sort of architectural feature

> *Collection of Judaica*, p. 23, no. 11; Barnett, *Catalogue of the Permanent and Loan
> Collections of the Jewish Museum*, nos. 488–94, table CX. This apparently was
> a common format; further study is required. Mention should also be made in this
> context of a manuscript illumination in the *Nuremberg Miscellany*, fol. 12v (36v),
> from Germany (1590), reproduced by Feuchtwanger, "The Coronation of the Virgin
> and of the Bride," p. 222, Fig. 14. In this illumination we see a wedding with a
> bride and groom under the wedding canopy, and to their left the rabbi who holds
> a sort of narrow-mouthed bottle of wine (see above, n. 45), that appears to be a
> double flask, with a narrow neck that splits into two mouths (see Fig. 19). This
> vessel most likely consisted of two adjoining bottles with two necks, linked for
> most of their length, that divide into two at their top. A. Feigel, in *Festgabe Prof.
> Georg Lenhart Ano Dom und Dioceze* (Mainz, 1939), p. 120, proposed that these
> two vessels are dictated by the halakhic requirement to use two cups (see above, n.
> 28), in accordance with the view of *Rosh* and others. This suggestion was rejected
> by G. Stein, in *Geschichte der Juden in Speyer, Beitrage der Speyer Stadgeschichte*
> 6 (Speyer, 1981), pp. 56–57; on the other hand, it was supported by Mann, in her
> article in *Artibus et Historiae, an Art Anthology ... in Honour of Rachel Wischnitzer*,
> pp. 18–22. The double cup has a long and fascinating history, as can be learned from
> the discussion by Mann. It originated in Christian cups, the earliest of which is that
> of St. Godehard (1038). Such vessels were called *Dopplescheur* or *Dopplekopf*. See
> H. Koppelhausen, "Die Doppelkopf: sein Bedeutung fur das Deutsche Brauchtum
> des 13 bis 17 Jahrhunderts," *Zeitschrift fur Kuntswissenschaft* 14, 1–2 (1960),
> pp. 20–25. Their use spread with the popularity of the imbibing of spirits in the
> Christian world in the thirteenth century, and among the Jews for halakhic needs
> (that also were formulated in that period following the rulings by the *Rosh* and other
> authorities). Such double cups would be given as wedding presents by Christians, in
> an additional linkage with the similar vessel used in the Jewish wedding ceremony.
> See H.M. von Erffa and D.F. Rittmeyer, "Doppelbecher," *Reallexicon zur Deutschen
> Kunstgeschichte* 4 (Stuttgart, 1958), pp. 168–69; P. Pechstein, "The Welcome Cup,"
> *Connoisseur* 199 (1978), p. 181; also mentioned by Mann, p. 24, notes. We learn
> from this of the long history of the use of these double cups, and of their artistic
> form; consequently, the fact that some are cask-shaped should not be directly linked
> to the Talmudic source.

48 In Kirchner, *Judisches Ceremoniel*; see below, n. 53.

49 Reproductions of these *huppah* stones appear in Hakohen, *Hayyei Adam: Kelulot*, on,

is mentioned in the Yiddish *Sefer Minhagim*: "The groom throws the cup against the star that is carved above the synagogue gate." Both collections of Worms customs[50] state that the cup is dashed against a stone in the shape of a lion's head,[51] while *Mahzor Vitri, Maharil,* and R. Moses Mintz state only that the cup is thrown against a wall, most probably because *huppah* stones constructed for this purpose were not in existence in their time, and stones distinctly fashioned as "targets" were produced only in later periods. The cup was thrown when it contained wine; as, for example, in Libya:

respectively, pp. 162, 160, 165; they are all from Germany, seventeenth-eighteenth centuries.

50 Kirchheim, *The Customs of Worms Jewry*, p. 79 (Hebrew); Schammes, *Wormser Minhagbuch*, Vol. 2, p. 40.

51 N. Feuchtwanger(-Sarig) has recently published two articles on the Traustein, one ("Interrelations between the Jewish and Christian Wedding in Medieval Ashkenaz") in *Proceedings of the Ninth World Congress of Jewish Studies*, D, Vol. 2 (Jerusalem, 1986), pp. 31–36; and the other ("Der Traustein an der Urspringer Synagoge — Beispiel fur einen weitverbreiteten Brauch") in *Das Projekt Synagoge Urspringen: herausgegeben im Auftrag des Landkreises Main-Spessart und des Forderkreises Synagoge Urspringen*, ed. H. Bald and K. Bingemheimer (Wurzburg, 1993), pp. 53–57, with a complete bibliography. She writes in the latter article that the first example of such a "marriage stone" is from the Mainz-Weisenau synagogue (1691). Others then appear in Bingen (1700), and in Furth (1705) (p. 53, and notes on p. 56). To these we should add the wedding stone in Wurttenberg; see *Judische Gotheshauser und Friedhofe in Wurttenberg* (Stuttgart, 1932), p. 109: a "wedding stone" from 1751, with a Star of David and the inscription קול ששון [= קש the sound of mirth] וקש [= וקול שמחה and the sound of gladness] מזל טוב [= מט *Mazal Tov*] קח [= קול חתן the voice of bridegroom] וקכ [= וקול כלה and voice of bride]." Some of these stones were set in the northern wall, or the northern corner of the synagogue. Feuchtwanger(-Sarig) also discusses the possibility of external influences in the fashioning of this practice. Her first article (p. 34) also contains eyewitness testimony by Schudt, *Judischer Merckwurdigkeiten*, Vol. 2, pp. 1031–32, to the conducting of a Jewish wedding in the courtyard of a non-Jew, after the great conflagration that razed the Frankfurt ghetto; during the ceremony, one of the guests drew a star (which, according to Feuchtwanger, was a symbol of propitious *mazal* [meaning both good luck and one of the signs of the Zodiac]) on one of the walls of the house against which the groom dashed the cup (see also Schudt, Vol. 2, p. 119). This star also appears on wedding canopies; see, e.g., the depiction of a wedding canopy on a wimpel reproduced by J. Ungerleider-Mayerson, *Jewish Folk Art: From Biblical Days to Modern Times* (New York, 1986), p. 111 (from the United States, 1929). The star also is connected to the use of the term "himmel" for the wedding canopy (see above, n. 28, and below, n. 53).

Following the Seven Blessings, the cup from which the bride and groom drank is smashed by the groom, when it is almost full of wine, that is spilled on the earth.[52]

This procedure is clearly visible in Fig. 17.[53]

52 Hakohen, *Hayyei Adam: Kelulot*, p. 176, the practices of Libyan Jewry.
53 This engraving is from Kirchner, *Judisches Ceremoniel*, with a similar illustration in the same work (reproduced in *Jewish Encyclopedia*, Vol. 5, p. 343), which portrays a wedding conducted next to the synagogue that I have learned is the synagogue in Furth (see above, n. 16). See the *Jewish Encyclopedia*, Vol. 5, p. 537: an engraving by Johann Alexander Boener (1705) of this synagogue; cf. p. 536. See also R. Krautheimer, *Mittelalterliche Synagogen* (Berlin, 1927), pp. 243–48 and Fig. 24; R. Wischnitzer, *The Architecture of the European Synagogue* (Philadelphia, 1964), pp. 81, 286 n. 10; C.H. Krinsky, *Synagogues of Europe: Architecture, History, Meaning* (Cambridge, MA and London, 1985), pp. 294–96. The synagogue of Furth appears in additional illustrations in Kirchner's book: in one depicting *Kiddush ha-Hodesh* (the blessing recited upon seeing the new moon), and in another that shows the interior of the synagogue from a different angle (Krautheimer, Figs. 96, 97). This model repeats itself in Bodenschatz, *Kirchliche Verfassung der heutigen Juden* (reproduced in *Jewish Encyclopedia*, Vol. 5, p. 345); it is unclear whether Bodenschatz relied upon Kirchner, or whether he had firsthand knowledge of the Furth synagogue. Some other synagogues with buttresses somewhat resemble the synagogue in Furth, such as those in Pinczow and Vodislov (Poland). See J. Cempla, *Avnei Kodesh (Holy Stones: Synagogue Remains in Poland)* (Tel Aviv, 1959), Figs. 9, 11. See also G.K. Lukomskii, *Jewish Art in European Synagogues (from the Middle Ages to the Eighteenth Century)* (London and New York, 1947), pp. 68 (Cracow), 70 (Pinczow, Szydlow), 72 (Kurow), 82 (Nieswiez), each with an external buttress. Of similar style is the church in the woodcut *The Collapse of the Church* by Matthias Gereng (1500–69), which appears in the monumental work by W.L. Strauss, *The German Single-Leaf Woodcut, 1500–1550* (New York, 1975), p. 306, Fig. 51. The influence of the architectural style of medieval German churches is noticeable in certain (external) architectural traits. See, e.g., K.R. Langewiesche, *Deutsche Baukunst der Mittelalters und der Renaissance* ... (Taunis and Leipzig, n.d.), no. 119: the church of Halle (fifteenth century); no. 174: the cathedral of Prenzlau (mid-fourteenth century); no. 179: the church in Peplin (from the first half of the fourteenth century) (see also Fig. 24).
   It should also be mentioned that we see in the bottom part of the canopy covering in the illustrations in Kirchner's book an embroidered or drawn sun, a motif that also appears in the *huppah* stone described above. This is also visible in the wedding canopy in Buxtorf's work (see esp. above, the end of n. 25) that appears in Pappenheim, *The Jewish Wedding*, p. 34; and also in an illustration from Amsterdam (1683), reproduced by Rubens, *A Jewish Iconography*, no. 1091 (our Fig. 9), where

The practice of spilling out the wine, even before that of smashing the cup, is mentioned in *Mahzor Vitri* (loc. cit.): "He pours more into it, recites the Seven Blessings, drinks, give to drink [to the bride], **pours out**, dashes the glass cup against the wall, and breaks it." *Raban* (Rabbi Eliezer ben Nathan of Mainz) asks in this regard: "I am puzzled by their custom of demeaning the cup of blessing, and spilling it all out and wasting it."[54]

We have already mentioned the desire for practice to accord with all the different halakhic views, which is finely exemplified by Fig. 25,[55] in which many of the customs mentioned above come together in a single wedding: a canopy on poles, a scarf over the groom and bride, and a veil covering the bride's face.[56]

Another fascinating type of wedding appears in Fig. 26 (by Picart) and the upper left corner of Fig. 27 (a *ketubah* from Amsterdam, 1848; detail: Fig. 28), in which the bride and her bridesmaids sit within a marquee that stands in a room of the house, and the groom comes to this marquee and

we also see a circular wedding canopy, as in a work attributed to Calmet; in the latter etching, however, it stands on four poles, while here it is suspended from the ceiling. On the underside of the canopy, in both depictions, we see the sun, the moon, and the stars (see above, nn. 18, 28, 51), as was already noted by J. Gutmann, *The Jewish Life Cycle* (Leiden, 1987), p. 16.

54 *Raban, Even ha-Ezer* 177. See Hakohen, *Hayyei Adam: Kelulot*, p. 166. See, e.g., the photographs in B.Z. Ophir, *Pinkas Hakehillot: Germany — Bavaria* (Jerusalem, 1972), pp. 201, 301, 460, 465, 513, 526 (Hebrew); Schammes, *Wormser Minhagbuch*, Vol. 2, p. 40 n. 110 (see below, n. 56). For the smashing of the cup, see Hozeh, *Sefer Toledot ha-Rav Shalom Shabazi u-Minhagei Yahadut Sharab be-Teiman*, p. 91, who writes that this is "a total mockery." See also *Noheg be-Hokhmah*, p. 127; Pinari, *Beit Hatanim*, pp. 41–42; see also A. Yaari, "The Safed Earthquake in 1760," *Sinai* 28 (1951), pp. 354–55 (Hebrew); Rabbi Isaac Wendrowsky, *Minhagei Beit Yaakov* (New York, 1907), p. 47; Werdiger, *Edut le-Yisrael*, pp. 36–37; Lauterbach, "The Ceremony of Breaking a Glass at Weddings," pp. 351–80; Hakohen, *Hayyei Adam: Kelulot*, pp. 165–66; R. Gladstein-Kestenberg, "The Breaking of a Glass at a Wedding," in *Studies in the History of the Jewish People and the Land of Israel*, Vol. 4: *In Honour of Azriel Schochat on the Occasion of His Seventieth Birthday*, ed. U. Rappaport (Haifa, 1978), pp. 205–208 (Hebrew).

55 Bodenschatz, *Kirchliche Verfassung der heutigen Juden* (1748).

56 Obviously, the view that the "acquisition" of betrothal is effected when the bride enters the groom's house cannot be expressed in any visual representation of the wedding. It would seem, nevertheless, that the people in the painting would customarily gather after the wedding for a banquet, as R. Joel Sirkes writes (*Bah*, para. 61).

betroths his bride. This was the reality of the wedding ceremony known to the artist, one that is to be found in the writings of the *Rishonim*, such as the following statement by R. Asher ben Jehiel (*Rosh*):

> It is the custom in Germany to erect a marquee to seat the groom and bride, and this is called the *huppah*.[57]

57 See Rashi, BT Megillah 5b, s.v. "*Ve-Netiyah*"; Ketubot 7b, s.v. "*Be-Veit ha-Hatanim*," that the *huppah* is in the groom's house. He apparently understands that the wedding canopy is unfurled there, as does *Ritba* (Rabbi Yom Tov Ishbili) on Ketubot loc. cit., and as is explained in *Eikhah Rabbati* 4:11: "The groom and bride sit there all the seven [days]." This resembles the statements by Maimonides and the other *Rishonim* cited above (n. 18), but they did not mention the marquee. And similarly, the pupil of *Rashba* cited in Stern, *The Order of Betrothal and Marriage according to Our Early Masters*, p. 69; and in *Beit Yosef*, in the name of *Ha-Ittur* and *Orhot Hayyim*, para. 61. See also *Be'ur ha-Gra, Even ha-Ezer* 52:9; Rabbi Isaac Nunis Belmonte, *Sha'ar ha-Melekh* (Salonika, 1771), "*Huppat Hatanim*," para. 9, in the name of a *Rishon*, a contemporary of *Rashba*; Abraham al-Nakawa, *Kerem Hemer* (Leghorn, 1869–71), para. 94, in the name of the rabbis of Fez. (Note should also be taken of the unusual shape of the wedding canopy in Crimea, as reported by E. Deinard, in *Massa Krim: The History of the Israelites in the Crimean Peninsula, and Especially the History of the Kuzars, the Karaites, and the Krimchaks* [Warsaw, 1878], pp. 141–42: "In [the bride's] chamber they prepare for her a bed, with pillows and comforters on which she is to sit all the seven days. Around the bed they hang sheets and veils, lest any male look at her through the window, either intentionally or carelessly. They call this bed '*huppah*.'") The groom is not sitting in this illustration, but after the betrothal he, too, sat with his bride under the wedding canopy. Hakohen, *Hayyei Adam: Kelulot*, "Customs of Persia," p. 180, relates: "The wedding is conducted at twilight in the house of the bride, at the expense of the groom," which may possibly explain why the bride is sitting: it is her house. It is also noteworthy that many houses boasted marquees, not necessarily in relation to any wedding ceremony. See also Werdiger, *Avodat Yisrael*, p. 55.

As regards the conducting of the wedding ceremony in a house, this was practiced, even according to the view that called for extending a cloth on poles; see Schammes, *Wormser Minhagbuch*, Vol. 2, pp. 32–33. For an overview of the different opinions regarding *huppah*, see Adler, *Nisu'in ke-Hilkhatam*, Vol. 1, pp. 243–48; G. Felder, *She'eilat Yeshurun* (New York, 1988), para. 35; *Enziklopedia Talmudit*, Vol. 16 (Jerusalem, 1980), cols. 417–22; Hakohen, *Hayyei Adam: Kelulot*, pp. 165–66; also see pp. 19–20. See also Werdiger, *Edut le-Yisrael*, pp. 20–25; A.S. Herschberg, "Betrothal and Marriage Customs in the Talmudic Period," *He-Atid* 5 (Berlin-Vienna, 1923), pp. 75–104 (Hebrew). Rabbi David Friedmann, *Piskei Halakhot* (Warsaw, 1898), Vol. 1, fol. 47, writes (in his *Yad David* commentary) that anything that shows that the woman enters the domain of her husband is valid, by Torah law, to serve as

The painter of Fig. 26, Bernard Picart, wrote under his painting (early eighteenth century) that it shows a man writing in a ledger the "charity" that is given at the wedding. R. Joseph Caro explains the nature of this "charity":[58]

> When a man marries a wife, it is the way of his friends and acquaintances to send him money, so that he will be able to withstand his expenditure for the banquet. These monies are called *shushvinut*. This *shushvinut* is not a complete gift that someone sent him, rather, if this [other person] were to take a wife, then he [the current groom] repays [by] sending [the sum of money] to him, just as he [the first giver] had sent to him [the groom]. Therefore, if [the second person] were to marry, but he [the current groom] were not to repay him the *shushvinut*, then he [the original giver] sues him and collects from him. There are several differing customs in this matter. Since it is not customary to file such suits at the present time, I saw fit not to discuss this subject at length.

This practice is mentioned in the sources relating to the Jews of Libya, some of whom arrived in this land after the Expulsion from Spain (similar to the individuals in the painting: Jews of Portuguese origin who found refuge in Holland).[59] A description of the Libyan practice follows:

huppah. As regards separation between men and women at the wedding ceremony, I have not found any illustration of such a separation by a physical partition; see Lewy, *Minhag Yisrael Torah*, Vol. 1, pp. 111–22; *Minhagei Yeshurun* (New York, 1988), p. 35: "When a wedding takes place in a Shul women are permitted on the main floor, seated separately." For art and wedding canopies see Gutmann, "Jewish Medieval Marriage Customs in Art"; *idem, Beauty in Holiness: Studies in Jewish Customs and Ceremonial Art* (New York, 1970); see also *idem, The Jewish Life Cycle*, pp. 10–18.

58 *Shulhan Arukh, Even ha-Ezer* 60.

59 See Schammes, *Wormser Minhagbuch*, Vol. 2, p. 30: "Everything is thrown into the same bowl, and everything is written in a *ztetel* [a note]." The editor refers (n. 56) to Rabbi Mordecai Halberstam, *Ma'amar Mordekhai* (Brno, 1789), para. 59, who wrote: "Go and see what is the practice of the people, the custom of Israel is Torah [i.e. it has the status of biblical law], [namely:] before the wedding ceremony two lists are drawn up from the *ein worf* [i.e. the throwing in of presents], what was given from the bride's side, and [what was given] from the groom's side. Each of them is given one list, for if some [untoward] occurrence were to happen, Heaven forbid, they would be able to know, demand, and collect what each [one's side] had

In the celebration that they hold in the house of the groom on the evening preceding the wedding, each one gives a sum of money, according to his ability. In this manner a considerable sum is collected that evening, and is given to the groom, to be used for the expenses of the wedding. All the contributions, including the meals, are written in the special family ledger that is earmarked for this purpose, and when the occasion arises for a celebration in the house of the contributors (a circumcision, a Bar Mitzvah, or a wedding), the groom is obliged to return to each, as the contribution that he had made to [the groom]. In the instance of evasion [of repayment] by the groom, the recipient of the [original] contributions, the claimant may bring a lawsuit by Torah law against him that will compel him to [re]pay what he had received.[60]

This explains the necessity for recording in a ledger the amount given by each, so that the groom will be able to return this sum to the "contributor" at the proper time. This was also common in the Caucasus region:

The presents to the young couple were given at a special banquet, the "*natar*" (gifts) banquet. The distinguished members of the community would sit next to the groom, who sat with bent head, looking at the ground. [...] To the left of the groom sat the scribe, who recorded the name and gift of each one.[61]

Hakohen also describes the custom in other lands. In Persia:

An orchestra plays for the event, and one of the musicians announces the "*shabash*" — the contributions in the form of gold coins, that are given in honor of the bride and groom, whose redemption [money] is later given to the musicians. (p. 180)

In Kurdistan:

The ceremony known as "*tzobah*" (*shabash*) is conducted on a Saturday night. The gifts are contributions of money, household items, kitchen

given." He also cites *She'eilot u-Teshuvot R[abbi] Y[edidyah] T[ayah] Weill, Even ha-Ezer*, para. 42: "The custom everywhere is to draw up a list at the time that the *ein worf* is given, and to record what the groom's side gives, and what the bride's side gives, in order to know in the lack [of a *huppah*, i.e. if the wedding is canceled] what is coming to each side." See also *Yosif Ometz*, para. 657; Schammes, p. 47 and n. 11.

60 Hakohen, *Hayyei Adam: Kelulot*, p. 176, the practices of Libyan Jewry.
61 Hakohen, op. cit., p. 195.

utensils, bedding, jewelry, and the like. [...] All the gifts are recorded, so that they will be remembered by the bride and groom (p. 183).

And in the Caucasus regions:

In Derbent and Kuba, it was also customary to approach the groom, and each one would kiss him on his forehead and put a few coins in his pocket (p. 195).

Like the Libyan practice that we described, a record was also kept in the ledger of the contributions of meals, and it was incumbent upon the groom to return them when the time came.[62]

This practice of reciprocal gifts is still observed among the Georgian Jewish community in Israel.

Interestingly, this motif also appears in the painting *Noce Juive au Maroc* (*A Jewish Wedding in Morocco* — Figs. 29, 30) by the noted French artist Eugene Delacroix. The painting, which was executed ca. 1837–41, was recently the subject of a rigorous examination by Cissy Grossman.[63] In this painting, which portrays the postnuptial celebrations during the evening following the wedding, which happened to be a Thursday night, the guests come and bring presents of silver and items for the new home. A person is sitting in the foreground of the painting, on a carpet, with an inkwell and pen before him on a low table. This figure is apparently the scribe who prepared the *ketubah*, "and has probably just completed writing a list of gifts and their donors."

The fact of the bride and groom's sitting under the wedding canopy is foreign to the Western observer, although this posture is mentioned by *Rosh* (loc. cit.): "to seat the groom and bride," and we find the couple seated on chairs even in pictures of weddings conducted under the wedding canopy

---

62 This poses a difficulty, since *Shulhan Arukh, Even ha-Ezer* 170 rules: "A person may not say to his fellow, 'Come and eat what you gave me to eat,' for this is the way of interest'"; see also *Shulhan Arukh*, loc. cit., 171:13, gloss; further study is required. This is similar to the laws of the *shushbinim* [the groom's/bride's "friends," or best men) in the Talmud (Bava Batra 144b); the term "*shabash*", also, is reminiscent of the term "*shushban*," from the root שבב, whose meaning in Syrian is fellow, friend, neighbor; see Herschberg, "Betrothal and Marriage Customs in the Talmudic Period," pp. 94–95.

63 C. Grossman, "The Real Meaning of Eugene Delacroix's 'Noce Juive au Maroc,'" *Jewish Art* 14 (1988), pp. 64–73.

with which we are familiar. In Figs. 31–32[64] we see a bride and groom sitting on chairs under a canopy, and in Fig. 33[65] we see chairs ready for their occupants under a canopy, which is the contemporary practice in the Strasbourg community. The members of this community explain that since the bride and groom have been fasting the entire day, and the rabbi will deliver a lengthy sermon, the couple need to sit. Sitting under the wedding conopy was accepted by the leading Torah authorities of the Franco-German center; even though they spoke of sitting in a marquee in the house,[66] the custom of sitting under a canopy that was under the open sky was adopted in some localities, in an apparent combination of elements from different practices.[67]

---

64 A wimpel from Alsace, France, 1881, reproduced in Ungerleider-Mayerson, *Jewish Folk Art*, p. 110.

65 From France, 1923, in Ungerleider-Mayerson, p. 96; and similarly, in an additional wimpel from Alsace(?), 1921, reproduced in Kirshenblatt-Gimblett, *Fabric of Jewish Life*, no. 169, p. 100. Incidentally, the round canopy is reminiscent of the *huppah* portrayed by Calmet (above, n. 25).

66 Cf. above, n. 12.

67 See *Minhagei Yisrael*, Vol. 2, p. 198; see also Werdiger, *Edut le-Yisrael*, p. 63; *She'eilot u-Teshuvot Rabbeinu Moshe Mintz*, para. 119: "The groom and the bride are made to sit under the bridal canopy," to which we should add the description appearing in A. Cohen, *An Anglo-Jewish Scrapbook, 1600–1840: The Jew through English Eyes* (London, 1943), p. 284, by S.E. Moryson (late sixteenth century), in which the bride sits on a high chair, decked in white and with her face covered by a white veil. See *Shakespeare's Europe: Unpublished Chapters of Fynes Moryson's Itinerary: Being a Survey of the Conditions of Europe at the End of the Sixteenth Century*, ed. C. Hughes (London, 1903), p. 491. The bride's wearing of white clothing is mentioned in *Shulhan ha-Ezer*, Vol. 2, fol. 27. It is the custom of some for the groom also to be attired in white; see *Orhot Hayyim, Hil. Kiddushin* (*Marriage Laws*), para. 21; *Kol Bo*, para. 71; *She'eilot u-Teshuvot ha-Radbaz*, section 1, para. 693; see also BT Shabbat 114a; Niddah 20b. In some places, the groom wears a *kittel* (symbolic white robe); see *Matteh Moshe, Hil. Hakhnasat Kallah*, para. 2; *Derekh Hayyim* prayerbook, the wedding ceremony. See also Rabbi Jacob Tenenbaum, *Naharei Afarsemon* (Paksa, 1898), *Yoreh Deah*, para. 23. Many explanations have been put forth for this practice. See Sperber, *Afarkasta de-Aniya*, Vol. 1, p. 392, para. 170, on whether a marriage ceremony was to be performed for someone who refused to wear white at his wedding. This same case was also discussed in Rabbi Moses Schick, *She'eilot u-Teshuvot Maharam Shik* (Munkacs, 1881–1904), para. 88; Rabbi Moses Nahum Yerushlimski, *Be'er Moshe* (Warsaw, 1901), Vol. 5, para. 166; *Naharei Afarsemon, Yoreh Deah*, para. 2; see also Adler, *Nisu'in ke-Hilkhatam*, Vol. 1, p. 365 and notes; for the wedding garments of the bride and groom in Moroccan Jewry, see also Ben-Ami, *Le Judaisme Marocain*, pp. 233–36.

1. Jewish wedding, Pietro Longhi, Venice, 18th century

2. Jewish wedding, Tunisia, end of 19th century (?)

3. Jewesses of Fürth in 1705

**4. Jewish wedding, Padua 1477,
Ms. Hamburg Cod. Hebr. 337
(Blessing of R. Meir Rothenburg)**

5. Jewish Wedding, Italy 1470,
Ms. Rothschild 24
Collection of the Israel Museum,
Jerusalem
Photo © The Israel Museum /
David Harris

6. Jewish Wedding, Italy, Pesaro 1481

7. Germany, Fürth 1705

Costume of Jews and their wives. Engraving by Boener.

The women in their distinctive Jewish ruffs with sleeves to match and cloaks. They seem to be wearing *frets* as head-dress. The man in the center wears a ruff but the one on the right (the rabbi?) is in a plain collar, a Jewish *barette*, a tunic buttoned down the front and a sleeveless cloak.

8. Latin Mishnah, Amsterdam 1700

9. Jewish wedding, Picard, Amsterdam 1721

10. Jewish wedding, Calmet, Amsterdam and Leiden 1725

11. Jewish wedding, Leusden, Utrecht 1672

12. Wedding girdle, 19th century

13. Jewish wedding
M. Oppenheim 1861

14. Jewish wedding
M. Oppenheim 1882

15. American *Ketubah*, 1864

16. Majolica plate, Italy ca. 1530

17. Jewish wedding, Kirchner, Nuremberg 1726

18. Double wedding wine cup, Germany, 18th century

20. *Huppastein*, **Germany, 17th century**

19. Jewish wedding, Nuremberg miscellany 1590 (?)

21. *Huppastein*,
Germany,
18th century

22. *Huppastein*, Germany, 18th century

23. *Huppastein*, **Germany, 17th century**

24. Engraving by Bohner, 1705

25. Bodenschatz, Erlang 1724

26. Jewish wedding, Picard, Amsterdam 1721

27. *Ketubah*, **Rotterdam 1658**

27a. Detail of Fig. 27

28. Detail of Fig. 27

29. Moroccan Jewish wedding, Delacroix 1837–41, Musée du Louvre, Paris

30. Detail of Fig. 29

31. Wimpel, Alsace 1881

32. Wimpel, Alsace 1881

33. Wimpel, Alsace 1881

**34. Raphael, *The Sposalizio*, 1504, Milan, Brera
Ministry for Cultural Assets and Activities**

35. Silver plate with Jewish wedding scene based on Oppenheim, Germany, 19th century

36. *Dextrarum Innuctio*, Roman relief

37. Lucas van Leyden, *The Fiancés*, ca. 1519
Strasbourg, Fine Arts Museum

APPENDIX

THE NATURE OF THE *HUPPAH*

R. Moses Isserles (*Rema*, d. 1572) writes in his glosses to the *Shulhan Arukh*:[1]

> According to one opinion, *huppah* does not consist of *yihud*, but rather it is any act of the groom bringing her to his house for the purpose of marriage (as was written by *Ran* [Rabbeinu Nissim], beginning of Ketubot); and according to another view, *huppah* consists of the unfurling of a handkerchief over their heads at the time of the blessing (brought by *Beit Yosef*); and yet another view maintains that *huppah* is effected when she goes forth in a veil, and for a widow, when they engage in *yihud* (*Tosefot*, first chapter of Yoma). **The current straightforward practice** is to call "*huppah*" the place where a cloth is spread over poles, under which the groom and the bride are brought in, in public, where he betroths, and where the betrothal and wedding blessings are recited; after which they are led to his house, and they eat together in a concealed place — **and this is the *huppah* that is practiced at present**.

This description of current practice is reiterated by R. David ha-Levi (1586–1667), the author of *Turei Zahav*:[2]

> **Now** "*huppah*" refers only to the betrothal [i.e. betrothal-marriage] of the bride under a cloth that is unfurled on poles, as is stated by *Rema* [...] for in the early generations, a *huppah* on poles was not done.

Isserles' survey teaches of the existence of many varying definitions of the essential nature of the *huppah* (i.e. the fundamental element of the

1   *Shulhan Arukh, Even ha-Ezer* 55:1.
2   *Turei Zahav, Even ha-Ezer* 57:4.

marriage ceremony),[3] while emphasizing that in the "**current** straightforward practice," a canopy is extended over four poles.

We see from the above[4] that the practice of unfurling a canopy over four poles was initiated shortly before the time of R. Isserles,[5] and was quickly adopted by various communities, mainly in Poland.[6] On the other hand, it was opposed by some, who claimed that this practice was erroneous, and was of no acquisitional significance.

This form of wedding ceremony was conducted by non-Jews in different lands. Thus, for example, we find a painting from 1417 of a Jewish delegation going to the Pope in Konstanz (Constance) in southern Germany, in which we see how the delegation passes under a canopy that appears just like the Jewish ceremonial canopy described by Isserles[7] (Fig. 1). And this is not the only such testimony: John Brand attests in the eighteenth century:[8]

3   See above, chap. 21, *Resh Kallah u-Mai Huppah*, pp. 34 ff.
4   See above, chap. 20, n. 28, for halakhic reservations regarding the understanding of "*huppah*" as such a canopy, and variant practices.
5   As was already noted by scholars. See, e.g., what was written by S.B. Freehof, "The Chuppah," in *In the Time of Harvest: Essays in Honor of Abba Hillel Silver on the Occasion of His 70th Birthday*, ed. D.J. Silver (New York, 1963), p. 187: "It is obvious from the note of Moses Isserles to Even Hoezer, 55:1, that the canopy [the *chuppah*] as we know it now was a novelty in his day." See what Silver further writes, pp. 188–93. Silver was followed by J. Guttmann, "Wedding Customs and Ceremonies in Art," in his collection, *Beauty in Holiness*, p. 317 n. 35 (first appearing in *The Jewish Marriage Anthology*, ed. P. and H. Goodman [Philadelphia, 1965]), with a reference to the apostate A. Margaritha, *Der ganz Judisch glaub* ..., second edition (Leipzig, 1713), p. 98, who already mentioned this practice in 1530 (when the book was first published, in Augsburg). See also S.B. Freehof, *Reform Jewish Practice and Its Rabbinic Background* (Cincinnati, 1944), Vol. 1, pp. 85–86; H. Schauss (Shoys), *The Lifetime of a Jew throughout the Ages of Jewish History* (Cincinnati, 1950), p. 164. Also worthy of close study is what was written by Hamburger, *Shorshei Minhag Ashkenaz*, Vol. 3 (Bnei Brak, 2004), pp. 486 ff. (Hebrew).
6   Hamburger, p. 489.
7   Hamburger, p. 493, from the *Chronik des Konstanzer Konzils, 1414–1418*, by Ulrich von Richental. The painting depicts a Jewish delegation walking under the canopy (seemingly resembling a Jewish *huppah*) to the Pope, who also appears, facing them with his entourage, on horseback, under the canopy.
8   J. Brand, *Observation on Popular Antiquities, chiefly illustrating the origin of our vulgar ceremonies and superstitions* (London, 1771). A second edition was published in London, 1900, with a number of additions by Sir Henry Ellis from 1813; the citation is from the second edition, pp. 380–81.

Care Cloth

With the Anglo-Saxons the nuptial benediction was performed under a veil, or square piece of cloth, held at each corner by a tall man over the bridegroom and bride, to conceal her virgin blushes: but, if the bride was a Widow, the veil was esteemed useless.

According to the use of the Church of Sarum,[9] when there was a marriage before mass, the parties knelt together and had a fine linen cloth, called the Care Cloth, laid over their heads during the time of mass till they received the benediction, after which they were dismissed.

The Hereford Missal[10] directs that, at a particular prayer, the married couple shall prostrate themselves, while four clerks hold the pall, i.e., the care cloth, over them. The rubric in the Sarum Manual is somewhat different; and the York Manual also varies here.

There is a curious wedding sermon by William Whately, preacher

---

9   I.e., the order of prayers and rites of the cathedral in Salisbury (also known as Sarum). See *Oxford Dictionary of the Christian Church*[2], ed. F.L Cross and E.A. Livingstone (Oxford, 1983), p. 1229:

> **Salisbury** or **Sarum**, Use of. The local medieval modification of the Roman rite in use at the cathedral church of Salisbury, traditionally ascribed to St. Osmund (d. 1099) but really much later. The Customary, i.e. the cathedral statutes and customs and a complete directory of services, were compiled by Richard Poore (d. 1237). The 'New Use of Sarum' was a further (14th-cent.) revision, effecting certain changes in the Calendar. In the later Middle Ages the Sarum Use was increasingly followed, in whole or in part, in other dioceses, and in 1457 started to be in use in nearly the whole of England, Wales, and Ireland. In 1543 the Canterbury Convocation imposed the Sarum Breviary on the whole province, and the books of the Sarum rite furnished the Reformers with their main material for the First (1549) BCP of Edward VI, in the Preface to which (the section now headed 'Concerning the Service of the Church') the Sarum Use appears as one of the local variations which the new standard order was to replace. In the years preceding the Reformation the output of Sarum books was enormous. The much increased knowledge which followed their discovery and re-editing in modern times led to the revival of Sarum customs and ornaments in many English cathedral and parish churches.

> See also W.H. Frere, *The Use of Sarum*, Vol. I: *The Sarum Customs as Set forth in the Consuitudinary and Customary* (Cambridge, 1898); C. Wordsworth, *Ceremonies and Processions of the Cathedral Church of Salisbury* (Cambridge, 1901).

10   A missal (Latin: *Liber Missalis*, or *Missale*) is a sort of prayerbook of the Christian Church. Its etymology comes from the connection between such a book of prayers and rites and the Mass.

of Banbury in Oxfordshire (1624) entitled A Care-Cloth, or a Treatise of the Cumbers and Troubles of Marriage. The etymology of the word "Care" used here in composition with "Cloth" is dubious.[11] Whately has given it the ordinary meaning of the word, but, as we think, erroneously. Like many other etymologists, he has adapted it to his own purpose.

Something like this care cloth is used by the modern Jews, from whom it has probably been introduced into the Christian Church. Modena's History of Jewish Rites[12] refers to "a square Vestment called Taleth, with pendants about it, put over the Head of the Bride-groom and the Bride together"; and Levi, in his work on the same subject, speaks of "a Velvet Canopy."[13]

Graphic depictions of such a canopy appear in Jewish literature beginning

11 See *Oxford English Dictionary, Compact Edition* (Oxford, 1971), Vol. 1, p. 339 (115c), s.v. "Care": "Obsolete. Some kind of stuff." The dictionary hesitantly connects this word with "cary" (p. 346, 143c): "Obsolete. Some textile fabric," and indeed, it is difficult to determine the source and meaning of this word. It apparently should not be connected with the "care-cakes" mentioned by M.M. Banks, *British Calendar Customs: Scotland*, Vol. 3 (London, 1941), p. 224; nor with "Care-Sunday"; see A.S. Palmer, *Folk-Etymology: A Dictionary of Verbal Corruptions or Words Perverted in Form or Meaning by False Derivation or Mistaken Analogy* (London, 1882 [photocopy edn.: New York, 1969]), p. 50. It is tempting to connect it with the Latin *carus* (French: *cher*; Italian: *caro*; Provencal: *car*), meaning beloved, i.e. the cloth or canopy of love, but this seems to be nothing more than an etymological homily. I recently found this word listed by J.O. Halliwell[-Phillipps], *A Dictionary of Archaic and Provincial Words ... from the XIV Century* (London and New York, 1924 [photocopy edn.: London, 1989]), p. 232b, s.v. "Care," who observes: "Palsgrave calls it carde clothe and seems to say it was then (1530) out of use." This would seem to imply that the practice is much earlier than this date, for by then the term was no longer current; this issue is worthy of further investigation.

12 The reference is to the famous book by R. Leone (Judah Aryeh) da Modena, *Historia dei Riti Ebraici* (Paris, 1637; Latin translation: Leonis Mutinensis Opusculum, *De Ceremoniis et Consuetudinibus Hodie Jedeos inter receptis ...* [Frankfurt a.M., 1693]). Brand undoubtedly used the English translation: Leon Modena, *The History of the Rites, Customes, and Manner of Life, of the Present Jews, throughout the World*, trans. E. Chilmead (London, 1650).

13 David Levi, *A Succinct Account of the Rites and Ceremonies of the Jews: as Observed by Them, in Their Different Dispertions ... at This Present Time ...* (London, 1781).

in the early seventeenth century, as in the *Minhag Bukh* by R. Simeon Levi Guenzburg[14] (Fig. 2), and afterwards in a Grace after meals booklet from Dyhernfurth (1692) (Fig. 3)[15] and in a Grace after meals from Amsterdam (1722) (Fig. 4);[16] and in more primitive fashion in the *Frankfurt Minhagim Book* (Fig. 5).[17] Such illustrations also entered the literature of the Christian Hebraists, such as the book by Johannes Leusden of the University of Utrecht, *Philologus Hebraeo-Mixtus* (first edition: Utrecht, 1663), which included eight woodcuts based on the *Minhagim* books, albeit not identical, but very similar to the illustrations in the latter (Fig. 6).[18]

Earlier than this, however, in various manuscripts, the wedding ceremony and the wedding canopy appear in a completely different fashion, in accordance with one of the views cited by Isserles. Thus, for example,

14 Venice 1601. See the small, but important, book by Ch. Shmeruk, *The Illustrations in Yiddish Books of the Sixteenth and Seventeenth Centuries* (Jerusalem, 1986) (Hebrew), p. 53:

> There is a pronounced [...] tendency by the artist who prepared the illustrations for the 1600 [or 1601] edition of the *Minhagim* book to expand the participation of children, and to extensively depict them. Indeed, the numerous editions added several children's figures [...] children holding the wedding canopy. [...] The shared element in the editions of the *Minhagim* book and the Pesah Haggadot is the desire to graphically illustrate the role of children in the observance of the commandments and to accustom them to the traditional pattern of life.

See the continuation of Shmeruk's instructive presentation.

15 *Seder Birkat ha-Mazon*, ed. M. Hovav (Jerusalem, 1977), p. 54.

16 *Benedicion despues de Comer*, ed. M. Hovav (Jerusalem, 1979), p. 72.

17 Frankfurt, 1708.

18 See N. Feuchtwanger-Sarig, "An Illustrated Minhagim Book Printed in Amsterdam," in *Bibliotheca Rosenthaliana: Treasures of Jewish Booklore, Marking the 200th Anniversary of the Birth of Leeser Rosenthal*, ed. A.K. Offenberg, E.G.L. Schrijver, and F.J. Hoggewoud (Amsterdam, 1994), p. 36, who asserts that between 1660 and 1992 Leusden worked in conjunction with Joseph Athias in the printing of the first Bible with verse enumeration, and that this relationship also continued afterwards. Thus, after Athias founded his printing house in 1662, he published a *Minhagim* book with new illustrations based on the traditional iconography that, Feuchtwanger-Sarig surmises, Leusden might have used afterwards in his own book. In our opinion, however, Leusden made new printing blocks resembling the traditional ones we have seen above. For Joseph Athias, see *Encyclopaedia Judaica* (Jerusalem, 1971), Vol. 3, cols. 819–820. The second edition of Leusden's book (Utrecht, 1682) contains entirely different illustrations that are considerably finer and more sophisticated metal etchings, in contrast with the former woodcuts (see Fig. 7).

in the second Nuremberg Haggadah (Germany, ca. 1470), there is no canopy supported by poles, but rather a long cloth that extends over the heads of the bride and groom (Fig. 8).[19]

Prof. Joseph Gutmann,[20] observing "the emergence of unique and novel Jewish customs centering around the Jewish involvement with medieval Germany,"[21] cites a series of customs, some connected with the marriage ceremony, such as, among others, the *Knas-Mahl* and the *Spinnholz*, which draw upon Christian practices. As regards the type of *huppah* under discussion, he writes:

> In medieval Germany the wedding ceremony was shifted to the synagogue and the *huppah* now consisted of spreading or covering the bridal couple with a cloth (*sudar*) or a prayer shawl (*talit*). It is worth noting that in Christian usage, during the nuptial Mass in the church, a cloth (*pallium, velum*) was also spread over the bridal couple. This Christian custom is already found in Germany in the early Middle Ages and it is likely that Jews adopted this practice.[22]

Gutmann's conclusion is confirmed by the testimonies cited above. Unlike

19 See Metzger, *Jewish Life in the Middle Ages*, p. 300, no. 345; Guttmann, "Wedding Customs and Ceremonies in Art," p. 331. This Haggadah is among the holdings of the Zalman Schocken Library, MS. 24087 (see Metzger, p. 303, no. 84, 89). Additional illustrations of mid-fifteenth century wedding ceremonies appear in *Resh Kallah u-Mai Huppah*, pp. 50–52. An extensive discussion of the *talit* as a wedding canopy is provided by Hamburger, *Shorshei Minhag Ashkenaz*, Vol. 3, pp. 418–86.
20 J. Gutmann, "Christian Influences on Jewish Customs," in *Spirituality and Prayer: Jewish and Christian Understandings*, ed. L. Klenicki and G. Huck (New York, 1983), pp. 129–38.
21 Ibid., p. 129. See also *idem*, "Jewish Medieval Marriage Customs in Art," pp. 47–62. See also above, chap. 21, n. 28, for the "himmel" held above the bride, that would seem also to come from Christian sources.
22 Gutmann, "Christian Influences on Jewish Customs," p. 133. On p. 137 n. 23 he refers to K. Ritzer, *Formen, Riten und religioses Brauchtum der Eheschliessung in den christlichen Kirchen des ersten Jahrtausends* (Munster, 1962), pp. 158, 176, 231 ff., and to J. Sauer, *Symbolik des Kirchengebaudes und seiner Ausstattung in der Auffassung des Mittelalters* (Freiburg, 1924), p. 210. See also Gutmann, "How Traditional Are Our Traditions?", in *Beauty in Holiness*, pp. 417–19. Incidentally, Muslims may well ask the same question, since they too sometimes use a canopy at their weddings. See Fig. 10, of an Arab-Muslim Wedding, copper engraving of the mid-nineteenth century.

Brand's assertion that the Jewish custom went over to the Christian church, the opposite is the case: the Jewish practice developed under the influence of the Christian procedure. This religious crossover can be dated to the late fifteenth–early sixteenth century, since before the time of R. Moses Isserles, "no *posek* mentioned the unfurling of a cloth on poles."[23]

What led to the emergence of a new form of *huppah* in Poland at the turn of the sixteenth century? Freehof suggests that the Jewish population in Poland, which greatly increased in Isserles' time, was impoverished, and thousands of young men married without any property to speak of. They did not have their own nuptial chamber in which they could engage in *yihud*, thus resulting in the quasi-room canopy that was extended over poles. Freehof summarizes his proposal as follows:[24]

> Many of the grooms were poor Talmudic students who married the daughters of relatively well-to-do merchants. It would be easy to set up the *chuppah* in the house of the bride, as Elijah of Vilna indicates. This would raise legal objections because one definition of the process of *chuppah* was that the bride should be handed over to the premises of the groom. Therefore it was held on the premises of the synagogue which were everybody's property. It was kept open-sided so that it should not be mistaken for the actual chamber of "acquiring." Since, however, the new symbolic canopy did somewhat resemble the old private wedding tent, the older custom of the Rhineland to conduct the wedding in the synagogue itself seemed no longer appropriate. Hence the ceremony was moved to the courtyard.

Freehof's thesis is intriguing, but unconvincing. More weight should be given to the explanation set forth by Hamburger, in the summation of his chapter on "A Cloth on Poles," which we shall cite in part:[25]

> Rabbi Elijah Bahur-Ashkenazi, who lived in Italy a generation before R. Moses Isserles, told of the existence of this [canopy] *huppah* in his land. He called it a "baldaquin,"[26] the non-Hebrew name of the canopy that is supported by poles that was borne over the Pope in the

---

23 Hamburger, *Shorshei Minhag Ashkenaz*, Vol. 3, p. 487.
24 Freehof, "The Chuppah," p. 193.
25 Hamburger, *Shorshei Minhag Ashkenaz*, p. 533.
26 See ibid., p. 491.

medieval period when he went to certain rites. It is known that the use of the "baldaquin" in a dignified procession spread from the Popes to the kings of Europe, and later, also to other societal strata in many European lands. The first use by Jews of a cloth on poles is known to us from a painting of a Jewish delegation to the Pope in 1417.

The canopy unfurled over poles was first used to adorn the processions of important individuals. Over the course of time, this practice also spread to many European Jewish communities, for the inauguration of a Torah scroll, and for the procession of *Hatanei Torah*[27] on Simhat Torah. [...]

In Germany and Poland the pole canopy was used to bring the bride to the betrothal and wedding ceremony. After the bride arrived at the site of the ceremony, it was the practice of some to remove the cloth [on the] poles, and to spread a *talit* over the heads of the groom and bride as a *huppah*. Once the *talit* had been spread over them, the canopy on poles remained behind, with no [further] use. [...]

In other *huppot* in Germany, the canopy on poles remained over the heads of the groom and bride even after the *talit-huppah* was extended over the heads of both and the betrothal and marriage ceremony began.

While in German communities the canopy on poles was used for the bridal procession, and at times to augment the *talit* canopy, the former became the sole *huppah* in Eastern Europe, with its gradual abandonment in the bridal procession, until it was reserved exclusively for the *huppah* requirement of the wedding ceremony.

Although the canopy on poles was used in Germany for the bridal procession, and in Poland for the *huppah* itself, it was unknown among Sephardic and Eastern Jews, not for the procession, and definitely not for the *huppah*. The use of the cloth canopy originated in European rites, and did not spread to the Islamic sphere.[28]

The relationship between the Italian *baldacchino* and the English Care Cloth has not been properly examined. It would seem that two elements converge here: the *baldaquin* of the bridal procession, as portrayed by Hamburger, and the Care Cloth of the Christian church, which played a role in weddings before the Mass; and the incorporation of these two elements, both under

27 See below, chap. 25 ("'How They Dance before the Bride'"), after n. 33.
28 However, see Fig. 9.

external influence, created the Jewish wedding canopy with which we are familiar today.[29]

29 Tangentially, it should be noted that in the article cited above Freehof draws our attention to a passage from *She'eilot u-Teshuvot Rabbeinu Moshe Mintz*, para. 109 (ed. Domb: Vol. 2, p. 575). Mintz, who lived in Germany and Poland, 1435–80 (see Domb, Vol. 1, pp. 10–12), writes: "After the *Main*, it is the practice in several communities to sit the groom and bride under a *kippah* that is made for this purpose, and this is our *huppah*" (for the *Main* and its meaning, see the discussion by B.S. Hamburger, in Schammes, *Wormser Minhagbuch* [written ca. 1648], Vol. 2, pp. 20–21 n. 5). Freehof has his doubts concerning the nature of this canopy, and whether it was supported on four poles. He states only that the couple sat under it, and that it was not the venue of any ceremony. He writes (p. 189): "Whether this *kippah* or pavilion is the antecedent of the East European *chuppah* is not more than possible." Although we cannot determine the relationship of this "*kippah*" to the wedding canopy under discussion, it most probably did not come with four poles, and was round (the regular meaning of the term *kippah* — dome). R. Mintz's statement, however, might constitute a source for a certain type of *huppah*, albeit later, that we found in another engraving, by Jan Luyken, in the translation into Dutch: Modena, *Kerk-zeeden en de gewoonten: die huiden ingebruik zyn onder de jooden*, facing p. 116, which depicts a Jewish wedding (Fig. 10). Here we see a round *kippah* hanging from the ceiling of the synagogue interior. The groom, who is wearing a *talit*(?) cloth(?), extends what seems to be a ring to his modest bride. The children hold torches, one adult holds what is probably a cup of wine, the bearded rabbi has a *ketubah* open in his hand, and the *kleizmerim* play in the background. In the windows of the synagogue we see portrayals of Moses and Aaron. Was this *kippah* a mere decoration, or did it fill some ceremonial function? Further study is required to answer this question, For the etchings of Luyken, see R.I. Cohen, *Jewish Icons: Art and Society in Modern Europe* (Berkeley and Los Angeles, 1998), pp. 38–43.

1. *Chronik der Konstanzer Konzils*, **1414–18**
Ulrich von Richental

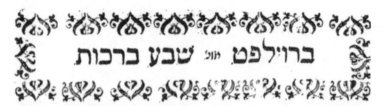

2. *Minhag Buch*, **Simeon Levi Guenzburg, Venice 1601**

3. Grace after meals booklet, Dyhrenfurth 1692

4. Grace after meals booklet, Amsterdam 1722

פֿדריילפֿט אונ' שבע ברכות :

5. *Minhagim* Book, Frankfurt 1708

6. Jewish wedding, Leusden, Utrecht 1663

7. Jewish wedding, Leusden, Utrecht 1682

**8. Nuremberg *Haggadah*,
Germany, ca. 1470**

9. Muslim Wedding, Paul Hardy, 19th century

10. Jewish wedding, Jan Luyken, Amsterdam 1725

22

THE WEDDING RING IN THE CUP OF WINE

Elsewhere we listed customs that have literary origins.[1] In this chapter we will present an additional example of this phenomenon: a strange practice that apparently emerged from a literary source. In the book *Even Sapir* by the famous traveler Jacob Saphir we find a description of a wedding in Cochin (southern India):[2]

> A cup of wine is brought, the silver coin of acquisition [i.e. by which the betrothal is effected] is placed [in the cup] and is tied with a white string. The cup is given to the groom, who holds the cup in his hand with the [ring attached to the] string:[3] one end [of the string] is in

1 *Minhagei Yisrael*, Vol. 2, pp. 203–26.
2 Joseph Saphir, *Even Sapir*, Vol. 2 (Mainz, 1874), p. 72.
3 The main purpose of tying the coin with a white string was undoubtedly to prevent the person who extracted the coin from the cup from dirtying his fingers in the wine (for the inhabitants of Cochin are fastidious and are very exacting regarding their personal cleanliness). This may possibly also possess a magical protective element (cf. *Shulhan Arukh, Orah Hayyim* 455:1, in the gloss; *Minhagei Yisrael*, Vol. 1, p. 16), but this is mere conjecture.

The Cochin custom might possibly call for two cups, one for the rabbi and the other for the groom (see below, n. 4), reflective of the fact that the ceremony entails two different types of cups: the cup of betrothal (containing the coin), and the cup over which the wedding blessing is recited. Another possibility is that the two cups are in remembrance of the view that requires one cup for the betrothal (*kiddushin*), and a second cup for the marriage (*nisu'in*). See *Hagahot Maimoniyot* on Maimonides, *Mishneh Torah, Hil. Ishut* (*Laws of Marriage*) 3:60, that Rabbenu Tam understood this to mean that two cups are required; see *Shulhan Arukh, Even ha-Ezer*, paras. 34, 62; see Werdiger, *Edut le-Yisrael*, pp. 31–33. A proof for the

the cup, and the other end is in his hand, with a full cup of wine. He recites [the introduction to the blessing] "With your permission,"[4] [...] and he says "Blessed are You, O Lord, who sanctifies Israel by *huppah* and betrothal. You are *meureset* to me, you are *mekudeshet* to me [both terms meaning "betrothed"], O virgin bride [...] with this beaker and this money, and everything that is in it, you shall come into my possession [...]."[5] The groom tastes, and then the groom takes **the ring of acquisition from the cup**, gives the cup to the bride, and recites: "With this you are betrothed." The bride tastes from the wine and returns the cup to the hand of one of those in attendance. The groom places the ring on the bride's right little finger, and says, "Come, my betrothed."

This puzzling custom of placing the ring in the cup also appears among the Mountain Jews of the Caucasus region, a Jewish community that was isolated from other Jewish centers. In his travelogue, J.J. Chorny depicts a wedding held in the city of Achalzaich:[6]

first proposal apparently is to be found in J.J. Chorny, *Sefer ha-Massa'ot be-Eretz Kavkaz* (*Book of Travels in the Caucasus*) (St. Petersburg, 1884), p. 129, the description of a betrothal ceremony in the village of Chinval: "While the sage was reciting the blessings over the cup, the groom's hand held a pottery cup with special wine, in which the coin of betrothal, as well, was placed. Upon the completion of the blessings, the groom would remove the coin from the wine in his cup, and he forcefully dashed the pottery wine-cup on the ground, so that it smashed into pieces." Clearly, the pottery cup held by the groom was different in nature from the cup held by the rabbi, over which the benediction of the wedding ceremony was recited; the purpose of the former was to serve as a receptacle for the coin. For the smashing of the pottery cup during the wedding, see Elzet, *Reshumot*, Vol. 1, p. 355. For a general discussion of the breaking of a cup during the wedding, see *Minhagei Yisrael*, Vol. 1, p. 11 n. 4, with a reference to the comprehensive article by Lauterbach, "The Ceremony of Breaking a Glass at Weddings," pp. 351–80; see above, chap. 22 ("*Huppah*").

4   For the assuming of permission, and many other details from the custom of Cochin, see Rabbi Shemtob Gaguine (the author of *Keter Shem Tov*), *The Jews of Cochin* (Brighton, England, 1953), pp. 60 ff. (Hebrew). According to the Cochin custom, "two cups filled with wine were brought; one cup was put in the hand of the groom, and the other, in the hand of the rabbi, and the rabbi recited the Seven Blessings" (p. 63). Gaguine further wrote (p. 63 n. 4) that he did not find this custom in the Jewish sources, nor did he offer a reason for this (see above, the preceding note).

5   Gaguine (p. 60) presents a slightly different version from the Cochin prayerbook.

6   Chorny, *Sefer ha-Massa'ot be-Eretz Kavkaz*, p. 160. During the twentieth century,

The groom betroths the bride in accordance with Jewish law, but while drinking of the cup of the blessing, **the groom places the ring within the cup of wine** and he gives to the bride to drink. When he receives the cup back from her, he takes the ring out again (I do not understand the reason for this).[7]

Moshe Yosefov describes a similar ceremony in the Caucasus:[8]

The rabbi takes a cup of wine, recites the blessing over it, drinks half of it, and gives the other half to the groom. The latter places within the cup a silver coin or a ring; he drinks, and gives to the bride. She imbibes of the wine, and takes the ring for herself. In some places it is the young man who takes the ring. This action obligates both parties, and afterwards release [from the marital bond thus forged] can be effected only by means of a writ of divorce.

At times, it suffices for the groom to sit in his house. The cup of wine and the coin within it are brought, the bride drinks, and she is thereby betrothed to him in full accordance with Jewish law.

Erich Brauer sets forth a similar wedding ceremony among the Jews of Kurdistan:[9]

however, the custom changed in character, and different communities developed differing ceremonial practices. See the Israel Museum catalogue: *Mountain Jews: Customs and Daily Life in the Caucasus*, ed. L. Mikdash-Shamailov (Jerusalem, 2002), pp. 96–97, on the custom in Azerbaijan; pp. 100–102, Dagestan.

7   Chorny continues: "Following the *huppah* [formal wedding ceremony], the groom seizes the bride with both hands and **raises her up**. He brings her into a small room close to the *bimah* [the raised platform from which the Torah is read] that is made out of a few synagogue curtains, where he sits her down. He then returns and stands once again in his original place on the *bimah*, and the rabbi and the entire congregation chant this song." The "raising up" of the bride gives the impression that it is another method of effecting "acquisition" of a person, that is, the groom acquires his bride by lifting her up(?). This might also bear some resemblance to the "leading" of the bride to *yihud* [the first seclusion of the bride and groom as husband and wife], which constitutes the bride's entry into the groom's domain to some degree. See Werdiger, *Edut le-Yisrael*, p. 65. Or, possibly, this may be parallel to the practice of raising the bride that is common among many non-Jewish peoples, and the current widespread practice of carrying the bride over the threshold. See Westermarck, *The History of Human Marriage*, Vol. 2, pp. 535–38 (esp. p. 537 n. 1). For the fashioning of the wedding canopy from synagogue curtains, see Werdiger, p. 205.

8   Yosefov, *Ha-Yehudim ha-Harariyim ba-Kavkaz uve-Yisrael*, p. 180.

The groom takes the wedding ring [*esiksit kadoshey*], that is made of silver and can also contain a precious stone, **dips it in wine**, and shows it to the witnesses, so that they will confirm that it "has the value of a *perutah*" [the minimum legal value for this] [or *ketoya kha para* — ed.]. The groom then places the ring on the bride's finger, while reciting the blessing. The bride is not veiled while this ceremony is conducted, for it happened more than once that another girl had been brought in place of the bride. The groom, who usually is modest and shy, is ordered [by the officiating rabbi] "to kiss her hand," "*dinshok idah*" [while laughing], and the women begin [ululating]: "*Kelililili*." The groom then smashes the cup of wine, the bride is led back to her room, and the men and women sit down to "*se'odit kadoshey*," the wedding banquet.

What is the common source of the practices of such distant and isolated Jewish communities? *Ha-Ittur* writes as follows:[10]

In some localities, the ring is placed in the cup, [the groom] recites the blessing over it, gives to the woman, and says: "Be betrothed to me with what is in it." And all is in accordance with the [accepted] custom.

The origins of this practice can be traced to the writings of the Geonim, for *Seder Rav Saadiah Gaon*[11] cites a tradition according to which the groom declared, before witnesses: "[You are] *arisat* [= *meureset*] to me and *mekudeshet* to me **with this cup and with what is in it**. This is also the

---

9 Brauer, *The Jews of Kurdistan*, p. 96. For various types of wedding rings, see the Brauer collection at the Hebrew University. The Jews of Kurdistan are especially fond of rings with black stones that symbolize the bride's beauty, following Cant. 1:5 (Brauer, p. 96 n. 10), and they apparently were not scrupulous in their avoidance of any addition of precious stones; see above, chap. 18, "Betrothal Rings." Further information on marriage customs of the Jews in Kurdistan may be found in M. Yona, *Kurdish Jewish Encyclopaedia* (Jerusalem, 2003), Vol. 1, pp. 206–11 (Hebrew). As for Bukhara, see Moshavi, "Customs and Folklore of the Nineteenth Century Bukharian Jews," pp. 160–61.

10 *Ha-Ittur*, section 2, p. 63, col. a; cited in Werdiger, p. 39 (but with the reference following the Lvov edition: section 2, 27 beginning of [c]); also cited in Lewin, *Otzar ha-Gaonim*, Vol. 8, Kiddushin, Responsa, p. 11, para. 29.

11 P. 93.

exact, word-for-word version in *Teshuvot ha-Geonim*.[12] This tradition made its way from Tannaitic and Amoraitic sources that discuss M Kiddushin 2:2. The Babylonian Talmud teaches:[13]

> Our masters taught: "Be betrothed to me with this cup" — one [*baraita*] taught: With it and with its contents; another taught: With it, but not with its contents; and yet another taught: With its contents, but without it. This, however, does not pose a difficulty: the first refers to water, the second, to wine, and the third, to *tzihara* [a translucent wine].

And in the Palestinian Talmud:[14]

> [If there is anything] "in this cup" — and if what is in it has the value of a *perutah*, she is [thereby] betrothed, and if not, then she is not betrothed. [According to the view that] she is acquired [i.e. betrothed] with it and with its contents, if its contents have the value of a *perutah*, then she is betrothed; and if not [she is not betrothed]. She is acquired only with its contents.[15]

Saul Lieberman[16] understood an unspecified "cup" as meaning a cup of wine, and "betroths with this cup" (of wine) means with the cup and its contents.[17] He added that it would seem

> that this case, as well, was taken from the reality. And even though, both in theory **and in practice** betrothal was effected with money and with anything of equivalent value [...], and also with a cup of wine [...], logic dictates that for a regular betrothal, that is with the consent of the family, in a festive manner, and with the betrothal blessing,

12 S. Assaf (ed.), *Teshuvot ha-Geonim* (Jerusalem, 1927; added title page in 1942 edn., Vol. 2: *Responsa Geonica*), p. 63, para. 45.

13 BT Kiddushin 48b.

14 PT Kiddushin, 2: beginning of 2, 62(c).

15 See Lieberman, *Tosefta ki-Fshutah*, Vol. 8: *Order Nashim* (New York, 1973), pp. 930–31, and in his glosses, whose version I followed in translating the text from the Palestinian Talmud.

16 Ibid., p. 931.

17 See Meiri on Kiddushin (ed. A. Sofer [Jerusalem, 1963]), loc. cit., p. 239, citing "*yesh mefarshim* [one interpretation]," copied by Lieberman, *Tosefta ki-Fshutah*, loc. cit.

> there undoubtedly was a fixed practice, in the well-known order, as to what was used to effect the betrothal.

It therefore appears that at times betrothal was effected with a cup of wine in which a coin had been placed. Traces of this are to be found in *Mahzor Teiman* (MS.),[18] with the version: "With the wine in this cup **and with the kesef that is in it**." The version of Persian Jews, likewise, reads: "With this cup of wine, and what is in it **of silver and of gold**."[19]

Betrothal with a cup of wine containing a coin was indeed practiced in Yemen by the Jews of Sharab, as is shown by the following description:[20]

> Afterwards the groom prepares a pure silver coin, that is called *anatain*, equivalent in value to the Italian *issar*, or it already was prepared. After he immersed the coin in a ritual bath so that it will be free of taste,[21] for perhaps the coin was impure, or it had been held by someone suffering from boils, or by an impure person, or the coin was under a spell: by washing and immersion, then the ring[!] is tested, because of the case of

18 Cited in *Seder Rav Saadiah Gaon*, p. 93; Lieberman, *Tosefta ki-Fshutah*, loc. cit. See also *Ha-Hillukim she-bein Anshei ha-Mizrah u-Benei Eretz Israel*, pp. 139–40.

19 See Margoliouth in *Ha-Hillukim*, loc. cit., based on E.N. Adler, "The Persian Jews: Their Books and Their Ritual," *JQR* 10 (O.S.) (1898), p. 618. The customs of Persian Jewry are deserving of a separate study. See H. Mizrahi, *The Jews of Persia* (Tel Aviv, 1959) (Hebrew). These versions were also current in the Land of Israel; see, e.g., M.A. Friedman, *Jewish Marriage in Palestine: A Cairo Geniza Study* (Tel Aviv and New York, 1981), Vol. 2, no. 10, p. 101: "[...] you, so-and-so daughter of so-and-so, are betrothed [*mekudeshet*] to me with this cup and with what is in it." See also M.A. Friedman, "Matchmaking and Betrothal Agreements in the Cairo Geniza," *Proceedings of the Seventh World Congress of Jewish Studies: Studies in the Talmud, Halacha and Midrash* (Jerusalem, 1981), pp. 157 ff. (Hebrew).

20 Hozeh, *Sefer Toledot ha-Rav Shalom Shabazi u-Minhagei Yahadut Sharab be-Teiman*, pp. 91–92.

21 Cf. Y.L. Nahum, *Mi-Tzefunot Yehudei Teiman (From the Secrets of Yemenite Jewry)* (Tel Aviv, 1962), p. 161: "Then the groom takes from his pocket a **clean and shiny silver** coin, **after it was cleaned by a silversmith** [emphasis added — D. S.] and gives it to the rabbi. The latter examines it, and shows it to two witnesses. After the examination, they nod their heads in agreement that the coin is fit, and a second cup is immediately filled with wine. The groom stands and holds it in his hand, with the rabbi supporting him [the groom]. Now, however, in addition to the cup, the groom places the coin of betrothal on his palm, **under the cup**" (the early practice was to place the coin of betrothal within the cup of wine, as is shown from the text of the betrothal ceremony).

the ass of Zeiri that is mentioned in the Talmud [BT Sanhedrin 67b]. The cup is poured for the betrothal blessing [...] that is "O virgin bride" [...] you shall become my wife with the wine in this cup **and with this money in it**[22] (**and now he places the coin in the cup**) by which you enter my possession [...] (the groom gives the bride the cup, within which is the coin, before the witnesses, and he says:) "Take your betrothal [money]" (and the bride accepts it from his hand and drinks from the cup). Then the rabbi takes the cup from the woman's hand and pours it out on the earth [...] the money of betrothal still remains within the cup. Then the rabbi rereads the *ketubah* an additional time. The rabbi takes the coin from the cup and wipes it off, he places the coin on the *ketubah* and gives it to the groom. The rabbi orders the bride to extend her hand to receive the money of her betrothal. He then says to the witnesses: "See the groom betrothing the bride by giving, directly from his hand to hers." (For if the witnesses did not see the money of betrothal, from the hand of the groom to the hand of the bride, she is not betrothed [...].) [...] the groom responds after him [i.e. the rabbi], word by word, as follows: "Take your betrothal, and your document of *ketubah*, and everything which is written in it for you, that with them you come into my possession, according to the law of Moses and Israel"; then the groom directly receives from the hand of the groom the *perutah*, that is (*anatain*, written in Arabic), and the *ketubah*, as was mentioned. Then they return to their place to recite the Seven Blessings.

This procedure effects monetary-value betrothal with a coin, and not with a ring.[23] The original purpose of the immersion in water of the coin was definitely to clean it, since it is then placed in the cup of wine from which the groom and bride drink, and coins pass from hand to hand and all manner of dirt and illnesses (as well as impurities and spells, a notion held by the members of the Sharab community) adhere to them. This form of the wedding ceremony is therefore close to those observed by the Cochin community[24] and the Mountain Jews.

---

22 And similarly in *Mi-Tzefunot Yehudei Teiman*: "and with the money in it."
23 Cf. Freimann, *Seder Kiddushin ve-Nissu'in Aharei Hatimat ha-Talmud*, pp. 285, 292.
24 The following description by the inhabitants of Sharab (Hozeh, p. 91) is instructive for our understanding of the Cochin practices: "Then the rabbi gathers four *tzitziyot*

Over the course of time, the effecting of betrothal with a ring, rather than money, or anything else of monetary value, became the universal Jewish

> [ritual fringes] from the groom's *talit* [prayer shawl], and he holds them from one side, and the groom, from the other. The rabbi says to the groom: 'With the *talit*, **including all manner of proviso and condition ad infinitum**,' and the groom responds: '[i.e. I swear] By my *talit*.' The rabbi [then] says: 'Have you accepted everything that is written concerning you in this *ketubah*?' [...] and the groom replies: 'I have accepted.' [The rabbi then says to the groom:] 'Have you accepted this acquisition [binding] by Heaven and earth, by severe oath upon your neck, with the consent of the Omnipresent, blessed be He, and with the consent of this holy congregation.[...]'" The practice of effecting acquisition by holding the *tzitziyot* was discussed by S. Scheiber, *Essays on Jewish Folklore and Comparative Literature* (Budapest, 1987), pp. 106–11, who shows that this procedure has its roots in the Geonic literature, is also mentioned in the Karaite sources, and survived in several Jewish communities until recent generations. Cf. also Kasher, *Torah Shelemah, Toledot*, Vol. 4 (Jerusalem, 1934), p. 1028, para. 165; Nahum, *Mi-Tzefunot Yehudei Teiman*, p. 162. (This possibly is to be linked to what is taught in *Maharil*, ed. Spitzer, p. 471; *Kol Bo, Hil. Ishut [Marriage Law]*, that the wearing of a *talit* by the groom is based on the injunction, "You shall make tassels" [Deut. 22:12] and its proximity to "a man marries a woman" [v. 13]. See *Minhagei Yisrael*, Vol. 3, pp. 60–64.)

In this connection we should draw attention to the interesting Alsace custom recorded by Daniel Stauben (1825–75) in his *Scènes de la vie juive en Alsace*, trans. R. Choron: *Scenes of Jewish Life in Alsace* (Malibu, 1994), p. 109:

> Now we reached the symbolic stage of the engagement. Reb Lippman took a piece of chalk from his huge pocket and traced a circle in the middle of the hall. Then he placed everyone present around it. Schemele [the groom] was facing Deborah [the bride] and Reb Lippman was standing in the middle of the circle. Holding one of his frock tails, he asked all witnesses to touch it one by one. He then turned to the chest of drawers on which a cup had been placed for the purpose. He took the cup and returned to the center of the circle around which the crown was still assembled. Lifting his arm high up, no doubt to increase the force of gravity, he dropped the cup, broke it into a thousand pieces, and then, at the top of his voice, shouted "*masel tof!*" In a chorus, the whole congregation repeated "*masel tof!*" and everybody picked up a fragment of the cup to take home. Thus the engagement was consummated. The circle traced in chalk indicates that from now on the couple may no more deviate from the road that they had entered. The touching of the frock tail by everyone present is, according to the Talmud, a sign of consent to any transaction concluded, whatever its nature. The broken cup, just as the bottle smashed on the wedding day, is a sort of *memento mori* in action: there is no joy without sorrow. And *masel tof*, last but not least, is a Hebrew expression for "good luck" or "congratulations."

practice. Thus we find in the passage from the Yemenite prayerbook cited above, after the wording "With the wine in this cup **and with the coin**

Here we have traces of the original practice of holding the *tzitziyot* (in this instance, a "frock tail"), coupled with the breaking of the cup (see above, chap. 16 ["The Breaking of Plates during the *Tena'im* Ceremony"]), within the symbolically drawn circle (that might have been, to some extent, for protective purposes, guarding against evil spirits).

Apropos the holding of *tzitzit*, Scheiber refers to *Raban* (R. Eliezer ben Nathan of Mainz), *Even ha-Roshah*, cited in *Kol Bo*, end of para. 126 (= N.N. Coronel, "*She'eilot u-Teshuvot Even ha-Roshah le-R. Eliezer bar Natan, z.z.l.,*" *Shomer Tziyyon ha-Ne'eman* 4, *Mikhtav* 193 [Altona, 1855 (photocopy edn.: New York, 1963)], fol. 385b): "A Torah oath: the person who is adjured takes a Torah scroll in his hand; and if he is a Torah scholar, *tefillin* suffice; and according to one opinion, even *tzitzit*." The procedure of a Torah scholar swearing by holding *tefillin* in his hand is based on BT Shevuot 38b: "From the outset, Torah scholars [are adjured] with *tefillin*" (see there). The latter option ("even *tzitzit*"), however, is not in the BT.

Rashi (s.v. "*Be-Sefer Torah*") writes: "In our time the *Rishonim* canceled the Torah oath, since it[s violation] carries a severe punishment, and they enacted the punishment of his being cursed before ten [people]." Rashi refers to a Geonic enactment; see Lewin, *Otzar ha-Gaonim*, Vol. 10 (Jerusalem, 1941), Gittin, Responsa, paras. 166–167, p. 66. *Rabad* (Rabbi Abraham ben David of Posquières), *Hasagot* on Maimonides, *Hil. Shevuot* (*Laws of Oaths*) 13:13, writes:

Abraham said: I heard that the Geonim instituted that a person is not to be adjured at the present time, neither with a [divine] Name nor with a substitute name, so that the world would not be destroyed by the sinners who have become numerous. Rather, he is placed under a ban and cursed. He is placed under the ban with *shofarot* [ram's horns], the extinguishing of candles, and the overturning of beds, to threaten him that if he will sin, he will sin against himself.

References to this enactment appear in the Geonic literature, such as a responsum by a certain Gaon, possibly Rav Natronai Gaon, cited in *Teshuvot Geonim Hemdah Genuzah*, para. 22, which reads: "Know, that by the Torah an oath is not administered for any real estate transaction, as was said by our master, Mar Rav Zadok Gaon, of blessed memory, in the academy, that this [mishnah, governing oaths of biblical authority] was taught [i.e. formulated] in the early generations, that they would administer a Torah oath with a Torah scroll [...] but now, on account of the deceivers [...] the courts refrain from administering oaths with a Torah scroll. [...] The courts realized that instances of taking a false oath have multiplied, and they bring punishments upon [the one who swears falsely] and upon the entire world; they refrained from imposing Torah oaths, and uprooted this entirely." See H. Tykocinski, *The Gaonic Ordinances* (Jerusalem, 1959), chap. 4, "The Cancellation of a Vow Taken by the Name of the Lord," pp. 58–68 (Hebrew); and the recent comprehensive work: I. Schepansky, *The Takkanot of Israel* (Jerusalem and New York, 1993), Vol. 3: *Geonic Enactments*, chap. 12, pp. 302–34 (Hebrew).

that is in it," the prayerbook continues: "it is customary that the *kesef* [i.e. monetary-value object] with which he betroths be **a ring**."[25]

Rif (R. Isaac Alfasi), however, is not party to this view, as we learn from the following passage by *Rashba* (Rabbi Solomon ben Adret) in his novellae on Shevuot 39b, para. 116: "Rashi wrote: 'the *Rishonim* canceled the Torah oath, since it[s violation] carries a severe punishment, and they enacted that [the offender] would be cursed; this means, this cursing is of the nature of taking an oath.' The *Rif* is not of this opinion, for he wrote in a responsum regarding a person who rejected the basic tenets of Judaism, that an equitable oath was administered to him, and after this a single witness testified against him, and he took an oath with an object in his hand [i.e. a full oath]." (Cf. *She'eilot u-Teshuvot Rabbenu Yitzhak Alfasi*, ed. D.Ts. Rothstein [New York, 1975], para. 44, pp. 139–40; see para. 49, pp. 146 ff.) Maimonides shares the view of Alfasi, his teacher's teacher (*Mishneh Torah, Hil. Shevuot*; see Rabbi Y.H. Sofer, *Zekhut Yitzhak*, Vol. 1 [Jerusalem, 1992], pp. 244–48).

For a Torah oath, "the person under oath holds a Torah scroll in his arm, and swears by the [divine] Name, or with a substitute name, or with an adjuration, either from his mouth or from the mouth of the judges. [...] If he held *tefillin* in his hand while the oath is administered to him, he need not take an oath again, for he is holding [a portion of] the Torah in his hand, and they are as a [Torah] scroll. [...] [As regards] Torah scholars, from the outset, he may have the oath administered to him while sitting, with *tefillin* in his hand" (*Hil. Shevuot* 11:8–12). The holding of the *tzitziyot* might possibly be a compromise between the position of the Geonim and that held by Alfasi and Maimonides. The holding of a Torah scroll or *tefillin*, that contain the Name of God, is the same as taking an oath with this Name (but is much more severe), and the taking of such an oath falsely places the entire world at risk. The holding of *tzitziyot*, in contrast, that do not contain the name of God, and are merely a reminder for the commandments (and without *tekhelet* [the azure hue mandated for the *tzitzit*], nor do they recall the Divine Presence), is merely a stringency. (For the difference between *tashmishei mitzvah* [objects for religious use, but without intrinsic holiness] and *tashmishei kedushah* [those objects with intrinsic holiness], that is, between *tzitzit*, on the one hand, and a Torah scroll and *tefillin*, on the other, see also *Shulhan Arukh, Orah Hayyim* 201:1; *Minhagei Yisrael*, Vol. 2, p. 196.) This means that, from one aspect, their being held represents the maintenance of the tradition of taking a religious object and the psychological intensity that this entails, while, from another aspect, it does not have the severity of the taking of an object that contains the Name of God (see *Minhagei Yisrael*, Vol. 1, chap. 3; Vol. 2, chap. 40, for the place of compromise in the fashioning of customs). This discussion leads us to conclude (not without reservations) that *Raban* (R. Eliezer ben Nathan) described two different practices, the one prescribed by Alfasi and Maimonides, of holding *tefillin*, and the other, the compromise that advocates the holding of *tzitziyot* as an interim measure.

The ring as a means of effecting betrothal is not mentioned by the Babylonian Talmud,[26] which speaks only of money, in accordance with M Kiddushin 1:1. Nor is the requirement of a cup of wine explicitly stated in the Talmudic literature, neither before the betrothal blessing, nor preceding that of marriage.[27] This topic first appears in the opening chapter of *Kallah*, with an allusion to the matter in the Palestinian Talmud.[28] Only the Geonic

The ties between Yemen and Cochin were recently discussed by M. Gavra, "18th-Century Yemenite Halakhic Sages," Ph.D. diss., Bar-Ilan University, 1992, p. 132 (Hebrew). A great deal of additional material is to be found in Freimann, *Seder Kiddushin ve-Nissu'in Aharei Hatimat ha-Talmud*, p. 107. See the recent illuminating article, Y. Qafih, "An Ancient Wedding Custom," *Tema* 4 (1994), pp. 42–54 (Hebrew).

It also should be noted that the Caucasian practice is far more rudimentary, and exhibits many signs of a lack of halakhic knowledge, as can be seen from a perusal of Chorny's book. The degree of accuracy, however, in Chorny's discussions is questionable, especially as regards the details of the Caucasian practices and the depth of his understanding of these customs. Further study should be devoted to the folkways of the Caucasus Jews.

25 Assaf, *Teshuvot ha-Geonim*, pp. 63–64 n. 13 (incidentally, he refers to *She'eilot u-Teshuvot ha-Geonim Shaarei Tzedek*, Vol. 3, *Sha'ar* 3, para. 1: "We see that she received the writ of betrothal and כוס of betrothal," and writes that the correct reading is: "וכוס [and the cup]." And in the Jerusalem 1966 edition [p. 36]: "and וכסף [the money] of betrothal," which he views as more reliable).

26 Werdiger, *Edut le-Yisrael*, pp. 38 ff. discusses the question at length, and his examination need not be repeated here; see *She'eilot u-Teshuvot ha-Rashba*, Vol. 1, responsum 1186, cited in *Orhot Hayyim*, Vol. 2, p. 57.

27 See the extended discussion: Werdiger, *Edut le-Yisrael*, pp. 28 ff.

28 PT Sotah 8:5. This issue requires further elaboration, since in Talmudic sources neither the betrothal ceremony nor the actual marriage ceremony required the recitation of a blessing over, and the drinking of, wine. See BT Ketubot 7b–8a:

Our masters taught: The blessing of the bridegrooms [i.e. the wedding ceremony] is recited among ten [people] all seven [days]. R. Judah said: On condition that new faces [i.e. individuals not present previously] come. What blessing does one recite? R. Judah said: [1] "Blessed are You, O Lord our God, King of the Universe, who has created everything for His glory"; and [2] "[...] the Creator of man"; "who has created man in His image, in the image of the likeness of His form, and He prepared for him, from Himself, an everlasting building, Blessed are You, O Lord, the Creator of man"; [4] "May the barren greatly rejoice and exult, at the ingathering of her children within her in joy, Blessed are You, O Lord, who gladdens Zion through her children"; [5] "Thoroughly gladden the beloved companions [i.e. the bride and groom] as You gladdened

literature explicitly states that the wedding ceremony demands a cup, in terms of strict legal requirements.[29] Consequently, the above passage in BT

> Your creatures in the Garden of Eden, in the East, Blessed are You, O Lord, who gladdens the groom and the bride"; [6] "Blessed are You, O Lord our God, King of the Universe, who has created joy and gladness, bridegroom and bride, rejoicing, joyous song, mirth, delight, love, and brotherhood, and peace, and companionship. Speedily, O Lord our God, may there be heard in the cities of Judah and the streets of Jerusalem, the sound of joy and the sound of gladness, the voice of the bridegroom and the voice of the bride, the shouts of joy of grooms from their bridal canopies, and of youths from their feasts of song, Blessed are You, O Lord, who gladdens the bridegroom with the bride."

The Talmud continues by relating that "Levi happened to come to the house of Rabbi, to the wedding feast of his son R. Simeon, [and] recited five blessings" (see below). This ("R. Judah said") appears to be the correct version; while in the version of *Kallah Rabbati* 1 ("and [as for] the seven blessings: what is recited? R. Levi said ...") the name of R. Levi was wrongly inserted, from the continuation of the Talmudic discussion; see M. Hirschler (ed.), *Ketubot*, ed. Makhon ha-Talmud ha-Yisraeli he-Shalem (the Complete Israeli Talmud Institute) (Jerusalem, 1972), pp. מ-מא, n. 1.

The introductory question in the Talmud (Ketubot loc. cit.) is "What blessing does one recite?", while *Kallah Rabbati* begins with "and [as for] the seven blessings: in what manner are they recited?" The list in BT Ketubot comprises only six blessings, while *Kallah Rabbati* enumerates seven, since it includes "... who creates the fruit of the vine." This blessing, however, is not mentioned in Ketubot, as Rabbenu Tam observes (*Sefer ha-Yashar*, ed. Rosenthal, para. 45:5, p. 82): "Even though we have not found the cup in the Talmud, but rather [only] six blessings, we must follow the simple path, since [the recitation of a blessing over] a cup is customary, and R. Yehudai instituted it." R. Jacob ha-Gozer (*Zikhron Berit le-Rishonim*, p. 88) similarly states: "It [the drinking of wine from a cup] is mentioned [in the circumcision blessing] only by the Geonim. R. Yehudai, R. Sherira, and other Geonim instituted it, in the manner of the 7 blessings of the cup of the groom." And, likewise, in R. Simeon bar Zemah, *Teshuvot ha-Tashbetz*, Vol. 3, para. 65:

> The cup of wine is not mentioned in any place in the Talmud, neither in respect to the blessing of betrothal and marriage, nor in respect to circumcision, nor in respect to the redemption of the [firstborn] son, as it is mentioned in respect to *Kiddush* [that sanctifies] the day or in respect to *Havdalah* in the chapter "These are the matters" in [BT] Berakhot [52b], and in the chapter "On the eve of Passover" ([Pesahim] 102b). Maimonides, of blessed memory, wrote, for some of these [halakhic practices that he mentions] the people customarily bring a cup of wine. And, similarly, in the first chapter of Ketubot [8a], when they spoke of the marriage blessing, they said "six blessings," and 7 blessings are not mentioned anywhere. Since they are not obligatory, as they are in *Kiddush*,

Kiddushin — that the woman is betrothed with the cup and with its contents — refers to the value of the latter, that is, the procedure by which betrothal

> they have the legal status of *birkot ha-nehenim* [blessings recited in relation to certain physical pleasures, such as eating, drinking, smelling spices, etc.] [i.e.] they are to be recited only by the one drinking from them [i.e. from the cup], as is mentioned in the chapter "If the Court saw it" ([Rosh Hashanah] 29a). Accordingly, the one reciting the blessing must himself imbibe of [the contents of] the cup, as regards the circumcision blessing, the betrothal blessing, and the marriage blessing. *Tosafot*, however, wrote [...], and, according to our opinion, we learn two things: one, that the one reciting the blessing need not imbibe [...]. Consequently, the obligation [regarding actual drinking from the cup] is fulfilled by the imbibing of the groom and the bride in the betrothal and marriage blessing, and this is not a blessing in vain, [even] if the one reciting the blessing does not imbibe.

We learn from this that the version in *Kallah Rabbati* dates from (or later than) the Geonic period, after the institution of the blessing over wine, when the concept of "seven blessings" came into force. According to one view, the tractate of *Kallah Rabbati* is attributed to the school of R. Yehudai Gaon. R. Levi undoubtedly did not recite the "... who creates the fruit of the vine" blessing, he rather "recited six blessings." The words "except for wine" is a later addition. In the Geonic period in the Land of Israel only three blessings (which have not been identified, since they have sunken into oblivion) were recited, as can be understood from *Ha-Hillukim she-bein Anshei ha-Mizrah u-Benei Eretz Israel*, para. 28, ed. Margoliouth, p. 143: "Those of the East [= Babylonia] bless the groom with seven blessings, and those of the Land of Israel, with three." This means that not only is the version of *Kallah Rabbati* from the Geonic period, it is solely from Babylonia, and not from the Land of Israel, as Margoliouth correctly observes (p. 144).

As regards the dating of the institution of the blessing recited over wine, Rabbenu Tam, as was noted above, maintained that this regulation was enacted in the time of R. Yehudai Gaon. Margoliouth (p. 144 n. 3), however, assigns it an earlier date, during the period of the Savoraim, finding its source in the Geonic responsum published by Harkavy (A. Harkavy, *Zikkaron le-Rishonim ve-gam le-Aharonim* [=*Studien und Mittheilungen aus der Kaiserlichen Oeffentlichen Bibliothek zu St. Petersburg*], Vol. 4 [Berlin, 1887], para. 65, p. 30), in which the "seven blessings" are cited in "the mouth of our early masters, the great ones of the world [...] and so we have learned as being the general [practice] of the rabbis," which, according to Margoliouth, are titles reserved for the Savoraim; see Harkavy's glosses: p. 345 on p. 7; p. 352 on p. 30 l. 16. See also Lewin, *Otzar ha-Gaonim*, Vol. 8, Ketubot, para. 91, p. 28.

Interestingly, the sources also report more than seven blessings. Both the *She'iltot* and Abudarham write, in the name of R. Saadiah Gaon, that blessings were recited, not only over wine, but also over spices, with the formulation "... who creates

is effected with something of monetary value; and at times it was customary to place the betrothal money within the cup, as we saw in the Yemenite prayerbook and in the Persian practice.

species of spices," or "... who creates spice trees" (*Otzar ha-Gaonim*, Ketubot, para. 76, p. 25; para. 77, in the name of *Kol Bo*).

The annals of the blessing recited over the cup of wine were thoroughly investigated by Werdiger, *Edut le-Yisrael*, pp. 28–33, who finds (p. 29) an allusion to the cup in the betrothal ceremony in PT Sotah 8:5 (22[d]), which states: "the wine has a sharp taste [...] and it [is used in the ceremony in which] the bride is betrothed" (based on Rabbi S.J. Zevin, in *Enziklopedyah Talmudit*, Vol. 4, col. 423 n. 44). See also the lengthy exposition by Tamar, *Alei Tamar, Nashim*, Vol. 4 (Tel Aviv, 1982), p. 244, who maintains that, even according to Rabbenu Tam, the blessing over a cup was performed in the Land of Israel already during the time of the Talmud. He uses as a proof-text Gen. Rabbah 8:13, on Gen. 1:28: "'God blessed them' — R. Abbahu said, The Holy One, blessed be He, took a cup of blessing and blessed them." Theodor comments, in his edition of the midrash (p. 66, on l. 7): "'And blessed them' — MS. Paris [149] adds 'seven blessings' in the verse, and the Rabbis instituted in accordance with this model" (this, obviously, is a later addition). See also L. Ginzberg, *Teshuvah bi-Devar Yeinot ha-Kesherim veha-Pesulim le-Mitzvah* (*A Response Concerning Wines that Are Fit or Unfit for Ritual Use*) (New York, 1922), pp. 21–22, concerning PT Sotah; and the version in his *Yerushalmi Fragments from the Genizah* (New York, 1909), p. 215 n. 3: "*u-me'arsin bo*" instead of "*mekadshin bo*." He also suggests in his *Teshuvah* that this refers to the same practice of betrothing "with a cup and its contents," i.e. a coin or a ring, but concludes (Ginzberg, *Teshuvah bi-Devar Yeinot*, p. 22) that we can hardly say that during the time of the Palestinian Talmud the act of betrothal was conducted with the recital of a blessing over a cup of wine (see below, chap. 22, "The Wedding Ring in the Cup of Wine"). He ends his discussion with the following proposal:

It therefore seems to me that the correct version in the Palestinian Talmud is "*u-mekadshin bo*" — or *alav* [over it]. The simple meaning is that Kiddush is recited over fermented wine [i.e. as opposed to grape juice] on Sabbaths and Festivals, as is stated in our [version of] the Talmud. The words "*et ha-kallah*" [the bride] were added by scribes who derived this from the adjoining passages: when, immediately following, it was stated that the mourner is consoled with it [the wine], they thought that *mekadshim* [which really means, in this context, consoling the mourner] refers to [the betrothal of] the bride.

If his analysis is correct, then this is a relatively early addition, from the Geonic period; as *Soferim* 19:9 (ed. Higger, p. 334; see the glosses ad loc.), which is from this period, attests: "our masters were accustomed to recite the grooms' blessing over a cup, in [the presence of] ten." Some *Rishonim* cite a teaching from the Palestinian

As time passed, however, all Jewish communities adopted the procedure of effecting betrothal with a (gold) ring,[30] together with the practice of both the groom and bride drinking from the wine that began in the Geonic period.[31] The literature and the early versions of the betrothal declaration that became enrooted in different Jewish communities notwithstanding, indicate that betrothal was also effected "with this cup and with its contents [i.e. the wine]," which they understood as referring to the cup of wine from which

Talmud that mentions the cup of betrothal and marriage, such as *Rokeah*, para. 352 (ed. Schneersohn, p. 339): "Palestinian Talmud, in [6:1] 'how is the blessing of the fruit of the vine performed' — how is wine different? Since it has many uses, for *Kiddush* and for *Havdalah*, it is [also used] for betrothal and for *huppah*." *Ravyah* (Vol. 1, para. 98, ed. Aptowitzer, p. 77) offers a similar explanation, with the editor observing (n. 16): "This entire teaching [...] is not in the extant Palestinian Talmud; its place is in Berakhot 6:1 [...] and it is from '*Sefer Yerushalmi*'" (for the latter book, see the gloss by Aptowitzer: p. 9 n. 17). Even, in "*Sefer Yerushalmi*," however, this is quite an early addition.

We learn from all this that although Midrash Rabbah, in the name of R. Abbahu, seemingly alludes to a Land of Israel practice (as early as the time of the Amoraim) to bless the couple over a cup of wine, it is unclear whether or not this was a fixed procedure until the Geonic period, according to *Soferim* and that "*Sefer Yerushalmi*." As long as we are uncertain of the version in PT Sotah, this issue cannot be definitively resolved.

In contrast, the wedding blessing was incontrovertibly not recited over a cup of wine during the Talmudic period in Babylonia, where it was instituted only during the time of the early Geonim.

29 See Werdiger, *Edut le-Yisrael*, pp. 28 ff.; *Mahzor Vitri*, p. 592.

30 Werdiger, pp. 37–41; Margoliouth, *Ha-Hillukim she-bein Anshei ha-Mizrah u-Benei Eretz Israel*, pp. 139–40. Coins were still used for this purpose in some localities. See, e.g., Chorny, *Sefer ha-Massa'ot be-Eretz Kavkaz*, p. 155: his description of a betrothal ceremony in the village of Soram: "The groom's father brought to the rabbi two gold coins and a few pearls, and put them in his hand **as [the means of] betrothal**, since the rabbi is to be his agent for conducting the betrothal of his son with the bride. [...] The rabbi gave one coin to the father of the bride as a sort of earnest money, or to seal the agreement. **He keeps the second coin in his hand as [the means of] betrothal**. [...] The rabbi approached her and gave in her hand the silver (gold?) coin, and said to her: 'I am the agent of the groom, behold, you are betrothed with this coin, on behalf of the groom, so-and-so son of so-and-so, in accordance with the law of Moses and Israel.' Then, when she received her coin and the betrothal was effected, she grabbed [...] the hand of the sage and kissed it."

31 Werdiger, *Edut le-Yisrael*, pp. 28–38.

the new couple drank. This, in turn, led to the strange development of placing the ring within the wine, sipping from it, and then removing the ring from the wine and giving it to the bride.

The picture that emerges from this discussion is that this practice, in the manner in which it was preserved by the Jews of the Caucasus and Cochin,[32] is enrooted in a literary source (either written or oral, as the version of the text recited by the groom) whose original purpose was no longer relevant, to be replaced by the refashioning of a practice of renewed significance, based on the early traditional version: "You are *arisat* and *mekudeshet* to me with this cup and with its contents."

---

32 The Mountain Jews of the Caucasus apparently received their custom via Persia, while the practice of the Cochin community came from Yemen.

23

THROWING A SHOE AT A WEDDING

We have already noted elsewhere[1] the difficulty in determining the direction of influence between Jewish and non-Jewish customs, that is, whether a certain practice that is observed both by Jews and non-Jews came from the Gentile world to the Jewish one, or the opposite. We have a strange custom, one that is quite widespread in non-Jewish culture: the throwing of an old shoe (or shoes) after the bride and groom. This custom is to be found in England, Scotland, Denmark, in the Rhine region, among the Gypsies in Transylvania, in Greece, Turkey, and other locations.[2] Thus, for example, Edward Westermarck attests to a Moroccan practice:[3]

1   *Minhagei Yisrael*, Vol. 1, p. 233.
2   Westermarck compiled a wealth of material in *The History of Human Marriage*, Vol. 2, p. 539; the following is a partial bibliography of the testimonies to this phenomenon. W. Gregor, "Some Marriage Customs in Cairaibuly in Inverallochy," *Folk-Lore Journal* 1 (London, 1883), p. 91 (Scotland); H.F. Feilberg, *Bidrag til en ordbog over jyske almuesmal*, Vol. 3 (Copenhagen, 1912), p. 642; *idem, Tellaeg og rettelser* (Copenhagen, 1911–12), p. 64 (Denmark); Samter, *Geburt, Hochzeit und Tod*, p. 189 (Rhineland); p. 198 (Greece); H. von Wlislocki, *Vom wandernden Zigeunervolke: Bilder aus den Leben der Siebenburger Zigeuner; geschichtliches, ethnologisches, Sprache und Poesie* (Hamburg, 1890), p. 189 (Gypsies); M.R. Cox, *An Introduction to Folk-Lore* (London, 1897), p. 18 (Turkey). See also Radford, *Encyclopaedia of Superstitions*, p. 218; Opie and Tatem, *A Dictionary of Superstitions*, p. 351. Additionally, see Westermarck, *Marriage Ceremonies in Morocco*, Vol. 1, pp. 257–58 n. 2. This practice crossed borders and continents, as can be seen by its observance in the United States. We find in Hyatt, *Folk-Lore from Adams County, Illinois*, p. 370, no. 7352: "The throwing of an old shoe after a newly wedded couple brings them good luck"; loc. cit., no. 7353: "If you throw an old shoe at a bridal pair and it hits one of them, they will be lucky"; p. 371,

In the Hiaina the bridegroom, accompanied by the *islan*, goes to the door of the house in which the bride is waiting. He is there left alone by his friends, and enters the house. He cuts with his sword the rope which has been tied from wall to wall in front of the bed; this is to cut off the *bas*. He gently slaps the bride on her forehead and shoulders with the flat of his sword, so as to expel evil spirits. He takes off her right slipper, removes the needle which her mother has put into it as a protection against *jnun*, and throws it away, at the same time throwing away the *bas*, and then puts the slipper back on her foot. He plaits the hair on the right side of her head, opens her *mansoriya* or *qaftan*, takes hold of her, and pulls her up to stand.[4] She now removes his slippers; there was said to be some magic in this, perhaps the bridegroom thereby hopes to become master.

There are many variations of this custom, such as that described by Bonnerjea:[5] "Old shoes are tied on to the bridal carriage for luck (Great Britain), or in Transylvania, to enhance the fertility of the union."[6] And similarly:[7]

Almost everyone is aware of the tradition of tying a pair of old shoes to the back of a newlywed couple's car. In ancient times, the father of the bride threw an old shoe to the couple. This signified that his daughter had now become the property of the groom.

no. 7378: "Let someone throw an old shoe among the guests at a wedding, and the person hit by the shoe will be the first one of that group to marry." See Hyatt's introduction, pp. xv–xvi, for the ethnic composition of the population in the region: "[...] British, [...] German, Dutch, [...] Celtic and Scandinavian descent." It would be appropriate here to mention another Jewish practice that apparently migrated all the way to Adams County. We know of the custom (albeit without knowledge of its origin) of dancing with a broom at the wedding of the youngest son in the family (the "*mezhinik*" in Yiddish). As this was practiced in that part of Illinois (ibid., p. 372, no. 7379): "Let the bridegroom hold a broom and stand on one side of the room and have the unmarried men line up at the opposite side of the room. At a given signal they must race towards the broom, and the first one to reach it will be the first to marry." For more on the broom, see Westermarck, *Ritual and Belief in Morocco*, Vol. 1, pp. 595–96.

3   Westermarck, *Marriage Ceremonies in Morocco*, pp. 236–37.
4   See above, chap. 18 ("Some Wedding Preparations").
5   Bonnerjea, *A Dictionary of Superstition and Mythology*, p. 228, s.v. "Shoe."
6   With a reference to E. Hartland, *The Legend of Perseus* (London, 1894), p. 171.
7   *Zolar's Encyclopedia of Omens, Signs, and Supersititions* (New York, 1995), p. 325.

In addition to the interpretation offered by Zolar, that the bride had passed from her father's domain to that of the husband, many other explanations have been presented, such as this being a remnant of the custom to kidnap the bride;[8] or that, in some way, it symbolized fertility;[9] that it served to drive away demons and destructive agents;[10] or was a gift to the latter.[11] All of these views are cited by Westermarck;[12] since none is in itself sufficient, he concludes:[13]

> It is probable that the various rites in which shoes are used owe their origin to more than one idea.

Each of these proposals might conceivably be partially correct for a certain time and place; that is, in a specific country in which this custom was common, it was understood as a means to be rid of demons, to increase fecundity, and the like.

All this, however, does not properly explain the origin of the practice, and how the throwing of a shoe has such a specific effect. The answer seemingly was formulated by Knowlson, who writes:[14]

---

8 J.F. McLennan, *Studies in Ancient History: Comprising a Reprint of Primitive Marriage: An Inquiry into the Origin of the Form of Capture in Marriage Ceremonies* (London, 1886), p. 14.

9 A. Sartori, "Die Schuh im Volksglauben," *Zeitschrift des Vereins fur Volkskunde* 4 (Berlin, 1894), p. 153; Aigremont (S. von Schultze-Gallera), *Fuss- und Schuhsymbolik und- Erotik: folkloristische und sexualwissenschaftliche Untersuchungen* (Leipzig, 1909), p. 55; E.S. Hartland, *Primitive Paternity: The Myth of Supernatural Birth in Relation to the History of the Family* (London, 1909), Vol. 1, p. 10; E.H.P.A. Haeckel (Heikel), *Sandalion: Beitrage zur antiken Zauberriten bei Geburt* (Helsinki, 1915), pp. 36 ff.

10 T. Zachariae, "Zum altindischen Hochzeitsritual," *Vienna Oriental Journal* 17 (1903), p. 138; W. Crooke, *The Popular Religion and Folk-Lore of Northern India* (Westminster, 1896), Vol. 1, pp. 33 ff.; H.O. Rosen, *Om dodsrike och dodsbruk i fornnordisk religion* (Lund, 1918), pp. 152 et seq.

11 E. Samter, "Hochzeitsbrauche," *Neue Jahrbuche fur die klassische Altertum Geschichte fur deutsche Literatur und fur Paedagogik*, Vol. 19 (Leipzig, 1907), pp. 134 et seq.; *idem, Geburt, Hochzeit und Tod*, pp. 201 et seq.

12 Westermarck, *Ritual and Belief in Morocco*, Vol. 1, pp. 540–41.

13 Ibid., p. 541; see the continuation of his discussion.

14 T. S. Knowlson, *The Origins of Popular Superstitions and Customs* (London, 1995), p. 104.

> It was in the sense of confirming a sale or exchange that the Jews understood the removal and giving of a shoe or sandal.

Knowlson's intent is to the historical explanation in Ruth (4:7): "Now this was formerly done in Israel in cases of redemption or exchange: to validate any transaction, one man would take off his sandal and hand it to the other. Such was the practice in Israel" — a practice that is reminiscent of the *halitzah* ceremony in Deut. 25:9: "His brother's widow shall go up to him in the presence of the elders, pull the sandal off his foot, spit in his face [...]." This biblical injunction is the source of the practice set forth in the Palestinian Talmud:[15]

> At first, acquisition was effected by the removal of one's shoe. This is [the meaning of] what is written: "Now this was formerly done in Israel in cases of redemption or exchange: to validate any transaction, one man would take off his sandal" [Ruth 4:7]. There they say: Rav and Levi: One says, The purchaser, and the other says: The seller, for this disagreement corresponds with the dispute in the following case, for it is taught: Boaz gave to the redeemer. R. Judah says: The redeemer gave to Boaz.[16]

15 PT Kiddushin 1:5.
16 Cf. Radford, *Encyclopaedia of Superstitions*, p. 218. For the passage in PT Kiddushin, see Rabbi I. Tamar, *Alei Tamar: Yerushalmi — Seder Nashim* (Jerusalem, 1982), pp. 409–10. Gaster, *Myth, Legend, and Custom in the Old Testament*, Vol. 2, para. 123, pp. 449–50, 540, discusses the reason and source for the removal of the shoe as signifying divorce, *halitzah* (see chap. 26, below), and the like. He then provides five suggestions, the first four of which he rejects before finally, and somewhat skeptically, proposing: "Not impossibly, the true explanation lies in the fact that the shoe was a symbol of authority; the ceremonial removal of it therefore indicated that such authority had been surrendered." According to this proposition (see the continuation of his discussion), the removal of the shoe may, possibly, also symbolize the removal of ownership, that is, an act of acquisition. See also E. Stern, s.v. *"Na'al [Shoe]," Enziklopedyah Mikra'it (Encyclopaedia Biblica)*, Vol. 5 (Jerusalem, 1965), col. 891: the removal of the shoe is related to the transferal of ownership, and "according to [E.A.] Speiser ["Of Shoes and Shekels," *BASOR* 77 (1940), pp. 15–18], this practice is mentioned in I Sam. 12:3, where the reading of the Septuagint is to be followed: 'ransom and a shoe? Testify against me, and I will return it to you,' instead of 'From whom have I taken a bribe to look the other way?'[?]. He interprets in a similar spirit Amos 2:6; 8:6, where, he contends, shoes symbolize the transferal of ownership from the pauper to the rich man; see the

That is to say, acquisition is effected by the removal of one's shoe, either by the seller or by the purchaser. The details of this ancient practice, that has not been followed for ages, and that has been superseded by the custom of "cutting off,"[17] and other manners of acquisition, are not known, thus resulting in the disagreement between Rav and Levi concerning the manner of its performance. Its memory, however, remained vibrant over the course of time, and was practiced in various forms by non-Jews as well, perhaps based on their understanding of the verses in Deuteronomy and Ruth. When, for example, in the early nineteenth century, King Vladimer desired to marry the daughter of Reginald, the latter responded: "I will not take off my shoe to the son of a slave."[18]

A remnant of this custom may have survived among the Jews of Kurdistan, as is reported by Erich Brauer:[19]

> The groom is also advised that, prior to the Seven Blessings, he is to remove one of his shoes, and during the recitation of the Seven Blessings [during the wedding ceremony], he is to slowly put his foot into the shoe, so that by the conclusion of the blessings, the shoe will once again be on his foot.[20]

It would therefore appear, in conclusion, that the ancient Israelite method of acquisition by the removal of one's shoe, which is hardly remembered in the various Jewish communities (with a possible trace remaining among the

commentary by R. David Kimhi on this verse. Speiser also finds a reference to this practice in the Nuzi documents, which tell of two unusual instances of the transferal of real estate, that were affirmed by the ceremony of the removal of a shoe."

17 PT Kiddushin 1:5; Ketubot end of chap. 2.
18 Knowlson, *The Origins of Popular Superstitions and Customs*, p. 104; Radford, *Encyclopaedia of Superstitions*, loc. cit. According to another tradition, however, she said: "I do not wish to take off the shoes of a coward." See Sokolov, *Russian Folklore*, p. 207. If so, then removing the man's shoes is a mark of her submission to him. See above, chap. 13, n. 7.
19 Brauer, *The Jews of Kurdistan*, p. 111.
20 See Frazer, *Taboo and the Perils of the Spirit* (Vol. 3 of *The Golden Bough*; New York, 1935), p. 300: "In some parts of the Highlands it was deemed enough that the bridegroom's left shoe should be without buckle or lachet, 'to prevent the witches from depriving him, on the nuptial night, of the power of loosening the virgin zone.'" This, however, ensues from a completely different notion. See also pp. 311–13, for Greek soldiers going forth to war wearing only a single shoe, and Frazer's interpretation of this custom.

Jews of Kurdistan), was observed in a different manner by several European peoples. Since the origin of their practice has not been unequivocally determined, differing reasons and explanations have been suggested, in accordance with their respective culture and beliefs.

24

"CONFETTI": THE THROWING OF WHEAT KERNELS AT WEDDINGS

In Bodenschatz's book[1] we see how wheat, or seeds, are thrown next to the wedding canopy, and children (!) collect them (see Figs. 1, 2). The same motif appears in a copper engraving from the eighteenth century attributed to Calmet.[2] The custom of throwing wheat is already mentioned by R. Eleazar ben Judah of Worms:[3]

> As for the practice of throwing wheat at the groom and the bride when they are brought early Friday morning, in accordance with "[He endows your realm with well-being,] and satisfies you with choice wheat" [Ps. 147:14]. And in [BT] Berakhot, the chapter "If Three Persons Have Eaten" [50b]: "Roasted ears of corn and nuts may be cast in front of them in the summer, but not in the rainy season."

Tosafot[4] explains the reason for this distinction:

> Even though the food inside nuts does not become loathsome, they nevertheless become loathsome when they fall in the mud. Now, however, when it is customary to throw wheat in the wedding room, care must be taken that they be thrown only in a clean place.

1   Bodenschatz, *Kirchliche Verfassung der heutigen Juden, sonderlich derer in Deutschland*, Vol. 4, fig. 11, opposite pp. 127c, the roundel in the upper left corner.
2   In the catalogue: Pappenheim, *The Jewish Wedding*, p. 39; see above, chap. 22, "The Wedding Ring in the Cup of Wine," p. 265.
3   *Rokeah*, para. 352, p. 239.
4   *Tosafot*, Berakhot 50b, s.v. *"Ve-Lo bi-Yemot ha-Geshamim."*

Based on this *Tosafot*, and additional *Rishonim, Shulhan Arukh*[5] rules:

> Those throwing wheat before grooms must take care to throw only in a clean place, and also that they [the wheat kernels] be swept away from there, so that they not be stepped on.

This law is cited by Buxtorf:[6]

> Tum sponsus sponsam acceptam semel quoque circumducit; populus autem in illos frumentum conjicit, et omnes conclamant: Pru urefu *Fructificate et multiplicamini*: Cavendum vero, ut frumentum nonnisi in locam mundam conjiciatur, et postea grana diligenter convenantur, ne pedibus conculcentur.

Buxtorf adds that wealthy Jews would occasionally include coins for the poor with the wheat. His description also is brought, in slightly different style, by Bodenschatz.[7]

The recitation of the blessing of *"Peru u-rvu"* ("Be fruitful and multiply") when the wheat is thrown is also mentioned by R. Jacob ben Moses Moellin:[8]

> When she [the bride] reaches the entrance of the synagogue courtyard, the rabbi and the dignitaries go and lead the groom to the bride. The groom takes her in his hand, and when they are together, all the crowd throws wheat on their heads, and they say three times: "Be fruitful and multiply."[9]

This blessing already appears in the writings of the *Rishonim*, such as *Mahzor Vitri* (p. 589): "Wheat is thrown upon them as a sign of blessing: 'Be fruitful and multiply with success in everything good,' and satisfies you with choice wheat." Here, however, all this follows the wedding ceremony, while in the other sources cited above they precede the ceremony.[10]

---

5 *Shulhan Arukh, Orah Hayyim* 171:5.
6 Buxtorf, *Synagoga Judaica*, p. 631.
7 Bodenschatz, *Kirchliche Verfassung der heutigen Juden*, Vol. 4, p. 124, para. 14; and, in abbreviated form, also in Leusden, *Philologus Hebraeo-Mixtus*[2], p. 174.
8 *Sefer Maharil*, p. 464.
9 And similarly, in *Sefer Minhagim de-ve Maharam ... me-Rotenberg*, p. 83; Schammes, *Wormser Minhagbuch*, Vol. 2, p. 25.
10 See Adler, *Nisu'in ke-Hilkhatam*, Vol. 2, chap. 18, para. 45, pp. 584–85, for the various views regarding the order of these practices. Cf. Werdiger, *Edut le-Yisrael*, p. 56.

R. Jousep Juspa Kaschmann adds,[11] after mentioning the practice, in the name of R. Jacob ben Moses Moellin, that "חלב חטים ישביעך [satisfies you with choice wheat] has the same numerical value as חתן וכלה [groom and bride]."[12] Schammes adds (ad loc.): "It is customary for the fathers of the groom and of the bride to bring them [the wheat kernels] in their hand, in a small bowl." This detail, however, does not appear in the illustration in Bodenschatz, nor in his verbal description; and it also is omitted from the book by Buxtorf (Bodenschatz's primary source).[13]

Intriguingly, although, as we saw above, the *Shulhan Arukh* prohibits trampling on the wheat kernels that are now scattered about, R. Jair Hayyim Bacharach (the author of *Havvat Yair*) wrote in his commentary *Mekor Hayyim*:[14]

> "and also that they be swept away" — this is also written in *Hagahot Maimoniyot*, **but this was not the practice**. The custom here is to throw wheat on the heads of the groom and bride on the morning of the wedding day, as they walk about in the special room known as the "Braut Haus,"[15] **and all the people trample, and do not refrain**.

11 Kaschmann, *Noheg ka-Tzon Yosef*, "Marriage," para. 7, p. 113.

12 This numerical-value equation also appears in an early manuscript cited in *Nahalat Shivah*, second edition, fol. 19a; Schammes, *Wormser Minhagbuch*, Vol. 2, p. 25 n. 20. See also the editor's gloss, *Sefer Maharil*, p. 464, n. 3, which provides additional sources; Schammes, loc. cit., nn. 20, 21.

13 Nor is it to be found in da Modena, *Historia dei Riti Ebraici* 4:3, pp. 85–88, which was often used as a source for many later authors. The book was most probably written ca. 1616. See Modena's autobiography: *Hayye Yehuda*, ed. A. Kahana (Kiev, 1911), p. 56, cited by S. Sabar, "The Beginnings of *Ketubbah* Decoration in Italy: Venice in the Late Sixteenth to the Early Seventeenth Centuries," *Journal of Jewish Art* 12–13 (1986/87), p. 99 n. 23.

14 *Shulhan Arukh Orah Hayyim im ha-Perush Mekor Hayyim* (*Shulhan Arukh, Orah Hayyim*, with the *Mekor Hayyim* Commentary), ed. E.D. Pines, Vol. 2 (*Kitzur Halakhot*), 171:5 (Jerusalem, 1984), p. 223.

15 For the "Brat Haus," see the editor's gloss, Schammes, *Wormser Minhagbuch*, Vol. 2, pp. 7–8, n. 48 (and p. 32 n. 66). This term means "the bride's house." Actually, this was a wedding hall, and is described in *Mekor Hayyim*, loc. cit., as "a special room known as *Braut Haus*." Other sources call it the "*Tanz Haus*" (dance house). Already in the period of the *Rishonim*, this place was the venue of the wedding ceremony and of dancing, as is indicated by *Sefer Hasidim*, ed. Margaliot, para. 4, pp. 53–54: "It once happened that a pietist was sitting in the wedding ceremony house, and he heard one of the singers in the dances." This hall belonged to the

Even if this was the custom in the community of R. Bacharach (1639–1702), that is, Worms in the second half of the seventeenth century, the illustration of Bodenschatz shows their care in not stepping on the kernels that they

community, as we learn from R. Meir of Rothenburg, *She'eilot u-Teshuvot Maharam ben Barukh mi-Rotenburg* (Prague ed.), para. 118, who mentions "the wedding house of the community." See also A. Berliner, *Hayyei ha-Yehudim be-Ashkenaz be-Yemei ha-Beinayim* (*The Life of the Jews in Ashkenaz in the Medieval Period*) = *Aus dem Leben der Juden Deutschlands im Mittelalter* (Warsaw, 1900 [photocopy edn. Israel 1969]), pp. 70, 79. This is not to be confused with *beit ha-kallah*, which was the actual bride's house. Incidentally, the description by Schammes, op. cit., p. 7, corresponds exactly to the illustration in Bodenschatz: "The bride goes first, with her two maids to her right and to her left, and all the maidens after them, with the *leitzanim* [here, musicians] preceding them with musical instruments, making music from the bride's house to the *Braut Haus*," just as this scene is portrayed in the illustration in Bodenschatz: we see her going forth from a wooden house, the house "of the bride," flanked by "her two maids," followed by the maidens, with the musicians preceding her, and the entire procession makes its way to the wedding canopy that is in the upper right roundel in the picture, next to the synagogue. In the picture we see that the private house, that of the bride, is of wood, as were most people's houses; only a number of public structures, such as the synagogue, were of stone construction, as in this illustration. See Pollack, *Jewish Folkways in Germanic Lands (1648–1806)*, p. 1.

26 For the custom, in non-Jewish cultures, of throwing seeds at the bride, or at the new couple, see Westermarck, *The History of Human Marriage*, Vol. 2, pp. 470–84. This, of course is the source for the practice of throwing confetti at the newlyweds, which began in Italy (Westermarck, p. 475; G. Pitre, *Usi e costumi credenze e pregiudizi del populo siciliano* [Palermo, 1889], Vol. 2, pp. 72 ff.; A. Bresciani, *Dei costumi dell' isola di Sardegna comparati cogli antichissimi populi italiano* [Naples, 1850], Vol. 2, p. 154; G. Faggiani, "Feste ed usanze della Sardegna," in D. Provenzal, *Usanze e feste del populo italiano* [Bologna, 1912], p. 232), continuing from there to many other lands. In a number of countries, including ancient and modern Greece, coins were sometimes among the items that were thrown (Westermarck, pp. 473–74).

We have already (above, chap. 21, "*Huppah*") pointed out a number of parallels between the Jewish wedding ceremonial customs and those of the Romans. Here we may note what appears in Smith, Wayte, and Marindin, *Dictionary of Greek and Roman Antiquities*, Vol. 2, p. 1441, s.v. "*Matrimonium, Nuptiae*": "The part of the bridegroom in the procession [after the marriage ceremony] was to scatter nuts for the boys in the crowd (Vergil, *Ecl.*, 8,30; Catullus 61,131). Though Catullus says that it shows the putting away of childhood, it is much more likely that the nuts symbolised the fruitfulness of marriage and plenty (cf. Plin. *N. H.* 15:86). The custom, which may be compared with the Greek καταχύσματα [sweetmeats

collected, with the throwing being performed in a clean place, next to the wedding ceremony, all in accordance with the verbal description given by Buxtorf, who in turn followed his rabbinic sources.[26]

poured on the wedded pair at the entrance to the bridegroom's house] (*supra* [Smith et al.], p. 136a), has its representative in the throwing of rice at the present day."

Of interest for this discussion is the painting by Stryjowki (Poland, mid-nineteenth century) that was in Budapest, disappeared after a robbery, and later resurfaced. In the reproduction in the *Jewish Encyclopedia*, Vol. 8, opposite p. 346 (Fig. 3), we see a woman throwing something from inside her apron, and children rolling on the ground in search of the wheat or candies that were thrown. All this happens next to the canopy for the wedding that is held outdoors, in front of the synagogue. This painting was the source of a silver wedding plate that appears in Kaniel, *A Guide to Jewish Art*, pp. 62–63. This painting was mentioned, without discussion, in H. Nelken, *Images of a Lost World: Jewish Motifs in Polish Painting, 1770–1945* (New York, 1991), pp. 114–15, with detail no. 194, characterizing this as a "wood engraving"(?). Attention should also be paid to the staircase ascending to the women's section in which women and children stand and gaze upon the ceremony; a similar set of stairs is depicted in Oppenheim's *Die Trauung* (see above chapter 21, Figs. 13, 14). It would appear that external staircases led to the women's sections of synagogues in both Germany and Poland. This was the case in the Neuschul synagogue in Frankfurt am Main (built in 1711), in which external stairs led to the three levels of the women's section (Oppenheimer himself lived in Frankfurt a.M.). See Wischnitzer, *The Architecture of the European Synagogue*, pp. 76–77. And, likewise, in the engraving by Bernard Picart, *Manière de conduire les Epaux de la loi chez eux*, which portrays the procession of the *Hatan Torah* and *Hatan Bereshit* to their homes from the synagogue, which has an external set of stairs leading up to the women's section; in the synagogue in Gwozdziec, Galicia, which dates from the seventeenth century (ibid., pp. 141–42); in Mogilev, Byelorussia, also from the seventeenth century; in Nasielsk, formerly in Poland; and in Lutomiersk. See Landsberger, "Jewish Artists before the Emancipation," p. 391, and fig. 12. For the throwing of wheat at weddings, see, recently, Dvorkes, *Bi-Shvilei ha-Halakhah, Shabbat u-Mo'adim*, pp. 97–99, 186–87.

1. Bodenschatz, Erlang 1748

2. Detail of Fig. 1

3. Stryowski, late 19th century

25

"HOW THEY DANCE BEFORE THE BRIDE"

Zvi Friedhaber[1] revealed that Jews in European communities engaged in mixed dancing at various social events, and especially at weddings, as we learn from the different warnings issued against this practice.[2] Men and women dancing together appear in an illumination from MS. Rothschild 24 (Italy, ca. 1470)[3] (Fig. 1). The custom of mixed dancing is explicitly permitted in the regulations of the community of Padua, in Italy:

> It was likewise enacted that men may not dance together with married women, no male with a married female, except on Purim. They may, however, dance with unmarried women, provided that the males will be dressed differently [from the women].[4]

---

1   Z. Friedhaber, "Religious-Ceremony Dances, Their History, Forms, and Dancers," *Dukhan: Journal for Jewish Music and Liturgy* 15 (eds. I.S. and A. Recanati) (2000), pp. 29–40 (Hebrew). See the entire book: Klein, *Wedding Traditions of the Various Jewish Communities*, which contains much diverse material concerning dancing among different communities.

2   Friedhaber, op. cit., pp. 30–31. For additional relevant sources, see S. Kats, *Kedoshim Tihiyu* (*Laws and Conduct in Society and the Youth Movement Concerning the Laws of Modesty*) (Jerusalem, 1979), pp. 47–57 (Hebrew).

3   See Hakohen, *Hayyei Adam: Kelulot*, p. 72.

4   From the community regulations of Padua (1507). See R. Bonfil, "Aspects of the Social and Spiritual Life of the Jews in the Venetian Territories at the Beginning of the 16th Century," *Zion* 41 (1976), p. 71 (Hebrew). See for bibliography on this topic: Y. Ahituv, "Modesty from Mythos to Ethos," in *A Good Eye: Dialogue and Polemic in Jewish Culture. A Jubilee Book in Honor of Tova Ilan*, ed. Y. Ahituv et al. (Israel, 1999), p. 245 (Hebrew); A. Grossman, *Pious and Rebellious: Jewish Women in Europe in the Middle Ages* (Jerusalem, 2001), pp. 254–55 (Hebrew).

Friedhaber pays special attention to the singular conception of R. Johanan Luria (late fifteenth-early sixteenth centuries) concerning dancing. Luria wrote, concerning singing and dancing by women:

> It is only for the maidens [literally, virgins] to entice men so that the latter shall seek them out — it is proper to protest against women who sing before brides in the presence of men. Only maidens are permitted to do so, to be endeared of the young men, so that they will jump after them for the purpose of matrimony.[5]

Such a tableau of a young woman dancing before the bride and groom after the wedding ceremony appears in a postcard from 1912 (Fig. 2),[6] and in a painting by the renowned artist Eugène Delacroix, *Noce juive au Maroc* (above chap. 21, Fig. 29).[7]

This practice, however, did not go unopposed. Thus, for example, the unequivocal formulation by R. Joseph Hayyim ben Elijah Al-Hakam, the author of *Ben Ish Hai*:[8]

> Even the dancing of women by themselves before men is forbidden, for this will arouse the evil inclination of the men who are watching. Several of the later rabbinical authorities cried out against such as this, that they do not have permission based on [the requirement to] cause the groom and bride to rejoice.

As depicted in the painting by Delacroix, dancing by women in front of the men at a wedding in North Africa apparently had been customary in previous generations, as well. In the eleventh century a sage from the community of Gabes, Morocco, directed a query to Rav Hai Gaon, in which he related:

> It is the practice in our places, that in the houses of the groom and the

An accurate artistic portrayal of these Purim parties, in which masked men and women danced together, appears in Porter and Harel-Hoshen, *Odessy of the Exiles*, p. 58.

5   Rabbi Johanan Luria, *Meshivat Nefesh*, MS. Oxford Opp. Add. 4091; Institute of Microfilmed Hebrew Manuscripts, Jewish National and University Library, no. 16726, *Beshalah*, fol. 81a.

6   See E. Duda, *Old Jewish Postcards from Marek Sosenko's Collection* (Cracow, 1998), fig. 93.

7   Oil on canvas (1837–1841), Louvre Museum, Paris.

8   *Ben Ish Hai, Shoftim*, para. 18.

bride, women beat on drums and engage in dancing, and non-Jews are brought to gladden with the music of the lyre, the timbrel, and the pipe.

In his response, R. Hai Gaon writes:

Regarding what you wrote [...] that women play on drums and engage in dancing: if this is in the company of men, there is nothing more unacceptable than this [...] and we place under the ban anyone who acts dissolutely in this manner.[9]

Avraham Grossman concludes from this: "In Babylonia, which was under the watchful eye of the Geonim, women did not participate together with men in wedding festivities, but this was customary in faraway northern Africa."[10] We learn from the prohibition in *Ben Ish Hai* that this custom did not cease following its prohibition by R. Hai Gaon, with visual evidence of its continuation provided by the painting of Delacroix.[11]

As regards the separation of the sexes at weddings, it is significant that I have yet to find a description of a partition between men and women at a wedding ceremony; to the contrary, in most instances, men and women are portrayed as mingling together at such ceremonies. The author of *Seridei Esh* writes:[12]

Only as regards the synagogue is there an early regulation to erect high partitions [...] but in voluntary gatherings, such as the time when a bride is brought under the wedding canopy or during speeches and sermons, stringency was never applied as regards partitions [...] and we have never seen that this matter [the partition] was strictly enforced in the lands of Lithuania and Poland, rather [this practice] by Israel was allowed; if they are not prophets, they are the sons of prophets.

Rabbi Mordecai Jaffe, the author of *Levush* (sixteenth century), wrote that in his time care was not taken to separate men from women at weddings:

9 Lewin, *Otzar ha-Gaonim*, Vol. 10, Gittin, *Responsa*, pp. 8–9.
10 Grossman, *Pious and Rebellious*, pp. 341–42.
11 For an additional depiction of a woman dancing before men at a wedding, see "A Jewish Wedding and a Dance," G. Beauclerk, on stone by Giles. Litho. 98 x 98. R.(III) pl. 94, in: A. Rubens, *A Jewish Iconography*, revised edition (London, 1981), p. 204.
12 Rabbi Jehiel Jacob Weinberg, *She'eilot u-Teshuvot Seridei Esh* (Jerusalem, 1961), Vol. 2, para. 8.

Possibly because now women are quite accustomed to be among men, and there is no sinful thought here at all [...] from their being so accustomed to be among us, and since they have become habituated to this [there is no longer any fear of such thoughts].[13]

Notwithstanding these halakhic statements, there are artistic depictions in which women stand on one side of the wedding canopy, and the men on the other.[14]

To return to Fig. 2, on the 1912 postcard: the woman dancer in the scene holds a large braided *hallah* (festive loaf) that also is mentioned by Friedhaber:[15]

Suddenly, R. Jozip would leave the groom and the bride standing, and go forth dancing before them, holding in his hands a huge braided *hallah*, with all those in attendance accompanying him with their clapping.[16]

An additional example of this custom comes from the town of Koznitz, where the "*hallah* dance" was performed by four pious women, who danced before every new couple while holding an enormous *hallah*.[17] In contrast

13 Rabbi Mordecai ben Abraham Jaffe, *Levush Malkhut* (Venice, 1620), Vol. 2: *Levush ha-Hur, Likkutei Minhagim* (*Collections of Customs*), para. 36. See also Rabbi Y.H. Henkin's article entitled "Ika d'Amrei/Others Say: The Significant Role of Habituation in Halakha," *Tradition* 34, 3 (2000), pp. 40–46.

14 Metzger, *Jewish Life in the Middle Ages*, p. 132. See recently, E. Fram, *Ideals Face Reality: Jewish Law and Life in Poland, 1550–1655* (Cincinnati, 1997), pp. 77–78, who refers to *Maharshal* (Rabbi Solomon ben Jehiel Luria), *Yam shel Shelomo*, Gittin 1:18; Ketubot 1:2, who vigorously protests against the custom of mixed dancing at weddings.

15 Friedhaber, "Religious-Ceremony Dances," p. 38. See Klein, *Wedding Traditions of the Various Jewish Communities*, p. 44, who writes that in Poland and Lithuania, following the wedding ceremony, "the mother of the bride goes forth to them with a large braided, yellow *hallah*, about a meter in length, in one hand, and a glass of wine in the other." See also Dalven, *The Jews of Ioannina*, p. 145, for the ceremony of the bride's baking *hallah* during the week following her wedding.

16 H. Fenester, "*Shtetl* Types," in *Yizkor Baranow: A Memorial to the Jewish Community of Baranow*, ed. N. Blumenthal (Jerusalem, 1964), p. 156 (article in Yiddish). Cf. Westermarck, *The History of Human Marriage*, Vol. 2, p. 481, for the bringing of bread to the bride in northern Africa.

17 Friedhaber, "Religious-Ceremony Dances," p. 39 (from H. Schapira, "Those by Lyre and Those by Trumpet," in *Sefer Koznitz* [Tel Aviv, 1970], p. 187 [Hebrew]). The

with the *hallah* dance, in the town of Neishtatel, the old woman Rohre Johnes would dance while holding a large cake that she raised up high. The townspeople believed that the cake symbolized livelihood.[18] Interestingly, this practice was also observed in Georgia, where it was known as the *kabaluli* dance, which was performed following the wedding. This dance symbolized the acceptance of the couple into the family (the name has its source in the Hebrew word *kabbalah*, acceptance). This act is somewhat reminiscent of the ancient practice mentioned in the Talmud:[19] "It was said of R. Judah bar Ilai that he would take a myrtle twig and dance before the bride, saying: 'Beautiful and graceful bride.'"

A photograph of this dance (Fig. 3) appears in the *Rimonim* journal,[20] in which a woman dances while waving a yeast cake with lit candles. In the postcard picture, behind the young woman stand *kleizmerim* (traditional Jewish musicians), who filled an important role at weddings, and especially for the dancing. These musicians are accompanied by a jester; some *kleizmer* groups had their own *badhan* (jester).[21] The role of the *badhan* was not always to amuse (*le-vade'ah*); some felt duty bound to deliver moral instruction, and the like.[22] A painting by an anonymous artist from Poland (twentieth century)[23] shows such a *badhan* standing on a chair, with all those around him weeping and holding handkerchiefs in their hands (Fig. 4). When the band had its own *badhan*, he would march at the head of the procession

roots of this custom can be traced to the Roman practice; see Z. Yavetz, *Augustus* (Tel Aviv, 1994), p. 31 of plates, with a relief of a maidservant (the fourth from the left) bearing a wheat cake (*far*), from which the name of the ceremony is derived. The ceremony reached its climax with the eating of the cake. There are also traces of such customs in ancient Greece. See Farnell, *The Cults of the Greek States*, Vol. 1, pp. 186, 254 (Samos).

18 Friedhaber, op. cit., p. 40.

19 BT Ketubot 17a.

20 R. Arbel, "Georgian *Ketubbot*," *Rimonim* (ed. S. Sabar), 6–7 (1999), p. 44 (Hebrew).

21 See J. Mazor, "The *Badhan* in Hasidic Society: Historical, Social, and Musical Aspects," in *Dukhan* 15 (2000), p. 47 (Hebrew). And earlier, *idem*, "The Place of Music in the Hasidic Wedding," *Dukhan* 11 (Hebrew), pp. 71–72, and pp. 70–71 for *kleizmerim*, following Stutschewsky, '*Klezmorim*' (*Jewish Folk Musicians*), "The *Kleizmerim* at the Wedding," pp. 159–80. See the recent A. Krasney, *Badhan* (Ramat Gan, 1999), pp. 71 ff. (Hebrew). For the *badhan* in the Jewish wedding, see also above, chap. 21 ("The '*Huppah*' — The Wedding Canopy/Ceremony"), n. 45.

22 See Mazor, op. cit., p. 50.

23 See Hakohen, *Hayyei Adam: Kelulot*, p. 24.

bringing the bride to the wedding ceremony, accompanied by the *kleizmerim*, with cymbals in his hands.[24]

In her discussion of Chagall's painting of a wedding, which depicts the procession of the bride and groom to their house, accompanied by singing and dancing (Fig. 5), Mira Friedman[25] is undecided as to the identity of the figure standing next to the violinist: whether he is a *badhan*, or "perhaps an additional *kleizmer* playing an organ, with his playing fingers visible above him."[26] This unclear figure also appears on another painting by Chagall.[27] The latter painting (Fig. 6) becomes more comprehensible from a comparison of these figures with the wedding procession that is described in the *Minhagim Buch* (Frankfurt a. M., 1714–18),[28] in which we clearly see this same figure, with other musicians alongside, and a portable organ on the figure's shoulder (Fig. 7).

Another fascinating motif in Chagall's wedding paintings is the rooster, which symbolizes love, and which frequently appears in his depictions of lovers.[29] Interestingly, the motif of the rooster at a wedding is an ancient one that originated in the Roman world.[30] It represents fertility, and served as the basis for the Talmudic practice of bringing roosters before the bride and groom, to say: be fruitful and multiply like roosters.[31]

---

24 Mazor, "The *Badhan* in Hasidic Society," p. 47. And see Fig. 14 by an unknown artist from Cracow, 1902.

25 M. Friedman, "Chagall's Weddings," *Rimonim* 6–7 (1999), pp. 69–86 (Hebrew).

26 Friedman, fig. 1.

27 Friedman, fig. 2.

28 See Hakohen, *Hayyei Adam: Kelulot*, p. 152.

29 Friedman, "Chagall's Weddings," p. 74, and n. 22.

30 See K.J. Dover, *Greek Homosexuality* (London, 1978), p. 6; ibid., figs. R348, R758.

31 See BT Gittin 57a. I found in Ungerleider-Mayerson, *Jewish Folk Art*, p. 83, a painting of a model from raffia cord by Baruch Mairantz, who was born in Wielun, Poland, and immigrated to Israel in 1935; Mairantz portrayed characters representing the life of the *shtetl* (small Eastern European Jewish community). In this picture we see the bride siting on a regal chair; to her left is a rabbi who sings and dances on a chair, and to her right are *kleizmerim*, above whom is a rooster(!). (The model is in the Eretz Israel Museum, Tel Aviv, Department of Ethnography.) (See Fig. 8.)

See Klein, *Wedding Traditions of the Various Jewish Communities*, p. 44, who tells of the custom in Poland and Lithuania that, after the wedding, the couple, accompanied by music, are led to the bridal suite, where people come forth with buckets full of water and roosters, and throw wheat kernels on the couple, and the like. This, apparently, is the intent of the model. For the buckets of water, see ibid.,

Shalom Sabar[32] noted that a few *ketubot* from Sana, Yemen, contain a schematic drawing of a pair of fowl or birds, and connected them to this

p. 47, that a waterdrawer from the town came with buckets of water towards them and proclaims: "That you should always have everything plentifully." Cf. ibid., p. 49, that in Russia, as well, people went forth to greet the new couple with full pails of water. See p. 97, for the custom in Afghanistan for women to come toward the bride with water (see below, chap. 27, "The Bride's Entry into the Bridal Suite"). For more on the rooster as symbolizing marriage and fertility, see BT Berakhot 57a: "If a person sees a rooster in a dream, he may expect male children." And in T Shabbat 6:4 (ed. Lieberman, p. 23): "and they tie up a chicken for her [the woman in childbirth], so that it לציַת"; and in another version: "לצות." Lieberman explains (p. 23 l. 13): "That is, for company [*le-tzavta*], so that she shall not feel lonely." See also what Lieberman observed in *Tosefta ki-Fshutah*, Vol. 3, pp. 84–85, that this is a sort of protective charm, with a reference to Aelian 4:29. It would, appear, however, that fertility also enters here. See Berger, *Jews and Medicine: Religion, Culture, Science*, p. 130: a charm for protecting babies, above which are two roosters, and a fish above a *hamsah* (the amuletic "hand of Fatimah" with five fingers). N. Berger, "*Therefore Choose Life...*" *Jews and Medicine: Religion, Culture, Science* (Tel Aviv, 1995), p. 130: an amulet for the protection of mother and baby, with two roosters and a fish in the upper part, over the *hamsah*.

See I. Scheftelowitz, "Das Stellvertretende Huhnopfer. Mit besonderer Beruecksichtigung des judischen Volksglaubens," *Religionsgeschichtliche Versuche und Vorarbeiten* 14, 3 (1914), p. 10; see the monumental work: Goodenough, *Jewish Symbols in the Greco-Roman Period*, p. 151. For the rooster in Chagall's iconography, see D. Rix, "Literal and Exegetical Interpretation in Chagall's 'Song of Songs,'" *Journal of Jewish Art* 6 (1979), pp. 125–26. For more on the rooster as a symbol of fertility and the connection between the latter and the wedding ceremony, see J. Hastings, *Encyclopaedia of Religion and Ethics* (New York, 1928), Vol. 3, p. 697b: the southern Slavs bring a rooster (symbolizing the groom) to the church during the wedding procession (F.S. Krauss, *Sitte und Brauch der Sudslaven: Nach heimischen gedruckten und ungedruckten Quellen* [Vienna, 1885], pp. 445 ff.) The rooster (or hen) plays a considerable role, in a number of different ways, in wedding ceremonies. See, e.g., *Sefer Maharil*, ed. Spitzer, *Hil. Nisu'in* (*Laws of Marriage*), p. 468: "*Mahari Segal* [Rabbi Jacob ben Moses Moellin] said, It is customary, following the blessing [i.e. the wedding ceremony] for the groom and bride together to eat an egg and a rooster." And similarly in Rabbi Juda Loew Kirchheim, *The Customs of Worms Jewry*, ed. I.M. Peles (Jerusalem, 1987), p. 79. In another collection of Worms customs, R. Jousep (Juspa) Schammes writes in *Wormser Minhagbuch*, Vol. 2, p. 41: "Afterwards one of his attendants comes with a bowl in his hand, in which is a cooked hen. He asks the groom if he desires to redeem the hen. The groom says: 'Yes,' he places the bowl with the hen on the table, and the hen is immediately set before the groom, who cuts from it a single

Talmudic tradition. A drawing of a rooster also appears at the beginning of a *piyyut* (liturgical poem) for Simhat Torah from Rome (1766) that was dedicated to Isaac Berachiah Raphael.[33] The connection between the

thigh. He returns it to the bowl, and then the hen is ownerless [i.e. free to all], and whoever is first to seize it gains possession of it. After this, the Seven [wedding] Blessings and Grace after Meals are recited." The editor comments (n. 124): "This custom of the redemption of the hen does not appear any other place, and it is like the redemption of *kaparot* [the fowl that is symbolically slaughtered to atone for a person] on the eve of Yom Kippur, see R. Moses Isserles, *Shulhan Arukh, Orah Hayyim* 605." The editor further refers (n. 122) to BT Gittin 57a, and to the dictum by R. Zeira in BT Ketubot 5a, that engaging in the first intercourse on the night following the Sabbath (i.e. Saturday night) is forbidden as a preventive measure, lest he come to slaughter a fowl on the Sabbath. Rabbi Menahem Meiri explains: "For it was their practice to feed the members of the household chicken on the night of the first intercourse, as a propitious sign that they shall be fruitful and multiply like roosters." *She'eilot u-Teshuvot Maharam Mintz*, ed. Domb, Vol. 2, para. 109, p. 551, mentions a different practice: "It was customary to throw a rooster and a hen over the heads of the groom and bride, above the wedding canopy, after the marriage blessing, with support for this from the aggadah in the chapter *Ha-Nizikin* [Gittin, chap. 5]" — and so we have yet another custom reminiscent of *kaparot*; this is deserving of more extensive treatment elsewhere. See also the prayerbook by Rabbi Jacob Emden, *Beit Yaakov* (Lemberg, 1904), fol. 159a, top of col. 2, "*Mitot Kesef*" 6:7, regarding the rooster and sexual relations. See below, n. 33.

32 S. Sabar, "A Jewish Wedding in 18th Century San'a: The Story of the *Ketubbot* of the Al-Eraqi and Al-Sheikh Families — Between Tradition and Innovation," *Rimonim* 6–7 (1999), p. 27 (Hebrew).

33 G. Cohen Grossman, *Jewish Art* (Southport, 1995), p. 208. See S. Weich-Shahak, "Wedding Songs of the Sephardic Jews from Bulgaria," *Dukhan* 12 (1989), pp. 195–96 (Hebrew), who describes a banquet on the second day after the wedding. As she puts it:

On that second day, that is called "the day of the sacrifice," *dea del zevah*, a large fish is purchased, and is placed on an *abilah*, a large platter, garnished with greens and colored ribbons, and the platter is set on the floor. The groom and the bride jump over the fish three times, in the belief that this will ensure fertility and prosperity for the young couple. Afterwards, the fish is cooked and a sumptuous banquet is prepared, to which guests are invited in two groups. First comes a group of guests from the groom's side, and they eat until the calls are issued: "Well, go, now, the group of the bride is coming." Then they leave the room, followed by the entrance of the bride's group, to whom food is served, until members of the groom's family burst in, and say: "*Heida, heida,* now go already, now the bride is ours." This moment, of the bride's separation from her mother, is an emotional one, accompanied by many tears, especially

wedding and the honors of *Hatan Torah* and *Hatan Bereshit* (the honorific titles given, respectively, to the "Groom of the Torah" and the "Groom of

the mother's. At this moment special songs are sung that speak of the moment of parting, and also the advice that a mother must give her daughter, so that she will be a good wife for her new family.

Weich-Shahak writes of the historical origins of these Jews (p. 181):

The Sephardic Jews came to Bulgaria after the Expulsion from Spain, and possibly even before, after 1396. They found in Bulgaria a Jewish community of Romaniot Jews who had dwelled there from the time of Byzantium, and of Ashkenazim, who had arrived from Hungary after 1376, and from Bavaria after 1470. The Sephardim, who had come to Bulgaria via Salonika and via Italy, greatly influenced both the Romaniots and the Ashkenazim, and instituted their customs and their Jewish language there. The three Jewish communities continued to maintain their distinctiveness in three separate frameworks until a joint chief rabbi was appointed for them [all] in 1640. Throughout that time the Sephardic Jews in Bulgaria maintained contact with other communities: with Turkey, Greece, and Walachia (Romania), with cantors and religious functionaries coming from [these countries] to Bulgaria.

A. Amer and R. Jacoby, *Ingathering of the Nations. Treasures of Jewish Art: Documenting an Endangered Legacy* (Jerusalem, 1998), p. 31, provides an interesting illustration of the entrance to a Jewish house in Djerba, in Tunisia. Next to the door, to its left, are fish and a *hamsah*, and to its right, a *menorah* and two *hamsot*, all painted blue. The editors explain that these paintings remain on the walls of the house during the first year of the marriage of the couple that lives there, to protect them from the *mezikim* (destructive agents/demons), and to afford them fertility.

The connection between fish and marriage can be easily understood in accordance with BT Ketubot 5a: "Come and hear: Bar Kappara taught: A virgin is married on Wednesday and the intercourse is conducted on the fifth day [i.e. Wednesday night], since the blessing for fish [Rashi: 'Be fertile and increase, fill the waters' — Gen. 1:22] was delivered on it." See also Yoma 75a:

"We remember the fish that we used to eat free in Egypt" [Num. 11:5] — Rav and Samuel [disagreed]. One said, [This means: real] fish, and the other said: [this refers to] illicit intercourse. The one who said fish [did so] because it is written, "that we used to eat"; and the one who said illicit intercourse [did so] because it is written "free" [i.e. such intercourse entails no financial responsibilities]. As for the one who said illicit intercourse, is it not written "that we used to eat"? It [the Bible] employed euphemistic language.

Cf. I. Scheftelowitz, "Das Fisch-Symbolik im Judentum und Christentum," *Archiv fuer Religionswissenschaft* 14, 1 (1911), pp. 1–53, 321–92, and esp. p. 377. See also *Semahot* 8:3, ed. Higger, p. 3: "Strings of fish and pieces of meat are scattered before grooms and brides [...] but not pieces of cooked fish [...]." See Schauss

Genesis" who are called up on Simhat Torah for the last Torah reading from the Book of Deuteronomy and the immediately following first reading from

(Shoys), *The Lifetime of a Jew throughout the Ages of Jewish History*, pp. 178, 218, who writes that immediately following the wedding the bride and groom would eat a fish meal, symbolizing fertility; and in Eastern communities, two fish were brought in a silver vessel to the wedding ceremony, where they were placed on the ground, close to the wedding canopy (see p. 318 n. 229 for references to the sources). See Klein, *Wedding Traditions of the Various Jewish Communities*, p. 97, that after the wedding ceremony the women go forth to the bride with water, and say: "be fertile [*tidgi*] like the fish [*dag*] of the water" (see above, n. 27). See also Schammes, *Wormser Minhagbuch*, Vol. 2, p. 49: "The night after the first act of intercourse, the groom purchases fish and holds a banquet. [...] He invites them to this banquet: '*Fisch Mahl* [= a fish meal].'" See the editor's gloss, n. 24, with a reference to *Rokeah*, para. 354; R. Moses Isserles, *Shulhan Arukh, Yoreh Deah* 391:2: "That fish banquet that is held after the wedding." And *She'eilot u-Teshuvot Sha'ar Efrayim*, para. 112: "And within the seven days of feasting, a fish banquet is held, as is customary after the first act of intercourse." And in Schammes, op. cit., p. 50 n. 28, the editor mentions that the practice in Nikolsburg is to hold the "Fisch Mahl" on the wedding day (following *Takanot Nikolsburg* [*Constitutiones Communitatis Judaeorum Nikolsburgiensis*], ed. E. Roth [Jerusalem and Tel Aviv, 1961], no. 65 [Hebrew]). An interesting variation of the "*Fisch Mahl*" was practiced in Tunis: see S. Sarfati, *Tunis "El Khadra" la Verte: Traditions ancestrales Legendes et Coutumes juives en Tunisie 1881–1948* (Lod, 1993), p. 108 (Hebrew). The passage in Sarfati in its entirety reads as follows:

> Upon the conclusion of the seven days of rejoicing and celebrations, relatives and friends were invited to the house of the bride and groom, for a ceremony called by the local inhabitants "*Kusan al Hutah*" = the cutting up of the fish. This ceremony was intended to undermine the new husband's dominion over his new wife, and to raise the young bride's esteem in the eyes of her husband.
>
> The ceremony was conducted thusly: a platter on which a gray mullet was placed was brought from the kitchen. It was set in the middle of the room, so that all those present could watch the ceremony. The bride and groom were invited to stand facing one another, with the fish between them. The groom stood in such a way that the head of the fish was directed towards him. Then, each one of the couple was given a knife, and they had to compete for the speedy cutting up of the fish. In order to aid the bride to prevail over the groom, a wooden stick was inserted in the fish's mouth, to make this more difficult for the husband, who stood at the side of the fish's head, and the bride was given a sharp knife, while a dull one was given to the groom. At the beginning of the competition, the couple were asked to prepare for the cutting up of the fish. When the agreed-upon sign was given, the couple cut up the fish. While the husband was struggling to carve up the head of the fish, the bride, in contrast, would easily, without difficulty, cut

the Book of Genesis), and the parallels between the details of these practices, were already noted by Guy Filk. This *ketubah* illustration may bear a trace

up the tail, to the delight of all in attendance. The women among those present would cheer, and all those present would call out "*Marato galavtaho*" — his wife bested him.

In Ioannina [in Greece], on the Friday of the wedding week the groom would purchase a live fish, return home with it and cast it, still alive, at his wife's feet, so that she would fear him in the same way that she feared the fish that was thrashing about at her feet — all this accompanied by much laughter. See the description in Dalven, *The Jews of Ioannina*, p. 145.

See also Goodenough, *Jewish Symbols in the Greco-Roman Period*, Vol. 5, pp. 3ff., for a complete treatment of the symbolism associated with fish, esp. pp. 44–50. See R. Eisler, "Der Fisch als Sexualsymbol," *Imago* 3 (1914), pp. 165–96; J.L. Weston, *From Ritual to Romance* (New York, 1957), p. 135.

This should possibly be linked with th practice of eating fish at the Sabbath meals. See *Be'er Hetev, Orah Hayyim* 242:1, based on BT Shabbat 118b: "With what does one delight in it [the Sabbath]? R. Judah son of R. Samuel son of Shilat said in the name of Rav: With a dish of beets, large fish, and heads of garlic." Many reasons have been advanced for this culinary delight. See Lewy, *Minhag Yisrael Torah*, on *Shulhan Arukh, Orah Hayyim* 274:1, pp. 88–89; Rabbi S.P. Gelbard, *Otzar Ta'amei ha-Minhagim* (*Compendium of the Reasons behind Customs*) (Petah Tikvah, 1998), pp. 188 ff. The inclusion of garlic apparently alludes to the obligation of *onah* (cohabitation; literally, season) on Friday night (see *Shulhan Arukh, Orah Hayyim* 280; *Mishnah Berurah* ad loc. [1]). See BT Bava Kamma 82a, that one of the regulations enacted by Ezra is that garlic be eaten on Fridays as an aphrodisiac, because of the requirement of *onah*, as it is written, "that yields its fruit in season" (Ps. 1:3). Cf BT Ketubot 62b: "R. Judah said: Samuel said: [The *onah* of Torah scholars] is every *erev Shabbat* [that can mean either Friday (before the Sabbath), or Friday night], for it is written, 'that yields its fruit in season.'" (See *Sefer Hasidim*, ed. Margliot, para. 390, p. 283.) An extensive discussion of this was provided by Schepansky, *The Takkanot of Israel*, Vol. 1, pp. 195–96, who also showed that, according to many *poskim*, "*erev Shabbat*" means Friday night. For the obligation of *onah* in the Kabbalistic literature, see E.K. Ginsburg, *The Sabbath in the Classical Kabbala* (Albany, 1989), index entry "Union, sexual"; it would appear that the chanting of the Song of Songs and "*Eshet Hayil*" ("Woman of Valor" — Prov. 31:10–31) on Friday night are related to this matter (see Elzet, "*Mi-Minhagei Yisrael* [On Jewish Customs]," *Reshumot*, p. 339), aside from the reasons from the Jewish esoteric teachings that call the Sabbath "the bride."

Some Sabbath platters contain depictions of fish, such as the plate in the lithograph by Alphonse Levy (Fig. 12), from *Scènes familiales juives* (Paris, 1903) (and not from the book by Leon Cahun, *La Vie Juive* [Paris, 1886], as is erroneously stated

of this parallelism (Figs. 9, 10). A practice similar to that mentioned in the Talmud, of placing fowl before the new couple, was conducted by the Jews of Afghanistan, who sent a bedecked hen to the bride in honor of her betrothal (Fig. 11).[34]

Along with the rooster, the fish is another motif that recurs in Chagall's paintings of wedding and love scenes, possibly also signifying fertility.[35] The geometric form in a *ketubah* from Yemen (1658), which Sabar presumes to

by Kanof, *Jewish Ceremonial Art and Religious Observance*, p. 117 [Fig. 13]. The engraving on the rim of the plate reads: "Sabbath fish" (the plate is among the holdings of the Jewish Museum, New York). For Alphonse Levy, see now Cohen, *Jewish Icons*, pp. 175–78, 299; E. Heyman, *Alphonse Levy: Peintre de la vie Juive* (Strassburg and Geneva, 1976). See also Westermarck, *The History of Human Marriage*, Vol. 2, pp. 484–85, that immediately following the wedding among Eastern Jews, the bride and groom would jump three times over a platter full of fresh fish; D.T. Lobel, *Hochzeitsbrauche in der Turkei: Nach eigenen Beobachtungen und Forschungen und nach den verlausslichsten Quellen* ... (Amsterdam, 1897), p. 287; M. Grunwald, s.v. "Marriage Ceremonies," *Jewish Encyclopedia* (New York, 1904), Vol. 8, p. 341b. Further study should be devoted to these matters. If all the above is correct, then the practice of eating fish on the Sabbath relates primarily to the Friday evening meal.

A pottery plate with a fish seal at its center already appears in the Byzantine period (based on the symbolic meaning of the fish in the Christian world). See the exhibition catalogue: Y. Israeli and D. Mevorah, *Erez ha-Natzrut (The Cradle of Christianity)* (Jerusalem, 2000), p. 116 (Hebrew).

34 In N. Baram-Ben-Yosef, *Bo'i Kallah: Betrothal and Wedding Customs of Afghanistan Jewry* (Jerusalem, 1997), pp. 48–49 (Hebrew). As the catalogue expresses this:

One common betrothal custom was the sending of a painted and decorated hen to the bride: in order to cheer the spirits of the bride, who was usually quite young, the groom's mother would be sure to send her a white hen whose eyes had been made up with kohl, whose beak was painted red, and whose feathers were painted red, green, and blue. White hens were rare in Herat (the local hens were of the dark-colored strain), and white could possibly have symbolized purity and virginity. The hen was also adorned with a mantle (a "small garment") and tiny trousers. Sometimes, a chain of silver coins was placed around its neck, silver bells were tied to its legs, and when it hopped about in the courtyard the ringing of the bells caused those present to laugh. A decorated hen would be sent before the formal betrothal, or on the Purim holiday that fell during the year of the betrothal. The bride would usually keep the hen until her first birth, when it would be slaughtered for the banquet held in honor of this event.

35 Based on Gen. 1:22. See, e.g., in his painting: *To My Wife* (1933/4), Musée National d'Art Moderne, Paris: a wedding canopy, a fish, and a rooster.

be a magical fertility symbol,[36] the origin of which has yet to be determined, may be perceived as piscine (Fig. 9).[37]

Finally, the most famous wedding dance is the so-called "*mitzvah tanz*," in which the bride and bridegroom dance together holding a handkerchief between them, showing that they are now together, on the one hand, yet apart since the marriage has not yet been consumated (Fig. 15).[38]

36 Sabar, "A Jewish Wedding in 18th Century San'a," pp. 26–27.
37 It might be appropriate at this juncture to add another observation concerning weddings. Chapter 18, above, contains a discussion of symbols connected to the remembrance of Jerusalem: "if I do not keep Jerusalem in memory even at my happiest hour" (Ps. 137:6), and especially (p. 166 pass.), the placing of burning ashes on the head of the groom, and/or the placing of a black cloth on his head, and the breaking of the cup, all as symbols of the mourning for the destruction of the Temple. Schammes, *Wormser Minhagbuch*, Vol. 2, p. 40, states that following the betrothal, "he immediately reverses the *mitron*, and wears it around his neck like a mourner" — yet another mourning practice, in commemoration of the destruction of the Temple. See Part 2, chap. 19, "A Kerchief around the Neck of the Mourner." Cf. Schammes, op. cit., p. 96: "The mourner sits with the *mitron* around his neck, on his head, and he sits and is silent." For the mitron, see Schammes, ad loc., nn. 69–70. See also above, n. 31, the eating of a hen and an egg; the egg might possibly also have an additional symbolic meaning, since it is the food of mourners. See *Shulhan Arukh, Orah Hayyim* 552:2, gloss by R. Moses Isserles; Schammes, *Wormser Minhagbuch*, Vol. 1, p. 121 n. 5; Vol. 2, p. 95, editor's glosses. For the egg as a symbol of fertility, see Patai, "Folk Customs and Charms Relating to Birth," *Talpioth* 9, pp. 240–41; *Minhagei Yisrael*, Vol. 2, p. 291. See also O. Melamed (ed.), *Annals of Iraqi Jewry* (= *Kehilot Yisrael, Iraq*), trans. E. Levin (Jerusalem, 1995), p. 125 in Iraq, following the wedding ceremony, the bride and groom would go to the groom's house, where a plate with a cooked hen, covered with a special embroidered cloth, would await them in their room.
38 Traditional Wedding Dance, painting by Alba, early twentieth century.

1. "Dancing", Ms. Rothschild, Italy ca. 1470

2. Dancing in front of the bride and bridegroom, Photograph, Poland 1912

3. Kabaluli Dance, 1970

4. Jester performing before the bride, Poland, 20th century

5. Russian Wedding, Marc Chagall, 1909
© **ADAGP, Paris 2007**

6. Wedding scene, Marc Chagall, 1909–1911
© **ADAGP, Paris 2007**

7. Wedding, *Sefer Ha-Minhagim*, Frankfurt 1714/18

8. Straw model of a wedding, Baruch Mairantz, mid-20th century

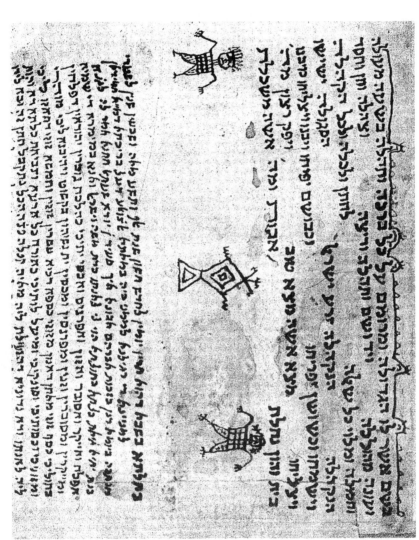

9. Yemenite *Ketubah*, 1658, Zucker Collection, New York

10. *Piyyut* for Simhat
Torah, Rome 1766

11. Decorated hen,
engagement present to a
bride, Jerusalem 1980,
Israel Museum

12. Plate with lithograph based on Alfonse Levy

13. Alfonse Levy, Paris 1903

14. *Badhan*

15. *Mizvah Tanz*, **Alba, early 20th century**

26

THE BRIDE'S ENTRY INTO THE BRIDAL SUITE

At times the direction of cross-cultural influences is the opposite of what is asserted by scholars. An example of such an erroneous attribution appears in the following description of a wedding practice of Libyan Jewry:[1]

> Before the bride enters the room that is designated for the groom and his wife, she takes from her bosom a hen's egg that the groom had brought her in a basket, and she throws it against the wall of the room from the outside. And when she enters, as well, she throws another egg inside the house, to dirty the walls of the room, inside and out, as a sign of mourning, in commemoration of the destruction of the Temple.

And further, when speaking of the Muslim Berbers and their customs:[2]

> Another practice is observed by them: before the bride's first entrance into the house of the groom, the bride takes from her bosom a hen's egg and throws it up on the wall, to dirty the wall of the house. This practice is observed among the Jews in the entire Tripoli district, as a sign of mourning for the destruction of the Temple [...] but I did not know how the Berbers adopted this custom, and what connection they have to mourning over the destruction of the Temple. Unless we were to say, that they mainly were a single clan of the Jews, but over

---

1   M. Ha-Cohen, *Higgid Mordecai: Histoire de la Libye et de ses Juifs, lieux d'habitation et coutumes*, ed. H. Goldberg (Jerusalem, 1982), para. 89, p. 277 (Hebrew).

2   *Idem*, para. 90, p. 281.

the course of time they were assimilated; or we were to say that they adopted this custom for some other reason.

We shall not address the issue of Berbers who converted to Judaism.[3] There can be no doubt, however, that this routine is of non-Jewish origin, and was adopted by Libyan Jews from some foreign source, since it is to be found in numerous non-Jewish cultures. Westermarck collected a great deal of material on this practice:[4]

> There are various rites that are intended to ensure or facilitate the consummation of the marriage. Among the Aith Yusi, a Berber tribe south of Fez, after the bride has been painted with henna, an egg enveloped in a kerchief is tied round her forehead; it is then broken by the woman who painted her, and is left there till she is washed. This is done in order that her hymen shall be broken by her husband as easily as was the egg. [...]
>
> In another Berber tribe, in the Rif, the bridegroom's mother places a mug upside down with a so-called *didli* (an ornament consisting of dollar or half-dollar pieces threaded on a string of horsehair and worn by women round the forehead) and an egg on the top of it, and the bridegroom then breaks both the mug and the egg with a kick, as I was told, "so as to destroy the evil." It is probable that "the evil" in this case meant any possible impediment to the consummation of the marriage. There is much fear in this part of Northern Africa of magic obstacles to sexual intercourse.
>
> The ceremonial breaking of eggs at weddings is found in other countries than Morocco. In a book on the 'Customs and Manners of the Persians' we read:— "Dadeh Bazm Ara says, the bride should take a hen's egg in her hand, and on getting up throw it against the wall to break it, keeping her face towards the Kibleh, or in the direction of Mecca. Kulsum Naneh thinks that a useless proceeding, and recommends a needle to be presented to her on her marriage."

3   See the lengthy discussion in H.Z. [J.W.] Hirschberg, *A History of the Jews in North Africa* (Jerusalem, 1965), Vol. 2, chap. 8, pp. 9–36 (Hebrew).

4   Westermarck, *The History of Human Marriage*, Vol. 2, pp. 457–59. We may add the following reference: John Aubrey, *Remaines of Gentilisme and Judaisme* (1686–87), ed. J. Britten (London, 1881), p. 110, no. 4, on breaking eggshells to prevent witchcraft.

Among the Tenggerese in East Java the bridegroom on the last day of the wedding breaks an egg which has been placed on a stone, after which the bride smears her feet with its contents. Among the Sundanese in West Java a hen's egg is placed before the door of the newly wedded pair; which appears to imply a similar rite of breaking it. In Bali an egg and a cocoa-nut are offered to the bride and bridegroom, who throw them on the ground so that they break, and then disperse the pieces in different directions as offerings to the *kalas*, or spirits. In France, in the seventeenth century, a bride, in order to be happy in her marriage, trod upon and broke an egg when she entered her new home on the wedding day. At Avola, in Sicily, on the bride's arrival at her new home, the bridegroom breaks two eggs with his foot. The use of eggs in marriage rites may, as we shall see, serve different purposes; but when the breaking of an egg plays a prominent part in the rite and the marriage is consummated shortly after, there is some reason to suspect that the original intention of the ceremony was to ensure the defloration of the bride, though the idea of promoting her fertility or other ideas may very well have been combined with it.

When this practice was embraced by the Jews, they gave it their own reason: as signifying their mourning over the loss of the Temple; and then expressed their wonder at the Berber tribes for acting like the Jews.

Westermarck then provides us with much material concerning another custom, that of breaking vessels during the wedding, which is reminiscent of the smashing of the cup at a Jewish wedding. As Westermarck describes the non-Jewish practices (pp. 459 ff):

> Earthenware vessels or objects of glass are often ceremonially broken at weddings both in Morocco and elsewhere. Thus in Andjra, after the bridegroom has been painted with henna, his best-man takes the bowl containing the rest of the henna-mixture, lifts it on his head, and begins to dance before the bridegroom. After a while he hands the bowl to another bachelor, who does the same; and thus all the bachelors present dance in turn with the bowl on their heads till the last one lets it drop down on the ground and break, which is supposed to remove the *bas*, or evil. In another tribe the girl who painted the bridegroom with henna puts the bowl on her head and dances with it, till at last she throws it on the ground so that it breaks, and thereby,

it is thought, rids the bridegroom of his *bas*. Among the Bogos of North-Eastern Africa the bridegroom, before he has intercourse with the bride, breaks an earthenware pot. In Armenia a plate is offered to the bridegroom, who throws it on the ground and tramples it to pieces. At Bajar, when the marriage contract had been made, it was the custom for the guests to throw the bottles of rose-water which they had brought with them against the wall.

The breaking of an earthenware vessel is a marriage ceremony among the Gypsies in Turkey, Moldavia, Transylvania, Spain, and Germany.[5]

Lauterbach,[6] in a classic article, traced the origins of this custom, and showed that originally it was intended as a preventative measure against evil spirits. But here, again, later Jewish authorities interpreted it as signifying the mourning over the loss of the Temple.

---

5   Cf. Gaster, *The Holy and the Profane*, pp. 119–21. For the observance of this custom among Yemenite Jewry, see J. Ratzhabi, "The 'Dardaim,'" *Edoth* 1 (1946), p. 168 (Hebrew); see above, chap. 21 ("The '*Huppah*' — The Wedding Canopy/Ceremony"), n. 54, with a reference to the instructive article by Lauterbach (see below, n. 6).
6   Lauterbach, "The Ceremony of Breaking a Glass at Weddings."

27

THE LIGHTING OF CANDLES AFTER THE WEDDING

Incidental to our examination of matters relating to weddings, the current chapter will discuss an additional aspect of the wedding ceremony. Some time ago, I was asked concerning the meaning of a sentence found in the prayerbook of R. Jacob Emden,[1] in which the text of the wedding ceremony is followed by two comments, the second of which states: "The bride may not light candles with a blessing after the wedding, except on Sabbath eve." The meaning of this prohibition eluded me, until the recent book *Zekhut Yitzhak* by R. Yaakov Hayyim Sofer[2] cited a responsum by R. Solomon Kluger,[3] who was asked concerning the lighting of candles by brides during the weekday, **with a blessing**. R. Kluger responds:

> There is no need [to comment] on this, since this is an instance of ignorance. As regards the reason written by someone, that this is her holiday, and also that there is an obligation to kindle lights during the wedding, this is quite preposterous, he mouths empty words [see Job 35:16], and it was not worthwhile for his exalted excellency [the one addressing the query] to have committed it to writing. That person fabricated this; let this matter sink [into oblivion], and not be stated. [...] As regards the lighting of candles by the bride on weekdays, this is to be judged favorably, for this is merely a manner of learning: she is taught how to perform [candle lighting]; this is like a teacher of small

1 Rabbi Jacob Emden, *Beit Yaakov*, Vol. 1, fol. 126a.
2 Sofer, *Zekhut Yitzhak*, Vol. 1, p. 249.
3 R. Solomon Kluger, *She'eilot u-Teshuvot Tuv Ta'am ve-Da'at*, third edn., Vol. 1 (Lemberg, 1884 [photocopy edn.: Bnei Brak, 1979]), end of para. 98, fol. 38b.

children, who is permitted to teach them the blessings. Consequently, this practice is not to be abrogated; only inform them that they tell the bride as an educational matter, how to recite the blessings on Sabbath and Festival, without having the intent [to perform this] for the sake of the blessing itself.

This lighting of candles with a blessing by the bride immediately following her wedding, on a weekday, was vigorously opposed by R. Solomon Kluger, echoing the view set forth by R. Jacob Emden.

Although I have not yet found the source of the custom, I thought to propose (as no more than conjecture) that the source of this practice is to be found in the non-Jewish world. Grimm writes in his monumental *Deutsche Mythologie*:[4] "At a marriage-feast they set two candles, before the bride and bridegroom; the one whose light goes out first of itself, is sure to die first."[5]

I later discovered that Benjamin Adler[6] gave the following reason for this (in the name of the book *Barukh Hashem*[7]): "This error ensues from the practice of many to conduct a wedding on Sabbath eve,[8] with the bride [then] kindling the Sabbath lights in the proper fashion."

This proposal is even more persuasive in light of what R. Samuel ha-Levi wrote in *Nahalat Shivah*:[9]

> The practice in Ashkenaz [= central Europe], to this day, is to conduct virgin weddings on a Wednesday, even though the reason that he [the husband] may go early to the court is not relevant, nonetheless, the custom remains in effect. [...] Possibly another reason is to be appended to this, since we are few in the land of Ashkenaz [= Germany], we have remained few of the many, and the people are greatly dispersed,

4 Grimm, *Teutonic Mythology*, Vol. 4, p. 1843, no. 17.
5 Cf. chap. 1 in Part 2, "Omens of Approaching Death," p. 359.
6 Adler, *Nisu'in ke-Hilkhatam*, Vol. 1, p. 372 n. 137.
7 *Barukh Hashem*, later edition, para. 41.
8 See above, chap. 19, "Wedding Dates," p. 171. Freimann, *Seder Kiddushin ve-Nissu'in Aharei Hatimat ha-Talmud*, p. 127, quotes R. Jonathan Treves, in the latter's commentary on the Rome festival prayerbook, *Kimha de-Avishuma* (Bologna, 1540), Vol. 2, pp. 284–85: "Those who lead her to the *huppah* on the Sabbath, recite the betrothal benedictions in advance on Sabbath eve [that is, Friday] because it is not allowed to betroth a woman on the Sabbath." See Sabar, "The Beginnings of *Kettubah* Decoration in Italy," p. 99.
9 *Nahalat Shivah*, para. 12, subsection 1(a).

solitary Israelites, one in the city and two in the state, the barest
remnants, by our numerous sins; and the host of the banquet must
call upon his helpmate to invite many people from other locations
and cities. Accordingly, on behalf of people [invited from] a distance,
so that each individual shall be able to return to his place before the
Sabbath, it was instituted that weddings be conducted in the middle
of the week. In the land of Poland, including Austria, Bohemia, and
Moravia, in the places of habitation of the praiseworthy congregations
of Israel until the advent of the Redeemer, such a fear is not relevant,
and therefore most weddings are conducted on Fridays. Although *Beit
Yosef* [i.e. R. Joseph Caro] wrote that many challenge this practice,
he himself nevertheless wrote that the simple practice is to conduct
weddings on Fridays. See *Teshuvot Rama*, para. 125; and he wrote in
the glosses on *Derishah*, para. 643, in the name of *Mordekhai*, that it
was the custom to conduct weddings on Fridays, due to the poverty
[of the populace].

In addition to the institution (apparently following the massacres of 1296) of
conducting weddings on Fridays, to reduce the wedding expenses,[10] *Nahalat
Shivah* therefore provides a demographic explanation[11] for the practice of
some communities to conduct weddings specifically on Wednesdays.[12]

10 See Schammes, op. cit., pp. 9–10 n. 1, who lists additional sources for this practice.
11 See *Minhagei Yisrael*, Vol. 3, pp. 106–11, for the demographic factor in the
    fashioning of the practice. See also Hamburger's gloss, Schammes, *Wormser
    Minhagbuch*, Vol. 2, pp. 34–35, that the conducting of the wedding ceremony
    by a rabbi was apparently among the enactments of Rabbeinu Tam, or from his
    period: "Notwithstanding this, in those places in which a rabbi was not present,
    such as small communities, a leniency was granted, to permit the conducting of the
    wedding ceremony, even by someone who was not a Torah scholar." And as R.
    Samuel ben David ha-Levi writes in *Nahalat Shivah* 12:4:
        By our numerous sins, we are few in the land of Ashkenaz [= Germany], the
        house of Israel is greatly dispersed in solitary fashion in the towns and villages,
        and they have no mentors; the smallest among a thousand wishes to be the
        mightiest of the mighty. Accordingly, at the very least, the conductor of the
        wedding ceremony must be authorized by a rabbi of the land.
    It further seems that many wedding practices in central Europe could have come
    into existence only as a consequence of the rarity of weddings in the sparsely
    populated Jewish communities. Thus, for example, the practice of calling to the
    Torah reading on the Sabbath following the wedding: "It happened that the Torah
    portion would be read two or three times" (Schammes, *Wormser Minhagbuch*, Vol.

R. Samuel ben David ha-Levi therefore indicates in *Nahalat Shivah* that the rabbis initially established Wednesday as the wedding day, which, for various reasons, was later changed to Friday. (In a further development, some communities reinstated Wednesday as the day for weddings, this time for demographic reasons.) Consequently, women may have become accustomed to kindling Sabbath lights immediately following their wedding, which then became a sort of fixed custom, one that persisted even after Wednesday was reinstituted as the wedding day, and the original reason for this lighting no longer existed. Although the reason was terminated, the custom remained, to the sorrow of the *poskim*.

2, p. 54 n. 36) would be inconceivable as a standard practice in a locality with frequent weddings. Due to the meager population of these communities, it also was not possible to fulfill the requirement of providing "new faces" (i.e. people who were not present at the wedding ceremony) during each of the weekdays of the seven days of the wedding celebrations. Therefore, in the Rhine communities, the *Sheva Berakhot* (the seven wedding blessings [and the accompanying banquet]) were recited during the week following the wedding only on the Sabbath, according to *Maharil* (R. Jacob ben Moses Moellin), "for we do not have new faces, except on the Sabbath day" (*Sefer Maharil*, ed. Spitzer, p. 468); and in the textual variants ad loc.: "as was instituted by *Mahari Segal* [= Moellin] in Mainz." R. Naphtali ben Isaac Katz, *Semikhat Hakhamim: Kedushah u-Berakhah* (Frankfurt a.M, n.d.), fol. 32 (on BT Berakhot 12a), writes: "New faces are an uncommon matter." See Schammes, *Wormser Minhagbuch*, Vol. 2, p. 59 n. 82.

12 This might possibly be somewhat related to the wedding rings (see above, chap. 22, "The Wedding Ring in the Cup of Wine") bearing the inscription "to light the Sabbath lamp." Wolf, "Rings," *Jewish Encyclopedia*, p. 430, writes: "These rings, which were to remind the women of one of their chief duties, the lighting of the Sabbath lamps, were in use early in the Middle Ages, as is shown by the fact that such a ring was found in Mecklenburg together with Anglo-Saxon coins and Arabic dirhems (Donath, "Gesch. der Juden in Mecklenburg," p. 78) [= L. Donath, *Geschichte der Juden in Mecklenburg* ... (Leipzig, 1874 [reprint Germany, 1974])]." I have not been able to confirm this report; such a ring appears in Kayser and Schoenberger, *Jewish Ceremonial Art*, pp. 152–53, no. 164 (but apparently with some error: the illustration accompanying the caption does not contain such an inscription, and it probably reads: "*Mazal tov*"; the illustrations apparently were interchanged); this requires further examination. See also Cohen and Horowitz, "In Search of the Sacred: Jews, Christians, and Rituals of Marriage in the Later Middle Ages," pp. 227–30, 236.

28

THE MORNING AFTER

There are some Jewish customs that have been completely forgotten, and must be rescued from oblivion, such as the following practice described in *Derekh Eretz Zutta* 7:2:[1]

> Just as the bride, so long as she is in her father's house, keeps herself in retirement, but when she is about to leave [her father's house] makes herself known, saying, "whosoever knows any evidence against me, let him come and testify."

This simile implies that at the time of the wedding the bride would prove her virginity, and was therefore entitled to receive the compensation set forth in the *ketubah* for a virgin. This practice, of bringing proof after the first act of intercourse of the bride's virginity prior to the consummation of the marriage, is known among non-Jewish peoples,[2] and also as a Jewish

1 My edition: *A Commentary on Derech Erez Zuta, Chapters Five to Eight, also called Derech Erez Ze'ira* (Ramat Gan, 1990), p. 99; cf. pp. 123–26.

2 Here we may refer to J. Selden, *John Selden on Jewish Marriage Law: The Uxor Hebraica*, trans. and commentary by J.R. Ziskind (Leiden, 1991), p. 290 (the *Uxor Hebraica* was first published in London, 1646):

   The African Moslems claim that the defloration of a virgin always happens at first embraces when blood appears, if John Leo is to be believed. While the couple is in the chamber, he said, "A banquet is prepared, and there is a certain woman who waits at the entrance, and when the bride is deflowered, the blood-stained linen is spread out and held in her hand, and she shows it to the guests. She cries out in a loud voice that up to now the bride was an uncorrupt virgin. First the groom's parents and then the bride's grandly receive her along with certain other women. But if by chance she was found to be a non-virgin, the marriage was

custom,[3] but not from the Talmudic sources.[4] The Byzantine-period *paytan* (composer of liturgical hymns) Amittai who lived in Oria, Italy (d. 886) writes in his *kedushata* (hymn) for the groom:

> And how fine for the groom on his wedding day **to show the purity of his wife's virginity, with head held high**,[5]

and only afterwards:

> for the signing of the witnesses to the *ketubah*, and to make his joy perfect.

This means that the witnesses sign the *ketubah* that is given to a virgin only after her worthiness to receive such a benefit has been demonstrated to them, which also is a major innovation.[6] Since we know of the close bond between the teachings of the early Italian *paytanim* and the teachings of the sages in the Land of Israel,[7] the practice depicted by Amittai may very well be reflected in *Derekh Eretz Zutta*, which was composed in the Land of Israel.[8]

> regarded as void, and to the great shame of everyone she is forthwith returned to her parents."

3   See, e.g., M. Ha-Kohen, *Higgid Mordecai* (*The History of Libyan Jews, Their Settlements, and Their Customs*), ed. H.E. Goldberg (Jerusalem, 1982), pp. 277–78 (Hebrew); Brauer, *The Jews of Kurdistan*, p. 116; N. B. Gamlieli, *Ahavat Teman: Arabic Poetry and Songs of the Yemenite Jewish Women*[2] (Tel Aviv, 1979), p. 215 (Hebrew); M. Ammar, "Wedding Orders and the *Ketubba* Text among Moroccan Jews since the XVIth Century," in Chetrit et al., *The Jewish Traditional Marriage: Interpretative and Documentary Chapters*, pp. 107–83, esp. p. 139 (Hebrew); M. Malul, "The *Sosbin* in the Wedding Ceremony in Morocco: A Study of the Sources of an Ancient Social Institution," in *The Jewish Traditional Marriage*, pp. 281–305, esp. pp. 286–87 (Hebrew).

4   See R. Kashani, R. Posner, s.v. "Marriage," *Encyclopaedia Judaica*, Vol. 11, col. 1045.

5   See *Megillat Ahimaaz: The Chronicle of Ahimaaz, with a Collection of Poems* ..., ed. B. Klar (Jerusalem, 1974), p. 94, and gloss, p. 169 (Hebrew); *The Poems of Amittay*, ed. Y. David (Jerusalem, 1975), p. 23 (Hebrew).

6   See E. Fleischer, "Aspects in the Poetry of the Early Italian Paytanim," *Hasifrut* 30–31 (1981), p. 144 (Hebrew); I. Ta-Shma, "Law, Custom and Tradition in Early Jewish Germany — Tentative Reflections," *Sidra* 3 (1987), p. 111 and n. 50 (Hebrew).

7   See Fleischer, pp. 131 ff., esp. pp. 141 ff.

8   As, however, Rabbi Moshe Raziel commented on this point:
    Derekh Eretz Zutta does not constitute proof that the obligation of the *ketubah* for

In the case of the newly wed woman accused of not being a virgin (see Deut. 22: 13–19), her father can counter this claim by presenting

> a virgin came into effect after her virginity was demonstrated. All that is stated there is totally congruent with what is stated in the Babylonian and Palestinian Talmuds [tractate] Ketubot, regarding "going forth [to the wedding ceremony] as a virgin." For the virgin went forth to the wedding ceremony while indicating that she is a virgin, so that if someone knows that she is not a virgin, he may come and testify against her. This is exactly like the procedure followed in the case of someone about to be executed, that the matter is publicized, so that anyone who has any information in his favor could come and so testify. Otherwise, the rule prohibiting the consummation of the marriage prior to [the groom's] writing her a *ketubah*, or, in pressing circumstances, effecting acquisition of movable property [to ensure his fulfilling his monetary obligation to her], that is a straightforward rule in the Talmud, would contradict this understanding. [...] As regards the [actual] practice, the custom in Judea of putting them together at the *erusin*, as well, ensued, at least according to the Palestinian Talmud, from the exigencies of the time; and even according to the Babylonian Talmud, the time when he wrote her the *ketubah* is unclear. Also, the practice in Libya [...] or the *piyyut* of Amittai show only that testimony would be given immediately after the first act of intercourse, possibly in order to prevent future disagreements and quarrels. The continuation of this *piyyut* cannot undermine the straightforward law that one may not consummate the marriage before writing the *ketubah* for his wife. This is especially so, since the early Tannaitic procedure was to pay her *ketubah* in its entirety before the wedding ceremony.
> We do, however, find examples of the *ketubah* being signed after the act of cohabitation. See *Arugat ha-Bosem*, ed. Urbach, Vol. 4, p. 44 gloss 28, citing *Or Zarua*, Vol. 1, para. 712, who describes a custom of writing the *ketubah* before the Sabbath, but signing it after the Sabbath, for a wedding performed on a Friday night (see above, chap. 19, "Wedding Dates").

9   Once again we shall refer to Selden, p. 293, who writes:

> The truly great Hugo Grotius speaks of the aforesaid linen or covering as being "examples" or "signs'" [Andeas Schott translates as "rags (Andreas Schott, 1552–1622, a Jesuit theologian and classicist)] of the soiled garments of women" (Grotius, Annotat. in V. T., 1, p. 1789). These are called by the Alexandrians the φυλακεῖα as we know from the life of the philosopher Isidore of Damascus found in Photius (Cod. 242, 338b.25) and Suidas (Lexicographi Graeci 1.3 no. 823). In the Photian excerpts there immediately follows, as mentioned in the previous book where the authentication of the marriage instrument by the hands of the priest of Isis is discussed (Cap. 28), the following words on the matter (to Deut. 22:17): "Among the Hebrews this is not done by priests but by attendants who are called *shoshvinim*"; as if the intention of the passage was to reserve to the priests the inspection of the sign of the soiled women's garments (as he says

the stained garment (*simlah*) before the elders of the city (v. 17). This *simlah* is probably to be identified with the *mapah shel betulim*, the "cloth of virginity" mentioned in BT Ketubot 16b,[9] and also in the sectarian literature.[10]

in the first intercourse). I certainly do not see how this matter applies to the duties of the priest. The more sharp-sighted would see this.

10 *Megillat Taanit: Versions, Interpretations, History*, ed. V. Noam (Jerusalem, 2004), pp. 72, 206 (Hebrew), in the Scholion, 4 Tammuz: the Boethusians would interpret "And they spread out the *simlah* before the elders of the town" (Deut. 22:17) as meaning an actual dress, in an apparent reference to the Talmudic *mapah shel bitulim*. Noam observes that M. Kister, "Studies in 4QMiqsat Ma'ase Ha-Torah and Related Texts: Law, Theology, Language and Calendar," *Tarbiz* 68 (1999), pp. 332–33 n. 69 (Hebrew), found a parallel to this Boethusian law in the Qumran writings. Noam also refers (n. 38) to the discussion of the Qumran sect's attitude to the claim of virginity by J.H. Tigay, "Examination of the Accused Bride in 4Q159: Forensic Medicine at Qumran," *JANES* 22 (1994), pp. 129–34; A. Shemesh, "4Q271.3: A Key to Sectarian Matrimonial Law," *JJS* 49 (1998), pp. 244–59. The practice of displaying the *mapah shel bitulim* was observed in many Jewish communities (see above). To this we should add M. Bar-Ilan, in his review article of the Noam edition (in press).

29

THE *REGEL REDUFIN* OF CAUCASUS JEWRY

In his description of the marital practices in the city of Achalzaich in the Caucasus mountains,[1] Joseph Judah Chorny also mentions the following procedure:[2]

> After a few days or months, or on a holiday, the bride and the groom are invited by the groom's relatives to the home of the bride's father and mother, and a lavish banquet is held for them. The bride's father is then obligated to give to his daughter and her husband an important gift of silver or gold, and the couple remain there for several days, and in some instances, for several weeks. This is the order of weddings among our fellow Israelites in the city of Achalzaich — strange and unusual customs, that have no basis in any source; they [simply] adopted them as their practice. Perhaps [they adopted these customs] from the early Ishmaelite and Georgian non-Jews in whose midst they dwelt from ancient times, and over the course of time, many follies that they learned from the actions of their neighboring non-Jews have proliferated among them. The reader can judge from this to what spiritual level they have reached, for the European man, if he will speak with them, will immediately realize that they are a bit intermingled *mit wildeheit* [with wildness] and their wild mentality. A wondrous thing!

1 See above, chap. 22 ("The Wedding Ring in the Cup of Wine").
2 Chorny, *Sefer ha-Massa'ot be-Eretz Kavkaz*, p. 161.

Chorny's description may very well be correct.[3] However, as regards the source of the custom that centered around the banquet in the home of the bride's father, it may be assumed that this is a residual from the ancient Talmudic practice known as *ha-regel redufin*, a reference to which appears in the midrash:[4]

> We are comparable to the daughter of kings who went for *regel redufin* to her father's house; eventually, she returned to her home safely.

This term is defined by R. Yose ben Bun in the Palestinian Talmud:[5]

> What is *regel redufin*? R. Yose ben Bun explained: this is the first *regel* [foot; here, one of the three pilgrimage festivals] on which her husband pursues her [*rodefah*] to her husband's house.

Even though the meaning of the passage in PT is unclear, this patently refers to some celebration, which most likely was held in the house of the bride's father a certain amount of time after the wedding, and in the course of which the bride returned to her father's house.[6]

3   Natan Eliashvili writes of these same Mountain Jews in his book *The Jews in Georgia and in the Land of Israel*, ed. G. Kressel (Tel Aviv, 1975), p. 40 (Hebrew):
    The Mountain Jews lived among the Turks, within the tribes of wild peoples, by whom their lives were greatly influenced, at home and in society. They are easily angered, they love to use firearms, and they are liable to murder for some petty reason. Revenge was present among them, as among the tribes of the East in general, as was also noted by Z. Anisimov in his article "The Mountain Jews" (*Ha-Shilo'ah*, vol. 18), that an entire town of Jews (Noga-Dir) were wiped out by each other due to revenge, until only a few of them were left.
    It is well-known, however, that Georgian Jews, including the above author, held the Mountain Jews in low esteem, as is patent in this passage. For a general treatment of the Mountain Jews, see Yosefov, *Ha-Yehudim ha-Harariyim ba-Kavkaz uve-Yisrael*, and especially on weddings, pp. 181–82 (he does not mention the practice depicted by Chorny).
4   Cant. Rabbah 8:10.
5   PT Pesahim 8:1.
6   See the discussion in my *A Dictionary of Greek and Latin Legal Terms*, p. 197, where I suggested that *redufin* is actually the Latin *repudium* (repudiation of a prospective spouse). See N.H. Torczyner (Tur-Sinai), "R. Johanan Said: They Taught in Regard to *Regel Redufin*," in *Commentationes Iudaico-Hellenisticae im Memoriam Iohannes Lewy* (*Jonathan Levy Memorial Volume*), ed. M. Schwabe and J. Gutmann (Jerusalem, 1949), pp. 59–64 (Hebrew); *idem*, "*Regel Redufin* and From

APPENDIX

SIMILARITIES BETWEEN THE ROMAN AND
JEWISH WEDDING CEREMONIES

The following table briefly summarizes some of the main parallels between Roman and Jewish wedding ceremonies, all of which have been alluded to, or discussed, in the preceding chapters, along with analyses of the directions of cultural influence. A fine description of the Roman ceremony is to be found in Smith, Wayte, and Marindin, *Dictionary of Greek and Roman Antiquities*, Vol. 2, p. 1441, s.v. "*Matrimonium, Nuptiae*," pp. 142–44.

Roman	Jewish
There was a ceremony of betrothal (*sponsalia*), which sometimes took place long before the wedding. On this occasion the prospective bridegroom gave his fiancee a ring that she wore on the third finger of her left hand. Sometimes guests were invited, and the bride-to-be received presents.	Equivalent to the *erusin* ceremony, in which a coin or (later) a ring was given by the bridegroom to the bride. Presents were received and recorded.

the Age of Twenty *Li-Rdof*," in *The Language and the Book*[2] (Jerusalem, 1955), Vol. 3: *Beliefs and Doctrines*, pp. 279–85 (Hebrew); E. Ben Yehuda, *A Complete Dictionary of Ancient and Modern Hebrew* (Jerusalem, 1951), s.v. "*Riduf*," p. 6447 n. 3, further suggests that *regel* in *regel redufim* is *regale repudium* (cf. the above passage in Cant. Rabbah), or *regel = legale repudium*. We understand *regel* in the Hebrew meaning, that of "period." The text in PT Pesahim is difficult (cf. BT Pesahim 87a); see the commentators ad loc. Tur-Sinai himself could not interpret the entire text ("R. Johanan Said," p. 64). Note that the teaching is delivered in the name of R. Johanan, who also used the term *dipurin* in the sense of *repudium*. (But cf. I. Ziegler, *Die Konigsgleichnisse der Midrasch, beleuchtet durch die romische Kaiserzeit* [Breslau, 1903], p. 361, who understands *redufin* as *repotio*, drinking after the wedding, the first festival after the wedding.) See also the more recent discussion by R. Kimelman, "Rabbi Yohanan and Origen on the Song of Songs: A Third-Century Jewish-Christian Disputation," *HTR* 73 (1980), pp. 590–91 n. 101. See also *Shulhan Arukh, Even ha-Ezer* 74:9.

Roman	Jewish
Great care was taken in the choice of the day for the wedding. Certain seasons, on account of the nature of the religious rites that fell within them, were regarded as distinctly inauspicious, namely, the month of May, the first half of June, the third week in February, the first half of March, and some other single days, including all Kalends, Nones, and Ides. Moreover, festival days in general were avoided.	Certain days were preferred for the wedding; so, too, certain times of the month and certain seasons: the Three Weeks, the period of the counting of the *Omer*, are unsuitable for weddings.
The wedding was preceded by a ceremony of parting the hair, arranging it into six locks, and more.	A variety of different customs relate to the bride's hair prior to the wedding: untying it, shaving it off, and the like.
Before the actual wedding ceremony, a marriage contract (*tabulae nuptiales*, or *tabulae dotales*) was signed before witnesses (*signatores*).	Before the wedding, the *ketubah* is written out and signed by witnesses.
The bride wore a veil over her head, and was crowned with a wreath of flowers. In the later period it was usual for the bridegroom also to wear a garland.	The bride wore a veil (*hinumah*) and a wreath or garland; the latter, however, was discontinued in the time of Titus (BT Sotah 49b).
In the rite of *confarreatio* they both partook of the sacred cake, *libum farreum*, so named because it was made of coarse wheat called *far*.	According to some customs, a loaf of bread was presented to the bride on her entry to her new home.
This took place in the presence of ten witnesses, with the Pontifex Maximus and the Flamen Dialis taking part in the ceremony.	The wedding ceremony takes place before a quorum of ten, and was usually (at a later date) officiated by a rabbi.

Roman	Jewish
Then the bride was led up to the bridegroom, and their right hands were joined together.	We have seen the joining of the hands in the wedding ceremony under the *huppah*.
Then came the wedding feast (*cena nuptialis*), in which a wedding cake (*mustaceum*) was cut up and distributed to the guests.	The wedding ceremony is followed by a feast, in which the Seven Blessings (*sheva berakhot*) are recited.
After the ceremony and the wedding feast, both of which generally took place in the house of the bride's father, there was a procession (*deductio*) to the new home (*in domum deductio*), with the participation of the general public, and not only the bridal party.	Prior to the procession, the couple were taken to a bridal place, where they stayed a short time in private (*yihud*), followed by the feast, after which they were led off to their new home.
The ceremony usually was held at dusk, whence arose the custom of having torches. Flute players and torchbearers went in front.	The use of candles plays a prominent part in the Jewish wedding ceremony, both in the procession leading up to the *huppah*, and in the ceremony under the wedding canopy. Musicians play instruments.
The part of the bridegroom in the procession was to scatter nuts for the boys in the crowd.	Nuts and grains of wheat were scattered during the marriage ceremony.

30

THE *HALITZAH* CEREMONY

1. THE TRANSLATION OF THE BOOK BY LEONE DA MODENA, AMSTERDAM 1724

The *halitzah* ceremony (the symbolic act in which the shoe of the brother-in-law of a widow childless from her late husband is removed, thus relieving him of the obligation to marry her, as prescribed in Deut. 25:5) is described, verbally and graphically,[1] in a number of non-Jewish sources from the sixteenth century on. Some of these depictions exhibit marked inaccuracy in the halakhic aspects of this act, such as the illustration in a book published in Amsterdam in 1744 entitled *Kerk-Zeeden en de Gewoonten, die huiden in gebruik zyn onder de Joden.* This book was a translation of the Italian work by R. Leone (Judah Aryeh) da Modena, *Historia dei Riti Ebraici* (Paris, 1637), which appeared in many editions and numerous translations. In the woodcut opposite p. 128 of the Amsterdam edition (Fig. 1),[2] we see

---

1   A Jewish illumination from an early fifteenth-century German manuscript: Parma, MS. Parma Biblioteca Palatine 2823–De Rossi 893, fol. 324v, is reproduced in Metzger, *Jewish Life in the Middle Ages*, p. 300, no. 345, in which we see the brother-in-law with his foot on a small chair(!), as the widow unties the straps of his shoe with her right hand; see below. A *halitzah* ceremony in southern France from 1747 is described by S. Mrejen-O'hana, "Pratiques et comportements religieux dans les 'quatre saintes communautés' d'Avignon et du Comtat Venaissin au XVIIIᵉ siècle," *Archives Juives* 28, 2 (1995), p. 9.

2   The woodcut was executed by "J. L." (= the acclaimed lithographer Jan Luyken). For the book by da Modena, its various editions, and aims, see R.I. Cohen, "The Visual Image of the Jew and Judaism in Early Modern Europe: From Symbolism to Realism," *Zion* 57 (1992), pp. 313–16 (Hebrew); M.R. Cohen, "Leone da Modena's 'Riti'; A Seventeenth Century Plea for Social Toleration of Jews," *Jewish Social Studies* 34 (1992), pp. 287–321.

a quasi-*halitzah* ceremony, but the *yabam* (brother-in-law) is **sitting** and presenting his **left foot**, while the *yevamah* (childless widow) is **kneeling** as she removes his shoe with **both hands**. In actuality, it is usually the **right** shoe that is removed,[3] the brother-in-law is required to **stand**,[4] the widow **does not kneel**,[5] and she removes the shoe using only her **right hand**. Nor does the manner in which the rabbinical judges and witnesses sit correspond to what is depicted in the Jewish sources of this ceremony (see below). Da Modena's explanation apparently lacked sufficient detail for the artist to provide an accurate halakhic reconstruction.[6]

2. THE LATIN MISHNAH (AMSTERDAM, 1700)

In contrast, the picture that adorns the front page of the Order of *Nashim* of the Latin translation of the Mishnah by Guilielmus Surenhusius, published by Gerardus & Jacobus Borstius (Amsterdam, 1700), in the roundel above the tractate of Yevamot (Figs. 2, 3), matches the Jewish sources on the *halitzah* ceremony in almost all its details. Thus, for example, the brother-in-law

---

3   See *Enziklopedia Talmudit* (*Talmudic Encyclopedia*), Vol. 15, s.v. "*Halitzah*," col. 765, following PT Yevamot 12:1. There is a disagreement as to whether this is merely a choice manner of performing the commandment, or whether it is a *sina qua non*. The definitive halakhah (*Shulhan Arukh, Even ha-Ezer* 169:30, in the gloss by R. Moses Isserles) is that the removal of the shoe by the woman's left hand or with her teeth is valid. From the outset, however, this action should certainly be performed with the right hand. As regards a left-handed widow, see the edition by S.E. Stern of the *seder halitzah* formulated by Rabbeinu Solomon for the Jews of Paris, *Kovetz Torani Zekhor le-Avraham* 1994–95), p. 10 n. 12 (Hebrew). I have not found any mention in the halakhic sources of the removal of the shoe with both hands.

4   A legal disagreement exists on this point, as well: may the brother-in-law sit during the *halitzah* ceremony, and is the act valid after the fact? The definitive halakhah, however, requires the brother-in-law to stand. See the detailed discussion in *Enziklopedia Talmudit*, op. cit., cols. 761–762.

5   This detail, too, is the subject of a difference of opinion, but the halakhah requires her to stand.

6   There might be some stylistic influence here from the motif in the New Testament of washing the feet. See, e.g., the woodcut by Durer in his *Kleiner Passion* (Nuremberg, 1511). See W. Worringer, *Die altdeutsche Buchillustration* (Munich, 1921), p. 125. This motif also bears comparison with depictions of the Jewish bathhouse. See, for example, the sixteenth-century woodcut reproduced in the *Jewish Encyclopedia*, Vol. 8 (New York, 1904), p. 589, which portrays the washing of the feet.

stands, leaning on a **board**[7] that rests on the wall. Compare this with the description by R. Michael Jozefs of Cracow[8] (para. 80): "The *yabam* is to

7   See L.I. Rabinowitz, "Levirate Marriage and Halizah," *Encyclopaedia Judaica*, Vol. 11, col. 130, that it was customary to have the brother-in-law lean against a board on which the dead were washed. This custom is mentioned by R. Yehuda Elzet, *Reshumot*, Vol. 1, para. 89, pp. 371–72, who sought a source for this in *Matamim he-Hadash*, "Halitzah," fol. 13a, which he quotes: "Since the soul of the deceased is located under the board on which the person undergoing *halitzah* leans" (at any rate, this is how he understood Rabbi Isaac Lipets, although this explanation is not explicit in *Matamim*), adding in parenthesis: "The simple explanation: because the community did not possess another board, and they were not desirous of purchasing an additional board[?]." He later expanded on this in his article: Y. Avida, "Strange Immersions," *Yeda-'Am* 3, 1 (1955), p. 10 (Hebrew), where he writes:

> In my childhood I recall [in the city of Zakrotchin (Zakroczym), Warsaw district], that they brought to the house that was designated for the conducting of the *halitzah* ceremony, the "purification board" (*taharah-bret*), that is, the plank on which the corpse would be washed and purified. They said that the deceased stands behind this board. Everyone was careful not to approach the board, to move it, or look at what was happening behind it, for they said that anyone on whom the chair would fall, would not complete the year.

He further comments (nn. 4, 5):

> This board would also be brought and stood up close to the place of the person to whom an oath was administered in civil cases, to intimidate him and to remind him of the day of [his] death. And, likewise, all the folktales in which the dead were either summoned to, or instituted litigation in, a *din Torah* [i.e. a case brought before a rabbinical court], such as in cases of the selling of the merit for the performance of commandments and of one's portion in Paradise, we were told, relate how the "*taharah-bret*" was brought to the court, and was stood up in a corner, or pitched against the wall, with the deceased standing beyond this board, so that no one would see this spirit and become alarmed. From this place the deceased would plead his case.

Elzet concludes: "I suspect that the author of *Seder Halitzah* [i.e. R. Teicher, see below, the following note] intentionally omitted this detail, that is so important for us, but he undoubtedly considered it to be 'an Amorite practice [i.e. idolatrous],' and concealed it. What he wrote: 'The simple practice is that a board is brought and placed against the wall' cannot be understood in any other sense." This practice could possibly be connected with what we mentioned in Part 2, chap. 8, "The Construction of the Coffin in the Cemetery," n. 49, that the will of R. Judah he-Hasid mandates: "When the corpse is purified, the board on which he is purified is not overturned; for this entails danger, lest someone die within three days."

8   (= R. Michael ben Joseph Teicher) (first published: Vilna, 1863), cited in *Shulhan Arukh, Even ha-Ezer*, beginning with the Vilna 1879 edition.

press his heel in the ground, **with his back to the board**, and he is not to lean excessively." Rabbi Moses Mintz specifies:[9] "The *yabam* shall come before the judges and stand next to a pole, a wall, or a **board**."

The widow stands on her feet, slightly stooped:[10] "Nonetheless, she is not to sit, nor kneel, **she rather is to stand, bending her body**, as she casts the footwear to the ground"; and she removes the shoe with her right hand.[11] The manner in which the judges and witnesses sit, and their number, however, does not correspond exactly with the descriptions by the halakhic authorities. The illustration from the Latin Mishnah has the rabbi-judge sitting in the middle, flanked by three people sitting on each side, while the halakhah requires only an additional two individuals on one side (who together with the rabbi constitute a court of three judges), and another two people — the witnesses[12] — on the other side. This illustration, however, adds an additional person on each side. It should be noted at this juncture that the presence of a quorum of ten people was usually preferred at the *halitzah* ceremony, thus requiring the presence of five more people, in addition to the three judges and the two witnesses.[13] This quorum, that is, for the purpose of making this act known in public,[14] is not an absolute requirement and its absence does not invalidate the ceremony, since it is not specified in the *Shulhan Arukh*.[15] In the background of this illustration we see a large crowd of spectators outside the gate, a scene that accords with the following description by R. Jacob ben Moses Moellin:[16]

9 *She'eilot u-Teshuvot Rabbeinu Moshe Mintz*, ed. Y.S. Domb (Jerusalem, 1991), para. 61. See I.S. Lange, "R. Meir of Padua as the Redactor of *Seder Gittin ve-Halitzah by Mahari Mintz*," in *Miscellanea di Studi in Memoria di Dario Disegni*, ed. E.M. Artom, L. Caro, and S.J. Sierra (Torina and Jerusalem, 1969), pp. 49–76 (Hebrew).

10 *Shulhan Arukh, Even ha-Ezer* 169:30.

11 As is mandated by the *Shulhan Arukh*; cf. above, n. 1.

12 *Shulhan Arukh, Even ha-Ezer* 169:1, 3.

13 See Rabbi Judah Ashkenazi, *Be'er Hetev*, para. 6, on *Shulhan Arukh*, loc. cit.; see below. The deliverance of a writ of divorce is also performed in the presence of a quorum of ten. See *Shulhan Arukh, Even ha-Ezer* 154:67: "A quorum is to be assembled, in order to give the writ of divorce in [the presence of] ten"; and similarly, *idem*, 133:3: "A writ of divorce is generally given in a quorum of ten."

14 See *Be'er Hetev*, loc. cit.; see also *She'eilot u-Teshuvot Rabbeinu Moshe Mintz*, p. 583, and n. 5.

15 *Even ha-Ezer* 169:1.

16 *Sefer Maharil*, ed. Spitzer, p. 514.

In the morning, when they left the synagogue, the rabbi told his two colleagues, the rabbinical judges: "Come, let us go to the place that we specified yesterday." **And all the congregation went with the brother-in-law after them**.

R. Moses Mintz continues in this vein:[17]

In the morning, after leaving the synagogue, the beadle shall immediately call in a loud voice: "Know, men and women, adults and minors, that *halitzah* shall now be performed."

R. Moses Isserles similarly writes:[18]

Consequently, it is the current practice for people to go and perform *halitzah* immediately after leaving the synagogue in the morning, **for then there is a multitude of people**, and the greatest among them says to his fellows: "Let us go to [witness] the *halitzah* in the place that we decided yesterday."

And as this is described by R. Jousep Schammes:[19]

And the following day, on the day of the *halitzah*, prior to the *halitzah*, the beadle proclaims all along the street, from one end to the other: "*Zu der halitzah* [to the *halitzah*]." **And all the people gather at the courtyard of that synagogue**. Then the rabbi says to his two colleagues the judges: "Let us go to the place that we decided yesterday."

The entire purpose of this arrangement was to publicize the matter (see above), as was that of the quorum of ten, and possibly, if a large public was in attendance, the need for a quorum was no longer relevant. In this illustration, we witness how "all the people gather at the courtyard," the site of the *halitzah* ceremony, and watch the rite, thus affording it the greatest possible publicity.

---

17 *She'eilot u-Teshuvot Rabbeinu Moshe Mintz*, ed. Domb, para. 61, p. 585; see the editor's gloss, n. 35.
18 R. Moses Isserles, "*Seder Halitzah*," para. 13.
19 *Wormser Minhagbuch*, Vol. 2, p. 124.

3. CALMET, AMSTERDAM 1731

Another example of a semiaccurate portrayal of *halitzah* is to be found in the Dutch edition of the monumental dictionary by Augustinius Calmet,[20] which contains an elegant engraving of the *halitzah* ceremony (Fig. 4). The seated brother-in-law[21] extends his right foot, and the widow, who is standing bent over, removes his shoe with her right hand.[22] Opposite them are three seaked judges, one of whom, apparently the most important, is writing the writ of *halitzah*. Behind the judges are the two witnesses, who, in contrast with the judges, are standing.[23] There is no quorum of ten, nor a crowd

20 Amsterdam and Leiden, 1731, Section 3, next to p. 378. The full title of this edition is: *Byvogzel tot het Algemeen Groot Historisch Oordeelkundig, Chronologisch, Geographisch, en Letterlyk Naam-en Woord-Boek van den Ganschen H. Bybel...*, translated and edited by Jacob van Ostade and Arn. Henr. Westerhovius.

21 See above, n. 3.

22 The widow is covered by a sort of long cloth, while the brother-in-law wears no special headwear. In contrast, see MS. Oxford 765, from a student of R. Joel Sirkes (cited in *She'eilot u-Teshuvot Rabbeinu Moshe Mintz*, editor's gloss, p. 587 n. 55), which attests:

> and in a location where engarbing is customary, the brother-in-law's head is wrapped, as a mourner, or as one under the ban, with his *mitron* [see Part 2, chap. 19, "A Kerchief around the Neck of the Mourner, and the Practice of Covering the Head," n. 18], and the widow is similarly enwrapped. In our place, where enwrapping is not customary, he nevertheless places a hat on his head, next to his eyes, as is the practice of mourners, and the woman also is enwrapped in a kerchief, as is done by mourning women.

The brother-in-law's hat in the portrait by Calmet, however, is not "next to his eyes." For the shape of the hat, see Rubens, *A History of Jewish Costume*, no. 184, a wedding (Nuremberg, 1731[?]).

23 For the number of religious judges, see BT Yevamot 111b; *Ravyah*, Vol. 4, para. 894, p. 30 and n. 273; the order of *halitzah* by R. Eliezer ben Samuel of Metz (the author of *Sefer Yere'im*), in E. Kupfer, *Teshuvot u-Pesakim me'et Hakhmei Ashkenaz ve-Tzorfat (Responsa et Decisiones)* (Jerusalem, 1973), p. 213; and even in "*Siddur Halitzah mi-Nimukei Rabbenu Shmuel ha-Levi*" (possibly R. Samuel ben Abraham ha-Levi of Worms), in Kupfer, loc. cit., p. 219. See below, n. 59. For the judges sitting, see BT Shavuot 30b; the order of *halitzah* by R. Eliezer ben Samuel of Metz, in Kupfer, p. 213; *Shulhan Arukh, Even ha-Ezer* 169:12; *Shulhan Arukh, Even ha-Ezer, Seder Halitzah* 46; *Shulhan Arukh, Even ha-Ezer, Perush Seder Halitzah*, para. 64. Cf. *Shulhan Arukh, Even ha-Ezer, Seder Halitzah*, para. 55, and *Shulhan Arukh, Even ha-Ezer, Perush Seder Halitzah*, para. 80, which imply that the others stand. And in the gloss by R. Moses Isserles on *Shulhan Arukh, Even ha-Ezer*

of spectators standing at the gate. Moreover, the footwear is not the shoe required for *halitzah*, because it lacks the required straps. Thus, the artist was not precise in the minor details, although he faithfully presented the other facets of the ceremony.

4. KIRCHNER, NUREMBERG 1724

The books by Kirchner (Nuremberg, 1724) and by Bodenschatz (Erlang, 1748)[24] contain both verbal[25] and pictorial descriptions. The latter are quite detailed, and the engravings that are based on the written descriptions are highly accurate (see Figs. 5, 6). See, for example, the engraving in Kirchner's book (by the engraver Pushner), which portrays the first stage in the process of *halitzah* (on the left side, outside the *halitzah* room), in which the brother-in-law is washing both his feet in a round vessel,[26] and the text[27] specifies: "und ihres vestorbenen Mann's Bruder muss vor der Kammer oder Stuben-seine strumpfe aufzeihen und seine fusse rein waschen," that is, the brother-in-law must remove his stockings and wash his feet. In similar spirit, the *Shulhan Arukh* rules:[28] "Some are careful that there be no mud within the shoe; for this reason, one opinion calls for washing the right foot very thoroughly."[29] Although some *poskim* (such as R. Samuel ben Uri Shraga Phoebus, in *Beit Shmuel*) wrote that this is a mere stringency, this custom was nevertheless presented as binding halakhah in the *Seder Halitzah* in

> 169:14: "Two valid witnesses are chosen, and they are told to stand next to the benches, for their examination regarding the brother-in-law and the widow, if they are fit to perform the *halitzah* ceremony." The witnesses, however, apparently were permitted to sit during the ceremony itself, as did the judges, but they were to be set apart from the latter.

24 Kirchner, *Judisches Ceremoniel*, pp. 198–204; Bodenschatz, *Kirchliche Verfassung der heutigen Juden*, pp. 148–58. Mention should also be made of Buxtorf, *Synagoga Judaica*, chap. 41, which, in great measure, followed da Modena.

25 There are scattered inconsistencies between the verbal description and the illustration (see below); generally speaking, however, the latter clearly relates to the verbal text.

26 Cf. *She'eilot u-Teshuvot Rabbeinu Moshe Mintz*, p. 586: "The rabbi must inform the beadle to take care that there be a **tub with water** [hot, or at least lukewarm], and a towel or sheet for washing [and drying] the foot of the brother-in-law."

27 Kirchner, *Judisches Ceremoniel*, p. 199.

28 *Shulhan Arukh, Even ha-Ezer* 169:26.

29 *Be'er ha-Golah refers to Mordekhai* (Yevamot 56), in the name of R. Eliezer ben Joel ha-Levi of Bonn (*Ravyah*), *Ravyah*, ed. Aptowitzer, Vol. 4, para. 894, p. 35.

the *Shulhan Arukh*;[30] in the *Perush Seder Halitzah*;[31] and in *Seder Halitzah* by R. Michael Jozefs of Cracow.[32] R. Jousep Schammes[33] reports (based on *Maharil*[34]): "And lukewarm water is there, immediately outside the yeshivah; the beadle washes the foot of the brother-in-law, and sees that nothing has adhered to it." The woodcut in Kirchner, however, has the brother-in-law washing **both his feet**, by himself (see below for an explanation). Kirchner maintains that the *parnas* (a community leader) or the attendant of the rabbi places his shoe(s) back on the brother-in-law: "und die Fursteher oder die Rabbiner Schuhe [in the plural!; in actuality, the widow removes only one shoe] an Diener thut ihn seine." It would appear from his account that both shoes are removed, but the woodcut shows the removal of only the left shoe, with the text and the picture seemingly contradicting one another. The removal of both shoes, however, is mandated in the case of a brother-in-law who favors his left foot.[35] As this is formulated by the *Shulhan Arukh* (loc. cit.): "[As regards] the left-footed one: according to one opinion, both [shoes] are removed, the right shoe by the right [hand], and the left shoe by the left [hand], while another opinion questions whether he is capable of performing *halitzah* [and the first view was followed; see *Perush*, para. 40]."[36] It is therefore plausible that Kirchner wrote his description based on a ceremony that he personally witnessed, or about which he had heard from his acquaintances: that of the *halitzah* of a left-handed brother-in-law, based on the Central European custom, in which both shoes are removed.[37]

Kirchner himself sensed the difficulty inherent in his verbal description, and mentioned in a footnote that it was usual for only a single shoe, the

30 *Shulhan Arukh, Even ha-Ezer, Seder Halitzah* 7, based on R. Yaacov Margolis, the author of *Seder Haget* (*Laws of Divorce*), ed. Y. Satz (Jerusalem, 1983) (Satz states in his introduction, p. 10, that "a comprehensive introduction to the book and the life of our master [i.e. Margolis] will appear in the beginning of the second volume").

31 *Shulhan Arukh, Even ha-Ezer, Perush Seder Halitzah*, para. 52.

32 R. Michael Jozefs of Cracow, *Seder Halitzah* (appended to *Shulhan Arukh, Even ha-Ezer*), para. 62.

33 Schammes, *Wormser Minhagbuch*, Vol. 2, para. 268, p. 123.

34 *Sefer Maharil*, ed. Spitzer, p. 518.

35 *Shulhan Arukh, Even ha-Ezer* 169:25; *Shulhan Arukh, Even ha-Ezer, Perush Seder Halitzah*, para. 40. See *Enziklopedia Talmudit*, "Halitzah," col. 758.

36 See above, n. 3.

37 For the order in which the shoes are removed, see *Enziklopedia Talmudit*, "Halitzah," cols. 758–760.

right one, to be removed,[38] citing PT Yevamot 12:1.[39] He further writes in the same note that the woman must remove the shoe with her right hand, and if perforce, as the result of an accident, she has no right hand, she unties the straps of the shoe with her teeth.[40] And, indeed, in the woodcut, the widow removes the shoe with her right hand (albeit from the left foot). According to our above proposal, this was only a part of the entire *halitzah* procedure, which also included removing the shoe from the brother-in-law's right foot.

What appears even more intriguing is Kirchner's text and woodcut regarding the form of the strap on the shoe. When I first saw this illustration from Kirchner's book, it seemed as if the shoe was attached to the floor by some sort of chain, which is quite puzzling, since the brother-in-law is required to walk at least four cubits before the actual act of *halitzah*.[41] When the book first came into my hands, and I read the description, I discovered something new, for which I have not found any source.[42] Kirchner writes that the *halitzah* shoe is flanked on each side by two long straps, each twelve and a half cubits in length(!). The straps are tied together with **139** knots, and they are to be untied by the brother-in-law, using only two fingers of his left hand.[43] Kirchner additionally warns that this untying must be done without contact by any other limb, and even without the extension of any other body part. If these conditions are not all met, the participants must repeat the entire ceremony, even if this were to take ten years![44] Since we have already learned from Kirchner that the shoe is removed by the **right hand of the widow**, and

---

38 P. 200: "Doch ist hierben zu erinnern das sonsten nur vor ausziehung eines einigen und zwar des rechter Schuhes gedacht wird."

39 See above, n. 2.

40 Based on PT, loc. cit.; *Shulhan Arukh, Even ha-Ezer* 169:31. See *Enziklopedia Talmudit*, "*Halitzah*," cols. 765–766.

41 *Shulhan Arukh, Even ha-Ezer, Seder Halitzah*, para. 43; Jozefs, *Seder Halitzah*, para. 67, and more.

42 Kirchner, pp. 200–202. My thanks to Dr. Michael and Dafna Mach for their aid in understanding the difficult German of these passages.

43 "Waran ein ziemlicher Riemen / welcher lang muss sein auf jeder Zeit des Schuhes in die zwolf und eine halbe Ellen / und die gedachte Riemen werden zusammen geknuft mit 139 Knoten da muss es gedachten Verstorbennen sein Bruder / welchen man den linken Schuhe hat angezogen / den verfnupten Schuh-Riemen mit zween Fingern dem linken Hand allein aufnupten oder aufmachen."

44 "[...] so mussen die gedachten ganzen Ceremonien wieder aufs neue angefangen werden / und wann auch zehen Jahr damit solte gebraucht werden."

not by the brother-in-law, we must understand this passage as referring to another act: a custom that we have not yet found in the Jewish sources. In other words, after the straps are bound around the shoe and the foot, as is the accepted practice (and as Kirchner concisely describes this on p. 201), the rest of the long straps are tied to **one another** with **139** knots, which the **brother-in-law** must untie with two fingers of his **left hand**. All of this must take place before the widow can untie the regular knots of the strap (two knots and a bow)[45] with her right hand, in order to perform the basic requirement of the commandment of *halitzah*. This is probably an additional obstacle that the brother-in-law must overcome before the *halitzah* itself, and the 139 knots (the word *ha-halutz*, i.e. the one who undergoes *halitzah*, has the numerical value of 139) may possibly allude to the severance of his ties with his dead brother and his sister-in-law.

We also see in Kirchner's illustration that the heads of the brother-in-law and the widow are covered with a black cloth or sackcloth; as the text describes this (p. 199):

> [...] und stellet sich mit einen schwarzen tuchenen oder leinwandenen Sacke uber seinen haupte / nur das etwas sehen kan [...] der gemeldten Frauen einen schwarzen Mantel uber ihr haupt decken.

This practice corresponds to that in Worms,[46] where the brother-in-law wore the mourner's *mitron*,[47] and for the widow, a "head covering of a *Sturz* or *sarbal* on the head of the mourning wife."[48]

---

45 See *Enziklopedia Talmudit*, "*Halitzah*," cols. 752–754. The compound manner of tying is in order to fulfill the requirements of the law in accordance with all the different views of the Amoraim. R. Zeira maintains that it is to be tied with two knots, while R. Haninah is of the opinion that it is to be tied with a bow. Consequently, two knots are made, with the bow over them (*Enziklopedia Talmudit*, ad loc., nn. 110–111). Cf. *Minhagei Yisrael*, Vol. 1, pp. 39 ff.; Vol. 2, pp. 23 ff. (See also *Minhagei Yisrael*, Vol. 6, chap. 2, pp. 9–16, regarding the binding of the hand *tefillin*.)

46 Schammes, *Wormser Minhagbuch*, Vol. 2, p. 124.

47 For this item of clothing, see Rubens, *A History of Jewish Costume*, p. 158. For the *sarbal*, see Rubens, p. 154.

48 Cf. *Shulhan Arukh, Even ha-Ezer* 169, *Seder Halitzah* 14; *She'eilot u-Teshuvot Rabbeinu Moshe Mintz*, p. 587, with additional sources in the editor's n. 55. The reason for this "mourning" is because the brother-in-law does not fulfill his duty to his dead brother, and is therefore as one in mourning and outcast. See *Hagahot Maimoniyot, Hil. Halitzah* (*Laws of* Halitzah) 4:9, cited in the editor's gloss, *She'eilot u-Teshuvot Rabbeinu Moshe Mintz*, loc. cit.

In this picture the widow is kneeling on one knee, a posture that would seem to be forbidden, since *halitzah* is to be performed while standing.[49] Other opinions, however, maintain that the widow need not stand,[50] since the biblical verse "If he insists [*ve-omad*, or: stood], saying ["I do not want to marry her"]"[51] refers exclusively to the brother-in-law, and not to the widow.[52]

5. BODENSCHATZ, ERLANG 1748

As regards the rabbis being seated and their location (which was already discussed above, in Kirchner's woodcut) we find six judges at the table, and an additional two people standing behind them. On the other hand, the illustration (by I.C. Muller) reproduced by Bodenschatz shows three people (the three judges)[53] on one side of the table, two others on the other side and a little removed from the three judges[54] — these are the witnesses,[55] and an additional five people standing behind them, for a total of ten people, besides the brother-in-law and the widow. And similarly in the *Seder Halitzah* of the *Shulhan Arukh*:[56]

> Other people are brought who shall be present during the *halitzah*, there shall be at least five, that [together] with the judges shall be ten.

49 *Shulhan Arukh, Even ha-Ezer* 169:12, 29; ibid., *Seder Halitzah* 46.
50 Such as R. Moses Parnas of Rothenburg, *Sefer ha-Parnas* (Vilna, 1891), para. 357, and more. See *Enziklopedia Talmudit*, "Halitzah," col. 762, n. 226.
51 Deut. 25:8.
52 *Enziklopedia Talmudit*, loc. cit.
53 See Schammes, *Wormser Minhagbuch*, Vol. 2, p. 124; Jozefs, *Seder Halitzah*, para. 11, and more.
54 The halakhic sources, such as Schammes, *Wormser Minhagbuch*, Vol. 2, p. 124, emphasize this separation between the judges and other people and the maintenance of a certain distance between the two groups. See *Sefer Maharil*, ed. Spitzer, pp. 514–15 and editor's n. 6, based on *Ravyah*, para. 894, Vol. 4, p. 32; and similarly in *Shulhan Arukh, Even ha-Ezer* 169, *Seder Halitzah*, para. 12; and in a *seder halitzah* in MS. British Museum Add. 2711.575: "And the judges sit there, that is, three judges, and two a bit away." See *She'eilot u-Teshuvot Rabbeinu Moshe Mintz*, p. 587 n. 19.
55 Schammes, *Wormser Minhagbuch*, loc. cit.; Jozefs, *Seder Halitzah*, loc. cit.; *Shulhan Arukh, Even ha-Ezer* 169, *Seder Halitzah*, para. 12.
56 *Shulhan Arukh, Even ha-Ezer* 169, *Seder Halitzah*, para. 13.

This law is then explained:[57]

> "Other people are brought ... that [together] with the judges shall be
> ten" — *Hagahot Maimoniyot*[58] writes as follows: "*Pirkei R. Eliezer*[59]
> states explicitly that ten are required, as it was said:[60] 'Go bring me a
> group of ten people, so that I may tell you in their presence.'"

R. Michael Jozefs rules:[61]

> There must be ten people: the three judges, the two additional ones, the
> two witnesses, the brother-in-law, and the beadle are included among
> the ten.

This count is clearly stressed by Kirchner:[62]

> Wenn sich nun diese 5 Personen gesetzet haben, so ruft man noch so
> viele herzu von dem haben sich versamletan Volke, damit es ihre 10
> werden, von welchen aber keiner sitzen darf auf denjenigen Platz, vo
> die Richter sitzen, und so lange die Chalizah wahret.

It should be noted that in the illustration in Bodenschatz (and also in that
in Kirchner), we do not see a crowd standing by the gate of the venue of
the *halitzah*, thus compelling the former to specify a quorum of ten, which
is not the case in the title page illustration in the Borstius Mishnah, which
does depict a large audience.

Bodenschatz also shows the next stage of the *halitzah* process (lower left
illustration), in which the widow spits before the brother-in-law. As this step
is described by R. Moses Mintz:[63]

---

57 *Shulhan Arukh, Even ha-Ezer* 169, *Perush Seder Halitzah*, para. 23.
58 *Hil. Yibum ve-Halitzah* (*Laws of* Yibum *and* Halitzah) 4:6.
59 *Pirkei de-Rabbi Eliezer*, ed. Luria, fol. 44b; see the gloss by Luria, n. 27. The text
   is distorted in *Be'er Hetev* 169:6, where it reads: "*R. Eliezer de-Milah*" (instead of
   Pirkei de-Rabbi Eliezer). See *Ravyah*, Vol. 4, para. 894, p. 54. See Stern, *Seder
   Halitzah* of Rabbeinu Solomon, p. 9 n. 1. This *Seder Halitzah* states: "It has become
   customary to conduct *halitzah* with five judges, and as it is [set forth] in *Tur, Even
   ha-Ezer* 168, in the name of *Baal Halakhot*: 'It is necessary for five to sit in that
   rabbinical court.'" See the order of *halitzah* by R. Eliezer ben Samuel of Metz, in
   Kupfer, *Teshuvot u-Pesakim me'et Hakhmei Ashkenaz ve-Tzorfat*, pp. 214–15.
60 BT Yevamot 67a; Bava Batra 142b.
61 Jozefs, *Seder Halitzah*, para. 20.
62 *Judisches Ceremoniel*, p. 152.
63 *She'eilot u-Teshuvot Rabbeinu Moshe Mintz*, p. 592.

> She stands upright facing the brother-in-law when she spits. It is necessary for the three judges, as well as the two [witnesses], to see the spittle emerge from the mouth of the widow, in front of the brother-in-law, until it reaches the ground.[64]

The picture in Bodenschatz conforms to this procedure: we see the shoe on the ground after the widow has removed it and cast it to the ground, and she stands upright facing the brother-in-law and spits before him in the presence of the three judges (and possibly also of the two other individuals, who are beyond the frame of the illustration).

Bodenschatz also provides an additional picture (lower right) that presents the *halitzah* footwear from different angles (Fig. 6), and which apparently is based on the picture in Kirchner[65] (Fig. 7). We shall not discuss the details of the shoe, since they are so numerous. We shall only observe that Kirchner himself, in a lengthy note (p. 201), provides a detailed description, but is not certain if all these details are mandatory. He also attests in a note on the preceding page that he received such a shoe to examine from his learned fellow Christoph Arnold, who was given it by the rabbi of Fuerth, Rabbi Mejer,[66]

64 Cf. *Shulhan Arukh, Even ha-Ezer* 169:38; *Shulhan Arukh, Even ha-Ezer, Seder Halitzah* 53, and more.

65 *Judisches Ceremoniel*, facing p. 226. We have already discussed the degree of Bodenschatz's dependence upon Kirchner. This illustration appeared in reverse in Buxtorf, *Synagoga Judaica*, p. 751, without a caption, and with additional minor changes, such as alterations in the size of the letters within the illustrations and the numeration. We have already seen this phenomenon in depictions of burial in the cemetery (see the Part 2, chap. 6 ["The Firstborn of an Animal in the Cemetery"], n. 15), the *sukkah* (see *Minhagei Yisrael*, Vol. 6, pp. 155–56), and the like.

66 Cohen, "The Visual Image of the Jew and Judaism in Early Modern Europe," pp. 336–40, has already shown that "a phenomenon that became enrooted within the German communities, visits by Christians in private and public synagogues" (p. 336), had begun in the time of Bodenschatz. In one of the latter's illustrations Cohen finds visual expression, not only of such a visit by a non-Jew, but also of Jewish openness to such interest by those not of their faith (pp. 337–38). Cohen's thesis is seemingly confirmed by the testimony of Bodenschatz, to which we should add the evidence of non-Jews who were present at Jewish ceremonies in Italy. An example of this is the visit in 1580 by the Frenchman Montaigne to a circumcision in Italy (albeit one conducted in a private house), who described the ceremony to the best of his understanding. See the book by Emmanuel Rodocanachi, *Le Saint-Siege et les Juifs: le ghetto à Rome* (Paris, 1891 [Bologna, 1972]), pp. 311–14; also cited in Bonfil, *Jewish Life in Renaissance Italy*, pp. 250–54.

who had this footwear from a *halitzah* ceremony. This picture of the shoe is quite similar to that in MS. British Museum Add 2711.575, in an abbreviated order of *halitzah* by an as yet unidentified author[67] (Fig. 8).

We learn from the above just how many halakhic details of the custom of *halitzah*, as practiced among Ashkenazic Jewry,[68] underlie these descriptions and pictoral representations, along with another custom, that of the 139 knots, which is unknown from any other source. Our intent in this chapter was not to provide an extensive and detailed explanation of all these Christian compositions, but only to exemplify our research methodology and to hint at the riches that are concealed in these sources — a veritable treasure trove that awaits further study.

---

67 See *She'eilot u-Teshuvot Maharil* (*Responsa of Rabbi Yaacov Molin — Maharil*), ed. Y. Satz (Jerusalem, 1979), p. 20; and also p. 12 (my thanks to Rabbi Y. Satz for drawing my attention to this source). See also Rubens, *A History of Jewish Costume*, p. 140, no. 202: a *halitzah* shoe from Austria (nineteenth century), which was in use in the Vienna community, and which resembles the footwear in our illustration. (This may be the same shoe reproduced in *Monumenta Judaica* [Cologne, 1964], E195, fig. 57: a *halitzah* shoe from the eighteenth-nineteenth centuries.) Additionally, I found a *halitzah* shoe from a community in Hungary, dated to the eighteenth-nineteenth centuries, which appeared in the catalogue of a Judaica auction in Jerusalem (October 20, 1988), item no. 775, which also is quite similar to the standard *halitzah* shoe. See also B. Kirschner, "Jewish Usages in Folk Art," *Yeda-'Am* 2, 2–3 (1954), p. 160 (Hebrew); Y.-T. Lewinski, "The Riddle of the Shoe and the Hebrew Inscription on a Flag from 1540," *Yeda-'Am* 4 (1957), pp. 56–58 (Hebrew).

68 Note should also be taken of the observation by Bodenschatz (p. 152) that *halitzah* is not conducted on a Friday (similar to the Ashkenazic custom not to hold divorce proceedings on this day). See *Terumat ha-Deshen*, para. 227; *Shulhan Arukh, Even ha-Ezer* 154:1; Schammes, *Wormser Minhagbuch*, Vol. 2, para. 265, p. 121 and n. 1. In *Shulhan Arukh, Even ha-Ezer* 169:6: "(According to one opinion, *halitzah* is not to be conducted on a Friday, and according to another view, it is customary [to do so on Friday])," based on the above passage in *Terumat ha-Deshen* (and not para. 257, as is printed in *Shulhan Arukh*). See *Pithei Teshuvah*, on *Shulhan Arukh, Even ha-Ezer* 169:10.

1. Luyken, Amsterdam 1744

2. Latin Mishnah, 1700

3. *Halitzah* **Ceremony (detail of Fig. 2)**

4. *Halitzah*, **Calmet 1702**

5. *Halitzah*, **Kirchner, 1724**

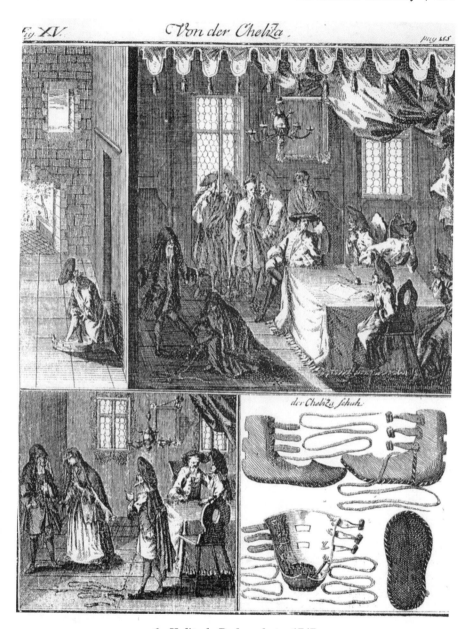

6. *Halitzah*, **Bodenschatz, 1747**

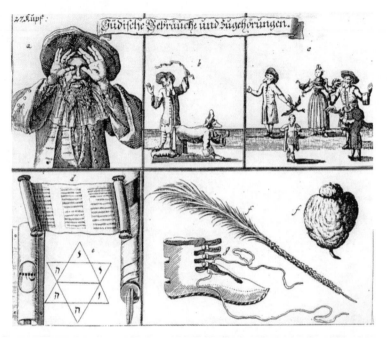

7. *Halitzah* **shoe, Kirchner, 1742**

8. *Halitzah* **shoe, Ms. BM 575**

31

ON DIVORCE

In the preceding chapter on *Halitzah* we saw how accurate graphic depictions of Jewish rituals can be, and how much we can learn from them. The degree of accuracy and detail in these illustrations is well reflected in the woodcut in which Bodenschatz portrays the giving of a writ of divorce[1] (our Fig. 1), where we see the husband holding the writ of divorce with his fingers, above the extended hands of the wife. This should be compared with the procedural rules of divorce set forth by R. Michael Jozefs of Cracow:[2]

> The writ of divorce is given to the husband, and [the judge] tells him: "Hold the writ of divorce in your hand, until I tell you to give it to her";

and in para. 223:

> She extends her hands, opens them, and brings them together, in order to receive the writ of divorce. Her hands must not be as a slope, so that the writ of divorce could fall from them, rather she merely raises her fingers, so that her hands shall not be within three handbreadths of the ground or of the table, and she opens her hands upward in order to receive the writ of divorce.

In para. 224:

> The rabbi cautions her not to clench her fists until he tells her to bring them together [to receive and clutch the writ of divorce].

1   *Kirchliche Verfassung der heutigen Juden*, next to p. 140.
2   R. Michael Jozefs of Cracow, *Seder ha-Get im Perush Birkat ha-Mayim*, ed. M. Hershler (Jerusalem, 1983), Vol. 1, para. 218, p. 277.

And last, in para. 232:

> The husband immediately releases the writ of divorce so that it gently falls into her hands.[3]

This also bears comparison with the verbal description by Bodenschatz (p. 141), in which he writes that, following this action, the husband says: "Here is your writ of divorce....":

> So bald nun der Mann diesen gesagt, so lasset er zugleich den Scheidenbrief der Frau in die hand fallen.

R. Moses Isserles adds:[4]

> The face of the wife is customarily covered, out of modesty, until the sage speaks with her and she receives the writ of divorce.

All this is presented in the woodcut. It also should be noted that the writ of divorce is not folded (although I am not certain of this).[5] It appears, however, that the procedure depicted in the illustration in Bodenschatz follows the opinion of *Mahari Mintz*. Additionally, in this woodcut the husband holds the writ of divorce in his left hand, while *She'eilot u-Teshuvot Rabbeinu Moshe Mintz* (p. 580; cf. p. 515) specifies that "he takes the writ of divorce in his right hand." The editor correctly comments (p. 515 n. 48): "I did not find this law in other orders of divorce." We obviously should stress the importance of the details in these illustrations, such as the handing over of the ink and the quill to the scribe,[6] and the knife on the table with which the parchment is cut.[7] All this leads us to conclude that Bodenschatz was present at these ceremonies and faithfully observed the procedure that was followed.[8]

---

3 See the editor's gloss ad loc.

4 *Shulhan Arukh, Even ha-Ezer* 154, *Seder ha-Get* 81, gloss.

5 See *Shulhan Arukh, Even ha-Ezer* 154, *Seder ha-Get* 84: "It is the practice of some to fold it as a letter when he hands it over [cf. *Shulhan Arukh, Even ha-Ezer* 131:1, gloss by R. Moses Isserles; *Pithei Teshuvah* 139:4]. Others wrote not to fold it, but rather to give it to her as it is. He writes on the outside, so that all will see that this is a writ of divorce [as can be understood from R. Judah Mintz, *She'eilot u-Teshuvot ma-ha-Ri Mintz* (Cracow, 1882), "*Seder ha-Get*," para. 69, fol. 37b, s.v. "*Amirah*"]." *She'eilot u-Teshuvot Rabbeinu Moshe Mintz*, p. 560, states explicitly: "Then he folds the writ of divorce as a letter and places it in the hand of the husband." Cf. p. 576, and n. 46.

6 Cf. *Shulhan Arukh, Even ha-Ezer, Seder ha-Get* 154:15; cf. 122:1.

7 *Shulhan Arukh, Even ha-Ezer, Seder ha-Get* 39.

8 See above, chap. 30 ("The *Halitzah* Ceremony"), n. 66. See also *Minhagei*

Another practice related to divorce is described by Rabbi Jacob Castro,[9] who writes that the participants immerse in a ritual bath following the divorce ceremony. This custom apparently was taken over from Muslim Egypt. Similar action was taken in Calcutta, India:[10]

When I was engaged with them in matters concerning divorce, I saw their practice and folly, how they fear the writ of divorce. They even are afraid of the smell of the writ of divorce, and they flee from it as from a contagious disease. They will not allow a divorce ceremony to be conducted in a house inhabited by people, lest an evil spirit from this adhere to them. They also close the windows that face the venue of the divorce ceremony, so that the sound and smell of the writ of divorce shall not enter. The clothing of the divorced man and woman are as impure to them as those of the one stricken by the plague; accordingly, as soon as the act of divorce is concluded, they hurry to the water, to immerse in a ritual bath. Whoever makes haste to the water, as the one bitten by an *arod* [a type of scorpion] (Berakhot 33a, in Rashi) is praiseworthy. And whoever is more powerful gives more to the ritual bath attendant, to let him in first. The garments that they remove before [entering] the water shall not be worn by them again, and they are declared free for the poor. When they emerge from the water, they don other garments, from foot to head. Consequently, they wear inferior clothing at the time of the divorce ceremony.

In response to my query, Prof. David Schulman of Jerusalem, an expert on India, could find no local Indian influence in all these happenings. For the present, the source of this custom remains an enigma.[11]

Yisrael, Vol. 6, pp. 146–49 n. 23, on the throwing of apples on Simhat Torah and Shavuot.

9 Rabbi Jacob Castro, *She'eilot u-Teshuvot Ohalei Yaakov* (Leghorn, 1783), para. 131; with reference in J.S. Spiegal, "R. Jacob Castro [Maharikas] and His Works," *Alei Sefer* (1990), p. 24. See the incisive article by Y. Avida, "Strange Immersions," *Yeda-'Am* 3,1 (1955), p. 9 (Hebrew).

10 See Ben Naim, *Noheg be-Hokhmah*, who cites the description by Jacob Saphir (*Even Sappir*, Vol. 2 [Mainz, 1874 (photocopy edn.: Jerusalem, 1970)], chap. 26, p. 104).

11 See Westermarck, *The History of Human Marriage*, Vol. 3, pp. 314–17, for divorce in the Indian religion. Cf. R. Mosheh Yehudah Kats, *Va-Yaged Moshe* (Brooklyn, 1980), p. 72.

1. Divorce proceedings, Bodenschatz, 1748

PART 2

DEATH

1

OMENS OF APPROACHING DEATH

Rabbinic sources give many examples of omens or portents that warn of
an incipient death or tragedy in the family, such as the case of candles that
go out by themselves (discussed below, Chapter 21). Here we shall limit
ourselves to a discussion of two such omens: the hen that crows, and the
sighting of incomplete shadows.

1. THE HEN THAT CROWED

Edward Westermarck writes in his book *Ritual and Belief in Morocco*:

> The uncanny feeling caused by an unusual event makes it bad
> *fal* [magic influence/omen]. If a hen is heard crowing like a cock
> somebody in the house will die, unless it is killed at once, in which
> case the *bas* [evil influence] will fall back upon the hen (Hiaina).[1]

This belief was not restricted to Morocco, and also was prevalent in Syria,
as Eijub Abela writes:

> Wenn ein Henne anfangt zu Krahen, so ist von schlimmer
> Vorbedeutung fur die leute, in deren Huhnerhof sie sich befindet.
> Auch wird sie Sifort getodtet, weil sie thut, was ihr nicht zusteht.[2]

This superstition, mentioned by Abela, is also described by H. Lewy in
his article on the ways of the Amorites, albeit without mentioning his

---

1   Vol. 2 (London, 1926), p. 32.
2   E. Abela, "Beitrage zur Kenntniss aberglaubischer gebrauch in Syrien," *ZDPV* 3
(1884), para. 25, p. 85 (cited by Westermarck, loc. cit.).

source.[3] He also found this phenomenon in Germanic folk beliefs, with a reference to Grimm,[4] and among the Slavs, as reported by Wuttke.[5] This superstition is likewise to be found in China,[6] Macedonia,[7] and Bengal. An entry in the dictionary of Opie and Taten also teaches of the spread of this notion in parts of Great Britain (testimonies beginning in the early eighteenth century).[8] As regards the phenomenon discussed in BT Shabbat 67b: "One who says, 'Kill this rooster, because it crowed in the evening,'" that is, because such crowing is a bad omen, there are testimonies of such practice from the early sixteenth century.[9] In other words, this notion was prevalent even in relatively recent times, in both the East and the West.

This matter is strongly reminiscent of what Rabbi Judah he-Hasid asserted in his testament: "If a hen crows like a rooster, it is to be slaughtered immediately." Margaliot notes that this apparently contradicts the express ruling in the Talmud (Shabbat 67b), that a person who says "Kill this hen, because it crowed like a rooster" is guilty of Amorite practices.[10]

Regardless of the wording of the description of this belief, whether or not it constitutes "the ways of the Amorites," the practice of slaughtering a hen that crows like a rooster was clearly already in effect in the Talmudic

---

3 H. Lewy, "Morgenlandischer Aberglaube in der romischen Kaiserzeit," *Zeitschrift des Vereins fur Volkskunde* 3 (1893), p. 31.

4 J. Grimm, *Teutonic Mythology*[4], ed. J.S. Stallybrass (New York, 1966), Vol. 4, Appendix: "Superstitions," nos. 83, 555, 1055.

5 A. Wuttke, *Der deutsche Volksaberglaube der Gegenwart*[3], ed. E.H. Meyer (Berlin, 1900), p. 269. This is also reported by B. Bonnerjea, *A Dictionary of Superstition and Mythology* (London, 1927), p. 124.

6 J. Doolitle, *Social Life of the Chinese* (New York, 1867), Vol. 2, p. 328.

7 G.F. Abbot, *Macedonian Folklore* (Cambridge, 1903), p. 106; and see J.C. Lawson, *Modern Greek Folklore and Ancient Greek Religion* (Cambridge, 1910), p. 314.

8 I.A. Opie and M. Tatem, *A Dictionary of Superstitions* (Oxford and New York, 1992), pp. 197–98.

9 E.g.: Thomas Moresinus, *Papatus: seu, depravatae religionis origo et incrementum* (Edinburgh, 1594), p. 21 (cited in Opie and Tatem, *Dictionary*, p. 91). See also E. and M.A. Radford, *Encyclopaedia of Superstitions* (New York, 1949), pp. 83–84: "If a cock crows at midnight, the angel of death is passing over the house (Cornwall). For a cock to crow late at night means a death in the family. (East Riding of Yorkshire.)"

10 *Sefer Hasidim*, ed. R. Margaliot (Margulies) (Jerusalem, 1970), pp. 26–27 and the extensive discussion in n. 67. See *Teshuvot Maharil* 111, who proposes the version: "This does not constitute Amorite practices." See also S. Lieberman, *Tosefta ki-Fshutah*, Vol. 3 (New York, 1962), p. 86.

period. In the final analysis, however, it would seem that we are to prefer the version of the majority of the manuscripts, that this does "constitute Amorite practices," despite the difficulty this poses in the dictum by Rabbi Judah he-Hasid (he possibly possessed a different version, that is not the original formulation).

In 1969 Yishaq Avishur published an important article on the section devoted to "the ways of the Amorites" in T Shabbat in which he (successfully) pointed to the Canaanite-Babylonian background of these laws pertaining to Amorite practices, "based on parallel material from the literatures of Canaan and of Babylonia."[11] For some reason, however, he did not discuss the dictum in the BT, despite its presence in T Shabbat 6:5 (ed. Lieberman, p. 23). We nonetheless may presume that this practice also found its way into the Babylonian period.[12] At any rate, the antiquity of this custom — greatly preceding the Tannaitic period — is not to be questioned.

We bear witness to a superstition that has its roots in the lands of the East, and which developed in medieval Ashkenaz, continuing in Syria and Morocco, and even Russia and England, in modern times. This is not surprising, because "signs" and folk beliefs are preserved over the course of time, such as the protection afforded by the use of iron described in T Shabbat in two places: 6:4 (Lieberman, p. 23): "He who ties a piece of iron to the leg of the bed of a woman in childbirth [...]"; and 6:13 (p. 24): "If one puts a rod of wood or iron under his head [...] but if he did so in order to guard them, then this is permitted." In addition to what Lieberman describes,[13] similar practices were recorded by Westermarck in modern-day Morocco.[14]

Not only was this practice preserved for many centuries, it gained force as a (halakhically recognized) *minhag* among the Jews, and appears in the testament of R. Judah he-Hasid.[15] The *Rishonim* (medieval authorities) already noted that this section of the testament seemingly stands in opposition to the dictum in Shabbat 67b (above). If so, how could R. Judah have ordered the performance of an act that is forbidden by the Talmud as an

---

11 Y. Avishur, *"Darkei ha-Emori," Sefer Meir Wallenstein (Studies in the Bible and the Hebrew Language Offered to Meir Wallenstein...)* (Jerusalem, 1979), p. 19 (Hebrew).

12 See Avishur, *"Darkei ha-Emori,"* pp. 24–28 on "omens."

13 S. Lieberman, *Tosefta*, Vol. 2: *The Order of Moed* (New York, 1962), p. 84.

14 *Ritual and Belief in Morocco*, Vol. 1, p. 306, for iron next to the bed; Vol. 2, p. 385, for iron for a woman giving birth.

15 Para. 3; see above.

Amorite practice?[16] This question was already discussed in his responsa by *Maharil*,[17] who proposes that the correct version of the Talmud is "this **does not** constitute the ways of the Amorites." He writes:

> I, in my humble opinion, **resolved the testament and the practice**, for R. Judah he-Hasid maintained that the version here is "this does not constitute [*ein zeh*] the ways of the Amorites," while Rashi was forced to write that in all versions the text is "this is [*harei zeh*] the ways of the Amorites," implying that there are books some of which read "*ein zeh*."[18]

The *Maharil* is willing to correct the text of the Talmud[19] rather than change anything in the testament of R. Judah he-Hasid. In the continuation of his responsa, however, he rejects his own proposal, since he found in "*Sefer ha-Kavod*" composed by R. Judah he-Hasid, that he himself wrote in his own testament:

> If someone were to say, why many matters have been reversed, such as a hen that crowed like a rooster [...] and similarly the crowing of

16 See *Sefer Hasidim*, ed. Margaliot, p. 316: "There are matters that are Amorite practices, but which nevertheless are permitted." See also Rabbi Moses Sofer, *She'eilot u-Teshuvot Hatam Sofer, Yoreh Deah* 138, who was asked concerning what is written in *Be'er Hetev* on *Yoreh Deah* 179, in the name of the testament of R. Judah he-Hasid (that is not in the extant text): "'regarding the danger of building a house with stones' [...] and people say to place in the house fowl, male and female, and to slaughter them there. This seems to the honored [author] as the ways of the Amorites." For the definitions of "the ways of the Amorites," see *Enziklopedia Talmudit (Talmudic Encyclopedia)*, Vol. 7 (Jerusalem, 1956), cols. 706–712, that the prohibition is because of *hukat ha-goyim* (distinctive Gentile practice), and because it hints of idolatry (Ran [R. Nissim ben Reuben Gerondi], Avodah Zarah 11b).

17 *She'eilot u-Teshuvot Maharil (Responsa of Rabbi Yaacov Molin — Maharil)*, ed. Y. Satz (Jerusalem, 1979), para. 111, p. 208.

18 Rashi, Shabbat loc. cit., s.v. "*Yesh bo mishum Darkei ha-Emori*," writes: "And similarly, all, until the end of the chapter, read 'this is [*harei zeh*] the ways of the Amorites,' and also in the Tosefta." Rashi obviously meant to say that the wording is not "*yesh bo mi-shum* [this somewhat constitutes]," but rather (the definitive) "*harei zeh*," that is closer to denoting a Torah prohibition. This is in fact the version of the Tosefta (Shabbat, chap. 6 [ed. Lieberman, pp. 25–27]).

19 See *She'eilot u-Teshuvot Maharil*, p. 232, regarding the version of the Talmud, that even though such versions exist in manuscripts and in the *Rishonim*, the current printed version is to be preferred; see Margaliot, op. cit., p. 27 n. 67.

the rooster [...] **although it is of the ways of the Amorites** to insist upon slaughtering the cock [...]. Thus, the *hasid* [i.e. Judah he-Hasid] himself attested that his version was *"harei zeh mi-darkei ha-Emori,"* and not *"ein zeh."*

The difficulties in the testament of R. Judah he-Hasid, especially concerning the command to slaughter that hen that crowed like a rooster, troubled many authorities. Y. Peles drew my attention to additional sources concerned with this issue, which we will cite in their entirety.

The first source is from the commentary by R. Judah ben R. Nathan Zak on **Sefer Mitzvot Gadol**:

"They slaughtered this hen that crowed like a rooster ..." — Although it is stated in the testaments attributed to R. Judah Hasid, of blessed memory, to slaughter [it], we must say that the pupils wrote in his name that which he did not write, for his statement is contradicted by the Talmud. And there are many additional things in his testament that are contrary to the Talmud: he wrote not to marry the daughter of one's sister or the daughter of one's brother, which is contrary to what is written concerning the one who has relations with his niece (Yevamot 62b) and concerning those punished by burning (Sanhedrin 76b). He also wrote that money is not to be buried in the ground, while [the rabbis] of blessed memory wrote in [Bava] Metzia (42a) that money can best be guarded by placing it in the earth. He wrote that a man is not to marry two sisters consecutively, but we found that Joseph ha-Kohen said, Go and provide livelihood for the sons of their sister. As regards the practice of killing the hen that crowed like a rooster, I heard from the distinguished Moses Sholhow, may he live long, in the name of my granduncle, the *Gaon*, our master, the rabbi Zalman Zak, may the memory of the righteous be for a blessing, in the name of the pietist, our master the rabbi Tevlin, of blessed memory, that the Talmud prohibited only when one states expressly that the killing is because of this crowing; if, however, he does so silently, this is proper. And it appears to me that we should not be concerned, for if one is concerned, it will befall him, for the beliefs of the non-Jews are vanity.[20]

---

20 Known as R. Zalkalai (Ashkenaz, ca. 1540), in *Sefer Mitzvot Gadol ha-Shalem* (Jerusalem, 1993), Negative Commandment 51, p. 88.

The second source is from the book of commentaries on the Torah *Meshivat Nefesh* by R. Johanan Luria, one of the leading sages of Ashkenaz (fifteenth-sixteenth centuries — 1450–1550).

> According to my opinion, the general principle ceased to be dangerous, as regards the matter of killing a hen when it crowed as a rooster. Some state in addition that this is the testament of R. Judah Hasid, may the memory of the righteous be for a blessing. All my life I wondered at this, since it is taught in the chapter of "With what may a woman" [Shabbat, chap. 6] that this is an Amorite practice, and for this reason I refrained from doing so. When, however, the members of the household are careful to remain silent, and say simply that the rooster crowed, I think that there is nothing prohibited in this if they killed it. If they say the hen crowed [like a rooster], and for this reason they were enjoined not to kill it, this certainly constitutes Amorite practices, for they said that even though this does not constitute divination, it is a distinguishing sign (Hullin 95b). Due to our many exiles, because of our numerous sins, and the paucity of Torah scholars, the masses were incapable of dividing and separating that which should properly be distinguished. May God, may He be blessed, illuminate our eyes with His Torah and His commandments.[21]

Reuven Margaliot devoted an extensive discussion to this topic in a lengthy footnote in his edition of the testament,[22] in which he cites different views seeking to resolve this contradiction. For example, *Maharsha* (Samuel Eliezer ben Judah ha-Levi Edels),[23] who attempts to distinguish between "one who says, Kill the hen that crowed like a rooster" and "the one who says to kill it without specification"; and *Shiltei ha-Gibborim*,[24] who wrote that, as regards divination, it seems to him that if one does not actually speak, but thinks this in one's mind, then it is permitted. This reason was given by Rabbi Moses Isserles[25] in the name of *Maharil*; the Vilna Gaon wrote on this: "His words are as difficult as vinegar to the teeth [following Prov. 10:26], to deceive the Omnipresent."[26]

---

21 Ed. Yaakov Hoffman (Jerusalem, 1993), on Gen. 24:45, pp. 53–54.
22 *Sefer Hasidim*, ed. Margaliot, pp. 26–27 n. 67.
23 Hullin 95b, s.v. "*Ke-Eliezer.*"
24 On Alfasi, *Avodah Zarah*, chap. 2 (Vilna ed., 9a).
25 *Shulhan Arukh, Yoreh Deah* 179:4.

Rabbi Abraham David Wahrmann of Buchach, the author of *Da'at Kedoshim*, discussed this question at length in his book *Mile de-Hasiduta*, and encountered great difficulty in resolving this issue, especially since

> it is accepted by your people the House of Israel that *Sefer Hasidim* is **totally holy**.[27] It is by the rabbi of all the Diaspora, Rabbi Yehudah he-Hasid, without any [foreign] admixture. He was more knowledgeable than those who succeeded him, and he knew what we will [never] know. Accordingly, **it is clear, that this *baraita* contains an error, and was not authored by someone from the school of Rav Ashi, nor was it taught by Rabbi Hiyya and Rav Ashi** [i.e. is not canonical]; the version has to be to permit this.

Once again we find that this great Torah scholar finds himself **obligated** to correct the version of the Talmud, and to state that the *baraita* "was not authored by someone from the school of Rav Ashi." He is not willing to change the passage in the testament, and say that "it was not authored by Rabbi Judah he-Hasid." Wahrmann himself, however, is apparently uneasy with this answer, and in the continuation of this passage he suggests alternative resolutions, such as:

> Accordingly, it is possible to explain the statements of these testaments that possibly, in his time, he knew that there was danger at that time, **for nature constantly changes as time passes**. And it is not the same in all places. Consequently, **from then on, all the world admits that this does not constitute an Amorite practice**. It possibly also could be said that in his time it was no longer reported that the Amorites were strict in this regard. Therefore, this prohibition was not taught from then on, because the inhabitants of any place have the freedom to establish laws and conventions amongst themselves, even if they lack sufficient reason. Everything that they enact as a preventive measure concerning prohibitions is not to be changed. We are to be strict in

---

26 *Shulhan Arukh, Yoreh Deah* 179:8.

27 *Mile de-Hasiduta* (*Mile Dachsidusu*, [Kolomea, 1890]), pp. 39–41. Rabbi Hayyim Palache (Palaggi) wrote in *She'eilot u-Teshuvot Hayyim be-Yad*, para. 24, s.v. "*Ibra*": "We, for our part, saw fit to be stringent regarding **all** the testaments of our master Judah he-Hasid, of blessed memory." He further wrote in *Tohahot Hayyim, Nitzavim* 250:5: "And care must be taken **with all the testaments** of *Sefer Hasidim*, for they are danger-fraught words" (cited in Y.H. Sofer, *Biur Moshe* [Jerusalem, 1990], p. 6).

this regard only under two conditions: when it is known for a certainty that this is an Amorite practice, and also when it is known that there is no known benefit from this. Only when these two negative conditions join together does the prohibition apply, and not otherwise. [...]

This is likewise so for what is written in the testament regarding the hen, that, in his place, at any rate, the Amorites had ceased to maintain this. Since then, it was permitted to speak thus within your people the House of Israel, and much study is required as regards many details of disagreements concerning halakhot. At any rate [...] nonetheless, this does not pertain to what is written in *Sefer Hasidim* [...] for we act in accordance with the presumption that he is a great man, all of whose statements [were uttered] after he realized that there is no fear of a prohibition here. [...] And in all such instances, either all the world acknowledges that we are not strict, or he knew that it is not the way of the Amorites to speak thus.[28]

The explanations by Wahrmann undoubtedly require much study, as he himself attests, and it would seem questionable to state that since nature has changed, a prohibited act has become permitted for us, and who would presume to say this? Rather, Judah he-Hasid and his testament, **and the prevailing practice**, are so very strong that rabbinical authorities sense the need to make a supreme effort to resolve it, whether by the emendation and changing of the texts, or by various logical arguments.

Our wonder at this is even greater, because the explanation could be advanced that this section of the testament was stated solely for the generation of Judah he-Hasid, or for his family, and not for the entire people of Israel and for all time. This possibility is, in fact, to be found in the headings of the testament in several manuscripts, such as: "There are some that he commanded for his family alone, and there are others that he mandated for all Israel";[29] "Some are for his offspring, some for the Israelites, and some for the nations of the world";[30] "It is doubtful whether it is for the entire world, or specifically for his offspring; seemingly for the entire world, and care must be taken."[31] This path was also followed by *Noda bi-Yehudah* (Ezekiel ben

28 See also the continuation of his lengthy discussion.
29 MS. Rome Casanatense 194/2734.
30 MS. Oxford Bodleian 4037.
31 MS. Oxford Trinity College 1849 (= 142/142), from the fifteenth-sixteenth centuries.

Judah Landau)[32] in his discussion of para. 23 of the testament "A person should not marry a woman if she has the same name as his mother, or if his [future] father-in-law has the same name as his; and if he marries her, he should change one name, perhaps there is hope" (p. 17, Margaliot). Landau writes:[33]

> And similarly, we find in the testament of Rabbi Judah he-Hasid **things that are almost forbidden for us to hear** [...] but the truth will show its way, for the *hasid* **commanded [them] for his offspring after him** for all generations, for he saw with Divine inspiration that his offspring would not succeed in these marital matches. [...] [And] we are obligated to make a supreme effort to resolve what he said [because of R. Judah he-Hasid's stature], that he spoke only for a specific time or for [his] family, whereas the dicta of the Talmud apply generally.[34]

32 *Noda bi-Yehudah*, Part 2, *Even ha-Ezer* 79.

33 For para. 23 of the testament, see the discussion based on most of the relevant sources: S. Munitz-Hammer, "People's Names — Practice and Law," Master's thesis, Bar-Ilan University (Ramat Gan, 1989), chap. 6, pp. 106–25 (Hebrew). Cf. *Sefer Hasidim*, para. 477; Rabbi Abraham Isaac Kook, *She'eilot u-Teshuvot Ezrat Kohen* (Jerusalem, 1969), paras. 5, 7; Rabbi Ovadiah Yosef, *She'eilot u-Teshuvot Yabi'a Omer* (Jerusalem, 1956), Vol. 2, para. 7; Rabbi Rahamim Nissim Isaac Palache, *She'eilot u-Teshuvot Yafeh la-Lev* (Izmir, 1846), Vol. 6, 47b; Rabbi Joshua Solomon Ardit, *Hina ve-Hisda* (Izmir, 1864–77), Part 2, 225a; Rabbi Hayyim Halberstam (of Zanz), *She'eilot u-Teshuvot Divrei Hayyim* (Lemberg, 1875), Part 1, *Even ha-Ezer*, para. 8. See the extensive discussion in Rabbi Hayyim Simeon Dov Harki, *Sefer Shiv'im Temarim* (Warsaw, 1900), paras. 26–27, pp. 34a–38a.

34 See *Shiv'im Temarim*, 1b–2a, regarding this approach, with references to other Torah scholars who adopt this view. R. Hayyim Simeon himself, however, totally rejects it. See, however, Rabbi Abraham Zevi Hirsch Eisenstadt, *Pit'hei Teshuvah, Even ha-Ezer* 50:14, who was undecided on this issue; see also Halberstam, *Divrei Hayyim*, Part 1, *Even ha-Ezer*, para. 8, who, despite the great esteem in which he held the *Noda bi-Yehudah*, criticized him for his position on this issue, which cast doubt concerning the testament. Rabbi Isaac Judah Jehiel Safrin of Komarno, *Zohar Hai* (Lemberg, 1875), *Mishpatim* 133d wrote: "I fulminate against the prodigy of the generation, the *Gaon*, our teacher and master, *Moharil* [= the *Noda bi-Yehudah*] of Prague, who differs with *Sefer Hasidim* and brings proofs from the Talmud." See Y.H. Sofer, *Or Moshe* (Jerusalem, 1990), pp. 9–10.

Also relevant to the approach of the *Noda bi-Yehudah* on such issues is the rule stated by Judah he-Hasid in his testament, para. 35 (ed. Margaliot, p. 22): "A person should not serve as *sandak* for his fellow's two sons, unless one died." And similarly, *Maharil*, Laws of Circumcision 1 (*The Book of Maharil: Customs by*

The author of *Mile de-Hasiduta*, on the other hand, maintains the holy (and therefore binding) status of *Sefer Hasidim* in its entirety (see above), and therefore found it easier to emend the Talmudic texts and develop theories of changes in halakhah and *minhag* over the course of time, than to change even a single letter in the testament.[35]

> *Rabbi Yaacov Mulin*, ed. S.J. Spitzer [Jerusalem, 1989], p. 476 [Hebrew]), in the name of Rabbi Peretz: "This is not done double, to give his sons twice or three times to one *baal berit* [= *sandak*, commonly translated as "godfather"], rather, he chooses another *baal berit* for each son" (the text of Rabbi Peretz's dictum is not extant, but is cited in his name also in the *Semak* of Zurich, Commandment 154, ed. Y.Y. Har-Shoshanim-Rosenberg, Vol. 2 [Jerusalem, 1977], p. 46 n. 47; see Spitzer, loc. cit., n. 4). Rabbi Moses Isserles also cites this (*Yoreh Deah* 265:11). The *Noda bi-Yehudah* writes on this (Part 1, *Yoreh Deah* 86):
>
> > I am reluctant to give an answer that is not enrooted in the Talmud, and the statement by Rabbi Peretz that *Maharil* cites at the beginning of the Laws of Circumcision is merely a sort of support, to give a reason why we refrain from honoring a single person with two sons. As for the essence of this, I question *Maharil*'s comparing this commandment to the one who offers incense. [...] At any rate, these matters have no Talmudic root or basis, and this is all in the manner of homily and allusion, and constitutes neither *ikuv* [necessary condition for the performance of a commandment] nor set *minhag*, and people are not strict in this respect in all the lands of Poland. And in many locations, the permanent rabbi is obliged to always be the *sandak*. We should not speak at any further length about something whose entire root is not from the Talmud, and this is sufficient for the present.
>
> See also Margaliot's comment on the testament, p. 22 n. 50; A.L. Gelman, *The Noda bi-Yehudah and His Teachings*[2] (Jerusalem, 1972), pp. 32–34 (Hebrew).

35 How different is all of the above from what appears in a responsum by Moses Provencal, who wrote:

> These testaments did not come from the mouth of Joshua, and they are not to be believed, and certainly no action is to be taken in accordance with them, in opposition to the tradition of [the Rabbis,] of blessed memory. If one transgresses the words of the Rabbis on their account, I apply to them [the verses] "who leave the paths of rectitude" (Prov. 2:13), "they have forsaken Me, the Fount of living waters" (Jer. 2:13). Nor is it certain that all these were spoken by the *hasid*, they rather were stated by others and attributed to him, or they were found in his estate and were believed to be his, but are not from him. This refers to what Maimonides wrote in the first [part] of the *Guide* (1:61) regarding the invented names in charms. This is sufficient for a discerning and wise one as yourself (quoted by M. Benayahu, *Studies in Memory of the Rishon Le-Zion R. Yitzhak Nissim* [Jerusalem, 1985], p. 293 [Hebrew], in accordance with MS. Jerusalem

The testament also contains other questionable omens, such as para. 44 (ed. Margaliot, p. 24): "And likewise, if a tree bears fruit twice in one year, it is to be cut down immediately and not left standing." Margaliot correctly commented (p. 24, n. 61):

> Our wonder at this is manifest, for the cutting down of a fruitbearing tree is **forbidden by Torah law**, and lashes are received for this (Makkot 22a), and yielding fruit twice in one year is excellent; Eruvin 18a: "What is *yufra* [Rashi: that is important]? Ulla said: A tree that bears fruit twice a year."

(And the prohibition of cutting down fruit trees is mentioned in a nearby section in the testament, para. 45: "A tree that bears fruit is not to be cut down.")[36] He attempts to resolve the dictum in the testament, commenting: "If the tree is intrinsically good [i.e. fruit-bearing], it is deleterious for those [trees] standing near it, and since it weakens [the others], it is permitted to cut

JNUL8° 1999, query 9, fol. 19a; recently published in *She'eilot u-Teshuvot Rabbi Moshe Provintzalo*, ed. A.Y. Yanni [Jerusalem, 1989], pp. 22–23).

It perhaps could be said that since these practices were not followed, and the testament did not spread greatly throughout Italy, it was easier for Provencal to express himself in such a manner. See the editor's note, *Provintzalo*, p. 23 n. 4, with references to *She'eilot u-Teshuvot Mahari Mintz* (Cracow, 1882); Rabbi Jacob Poppers, *Shav Ya'akov* (Frankfurt am Main, 1742), *Even ha-Ezer* 22; Rabbi Moses Sofer, *Hatam Sofer, Yoreh Deah* 138; Menahem Mendel Schneersohn (of Nikolsburg), *She'eilot u-Teshuvot Tzemak Tzedek* (Brooklyn, 1964, and many other editions), *Even ha-Ezer* 143, 323, who wrote at length on this question, whether these testaments are to be attributed to R. Judah he-Hasid and are to be relied upon. See the excellent article by Y.H. Sofer in *Or Moshe*, 1, pp. 3–21, "On the Matter of Taking Care regarding the Testament of Our Master Judah he-Hasid, May His Merit Protect Us, Amen" also regarding Sephardic Jews, for which we possess a plethora of testimonies from the Spanish Torah scholars, who also maintained that the testament is to be observed. He cites Rabbi Hayyim Benvenist[e], *Keneset ha-Gedolah* (Izmir, 1731); *Hida* (Rabbi Hayyim Joseph David Azulai); Rabbi Hayyim Palache; Rabbi Eliezer Papo; Rabbi Solomon Ardit, and more. Nor did Sofer ignore the Ashkenazic sages, to share with us his wealth of knowledge in the rabbinic literature.

36 For the uprooting of nonfruitbearing trees, and fruitbearing trees for the building of a house, see Sofer, *Or Moshe*, p. 6 (such as Rabbi Hayyim Palache, *Tokhahot Hayyim* [Furth, 1841], *Nitzavim* 250:5), who also mentions *She'eilot u-Teshuvot Afarkasta de-Aniya* by my late grandfather, Rabbi David Sperber, Vol. 1 (Satu-Mare, 1940 [photocopy edn., with additions: Jerusalem, 1981]), para. 35, p. 52a; para. 121, p. 105b.

it down; see Bava Kamma 96a." The forced nature of this is obvious to any reader. The author of *Mile de-Hasiduta* explains: "His intent is to uproot it from there and replant it elsewhere, for it is forbidden to cut down a fruit tree, unless his intent is to a tree that could be replanted if cut down. [...] He removes it with its root, and he plants it elsewhere." According to what he writes, this foremost thought is missing from the book, and does not appear in the language of the testament, which merely states "it is to be cut down."[37]

We see how the leading *poskim* (decisors of Jewish law) were undecided regarding the sections of the testament that seemed to them as explicitly contradictory to the Talmud, or those sections that raised formidable difficulties for orderly and normal life, such as all the restrictions that the testament imposes on marital matches.[38] And even when there were several reasons to be lenient,[39] they nonetheless had reservations. Of special interest is the observation by the author of *Misgeret ha-Shulhan*, Rabbi Hayyim Isaiah ha-Kohen Halbersberg, in his book *Keter Torah*: "But what we see **exceeds the law**."[40] The fact that rules in the testament are contradicted by the Talmud served as an argument to **strengthen** the former's standing, and not to weaken it, as we see in *Sedei Hemed*:

> The more proofs that are brought from the cases in the Talmud unlike his [Judah he-Hasid's] statements, **enables us to judge him favorably**, for he was not a reed-cutter in a lake [i.e. a worthless person]. Far be it from us to say of him that he did not know, and that what was hidden from him is revealed to us, or that [he was unfamiliar with] an explicit Talmudic passage that we possess, and not only in a single place. We are forced to take strenuous measures to establish his words, so that the words of the sages will endure.[41]

Rabbi Judah he-Hasid's special standing undoubtedly imparted singular force to his testament. In the words of Rabbi Hayyim of Zanz:

37 On para. 45, in ed. Margaliot, p. 38. See *Shiv'im Temarim*, para. 52, pp. 55b–61a.
38 Paras. 24–31.
39 Such as those mentioned in *Pit'hei Teshuvah, Yoreh Deah* 116; *Even ha-Ezer* 2, 50.
40 *Keter Torah* (Lublin, 1901, and other editions), p. 55b, "*Zer Zahav*" 9:1; brought by Sofer, *Or Moshe*, pp. 17–18.
41 Rabbi Hayyim Hezekiah Medini, *Sedei Hemed, Hatan ve-Kallah* 5, brought by Sofer, *Or Moshe*, p. 12.

It is known that our master, Judah he-Hasid, was the teacher of the *Semag* [*Sefer Mitzvot Gadol*, authored by Moses of Coucy] and [Rabbi Isaac] *Or Zarua*, with all of our teachings and practices in the land of Germany and France following them. Accordingly, their discourse is undoubtedly better than the teachings of the later authorities.[42]

Notwithstanding this, it would appear that the testament enjoyed greater standing **where its rules were regarded as binding halakhah,** to the extent that the contradictions with the Talmud were not considered a reason to negate *he-Hasid*'s dicta. There were many and varied reasons for the spread of the testament throughout the Jewish world. Thus we find, for example, that Rabbi Rahamim Isaac Palache responded to a query that in early times this testament was not followed in his city (Izmir); one great rabbi married his daughter to a groom with the same name as his, and before long the groom became weak. The blame for this was placed on their not honoring the words of the *hasid*, and, since then, the testament was widespread and strictly observed, to the extent that even a great monetary loss would be suffered to separate a couple for this reason.[43]

---

42 *Mile de-Hasiduta*, p. 38.

43 *She'eilot u-Teshuvot Yafeh la-Lev*, Vol. 6, p. 46b, brought by Sofer, *Or Moshe*, p. 9. Cf. Ardit, *Hina ve-Hisda*, Vol. 2, 225b; Medini, *Sedei Hemed, Hatan ve-Kallah* 6, s.v. "*Ve-ha-Rav.*" See R. Amar, *Minhagei ha-Hida* (*Customs of the* Hida) (Jerusalem, 1990), Vol. 1, p. 26, who mentions the view of Rabbi Hayyim Palache (*Masa Hayyim*, para. 213), that *minhagim* relate to positive commandments, and not to prohibitions, and that, according to Maimonides, they have the standing of Torah law:

> The observance of the *minhag*: the main principle and root of this is what Maimonides wrote in the first chapter of *Hil. Mamrim* [*the Laws of Rebels*], that the [members of the] Great Court in Jerusalem [i.e. the Sanhedrin] are the pillars of instruction, and about them it is written, "[you shall act] in accordance with the instructions given you" [Deut. 17:11], and it is written, "you must not deviate" [ibid.]. That is to say, this entails a positive commandment and a prohibition. He [Maimonides] also wrote that the regulations instituted by them are a fence around the Torah: these are decrees, ordinances, and customs. It is a **positive commandment** to heed them. (This is the end of the citation from Rabbi Hayyim Palache.) This is also the view of *Terumat ha-Deshen*, para. 281, who wrote, in the name of *Sefer Mitzvot Gadol*, that communal regulations are of Torah force. And from this we learn regarding the *minhag*.

Cf. also Amar, op. cit., pp. 34–35, who cites, inter alia, R. Simeon bar Zemah, *Teshuvot ha-Tashbetz*, Vol. 1, paras. 49, 153: "Even if you were able to say that, by

This situation seems to parallel what we showed elsewhere regarding the general nature of *minhag*: where it spread and became enrooted, its standing is even stronger than what is written in the Talmud. As Rav Hai Gaon asserts:

> Greater than any other proof is to go out among the people and see how they act, "go out and see the custom of the folk" [Ber. 45a, as regards matters of ritual]. [...] **Only afterwards** do we examine all that has been discussed in the Mishnah or Gemara about this issue. All conclusions derived from them which are compatible with how we are minded is perfectly fine, but if there is anything which is not quite in keeping with our understanding — and cannot be clearly proven — it cannot uproot the roots.[44]

In the final analysis, it is the act and not the exposition that is principal: the *minhag*, as practiced by the people, whether in accordance with sources to which the people adhere, or whether due to other reasons. This is the Jewish way of life, by which we conduct ourselves and by which we explain and understand the sources.[45]

Talmudic law, they should act in a certain manner, nevertheless, since the generations have conducted themselves in accordance with this practice, **we are not empowered to change their practice at all**, since this is according to the rule of the *minhag*, that wherever there is no prohibition, **even if the practice is improper, we allow it and do not remove it**." Amar, op. cit., p. 3, also cites *She'eilot u-Teshuvot Shemesh ve-Tzedakah* by Rabbi Samson Morpurgo (Venice, 1742–43), para. 24, who writes: "Only this shall one call to mind, to take exceeding care not to change the custom of his fathers as the point of a needle; **not to exchange it, nor to replace it, [not] even bad with good**." Amar, loc. cit. also lists additional sources.

44 Rav Hai Gaon, *Tamim De'im*, para. 119, from the translation of T. Groner, *The Legal Methodology of Hai Gaon* (Chico, California, 1985), p. 17. For an additional example of a seeming contradiction between the Talmudic halakhah and the secure standing of a *minhag*, see J. Katz, "'Alterations in the Time of the Evening Service': An Example of the Interrelationship between Religious Costum [sic], Halacha and Their Social Background," *Zion* 35 (1970), pp. 35– 60, and esp. pp. 42–49 (Hebrew).

45 A fine and instructive characterization of *minhag*, in its general meaning of "custom," appears in the important book by the Belgian philosopher Chaim Perelman, *Justice* (New York, 1967), pp. 9–12. Due to the importance of his representation, we cite at length from his book (my thanks to Dr. J. Woolf, for drawing my attention to this):
> According to a great many writers, the law draws its authority from the source whence it emanates. The least contested source of moral and juridical norms is custom. When a given social arrangement has been accepted — either explicitly

2. EXAMINING A PERSON'S SHADOW IN THE LIGHT OF THE MOON ON THE NIGHT OF HOSHANA RABBAH

In his finely printed book,[46] Adolph Kohut brings a picture (Fig. 1) from the book by Johannes Leusden, *Philologus Hebraeo-Mixtus*,[47] adding the caption: *"Bergrussen des Neumonds"* (blessing the new moon). The *Jewish Encyclopedia*[48] similarly understands the picture, writing: "Blessing of the New Moon."[49] Although it might seem as if the picture is portraying a group of people who bless the moon and point to it, the question arises, why are they holding *lulavim* (palm fronds) in their hands, and, even more surprisingly, the individual on the right side of the picture **lacks a head**.

> or, as is more frequent, implicitly — and when people have conformed to it long enough to have made it customary or traditional, then it is regarded as normal and just to adhere to this arrangement and unjust to deviate from it. A mode of behavior that has been adopted without protest creates a precedent, and no one will object to actions that conform to precedents. The principle of inertia transforms every habitual way of thinking even for small children, and it is the basis for the rules that develop spontaneously in any given society. A customary form of behavior, one which conforms to the expectations of the members of the group, needs no justification; it will be accepted spontaneously as just, because it is as it should be. [...] But no logical deduction is made when one is dealing with behavior that is customary, or with a situation that is traditional. It is only when someone maintains that what ought to be is different from what is that proof has to be supplied. Proof is incumbent upon the man who asserts that the customary action is unjust, not upon him who acts in accordance with custom. It is presumed that what is, is what ought to be: Only in upsetting a presumption must proof be given. The principle of inertia thus plays an indispensable stabilizing role in social life. This does not mean that what is must remain forever, but rather that there should be no change without reason. **Change only must be justified**.
>
> To this we should add the fine formulation by my father, S. Sperber, *Ma'amarot* (Essays), ed. D. Sperber (Jerusalem, 1978), pp. 266–67: "Every practice in the world, every phenomenon, upon its initial appearance seems to us to be exceptional. Since it is repeated frequently, it establishes itself in the reality and in thought as an existing and fixed custom; we no longer wonder about it, we do not explain it intermittently and irregularly, we rather seek to understand it within itself, with its regularity."

46 A. Kohut, *Geschichte der deutschen Juden* (Berlin, 1898), p. 340.

47 Second edn., Utrecht 1682 (although Kohut [p. 316] writes "Utrecht 1657," there is no edition from this year; see below), next to p. 274.

48 (New York, 1905), Vol. 8, p. 243.

49 Apparently relying on Kohut, without seeing the original, because the *Jewish Encyclopedia* also gives the date as 1657.

The truth be told, however, there is nothing puzzling about the picture, because the caption given in the book by Leusden quite clearly specifies: "Viri exuent ad radios lunares" (people going forth toward moonbeams). The explanation of the picture on p. 278 states expressly:

> Hic conspiciuntur duo Judaei, qui una cum fasciculis ad lunae radios excurrunt, expiscaturi totius anni eventa: sed unius caput latitat, et in umbra non conspicitur: inde concludit se hoc anno esse moriturum.

In other words, there are **two people** (duo Judaei) who go forth in the moonlight, with bundles (cum fasciculis), and a headless one **and [i.e. because] it [the head] is not seen in the shadow** (et in umbra non conspicitur), which is a sign that he will not live out the year. This description, however, does not correspond at all with the picture, since the latter contains more than two people, and there is no **shadow** that lacks a head, but rather an actual person who has no head. Moreover, the entire explanation relates to the semiholiday Hoshana Rabbah (which falls on the 21st day of Tishrei).[50] Although the caption does not explicitly state this, in the continuation of the explanation the headlessness is elucidated with a lengthy quotation from J. Buxtorf, *Synagoga Judaica*,[51] which states that on the night of Hoshana Rabbah Jews go outside to examine their shadow by moonlight; if their shadow lacks a head, they know that they will die during that year.

Furthermore, the lack of other limbs is a sign of the death of different relatives, such as: "si manus dextra, filius; si sinistra, filia cum morte vitam commutabit," that is, if the right hand is missing, the person's son will die; if his left hand, then his daughter is doomed, and so forth. Since this is the night of Hoshana Rabbah, people go forth with *hoshanot* (willow branches used on Sukkot) in their hands[52] to examine their shadows in the moonlight.

50 J. Leusden, *Philologus Hebraeo-Mixtus*[2] (Utrecht 1682), p. 278. The dark part of the moon teaches that the picture depicts the last quarter of the moon, and not its beginning, for then the dark part is towards its left, while at the end of the month it is to the right.

51 J. Buxtorf, *Synagoga Judaica*[3] (Basel, 1712), chap. 21.

52 It is not clear whether they actually went out with *hoshanot*, a detail that I did not find in the sources, or whether this is an artistic convention to show in graphic fashion that this took place on Hoshana Rabbah.

This belief is well-known from the *Rishonim*. Especially prominent is the assertion by Nahmanides in his commentary on the Torah:[53]

> "Only you must not rebel against the Lord" — [...] They [Moses and Aaron] continued: "have no fear then of the people of the country, for they are our bread" [...] **"their shadow is removed from them"** [...] "the Lord is with us," therefore "have no fear of them."

Nahmanides writes on this:

> But it is possible that Scripture is alluding to the well-known fact that there will be no shadow over the head of a person who is [destined] to die that year, on "the night of the seal" [= Hoshana Rabbah night]. Therefore it says: "their shade is [already] removed from them," meaning that death has been decreed for them.

Nahmanides' teaching is brought by Rabbeinu Bahya on this verse, in slightly different language:

> Nahmanides, of blessed memory, interpreted: "Their shadow is removed from them," that their shadow was removed from their head, for on the great night of the seal[54] of Hoshana Rabbah, that is

---

53 Translation based on *Commentary on the Torah*, Num. 14:9, trans. C.B. Chavel (New York, 1975), *Numbers*, pp. 135–36.

54 The nature of Hoshana Rabbah as "the day of the seal" is based on M Rosh Hashanah 1:2: "On Rosh Hashanah all that come into the world pass before Him like flocks of sheep [...] and on the Festival [of Sukkot] they are judged for water." We also found in *Shibbolei ha-Leket ha-Katzar*: "And I heard that there are holy communities that recite on Hoshana Rabbah [the High Holy Days prayers:] 'Remember us for life,' 'Who is like You [... who remembers Your creatures for life],' [...] 'Remember Your mercies,' and 'Our Father, our King'" (which is the custom of Romaniot Jewry). There are *mahzorim* (holiday prayerbooks) from the fifteenth century with instructions to recite in *U-Netaneh Tokef*: "On Rosh Hashanah they will be recalled, on the fast of Yom Kippur they will be inscribed, and on Hoshana Rabbah they will be sealed" (see B. Vichleder, "The Glosses of Rabbi Solomon Rocca, May the Memory of the Righteous Be for a Blessing, and the Customs of the Holy Community of Urbino," *Kobetz Torani Zekhor le-Avraham* [1993], pp. 493–98 [Hebrew]). Rabbi Moses Isserles states (*Orah Hayyim*, 664:1): "It is the practice of some to wear the *kittel* [symbolic white robe] [on Hoshana Rabbah] as on Yom Kippur." (According to *Magen Avraham*, *Maharil* wore a *kittel*.) *Knesset ha-Gedolah*, *Orah Hayyim* 664 states: "It is customary to designate an important person for the *Mussaf* prayer, as for Rosh Hashanah and for Yom Kippur. In the *Mussaf* prayer we recite 'Remember

the twenty-sixth day of the Creation of the universe, a shadow **will not be found** for whoever is destined to die in that year. This is as if he said: death has already been decreed for them. This is his intent, even if not his wording. This appears to be the intent of Scripture, which said "When the day declines and the shadows flee" (Song of Songs 2:17); he [Nahmanides] said: when the time comes that man declines and the breath leaves his mouth, then his shadow will depart.

A detailed description of the "ceremony" of the examination of the shadow is provided by Abudarham, *Laws of Hoshana Rabbah*:[55]

There are people who are accustomed on Hoshana Rabbah night to enwrap themselves in a sheet[56] and to go out to a place illuminated by the light of the moon. They remove the sheet and remain nude,[57] and they spread out their limbs and their fingers. If one finds his shadow there, this is good. But if the shadow is lacking, he is doomed. If the shadow of one of his fingers is lacking, this is a sign regarding one of his relatives. The right hand is a sign for his male sons, and the left hand is a sign for the females. Nahmanides similarly interpreted.[58]

There are also special hours for this inspection. Rabbi Issachar [Ibn] Susan of Safed, writes:[59]

us for life,' 'Who is like You,' 'And therefore instill Your fear, and therefore instill Your glory, and therefore the righteous'; one recites [the Festival addition] 'You have chosen us' [...] and concludes '[...] For good life' and 'In the book of good life.'" And similarly, in the Festival prayerbook of Romanian Jewry: "We observe several of the practices of the High Holy Days on the day of Hoshana Rabbah."

55 (Jerusalem, 1967), p. 298.
56 Possibly an allusion to shrouds(?). See *Sefer Hasidim*, ed. Margaliot, para. 452, p. 311.
57 See below, the view of Rabbi Hayyim Vital that one must be completely nude.
58 Cf. Rabbi Eleazar ben Judah of Worms, *Rokeah*, ed. B.S. Schneersohn (Jerusalem, 1967), Laws of Sukkot, para. 221, pp. 123–24; *idem, Rokeach: A Commentary on the Bible*, ed. Ch. Konyevsky (Bnei Brak, 1986), Vol. 3, p. 51; *Kol Bo*, para. 52: "There is support for this practice from what appears in the *Haggadah* on the verse 'their shadow is removed from them,' that it is written in the *Haggadah* that the shadow of their head is not seen on the day of the *aravah* [willow, i.e. on Hoshana Rabbah]"; cf. Rabbi Eleazar of Worms, *Hokhmat ha-Nefesh* (Safed, 1913), p. 20a (also cf. p. 21a), quoted in Menahem Ziyyoni, *Ziyyoni*, and the Tosafist Rabbi Isaac ben Judah ha-Levi, *Pa'ne'ah Raza* (Warsaw, 1928) on Num. 14:9.
59 *Ibbur Shanim (The Incalcation of Years)* (Venice, 1578), p. 124.

To be known that the hour and the minute to see yourself in the moon on Hoshana Rabbah night: if the day of Hoshana Rabbah is Sunday — for eight hours; if on Monday — for five hours; if on Wednesday — for six hours; and if on Friday — for seven hours. I found [this] written correctly and accurately.[60]

Moses of Przemysl relates (in the name of Menahem ben Benjamin Recanati) in *Matteh Moshe*:[61]

I heard that some experimented with fowl[62] that they wanted to slaughter for the following day, and on Hoshana Rabbah night they had no shadow. The reason for this was given by some masters of the Kabbalah,[63] but I did not receive this tradition. Thus far his statement.

Sefer Hasidim[64] writes of this practice:

If a person did not see the shadow of his head on Hoshana Rabbah

60 Cited by K. Wilhelm, "The Orders of *Tikkunim*," in *Alei Ayin: The Salman Schocken Jubilee Volume* (Jerusalem, 1948–52), p. 139 (Hebrew). For more regarding the hour, see the extensive article by I. Weinstock, "Gazing upon Shadows on Hoshana Rabbah Night," in his book, *Studies in Jewish Philosophy and Mysticism* (Jerusalem, 1969), pp. 259–61 (Hebrew).

61 Ed. M. Knoblowicz (London, 1958), para. 957, pp. 182–83. Recanati's commentary is on the Torah portion of *Shelah*.

62 The experiment with fowl is possibly related to the practice of slaughtering on Hoshana Rabbah the fowl used for the *kaparot* (the fowl that serve as an "atonement" for people's sins, in a ceremony performed on the eve of Yom Kippur), as is stated in the book *Nahar Mitzrayim* by Rabbi Raphael Aaron ben Simeon (Thebes, 1908), Laws of Yom Kippur, para. 2, p. 43a: "There are those who do not perform the *kaparot* on the eve of Yom Kippur, but slaughter their *kaparot* on Hoshana Rabbah night — the night of the sealing, and their practice also is a fine one" (although he refers to the night of Hoshana Rabbah, and not to the following day). And similarly in *Kimha de-Avishuna* by Rabbi Johanan ben Joseph Treves, on the *Mahzor* of the Jews of Rome, Yom Kippur Eve (Bologna, 1540). This custom is connected with a series of practices that impart to Hoshana Rabbah a certain resemblance to the High Holy Days; see above, n. 52.

63 See Rabbi Moses Cordovero, *Pardes Rimmonim* (Salonika, 1584), *Sha'ar ha-Neshamah* 4; Rabbi Hayyim Vital, in H. Zemah, *Nagid u-Metzaveh* (Constantinople, 1726), Order of Hoshana Rabbah Night, 81b (cited in R. Margaliot, *Nitzotzei Or* [Sparks of Light] [Jerusalem, 1965], on Horayot 12a, p. 195).

64 Ed. Margaliot, para. 452, p. 312 (= ed. J. Wistinetzky [Berlin, 1891–94], para. 1144, pp. 378–79).

night, he and those who love him are to observe many fasts, and give much charity, and [then] he will live several years after this, as it is written, "But charity saves from death" [Prov. 11:4].

This entire matter appears in the *Shulhan Arukh*, in the gloss by R. Moses Isserles:

> The early ones, of blessed memory, wrote that the shadow of the moon on Hoshana Rabbah night contains a portent for what will happen to a person or to his relatives during that year. One wrote that a person should not be exacting regarding this, so as not to adversely affect his luck. Also, many do not understand this matter thoroughly. And it is better to be innocent and not to examine the future, and so it also seems to me.[65]

The *Zohar* also relates to this topic:

> Rabbi Isaac was sitting downcast one day at Rabbi Judah's door. [...] He said to him: Why do you ask this [thinking that you will die]? He replied: [...] Furthermore, when I am praying and come to "hearkens to prayer," I look for my shadow on the wall and I do not see it. I believe that since the shadow had disappeared and is no longer seen, the herald must have already gone out to issue the proclamation, for it is written, "Man walks about as a mere shadow" [Ps. 39:7] — as long as his shadow remains with him, a "man walks," and his spirit resides within him. But when a man's shadow disappears and is no longer seen, then he disappears from the world.[66]

Some authorities have sought to find a basis for this in the Talmud, in Horayot 12a:

65 *Shulhan Arukh, Orah Hayyim* 662:1. Cf. Rabbi Hayyim Palache, *Kaf ha-Hayyim* on *Orah Hayyim* loc. cit., para. 19, who also cites Rabbi Hayyim Vital (*Peri Etz Hayyim*, 150b): "that one must be actually completely nude when one looks in the shadow [cast by] the moon to see [his] shadow. There also must be a special hour for the moon" (cf. above, n. 60). Rabbi David ben Zimra (*Radbaz*) argues against this in his book *Migdal David* (Lvov, 1883), 29a, that it is forbidden to stand nude (see Wilhelm, "The Orders of *Tikkunim*," p. 139).

66 *Va-Yehi* (I, 217b); translation based on F. Lachower and I. Tishbi, *The Wisdom of the Zohar*, trans. D. Goldstein (Oxford, 1989), I, p. 135. For the teaching by the *Zohar* on this subject, see Weinstock, "Gazing upon Shadows," pp. 255–59.

One who desires to set out on a journey and wishes to learn whether or not he will return home should station himself in a dark house. If he sees the reflection of his shadow, he will know that he will return home again. This, however, is not a proper thing to do.[67]

I already alluded[68] to the fact that this belief appears in Roman sources, as in the description by Pausanius (second century CE):

Among the marvels of Mt. Lycaeus the most wonderful is this. On it is a precinct of Lycaean Zeus, into which people are not allowed to enter. If someone takes no notice of the rule and enters, he must inevitably live no longer than a year. A legend, moreover, was current, that anything alike within the precinct, whether beast or man, cast no shadow.[69]

Christians in the medieval period also believed in this superstition. Lynn Thorndike reports in his major work, *History of Magic and Experimental Science*:[70]

If one's head cast no shadow on the wall at the feast of Epiphany (= January 6), one would not live out the year.[71]

67 Cited in *Rokeah*, ed. Schneersohn; Buxtorf, *Synagoga Judaica*; Leusden, *Philologus Hebraeo-Mixtus*. See the references in R. Margaliot, *Nitzotzei Or*, on Horayot 12a, p. 195. For more on the passage in Horayot, see Weinstock, "Gazing upon Shadows," pp. 261–62.

68 *Minhagei Yisrael*, Vol. 1, pp. 15–16, with an extensive bibliography. Mention should also be made of D. Goldshmidt, *On Jewish Liturgy: Essays on Prayer and Religious Poetry* (Jerusalem, 1978), pp. 392–94 (Hebrew); and E. Horowitz, "Religious Practices among the Jews in the Late Fifteenth Century — According to Letters of R. Obadia of Bertinoro," *Pe'amim* 37 (1988), pp. 37–38 (Hebrew), with a reference to Wilhelm, "The Orders of *Tikkunim*," pp. 134–36, who argued that the practice of observing one's shadow came into being only in the sixteenth century within the circle of Safed Kabbalists; while M. Artom ("On the Letters of R. Obadiah of Bertinoro," *Yavneh* 3 [1960], pp. 112–24 [Hebrew]) maintains that there is no testimony to such a practice before the time of R. Obadiah of Bertinoro; and Horowitz concludes: "All of the above testimonies can be combined, to indicate that the Palermo custom was possibly the connecting link between the earlier practice of the thirteenth-fifteenth centuries and the later custom of the Safed Kabbalists" (p. 37); see the continuation of his instructive article.

69 Pausanias, *Description of Greece* 8:38:6 (trans. W.H.S. Jones, *LCL* [London-Cambridge, Mass., 1945], Vol. 4, pp. 93–95).

70 (New York, 1934), Vol. 4 (fourteenth-fifteenth centuries), p. 275.

This is paralleled by what is related by Strackerjan:[72]

> He who does not throw a shadow on Christmas Eve, will surely die in the next year.

And now, to return to our picture, which does not correspond to its explanation in the book by Leusden: it does not contain two people, but rather four (or five, counting the feet); moreover, the headless figure is not the shadow of the person standing opposite it, since the movements of the hands are not identical, nor is the direction of the *hoshana* the same, and there are other discrepancies. In other words, the figure on the right side is not a mirror image of the opposite one on the left side (in both, the left hand holds the *hoshana*).

The solution to this puzzle is to be found in the first edition of Leusden's book, which was published in Utrecht in 1663. This edition contains a much more primitive representation, a woodcut, instead of the copper engraving in the second edition. The picture in the first edition is set within the text of the explanation, and bears the caption "De Feste Pentacostes et Tabernaculorum." **Two figures** stand there, opposite each other, with the

---

71 Following the fifteenth-century author A. Digot, *Histoire de Lorraine* (Nancy, 1856), III, p. 182.

72 L. Strackerjan, *Aberglaube und Sagen aus dem Herzogthum Oldenburg* (Oldenburg, 1867), I, p. 32; quoted in Bonnerjea, *Dictionary of Superstition and Mythology*, p. 225. See also Opie and Tatem, *Dictionary of Superstitions*, p. 347, s.v. "Shadow, Headless," with a reference to R. Blakeborough, *Wit, Character, Folklore & Customs of the North Riding of Yorkshire* (London, 1898), p. 62 in a note: "should anyone cast such a shadow (shadowless head), it is held they will die ere next Christmas eve comes round." And also in M. Trevelyan, *Folk-Lore and Folk-Stories of Wales* (London, 1909), p. 30: "When the Christmas log is burning you should notice people's shadows, on the wall. [...] Shadows that appear without heads belong to persons who are to die within the year." See also what J.G. Frazer writes in his basic book *The Golden Bough, Taboo and the Perils of the Spirit*[3] (New York, 1935), p. 88: "In Lower Austria on the evening of St. Sylvester's day — the last day of the year — the company seated round the table mark whose shadow is not cast on the wall, and believe that the seemingly shadowless person will die next year. Similar presages are drawn in Germany both on St. Sylvester's day and on Christmas Eve," with references to Th. Vernaleken, *Mythen und Brauche des Volkes in Osterreich* (Vienna, 1859), p. 341; O.F. von Reinsberg-Duringsfeld, *Das festliche Jahr* (Leipzig, 1863), p. 401; Wuttke, *Der deutsche Volksaberglaube der Gegenwart*[3], p. 207, sect. 314.

one on the left being a mirror image of the person on the right, but lacking a head (see Fig. 2). Although this is not an actual shadow, in the regular sense of a shadow reflected on a wall and the like, it would appear that this is the manner chosen by the artist to depict this motif of a person and his shadow. This picture later appears, with minor variations, in the books of *minhagim*, such as the one published in Frankfurt in 1608[73] (Fig. 3).

In Leusden's third edition (Utrecht, 1862), the woodcuts are replaced by skillfully executed copper engravings. The illustrations appear on separate pages that were inserted between the printed pages, and do not adjoin the explanatory pages. Above each illustration is a reference to the relevant page. Thus, for example, our picture is next to p. 274 (and was bound around pp. 275 and 278), with a reference to p. 279. The artist who executed this fine illustration apparently did not fully comprehend its meaning, and based his work on the motif found in the various collections of *minhagim* (Figs. 4–7)[74] that depict *kiddush ha-levanah* (the blessing of the new moon/month),[75] which usually contain a group of people looking, and at times also pointing, at the moon. This assemblage includes a group of people on one side, and a lone individual on the other side.[76] Our artist added *hoshanot* in the hands of

73 The direction of the dark part of the moon is not correct in Fig. 2 (see above, n. 49), and was corrected when reversed in Fig. 3.

74 Fig. 4, from the *Amsterdam Minhagim Book* (1662), later appears in the *Amsterdam Minhagim Book* (1768) (in A. Rubens, *A Jewish Iconography*, revised edition [London, 1981], p. 42, no. 417). Fig. 23, brought by Rubens from *Amsterdam Minhagim* (1707) (p. 38, no. 371), and by Kohut, *Geschichte der deutschen Juden*, p. 301, from the Amsterdam Haggadah of 1695. The attributions to the latter are certainly incorrect. See Y.H. Yerushalmi, *Haggadah and History* (Philadelphia, 1975), Pls. 59–62, for this Haggadah; Fig. 24, Frankfurt 1708 (Rubens, p. 41, no. 410) = the Wilhermsdorf Haggadah (1687), ed. M. Hovav, *Seder Birkat Hamazon* (*Bendicion Despues de Comer*) (Jerusalem, 1981), p. 21.

75 He, nevertheless, knew enough to reverse the direction of the dark part of the moon, so that it would correspond to the end of the lunar month, and not its beginning. See above, n. 49. The direction in Fig. 8 is incorrect.

76 *Seder Birkat ha-Mazon*, ed. M. Hovav (Jerusalem, 1977), p. 14 is from *Minhagim* (Dyhernfurth, 1692) (Rubens, p. 33, no. 308); see our comments, n. 70, above. This is the place to expand upon the figure appearing in the *Venice Haggadah* (1601), next to the words "Terah, father of Abraham" (Josh. 24:2): a person facing to the right, pointing to the moon with his left hand, above which is the caption, "The image of Terah showing his sons the moon, and in its worship he would give his life for a *maneh* [a monetary amount]" (Fig. 9); and previously, on the bottom left of the title page, as one of Pharaoh's astrologers (Fig. 10) (see Yerushalmi, *Haggadah and*

his characters, following the example in the first edition, and changed the direction of the dark part of the moon, also in order to show that this scene is

History, for his Fig. 40, who was not precise in his translation). This figure is copied from the *Mantua Haggadah* (1568) (Fig. 11, bottom left) where it appears next to the words "*Yakhol me-Rosh Hodesh* [One might have thought (that the telling of the Exodus) should begin at the beginning of the month]," portraying an individual engaging in *kiddush ha-levanah*. This is paralleled by, albeit not identical to, the figure similarly occupied in the *Prague Haggadah* (1526), with the caption "*Hiddush ha-Levanah* [= *kiddush ha-levanah*]" (Fig. 12). The depiction of the wicked son in the *Prague Haggadah* (Fig. 13), on the other hand, was undoubtedly the model for the similar scene in the *Mantua Haggadah* (Fig. 14). The two figures in the *Venice Haggadah* who are pointing to the moon are not Jews (Terah, Pharaoh's astrologer), and it therefore is not surprising that they are bareheaded, in contrast with the other figures in this Haggadah. The head of the individual who is engaged in *kiddush ha-levanah* in the *Prague Haggadah* is covered, while the figure in the *Mantua Haggadah*, who is a **Jew** performing *kiddush ha-levanah*, is nevertheless — to our great surprise — bareheaded, unlike the majority of individuals portrayed in this Haggadah. The answer to this puzzling question apparently lies in the fact that the artist based his illustration (= woodcut) on a model from the Christian world, such as the woodcut by Hans Holbein the Younger to Habakkuk 1 (Fig. 15) in his *Icones Historiarum Veteris Testamenti*, which was first published in Lyons in 1538 (some thirty years before the publication of the *Mantua Haggadah*), and, over the course of the following eleven years, in seven additional editions, in Latin, French, Spanish, English, etc. The familiarity of the artist of the *Mantua Haggadah* with Holbein's work is patently evident from the image of the simple son with a weather vane (Fig. 16; cf. above, Fig. 11) that is copied (in reverse) from the latter book's illustration to Ps. 53:2 (numeration from new JPS trans.): "The fool says in his heart: 'There is no God'" (see R. Bonfil's introduction to the facsimile edition of the *Mantua Haggadah* [1560 (1568!)] [Tel Aviv, 1970], p. 3 of the introduction. This was already noted by Rachel Wischnitzer-Bernstein in her pioneering work: *Symbole und Gestalten der Juedischen Kunst* [Berlin, 1935], p. 97. See also the instructive article: M. Friedman, "Transplanted Illustrations in Jewish Printed Books," *Jewish Art* 14 [1988], pp. 44–55). See also Z. Hanegbi, "Purim Customs in Halakhah and in Art," in *Minhagei Yisrael*, Vol. 6, pp. 192–205 (see Fig. 17). Our difficulty, however, has not been completely resolved: why is this individual not wearing a hat? See *Minhagei Yisrael*, Vol. 4, pp. 162–63 n. 3; 176–79, when Michelangelo's *Jeremiah* is transformed in the *Mantua Haggadah* into an "old man who has acquired wisdom," and who has had a hat placed on his head (that was not worn by the *Jeremiah* of Michelangelo).

Admittedly, R. Leone (Judah Aryeh) Modena permitted bareheadedness, and even attested that "most of the Italian [Jews] are permissive in this matter, especially here

suitable for Hoshana Rabbah. Due to his lack of understanding of the content of his picture, he beheaded the figure that stands on the right, opposite the group to the left, once again in accordance with the illustration in the first edition, and thus transformed the "shadow" into a headless person.[77]

in the ghetto, and I, as well, when I speak with princes [i.e. am bareheaded] or when it is very hot." See I. Rivkind, "A Responsum of Leo da Modena on Uncovering of the Head," *Louis Ginzberg Jubilee Volume* (New York, 1949), Hebrew section, pp. 401–23 (the quotation is from p. 422). This still does not completely resolve our problem, in light of the fact that, as was already noted, most of the figures reproduced in this article have some sort of head covering; more study is required.

It should also be noted that illustrations of *hiddush ha-levanah* bear a slight resemblance to the depictions of "the Jewish astronomer." See, e.g., the woodcut from Louvain from 1528 in the book *Tabua Perpetua* (Fig. 18), reproduced in A. Rubens, *A History of Jewish Costume* (London, 1967), no. 132, p. 100. Cf. also the woodcut by Heinrich Vogthur, *The Banishment of the Astronomers from the Koppel Bible* (Strassburg, 1530), reproduced in *Print Quarterly* 4, 3 (1987), p. 281, fig. 196.

77 The shape of the moon in these pictures is a convention — a crescent, with its interior in profile. See, e.g., the woodcuts by Durer in *The Complete Woodcuts of Albrecht Durer*, ed. W. Kurth (New York, 1963), nos. 87, 88, 110, 125, ca. 1495–1500 (see Fig. 20). For an additional, and somewhat more sophisticated, woodcut, see Gerard Leeu, *Dialogus creaturarum* (Gouda, 1480), reproduced in N. Levarie, *The Art and History of Books* (New York, 1968), p. 153 (Fig. 21). This convention continued into the eighteenth and nineteenth centuries, and it is to be found on playing cards from that period. See R. Tilly, *A History of Playing Cards* (New York, 1973), pp. 40, 42. See also John Aubrey, *Remaines of Gentilisme and Judaisme* (1686–87), ed. J. Britten (London, 1881), p. 112, no. 15: "The sun and moon are usually described with humane faces; whether herein these be not a Pagan imitation, and these visages at first implied an Apollo and Diana, we may make some doubt, and we find the statue of ye sun was framed with raies about the head, such were indeciduous and unshaven locks of Apollo."

In actuality, however, such a crescent appears only in the first quarter of the lunar month, that is, until the third or fourth day after the *molad* (appearance of the new moon; see Fig. 19). The blessing for the new month, however, is usually conducted at a later time in the month. This issue was recently discussed extensively by Y. Gartner, *The Evolution of Customs in the World of Halacha* (Jerusalem, 1995), chap. 12, pp. 192–209 (Hebrew). Gartner demonstrates the development of the prevalent custom, following the view expressed in the ruling by Rabbi Joseph Caro in *Shulhan Arukh, Orah Hayyim* 426:4, and also held by Rabbi Isaac Luria, and among the Hasidim, not to bless the new moon until seven days have passed from the *molad* (see Gartner, pp. 202–209). At that time of the month, i.e. after the first quarter, the moon becomes fuller, and half or more of it is revealed. This is also attested by Paul Christian Kirchner, *Judisches Ceremoniel* (Nuremberg, 1724), p. 77, and

3. SNEEZING

It is generally accepted among Jews that if someone sneezes, other people respond by saying "*asia*" (Aramaic for "doctor"), or, more correctly, "*assuta*" ("health" or "remedy" in Aramaic); or the Yiddish "*zu gesund*" or "*Gesundheit*" ("for your good health").[78] The practice has early antecedents, and apparently arose out of the understanding that, just as life comes to a person by breathing in the soul through the nostrils (based on Gen. 2:7: "He blew in his [Adam's] nostrils the breath of life, and man became a living

Johann Bodenschatz, *Kirchliche Verfassung der heutigen Juden, sonderlich derer in Deutschland* (Ellangen, 1748), p. 169, that the Jews would bless the new moon only after seven days had passed. In their illustrations (Figs. 22, 23), however, they were not precise, and they portrayed the moon in its beginning phase. In Fig. 7, on the other hand, the moon appears in its fullness, that is, in the middle of the month, which is halakhically possible (see *Shulhan Arukh, Orah Hayyim* 426:3: "Until when is the blessing for it recited? Until the fifteenth [day] from the day of the *molad*, not including the fifteenth"), but not usual (with the possible exception of the month of Tishrei, when the blessing ceremony is conducted on the night following Yom Kippur — Rabbi Moses Isserles, *Orah Hayyim* 602; see A. Berger, "The Blessing of the New Moon before Yom Kippur or on the Night after Yom Kippur," *Kobetz Torani Zekhor le-Avraham* [1995], pp. 421–29 [Hebrew]). But even in this picture from the *Minhagim Book*, however, we should not seek precision. We rather are to regard this, once again, as a convention governing the artistic depiction of the moon. (See, e.g., the front page of the book by Johannes de Sacro Busto, *Sphaera Mundi* [Venice, 1488], reproduced in A.M. Hind, *An Introduction to a History of Woodcut* [New York, 1963], Vol. 2, p. 465. For this book, see Hind, op. cit., pp. 463–64; Kurth, *Complete Woodcuts*, p. 88.) An additional proof for the blessing of the new moon when the moon is full is possibly to be brought from the woodcut by Giovanni Andrea dalle Piane (1679–1750), of the blessing of the new moon in Venice, with a full moon (Rubens, p. 60, no. 620); Rubens, *A Jewish Iconography: Supplementary Volume* (London, 1982), p. 33.

78 Interestingly, this custom is listed by M.M. Hyatt, *Folk-Lore from Adams County, Illinois* (New York, 1935), p. 156, no. 3282: "When anyone sneezes, say 'Gesundheit (Health).' The person who has sneezed must answer 'Gesundheit ist besser wie krankheit (health is better than sickness).'" See Hyatt's introduction, p. 15, that in this region "Greeks, Italians and Jews scarcely exceeded the hundred mark, are new-comers, and have not been approached for folklore." And in a footnote, the author adds: "Two or three items given as Jewish were also known to several non-Jewish informants. Lore definitely Jewish was excluded." See part 1, chap. 23 ("Throwing a Shoe at a Wedding"), for similar phenomena.

being"), so, too, sneezing carries the danger of breathing out the soul. In this vein we read in *Pirkei de-Rabbi Eliezer*:[79]

> From the day the heavens and earth were created, no man was ever sick. Rather, when he was strolling through the marketplace he would sneeze and his soul would depart through his nostrils. Such was the situation until the time of our father Jacob who prayed and beseeched mercy [of God], saying to Him: "Lord of the Universe, do not take away my soul from me until I have charged my children and household." And the Lord hearkened to his request, as it is written, "Some time afterward, Joseph was told: 'Your father is ill'" [Gen. 48:1]. When the local citizens heard this, they were amazed, for there had never been a situation such as this from the time of the creation of the heavens and earth. Therefore, a person is duty-bound to say upon his sneezing, "*Hayyim* [life]," for his death has been changed to light, as it is written, "His sneezings flash forth light" [Job 41:10].[80]

This teaches that a sneeze warns of impending death; and to avert it, and reverse the divine pronouncement, one calls out "life," meaning, "May I[81] be granted life."

Yelamdenu, an ancient Jewish midrash, cited in the *Arukh* (an eleventh-century Talmudic dictionary),[82] states:

> [...] for so it is when a man sneezes, he [i.e. another person] says to him: "*Le-hayyim tovim*" [for good life], from which we may see that originally [i.e. before Jacob's time] he would die. [But] Jacob arose and prayed.

79 Chap. 52, based on *Pirkei de-Rabbi Eliezer*, ed. D. Luria (Warsaw, 1852), fol. 125b.
80 Cf. *Yalkut Shimoni*, Genesis, para. 77. According to this reading, the one who sneezes says this to himself.
81 See the preceding note.
82 *Aruch Completum (Arukh ha-Shalem)*, ed. A. Kohut (Vienna, 1878–92 [reprint: New York, 1955]), Vol. 6, p. 191a, s.v. "עטש." The *Arukh* translates: אישטרנוטרי, which Kohut explains (n. 4) as *sternutare*, a late Latin form of *sternuere*, to sneeze. The noun in Latin is *sternutatio* in Vulgar Latin, and, assuming that verbs formed from nouns generally end in –*are*, hence *sternutare* (see G.H. Grandgent, *An Introduction to Vulgar Latin* [New York, 1962], p. 16). This, however, is unnecessary, since *sternutare* means "to sneeze repeatedly, or violently," as opposed to *sternuere*, which means merely "to sneeze." See *Oxford Latin Dictionary*, ed. P.G.W. Glare (Oxford, 1976), p. 1819b, s.v. "*sterno*," "*sternuto*."

Yalkut Talmud Torah[83] cites *Pirkei de-Rabbi Eliezer* slightly differently:

> Therefore a person is duty-bound **to say to** his fellow, when he sneezes, ["to life," for] death has been turned into light.

According to this reading and the passage from *Yelamdenu*, it is not the sneezer who makes this utterance to himself, but rather someone else who sees or hears him sneezing.

PT Berakhot (6:6), in contrast, tells us:

> One who sneezes while eating may not say [to himself] ס׳י [= ἴασις ζῆθι = "for good health"], for this may endanger his life.[84]

Similarly, the *Arukh*[85] cites this passage in PT Berakhot as reading: "One should not say [to him][86] זט [= ζῆθι, "(to) life"].[87] The Palestinian Talmud

---

83 Cited in Kasher, *Torah Shelemah, Va-Yehi*, Vol. 7 (New York, 1950), p. 1739, para. 12.

84 See Rabbi I. Tamar, *Alei Tamar*, Vol. 1: *Zeraim I* (Givatayim, 1979), p. 228, who notes that many early authorities have the reading: "he may not say **to him**," i.e. another may not say to the sneezer. Lieberman, *Tosefta ki-Fshutah* (Vol. 3, p. 94 nn. 19, 25), however, demonstrates conclusively that this is not the correct reading.

85 *Aruch Completum*, Vol. 3, p. 282a, s.v. "זוטא"; and cf. *Additamenta as librum Aruch Completum*, ed. S. Krauss (Vienna, 1937 [reprint: New York, 1955]), p. 170, s.v. "זיטא," for additional variant readings in early authorities.

86 Delete the text within the brackets; see above, n. 84, and below.

87 Lieberman, *Tosefta ki-Fshutah*, Vol. 3, p. 94 n. 20, following *Additamenta as librum Aruch Completum*, cites further variants: MS. Vatican of the Palestinian Talmud has זס = σῶς; Rabbi Eliezer ben Joel ha-Levi of Bonn (*Ravyah*), Ravyah, ed. V. Aptowitzer (Jerusalem, 1938 [Jerusalem, 1965]), Vol. 1, para. 120, p. 102: זיזם (= זוז) = σῷζων, "save." See also Grimm, *Teutonic Mythology*, p. 1116, who writes: "The Greeks saluted the sneezer with ζῆθι, Ζεῦ, σῶσον," suggesting, as indeed does Lieberman, loc. cit., that we should read σῶσον (rather than σῷζον). See below, the citation from Anth. Graecia. See also Lieberman's n. 26, citing J. Preuss, *Biblisch-talmudische Medizin ...* (Basel, 1923), p. 84 (English trans. by Fred Rosner: *Biblical and Talmudic Medicine* [New York, 1978], p. 75), who (English, p. 76 n. 548) rejects some of these readings. He further notes that "the exclamation *zethi* ('live long') for sneezing is mentioned by Olympiodor (Scholia in Platonis *Phaedon*, ed. Finckh p. 30) but to equate *zt* with *zethi* is impossible." See also P.W. van der Horst, *Ancient Jewish Epitaphs: An Introductory Survey of a Millennium of Jewish Funerary Epigraphy (300 BCE–700 CE)*[2] (Kampen, the Netherlands, 1996), who writes (p. 40): "In order to ensure that they would be remembered, people sometimes erected and engraved their own tombstones already during their lifetime. This is

continues by explaining that if a person sneezes while eating he may choke. According to this understanding, someone else may wish him "life"[88] or "good health."[89]

T Shabbat,[90] however, reads:

> If one says *Marpe* [good health, cure], this is the way of the Amorites.[91] R. Eleazar be-R. Zadok says: One does not say *Marpe*, because this detracts from Torah study.[92] The School of R. Gamaliel did not say *Marpe*, because of the way of the Amorites.

Lieberman[93] has shown that some versions read "this is **not** the way of the Amorites," and he adds that the texts cited above, which encourage such an utterance, clearly must have had such a reading. He further explains why some sought to exclude this from the list of forbidden acts and formulas, while others included it. Leiberman refers us[94] to Pliny, Hist. Nat. 28:5:23, who talks of the practice of blessing one who sneezes.[95] He further cites Petronius[96] (d. 66 CE), but remarks that, for our purposes, the more

---

often indicated on the stones by the word Ζῶν / Ζῶσα / Ζῶντες / Ζῆ or *vivus*, etc." Perhaps they saw this as a *segulah*, a nostrum for long life.

88 See Lieberman, *Tosefta ki-Fshutah*, Vol. 3, p. 93 n. 18, referring us to Pliny, Hist. Nat. 28:6:86, that this was a Roman custom, too.

89 One may not, however, do so in the study hall, for this detracts from study; BT Berakhot 53a: it was not customary to say "*Marpe*" ("good health," "cure") in the study hall. See Rashi, ad loc., who substitutes the Aramaic *assuta* for *marpe*. See below, the citation from T Shabbat.

90 T Shabbat 7:5, ed. Lieberman, p. 26. See above, the preceding note.

91 See Avishur, "*Darkei ha-Emori*," pp. 17–47; M. Hadas-Lebel, "Le paganisme à travers les sources rabbiniques des II et IIIe siècles. Contribution à l'étude du syncretisme dans l'empire romain," in *Aufstieg und Niedergang der Romischen Welt: Geschichte und Kultur Roms im Spiegel der neuren Forschung*, ed. H. Temporini and W. Haase (Berlin, 1972–98), Vol. 2, 19:2, pp. 454–77; see also Lewy, "Morgenlandischer Aberglaube in der romischen Kaiserzeit."

92 See above, n. 89.

93 Lieberman, *Tosefta ki-Fshutah*, Vol. 3, pp. 93–94; cf. above, nn. 13, 18.

94 Lieberman acknowledges his debt to Heinrich Lewy's article, "Morgenlandischer Aberglaube in der romischen Kaiserzeit," p. 132.

95 "Why do we say 'Good health' to those who sneeze? [cur sternuentes salutamus]." See Pliny, *Natural History*, trans. W.H.S. Jones, *LCL* (London-Cambridge, MA, 1963), Vol. 8, pp. 16–17 (Book XXVIII, v. 23); cf. pp. 18–19 (ibid., v. 26).

96 *Satyrica* (not *Satyricon*), *Cena Trimalchionis* 98.

significant reference is to the *Anthologia Graeca* 11:268,[97] an anonymous epigram that runs thus:

> Proclius cannot wipe his nose with his hand, for his arm is shorter than his nose; nor does he say "Zeus preserve us"[98] (Ζεῦ σῶσον[99] when he sneezes, for he can't hear his nose, it is so far away from his ears.

And in later times, Christians would say: *"Deus te adiuvet,"* "God help you," substituting "Deus" for "Zeus."[100] And to this day in England one says to the sneezer "Bless you" or "God bless you."[101]

The Radfords believed that:

> The ejaculation — "God bless you," still used on hearing a person sneeze, is not a superstition. Its origin was in the great Athenian plague, a sneeze being so frequently the first indication that a person had contracted plague.[102]

The Romans practised the "blessing" and brought it to Britain.[103]

---

97 *LCL* edition: *The Greek Anthology*, trans. W.R. Paton, Vol. 4 (London, 1918), pp. 196–97.

98 Paton renders this as "God preserve us," but this misses the point. See further Preuss, *Biblical and Talmudic Medicine*, p. 75 n. 51: "Ammianos ridicules a Proklos who had such a long nose that he did not call out *Zen* [should read *Zeu*] *soson* when he sneezed because he didn't hear it since his ear was too far away. *Florig. Divers. Epigramat. Vet.*, ed. Henry Stephanus. Book 2 c. 13, p. 141."

99 Cf. above, n. 87.

100 Grimm, *Teutonic Mythology*, p. 1116: "Nu helfin Got! Christ in halfe!"

101 See Opie and Tatem, *A Dictionary of Superstitions*, pp. 364–65, with a wealth of references. See also Aubrey, *Remaines of Gentilisme and Judaisme*, pp. 103–104, 150, 177, 194; see also below, the Appendix to this chapter.

102 Radford, *Encyclopaedia of Superstitions*, p. 222.

103 Preuss, *Biblical and Talmudic Medicine* (n. 75) discusses this view at length, and we shall do best by citing him in extenso:

> The ancient historians such as Sigo (Carol. Sigonu. *Historiar. de regno Italiae.* Book 15 Basel 1575 p. 31. *ad anum* 590) and Urbini (Polydorus Vergilius Urbinatus. *De Rerum Inventoribus.* Book 8. Amsterdam 1671. Elzevir [preface in August 1499]. Book 6 c. 11 p. 410), as well as clerics (Guil. Durandus. *Rationale Divinor. Officior.* Lugdun. 1605. Book 6 c. 102 p. 393), report that the origin of this use of sneezing as a sign of great danger is the bubonic plague which raged in Rome in the year 590 and in which people suddenly died while sneezing or yawning. Pope Pelagius also died in this epidemic. As a result, it became customary to call out *"deus te adjuvet"* to someone

This explanation, however, seems unlikely, in view of the fact that we find this practice also in far-off lands, even as distant as India. Indeed, as Biren Bonnerjea writes, in his *Dictionary of Superstitions and Mythology*:[104]

Sneezing is due to demoniacal influence (India). [...] Sneezing is considered to be a call of death; therefore the middle finger and the thumb are snapped as a charm (India).[105]

Likewise, E. Westermarck, in his *Ritual and Belief in Morocco*,[106] relates that, in Hiaina:

[...] if a woman sneezes while engaged in weaving, a member of the household will die before long.

Westermarck continues, in a different spirit:

The Prophet is related to have said that God loves sneezing, and that

who sneezed. A Jewish chronicler of the sixteenth century, David Gans, **also fell victim to this assertion** [emphasis added — D. S.] (D. Gans, *Tzemach David*. Sedilkow 1834 p. 51b: until the year 590). The much older usage of this belief that sneezing heralds great danger is mentioned by Caesar Baron (Baronius. *Annales Ecclesiast.*: until the year 590. ed. Theiner. Vol. 10 p. 451 b), who cites as proof the aforementioned quotation from Plinius. From the report of the Dutch physician Isbrand Van Diemerbroeck who describes the plague in Nijmegen, one might perceive that the above narrative (of Plinius) might nevertheless be based on a true occurrence: *cum crebis sternutationibus neminem evadisse vidimus* (Diemerbroeck. De Peste. Amsterdam 1665, p. 101).

Dioscorides also reports that during the time of Valerius Flaccus cases were known in which epilepsy occurred following copious sneezing. Naturally, the modern German "bacteria-fanatic" knows that sneezing is "an attempted reaction of the nasal membrane against penetration by microbes." To him, the traditional *"prosit"* or *"zur Gesundheit"* ("bless you") is equivalent to saying to the person: "I wish you luck and hope that you rid yourself of the bacillus or bacilli" (Rivnus who is the same as Dr. Franz Bachmann. *War ist Krankheit?* Birnbaum 1892 p. 24)!

We see from the above that this was a widely-held assumption, but Preuss, rightly, I believe, rejected it.

104 B. Bonnerjea, *Dictionary of Superstitions and Mythology* (London, 1927?), pp. 235–36.

105 He refers to W. Crooke, *The Popular Religion and Folk-Lore of Northern India* (Westminster, 1896), p. 240; and to A.M.T. Jackson, *Folklore Notes*, ed. R.E. Enthoven (Bombay, 1915), Vol. 2, pp. 54 et seq.

106 Vol. 2, pp. 34–35. This was already noted by Preuss, p. 75.

if a person sneezes and immediately afterwards says, as he should do, "God be praised," it is incumbent upon everybody who hears it, or at least one of the party, to exclaim, "God have mercy on you."

In light of the above, Zolar's explanation seems the more convincing. As he writes in his *Encyclopedia of Omens, Signs, and Supersititions*:[107]

The common practice of saying "God bless you" when another person sneezes comes from the ancient belief that the soul leaves the body when a person sneezes, and only a blessing can bring it back.

He adds that "when a Hindu sneezes, those nearby say 'live,' to which he replies 'with you.'" This very closely parallels the Hellenistic-Roman and Judaic traditions, as we have seen above, and surely reflects a common belief in the soul entering and exiting through the nostrils.[108]

This widespread belief led to an ambivalent attitude to sneezing, for the soul could either enter or leave the body through the nostrils. Thus we read in *Funk and Wagnalls Standard Dictionary of Folklore*, in the entry on sneezing:[109]

Whether sneezing is a good or bad sign depends on the culture you happen to belong to. It may also be the sign that a devil or evil spirit

107 *Zolar's Encyclopedia of Omens, Signs, and Supersititions* (New York, 1995), p. 332.

108 We are not suggesting any mutual influences, but rather structuralist similarities, since all humans breathe through their noses.

109 M. Leach (ed.), *Funk and Wagnalls Standard Dictionary of Folklore, Mythology and Legend* (New York, 1949), p. 1031, entry by R.D. Jameson. Preuss, *Biblical and Talmudic Medicine*, p. 74, writes as follows:
Sneezing was considered a noteworthy occurrence by the ancients. Aristotle explains it as a holy, Divine sign which has great significance: *ton Ptarmon theon egoumetha einai* (Aristotle. *Problem Sect.* 33:7). He simultaneously raises the question (*ibid. problem* 9) as to why the other types of air which emanate from the body (so too in *Hist. Anim.* 1 c. 11, where Aubert and Wimmer misunderstood the word *pneumaton* of the text), flatus and ructus, are not considered to be holy. He answers that only sneezing comes from the principal and most Divine organ. Already in Homer, Penelope is happy that her son Telemachus sneezes when she expresses a wish (Homer. *Odyssey* 17:545). When someone sneezed at the precise moment that Kleanor declared that the situation of the 10,000 was not hopeless, the entire army *mia orme* offered prayers to the god on high (Xenoph. *Anab.* 3 Chapt. 2:9).

is trying to get out of the body. [...] The Koita of British New Guinea believe that sneezing in sleep is a sign that the soul has come back to the body. [...] In North Carolina, you will hear of a death if you sneeze at a meal. [...] The ancient Persians uttered prayers when they sneezed because a fiend in the body was coming out and persons who heard the sneeze also prayed, presumably to keep the fiend out of their own bodies. The Hindus also believe sneezes have to do with spirits entering or leaving by way of the nose.

And, since the sneeze could be regarded either as auspicious or ominous, in some cultures we find that it was viewed differently under differing circumstances. Thus, Eustathius, in his commentary on Homer,[110] observed long ago that "sneezing to the left was unlucky, but prosperous to the right."[111]

110 Eustathius (twelfth century CE) wrote a commentary on the *Iliad* and the *Odyssey*: Παρεκβολαὶ εἰς τὴν ‘Ομήρου ’Ιλιάδα (’Οδύσσεια), ed. G. Stollbaum, 1825–31: *Commentarie ad Iliadem et. Odysseum*, b.xviii. Cf. Catullus, Epig. 45: "Dextram sternuit ad probationem"; cited in W.C. Hazlitt, *Dictionary of Faiths & Folklore: Beliefs, Superstitions and Popular Customs* (London, 1905), p. 553a.

111 Cf. *Zolar's Encyclopedia of Omens, Signs, and Supersititions*, p. 333: "Should you sneeze from the right nostril, good luck is forthcoming; but from the left, expect bad luck." This is not as implausible as it would initially seem. Yoga, for example, places great emphasis on breathing techniques, in an advanced stage of which the devotee is to breathe through one nostril or another. *Pranayama*, the control of the *prana* (in this context, breath; see below), or "the practice of ordered breathing" (E. Wood, *Yoga* [Harmondsworth, Middlesex, 1962], p. 255) is the fourth of the eight stages of the Yoga process (*The New Encyclopaedia Brittanica* [1992], *Micropaedia*, s.v. "Yoga," Vol. 12, p. 846). This, together with the preceding step of *asana* (posture), "give the student [of Yoga] physical fitness for further Yogic practice" (Swami Nikhilananda, s.v. "Yoga," *Encyclopedia Americana* [1984], Vol. 29, p. 681). Swami Vivekananda, *Vedanta Philosophy: Raja Yoga* (New York, 1920), defines *Hatha Yoga*, of which *pranayama* is a part, as "the science of controlling body and mind, but with no spiritual end in view, bodily perfection being the only aim" ("Glossary," p. 243; but see below, for the use of these techniques in the worship of various deities). On this level, Yogic sources are effusive in their emphasis of the importance of Yogic breathing (which Yogi Wassan, *Secrets of the Himalaya Mountain Masters and Ladder to Cosmic Consciousness* [Punjab, 1927], p. 154, defines as "scientific breathing") and are quite detailed in the health benefits to be obtained by following this regimen. The first effects, after a few month's practice of only the initial breathing exercise: "the face will change; harsh lines will disappear; with this calm thought calmness will come over the face. Next, beautiful voice will come. I never saw a *Yogi* with a

Of course, the left (*sinistra* in Latin) was always more sinister, while the right

croaking voice" (Vivekananda, *Vedanta Philosophy*, p. 56). As is to be expected from a breathing exercise, *Dirgha anayama* "oxygenates the blood and purges the lungs of residual carbon dioxide" ("The Yoga Site: The Online Yoga Resource Center," at www.yogasite.com/pranayama.htm); Yogic hyperventilation is said to relieve hyperacidity (R.R. Javalgekar, *The Yoga-Science [for Everyone]* [Varanasi, India, 1990], p. 123). In an advanced stage, "these exercises will also give power for conquering the climate, so that rain, snow, wind, or storm will not bother. It will give power for resisting encroachment of any germs that may be breathed into the body, or taken into the body with food" (Wassan, *Himalaya Mountain Masters*, p. 158). Dr. Satyendra Prasad Mishra, *Yoga and Ayurveda: (Their Alliedness and Scope as Positive Health Sciences)* (Varnasi, India, 1989), p. 81, goes so far as to claim that "the practitioner of *Pranayama* is relieved of all diseases," while "those who are devoid of *Pranayama* suffer from all kinds of diseases," many kinds of which "are caused by the ill-regulation of the *Vayu* [air]." In Yoga exercises in general, "we collect a gigantic amount of energy" that "gives us an immense reserve of power" (S. Yesudian and E. Haich, *Yoga and Health*, trans. J.P. Robertson [(New York, 1953], p. 68). But see M.P. Gupta, *Dictionary of Indian Religions, Saints, Gods, Goddesses, Rituals, Festivals and Yoga Systems* (Agra, India, 2000), p. 386, s.v. "*Pranayama* mantra," who denigrates "the obstinate *hatha yogi*" who will waste his time and energy on inhalation, retention and exhalation in a bid to strengthen his body, "as contrasted with 'the self-controlled ascetic,' who is to contemplate upon the supreme Brahman by means of *Pranava* [the use of OM; see below]."

Going beyond the purely physical, *pranayama* also positively affects one's mental state. V.H. Date, *Brahma-Yoga of the Gita* (New Delhi, 1971), p. 284, asserts that control over the breath automatically brings mastery over the mind, and identifies *Pavana* (the mind) with *manus* (breath). T.S. Rukmani, *Yogavartikka of Vijnanabhiksu*, Vol. 1: *Samadhipada* (New Delhi, 1981), p. 191, explains that it should be understood as "the means for stabilizing the state of steadiness of the mind." Javalgekar adds to the mental benefits the relieving of tension (p. 130), overcoming a lack of concentration (pp. 130–31), and relieving general debility (p. 131).

On a more profound level, however, *pranayama* is thought to transcend the purely physical sphere, or even the realm of mental well-being. Swami Vivekananda, who, as we have seen, stressed the physical utility of this discipline, discusses it in a chapter revealingly entitled "The Control of Psychic Prana" (*Vedanta Philosophy*, pp. 55–61). *Prana*, we learn from Vivekananda, is "the sum total of the cosmic energy, the vital forces of the body" ("Glossary," p. 253), and *pranayama*, then, is the means of harnessing these forces, by awakening "a peculiar force which is dormant about the navel [...] which is the source of all occult power" (Manilal Drividi, *Yoga Sastra*, p. 32, cited by T.I. Tambyah, *Psalms of a Saiva Saint ... from the Writings of Tayumanaswamy* ... [London, 1925], p. 173). See, e.g., Bharatan

Kumarappa, *The Hindu Conception of the Deity* (London, 1934), pp. 27–28: "in the early theories the ultimate Principle was [...] described as Breath and as Food, for it is by means of these that creatures live." On a cosmic level, *prana* is "the life-giving breath of Brahman, whose out-going is creation and whose in-drawing is destruction" (W.J. Flagg, *Yoga or Transformation* [see below for details], p. 190; cf. below, the *Zohar*'s depiction of the removal of life by the divine breath), a process that is reflected in exhalation and inhalation by the Yoga practitioner. Indeed, in a presumably scientific-medical tract, Rammurti S. Mishra, M.D. (Shri Brahmananda Sarasvati), claims in his *The Textbook of Yoga Psychology: The Definitive Translation and Interpretation of Patanjali's Yoga Sutras for Meaningful Application in All Modern Psychologic Disciplines*, ed. A. Adman (New York, 1987), pp. 381–82, that "all energy, whatever its form" is included within the concept of *prana*. Hence the ultimate importance of proper breathing:

> All motions are forms of *prana*. Energy of every cell and tissue, of sensory and motor organs and mindstuff is manifestation of *prana*. By means of motion of respiratory organs, breathing, one can reach the unity of motions of the entire organism, By means of the unity of the entire individual organism, one reaches cosmic energy. This expansion of individual energy into cosmic energy is called *pranayama*. [...] Hence one can understand the significance of breathing.

Cf. the general definition of these and other actions (see below) by H. Zimmer, *Artistic Form and Yoga in the Sacred Images of India*, trans. and ed. G. Chapple and J.B. Lawson (Princeton, NJ, 1984), p. 43: "The magical acts that follow upon external ritual purification consist of uttering significant syllables, of meaningful gestures and breathing exercises" (n.: "These arts are mantra, *mudra*, and *pranayama*").

Especially relevant to the question at hand are the exercises in which the practitioner inhales and/or exhales through only a single nostril, in one of two variants (as prescribed in "Yoga breathing exercises (pranayam) for a calmer you," at ga.essortment.com/yogabreathinge_rrec.htm): one-nostril breathing, in which one nostril is closed with a finger, and the practitioner inhales and exhales through the other nostril a number of times, before switching to the other; and alternate-nostril breathing, in which the right nostril is closed with the thumb, and the practitioner breathes in through the left nostril, and exhales through the right. This is followed by inhaling through the right nostril, and breathing out through the left. In addition to specific nasal and respiratory improvements, the benefits to be gained, either alone or in conjunction with a certain neck posture, include "Volitional Control" over breathing, endocrinal equilibrium, and improvement of cerebral circulation, the "functions of the Vital Organs," the body metabolism, and the like (Javalgekar, *Yoga Science*, pp. 84–86). Wood, *Yoga*, p. 92–93, offers a description of "a simple form of the alternate nostril breathing" from the *Shiva Sanhita*, and promises us that if "the wise man" practices this for three months, together with other requirements of this regimen, "the channels of the body will have become purified. [...] the body becomes healthy and likeable and emits a pleasant odour, and there will be good appetite and digestion, cheerfulness, a good figure, courage, enthusiasm, and strength." Sri Swami Sivananda, *Kundalini Yoga* (at sivanandadlshq.org/download/kundalini.pdf, "Pranayama," p. 48), states categorically: "The practice of Suryabheda Kumbhaka [a form of alternate-nostril breathing] destroys decay and death." Furthermore, practitioners of *pranayama* "can impart their Prana [to others] for healing morbid diseases" (ibid., p. 49; see *passim* for the healing powers and other benefits attaining to the practitioner of *pranayama*). For the importance of this directional breathing, see also D. Frawley, *Tantric Yoga and the Wisdom Goddesses: Spiritual Secrets of Ayurveda* (Delhi, 1999), p. 210.

One- or alternate-nostril breathing is based on a holistic conception of the human body, the elements of which are the following: (1) nerve-currents on the right and left sides of the spinal cord, known, respectively, as *Pingala* and *Ida* (terms that also refer to the nostrils themselves). These respective channels-forces are the "Positive and Negative Terrestrial magnetic forces" (Wassan, *Himalaya Mountain Masters*, p. 152). *Pingala* represents the solar-masculine aspect, and *Ida*, the lunar-feminine aspect; (2) the *Susumna*, the passage through the center of the spinal cord (Vivekananda, *Vedanta Philosophy*, p. 59); (3) *Kundalini*, "lit. 'the coiled-up,' the residual energy, located according to the Yogis at the base of the spine, and which in ordinary men produces dreams, imagination, psychical perceptions, etc., and which, when fully aroused and purified, leads to the direct perception of God" (Vivekananda, *Vedanta Philosophy*, "Glossary," p. 247). For a popular, but lucid, description of these elements and one understanding of the goal of Yoga discipline, see J. Bailey, "Balancing Act," at www.yogajournal.com/wis-dom/927_1.cfm.

In most of these exercises, one-sided or alternate breathing is manually controlled. One Internet site, however, speaks of "psychic alternate nostril breathing," in which the practitioner is to breathe normally, but to "imagine you are breathing in through the left nostril and out the right." It is claimed that "after practicing regularly you may find that you can actually control the breath moving in the nostrils without using your hands — so that you are actually breathing in and out through alternative nostrils. If you focus your attention behind the nose above the upper palate you can find the switch that controls this (it's a subtle muscular contraction)" (at yoga.com.au/Infosheets/Alternative%20nostril%20breathing.pdf). Once this level of proficiency has been attained, presumably one-sided sneezing, as well, would be possible.

When approaching the question of parallels and possible influences between the Eastern tradition of Yoga and Jewish mystical traditions, we can do no better than quote Rudolf Otto, who addressed this issue in *Mysticism East and West: A Comparative Analysis of the Nature of Mysticism*, trans. B.L. Bracey and R.C. Payne (New York, 1932). Otto asks: "Are the thought worlds of East and West so different and incomparable that they can never meet and therefore at bottom never understand each other?" (p. xv). He concludes (p. xvi) that

in mysticism there are indeed strong primal impulses working in the human soul which as such are completely unaffected by differences of climate, of geographical position or of race. These show in their similarity an inner relationship of types of human experience and spiritual life which is truly astonishing. Secondly, we contend that it is false to maintain that mysticism is always just mysticism, is always and everywhere one and the same quality. Rather, there are within mysticism many varieties of expression which are just as great as the variations in any other sphere of spiritual life [...]. Thirdly, we affirm that these variations as such are not determined by race, or geographical situation, but that they may appear side by side, indeed that they may arise in sharp contrast to one another, within the same circle of race and culture.

For an overview of breathing in Jewish sources, with emphasis on Jewish meditative techniques, see M. Verman, *The History and Varieties of Jewish Meditation* (Northvale, NJ, 1996), pp. 111–29, and esp. 122– 24, for the significance of each of the nostrils.

The cardinal importance of breath, paralleling the Yoga conception, is already established in the biblical depiction of the Creation, as God infused man with the life-force when He "blew into his nostrils the breath of life, and man became a living being" (Gen. 2:7). The dimensions of this process are set forth in the *Zohar*. In *Aharei Mot*, para. 219 (the paragraph numbering for the *Zohar* follows Ashlag) it maintains that this life-giving process was conducted for all the heavenly hosts: "When the Holy One, blessed be He, blew breath into each of the hosts of heaven, all the hosts were made and stood complete. This is the meaning of [Ps. 33:6]: '[by the word of the Lord the heavens were made,] by the breath of His mouth, all their host.'" In *Bereshit*, para. 388, in the name of R. Isaac, it expands this concept, and asserts that the continued existence of the heavenly host, as well, is dependent upon the divine breath; and indeed, as is all of creation: "The Holy One, blessed be He, made the world by a breath, and by a breath [of Torah study] it is preserved" (*Zohar, Bereshit* B, para. 177); and not only by the breath of study: R. Isaac maintains (*Tazria*, para. 99) that "the world is maintained by breath [*hevel*], for were no breath to come from the mouth, it would not exist even for a single moment." Cf. *Vayetze* 191, which draws a distinction between these two terms, which are nonetheless intertwined: "'the word of the Lord' is speech [Ashlag: that is the *Nukva*, that illuminates with *Hokhmah*], and 'the breath of His mouth' is the spirit [Ashlag: this is the *Zeir Anpin*, which illuminates with *hasadim*]. One cannot exist without the other, and are included one within the other." Ashlag explains, on *Vayikra* 317, that the *Nukva* (lit., the female) is *Malkhut*, and the male is *Zeir Anpin*. (Cf. *The Revised English Bible* [Oxford and New York, 1989] on this verse, which equates the breath of the Lord with His command: "all the host of heaven were formed at his command"). The drawing of a parallel between this dual aspect (which is connected with spirit-breath) and the Yoga identification of the right *nadi* with the masculine aspect and the left with the feminine would be extremely forced.

The effect of the breath connecting Heaven and earth can also travel in the opposite direction: *Beshalah*, para. 320, states that when a person does good deeds in this world, and seeks to be occupied with the service of the Holy King, "the good deed that he does is transformed into a breath [*hevel*] above; and every breath from which a voice ascends becomes an advocate before the Holy One, blessed be He." Conversely, all that a person does that is not in the service of the King turns into a breath that "rolls him through the world" (ibid., para. 321).

Behar, para. 42: the breath of the nose (*reiha de-hotama*) is one of the "limbs of the King's body" from which superior prophecy originates, giving as a proof-text Ezek. 2:2: "[As He spoke,] a spirit [*ha-ruah*] entered into me," reminiscent of the Yoga notion that different parts of the body are the receptacles of different modes of energy (see also below, the reference to Regardie).

The *Zohar* states quite simply (*Bo*, para. 143) that "everything in the world is made of breath," and in another place (*Mishpatim*, para. 530), links the divine breath to the integration of all the aspects of the Godhead, using as a proof-text: "by the breath of His mouth, all their host" (Ps. 33:6). This same verse is also used as a proof-text for the Lord's forming and ordering the supernal holy angels with the breath that issued from His mouth (Tzav 18, para. 125). Cf. A. Wayman, *Yoga of the Guhyasamajatantra: The Arcane Lore of Forty Verses, A Buddhist Tantra Commentary* (Delhi, 1980), p. 198, the all-inclusive nature of the ten winds comprising *prana*: "Cooperating with *vijnana* [the ideal mind, consciousness] the five basic winds perform all deeds and the five secondary winds perceive all things."

In a clear parallel to the concept of the right-left aspects and their differing energies that underlies single- and alternate-nostril breathing, the *Zohar* explains (*Vayehi*, para. 534, with *Ha-Sulam* commentary in brackets): "Spirits and souls issue forth [from *Malkhut*] to receive their shapes [...] [*Malkhut*] receives from one side, and gives on another." Rabbi Yehudah Ashlag (*Ha-Sulam*, Vol. 7 [Jerusalem, 1950], p. 168) explains: "Although *Malkhut* receives from all three sides of *Zeir Anpin* [...] at first it receives only from the left side [...] and then it has the first three aspects of *Hokhmah*, but without *hasadim* [...]; its lights are frozen within it, and it cannot illuminate." Moreover, a direct connection is drawn (*Hukat*, para. 33) between breath and the adverse (to the extent of being fatal!) left side: "'Take away their breath, they perish' [Ps. 104:29], for another spirit stirs from the left, and a spirit of uncleanness rests upon people, on those who died [...] and on all other humans"; we are told that Adam's sin with the Tree of Knowledge consisted of his separating the right (= *neshamah kedoshah*) from the left (= *nefesh hayah*) of the two *ruhot* that descended with man upon his creation (*Tazria*, para. 116, following the interpretation of *Ha-Sulam*, Vol. 13 [Jerusalem, 1952], *Tazria*, p. 41).

The divine breath, however, like the in-drawing of the Brahman's breath (see above), can also be destructive, as is attested by *Zohar, Lekh Lekha*, para. 411: "But if a person is not deserving, because he did not preserve this sign [of the covenant, i.e., circumcision] [...] it is written: 'They perish by a blast [*me-nishmat*, i.e., breath] from God, are gone at the breath of His nostrils' [Job 4:9]." (See also *The Zohar*, ed. M. Berg [New York, 2003], Vol. 23, pp. 59–60, Index entry for "Breath.")

We see, therefore, distinct parallels between Yoga breathing techniques and the philosophy on which they are based, on the one hand, and the *Zohar*, on the other. The quest after influences between these two belief-systems, which had no contact during their formative periods, should not have been initiated, but, unfortunately, this is not the case. William J. Flagg, e.g., confuses the question of Jewish-Yoga linkage by devoting chapters of his book, revealingly entitled *Yoga or Transformation: A Comparative Statement of the Various Religious Dogmas concerning the Soul and Its Destiny, and of Akkadian, Hindu, Taoist, Egyptian, Hebrew, Greek, Christian, Mohammedan, Japanese and Other Magic* (New York and London, 1898) to "Hebrew Yoga" (pp. 239–53) and "Yoga of the Essenes" (pp. 254–55), in which he includes, inter alia, Elijah, Elisha, and Jesus (!), due to their use of magic, prophetical powers, and performance of miracles. For a contemporary "Introduction to Qabalistic, Magical and Meditative Techniques" (which draws mainly on non-Jewish sources) that further muddies the waters, see the directions for performing the "Qabalistic Cross"(!), that link various parts of the body with divine attributes and beings, along with references to Sanskit terms and concepts: I. Regardie, *Foundations of Practical Magic* (Wellingborough, 1979), pp. 14–15.

The current "New Age" inclination to incorporate Yoga and Kabbalah, inter alia, into a single holistic system, based on, at best, scanty knowledge, as exemplified by Regardie, is perhaps the most unsubstantiated attempt to link these two systems. Due to the extent of this contemporary phenomenon, it is worthy of examination. As regards the dimensions of this phenomenon: a word on methodology would be appropriate here. The use of Internet searches as an aid in research is increasingly common at present. In addition to gleaning specific information, these searches can provide (albeit imprecise) information regarding the general dimensions of a specific phenomenon. A search conducted on August 13, 2004, with the Google search engine for the two terms "Yoga" and "Kabbalah" returned 37,600 Web pages; a total of 155 pages contained the specific phrases "Yoga and Kabbalah" or "Kabbalah and Yoga"; and a Boolean search for the specific phrase "Torah Yoga" yielded a total of 14,500 pages. Obviously, this technique makes no claim to quantitative accuracy, and many factors may influence the inclusion of irrelevant Web pages (such as the independent listing of both Kabbalah and Yoga under the heading of "Meditative Techniques" on the "Wikipedia: The Free Encyclopedia" site). Nonetheless, these results are indicative of the clear linkage between these terms, at least in the contemporary popular consciousness. Revealingly, the web site of the "Book Store of Spirit Dimension" found it necessary to include, in its offering of the book *A Golden Mind, a Golden Life: A Book of Contemplations* by Swami Chidvilasananda, the following caveat (a review of the book on the Amazon.com site: www.amazon.com/exec/obidos/tg/detail/-/0911307826/002–1103307–7276865): "This book is NOT by Rabbi Nachman [of Bratslav]. It is a publication of Siddah Yoga [...]. This book is a compilation of contemplations by Eastern Religious Swarmis [sic] and Gurus. There is ONE quote by Rabbi Nachman in the book, but other than that, this book has no connection with Rabbi Nachman" (see spiritdimension.com.hinduism ...).

One of many examples of the purported connection between Kabbalah and Yoga is the "Nefesh Haya School of Ophanim and Prophetic Jewish Meditation," directed by Zvi Zavidowsky (at www.angelfire.com/pe/ophanim, from which the following quotations are taken), which claims that this "'Yoga' of the Kabalah" is "based on the fundamental teachings of the Hebrew alphabet attributed to Abraham, unifying body-breath-mind-soul through embodiment of the sacred 'signs' of the Hebrew alphabet and meditation with and breathing the Name of God." This system offers "the return of a form of 'yoga' or unification of soul, body and world which, according to the Kabalists, goes back to the creation of man and is considered to be part of the universal heritage. Ophanim has similarities with many eastern systems of yoga [...] and internal energy [cf. the concept of *Kundalini*, above], but it is clearly rooted in the ideas of the Jewish mystical tradition," claiming the postures it uses come from no less than *Sefer Yetzirah*. This system's breathing techniques are particularly revealing: it recommends inhaling to a count of ten and then exhaling to a count of five. Since these are the numerical values for the Hebrew letters *yud* and *heh* (that spell one of the names of God), "the tradition of our teachers holds that [10–5 breathing] is the original human breathing rhythm, which, in itself, is 'calling' the name of God."

In another extreme formulation, Bill Heilbronn claims in *Jacob's Ladder and the Anatomy of Meditation* (a booklet written for a community weekend of the Birmingham Progressive Synagogue), in regard to the first two steps of Raja Yoga: *Yama* ("concerned with the laws of personal restraint") and *Niyama* ("[...] obedience to the spiritual laws governing mastery of the instincts and emotions"), that "their counterparts in the Jewish tradition are to be found in the Ten Commandments and the Priestly Code (Leviticus 19)" (see yogamosaic.org/heilbronn.content.pdf).

The following is an example of an attempt to create a Jewish mantra that is obviously based on Eastern meditative and breathing techniques, but which, in effect, trivializes both traditions. Rabbi Lawrence Kushner ("Rabbi-in-Residence at Hebrew Union College-Jewish Institute of Religion"; Kushner's publisher at *Jewish Lights*, which caters to New Age sensibilities, told me several years ago that Kushner's books have a guaranteed, and growing, readership), in a short essay entitled "Breathing," first quotes the passage in I Kings 19: 11–12: "[...] but the Lord was not in the wind [...] And after the fire, the soft barely audible sound of almost breathing." He then proceeds to reduce the Tetragrammaton to a vocal exercise:

> The letters of the name of God in Hebrew are *yod, hay, vav*, and *hay*. They are frequently mispronounced *Yahveh*. But in truth they are unutterable. Not because of the holiness they evoke, but because they are all vowels and you cannot pronounce all the vowels at once without risking respiratory injury.
>
> This word is the sound of breathing. The holiest Name in the world, the Name of the Creator, is the sound of your own breathing.
>
> That these letters are unpronounceable is no accident, Just as it is no accident that they are also the root letters of the Hebrew verb "to be."

In a section entitled "Living Spiritual Talk — *Kavanah*," Kushner concludes by reversing the Yoga practice of chanting a holy name or word as part of a meditative breathing exercise, suggesting instead that simple breathing expresses divinity: "If God's name is the Name of Being, then perhaps breathing itself is the sound of the unpronounceable Name. Find a place and a time that are quiet enough to hear the sound of your own breathing. Simply listen to that barely audible noise and intend that with each inhalation and exhalation you sound the Name of Being. It may be no accident that this exercise is universally acknowledged as an easy and effective method for focusing and relaxation" (*The Jewish Lights Spirituality Handbook: A Guide to Understanding, Exploring Living a Spiritual Life*, ed. S.M. Matlins [Woodstock, VT, 2001], pp. 39–40). Cf. the Yoga meditative mantra exercises using such sounds as "OM," "HUM," and the like: e.g., H. Zimmer, *Philosophies of India*, ed. J. Campbell (New York, 1953), pp. 584–85; the distinctive elements of *Ujjayi Pranayama*, the "Hissing Type," consist of inhaling "by producing a high pitched (Sibilant) sound" and exhaling with a "hissing sound": health benefits are claimed, but without any spiritual pretensions for this breathing exercise that lacks any message (Javalgekar, *Yoga-Science*, p. 87).

The first, and it would seem insurmountable, obstacle to this New Age syncretic attempt is the extent to which Yoga is intimately intertwined with paganism, and Judaism's total ban of idolatrous practices (see, e.g., Exod. 20: 3–4; Deut. 16: 21–22; 18: 9–14). Two examples of the former will suffice: a meditative breathing exercise from the *Gheranda-Samhita* set forth in *The Original Yoga: as Expounded in Siva-Samhita, Gheranda-Samhita and Patanjala Yoga-sutra*, trans. and ed. Shyam Ghosh (New Delhi, 1980), pp. 174–75, begins with the instruction to sit in a certain posture, meditate upon "Brahma the Creator," breathe in through the left nostril, and then "meditate upon Visnu the Preserver," followed by meditation upon "Siva the Destroyer." H. Zimmer (*The Art of Indian Asia: Its Mythology and Transformations*, completed and ed. J. Campbell [New York, 1955], Vol. 1: Text, pp. 318–19) cites "an illuminating statement [for our purposes, as well, since it clearly links *pranayama*, breathlike mantras, and idolatry — E.L.] in the *Gandharva Tantra* concerning the act of worship":

> After having controlled his breath through *pranayama*, the initiate [facing the image] should take up a handful of flowers. The goddess should never be invoked without a handful of flowers. The initiate, **having controlled his breath** [emphasis added — E. L.], should then meditate on the supreme mistress in his heart; and beholding in his heart, by her grace, that image, the substance of which is consciousness, let him think of the identity of the image manifested within and the image without. Next, the effulgent energy of the consciousness within is to be conducted without by means of the mystic, magic seed-syllable denoting Wind [the life-breath of the organism], which is, namely YANG [... the initiate must mutter the syllable YANG, which contains and evokes the force of the microcosmic wind-god who dwells within him]; and directing this, with the outgoing breath, along the nostrils, he will infuse it into the handful of flowers.

A query was addressed to Midreshet B'erot Bat Ayin concerning the "Yoga and Kabbalah" in the course description of "Meditative Movement," out of concern that "various positions and movements in yoga are signs of obeisance to various Eastern deities." The response from this Orthodox educational institution gives a number of answers from "various Rabbinical authorities." The wife of Rabbi Mordechai Goldstein (Diaspora Yeshiva), in consultation with her husband, states: "The main thing is your *kavanah* (intention). Our intention is purely physical: health, breathing and exercising every limb." Rabbi Mordechai Becher (Ohr Sameach), distinguishes between the exercises and the philosophy; he rejects the latter, as being "*Avodah Zara* [idolatry] without doubt," while the exercises "have clear physical benefit and are based on rational ideas." In support of this position, he cites *Rema on Shulhan Arukh, Yoreh Deah* 178:1, regarding the prohibition of following the ways of the pagans: "But this is only forbidden in regard to customs of the pagans that are based on sexual immorality ... or a statue of their religion that has no logical reason, in which case we suspect that it is blemished with pagan [symbolism] ... but other customs of pagans that have [tangible physical] benefit are permitted." Accordingly, Yogic exercises are permitted, but not studying Yogic philosophy or using Yogic mantras in meditation. The last, and different, reply is given in the name of Rabbi Yit[z]chak Ginsburgh, a leading disseminator of Kabbalistic teachings. Because of his categorical rejection of any Jewish connection with Yoga, and his reply to the frequent use of Gen. 25:6 ("But to Abraham's sons by concubines Abraham gave gifts while he was still living, and he sent them away eastward to the land of the East") as a proof-text that Eastern teachings (such as Yoga) actually originated with Abraham, we cite a large portion of his response.

> All wisdom must derive from the Torah. Yoga has negative energy which is connected to *Avodah Zarah*, and is thus *pasul* [invalid], even if the person practicing does not have these negative thoughts. The "claim" to be one of the ancient teachings that Avraham Avinu [the Patriarch Abraham] sent east with his non-Jewish, idolatrous sons (of his maid-servant Ketura) were in fact "impure names [mantras]," i.e., names and practices for the spiritually impure. They are certainly not for Jews ([...] that in order that he not mix with them and learn from them, Avraham sent his other, foreign sons away). Surely, everything on "the other side" [the *Sitra Ahra*, symbolizing evil] has its parallel in the "side of holiness."

He then objects to the use of the term "Yoga" in a Jewish context:

> In addition to the spiritual (and physical) practices and disciplines which we have received directly from our forefathers and from Sinai, one of the essential powers inherent in our Torah is its ability to "clarify" and "redeem" fallen, Divine sparks, scattered throughout reality, especially in the foreign garb of non-Jewish wisdoms and spiritual practices. The beginning of any "clarification" process based upon Torah [...] is renouncing the non-Jewish "name" (in which inheres the spiritual source) attached to and identified with the wisdom or practice to be clarified. A "name" implies a total "way" and philosophy. Therefore, the very usage of the name "yoga," whether prefaced with the word "Jewish" or not, does not allow for true clarification (in fact the juxtaposition of the two terms "Jewish yoga" is *shatneiz* [i.e. a forbidden admixture])" ("Response to a Question Regarding Yoga and Kabbalah," at www.berotbatayin.org/yoga.htm).

A fascinating restatement of this opposition comes from an unexpected source: the Internet site of Shalach Ministries, a site "Dedicated to the Salvation of The Jewish People," whose declared mission is "to communicate to all Jews in the State of Israel regarding the necessity of accepting Yeshua [i.e. Jesus] as their personal

(*dextra*) was more propitious. Bonnerjea[112] tells us that in India sneezing to the West was auspicious, but while at work inauspicious, or that such an act in the morning is lucky, but at night ominous.[113]

The Jewish tradition, as we have seen, does not fear evil spirits flying in and out of our noses, but it does view the sneeze as ominous, either as a portent presaging eminent death, which had to be combated by the exclamation "Life," or as a threat to one's state of health that mandates a wish, prayer, and/or blessing for one's good health and recovery. Whichever way it might be interpreted, it was regarded with the greatest of gravity,

Lord and Savior." The site includes a 13–page section devoted to "Judaism and the Dangers of 'Torah Kabbalah or Torah Yoga,'" which launches a frontal attack on Kabbalah, which it categorizes as a mixture of "demonic activity, pagan philosophy, gnosticism and the Hebrew Bible." The article rejects the Kabbalistic attempt to actively influence God (and bring the Messiah), and cites *The New Standard Jewish Encyclopedia*, s.v. "Magic," p. 619: "Jewish religion is in principle opposed to magic because the ultimate source of everything is the absolutely free and sovereign will of God which can never be coerced. The only proper attitude is therefore prayer." The basic reason for the animosity to Jewish mysticism by this fundamentalist Christian ministry (based in West Virginia) appears to be the fear of competition, and a lack of recognition of Jesus by Kabbalists: "if they [Kabbalists] were really 'in touch' with Yahveh, there would be no need to 'hasten the advent of Messiah,' as they would declare that Yeshua came and will come again." The site then describes Yoga as a descent into the demonic and the occult that is fraught with danger. Echoing Jewish concerns (see above, the Midreshet B'erot Bat Ayin responsum), it notes that "it is difficult, if not impossible, to separate Yoga practice from Yoga theory." The sole hint of this ministry's true fear (again, of competition) appears in only a single sentence: "Around the world promoters of Yoga make such claims as, 'Yoga and Christianity are founded upon a similar base of wisdom' [...]" (at www.shalach.org/Torah Yoga/Yoga Warning.htm).

In summation, as we have indicated, there are numerous Jewish-Yogic parallels regarding breath and breathing exercises. No far-reaching conclusions, however, should be drawn from these similarities, for two reasons: the first, the totally opposing belief-systems on which the two traditions are based; and the second, as M. Lask observes in *Ecstasy: A Study of Some Secular and Religious Experiences* (London, 1961), pp. 252–53, in general, "control of breath" is one of the methods generally employed (i.e. in all cultures) to induce mystical experiences (note by Edward Levin).

112 Again citing Jackson, *Folklore Notes*.

113 Citing Crooke, *The Popular Religion and Folk-Lore of Northern India*; cf. Hazlitt, *Dictionary of Faiths & Folklore*, loc. cit.

for it indicated some form of threat. Thus, we find in *Zayit Ra'anan*,[114] by Rabbi Abraham Abele ben Hayyim Gombiner,[115] a commentary on *Yalkut Shimoni*:[116]

> And now we are accustomed to say [after sneezing] "I wait for Your deliverance, O Lord" [Gen. 49:18].

And, to the present day, the practice among Moroccan Jewry is:[117]

> When someone sneezes, they say to him *"Asuta"* [Remedy], and he replies *"Le-hayyim tovim"* [Good life], and afterwards they say "I wait for Your deliverance, O Lord."

---

114 Rabbi Abraham Abele ben Hayyim Gombiner, *Zayit Ra'anan* (Dessau, 1704; Vienna, 1743).

115 The author of *Magen Avraham*, the major supercommentary on the *Shulhan Arukh, Orah Hayyim*. See further *Shulhan Arukh, Orah Hayyim* 170:1, with supercommentaries. Note that Rabbi Jacob Hayyim Sofer, *Kaf ha-Hayyim* (first edn.: Jerusalem, 1910–26), *Orah Hayyim* 170, n. 3, has his reservations about this exclamation.

116 Genesis, para. 77.

117 Rabbi Yossef Ben Naim, *Noheg be-Hokhmah*, ed. M. Amar (Israel, 1987), p. 151.

APPENDIX

SNEEZING

John Brand, in his *Observation on Popular Antiquities*,[1] has a characteristically learned discussion on sneezing which, because of its rich sources, I shall cite in full:

SNEEZING

From the remotest antiquity sneezing has been held to be ominous. Thus we read in the Odyssey —

"She spoke: Telemachus then sneez'd aloud;

Constrain'd, his nostril echo'd through the crowd.

The smiling queen the happy omen blest:

So may these impious fall, by Fate opprest;"

the comment of Eustathius being that sneezing to the left was unlucky, whereas sneezing to the right was propitious.

Xenephon having ended a speech to his soldiers with the words, "We have many reasons to hope for preservation," one of his hearers sneezed; whereupon the whole army, accepting the omen, forthwith paid adoration to the gods, after which Xenephon resumed his discourse with the observation, "Since, my fellow-soldiers, at the mention of your preservation Jupiter has sent this omen," &c.

"Two or three neses," we read in the Vulgaria of Hormannus, "be holsom: one is a shrewd token;" and, according to Scot, if any one sneezes twice a night for three nights in succession, it is to be accepted as a sign that one of the members of the household is on the point of death, or that some other loss is about to occur, or some very striking advantage.

Prometheus, we learn from Ross's Arcana Microcosmi, was the first that wished well to the sneezer, when the man he made of clay fell into a fit of sternutation upon the approach of the celestial fire he had stolen from the sun; and this, says Ross, is the origin of the Gentile custom of saluting the sneezer. "They used to worship the head in sternutation, as being a divine part and seat of the senses and cogitation."

One of Aristotle's problems is, why sneezing from noon to midnight

---

1   J. Brand, *Observation on Popular Antiquities, chiefly illustrating the origin of our vulgar ceremonies and superstitions* (first edition: London, 1771, New Edition, with additions by Sir Henry Ellis [1813; London, 1900], pp. 650–52.

is good, but from night to noon unlucky; and St Austin tells us that the ancients were wont to go to bed again if they sneezed in the act of pulling on their shoes.

The rabbinical account of sneezing is very singular. According to Buxtorf's Chaldee Lexicon, it was a mortal sign even from the first man, until it was taken off by the special supplication of Jacob; "from whence, as a thankful acknowledgment, this salutation first began and was after continued by the expression of Tobim Chaiim, or Vita Bona! by standers-by, upon all occasions of sneezing."

When Themistocles sacrificed in his gallery on the eve of battle with Xerxes, one of the assistants on his right hand sneezed. Thereupon, says Plutarch, the soothsayer Euphrantides presaged the overthrow of the Persians.

There can be no doubt that the custom of invoking blessings on those who sneeze has been derived from the Christian world, where it generally prevails, from heathenism. Sigonius, absurdly enough, inclines in his History of Italy to deduce it from a pestilence that broke out in the time of Gregory the Great, which proved mortal to all who sneezed.[2] But there is ample evidence of its superior antiquity. Apuleius mentions it three centuries before, as also does Pliny in his problem Cur sternutantes salutantur; Petronius describes it; Coelius Rhodiginus has an example of it among the Greeks in the time of the younger Cyrus; it occurs as an omen in the 18th idyl of Theocritus; and it is alluded to in an epigram in the Greek Anthology.

Of the Emperor Tiberius it is recorded that, though otherwise a very sour man, he was most punctual in his salutations of others, and that he expected the same attention to himself; and, when the ten thousand were assembled in consultation about their retreat, a sneeze had the effect of making the warriors instantly evoke Jupiter Soter.

Indeed, the prevalence of the practice in the remotest parts of Africa and the East is attested by our earliest navigators. When the King of Mesopotamia sneezes, acclamations ensue throughout his dominions;

2   In Langley's Abridgement of Polydore Vergil we read: "There was a Plage whereby many as they neezed dyed sodeynly, whereof it grew into a Custome, that they that were present when any man neezed should say, God helpe you. A like deadly plage was sometyme in yawning, wherefore Menne used to fence themselves with the Signe of the Crosse; bothe whiche Customes we reteyne styl at this day."

and the Siamese tender the salutation, "Long life to you!" their belief
being that one of the judges of hell keeps a register in which is recorded
the duration of men's lives, and that when he opens it and inspects any
particular leaf, all those whose names happened to be entered thereon
never fail to sneeze immediately. So also of the Persians; Hanway
tells us that sneezing is reckoned a happy omen, especially when often
repeated; and we read in Codignus that, as in Mesopotamia, the sneeze
of the Emperor of Mesopotamia evoked the acclamations of the city.

In Portugal the observance of the custom is universal, and its
omission would be regarded as a grave breach of good manners; and
as regards ourselves, Bishop Hall, in his Characters (1608), affirms of
the superstitious man that, when he "neeseth," he "thinks them not his
friends that uncover not"; uncovering the head being at that period the
form of salutation.

What we have advanced above on this topic is set forth more
copiously in the Gentleman's Magazine for April 1771; the remarks
being founded upon Velley's History of France —

The Year 750 is commonly reckoned the era of the custom of
saying God bless you! to one who happens to sneeze. It is said
that in the time of the pontificate of St Gregory the Great the air
was filled with such a deleterious influence that they who sneezed
immediately expired. On this the devout pontiff appointed a form
of prayer, and a wish to be said to persons sneezing, for averting
them from the fatal effects of this malignancy. A fable contrived
against all the rules of probability, it being certain that this custom
has from time immemorial subsisted in all parts of the known
world. According to mythology, the first sign of life Prometheus's
artificial man gave was by sternutation. This supposed creator
is said to have stolen a portion of the solar rays; and filling
with them a phial, which he had made on purpose, sealed it up
hermetically. He instantly flies back to his favourite automaton,
and, opening the phial, held it close to the statue; the rays, still
retaining all their activity, insinuate themselves through the pores,
and set the factitious man a-sneezing. Prometheus, transported with
the success of his machine, offers up a fervent prayer, with wishes
for the preservation of so singular a being. His automaton observed
him, and, remembering his ejaculation, was very careful on the like

occasions to offer these wishes in behalf of his descendants, who perpetuated it from father to son in all their colonies.

The Rabbis, speaking of this custom, do likewise give it a very ancient date. They say that, not long after the Creation, God made a general decree that every man living should sneeze but once, and that, at the very instant of his sneezing, his soul should depart, without any previous indisposition. Jacob by no means liked to precipitate a way of leaving the world, as being desirous of settling his family affairs, and those of his conscience; he prostrated himself before the Lord, wrestled a second time with him, and earnestly intreated the favour of being excepted from the decree. His prayer was heard, and he sneezed without dying. All the princes of the Universe being acquainted with the fact, unanimously ordered that, for the future, sneezing should be accompanied with thanksgivings, for the preservation and wishes for the prolongation of life. We perceive, even in these fictions, the vestiges of tradition and history, which place the epocha of this civility long before that of Christianity. It was accounted very ancient even in the time of Aristotle, who in his Problems has endeavoured to account for it, but knew nothing of its origin. According to him, the first men, prepossessed with the highest ideas concerning the head, as the principal seat of the soul, that intelligent substance governing and animating the whole human system, carried their respect even to sternutation, as the most manifest and most sensible operation of the head. Hence those several forms of compliments used on similar occasions amongst Greeks and Romans: *Long may you live! May you enjoy health! Jupiter preserve you!*

Relying on the authority of Hippocrates, Sir Thomas Browne says that "sneezing cures the hiccup, is profitable to parturient women, in lethargies, apoplexies, catalepsies. It is bad and pernicious in diseases of the chest, in the beginning of catarrhs, in new and tender conceptions, for then it endangers abortion." As to the ground upon which the custom of salutation is based, he supposes it is the opinion entertained of sternutation by the ancients, who generally regarded it as either a good sign or a bad; using accordingly "Salve" or Ζεῦ σῶσον as a gratulation in the one case and a deprecation in the other. Sneezing, writes Sir Thomas, "being properly a motion of the brain suddenly expelling

through the nostrils what is offensive to it, it cannot but afford some
evidence of its vigour; and therefore, saith Aristotle, they that hear it
honour it as something sacred and a sign of sanity in the diviner part;
and this he illustrates from the practice of physicians, who in persons
near death use sternutatories (medicines to provoke sneezing), when,
if the faculty arise and sternutation ensue, they conceive hopes of life
and with gratulation receive the sign of safety."

1. *Hoshana Rabba* night, Leusden, Utrecht 1682

De festo Pentecostes & Tabernaculorum. 279

,, mortis vitandæ spes est , &
,, si iter facere constituerit, si-
,, gnum est , nunquam do-
,, mum reversurum,&c. Hoc
,, Rabbini ex verbis *Numer.*
,, 14. 9. *Recessit ab eis umbra*
,, *eorum*, demonstrant. Scri-
,, bunt verò, non intelligi de
,, umbra simplici, eò quòd
,, fieri non possit, ut quis ad
,, splendorem Lunæ suam
,, umbram non videat ; sed
,, de umbrâ umbræ. Si enim
,, rectè attendatur, duplicem
,, observari umbram,quarum
,, altera sit à reflexione um-
bræ prioris, Rabbini vocant באואה דבכואה *Umbram Umbræ.*

9. Dies octavus, sive primus post festum, etiam ipsis secundùm legem facer est, vocaturque ab ipsis שמיני עצרת *Octavus detentionis* ; forsan ideo sic vocatur, quia amicos suos, quos per septem dies secum habuerant, & conviviis lautioribus exceperant, die quoque octavo non dimittunt. Hic octavus dies incidit in diem 22. Tisri, sive Septembris. *Vide Buxt. in Synag. cap.* 21. Sacrificia hoc die offerenda describuntur Num. 29. 35. 36. 37. 38. *Die ipso Octavo, interdicti dies esto vobis : opus nullum servile facitote. Sed offeretis holocaustum, juvencum unum, arietem unum, agnos anni-culos septenos*, &c. *Quæritur* ; Quare Deus hunc octavum diem institue-rit ? *Resp.* Judæi incerti sunt quare hic dies octavus festo Tabernaculo-rum fuerit additus : ideoque varii varias rationes excogitarunt. 1. Non-nulli putant ideo fuisse institutum, ut peractis septem diebus populus per hunc diem etiam detineretur. 2. Vel ne dimissi hoc die laborarent, & negotiis suis domesticis vacarent. 3. Vel ut populus hoc die contribue-ret pecuniam in usus sacrificiorum. 4. Vel ut hic solennis dies esset typus & figura collectionis omnium gentium, vel electorum tantùm ad regnum cœlorum. 5. Vel ob collectionem frugum, ut hoc die serotinarum fru-gum primitiæ afferrentur, & pro iisdem Deo gratiæ agerentur. Sed ple-raque sunt incerta.

10. Die nono, h. e. die 23. mensis Tisri sive Septembris celebratur festum, à Judæis institutum, quod vocatur festum שמחת תורה *Lætitiæ Legis.*

2. *Hoshana Rabba* night, Leusden, Utrecht 1683

3. *Hoshana Rabba* **night**
Sefer ha-Minhagim,
Frankfurt 1708

4. *Kiddush ha-levanah*
Sefer ha-Minhagim, **Amsterdam 1662**

ודן יצער בון פרשת ההדש היכטאו אית זה החדש׃ רו ולה אל עשת
נפלאת ׃ (אין פון אוז תיהט אעלודהן) וגט אן אופן כב רו
מטנהים ׳) ריא קרונץ היבט און צתיח עת דורם אוז היבט אוז לוויא הפרץ
תורה אמיט אינגער ערטן ריא וואלכן סרדא ׳רופט ׳ וכן און ׳הלב קר ש׳
אוו׳ רופ ערריא הפטרה ׃ גט אמייט און אין ער אגרדן ספר תורה אין בא
אל פדעה היכטא און ויאמר יי אל משה וגל אדרן בארץ בצרים לצבר ׃ החדש
הוה לכס ׃ כי צא און בכל משכוחיכס תאכלו בצא ׳ אוו ׃ גט ריא הפטרה און
יהבצל היבט און כה אמר יי נראשן כאהר להרש ׳ און מי צ גיט סוכיר ושטיח ׳
צו כעלגט ראש רדש ניטן ׃ צו׃ כיצף וגט און אין קרוגץ היכטאן ראשן
אמצא ׃ צו מנחה וגט און וואל צדקתך ׃   כב כ ב גג און ועון

5. *Kiddush ha-levanah*
***Sefer ha-Minhagim*,**
Venice 1601

6. *Kiddush ha-levanah*
***Sefer ha-Minhagim*,**
Amsterdam 1707

דיא.לבנה מקדש זיין· טו

צן אנדה וזמגט אין ניט לדקתך חוג' וומזו אין ניט תחיינת וזמגט ותון עס
חן דער וומזלן ווער · נח וזמגט אין חך ניט לדקתך מם סבת:

דיא לבנה מקדש צו זיין

מן מיו חו חדש
דיה גייח לבנה
חקרט אין אוו חויך
ריח לימן סטין
רען עם מיז גלייך
חז גינגן איר דר
(שלינה) חלטגיגן
דרום רומדן אן חן
חולטור קיינם טמך
סטין · דען עם
עעלט מין טואחה
חונטור דיצם טמך

7. *Kiddush ha-levanah, Sefer ha-Minhagim,* **Frankfurt 1708**

8. *Kiddush ha-levanah, Sefer ha-Minhagim,* **Frankfurt 1740**

9. *Haggadah*, Venice 1601

10. *Haggadah*, Venice 1601

11. *Haggadah*, Mantua 1568

12. *Haggadah*, Prague 1526

13. *Haggadah*, Prague 1526

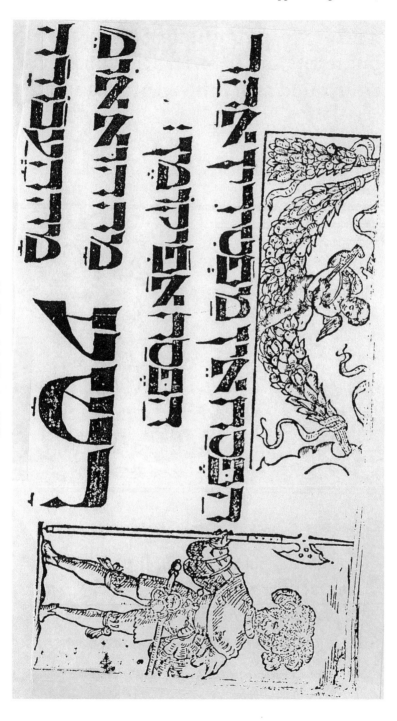

14. *Haggadah*, Mantua 1568

H ABAC VC pulmentum & panes meſſori-
bus ferens, in perſona ſanctorum piè cōque-
ritur, quòd mali iuſtos perſequantur.

HABACVC   I.

Portant des pains Habacuc le prophete
Aux moiſſonneurs & laboureurs des champs,
Se plaingt à Dieu de ce que iniure eſt faicte
Aux gens de bien par les felons meſchantz.

15. *Historiarum Veteris Testimenti Icones*, Hans Holbein the Younger, 1538

16. *Haggadah*, **Mantua 1568**

PSALTES contra Iudæos excãdeſcit, ac eos
qui CHRISTVM Meſsiam DEVM in le-
ge promiſſum infideliter & impiè negant,
inſipientes uocat.

PSALM. LII.

Folʒ ſont ceulx là (comme eſcrit le Pſalmiſte)
Qui en leurs cœurs dient que IESVCHRIST
N'eſt Meſſias : Dauid tant ſen contriſte
Qu'en pluſieurs lieux encontre culx l'a eſcrit.

17. *Historiarum Veteris Testimenti Icones*, **Hans Holbein the Younger, 1538**

18. *Tabula Perpetua*, **1528**

המולד

סהר
מתמלא

רביע
ראשון

ירח
מתמלא

ירח
מלא

ירח
מתמעט

רביע
אחרון

סהר
מתמעט

19. Phases of the moon

20. Albert Dürer, ca. 1500

21. *Dialogus creaturarum*, **Gouda, Gerard Leau, 1480**
Pierpont Morgan Library, New York

22. Blessing the New Moon, Kirchner, Nuremberg 1724

23. Blessing the New Moon, Bodenschatz, Erlang 1748

2

THE MANNER OF SITTING WHILE VISITING
THE SICK

Rav Ahai Gaon writes, in his *She'iltot*:[1]

> When a person enters to inquire about the health [of a sick person],
> he should sit neither on the bed nor on the mattress,[2] for Rabba said:
> One who visits the sick must not sit on the bed or on a chair or stool,
> but rather before him, on the ground, because the Divine Presence rests
> above the sick person's bed. And the Angel of Death is above his feet,
> [for we learn from Rabbi Joshua ben Levi that the Angel of Death
> commanded five things. He said to him: Take care ... When you enter
> the presence of a sick person, do not sit, neither at his head nor at his
> feet, neither on the mattress nor on the bolster, but rather on the ground,
> facing him, because the Divine Presence is at his head, and I am at his
> feet, with my drawn sword in my hand.][3]

This entire dictum is based on BT Nedarim 40a, as follows:

> Ravin said in the name of Rav:[4] From where is it derived that the
> Divine Presence rests above the bed of a sick person? As it is said: "The
> Lord will sustain him on his sickbed" [Ps. 41:4]. He also taught thusly:
> When a person enters to inquire about the health [of a sick person],

1 Rav Ahai Gaon, *She'iltot, Aharei Mot*, no. 93 (and in the edition of S.K. Mirsky
   [Jerusalem, 1966], no. 110, pp. 154–55).
2 In the printed editions, these two words: *apurya* (bed) and *amatzata* (mattress) are
   replaced by the corruption: *apahya* and *amtzanita* (see Mirsky, loc. cit.).
3 The addition in brackets is based on MS. Sassoon, cited by Mirsky, loc. cit. (see
   below).
4 And in *She'iltot*, as we have seen: "For Rabba said."

he should sit neither on the bed, nor on the mattress, nor on a chair. He rather enrobes himself and sits on the ground, because the Divine Presence rests above the sick person's bed, as it is said: "The Lord will sustain him on his sickbed."[5]

The simple meaning of this passage is that the Divine Presence rests above the sickbed, as was learned from the verse: "The Lord will sustain him on his sickbed." Therefore, it is forbidden to sit on the bed, a couch, or a chair, because then one is above the height of the bed in the physical area and realm in which the Divine Presence, as it were, is to be found. This dictum does not relate to the question at which end of the bed it is preferable to sit, at the feet of the sick person or at his head. All that is stated here is that the visitor must be lower than the level of the bed. This, however, is not how this instruction was understood over the course of time, as we see from the above *she'ilta* (query), which draws a parallel between "the Divine Presence rests above the sick person's bed" (based on the passage in Nedarim) and "the Divine Presence is at his [the sick person's] head" in the continuation of the *she'ilta*.

A proof for the Talmud's disregard of the location of the Divine Presence at the sick person's head may possibly be found in BT Avodah Zarah 20b:

> It is said of the Angel of Death that he is full of eyes. When a sick person is about to expire, he stands **above the head of his bed** [*me-ra'ashotav*], with his sword drawn in his hand and a drop of gall suspended from it. When the sick person beholds this, he trembles and opens his mouth; he casts this into his mouth. Is it from this that he dies, from this that [the corpse] becomes putrid, from this that his face turns green? [In those cases, the cause may have been a man and a woman suddenly encountering one another] when turning a corner.

In other words, the Angel of Death is at the sick person's head.

For some reason, however, this Talmudic exposition was understood differently, and the Angel of Death was moved to the patient's feet. Rabbi Naphtali Zevi Judah Berlin (*ha-Netziv*) already noted that the words "And the Angel of Death is above his feet" are not in the Talmud, and in *Ha'amek Sh'elah*[6] he refers us to the *Zohar:*[7]

---

5   Cf. Shabbat 12b.

6   Rabbi Naphtali Zevi Judah Berlin, *Ha'amek Sh'elah* (Vilna, 1864), p. 155, para. 10.

7   *Zohar, Pinhas* 234b, citing the *Ra'aya Meheimna*.

For this reason the author of the *baraita* established: The one who visits a sick person shall not sit at his head, because the Divine Presence is above his head, and not at his feet, because the Angel of Death is at his feet.[8]

Berlin already realized that the *Zohar* was not the source of the *she'ilta*, because "it is known that the light of this exposition [i.e. the] *Zohar* had not yet been revealed in the time of our master [R. Ahai Gaon]." He therefore proposes:

> It seems that this was the version of our masters in the Talmud, and the deficiency in Nedarim is evident, since it quotes a *baraita* as follows: "One who enters to visit the sick person [..] sits on the ground, because the Divine Presence rests above the sickbed...." This is not a reason that one sits on the ground, because of the Divine Presence, [...] rather, the primary version is: and he sits before him on the ground. And thus it is in Shabbat 10. The reason, "because of the Divine Presence," is based on the precise wording "before him [*lifanav*]," and not "at the head [*me-ra'ashotav*]" nor "at the feet [*margelotav*]" of the sick one. [...] There is no reason [for not sitting] "at the feet," and the [reason given] in the version of our master [R. Ahai Gaon] is because [of the presence there of] the Angel of Death.

It is our opinion that what is missing in the text of the Talmud is to be supplemented in accordance with the *she'iltot*. According to what we noted above, there is no basis for the difficulties raised by the *Netziv*. Furthermore, a study of *Dikdukei Soferim*[9] reveals that the early source for this addition has not yet been revealed. Mirsky, however, is of the opinion that he found the source in the lengthy addition in MS. Sassoon of the *she'iltot*, cited above in brackets.[10] The statement by the Angel of Death to Rabbi Joshua ben Levi appears in part in BT Berakhot 51b, and MS. Munich[11] contains additions not in the Talmudic text; it lists seven things of which the Angel of Death speaks, and not three (as in the Talmud) or five (as in *she'iltot*, MS. Sassoon). Mirsky further refers to *Midrash Ma'aseh Torah*:[12]

8 The version in *Ha'amek Sh'elah* is to be amended accordingly.
9 *Dikdukei Soferim ha-Shalem*, in *The Babylonian Talmud with Variant Readings* (Jerusalem, 1985), *Nedarim*, Vol. 1, p. 352 n. 109.
10 See the textual variants in Mirsky, p. 155, ll. 34–44.
11 See *Dikdukei Soferim ha-Shalem*, op. cit., p. 271, para. *shin*.

Rabbi Joshua ben Levi asked the Angel of Death three things. He [the Angel of Death] said to him [R. Joshua ben Levi]: And when you come in to a sick person, how do you sit? He replied, At his head. [The Angel of Death:] Do not sit before him, because I sit before him.[13]

That is, even if we do not know the exact time of the appearance of this additional passage, of the Angel of Death at the foot of the patient, it is quite early, and dates at least from the time of the Geonim or the *Rishonim*.

These laws, which pertain to the manner of sitting next to a sick person, appear in the writings of the *poskim*.[14] As regards the prohibition of sitting on a chair or a bench, Rabbi Moses Isserles wrote in his gloss:[15]

This [prohibition] applies specifically when the patient lies on the ground, in which case the one sitting is higher than him. If, however he [the sick person] is sitting on the bed, then one is permitted to sit in a chair or on a bench.[16]

Bodenschatz cites the view of Isserles,[17] and the illustration he provides[18] depicts people sitting on chairs next to the dying person.

---

12 In A. Jellinek, *Bet ha-Midrasch*, Vol. 2 (Jerusalem, 1938), p. 94 (Hebrew).

13 See *Huppat Eliyahu Rabbah*, at the end of *Reshit Hokhmah* by Rabbi Elijah ben Moses De Vidas (Jerusalem, 1972), *Sha'ar* 6, 271a: "... And not at his feet [...] I am at his feet, and my sword is drawn in my hand"; and in the edition of *Huppat Eliyahu Rabbah* by Ch.M. Horowitz: *Kavod Huppah* (Frankfurt am Main, 1888), p. 49, para. *nun*; *Pirka de-Rabbeinu ha-Kadosh*, in *Sheloshah Sefarim Niftahim* (*Three Books Opening*), ed. S. Shonblum (Lemberg, 1877), 17b; Rabbi Israel al-Nakawa, *Menorat ha-Ma'or*, ed. H.G. Enelow, Vol. 4 (New York, 1932), pp. 424, 482, 583, and the editor's glosses, p. 482 on l. 1; *Kol Bo*, para. 118, and more. See above, the passage in Avodah Zarah 20b, on which the passage in *Huppat Eliyahu* is based. In all these sources, however, the Angel of Death is positioned at the foot of the corpse; this point requires further study. For such "things that sages enumerated in a list," see my book, *Masechet Derech Eretz Zutta and Perek ha-Shalom* (Jerusalem, 1994), pp. 180–81. For this phenomenon of proximate sources with different numbers, of which there are many examples, see ibid., pp. 82–83.

14 See Maimonides, *Mishneh Torah, Hil. Avel* (*Laws of the Mourner*) 14:6; *Shulhan Arukh, Yoreh Deah* 335:3.

15 *Shulhan Arukh*, loc. cit.

16 In the name of *Beit Yosef*, based on *Ran*, Nedarim 40a. Isserles correctly concludes: "And this is the practice" (see above), for when the bench or chair is at the same height as the bed (and the extant illustrations show that they generally were lower), the one who sits on them does not enter the "realm of the Divine Presence," that is **above** the bed.

The question of sitting at the feet of the sick person was also extensively discussed in the halakhic literature.[19] *Ma'avar Yabbok* states simply that one is not to stand at the foot of a deathbed.[20]

As was noted above, the notion that the Angel of Death stands at the feet of the sick person originates in the period of the Geonim or, at the latest, in the time of the *Rishonim*. Similar folk beliefs are also to be found in the non-Jewish world. Jacob Grimm[21] brings the legend of a young and successful physician who has the ability to see the arrival of the Angel of Death. The physician became very wealthy, knowing that when the Angel of Death stands at the head of the patient,[22] the latter will die with certainty; if the angel stands at his feet, then the patient will probably recover. Accordingly, the physician would at times turn the patient around, so as to "confuse the Devil." In the continuation of the tale, the Angel of Death takes his revenge on the physician, and when the latter is distracted, he "snuffed out the light [of his life]."[23] Grimm[24] finds an allusion to this in the writings of the Roman scholar Pliny (mid-first century CE). In his book *Natural History*, Pliny writes:

> They also consider the tick a prognostication of life or death, for if the patient at the beginning of his illness responds when he who has brought in with him a tick [*ricinus*], standing at his feet [*a pedibus*

---

17 *Kirchliche Verfassung der heutigen Juden*, p. 167.

18 Bodenschatz, op. cit., next to p. 178; see Fig. 1.

19 See the summation in Z. Metzger, *Ha-Refuah le-Or ha-Halakhah* (*Medicine in Light of the Halakhah*), Part 1: Bikkur Holim (*Visiting the Sick*) (Jerusalem, 1984), chap. 22, paras. 3–4, pp. 66–68.

20 Rabbi Aaron Berechiah ben Moses of Modena, *Ma'avar Yabbok* (first edition: Mantua, 1526), *Siftei Rananut* 6. Cited in M. Klein, *Zikhron Shai* (Simluel-Silvaniei, 1923). (For *Ma'avar Yabbok*, see the recent article: A. Bar-Levav, "Books for the Sick and the Dying in Jewish Conduct Literature," in *Joseph Baruch Sermoneta Memorial Volume* [*Jerusalem Studies in Jewish Thought* 14, ed. A. Ravitzky (Jerusalem, 1998)], pp. 346–48, 357–76 [Hebrew].) See also Y.Y. Lerner, *Shmiras Haguf Vihanefesh* (*Guarding the Body and the Soul*) (Jerusalem, 1988), Vol. 2, para. 182:2, pp. 535–36 and note.

21 Grimm, *Teutonic Mythology*[4], Vol. 2, p. 853.

22 Which is the belief expressed in Avodah Zarah 20b (see above).

23 For the motif of the extinguishing of the light, see Grimm, loc. cit; cf. what I wrote in *Minhagei Yisrael* (*Jewish Customs: Sources and History*), Vol. 3 (Jerusalem, 1994), pp. 140 ff.

24 *Teutonic Mythology*, Vol. 3, p. 1181.

stanti] inquires about the illness, there is sure hope of recovery; should no reply be made, the patient will die.[25]

Although the connection is not sufficiently clear, there may be some linkage between the Roman passage and the medieval Christian folk belief.

Obviously, Jewish popular belief does not allow for the Angel of Death at the head of the bed, since this is the place, as it were, of the Holy One, blessed be He, and the Angel of Death was moved to the foot of the bed. This conception, however, also is to be found in medieval Christianity, as is shown from an illustration in a fifteenth-century French manuscript, *La Science de Bien-Mourir* (*The Science of a Fine Death*).[26] In this picture, we see the patient lying on his deathbed, with the Angel of Death standing at his head, and the Devil at his feet,[27] with a fishing rod in his hand,[28] with which he expects to ensnare the soul of the dying man if he expires without grace.

---

25 Pliny, *Natural History* 30:24:83, *LCL*, Vol. 8, p. 333.

26 MS. Gall. 28 fol. 5v, Bayerische Stadtsbibliotek, Munich. Brought by T.S.R. Boase, *Death in the Middle Ages: Mortality, Judgment and Remembrance* (New York, 1972), p. 120, Fig. 103.

27 This depiction of the Devil, as a sort of monster with horns, bird's feet, and a tail, is quite a well-known model. See, e.g., *Speculum humanae salvationis*, first Latin edition, ca. 1468, chap. 13; A. Wilson and J.L. Wilson, *A Medieval Mirror: Speculum humanae salvationis, 1324–1500* (Berkeley-Los Angeles-London, 1984), p. 166 (Fig. 3); cf. *idem*, pp. 142, 181; *La Miroir de l'humaine salvation*, chap. 20 (Woodcut of *The Devil Smiting Job*), Musée Condé, Chantilly MS. Fr. 139, p. 82 (ca. 1600). Cf. also *Envy and Sloth*, by Antwerp Master, ca. 1490–1500, Musée Royal de Beaux Arts in Antwerp, reproduced in R. Klibansky, E. Panofsky, and F. Saxl, *Saturn and Melancholy: Studies in the History of Natural Philosophy, Religion and Art* (Cambridge, 1964), Ill. 93. This portrayal also appears on playing cards from the eighteenth and nineteenth centuries. See Tilly, *A History of Playing Cards*, pp. 41, 43, 44 (*Le Diable*). See also L. Link, *The Devil: The Archfiend in Art from the Sixth to the Sixteenth Century* (London, 1995; New York, 1996), p. 143; Grimm, *Teutonic Mythology*[4], Vol. 3, p. 994; Vol. 4, pp. 1603–1604.

28 For the motive of the fishing rod, see Grimm, ibid., Vol. 2, p. 845. The motif of the Devil with a fishing rod seeking to ensnare souls is a common feature of medieval art, a fine example of which appears in the English-Norman *Holkham Bible* (ca. 1370), in which we see the Devil with a long fishing pole, and lost souls imprisoned on his back (Fig. 4).

(This latter motif, of lost souls piled up in a large sack on the Devil's back, may possibly be the inconographic source of the theme in the caricature by the Englishman James Gillray from 1795, *The Prophet of the Hebrews — **The Prince***

The patient and his visitor, who stands close to the bench next to the bed, do not see these beings, and their faces are therefore turned away from the angels (Fig. 2,[29] and Fig. 5, Prague 1780).

of Peace — *conducting the Jews to the Promised Land*, which depicts the false Messiah Richard Brothers [1757–1824] with a sack of people on his back that bears the inscription: "**Bundle** of the **Elect**." See the catalogue of the exhibition: *The Jew as Other: A Century of English Caricature, 1730–1830*, ed. F. Felsenstein and S.L. Liberman Mintz [New York, 1995], pp. 43–44. My thanks to Ms. Liberman-Mintz for drawing my attention to this important material.) See R. Mellinkoff, *The Devil at Isenheim: Reflections of Popular Belief in Gruenewald's Altarpiece* (Berkeley-Los Angeles-London, 1988), Ill. 24 (p. 43, and also p. 29). See also W.O. Hassel, *The Holkham Bible Picture Book* (London, 1954), 11b, with commentary: pp. 84–85; F.P. Pickering (ed.), *The Anglo-Norman Text of the Holkham Bible Picture Book* (Oxford, 1971), pp. 19, 84 (cited by Mellinkoff, op. cit., p. 97 n. 72). For the opposite of this conception, namely, the beneficent God trapping Satan, see the collection: M. Schapiro, *Late Antique, Early Christian and Mediaeval Art* (New York, 1979), p. 7 (the article first appeared in *Art Bulletin* 27 [1947], pp. 182–87). Many scholars have commented on this article and on Schapiro's interpretation of the *Merode Altarpiece*, but they did not disagree with him on this point. As Mellinkoff puts it: "None of the literature suggests that Schapiro's thesis concerning the devil's bait is incorrect." Cf. also Grimm, *Teutonic Mythology*[4], Vol. 3, p. 996.

29 See also Wuttke, *Der deutsche Volksaberglaube der Gegenwart*, p. 458. Toward the end of the sixteenth century an illustrated work called *Ars Moriendi* (*The Art of Dying*) was published in numerous languages. It depicted the war between the forces of good and the forces of evil at the time of a person's death, with the motif of the Devil at the head of the bed, waiting to catch the soul of the deceased (as in *Art del Bene Morire* [Florence, ca. 1495] or the French *Ars Moriendi* [1465]). See E. and J. Lehner, *Picture Book of Devils, Demons and Witchcraft* (New York, 1971), p. 84, no. 123; p. 85, no. 124; for additional illustrations of the Devil, *idem*, pp. 71– 72. For Death at the foot of the bed, see R. Van Marle, *Iconographie de l'Art profane au Moyen Age et à la Renaissance, et la Décoration des Demeures*[2] (New York, 1971), Vol. 2, p. 377, no. 411, "Le Mort et la Duchesa de la Dance Macabre de Holbein (Die Herzoginn)" (fifteenth century); p. 404, Ill. 438, by Behan (sixteenth century). This motif, of "Death at Head & Foot of Bed," appears in S. Thompson, *Motif-Index of Folk Literature* (Bloomington, Indiana, 1933), D1825.3.1, with a reference to BPI.377H (= J. Bolte and G. Polivka, *Ammerkungen zu den Kinder- und Hausmarchen der Bruder Grimm* [Leipzig, 1913–30]). See Opie and Tatem, *A Dictionary of Superstitions*, p. 117, in a source from Sompting, Sussex, in 1820: "You should never stand at the foot of a bed when a person is dying." The reason given there, however, is different: "The reason, I ascertained, was because it would stop the spirit in its departure to the unknown world." It would seem, however, that this is not the original reason, but rather, as we explained, that this is the place of the Angel of Death.

1. Visiting the sick,
Bodenschatz,
Erlang 1748

2. Visiting the sick
Ms. Gall. 28 fol. 5v,
Bayerische Stadtbibliothek,
Munich, 15th century

3. *Speculum humanae salvationis*
First Latin edition, ca. 1465

4. Holkham Bible, ca. 1330

5. Visiting the sick, Prague 1780

3

THE MOMENT OF DEATH[1]

In the lower right-hand corner of a woodcut reproduced by Bodenschatz,[2] we see a depiction of a room with a corpse, immediately following his death. The body lies on the floor,[3] on a layer of straw, with a candle burning by his

1 The recently-published exhibition catalog of the Library of the Jewish Theological Seminary of America: E. Deitsch, S. Liberman Mintz, W.M. Light, and D. Wachtel, *From This World to the Next: Jewish Approaches to Illness, Death* (New York, 1999) contains much material relevant to this chapter.

2 *Kirchliche Verfassung der heutigen Juden*, Vol. 2, next to p. 178.

3 Cf. also Buxtorf, *Synagoga Judaica*, chap. 49, p. 699. The earlier editions of this book provided a basis for much of what appears in later Christian books portraying Jewish customs. See Rabbi Isaac Alfayah [born Aleppo 1878, died Jerusalem 1955], *Kunteres ha-Yehieli*, Vol. 2 (Jerusalem, 1975 [first edition: Jerusalem, 1928]), chap. 15, para. 13, fol. 44a–45a, which attests to the laying out of the body "actually, with nothing intervening." For the reason for this practice, see Aaron Berechiah ben Moses of Modena, *Ma'avar Yabbok, Siftei Rananut* 15, fol. 105a. The practice of placing the corpse on the ground (see M Shabbat 23:5: "They may make ready [on the Sabbath] all that is necessary for the dead [...] and let it lie on sand so that it will remain [i.e. from deteriorating]") was already observed by the Romans. See A. Adam, *Roman Antiquities* (Philadelphia, 1872), p. 336, with a wealth of sources. For a description of Roman burial practices in general, see Adam, op. cit., pp. 335–48. The purification process of the corpse as described in the Jewish sources resembles that of the Romans, including the closing of the eyes, the binding of the chin (M Shabbat, loc. cit.), the wrapping in a linen sheet, etc.; see J. Hastings, *Encyclopaedia of Religion and Ethics* (New York, 1928), Vol. 4, p. 473b; for the binding of the feet, see op. cit., p. 432a. Similar customs are found among the Muslims; see E.W. Lane, *Arabian Society in the Middle Ages: Studies from The Thousand and One Nights* (London, 1883), p. 259, who also mentions binding together the ankles or the toes of the corpse. For the manner of the closing of the hand, see *Minhagei Yisrael*, Vol. 2,

head and a bowl of water next to his hand. Two mourners sit on the ground, their heads covered by a *matron* (a sort of headwear), one on each side of the corpse. On the wall is a piece of cloth, probably a towel.[4] At the right

pp. 276–77; Buxtorf, loc. cit.; Rabbi Abraham Danzig, *Hokhmat Adam*, "*Matzevet Moshe*," end of *Hil. Avelut* (*Laws of Mourning*), para. 9; W. Smith, W. Wayte, and G.E. Marindin, *Dictionary of Greek and Roman Antiquities*[3] (London, 1890), Vol. 1, p. 889. Also see *The Precious Legacy: Judaic Treasures from Czechoslovak State Collections*, ed. D. Altshuler (New York, 1983), p. 154, Ill. 140: the placing of a corpse directly on the ground (Prague, ca. 1780).

4   See the explanation in Bodenschatz, *Kirchliche Verfassung der heutigen Juden*, p. 178; see A.I. Sperling, *Sefer Ta'amei ha-Minhagim u-Mekorei ha-Dinim* (*The Book of the Reasons for Customs and the Sources of Laws*) (Jerusalem, 1982), para. 1039, and more. Cf. Kirchner, *Judisches Ceremoniel*, p. 215; Bodenschatz, p. 178, that the water and the towel are to ward off the Angel of Death and his sword. See J. Trachtenberg, *Jewish Magic and Superstition: A Study in Folk Religion* (Philadelphia, 1961), p. 180, thus enabling us to understand what Rabbi H.E. Shapira of Munkacs wrote in *Darkei Hayyim ve-Shalom*, ed. Y.M. Gold (Jerusalem, 1970), p. 457, para. 994, regarding the custom of placing a bowl of water with a piece of white tablecloth in the house of the deceased for all seven(!) days, that it had no source and that he protested against such a practice in his home. In n. 1 there, Gold cites *Ta'amei ha-Minhagim*, and comments that the latter did not see in the book *Hokhmat Adam*, "Behavior of the Burial Society and the Mourner," para. 13, that the placing of a bowl with water with a tablecloth constitutes Amorite practices, and that the custom is to be abrogated. Preceding this, Rabbi Zevi Hirsch ben Azriel of Vilna wrote in *Bet Lehem Yehudah*[2] (Furth, 1747), *Yoreh Deah* 376:3, that this is "a practice that should not be done in Israel." Others, however, sought to defend this custom, such as Rabbi Solomon Schuck, *Szidur Haminhagim* (Munkacs, 1888), paras. 18–19; Rabbi J. ha-Kohen Schwartz, *Moed le-Kol Hai* (Grosswardein, 1925), p. 3; Rabbi Benjamin Ze'ev (Wolf) Boskowitz, *Ma'amar Esther* (Ofen, 1822), *Derush* 6, *Ma'amar* 2, and more. Also see Klein, *Zikhron Shai*, 42a, in the name of *Sefer Har Abel*. See Y.H. Zlotnik, "Some Sabbath Aggadot and Customs," *Sinai* 25 (1949), pp. 21–23 (in a separate printing) (Hebrew). We have seen, therefore, that according to some authorities, the placing of a bowl of water (with a tablecloth) comprises "Amorite practices," and that it is "a practice that should not be done in Israel." It appears that this custom is based on the assumption that the soul is as thirsty as when it exists in the body, and needs to drink. This is probably the reason why some Semitic tribes bury their dead near sources of water, such as pits and springs. See the material collected by J. Morgenstern, *Rites of Birth, Marriage, Death and Kindred Occasions among the Semites* (New York, 1973), pp. 122, 246 nn. 20–24. Of interest is the statement by P.J. Baldensperger, "Peasant Folklore of Palestine," *PEFQS* 1893, p. 217, Question 30, that the Fellahin in Palestine leave a hollow scooped in the top of their tombs, so that the rainwater would gather there,

end of the picture two people stand and talk with each other, one holding a bowl containing two eggs (Fig. 1).[5]

The explanation of this picture[6] states:

> So bald der Kranjke verstorben [...] hier auf nummt man den Todten aus dem Bette, lest ihm auf langes Stroh, welches nach derlange gelegt ist, und dekt ihn mit einen Schwartzen Tuch uber dem Kopf zu,[7]

and the dead buried underneath could drink (cited by Morgenstern, loc. cit., n. 22). See also Westermarck, *Ritual and Belief in Morocco*, Vol. 2, p. 532; on p. 499 he writes that in ancient Babylonia and in Arabia a small vessel filled with water is placed next to the grave, alongside the head of the dead. Cf. F. Legey, *The Folklore of Morocco*, trans. L. Hotz (London, 1935), pp. 230–31, 239. For the thirst of the dead as perceived by the Romans, see F. Cumont, *After Life in Roman Paganism*[2] (New York, 1959), pp. 50–53; cf. P.J. Baldensperger, "Morals of the Fellahin," *PEFQS* 1897, p. 132. In this context we should perhaps discuss the practice of pouring out water in the vicinity of the deceased, for which many reasons have been given. See Rabbi Isaac Lipets of Siedlce, *Matamim* (Warsaw, 1899), paras. 11–17; Ashkenazi, *Avnei Hen*, pp. 333–37, chap. 37 ("The Pouring Out of Water after the Death of a Person"); Trachtenberg, *Jewish Magic and Superstition*, pp. 176–77; A.P. Bender, "Death, Burial, Mourning," *JQR*, Old Series 7 (1895), pp. 106–18. We will merely note here that this custom was quite widespread in eastern Europe (and in other cultures as well), as can be learned from Hastings, *Encyclopaedia of Religion and Ethics*, Vol. 4, pp. 415b, 427a; A.S. Rappoport, *The Folklore of the Jews* (London, 1937), p. 103. This matter might also be related to the habit of covering mirrors (see Rabbi Yehuda Elzet [Yehuda Leib Zlotnik-Avida] *Reshumot*, Vol. 1 [Odessa, 1918], p. 371, para. 87); Bender, op. cit., p. 117; Rappoport, op. cit., pp. 102, 104; and recently, E. Zimmer, "The Overturning of the Bed during Mourning and the Evolution of the Halakhah and Its Practice," *Sinai* 115 (1994/5), pp. 249–51 (Hebrew). I hope to expand on this issue elsewhere. As regards mirrors, see also S.B. Freehof, *Recent Reform Responsa* (Cincinnati, 1963), pp. 179–82, and also 149–53; and see further G. Roheim, *Spiegelzauber* (Leipzig and Vienna, 1919), pp. 207ff., cited by T. Reik in his interesting, albeit problematic, book, *Pagan Rites in Judaism: from Sex Initiation, Magic, Moon-Cult, Tattooing, Mutilation, and Other Primitive Rituals to Family Loyalty and Solidarity* (New York, 1964), pp. 64–65 (and in Reik's prologue).

5   This drawing is based on the 1729 Frankfurt and Leipzig edition of Buxtorf, *Synagoga Judaica*, p. 677 (Fig. 2) in reverse, that in turn is based on Kirchner, *Judisches Ceremoniel*, p. 207 (Fig. 3).

6   P. 171, para. 2.

7   For the covering of the head, even before the burial, and before the laws of mourning apply to the bereaved, and for the type of head covering, see the extensive discussion in the important book by E. Zimmer, *Society and Its Customs: Studies in*

zundert ein Licht an,[8] und stellt es zu seinem haupten, Fig. XVI num. 4. [translation: immediately after the death of the patient, the corpse is taken down from the bed and is laid on straw ... and it is covered with a black cloth over its head, and a candle is lit and placed at its head.]

In the picture, the face of the deceased has not yet been covered with a black cloth, but the corpse already lies on the straw.

Bodenschatz's depiction is close to what we find in the Worms *Minhagim Book*,[9] which relates that, immediately following the departure of the sick person's soul:

Straw is placed opposite the entrance to the house,[10] or alongside

the History and Metamorphosis of Jewish Customs (Jerusalem, 1996), pp. 200–201, 210 (Hebrew) (see also below, Part II, chap. 19).

8 Buxtorf, *Synagoga Judaica*, loc. cit.; cf. Leusden, *Philologus Hebraeo-Mixtus*, p. 457; Buxtorf, chap. 49; Trachtenberg, *Jewish Magic and Superstition*, p. 175. See below, the end of the current chapter; *Kunteres ha-Yehieli*, para. 14, 45a. Most of these practices were observed by Christians in medieval Germany; see Wuttke, *Der deutsche Volksaberglaube der Gegenwart*, pp. 457–58. Thus, Christians would light a candle at the head of the corpse; see the illustration in *Breviary f. Grimani*, 449v, in the Biblioteca Marciana, Venice (Flemish, 1480–1520), reproduced in Boase, *Death in the Middle Ages*, p. 121, Ill. 115; cf. p. 128. See J.M. Tykocinski, *Gesher ha-Hayyim*[2] (Jerusalem, 1960), Vol. 1, p. 116; *Shulhan Arukh, Orah Hayyim* 298:11. For the candle as symbolizing the soul, see what I wrote in *Minhagei Yisrael*, Vol. 3, pp. 140–55. This symbol was common in many cultures; see, e.g., H. Masse, *Persian Beliefs and Customs* (New Haven, 1954: translation of *Croyances et Coutumes Persanes suivies de Contes et Chansons Populaires* [Paris, 1938]), pp. 81, 98, 272; cf. ibid., p. 102, that for a number of days the soul hovers between the grave and the home (cf. *Minhagei Yisrael*, Vol. 3, pp. 145 ff.); see also below, the end of the current chapter.

9 R. Jousep (Juspa) Schammes, *Wormser Minhagbuch*, ed. B.S. Hamburger and E. Zimmer, Vol. 2 (Jerusalem, 1992), p. 90 (Hebrew).

10 Cf. Grimm, *Teutonic Mythology*, Vol. 4, p. 389. The *Wormser Minhagbuch* further specifies: "And one places a handful of salt at the threshold of that house." In n. 7 in the *Minhagbuch*, the editor comments: "I did not find the matter of the salt in any other source. Possibly this was practiced only in Worms." We did find, however, a similar custom among non-Jews in medieval Germany. See Grimm, op. cit., p. 1812, no. 846 (from Bielefeld): "A corpse is set down thrice on the threshold by the bearers; when it is out of the homestead the gate is fastened, **three heaps of salt are made in the death chamber**, it is then swept, and both broom and sweepings thrown in the fields; some also burn the bed-straw in the fields" (emphasis added); see also below, n. 15. For salt, see Legey, *The Folklore of Morocco*, p. 230.

it. Those standing there when the soul departs place the corpse on the straw, placing the feet of the corpse opposite the entrance to the house.[11] The corpse is covered with a black garment; it is customary to cover it with a cloak that he wore during his lifetime. They place a lighted candle up above, next to his head, until it [the corpse] is purified.

Cf. the Worms custom:[12]

It once happened that a person died here, in the holy community of Worms, at night, and after his soul departed they would place him on

It should further be noted that the *Wormser Minhagbuch* states (p. 89): "Immediately after his soul has departed, the windows of the room in which the corpse rests are opened." And similarly in *Ma'avar Yabbok*, section 1, chap. 26; *Hokhmat Adam*, "*Matzevet Moshe*," end of *Hil. Avelut*, para. 3; Gamaliel ben Pedahzur, *The Book of Religion, Ceremonies, and Prayers of the Jews* (London, 1738), p. 9. Cf. Grimm, op. cit., p. 1785, no. 191; p. 1804, no. 664 (from Wurtemberg). See also Radford, *Encyclopaedia of Superstitions*, p. 98; Tatem, *Dictionary of Superstitions*, p. 116; Hastings, *Encyclopaedia of Religion and Ethics*, p. 415b, who asserts that this was a widespread custom throughout Europe. Cf. Legey, *The Folklore of Morocco*, p. 228.

11 And similarly in the passage (below) from Pedahzur, loc. cit. Cf. Grimm, op. cit., p. 1804, no. 679; p. 1809, no. 779; Wuttke, *Der deutsche Volksaberglaube der Gegenwart*, p. 460. We see in Bodenschatz's illustration how the corpse lies with his feet pointing toward the entering visitors, who, we may assume, are coming from the entrance to the house. In other words, in this picture as well, the corpse lies with his feet facing the entrance. This, indeed, was the practice, as is attested by Elzet, *Reshumot*, Vol. 1, p. 370, para. 82: "One should take care neither to sleep, nor to lie down, with one's feet pointing to the entrance, because the corpse is placed on the ground with his feet towards the entrance." (See *Matamim*, "*Bar-Minan* [Mortal Man]," para. 7 [fol. 7b: "The reason why the corpse is placed on the ground with his feet towards the entrance is to allude that he is ready to go forth through this entrance to his resting place, and thereby save all entrances from the status of impurity."] And, thus, the popular curse: "May it be His will that you lie with your feet toward the entrance.") This custom, as Lipets attests, is related to the practice of taking the dead person out of the house feet first, a custom that was common in Christian Europe. See the extensive material in Hastings, op. cit., p. 426b. This was a custom already observed by the Romans; see Bender, "Death, Burial, Mourning," p. 105. In certain Muslim societies, however, the corpse was taken out head first; see Legey, *The Folklore of Morocco*, p. 234.

12 Rabbi Juda Loew Kirchheim, *The Customs of Worms Jewry*, ed. I.M. Peles (Jerusalem, 1987), "*Likkutim*," p. 303 (Hebrew).

the *gil*[13] and they covered him with his cloak, and they lit a candle up above, at his head.

The practice of placing the corpse on straw[14] is explained in the Jewish sources as being done so that it would not appear as if the dead person was

---

13 Straw; see the editor's note, p. 303 n. 8.

14 This also appears in Kirchner, *Judisches Ceremoniel*, pp. 214–15: "und legen den Todten auf ein Gebund Stroh neben dem Bette auf die Erden. Die Todten nun lassen sie auf gedachtem Stroh drie Stunden liegen"; while Buxtorf, loc. cit., makes no mention of this. Peles (*Customs of Worms Jewry*, p. 90 n. 11) lists many sources for this tradition. Lipets writes in *Matamim*, para. 8: "The reason why **seven** straws are placed under him on the ground is to allude to the fact that seven harsh judgments await him before he comes to his repose." (See also below, Chapters 14–15.) See Kirchheim, *Customs of Worms Jewry*, p. 310. Another possible reason for the use of straw was because the houses in rural areas had dirt floors, which were covered with straw. In this instance, fresh straw was laid down for the cleanliness of the corpse. See F. and J. Gies, *Life in a Medieval Village* (New York, 1991), p. 91; see also M. von Boehn, *Modes and Manners* (= *Die Mode*), trans. J. Joshua (1932 [photocopy edn.: New York, 1971]), Vol. 1, p. 262, that in medieval Europe "Floors were strewn with straw, or in summer with fresh greenery; the poets are giving free reign to their fancy when they scatter them with roses. As late as the fourteenth century Froissart, in describing the dwelling of the Count of Foix, mentions that rushes and grass were strewn on the floors." This is also implicit in *Turei Zahav, Orah Hayyim* 337, and the commentaries. See Rashi, BT Shabbat 124b, s.v. "*Shel Tamarah*." See the note by E. Shereshevsky, *Rashi, the Man and His World* (New York, 1982), pp. 217, 230, who thus explains the commentary by Rashi on BT Shabbat 47a, s.v. "*Malbenot ha-Mitah*": a sort of small hollow legs ("coasters"), in which the legs of the beds were placed "**to prevent them from being rotted**." Of interest is the observation by R. Patai, "Folk Customs and Charms Relating to Birth," *Talpioth* 6, 1–2 (1953), pp. 267–68: "To the present the custom of spreading a bit of straw on the earth and placing on it the woman giving birth is prevalent among many peoples. In the Kiurinsk district in Russia, in the village of Mamarus, Chorny heard that the Jewish women would give birth on the ground in a special room, on straw. It was also customary among the Jews of Bessarabia to lay down the woman about to give birth on straw on the ground, especially in remote villages, in which there was no physician, and only a midwife cared for the women in labor." See his discussion of the practice there, n. 19. I do not know if there is any connection between this practice and that relating to the corpse. In the continuation of this article (*Talpioth* 6, 3–4 [1955], pp. 686–94), Patai discusses the practice of "placing the newborn on the ground," an act that is reminiscent of setting the corpse on the ground.

As regards the matter of three hours, cf. *Minhagei Yisrael*, Vol. 6, p. 98, that the burial party waited a few hours after the death before proceeding with the burial.

being stoned, by being placed directly on the floor,[15] and this is also mentioned by Christiani:[16]

> Der Todte wie er in Leinwand[17] gewickelt auf dem Stroh liegt.
> [translation: the corpse, enshrouded in cloth, in laid on the straw.]

15 See, e.g., *Yesod ve-Shoresh ha-Avodah* (Jerusalem, 1968 [first edition: Novy Dvor, 1782]) by Rabbi Alexander Susskind (d. 1794), pp. 493–94:
> Immediately following the expiration of my soul from my body to its root [...] the burial society is to subject my body to the four forms of capital punishment of the Court. Since stoning is the most serious of them all, all of the forms of capital punishment are to be effected by stoning [...] and they are to inflict upon me the actual procedure of stoning, and thus they are to do: several people are to lift me up, right to the ceiling, and they are to dash me to the earth, specifically, with great force, **without any intervening sheet or straw**. Thus they are to act, seven times consecutively. [...] Even after the performance of the procedure of stoning described above, they are not to place me **on straw**, but only on the actual ground.

Rabbi Hayyim Hezekiah Medini (d. 1908), the author of *Sedei Hemed*, also wrote in his will (Vol. 14 of *Sedei Hemed*), that the order of the four forms of Court-imposed capital punishment be inflicted upon him:
> If the room in which I expire will be the bottom of the house, the actual ground, that is: a floor of stones or of dirt, my body is to be placed on the actual ground, without a sheet, with only my nakedness covered, out of respect, and also, if people desire, with my body covered by a sheet. At any rate, the side that is placed on the earth must be actually on the ground, without anything intervening. And if the floor of the room will be covered by sawdust, let much earth be brought and spread on the floor of the room, and [then] I am to be laid on the earth.

See the detailed discussion by S. Ashkenazi, *Avnei Hen: Topics in Jewish Customs* (Tel Aviv, 1990), pp. 306–19, chap. 34 ("The Posthumous Four Court-Imposed Capital Punishments") (Hebrew). This description of lying directly on the ground, with nothing separating the back from the earth, is brought by Tykocinski, *Gesher ha-Hayyim*, Vol. 1, p. 45, as the Land of Israel practice; he explains that this is because of "the sanctity of the earth," as it is written "Your servants take delight in its stones" (Ps. 102:15). Tykocinski adds: "And outside the Land of Israel, it is the practice to spread a bit of straw on the ground. A sheet is spread diagonally over the straw, and a pillow for his head. But it is also written in *Derishah* and in *S[iftei] K[ohen]* that he should not lie on his back on anything else, because this causes heat, leading to putrefaction. According to this [reason], this practice should be followed, even outside the Land of Israel." His argument does not seem to be decisive, but an exhaustive discussion would exceed the purview of the current work.

16 Friedrich Albrecht Christiani, *Der Juden Glaube und Aberglaube* (Leipzig, 1705), p. 153.

The apostate Gamaliel ben Pedahzur[18] (whose real name was Abraham Mears), provides a similar portrayal:

> As soon as the Soul is departed from the Body, the Corps with only a Shirt or Shift on, is lay'd on **clean Straw** on the Floor with the Feet towards the Chamber-Door, and cover'd over with a Sheet, and the Windows set open, and a Person left with the Corps to watch it from all Kind of Vermin till it is carried to their Burying-Ground.

This procedure was also followed by Christians in medieval Germany, as Grimm reports:[19] "If a corpse sigh once more when on the straw if it open its eyes (todten blick), then one of its kindred will follow soon."[20] Grimm further specifies:[21] "The straw on which the sick man died is carried out and burnt."[22]

17 Cf. Grimm, *Teutonic Mythology*, Vol. 4, p. 1799, no. 551; p. 1804, no. 665; p. 1806, no. 709. Cf. also *Rokeah*, para. 316: "It was the practice to prepare flax garments, without a border, and threads **without any knot**, and they dress him in trousers, shirt, [...] and they gird him with a flax girdle, and a belt for the trousers, also of flax." As regarding the refraining from knots, see Danzig, *Hokhmat Adam*, "*Matzevet Moshe*," end of *Hil. Avelut*, para. 5, based on *Rokeah*. Cf. Radford, *Encyclopaedia of Superstitions*, pp. 158–59: "If all the knots in a shroud are not loosened when a body is confined, the departed spirit will not rest"; Opie and Tatem, *A Dictionary of Superstitions*, pp. 222–23.
18 Pedahzur, *The Book of Religion, Ceremonies, and Prayers of the Jews*, p. 9.
19 *Teutonic Mythology*, Vol. 4, p. 1811, no. 828.
20 This practice is depicted by Wuttke, *Der deutsche Volksaberglaube der Gegenwart*, pp. 457, 460; cf. Grimm, p. 1782, no. 113; p. 1912, no. 846; p. 1827, no. 1124.
21 *Teutonic Mythology*, Vol. 4, p. 1844, no. 40.
22 Cf. Grimm, *Teutonic Mythology*, Vol. 4, p. 1788, no. 268; Wuttke, *Der deutsche Volksaberglaube der Gegenwart*, p. 466. This custom should perhaps be connected with the Lithuanian practice of burying the dead in straw sheaves; see V.J. Bagdanavicius, *Wellsprings of Folktales*, trans. from the Lithuanian by J. Zemkalnis (New York, 1970), p. 121 (with a reference to folkloristic stories in J. Basanavicius, *Lieturiskos pasakos yvairios* [Shenandoah, Pa., 1898], Vol. 2, pp. 255, 282–83). Bagdanavicius concludes (loc. cit.): "All these phenomena would be incomprehensible, if once there had not existed a custom of burying people in a sheaf" (in the final analysis, however, his presentation is less than convincing). Should we relate this to the custom of announcing a death in a roundabout way by placing a truss of straw in the street; see Rappoport, *The Folklore of the Jews*, p. 103 (citing D. Dergny, *Usages, Coutumes et Croyances ou Livre des choses Curieuses* [Paris, 1882], pp. 53–58).
    It should further be noted that the practice of laying the corpse on straw apparently was not observed in Italy, since the Italian apostate Paolo Medici, *Riti e Costume*

The two people standing to the right in Bodenschatz's picture appear to be the burial society members who have come to engage in the purification of the corpse. They will use the water to bathe the body, and the beaten eggs in their shells will be smeared on his head and face.[23]

degli Ebrei Confutati[5] (Venice, 1757), mentions the placing of the dead on the ground, but is silent regarding the use of straw.

23 See *Magen Avraham, Yoreh Deah* 4; cf. *Kol Bo*, para. 114 (= *Orhot Hayyim*, Vol. 2, p. 572):

This the practice in which Israel engaged regarding the dead and burial. [...] They smear him to remove his uncleanness, so that the people would not loathe him when they bear him, and they coat his head with eggs beaten in their shells. [No mention is made here of the wine of which *Rokeah* speaks; see what *Hokhmat Adam*, "*Matzevet Moshe*," end of *Hil. Avelut*, para. 8, comments, that in a place where wine is expensive, or cannot be obtained, water is used in place of wine. He further notes that the custom has been corrupted, and a bit of water is dashed on the corpse, and this is said to be the main element of the purification: "But this is none other than non-Jewish practices, and a very repellent custom, and it should be canceled. Rather, they wash his head with (water), and this bears no relation to the purification at all."] This was the ancient practice for marking. Since they would transport him outside the city for burial, so that the grave diggers would know that he is an Israelite, they would make this mark on him. The reason for the eggs is that this [life] is a cycle [...].

Y.Y. Greenwald, *Kol Bo al Avelut* (*Compendium on Mourning*) (Jerusalem and New York, n. d.), chap. 1, p. 86 n. 5, wrote that he did not understand his intent (regarding the making of a distinctive marking). There may be an omission here, with the reference to a symbol that the Jews were required to wear during their lifetime. See my comment in *Minhagei Yisrael*, Vol. 4, chap. 17, and the monumental work by S.W. Baron, *A Social and Religious History of the Jews*, Vol. 9 (New York and London, 1965), pp. 23–42; Vol. 11 (New York and London, 1967), pp. 96–106, but this still remains within the realm of conjecture. See also Leusden, *Philologus Hebraeo-Mixtus*, p. 457; Buxtorf, *Synagoga Judaica*, chap. 49. The caption to the picture in Kirchner states: "die Freunde bey einen verstorbenen Juden in der Trauer," implying that this is the *seudat havra'ah* (the mourner's meal following the funeral), which also features hardboiled eggs and lentils (see Bodenschatz, *Kirchliche Verfassung der heutigen Juden*, p. 878). See Sperling, *Sefer Ta'amei ha-Minhagim u-Mekorei ha-Dinim*, para. 1036. It is conceivable that Kirchner did not understand the scene depicted in the engraving. On p. 216, n. a, Kirchner cites the topic of eggs and wine from the book by (the apostate) Margaritha, but without much detail. (The intent is to Anton Margaritha, *Der ganz Judisch glaub* ... [Augsburg, 1530; second edition: Leipzig, 1713]. Kirchner apparently used the second edition, without specifying the year of publication in his introduction, where he calls it "*Juden Glauben*"). Cf. also Buxtorf, loc. cit.

This is corroborated by Bodenschatz's description:[24]

> [...] die heilige Gesellschaft [...] waschet ihn erstlich mit warmes wasser ganz zauber ab [...] nimmt Eyer, bricht solche auf, zusamt der Schalen, und schmieret seinen Kopf und Geschicht damit. [translation: (...) the burial society first of all washes the body in warm water, until it is completely clean (...) they take eggs beaten in their shells and smear them on the head and on the face.]

Cf. the process described in *Rokeah*:[25]

> Water is brought and heated, and his entire body, his limbs, and his head are washed. After this eggs and wine are brought, they are beaten together, and [with this]`mixed together, his head is washed.

It is noteworthy that in this picture, the coffin is closed; this may well also have been a prevalent custom, although I have not found sources for it.

Incidental to our mention of beds, attention should be directed to the important article by E. Zimmer,[26] in which he examined the fact that the practice of overturning one's bed, which was a central component of the laws of mourning in the time of the Talmud, almost completely disappeared over the course of time. Zimmer offers two reasons for this change: (1) during the period when superstitions were at their peak, the charges of sorcery connected with this custom intensified; and (2) the change in the physical shape of beds made their overturning more difficult. Thus, for example, *Ribash* (Rabbi Isaac ben Sheshet Perfet), when he was in Algiers after his exile from Spain in 1391, writes in his responsa:[27]

> The beds that were in use in our land were not fashioned as their beds, and they cannot be overturned. This is certainly the case for those [beds] in this land that are affixed to the walls.[28]

24 Bodenschatz, *Kirchliche Verfassung der heutigen Juden*, p. 171.
25 *Rokeah*, ed. Schneersohn, para. 316, p. 194.
26 "The Overturning of the Bed during Mourning, and the Evolution and Practice of the Halakhah," *Sinai* 158 (1995), pp. 228–53 (Hebrew).
27 Rabbi Isaac ben Sheshet Perfet, *She'eilot u-Teshuvot ha-Ribash* (Constantinople, 1546), para. 69.
28 See Zimmer, op. cit., p. 253, the picture of a bed from the fifteenth century, which closely resembles that which appears in Bodenschatz (Fig. 1), which certainly could not be overturned, due to its structure, size, and weight. (See the depictions of beds in the illustrations of circumcisions, as in Kirchner, *Judisches Ceremoniel*, p. 49, etc.)

1. Deathbed, Bodenschatz, Erlang 1748

2. Death and burial, Buxtorf, Frankfurt and Leipzig 1729

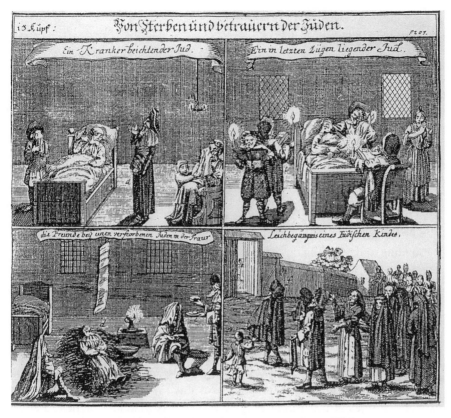

3. Death and burial, Kirchner, Nuremberg 1724

4

ASKING POSTHUMOUS PARDON OF THE DEAD

The book by Gamaliel ben Pedahzur[1] contains the following portrayal of an astounding and puzzling custom:

> If any Person desires to ask Pardon of the dead for any Differences that were between them in his Life Time, which very often happens, the Person who asks Pardon, must stand at the Feet-End of the coffin, and with his Finger and Thumb of each Hand, take hold of each first or great Toe of the dead, through the Stockings, which the dead has on, and say thus: "I do pray thy forgiveness, if I have committed any Offence towards thee, pray forgive me." And the Jews affirm, that oftentimes at the asking Forgiveness in this Manner, the dead Person has fell a bleeding violently at the Nose, which they take as a Token of some great Offence or Injury that has been given to the Deceased, by the Person surviving, that asks his Forgiveness.

Prof. Cecil Roth commented on this strange custom, which is so different from all that appears in the halakhic sources:[2]

> This must have been a very wide-spread practise: I have now seen it depicted in an engraving of Venetian Jewish life by Giovanni la Pian (eighteenth century).[3]

---

1. *The Book of Religion, Ceremonies, and Prayers of the Jews*, p. 11.
2. E.g., *Shulhan Arukh, Orah Hayyim* 606:2.
3. C. Roth, *Personalities and Events in Jewish History* (Philadelphia, 1953), p. 88 n. 3. His intent is to Giovanni Andrea dalle Piane (1679–1750); the engraving is listed in Rubens, *A Jewish Iconography*, p. 60, no. 619, and in *idem, A Jewish Iconography: Supplementary Volume*, p. 32* (Fig. 1).

In the engraving we see a woman on bent knees. In her right hand she holds the right large toe of the deceased, who is completely covered by a sheet and who lies on the floor. Below, in the second line of the inscription, we are told that this is the manner in which relatives request pardon, for possibly having offended the dead in some manner. Incidentally, the corpse lies with its feet pointing to the stairs, which probably lead to the entrance of the house.[4]

Roth concludes his note as follows: "once again, there is no need to stress the analogies: it is enough to think of the story of Richard I at his father's bier." I could not understand this reference, since Richard played no role at all in the funeral of his father, Henry II, and certainly did not ask for forgiveness from his late father.[5]

An additional reference to this practice appears in the book by the apostate Paolo Medici (1672–1738), *Riti e Costume degli Hebraei*:[6]

> Mentre il Cadavero e disteso in terra, vengono alcune Donnee appena entrate in quella stanza, toccano Colle mani giunte e piedi di quel Cadavero in contrassegno di addimandargli perdone se mai in vita l'avessero offeso in qualche cosa.

That is, after the corpse has been placed on the floor, a group of women come, and with arms linked, they touch the feet of the dead one to ask for forgiveness, lest they had offended him in his lifetime.

Most astounding, however, is what Masse writes:[7] "When anyone sees a dead person in a dream, the deceased has to be seized by the big toe and made to speak of the other world." Once again, we have the seizing of the corpse's big toe as a means of reconciliation(?) with the deceased.

This should be understood in connection with what we found in Wuttke's book,[8] that if the corpse stretches, the big toe of its left foot is to be kissed, otherwise the dead one will find no repose.[9] Interestingly, traces of this custom

---

4   See above, Part II, chap. 3, n. 11.
5   See J. Gillingham, *Richard the Lionheart* (London, 1978), p. 124. (My thanks to Prof. Avrom Saltman, for referring me to Gillingham's book.)
6   Medici, *Riti e Costume degli Ebrei* (Madrid, 1737 [= Milan, 1738], and other editions), p. 207.
7   Masse, *Persian Beliefs and Customs*, p. 96.
8   Wuttke, *Der deutsche Volksaberglaube der Gegenwart*, p. 467, para. 735.
9   Based on J. Grohmann, *Auberglauben und Gebrauche aus Bohmen und Mahren*, Vol. 1 (Prague, 1864), p. 190.

are also to be found in the Converso community, as we see in the following passage:[10]

> For this Crypto-Jew having acted as the religious leader of the community, the Catholics of the village used to say to the Crypto-Jews, with certain amusement: "Go to the **ceremony of the foot kisser** [emphasis added — D. S.], to the house of your Carlos!"

Carlos was Carlos Diogo Henriques, the elder of the community of Belmonte in Portugal, who "directed the ritual and sought uniformity in what had to be done by the members."[11] I was puzzled by the epithet "foot kisser," until my attention was drawn to this passage in *Sefer Hasidim*:[12]

> A man and his son arrived in a certain city, and the father ordered his son that when he [the father] would be called up to read from the Torah, he [the son] should not go on his knees to kiss [the father], since there were many [people there] who were childless. He ordered him not to kiss his knees, so that they [the childless] should not suffer distress.

Apparently it was the custom for the son to kiss his father's feet while the latter read from the Torah; it further seems that this practice persisted through many generations, even to the Crypto-Jewish community of the sixteenth century and later.

An allied practice is described by Rabbeinu Nissim:[13] "He fell upon his face in humbleness, and kissed their feet, saying [...]." This custom is still observed in certain Oriental Jewish communities,[14] and may be hinted at in Rashi's commentary to BT Avodah Zarah 17a, s.v. "*Abei Hadayahu*":

> See the way of people when they exit the synagogue: [the son] immediately kisses his father and his mother and whoever is senior to him on their knees or on the palm of their hand.

---

10 D.A. Canelo, *The Last Crypto-Jews of Portugal*[2] (1990, n.p.), p. 142 n. 4.
11 Ibid., p. 68.
12 *Sefer Hasidim (Das Buch der Frommen)*, ed. J. Wistinetzki and J. Freimann (Frankfurt a.M., 1924 [photocopy edn.: Jerusalem, 1969]), para. 937, p. 231.
13 H.Z. Hirschberg (ed.), *Rabbenu Nissim b. R. Jacob of Kairouan: Hibbur Yafeh me-ha-Yeshu'ah* (Jerusalem, 1970), p. 26.
14 See S.D. Goitein, *A Mediterranean Society*, Vol. 3: *The Family* (Berkeley, 1978), pp. 240, 478 n. 116.

The more usual procedure, however, was to kiss the hand.[15] Kissing feet was, then, an accepted manner of showing respect, and possibly also of begging forgiveness. The "foot kissers" were those who practiced such a custom.

Indeed, even in the latter half of the nineteenth century we find such a custom relating to the dead in Alsace. Daniel Stauben records such a procedure:[16]

> One by one, the desolate people bent down to the deceased and, lifting the shroud around him, they held his two cold feet in their hands, while with a choking voice they muttered the prescribed formula, imploring him to forgive them in heaven, whatever pain they may have caused him on earth. The casket was then temporarily nailed and carried to the cemetery, followed by all of us.

It therefore seems that, according to the popular belief, the kissing of the corpse's left big toe brings peace to the deceased, and apparently is also the way to conciliate him and win his pardon. This entire matter requires further study.[17]

15 See Rabbi Ovadiah Yosef, *She'eilot u-Teshuvot Yehaveh Da'at*, Vol. 4 (Jerusalem, 1981), para. 12, pp. 59–62, with the copious sources that he cites.

16 D. Stauben, *Scènes de la vie juive en Alsace*, trans. R. Choron: *Scenes of Jewish Life in Alsace* (Malibu, 1994), p. 49.

17 For the response of the body of the dead person to something that disturbs him, see M. Guedemann, *Ha-Torah ve-ha-Hayyim ... (Geschichte des Erziehungswesens und der Cultur der abendlandischen Juden wahrend des Mittelalters)*, Vol. 1 (Warsaw, 1897 [photocopy edition: Jerusalem, 1972]), p. 158, who cites *Sefer Hasidim* (Bologna ed., para. 1149): "When a person is killed, if the murderer comes to him, the wound will reopen" (the thoughtful observation of Avri Bar-Levav). For the kissing of a corpse in general, see A. Kosman, "Kissing the Dead — Transformation of a Custom," *Tarbiz* 65 (1995–96), pp. 484–508 (Hebrew), esp. p. 501 n. 82, that in the Salonika community, "before the closing of the coffin, the sons would ask forgiveness, and they would kiss the hand of the deceased" (based on I.S. Emmanuel, *Precious Stones of the Jews of Salonica* [Jerusalem, 1993], p. 13 [Hebrew]). For the reasons why kissing the corpse is prohibited, see Kosman, op. cit., pp. 497, esp. p. 500; this matter requires further investigation. An interesting addition appears in the article by E. Horowitz, "On Kissing the Dead in the Mediterranean World," *Tarbiz* 67 (1997), pp. 131–34 (Hebrew); Horowitz quotes a description of the funeral of Rabbi Samuel Aboab in Venice (1694) by his son and successor Jacob. According to the latter, immediately following his father's death "when his sons and pupils who stand over him saw that their mighty one has died, they fell on their faces, rent their garments, wept, **and kissed his feet**" (Jacob ben Samuel Aboab,

Lorsche un Ebreo e morto, si stende il Cadavere in terra involto in un lenzuolo i Parenti più stretti gli stanno intorno, piangendolo, ed encomiando le sue buone qualità ·
i conoscenti accorono baciandogli le dita di piedi e chiedendogli perdono, se mai l'avessero offeso. Le donne per più cautione presentano una comacie, le montando, e un cuscechetto di
Il Padrone muova in humesse largo il Cadavere per piedi le Cossa, e mentre lavato con acqua calda, e nascosti di Cosa a porte pangono lo di dia perduta

1. Giovanni Andrea delle Piane, 18th century

Introduction, *She'eilot u-Teshuvot Devar Shemuel* [Venice, 1702 (photocopy edn.: Jerusalem, 1983)]; also cited by M. S. Gerondi and H. Nippi, *Toledot Gedolei Yisrael be-Italiah* [*Annals of Jewish Sages in Italy*] [Trieste, 1853 (photocopy edn.: Brooklyn, 1993)], p. 386). Horowitz comments on this that "this instance refers to the public funeral of one of the city's rabbis, and to the personal testimony by one of the kissers. This, then, clearly refers to an actual occurrence, and to an action that was accepted among the Jews of northern Italy." Horowitz further draws our attention to the fact that "Cecil Roth omitted the description of the kissing of the rabbi's feet from the portrayal of the death and funeral of Aboab in his book on the Jews of Venice; Roth may possibly have thought that the statement by the rabbi's son was simple exaggeration. See C. Roth, *Venice*, Philadelphia 1930 (reprint New York 1975), p. 235." The material we have brought confirms that this was not mere hyperbole, and that this was indeed the Italian practice. For additional information concerning the kissing of the dead, see B.S. Puckle, *Funeral Customs: Their Origin and Development* (London, 1926), p. 75. Cf. *Minhagei Yisrael*, Vol. 6, p. 91 n. 14.

5

THE CUSTOM OF THE DECEASED'S WIFE PASSING UNDER THE BIER

It is related that among the Jews in Libya:

> When a man dies and leaves a pregnant wife, it is customary for the bearers of the bier to stand with the bier at the entrance of the room from which the corpse was taken out, and the widow passes under the bier, in the view of the congregation of those escorting [the funeral procession].[1]

Westermarck notes, regarding a similar practice in Morocco:[2] "If the deceased was a married man and his widow is with child, she passes once underneath the bier when it is raised, so that people may know that the child to which she will give birth was begotten by her husband." Westermarck further comments[3] that in some places in Morocco the widow passes under the bier three times.[4]

The symbolism of the pregnant widow walking under the bier is to be understood on the basis of the description by Patai[5] that direct or indirect contact with the corpse will likely have a beneficial effect on the fertility

---

1   *Yahadut Lub* (*The Book of Libyan Jewry*) (Tel Aviv, 1960), p. 396 ("Life and Customs").
2   *Ritual and Belief in Morocco*, Vol. 2, p. 454.
3   Op. cit., p. 455.
4   See Lerner, *Shmiras Haguf Vehanefesh*, para. 237:5, p. 692: "One is not to look upon those who have been killed or crucified, not even from a distance of one hundred cubits (*Ari* [Isaac Luria], of blessed memory)." This injunction may possibly be directed against this practice.
5   Patai, "Folk Customs and Charms Relating to Birth," p. 248.

of a woman. As Patai reports: "The barren Jewish and Muslim women in Tripoli in Africa drink from the water with which the corpse was washed." He continues[6] by observing that "in Egypt barren Muslim women would pass under the stone on which the bodies of criminals who were killed by the sword were washed. They would then wash their faces in the bloody water. Others would shriek above the body of a person who had been beheaded."[7] In Syria, the barren woman was counseled to stand **under** a hanged man.[8] In India, barren women bathe under a hanged man. Patai continues:

> It was the practice among the Jews of Baghdad to ensure the fertility of women, already at the time of the wedding. The bride would go in to the corpse after it had been washed, and walk three or four times above the body of the dead person, so that she would conceive.

Patai further relates of the charms made from the water in which the corpse was washed.

Based on the above, the passing of the widow under the corpse relates to the motif of fertility, and therefore is suitable for a woman who desires to publicly display her state of pregnancy.[9]

---

6 Ad loc., n. 38.

7 See E.W. Lane, *The Manners and Customs of the Modern Egyptians* (London, 1871), Vol. 1, pp. 325 ff.

8 See Abela, "Beitrage zur Kentniss aberglaubischer gebrauch in Syrien," p. 114.

9 For her going three times, cf. Patai, op. cit., p. 260, that the passing three times **under** something is also a well-known motif: "Enter under the stomach of a pregnant mare, go forth from side to side three times, what [danger] was in the woman, will pass to the mare, and the woman will not miscarry" (Rabbi Raphael Ohana, *Mareh ha-Yeladim* [Jerusalem, 1928], 16a, as related by Rabbi Abraham Yaluz).

6

THE FIRSTBORN OF AN ANIMAL IN THE CEMETERY

One of the strange phenomena we find in medieval cemeteries is the presence of livestock roaming freely in them. In order to understand this phenomenon, we have to understand the rabbinic laws pertaining to the firstborn of clean animals, which in Temple times were offered as sacrifices, and that "in these times" (i.e. after the destruction of the Temple) are given over to a *kohen* (one of the priestly class). Jewish authorities over the ages have expressed differing views regarding the status of the firstborn of a clean animal outside the Land of Israel. According to one opinion, the law of the animal firstborn does not apply outside the Land of Israel; others maintain the opposite, that this law is in force; while yet others assert that it is applicable by rabbinic law.[1] Most of the *poskim* concur that *kohanim* are obligated to receive the

---

1   See *Enziklopedyah Talmudit* (*Talmudic Encyclopedia*), Vol. 3, pp. 285–87; Medini, *Sedei Hemed*, Introduction to *Bekhor Behemah* (*Animal Firstborn*), Vol. 6, pp. 353–54; Rabbi M.M. Kasher, *Torah Shelemah* (New York, 1948), Vol. 12, *Bo*, pp. 191–92. See Maimonides, *Mishneh Torah, Hil. Bekhorot* (*Laws of the Firstborn*) 1:5: "The commandment regarding the firstborn of a clean beast applies both in the Land of Israel and outside the Land." This is the correct version, according to *Kessef Mishneh*, and according to Rabbi Eliezer ben Judah of Worms, *Maaseh Rokeah* (Sanok, 1912), who wrote: "I found it written in a manuscript that the commandment of the firstborn of a beast applies in the Land of Israel and outside the Land. I also saw in manuscripts that are here in Egypt [...] that a copy was discovered in a corrected version, signed by our master [i.e. Maimonides]." Several versions of the *Mishneh Torah*, however, read: "The commandment regarding the firstborn of a clean beast applies only in the Land of Israel." This was the version available to *Rabad* (Rabbi Abraham ben David of Posquières), Nahmanides, *Rashba* (Rabbi Solomon ben Abraham Adret), and *Ran* (Rabbi Nissim ben Reuben Gerondi), and they all questioned it. See *Sefer ha-Mitzvot*, Commandment 79. At the present, post-Destruction, time, we wait until the firstborn of a clean animal acquires a

animal firstborn, and that even outside the Land of Israel they must care for them until they exhibit some blemish (which thereby disqualifies them for use as sacrifices), even if this care entails great expense. There are various references in the halakhic literature to the custody of these firstborn, such as care being taken of a firstborn for several months in the "Braut Haus" (bride's house) in Erfurt.[2]

In Worms,[3] the practice was

> to give the animal firstborn to a non-Jew who lived over the graves,[4]

blemish (that disqualifies it as a sacrifice), and it may then be slaughtered (but such a blemish is not to be inflicted by human agency). According to *Tosafot* (Avodah Zarah 62b, s.v. "*U-le-Kavrinehu*"), if it died unblemished, it is to be buried in a cemetery, "and it seems that it is to be buried at somewhat of a depth, lest [animals] come to root after them." In the excavations conducted at Tel Baruch, Israel, in 1952, Yossi Kaplan found, at the end of the cemetery, a large grave full of animal bones. On November 2, 1952, the *Haaretz* newspaper printed a report about an immigrant from Tripoli who sought to bury the carcass of a firstborn goat in a human cemetery. He was charged by the police, and argued in his defense that he was acting "in accordance with the accepted law we follow from generation to generation." Rabbi Jehiel Michael Tykocinski rejected this custom, while Rabbis Zevi Nahir and Menahem Ehrenberg of Tel Aviv required its observance (see the *Ha-Zofeh* newspaper, November 13, 1952; November 28, 1952). See *Kol Torah*, Kislev-Tevet 5713 (= November 1952–January 1953), p. 14; Nisan-Iyyar 5713 (= March-May 1953), p. 16. Apparently basing his opinion on these newspaper articles, Kaplan determined that this large grave contained the carcasses of pure animal firstborn. See D. Brilling, "Sheep and Cattle Firstborn in Frankfurt am Main," *Yeda-'Am*, 3, 1 (1955), pp. 15–17 (Hebrew); cf. J.H. Lask, "This is the Story of 'He-Goat of the Community,'" *Yeda-'Am* 2 (1954), pp. 154–59 (Hebrew).

2   Rabbi Israel ben Hayyim Bruna, *She'eilot u-Teshuvot Mahari Bruna* (Salonika, 1788, and additional editions), para. 162. See Schammes, *Wormser Minhagbuch*, Vol. 2, p. 7 n. 48.

3   *Wormser Minhagbuch*, p. 86. This gloss, which comes from a manuscript, is an addition by Schammes himself, from the short MS. of his *Minhagbuch* (MS. Worms). See *Wormser Minhagbuch*, Introduction to Vol. 2, p. 9.

4   It was customary in Germany to entrust the guarding of cemeteries to non-Jews. See H. Dicker, *Die Geschichte der Juden in Ulm* (Rottweil, 1937), cited in S. Eidelberg, *Jewish Life in Austria in the XVth Century as Reflected in the Legal Writings of Rabbi Israel Isserlein and His Contemporaries* (Philadelphia, 1962), p. 75; see the additional sources brought by Eidelberg. See the comment by I. Klausner, *Korot Beit ha-Almin ha-Yashan be-Vilna* (*History of the Old Cemetery in Vilna*) (Vilna, 1935 [photocopy edn.: Jerusalem, 1972]), p. 30.

to raise it from the grass and herbs of the graves.[5] The *kohanim* give the non-Jew his wages for caring for it, and all the expenses that he will incur for it. Even if there will be more than one or two firstborn here, they will all be [incumbent] upon the *kohanim*, to raise them and to pay all the expenses from their pocket.

The editor of the *Minhagim Book*[6] referred to what *Hatam Sofer* wrote in his responsa:[7]

It was always the custom of our forefathers in the holy community of Frankfurt a. M. that firstborn beasts graze over the graves, and attendants and watchman are hired, and they [the animals] are fed.[8]

5   This would seem to be prohibited, since BT Megillah 29a teaches: "Cemeteries may not be treated disrespectfully. Cattle are not to be grazed in them." A similar injunction appears in *Semahot* 14:1 (*Treatise Semahot*, ed. M. Higger [New York, 1937], p. 204), and is brought as the law in *Shulhan Arukh, Yoreh Deah* 368:1, where Rabbi Moses Isserles writes, based on *She'eilot u-Teshuvot Terumat ha-Deshen*, para. 284: "And it is permitted to derive benefit from the grass over the graves [...] for the needs of the graves, for example, the pagan ruler grazes beasts over the graves, and it would not be possible to protest against this without incurring great expense, that is beyond the reach of the community." *Pit'hei Teshuvah* on *Yoreh Deah*, loc. cit., para. 2, refers to *She'eilot u-Teshuvot Hatam Sofer, Yoreh Deah*, para. 327, who wrote that in a place where all the living are cognizant that this is the practice, knowing that this will happen when they die, and they forego the respect due them, then all this is permitted, since it is not the deriving of benefit that is prohibited, this rather was enacted out of respect for the dead. (The reference in Isserles to the responsa of Rabbi Jacob ben Judah Weil is apparently to para. 94.). Here, in contrast, we are speaking of grass that grows in the cemetery, and not on the actual graves, from which, according to most opinions, benefit may be derived, even if not for the needs of the graves themselves. See *Haggahot Rabbi Akiva Eiger on Yoreh Deah*, op. cit. 62; Greenwald, *Kol Bo al Avelut*, Vol. 1, p. 168; Rabbi Shlomo Helma, *Avel ha-Shittim*, ed. I. Koenig (Jerusalem, 1980), pp. 34–35.

6   Schammes, *Wormser Minhagbuch*, Vol. 2, p. 86 n. 20.

7   *She'eilot u-Teshuvot Hatam Sofer, Yoreh Deah*, para. 302.

8   The *Hatam Sofer*, Rabbi Moses Sofer, was born in Frankfurt am Main in 1762, and left the city in 1781. The Jewish cemetery in the city, the Borneplatz, was closed in 1829. This responsum was most likely written at the beginning of the nineteenth century, possibly close to Sofer's appointment as rabbi in Pressburg in 1806. I found interesting testimony confirming the report by Sofer, that this was the long-standing practice in Frankfurt, in the book *Frankfurt*, by A. Freimann and F. Kracauer (Philadelphia, 1929), p. 227:
     Several decades pass without any word in regard to the cemetery. In 1640

At the beginning of the seventeenth century, when the Jews of Frankfurt were expelled by Vincent Fettmilch, the firstborn beast in the cemetery also fell prey to the anti-Semites. Stanza 56 of the Yiddish *Vincnetz* [= Vincent] *Lied*, a song composed by Elhanan ben Abraham of Frankfurt to celebrate the return of the Jews after their expulsion in 1616, relates:

> The firstborn of an ox was in the cemetery
> And was there for some time.
> They caused it great tribulations, they smote it with their sword
> Its flesh they gave to the innkeeper
> So that he [the innkeeper] would remember the day
> And that a buyer would come and desire to drink wine
> And they would give him a fine portion of ox-meat.

The Christian scholar J.J. Schudt (1664–1722) writes:[9]

> And if a firstling [of a clean beast] is born to the Jews in the vicinity of the city [Frankfurt] within a distance of many miles, it will be led here by a Christian or by a Jew, they will hang from its neck a sign on which will be written "This is the firstborn," they will tie it by the cemetery of the Jews, and they will leave it there.

Schudt further relates:

> I remember that I heard from my late father, Conrad Schudt, who for about twenty years, 1660–1680, was a gospel preacher in the province and in this city [Frankfurt am Main], that in his childhood such a firstborn ox gored a person who was working at the erection

> it was the object of a curious private complaint. Next to the cemetery lay a large bleaching field belonging to an alderman Volker, which he leased to a master-glazier living near the Allerheiligentor. The lessee had been given the keys to the wicket in the city wall and also to the cemetery gate, so that he could more readily get to his plot of ground. It happened that according to old custom an ox grazed in the cemetery and evidently often became pretty troublesome to the master-glazier on his way through. He asked the Council to order the Jews to get rid of the ox or lock it up so that he could walk through undisturbed. The Jews refused, and the case was decided in their favor.

See also H. Baerwald, *Der Alte Friedhof der israelitischen Gemeinde zu Frankfurt a.m.* (Frankfurt am Main, 1883).

9   J.J. Schudt, *Juedische Merckwuerdigkeiten* (Frankfurt and Leipzig, 1714).

of tombstones in the cemetery, and it killed him. The authorities demanded that the ox be handed over to them, and when they encountered difficulties, they sent several soldiers to shoot it in the cemetery. Afterwards, to the great sorrow of the Jews, the executioner placed it on his wagon, and led it through the *Judengasse* to the "carcass square," where he treated it like the other animal carcasses.

During the great conflagration that swept the Jewish quarter in 1711, the Jews of Frankfurt, according to Schudt, attempted to save the life of the firstling and pushed it to the house of Christians. There, however, it was set upon by dogs, who wounded it in its ear. This injury was not considered to be a "blemish," and did not rob the firstling of its "firstborn" status. In 1714 Schudt visited the "firstlings" in the cemetery, and portrayed them as follows:

> Now, in August 1714, the Jews keep [in the cemetery] an ox that is still young in age, and four he-goats. The eldest of the oxen, that was more than twenty years of age, died this year on Passover eve, and was buried three days later, wrapped in a white cloth, close to its cattle shed next to the cemetery, behind the fence. It was a very strong animal, with a large head, a fat and broad neck, and thick skin. In its lifetime the firstling swallowed much paper, as I saw with my own eyes: it swallowed an old, large book that was printed with Hebrew letters — albeit without its cover — as well as a silk handkerchief, with colored bands.

The noise made by the oxen and he-goats that grazed in the cemeteries interrupted the sleep of the Jews who lived nearby. This is attested by the poet Heinriche Heine in his book *Ludwig Borne*:[10]

> [...] my dear Doctor; tell me rather, what has become of the big oxen which my father once told me used to roam about in the Jewish burial-ground here at Frankfurt, and bellowed so terribly at night, that the peace of the whole neighborhood was disturbed?
> "Your good father," cried Borne, laughing, "really told you no untruth. There once existed the custom for all Jewish cattle-dealers to dedicate the first male offspring of their cows to God, as laid down in the Bible,

10 Heinrich Heine, *Ludwig Borne: Recollections of a Revolutionist*, abridged and trans. T.S. Egan (London, 1881), pp. 39–40.

and for that purpose they brought them from all parts here to Frankfurt, where to such dedicated cattle the Jewish burial-ground was allotted for pasture, and where they wandered about to their happy end, and really often bellowed frightfully."[11]

We therefore see that the practice of German Jews, in the communities of Worms and Frankfurt, was to keep the firstling in the cemetery, where it would graze until it became unfit for sacrifice. Three engravings from books by Christians that portray the customs and way of life of the Jews, all from the first half of the eighteenth century, depict burial in a Jewish cemetery: the first (Fig. 1), by J.G. Puchner;[12] the second (Fig. 2), by Jan Luyken;[13] and the third (Fig. 3), by G.P. Nusbiegel.[14] These engravings resemble one other, draw upon each other in terms of style, and actually almost constitute copies of each other.[15] Among their common elements is

11 All the above sources are cited by Brilling, op. cit., p. 16. For Heine's knowledge of Jewish topics, see I. Tabak, *Judaic Lore in Heine: The Heritage of a Poet* (Baltimore, 1948), esp. pp. 125 ff. For his time in Frankfurt, see Tabak, p. 19. Heine was familiar with Schudt's book (see Tabak, p. 47), and he quotes Ludwig Borne a number of times, but does not relate to the issue at hand.

12 Taken from Kirchner, *Judisches Ceremoniel.*

13 Buxtorf, *Synagoga Judaica.*

14 Bodenschatz, *Kirchliche Verfassung der heutigen Juden*, Vol. 4, next to p. 179. See further Brilling, "Sheep and Cattle Firstborn in Frankfurt am Main." Some illustrations are signed "*sculp[sit]*," while others are signed "*invenit [...] et sculpsit*," with "*invenit*" meaning designed, fashioned, painted, while "*sculpsit*" has the meaning of etched, engraved. When only "*sculp*" appears, this may mean an engraving that was executed on the basis of a painting by another artist, but when "*invenit et culpsit*" is used, then this is an entirely original creation by the artist. In this instance, Bodenschatz writes "*G. P. Nusbiegal sculp*," omitting the term "*invenit*," for the original idea was not his. See the important book by A.M. Hind, *An Introduction to a History of Woodcut* (New York, 1963), Vol. 1, p. 26. Cf. Hind, p. 30: "The draughtsman seldom finished his design in detail as he intended it to appear on the copper plate. He left his engraver to translate his more expeditious methods of shading in chalk or wash into the formal convention of line-engraving."

15 The etching in Buxtorf is the reverse of that in Kirchner, but is not an exact copy, although the two works are very similar. See Hind, *An Introduction to a History of Woodcut*, p. 17: "Very exact copies might be made by methods of transfer, but seldom so exact as not to disclose differences in detail, which would rule out the possibility of a cast. Most of the poorer copies are in reverse, the natural result of the easiest method, i.e. of copying an impression directly onto another block." In the engraving reproduced in Bodenschatz we see more artistic freedom. Rubens,

a seemingly marginal detail, namely, the beast that stands next to the fence and grazes on the cemetery grass, precisely as Juspa Schammes described. The cemetery portrayed in these engravings is most likely that of the city of Furth, as can be shown by a comparison with the illustration by Johann Alex Boener from 1705 (Fig. 4) in his series of paintings in the Kurzer Bericht von der alterhum und Freyheiten des freyen Hof-Markts Furth.[16] This cemetery,

> *A Jewish Iconography*, p. 52, nos. 539–567, writes that most of the illustrations in Kirchner are based on Buxtorf, nos. 250–276. (Rubens used the Nuremberg 1734 edition, with reference to the Frankfurt 1728 edition of Buxtorf.) The works by Luykens already appear in the 1702 edition of Buxtorf (entitled *Schole der Juden*). Kirchner's book was printed a number of times within a short period: Nuremberg 1720 (first edition), 1724, 1726, 173[4].

16 The synagogue that appears in the books by Kirchner and Buxtorf also appears in Furth; see the extended discussion on this issue in *Minhagei Yisrael*, Vol. 4, chap. 16. Incidentally, it is noteworthy that the tombstones are erect in the cemetery that is depicted, in accordance with the Ashkenazic practice. This is in contrast with the Sephardic practice of tombstones that lie flat. See H.J. Zimmels, *Ashkenazim and Sephardim* (London, 1958), p. 186, who refers to L. Zunz, *Zur Geschichte und Literatur*[2] (Berlin, 1919), p. 393. See *Or Zarua*, cited in *Haggahot Asheri* on Moed Katan, chap. 3, para. 126. See also P. Ehl, A. Parik, and J. Fiedler, *Old Bohemian and Moravian Jewish Cemeteries*, trans. G.S. Matouskova and Z. Joachimova (Prague, 1991), pp. 14 ff. It should further be noted that the building in the cemetery is covered by an attic, which the sources refer to as a *"Boiden."* See, e.g., *Pinkas Hekhsharim shel Kehilat Pozna (Acta Electorum Communitatis Judaeorum Posnaniensium)*, ed. D. Avron (Jerusalem, 1967), p. 147, para. 779; p. 167, para. 954. The building itself is called *"beit taharah"* (purification chamber). See Greenwald, *Kol Bo al Avelut*, Vol. 1, p. 87, para. 3; M. Hildesheimer, *Pinkas Kehillat Schnaittach (Acta Communitatis Judaeorum Schnaittach)* (Jerusalem, 1992), p. 62, who mentions that a well, the likes of which we see in these illustrations, was dug in the cemetery of Steinach, and a building for the guarding and purification of the corpse was constructed there. Hildesheimer refers to E.M. Fuchs, *Uber der ersten Niederlassungen der Juden in Mittelfranken* (Berlin, 1909), p. 16. The building is the *beit taharah*; of interest here is the observation by Joseph Yuspa Hahn, *Yosif Ometz* (Frankfurt, 1723 [photocopy edn.: Jerusalem, 1965]), p. 93, para. 455:

> > If one actually sees Jewish graves, he recites: "Blessed are You, O Lord our God, King of the universe, who created you justly, sustained you justly, kept you alive justly, and caused you to die justly, and who will revive you justly, and who knows the number of you all, and who will remove the dust from your eyes and revive you. Blessed are You, O Lord, who revives the dead." This is the version [of the blessing]. Even though I have not found it formulated by any *posek*, I nevertheless chose it because it was engraved with an iron and lead quill on a stone designated for this in the *beit taharah* from 1321.

which was established in 1607,[17] had been in use for more than a century when Boener used it as a model for his paintings. We have therefore found

The reference is to the *beit taharah* in Frankfurt am Main. Rabbi Moses Mintz elaborates, in his *Haggahot* (cited in a note in *Yosif Ometz*): "This stone was uprooted from the old *beit taharah*, and currently stands in the new cemetery. I copied it on 24 Heshvan 5597 [= 1737], and I found it, word for word, as written above, but I did not find the year '[5]181 [=1321]' on it." This blessing is based on BT 58b and its parallels. *Dikdukei Soferim ha-Shalem*, Berakhot 58b, p. 166, para. 1, comments: "And I found in the *Rishonim* twenty versions of this blessing." This blessing is being examined by my pupil, Rabbi Yehezkel Lichtenstein, and we therefore will not discuss it at length here (see below, Part II, chap. 7, n. 3). Another type of erect cemetery stone is to be found in Kurdistan.

If rain does not fall after a week of communal prayers, a Torah scroll is taken out and bedecked in a black cover, and the rabbi sprinkles cinders over the Torah scroll and over his own head. At this sight, he and the community burst into tears. After this, they march to the cemetery, to the section where the righteous are buried. At a small distance from the graves is a table-like stone that is called "*kippat sefer Torah*" [the Torah scroll dome]. The Torah scroll is placed on this stone, prayers and *selihot* [penitential prayers] are recited, and they read from the Torah (Deut. 4:5–30, and the Book of Jonah as the *haftarah* — supplemental reading from Prophets). If rain still does not fall, three Torah scrolls are taken to the cemetery, cinders are sprinkled over the heads of the seven elders of the city, they pray, etc.

See E. Brauer, "Rites and Customs in Times of Drought among the Jews of Kurdistan," in *Magnes Anniversary Book*, ed. F.I. Baer et al. (Jerusalem, 1938), pp. 51–52 (Hebrew). The well was both for the bathing of the corpse and for the various types of hand washing in the cemetery (see Schammes, *Wormser Minhagbuch*, Vol. 2, p. 94 n. 45; p. 95 n. 56; see also Trachtenberg, *Jewish Magic and Superstition*, p. 179). See Altshuler, *The Precious Legacy*, p. 158, Ill. 151: the picture of the Prague cemetery ca. 1780, for the use of the well for washing the hands, that is outside the bounds of the cemetery, near the gate; and in the catalogue of the exhibition in Manchester: C.R. Dodwell (ed.), *Jewish Art Treasures from Prague* (London, 1980), end of no. P14, the date 1697 appears above the pump (see Fig. 5).

17 See Hildesheimer, *Schnaittach*, loc. cit., that until then they had used the cemetery in Steinach, because only the major communities had been permitted to maintain a special place for burial. See A. Berliner, *Hayyei ha-Yehudim be-Ashkenaz be-Yemei ha-Beinayim* (*The Life of the Jews in Ashkenaz in the Medieval Period* [= *Aus dem Leben der Juden Deutschlands im Mittelalter* (Berlin, 1937)]) (Warsaw, 1900), p. 68; S.W. Baron, *The Jewish Community: Its History and Structure to the American Revolution*, Vol. 1 (Philadelphia, 1942), pp. 283 ff.; E. Zimmer, "The Kehillah: The Communal Life and Organization of Ashkenazi Jewry," in G. Hirschler, *Ashkenaz: The German Jewish Heritage* (New York, 1988), p. 155; M. Weinberg, *Geschichte der Juden in der Oberplatz*, Vol. 3: *Der Bezirk Rothenberg* (Salzburg, 1909), p. 15;

an additional German community that observed the practice of letting beasts graze in the cemetery.[18]

1. Burial, Kirchner, Nuremberg 1724

B.Z. Ophir (ed.), *Pinkas Hakehillot, Germany — Bavaria* (Jerusalem, 1973), p. 342 (Hebrew) (all with references in Hildesheimer).

18 This was addressed by R.I. Cohen, in his excellent article, "The Visual Image of the Jew and Judaism in Early Modern Europe: From Symbolism to Realism," *Zion* 57 (1992), pp. 329–30 (Hebrew), with a reference (p. 329, end of n. 99) to B. Deneke (ed.), *Siehe der Stein schreit aus der Mauer: Geschichte und Kultur der Juden in Bayern* (Nuremberg, 1988) p. 247. See Cohen, pp. 321 ff., for a general discussion of Boener.

2. Burial, Buxtorf, Frankfurt and Leipzig 1729

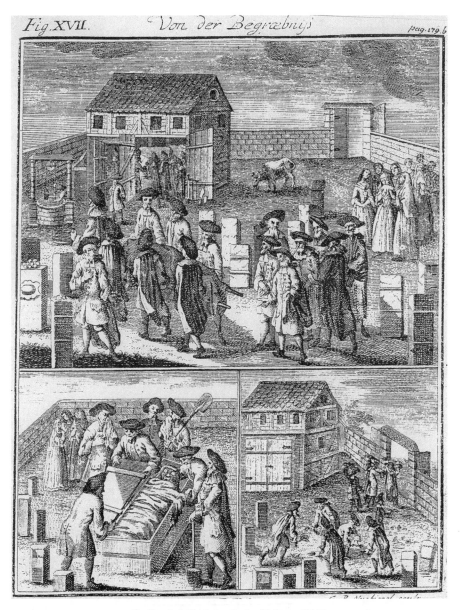

3. Burial, Bodenschatz, Erlang 1748

4. Cemetery, J. A. Boener, 1705

5. Handwashing, Prague 1780

7

OPENING THE COFFIN BEFORE BURIAL

In the preceding chapters we saw a number of illustrations of funerals in which an open coffin lies on the ground, with its cover on the side. This motif, as well, appears in the customs of Worms:[1]

> The ones who perform the purification are the ones who bear the coffin to the graves, for man and woman alike. This is their manner: They bear it until the Neu Pforte [the new gate], where they place it on the ground. They wait a while, until the women also arrive there. Then they resume bearing [it] over the graves into *beit Zur Tamim* [literally, the place of the perfect Rock = God],[2] where they place it on a rock that has been made ready for this.[3] The mourner recites *Ha-Zur Tamim* [a part of the standard funeral service], and at the conclusion of *Ha-Zur Tamim*, they bear [the coffin] to its grave. They place [the deceased] alongside the grave, **and they open his coffin**. The mourners who are obligated to rend [their garment], come and rend for their dead.[4]

1 Schammes, *Wormser Minhagbuch*, Vol. 2, p. 101.
2 See the comments by the editors, p. 92 n. 27, that this is "the place in which they recite *tzidduk ha-din* [the justification of the divine judgment, which begins with the words '*Ha-Zur Tamim*']"; for the Neu Pforte, see Schammes, op. cit., p. 101 n. 21.
3 See above, Part II, chap. 6, n. 16. Cf. Rabbi Juda Loew Kirchheim, *The Customs of Worms Jewry*, ed. I.M. Peles (Jerusalem, 1987), p. 309 (Hebrew).
4 Cf. Schammes, *Wormser Minhagbuch*, Vol. 2, p. 94: "They open his coffin, and they show the dead to the mourner at the time of rending." For this practice cf. Masse, *Persian Beliefs and Customs*, p. 100. The *Minhagbuch* then relates, regarding the rending (p. 101): "For a man, another helps him, and in his hand is **a reversed knife**: the helve opposite the mourner, and the blade in his hand." (In *Minhagbuch*, p. 101 n. 24, the editors refer to Rabbi Jair Hayyim Bacharach, *Mekor Hayyim*, Vol.

A similar portrayal is provided by Gamaliel ben Pedahzur:[5]

> The Corps is set down on one Side of the Grave [...] and the Lid of the Coffin opened on one of the Sides, to see if the Shrouds are tumbled, or if any Part of the Dress wants setting right again,[6] and then a small Quantity of Earth [...] which comes from the Land of Promise, [...] which is Jerusalem [...] they put [...] into a little Linnen Bag under the Head of the Corps.[7] [...] After that, any Relation and Friend is admitted to view the Corps, or to ask Forgiveness [...].

2 [Jerusalem, 1984], p. 321, para. 170, end of subpara. 2, who wrote: "Care is also taken so the knife will not rest with its point facing upwards"). And similarly in Pedahzur, *The Book of Religion, Ceremonies, and Prayers of the Jews*, p. 14: "the Priest or any other Jew, takes a Knife and holds it by the End of the Blade." *Kos Zekhukhit* of the Prague burial society (1713), which is described by Y. Shahar, "'For Drinking and for Rejoicing, for Drinking One's Fill of Love' — Burial Society Cups and Jugs from Bohemia and Moravia," *Hadshot Muzeon Yisrael* (*Israel Museum Bulletin*) 9 (1972), pp. 22–49 (Hebrew), contains an illustration that Shahar (p. 25) describes as follows: "Alongside the youth stands a Jew who gives, with his right hand, a knife for the rending to the one accompanying the dead behind him (**and he holds the knife by its blade**: we clearly see the ring that connects the blade to the helve, the nails in the helve, and the loop at its end)." We, then, have the Worms custom in the *Kos Zekhukhit* from Prague (cf. Trachtenberg, *Jewish Magic and Superstition*, p. 298 n. 5, regarding the common and self-understood belief that the knife is not to be placed with the cutting edge up. See Masse, *Persian Beliefs and Customs*, p. 273: "You should [...] never give a person an open knife nor offer it point foremost [for "the devil will lengthen it"]). As regards the opening of the coffin, this most likely was not observed in Italy in the sixteenth century. A close reading of *Ma'avar Yabbok, Siftei Rananut* 18 (ed. Vilna, 1927, p. 216) reveals that the coffin remained closed during the entire burial procedure.

5 *The Book of Religion, Ceremonies, and Prayers of the Jews*, pp. 12–13.

6 See below, n. 22.

7 The practice of placing earth from the Land of Israel in the grave has its source in *Haggahot Maimuniyyot, Hil. Melakhim* (*Laws of Kings*) 5:4, who cites a passage from the PT (Ketubot 12:4, 35b): "He [Rabbi Eleazar] said to him [Rabbi Bar Karia]: When they came to the Land of Israel, they would take a clod of earth and place it on their coffin, as it is said: 'His land will atone for His people' [Deut. 32:43]." *Haggahot Maimuniyyot* writes on this: "From this we see support for their practice of placing earth from the Land of Israel on the dead, even though the [narrative] in the Palestinian Talmud occurred in the Land of Israel." Rabbi M.M. Honig of Monsey, New York, drew my attention to E. Kupfer, *Teshuvot u-Pesakim me'et Hakhmei Ashkenaz ve-Tzorfat* (*Responsa et Decisiones*) (Jerusalem, 1973), para. 70, pp. 115–16, that quotes a responsum from *Sefer Rav Sherira Gaon* relating to this

This is followed by the rending of the garment, and then (p. 14):

After the Ceremony is over, the Coffin is nailed up, and put into the

practice; but see I.M. Ta-Shma, "The Attitude to *Aliya* to Eretz Israel (Palestine) in Medieval German Jewry," *Shalem* 6 (1992), pp. 317 ff. (Hebrew); I am grateful to Rabbi Honig for his instructive comment. *Sedei Hemed* adds that this provides some support for the practice of placing earth from the Land of Israel on the dead, even if they are buried outside the Land, for they nevertheless profit somewhat (cited in Klein, *Zikhron Shai* 16b, para. 19). It seems that the practice developed of placing the Land of Israel earth under the head of the deceased, in a small bag, similar to the custom described below (n. 22), of placing "a sack full of earth [...] under the head of the deceased"; in this latter practice, however, the earth is taken from the grave. It is explicitly stated by Kirchheim, *The Customs of Worms Jewry*, p. 310, that "the women take the little sack, fill it with **earth from the grave**, and place it under the head of the dead one" (see gloss 3, ad loc.). The reason for this practice is inexplicable, unless it is an erroneous development of the practice to use earth from the Land of Israel. (For the placing of earth under the head of the corpse, see S. Eidelberg, "Holy Earth: The Development of Two Customs," *PAAJR* 59 [1993], pp. 1–7 [Hebrew], for a comprehensive discussion of the topic and the sources.) In any event, it would seem that the placing of the head on a bag of Land of Israel earth was influenced by the custom of placing the head on earth from the grave. It was common in the medieval Christian world to put a bag under the head of the deceased. See Boase, *Death in the Middle Ages*, the illustrations on pp. 60–61, 64, 69, 72, 76–79, 81, 84–85, 94, 95, 123; and Pedahzur, *The Book of Religion, Ceremonies, and Prayers of the Jews*, p. 11, states that people would place "a little Pillow of Bran under the Head"; I have not yet found the source for this. Incidentally, since we have mentioned Pedahzur, the following is a depiction by him of a charm for a family that has lost many of its members (p. 17): "If there happens many Buryings out of one Family, soon after one another, the surviving Relation of the nearest Affinity in the Blood, takes a Padlock, and locks it, when the Coffin is put in the Ground, and then he flings the Lock in the Grave with the Corps, and flings away the Key above Ground, which is to put a Stop to Mortality in the said Family." Although I have not found such a procedure in the Jewish sources, the basic underlying concept appears in various cultures in the world. Cf. Frazer, *The Golden Bough*, Vol. 2: *Taboo and the Perils of the Spirit*[3], p. 309; more relevantly, in Wuttke, *Der deutsche Volksaberglaube der Gegenwart*, p. 468, para. 744; cf. p. 478, para. 762. See also F. Grunberg-Guggenheim, "A Lock in Grave as Means to Stop a Pestilence," *Yeda-'Am* 5, 1–2 (1958), p. 8 (Hebrew), on the burying of a lock together with the deceased, and the casting away of the key, in order to lock against the *mazikim* (destructive agents) and put a stop to plagues. Grunberg-Guggenheim also refers to the work by A. Rappaport, *Schlussel und Schloss* (Vienna, 1937). See also *Treatise Semahot*, ed. Higger, p. 152: "He said to him: We hang the key and writing tablet of the deceased because of the sadness of the soul. When Samuel

Grave, and the nearest of Kin in their Turns, fling three Spades full of Earth over it.

What we see in these engravings, therefore, is the stage preceding the burial, in which the coffin was opened before the rending of the garments, which was the practice in the time of *Maharil* (Rabbi Jacob ben Moses Moellin), since he states in his book of customs[8] that "he would protest to his sons, that they not gaze into the coffin[9] when it was opened to inter the dead, as it was

the Small died, they hung his key and his writing-tablet in his coffin, **because he had no son**" (see the reference by Higger to the sources, n. 39, ad loc.). See what D. Zlotnick wrote about this in his introduction to the translation: *The Tractate "Mourning"* (New Haven and London, 1966), pp. 16–17, in his presentation of the various theories (by Yeivin, Alon, and himself) regarding the source and reason for this custom. The passage from *Semahot* is cited by *Tur, Yoreh Deah* 306, but *Bah* (Rabbi Joel Sirkes) comments: "But now it is not customary to do so, and we prevent anyone who comes to change the [current] practice." The reverse of this process is to be found in Opie and Tatem, *A Dictionary of Superstitions*, p. 92, that in northern England, after the coffin has been lowered into the ground, the nails used to fasten its lid are removed, to facilitate the exit of the soul at the resurrection of the dead. Cf. Puckle, *Funeral Customs: Their Origin and Development*, p. 39, for the same practice in Ireland.

8 *The Book of Maharil: Customs by Rabbi Yaacov Mulin*, p. 606.

9 *Matamim*, p. 14, paras. 3–4, writes: "The reason why the face of the deceased is covered as soon as the soul departs is to prevent the accusers from gazing at his face and forehead, lest they increase his suffering (*Shibbolei ha-Leket*)." Another reason why a person should not look at the face of the dead is so that he would not be disgraced in the eyes of the beholder (*Ma'avar Yabbok*). See BT Horayot 13b, that looking at the face of a dead person is one of the ten things that adversely affects one's study. *Mishnah Berurah* 2:2 asserts that this causes one to forget his studies; and similarly in *Peri Megadim, Eshel Avraham* 2:1; *Peri Hadash, Likkutim*, beginning of para. 12. *Huppat Eliyahu Rabbah, Sha'ar* 2, writes that looking at the face of a corpse causes one's eyesight to dim; see Lerner, *Shmiras Haguf Vihanefesh*, para. 240, p. 699 n. 1; para. 237, p. 691 n. 7; and Lerner's introduction, p. 99.

This is the place to mention the matter of placing earth on the eyes of the corpse. See *Zohar*, 1, 226a, on the verse "and Joseph's hand shall close your eyes" (Gen. 46:4): "Certainly Joseph, for he was the firstborn [in intent] [...] 'His hand shall close your eyes' — to what does this relate? Rav Jesse said, As a mark of honor for Joseph. [...] I have seen in the chapter of Rav Jesse the Elder: Regarding worldly customs, if a person has a son, when he dies the son should put earth on his eyes at the time of his burial, for this is a mark of respect for him, being a sign that the world is now concealed from him." See Kasher, *Torah Shelemah*, Vol. 7 (*Va-Yigash*), p. 1675, para. 37, for the closing of the eyes of the dead. See *Shakh* (Rabbi Shabbetai

instituted." A variant reading by Spitzer states: "When they opened it to see if he is lying [i.e. that he was actually dead] [...] and to arrange the shrouds properly."[10] This procedure was also followed in seventeenth-century Italy, for as Rabbi Judah Aryeh (Leone) Modena relates, in his detailed description of the burial ceremony:[11]

> When they arrive at the cemetery, they place the coffin on the ground. If the dead person was an important person, a rabbi stands and delivers a eulogy in praise of the deceased. After this, they recite the supplicatory prayer that begins with "The Rock! His deeds are perfect, yea, all His ways are just" [Ha-Tzur Tamim — Deut. 32:4] that is called tzidduk ha-din [the justification of the Divine judgment]. They then place a shroud with earth under the head of the deceased. They **close the coffin** and bear it to the grave that has been dug according to his measure. It is customary for every person to prepare a grave for himself next to the graves of his forefathers and relatives.[12]

It seems that it was the fashion of some to lower the coffin into the grave while open, and possibly to place earth on the face of the deceased, and only then to close the coffin with its lid, as can be seen from one of a series of fifteen illustrations executed for the Prague burial society ca. 1780. In this picture we see the members of the burial society lowering the coffin on ropes into the grave. One of them holds the coffin lid, ready to lower it and cover the coffin.[13] Our suggestion is corroborated by the picture that appears in the

ben Meir ha-Kohen), *Yoreh Deah* 362:1, that in our time clay is placed on the deceased's mouth and eyes, in place of earth. Similarly in Roman times, earth was thrown upon the face of the dead (Cicero, *De legibus* 22:57).

10 See Pedahzur, above; see also n. 7, above.

11 *Historia de'riti Ebraice* (Paris, 1637; translation based on the Hebrew translation by S. Reuven [Vienna, 1827], in which this is Part 5, chaps. 6–7).

12 For the burial ceremonies in Italy in the Renaissance period, and their symbolism, see R. Bonfil, *Jewish Life in Renaissance Italy* (Berkeley, Los Angeles, and London, 1994), chap. 11, pp. 265–84.

13 See Fig. 1. Cf. Rabbi Moses Isserles, *Haggahot*, p. 95; and similarly in *Darkhei Moshe, Yoreh Deah* 359. See ad loc., n. 41, by the editor of *Darkei Moshe (Maharil)*, citing *Yosif Ometz*, p. 327, who wrote: "Extreme care is required, to part from the women when they go and return from the dead. [...] I heard that in the holy community of Worms people are accustomed to avert their faces, toward the side of the wall, when the women come." Rabbi Mendlen Rothschild, the head of the Worms rabbinical court, enacted that women are not to go at all to the grave. See

book by Medici,[14] where we see how two members of the burial society use ropes to lower the open coffin into the grave. The picture above it shows the

the gloss by Rabbi Sinai Luantz on Rabbi Juda Loew Kirchheim, *The Customs of Worms Jewry*, p. 310, gloss 3, that Rabbi Menahem Mendlen Rothschild enacted that women were not to go to the grave "to fill the little bags" with earth, and only the beadle was to take earth from the soil of the grave to put in a single vessel. He would then go to the women, who would take the earth, put it in their little sacks, and give them back to this beadle. He would give this to the members of the charitable society, while the women would immediately leave the cemetery, and they did not need to hear the *Kaddish*, so that men and women would not mingle together. For the separation of men from women during the funeral, see J.R. Marcus, "The Triesch *Hebre Kaddisha*, 1687–1828," *HUCA* 19 (1945–46), pp. 180–81, that the role of the *shammash* was to separate between them, even going so far as to throw stones to this end. Because of the intriguing nature of this practice, we cite Marcus' description in its entirety:

> One of the duties of the *shammash* in 1687 was to put an end to the "danger" (*sakkanah*) of men and women mixing together at the time when the dead were carried to the cemetery and when the people returned home after the burial. The beadle was enjoined to keep the two groups separate, to walk between them, to use every effort to keep them apart, and, if necessary, in order to accomplish this, to throw stones at the offending parties. This physical meeting of men and women was looked upon as something immoral, and a great danger which might cost one his life. Four years later, in 1692, the Prague fraternity had to cope with the same problem. To avoid the danger of men and women meeting and associating together, some of the pious of the Prague society even refused to participate in the burial. The women, therefore, were warned to keep their distance from the men. If they refused to heed the warning, special officers, who had been appointed for this purpose, were commissioned to exact pledges of good conduct from them, to tear off their cloaks and to give them to the poor, and finally the executives were even instructed to buy two sprinklers and to douse the people the (women?) who did not know their place! (His reference is to: Prague, 1692, para. 25, in *Judische Centralblatt* 8 (1889), pp. 51–52; cf. also *MGWJ* 21 [1930], p. 224.)

These cautionary measures trace their origin to authoritative halakhic works: *Ha-Pardes* 19b (ed. H. J. Ehrenreich [Budapest, 1924], p. 72) states:

> It is forbidden for women to mingle among men, either in a meal, dancing, or in any matter, rather, the women by themselves, and the men by themselves. We learn this from a *kal ve-homer* [a minori ad majus inference]: it is written, regarding the period of mourning: "The House of Israel shall mourn [this should read: 'The land shall mourn'], each family by itself: the family of the House of David by themselves, and their womenfolk by themselves" [Zech. 12:12] — banquet and rejoicing, certainly so, because the Evil Urge entices them. (Cf. BT Sukkah 52a; PT Sukkah 5:55b.)

exposed face of the corpse, while the explanation[15] reads: "*Das Schweitstuch uber das Geschicht*," that is, the face is covered. Of interest in this context is the description by the English authors Bonar and Murray[16] of a funeral in Lemberg:

> Arriving at a small portico or covered wall in the graveyard, they set down the bier, and uncovered the face of the dead. All the relations gathered round, and bending over the corpse, till their lips almost touched the lips of the deceased, entreated her to forgive them if they injured her[17] in any way.[18] After this they proceeded to the grave, and the body alone was lowered down into it, with the face uncovered.

This might possibly be connected with the practice of several German communities to delay the funeral for several hours after the death, in the event that the departed was actually still alive.[19] As this was expressed in *Yosif Ometz* (p. 327):

> If it is necessary to leave him overnight for his honor, this is permitted. In any event, he is not to be taken out close to the death, perhaps there still is the spirit of life in him, as happened several times. It has been reported that it happened in our time, that after the funeral the

This has its source in *Sefer Ma'asim le-Benei Yisrael* (see B.M. Levin, "*Sefer Ma'asim le-Benei Yisrael*," *Tarbiz* 1,1 [1930], p. 82 [Hebrew]):

> just as, regarding dancing, men and women may not dance together, but rather, the men by themselves and the women by themselves, [so, too,] regarding the time of mourning, when people weep with lamentation and crying, it is written, "The land shall mourn, each family by itself" — then decidedly during time of rejoicing and banquet, when they laugh and the Evil Urge is present, they certainly should weep, these by themselves, and these by themselves, so that their [Evil] Urge will not contemplate transgression, in the merriment of rejoicing.

14 Medici, *Riti e Costume degli Ebrei Confutati*, Ill. VIII, p. 153 (cf. Fig. 2 by Christiani, Leipzig 1705).

15 P. 153 (cf. Fig. 7).

16 A.A. Bonar and R.M. MacCheyne, *Narrative of a Mission of Inquiry to the Jews from the Church of Scotland in 1839* (Philadelphia, 1844), pp. 465 ff. Cited by A. Cohen, *An Anglo-Jewish Scrapbook, 1600–1840: The Jew through English Eyes* (London, 1943), p. 296. Cf. the passage from Pedahzur, above.

17 See above, chap. 4.

18 See below, n. 22.

19 See above, chap. 3, n. 14.

buried one recovered; because the grave had to be evacuated due to an overflowing river, they then found the coffin full of inscriptions in blood, with the head full of wounds from the grief of the interred. Recently, a regulation was enacted that the deceased is not to be removed from the house until three hours have passed before his funeral.

And in Worms:[20]

Rabbi [Samson] ordered, with the agreement of the *parnasim* [community leaders], that from this day forth no dead person is to be purified until two hours after his death.[21]

Accordingly, the main reason for the opening of the coffin and revealing the face of the deceased might have been to ensure that the dead person had in fact expired.[22]

---

20 Cf. the glosses in Kirchheim, *The Customs of Worms Jewry*, p. 91.

21 See the editor's gloss, Kirchheim, loc. cit., n. 24.

22 I received the following valuable comment from the scholar Tuvia Preschel regarding the reason for revealing the face of the dead before the funeral: Rabbi Judah, the son of *Rosh* (Rabbeinu Asher), relates in his testament (I. Abrams [ed.], *Hebrew Ethical Wills* [Philadelphia, 1926], Vol. 2, pp. 186–87), concerning the burial of his father: "Later (during the middle days of Tabernacles) my grandfather died and great honor was shown unto him at his death, people from neighboring places attending his funeral. Now it is the **practice** [emphasis added — D. S.] in Germany to set the coffin on a stone appointed for the purpose near the cemetery [cf. *Minhagei Yisrael*, Vol. 6, p. 97 n. 25; p. 98], and to open it to see whether the body has been dislocated by the jolting of the coffin." It has come to my attention that it is the practice of Christians in Russia to open the coffin at the time of the funeral, and relatives take their leave of the deceased with a kiss, and so forth. (For kissing the dead, see Kasher, *Torah Shelemah*, Vol. 2, p. 923, para. 26.) See Kosman, "Kissing the Dead — Transformation of a Custom," and the instructive comments on Kosman's article by E. Horowitz, "On Kissing the Dead in the Mediterranean World," *Tarbiz* 67 (1998), pp. 131–34 (Hebrew). This practice might be related to what we find in *Semahot* 8:1 (ed. Higger, pp. 148–49): "They go forth to the cemetery and examine the dead within thirty days, and we do not fear [that this is considered] Amorite practices. It once happened that one was examined after thirty days, and he lived for twenty-five years and then died. And another begat five children and then died." A variant text reads "three days" instead of "thirty days." See the textual variants in Higger; and in Zlotnick, *The Tractate "Mourning"*, pp. 11–12; see also below, the Appendix to chap. 15. See Rabbi Eliezer ben Joel ha-Levi of Bonn (*Ravyah*), *Ravyah*, Vol. 3, p. 565, who cites *Semahot* (= *Avel Rabbati*, loc. cit.) with the version

The pictures reproduced by Buxtorf and by Kirchner also show the preceding stage (since they usually included several, chronologically

of "three days" (see *Ravyah*, loc. cit., n. 3), adding that "it was the custom to open the grave of the deceased on the third day." Aptowitzer (n. 6) cites *Ha-Perishah, Yoreh Deah* 394: "This was specifically in their time, when the dead were interred in loculi [*kukhin*], and it was possible to uncover the corpse and see it." We perhaps should add to this what is taught by *Sefer Hasidim*, para. 451 (ed. Margaliot, pp. 410–11): "When there is plague in the city, those corpses are searched, for perhaps in some instances the corpse swallowed the shroud, which is dangerous [i.e. for others]." See Margaliot's glosses ad loc.; cf. the above passage from Pedahzur, *The Book of Religion, Ceremonies, and Prayers of the Jews*. The matter of the swallowing of the shroud is to be related to what Grimm records (*Teutonic Mythology*, Vol. 4, p. 1799, no. 551, from Worms and its environs): "If a garment or linen come before a dead man's mouth, one of the family will die." And additionally, op. cit., p. 1806, no. 709: "They put turf or a little board under the dead man's chin, that he may not catch the shroud between his teeth, and draw his relations after him." That is, the danger entailed in the swallowing of *ha-beged* [literally, the garment; translated as "shroud"] by the deceased is that his relatives also will die. Cf. Grimm, op. cit., p. 1811, no. 828. A similar superstition is held by the Persians: see Masse, *Persian Beliefs and Customs*, p. 100: "If the shroud falls into the mouth of the deceased, this is an extremely bad omen."

The spread of this belief is intriguing, for I found in Hyatt, *Folk-Lore from Adams County, Illinois*, no. 10322, p. 592: "If you bury anyone with a veil over their face and the veil gets in their mouth, they will call the family away." It then is related that some forty years previously (that is, ca. 1895) the aunt of the narrator's mother was buried with a handkerchief over her mouth, and members of the family began to die one after the other, until five had died. Then they examined the mother's aunt, and found the handkerchief stuck in her mouth. They removed the handkerchief, and no more family members died. The population of the region was of German, Dutch, and French descent (see Hyatt, Preface).

It seems, according to Kirchner, *Judisches Ceremoniel*, p. 218 n. 1, that when the corpse is already lying in the grave, in an open coffin, a sack with earth is placed under his head. See *Be'er Hetev, Yoreh Deah* 362:1. This procedure also appears in the above passage from Pedahzur. See Schammes, *Wormser Minhagbuch*, Vol. 2, p. 94: "Afterward they bear the dead to his grave. The women fill a sack with earth, and the men take it from them and place it under the head of the deceased [...] and they arrange the corpse in the coffin as is customary." See the editor's n. 51. It is not clear from the *Minhagbuch* when this was done, before or after the deceased was laid in the grave (see op. cit., n. 50). Cf. Kirchheim, *The Customs of Worms Jewry*, p. 310; see above, n. 7. Kirchheim continues: "They throw earth, both men and women, on the grave of the deceased **at least three times**, and I cast seven times, corresponding to the seven [days of the mourning week], thus I received

consecutive, stages within a single illustration), namely, that of the funeral procession, in which the bier is carried on the shoulders[23] of men, with

[this] from the early ones." This also appears in the description by Pedahzur (above; see chap. 3, n. 11). Cf. Schammes, *Wormser Minhagbuch*, Vol. 2, pp. 98–99: "The practice has already spread of the mourner being the first to cast earth on the coffin, followed by all the rest of the people, first the women and then the men. The woman takes a handful **three times**, the man with a spade **three times**, and then they go." An editor's note (n. 9) refers to the "three times": "and similarly in *Darkei Noam* (Gottlieb), 276:8" (Rabbi Menaham Gottlieb, *Darkei Noam* [Hanover, 1896–98]). To this we may add Kirchner, *Judisches Ceremoniel*, p. 218. And, here, we find in Grimm, *Teutonic Mythology*, Vol. 4, p. 1805, no. 699 (from the Ansbach area): "It furthers the dead man's rest if every one that stands round the grave throws **three clods** in"; cf. Wuttke, *Der deutsche Volksaberglaube der Gegenwart*, p. 468. And among the Romans, if anyone found an unburied body (the equivalent of the Jewish *met mitzvah* — a corpse of unknown identity, whose burial is incumbent upon all), he was required to cast dirt upon it three times (Horace, *Odes* 1:28; Quintilian, *Declamationes* 5:6; Petronius 114; Smith, Wayte, and Marindin, *Dictionary of Greek and Roman Antiquities*, Vol. 1, p. 889b). I have not yet determined the direction of this cross-cultural influence; see below, chap. 16, n. 5. As regards the throwing seven times, see *Minhagei Yisrael*, Vol. 1, pp. 217–21. The casting of earth a number of times also is practiced in Morocco: see Westermarck, *Ritual and Belief in Morocco*, Vol. 2, p. 459: "There (Tangier) some persons acquire merit [...] by throwing three handfuls of earth in the grave." See also op. cit., p. 516: "Relatives and friends throw three handfuls of earth into the grave before it is filled." An interesting comparison is provided by Puckle, *Funeral Customs: Their Origin and Development*, p. 162: "[...] the Roman custom of thus covering a body found unburied with at least three handfuls of earth." Incidentally, we learn from Westermarck (pp. 458–59) that care was taken in Morocco that the number of brick slabs covering the corpse in the grave would be odd, such as three, five, or seven, even if four would have sufficed. E.g., for the small body of a child, they would add one more slab. According to the superstition maintained by the tribes in Morocco, if the number was even, an additional death would occur. This, then, is the same fear of even numbers with which we are familiar from the Talmud (BT Pesahim 110b). This perhaps is how we are to understand the following passage in A. Ben-Yaacob, *Babylonian Jewish Customs*, Vol. 2: *The Life-Cycle in Babylonian Jewish Customs from Birth to Burial* (Jerusalem, 1993), p. 316, para. 9 (Hebrew): "According to a popular belief, one is not to visit the house of a mourner twice, but rather once or three or more times. If a person finds himself compelled to visit the mourner's house a second time, he is to go out into the street for a few minutes, and then to reenter, the third time; only after this can he go home and return to visit the house of that mourner as he pleases." Regarding the fear of even numbers, see Lerner, *Shmiras Haguf Vihanefesh*, Vol. 1, para. 28, pp. 89–93.

the women following behind. In the order followed in Worms:[24] in funeral processions, the men go first, and then the women.[25] When the bier is being

The illustrations in the books by Buxtorf and by Kirchner also bear comparison with the pictures depicting the burial of Jesus, as regards the shape of the grave, the covering of the face (see above, n. 4), and the like. See, e.g., the woodcut by Stephen Arndes from the *Lubecker Bible* (Lubeck, 1494); see W. Warringer, *Die altdeutsche Buchillustration* (Munich, 1921), p. 111, Ill. 68 (for the *Lubecker Bible*, see Hind, *An Introduction to a History of Woodcut*, pp. 364–67. See also R.P. Lamy, *Introduction à l'Ecriture sainte* [Leon, 1699; translation from the Latin], next to p. 20a: a corpse wrapped in shrouds in a unique fashion).

23 See Maimonides, *Mishneh Torah, Hil. Avelut* (*Laws of Mourning*) 4:2: "The dead one is borne on the shoulders to the cemetery." *Kessef Mishneh* writes regarding this: "He spoke of the [usual] way of the world. If, however, they desire to carry him on their hands, they may do so." *Kol Bo, Hil. Avelut*, para. 114 (85d) (*Orhot Hayyim*, Vol. 2, p. 571), writes: "The mourner and the other relatives take him on their shoulders." Rabbi Jacob ben Jehuda Hazan of London, *The Etz Hayyim*, ed. I. Brodie (Jerusalem, 1962), Vol. 1, p. 390: "They bear him on their shoulders to the cemetery"; and similarly in Pedahzur, *The Book of Religion, Ceremonies, and Prayers of the Jews*, p. 12; Aaron Berechiah ben Moses of Modena, *Ma'avar Yabbok*, "*Siftei Rananut*," chap. 15, fol. 107b; "*Imrei Noam*," chap. 28, fol. 40a. See Alfayah, *Kuntres ha-Yehieli*, Vol. 2, para. 35, fol. 59a. Before this, *Kol Bo* (*Hil. Avelut*, 73) wrote: "It is a positive commandment by their [i.e. the rabbis'] words to engage in all the needs of the burial, to bring out the deceased, to bear him on the shoulder, to walk before him, etc." A question was raised on the *Kol Bo* by Rabbi Shemtob Gaguine, *Keter Shem Tov* (Kaiden, 1934), p. 664, as follows: "I do not know where the rabbi of the *Kol Bo* found [that it is] a positive commandment to bear the dead on the shoulder," and cited the statement by *Kessef Mishneh*. It would seem, however, that *Kol Bo* did not mean that it is the bearing the dead on the shoulders that is a rabbinic positive commandment, but, rather, the occupation with the burial of the dead, in all its details, is such a rabbinic obligation. The practice described by the author of *Keter Shem Tov* himself (p. 863) is to bear the corpse on the shoulders, as in the woodcut in the *Frankfurt Minhagim Book* (Frankfurt, 1708) (in which the bier is covered by a black cloth[?]); in M. Hovav, *Bendicion Despues de Comer* [= *Birkat ha-Mazon*, Amsterdam 1723] (Jerusalem, 1979), p. 81; and in an illustration in a late fourteenth-century manuscript from Spain: MS. A, Hungarian Academy of Sciences, Budapest, fol. lv, 433 bottom, which is reproduced in T. and M. Metzger, *Jewish Life in the Middle Ages: Illuminated Manuscripts of the Thirteenth to the Sixteenth Centuries* (New York, 1982), p. 83, Ill. no. 116. Incidentally, we see there that the grave is prepared only when the coffin is brought, and not before (see below, chap. 8, n. 3). See also Metzger, p. 79, Ill. no. 109, from a late fifteenth-century Italian manuscript: MS. Garret 26, fol. 57v, Princeton University Library. This was also customary among Christians in the medieval period; see Boase, *Death in the*

carried, it is covered by a black shroud, similar to the practice in Ashkenaz of covering the corpse itself with a black sheet.[26]

Middle Ages, pp. 84–85, Ill. no. 70: "Stone funerial monument of Philippe formerly in the Abbey of Citeaux, Cot-d'Or, Pot Paris, Louvre, c. 1493." See also Altshuler, *The Precious Legacy*, p. 161, Ill. no. 155, from Prague and Mikulov 1724/5; p. 225, no. 162, the cover of a burial society cup, with a statuette of four people bearing on their shoulders the bier, on which lies the deceased (this demonstrates external stylistic influences, but this is not the place for a discussion of this point). The dead, however, were not always borne on the shoulders (as is attested by the picture in Bodenschatz, *Kirchliche Verfassung der heutigen Juden* (our Fig. 3), but below, in the pallbearers' hands, in contrast with Figs. 4–11. As Bodenschatz writes (p. 172): "Sie gehen namlich mit dem Todten, welcher auf der einem Bret liegt [...] von etlichen Juden, nicht auf der Achsel, wie unsere Zeichen, sondern ganz niedrig in den handen getragen wird, auf den Begrabnissorten" (translation: they go with the corpse lying on a board. [...] Among some Jews, not on the shoulders, as it appears in our illustration, but held rather low, in the hands). In the picture, however, we see that they carry the deceased held low, in their hands, and not on their shoulders, in a glaring inconsistency between the text and the illustration itself.

There might possibly have been different customs for the bearing of a coffin and for the carrying of a bier, that even in a locality where the coffin was borne on the shoulders, the bier was held below, in the hands, but this is not necessarily so, nor was this always the case. See, e.g., the depiction of a funeral in Tiberias from J.S. Buckingham, *Travels in Palestine*[2] (London, 1822), Vol. 2, p. 371 (cited in Cohen, *An Anglo-Jewish Scrapbook*, pp. 294–95): "The corpse followed wrapped in linen, without a coffin, and slung on cords between two poles borne on men's shoulders, with its feet foremost"; this matter is deserving of further study.

24 Schammes, *Wormser Minhagbuch*, Vol. 2, p. 93, in the glosses.

25 See Altshuler, *The Precious Legacy*, p. 157, no. 149 (Altshuler, catalogue no. 188, p. 259). The description given there is "Lowering the Body into the Grave," thereby implying that the corpse was not in a coffin. If so, then the board held by the man standing there is not a cover for the coffin, but for the grave itself, over which the earth is placed. It does not seem, however, that the dead were buried there without a coffin at all. In Ills. 145 (p. 156) and 147 (p. 157) in Altshuler (our Figs. 4 and 5), the corpse is carried on a board, and not on the bier in Ill. 148 (see our Fig. 7). Is this the board in Ill. 144 (p. 156; our Fig. 12), even though it does not appear to be identical with that in Ill. 147 in Altshuler? When the deceased is laid down for the eulogy, it seems that the board is placed over the bier (Altshuler: no. 146, p. 156, cf. our Fig. 13). This question requires further examination, and I hope to clarify this matter elsewhere. See also Dodwell, *Jewish Art Treasures from Prague*, at the end of the descriptions for Ills. P6–P14.

It should also be noted that in Altshuler, Ill. 141 (p. 157), we see women sewing the shrouds. And similarly in Schammes, *Wormser Minhagbuch*, Vol. 2, p. 91: "The

APPENDIX

Due to the importance of Avraham Steinberg's article for the topic of examining the coffin on the thirtieth day, we are citing a portion of his essay:[1]

women come and sew shrouds; at times they sew them in the death chamber, and at times in a room facing the Women's Section [in the synagogue], wherever the women desire (see n. 17 ad loc.). In our picture, they are engaged in this activity outdoors, next to the graveyard. Cf. Kirchner, *Judisches Ceremoniel*, p. 217.

26 Schammes, *Wormser Minhagbuch*, Vol. 2, p. 90 n. 13. Cf. Bodenschatz, *Kirchliche Verfassung der heutigen Juden*, Vol. 3, p. 172: "Sie gehen namlich mit den Todten, welcher auf einen Bret liegt, und einem schwarzen Tuch zugedekt." The black shroud appears in the lower part of the frontispiece illustration of the ledger of the Janoshaza burial society (see our Figs. 6, 7). In this picture the deceased is not in a coffin, but lies on a bier. See the discussion of this in Tykocinski, *Gesher ha-Hayyim*, Vol. 2, chap. 7, pp. 82–88; *Kuntres ha-Yehieli*, chaps. 7–8, fol. 13b–18b; chap. 11, fol. 24a–29b. This picture is reproduced in I. Benoschofsky and A. Scheiber, *The Jewish Museum of Budapest*, trans. J.W. Weisenberg (Budapest, 1987[?]), pp. 214–15; and on a drinking cup of the burial society in Mikulov, Moravia, from 1836. See Altshuler, *The Precious Legacy*, p. 159 (our Fig. 8); see Shahar, "For Drinking and for Rejoicing, for Drinking One's Fill of Love," Ills. 1a, 2b, 5c, 6, 10b, 11b. See the painting by H.G. Burgers (mid-nineteenth century) in the Rijksmuseum in Amsterdam (see *Memorboek: plateratlas van het leven der joden in Nederland van der middeleeuwen tot 1940 door Mozes Heiman Gans* [Baarn, 1971], p. 401). See the illustration by Giovanni della Piane (1650–79), a copper etching executed in Venice in the seventeenth century that depicts the funeral of the deceased and his transferal to a gondola in a canal. The coffin is draped with a black covering(?). (See V.B. Mann [ed.], *I TAL YA'*: Isola della rugiada divina, Duemila anni di arte e vita ebraica in Italia [Milan, 1990], pp. 188–89 [no. 75].) The draping of the coffin with a black shroud was also a medieval Christian practice (see the example in Gies, *Life in a Medieval Village*, p. 127 [Fig. 11]), although the coffin was not always covered. See Leusden, *Philologus Hebraeo-Mixtus*, Ill. 9; see, e.g., the illustration from Mainz (1710), in P. Arnsberg, *Die judischen Gemeinden in Hessen* (Darmstadt, 1973), p. 136 (Fig. 10). A precise examination of the material in these drawings will be extremely instructive concerning the types of biers, caskets, and coffins in use in different periods and by various communities. See, e.g., Fig. 2 (from Bodenschatz, *Kirchliche Verfassung der heutigen Juden*, Fig. 17, opposite p. 179); and in *Memorboek*, p. 106 (bottom right), the painting by Romeyn de Hooghe (1645–1708) from the late seventeenth century (who also executed additional paintings of the Sephardic cemetery in Amsterdam; see the recent work: E.R. Costello and U. Macias, *The Jews of Europe* [New York, 1994],

An extensive controversy regarding this issue arose in the eighteenth century with immediate implications for the burial of the deceased. In 1772 the Duke of Mecklenburg issued a decree forbidding speedy and premature burial, with the requirement of a three-day interval between the clinical determination of death and the interment. The distinguishing marks of death that were required were the decomposition of the flesh and the appearance of discoloration caused by death. The goal of this edict was to prevent the burial of people who were still alive. The ruling aroused heated opposition among the rabbis, who regarded this as an infringement upon the laws of the Jewish religion, since

p. 57); the frontispiece, *Takanot de-Hevrah Kadisha Gemilut Hasadim de-K[ehilah] K[edoshah] Ashkenazim be-Amsterdam* (Regulations of the *Gemilut Hasadim* Burial Society of the Ashkenazic Community in Amsterdam), 1776 (Fig. 14); *Ascamoth da Sta. Irmandade Hesed veEmeth* (Amsterdam, 1748); *Memorboek*, p. 187 (Fig. 15); and the well-known painting by Bernard Picart, Amsterdam 1723, in *Memorboek*, p. 129 (Fig. 16). Incidentally, ship sails can be seen in the background, since the Sephardic cemetery in Amsterdam (Ouderkerk) was located close to the Amstel River (see the drawing by Romeyn de Hooghe, *Memorboek*, p. 126. For a discussion of seventeenth-century representations of this cemetery, see, most recently, M. Zell, *Reframing Rembrandt: Jews and the Christian Image in Seventeenth-Century Amsterdam* (Berkeley, Los Angeles, and London, 2002), pp. 34–40, 206–207. (For the history of the Ouderkerk cemetery, see the booklet by L.A. Vega, *Het Beth Haim Ouderkerk* [Assen, 1979], esp. pp. 13 ff. This cemetery was established in 1614, initially in a small area, with additional lands added over the course of time. Bodies that had been buried in the cemetery in Groet were reinterred in Ouderkerk on the closure of the former in 1634 [Vega, op. cit., p. 15].) In the later drawing by Francisco Novelli, however, which appeared in *Racolto deiriti ... di tutti populi del mondo ...* (Venice, 1789), and in the etching by A. Barratti, the sails have vanished. See the last illustration in *Bilder aus dem Leben der Juden in Venedig ausgangs des XVIII Jahrhunderts* (Berlin, 1927). (For the dwarf in the drawing by Novelli, cf. the etching by Giovanni della Piane, depicting the transport of the corpse by gondola to the Venetian cemetery on the island of San Nicolo' di Lido [ca. 1784]. See the catalogue: V. Mann [ed.], *Gardens and Ghettos: The Art of Jewish Life in Italy* [Berkeley, Los Angeles, and London, 1989], pp. 18, 259 n. 1 [no. 89]. My thanks to Prof. Shalom Sabar for drawing my attention to this drawing.) For the bearing of the corpse on a bier of two wooden poles connected by iron locks, in the shape of a ladder, see Gaguine, *Keter Shem Tov*, pp. 663–64, para. 782. A similar model was used by Christians in the medieval period; see Ill. 23, Walters Art Gallery, *Psalter and Book of Hours*, Ms. 102 f. 76v–77, reproduced in Gies, *Life in a Medieval Village*, p. 127.

the halakhah mandates the burial of the deceased as soon as possible after the moment of death, without any unnecessary delay. Moses Mendelssohn (1729–1786) was among the supporters of the order by the Duke, and published a justification of the edict on halakhic grounds, albeit anonymously.[2] Rabbi Jacob Emden (1697–1776) wrote an important epistle to Mendelssohn on 2 Tammuz 5532 [1772],[3] that reflected the rabbinic opinion of his time, in which he rejected all of Mendelssohn's proofs justifying the edict. Rabbi Judah Leib Margolioth[4] also dismissed the reasons for delaying the determination of the time of death and the burial of the corpse. [...]

During this period many states included in their criminal statutes the prohibition of burying the deceased on the day of his death, and this decree was slowly accepted by the Jews as well.

The issue reawakened during the time of Rabbi Moses Sofer (1762–1839), who wrote:[5] "It seems to me that since in the state of the emperor they became accustomed to delay [burial] by order of the king and his mighty ones, this reason was forgotten, until it was regarded as Torah law." He consequently reexamined the halakhic principles for determining the time of death, rejected all of Mendelssohn's proofs, and ruled that the deceased must be buried close to the time of his clinical death. Sofer vigorously defended this ruling, and wrote: "Accordingly, this is the rule regarding all instances of death, that this is the accepted standard that we possess since the congregation of the Lord became a holy people, and even if all the winds in the world will blow their mightiest, they shall not move us from the place of our holy Torah."

1   A. Steinberg, "The Determination of the Time of Death — Part 1: Historical, Philosophical, and Medical Aspects"; *idem*, "Part 2: Halakhic Aspects," in *Sefer Assia*, ed. A. Steinberg (Jerusalem, 1982), pp. 393–94, 402, 411–14 (Hebrew).
2   *Ha-Me'assef*, Adar (February–March) 1785, reprinted in *Bikkurei ha-Ittim*, 1823, p. 82; in 1797 Isaac Euchel, the editor of *He-Me'assef*, published a booklet in German, in Hebrew transliteration: *Is Delaying the Burial of the Dead Truly Forbidden by the Laws of Israel?* containing a summary of the opinions after Mendelssohn.
3   *Bikkurei ha-Ittim*, 1824, pp. 229–32.
4   Published in Naphtali Hertz Schlezinger, *She'eilat Hakham* (Frankfurt on the Oder, 1797), p. 20.
5   *She'eilot u-Teshuvot Hatam Sofer, Yoreh Deah* 335 (this was written in 1837).

An additional passage that seemingly relates to the time of death, and that constituted a basis for the historical debate concerning the postponing of burial, is the halakhah in Tractate *Semahot*:[6] "They go forth to the cemetery and examine the dead within three days,[7] and we do not fear [that this is considered] Amorite practices. It once happened that one was examined after thirty days, and he lived for twenty-five years and then died. And another begat five children and then died."[8] This was Mendelssohn's second proof that the halakhah mandates delaying the burial for three days, until the appearance of discoloration, and we are not to hastily engage in burial immediately following the appearance of the classical signs of death.[9] This argument was

---

6 *Semahot* 8:1.

7 The *Prishah* on *Tur, Yoreh Deah* 394 writes that specifically in their time, when the deceased were buried in loculi, it was permitted to examine the dead within three days; now, however, when it is the practice to bury in the earth, such examinations are not conducted. Incidentally, this matter is mentioned in a disagreement between Mendelssohn and Rabbi Jacob Emden. Mendelssohn, who insisted upon postponing the burial for three days, proposed the erection of a sort of artificial cave next to the synagogue, where the dead would be purified and undergo examination during the three days, to be followed by the burial. Emden vigorously rejected this suggestion, and wrote: "Do not even think of this, because none of the great ones throughout the generations even mentioned it."

8 The reading in *Tur, Yoreh Deah* 394 is: "It once happened that one was examined after thirty days, and he lived for twenty-five years and begat five children and then died." In other words, *Tur* omits the word "another," thus implying that this depicts a single incident. According to the above reading, on the other hand, there were two cases: one who lived for twenty-five years after his grave was examined, and another who begat five children after the examination.

9 Incidentally, an additional proof brought by Mendelssohn is a law in *Shulhan Arukh, Yoreh Deah* 357:1, that it is permitted to delay the burial of the deceased if this is to his honor, e.g., in order to bring a casket, shrouds, professional lamenters, and the like. Mendelssohn writes: "If they permitted delaying for such a minor matter as this, this is certainly the case if there is any trace of doubt whether he remains alive, then he is not to be buried, and nothing stands in the way of saving life." Clearly, however, this argument has no basis if we assume that there is no possible doubt that the person is indeed not alive, when the halakhically accepted signs of death appear.

Mendelssohn further wrote: "Here, all the sages of medicine will testify and tell that there is no clear sign of death, and at times a person will faint [so strongly] that the pulse will fall silent and breathing will completely cease; those watching will think that he is dead, but this is not so." Emden rejected this argument, asserting that "Far be it from us to heed them as regards definite Torah laws." *Hatam Sofer*

already rejected by Emden, who wrote: "When, however, they acted properly with him [the deceased], with deliberation and proper supervision, as is the practice of the burial societies in those times and in peacetime, we have absolutely no fear regarding the most remote and infinitesimal possibility. [...] Undoubtedly, however, there is a difference between slightly probable and generally not probable, save for a miraculous manner, that also is to be regarded as impossible, and which we do not fear." In other words, the principle is that the criteria of death are determined on the basis of an absolute majority of cases, while it is clear that there are rare and exceptional instances, but they are not to be taken into account because of their extreme uncommonness.

Rabbi Zevi Hirsch Chajes[10] delved into this matter more deeply, proving that although a mere majority of cases is not sufficient for not taking measures that may potentially save life, we nevertheless are not to consider those rare cases in which people continued living despite their being defined as dead by the accepted criteria. This is "because the exceptions are one of a myriad of myriads of human beings, consequently, this is an insignificant minority, which, according to the entire world [i.e. all opinions], we are not to fear."[11]

expanded on this point in his responsa, based on the assumption that the criteria established by the halakhah are absolute, and are to be relied upon. Additionally, modern medicine does not maintain the opinion that Mendelssohn attributes to the physicians of his time, and that precise signs of death can definitely be determined by clinical and technological means.

10 *She'eilot u-Teshuvot Maharaz Chajes*, para. 52.

11 In his responsa Chajes cites BT Shabbat 152b: "For twelve full months his body exists and his soul ascends and descends" — and obviously, the burial is not to be postponed for a year. Consequently, all the issues of this type do not belong to the definition of the moment of death. See also I. Jakobovits, *Jewish Medical Ethics* (New York, 1959), pp. 157–58. Cf. also the interesting work by J. Bondeson, *A Cabinet of Medical Curiosities* (New York and London, 1991), "Apparent Death and Premature Death," pp. 96–121.

1. Lowering the dead into the grave, Prague 1780

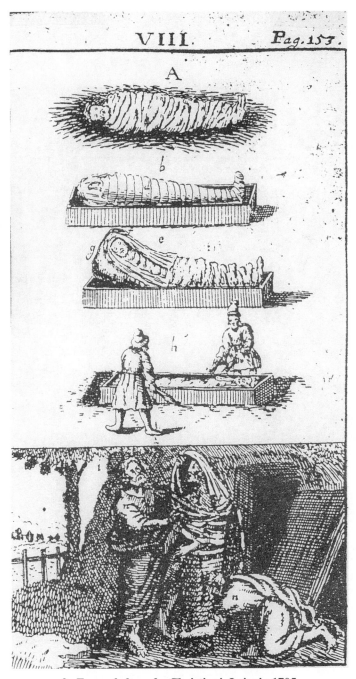

2. Funeral shrouds, Christiani, Leipzig 1705

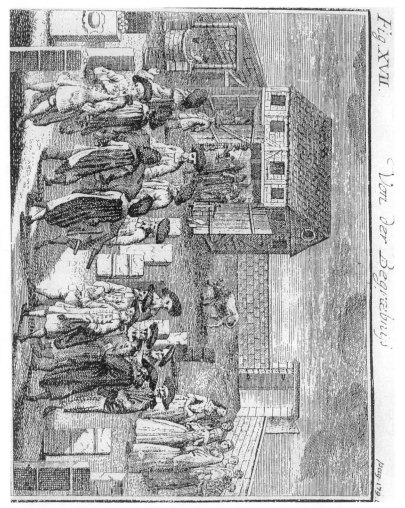

3. Bearing the bier, Bodenschatz, 1748

4. Bearing the bier, Prague 1780

5. Bearing the bier, Prague 1780

6. *Hevra Kadisha* book, 1802

7. **Detail of Fig. 6**

8. *Hevra Kadisha* jug, Moravia 1836

Sepultura Judæorum. 457.

9. Bearing the bier at a Jewish funeral, Leusden, Utrecht 1682

10. Jewish funeral, Mainz 1710

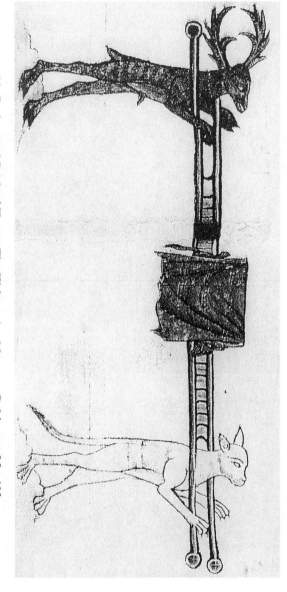

11. Psalter and Book of Hours, The Walters Art Museum, Baltimore, Ms. 102

12. Digging the grave, Prague 1780

13. The eulogy, Prague 1780

14. Rule-book of the Burial Society,
Gemilut Hasadim, **Amsterdam 1776**

15. Rule-book of the Burial Society,
Hesed ve-Emet, **Amsterdam 1748**

16. Digging the grave, Picart, Amsterdam 1728

8

THE CONSTRUCTION OF THE COFFIN
IN THE CEMETERY

When we look at the illustration by Bodenschatz (Fig. 1) we see what looks like a saw resting next to the right door of the purification chamber, seemingly attesting to the fashioning of the coffin in the cemetery. *Maharil* attests[1] that: "in most of the places where [the corpse is taken out in a bier][2] the coffins are made in the cemetery."[3] Further testimony to this practice

1 *The Book of Maharil: Customs by Rabbi Yaacov Mulin*, p. 601.
2 See above, chap. 7, n. 23.
3 We are to be precise in our reading of *Maharil*, loc. cit., p. 601, para. 8: "All cease Torah study to take the deceased forth from the city, and to make the coffin." In Worms itself, however, the coffin was made in the city (*Maharil*, loc. cit.); Schammes, *Wormser Minhagbuch*, Vol. 2, p. 99, states that it was fabricated in the synagogue courtyard; see the editor's n. 1, with references to the *Rishonim* who advocate this (cf. above, chap. 7, n. 23).

It would be appropriate here to mention the dictum that appears in the testament of R. Judah he-Hasid, para. 2 (ed. Margaliot, pp. 10–11): "A grave is not to be dug and left open if the deceased is not to be laid in it that same day; if it is left open until the morning for a few days [until 16 days], one of the townspeople will die." Margaliot (n. 2) refers to Rabbi Jeroham (ben Meshullam), *Toledot Adam ve-Havvah* (Constantinople, 1516), para. 28, who quotes R. Judah he-Hasid, to R. Moses Isserles, *Yoreh Deah* 339:1, and R. Abraham Zevi Hirsch Eisenstadt, *Pit'hei Teshuvah, Hoshen Mishpat* 73:14; 190:16. Margaliot questions this, based on many sources that indicate that numerous graves were dug at the same time, so that they would be ready when needed; he also drew a distinction between the digging of a cave and that of a grave; see his lengthy discussion ad loc. Rabbi Yehoseph Schwarz attests that this was the practice in Jerusalem some 150 years ago; see M. Schwartz, "R. Yehoseph Schwarz on the Customs of the Land of Israel 150 Years Ago,"

appears in a series of drawings of the Prague burial society, in which we see the members of the burial society using a large saw next to a small building in the cemetery, close to the tombstones.[4]

Ha-Ma'yan 35, 3 (1995), p. 41 (Hebrew) (cf. *Tobit*, chap. 8; this, however, poses no difficulty, because the ruling by Rabbi Daniel Tirni, in *Ikkarei ha-Dat* (Vilna, 1904), forbidding the digging of a grave on one day for the next, refers specifically to digging during the daytime. Engaging in this activity, however, from the beginning of the night for use the next day, as is the case in *Tobit*, is permitted, because this is considered to be the same Jewish calendric day, as is stated in Klein, *Zikhron Shai* 18b, para. 44). Cf. the testament with Grimm, *Teutonic Mythology*, Vol. 4, p. 1817, no. 935: "The sexton does not dig the grave till the day of the burial, else you'd have no peace from the dead." See Trachtenberg, *Jewish Magic and Superstition*, pp. 175–76; 301 n. 49. For the spread of this belief, see Hyatt, *Folk-Lore from Adams County, Illinois*, no. 10330, p. 593: "A grave must not be dug except on the day of burial, for if a grave be left open overnight, there will be another death" (see above, chap. 7, n. 22). Note should be taken of what R. Moses Isserles rules (*Yoreh Deah* 339:1) that it is forbidden to cause someone to die more quickly, for example, if someone is dying for a long period of time, and is not taking his leave of this world, it is forbidden to remove the bolster or cushion from under him, based on what people say that the feathers from some fowl are responsible for this (i.e. delaying the departure of the soul). "What people say" indeed appears in Grimm, op. cit., p. 1788, no. 281: "If a sick or dying man has **hen feathers** under him, he cannot die" (emphasis added); and similarly in Wuttke, *Der deutsche Volksaberglaube der Gegenwart*, p. 456. Cf. Trachtenberg, *Jewish Magic and Superstition*, pp. 174, 301 n. 47; Elzet, *Reshumot*, Vol. 1, p. 371, para. 88; Radford, *Encyclopaedia of Superstitions*, p. 98, "Pigeon feathers." For the superstition that a person cannot die as long as there is a pillow with feathers under his head, and that the pillow must be removed in order to alleviate his passing, see T.H. Gaster, *The Holy and the Profane* (New York, 1955), p. 157, and his references to the literature, p. 242. Interestingly, a scholar in Jena wrote an entire treatise on this in the late seventeenth century: C. Questel, *De pulvinari morientibus non subtrahendo* (Jena, 1698) (reference in Gaster, loc. cit., n. 8). After the person dies, however, the determination of whether the person has actually expired is conducted by placing a hen's feather on his nose. See Danzig, *Hokhmat Adam*, "*Matzevet Moshe*," end of *Hil. Avelut*, para. 3. The testament further states (para. 6, p. 12): "When the corpse is purified, the board on which he is purified is not overturned; for this entails danger, lest someone die within three days" (and similarly in Rabbi Jeroham, *Toledot Adam ve-Havvah*, loc. cit.; *Hokhmat Adam* 157:8). This could possibly also be compared with the superstition recorded by Grimm, *Teutonic Mythology*, Vol. 4, p. 1828, no. 1060: "If by mistake the pall be laid over the coffin wrong side out, another in the house will die."

4   See Fig. 2. See Altshuler, *The Precious Legacy*, p. 159, Ill. 148 (Altshuler, catalogue no. 187, p. 259). In the same painting we see two members of the burial

The order of the pictures in Bodenschatz shows that the deceased was brought from his house to the cemetery on a bier, and in the cemetery he was transferred to a casket, which was prepared there, and in which he was buried (see above, n. 3).

1. Making the coffin, Bodenschatz, 1728

2. Making the coffin, Prague 1780

society carrying an empty bier; cf. above, chap. 7, n. 9. Incidentally, in the next chapter, I discuss the practice of making the coffin for a sage from his table, to which we should add what also is written in Schammes, *Wormser Minhagbuch*, Vol. 2, p. 100: "If a woman was accustomed to make wax candles for the synagogue, the plank on which she made the candles is used as a plank for her coffin, within the boards of the coffin." See ad loc., n. 8.

9

THE TABLE FOR THE COFFIN

Menorat ha-Maor[1] tells of an interesting custom:

> I heard that the great ones of France and the hospitable wealthy ones observed a very honorable custom that had spread among them from early times: they would make from the table, on which they would feed the poor, planks and a coffin, in which they would be buried.

This tradition is also mentioned by Rabbeinu Bahya.[2] It is similarly related that the coffin was made for Rabbi Isaac Lampronti (the author of *Pahad Yitzhak*) from an old table on which he engaged in Torah study.[3] This custom was followed not only in Spain (Rabbeinu Bahya, al-Nakawa) and Italy (Lampronti), but also in Libya:[4]

---

1 Ibn al-Nakawa, *Menorat ha-Maor*, Vol. 1, p. 35.
2 *Shulhan shel Arba*, in *Kitvei Rabbeinu Bahya* (*Writings of Rabbeinu Bahya*), ed. C.B. Chavel (Jerusalem, 1969), p. 474; and in brief, in his commentary on Ex. 25:23 (ed. C.B. Chavel [Jerusalem, 1967], p. 279).
3 Ch. Knoller, *Davar Yom be-Yomo* (Przemysl, 1933), for 12 Kislev, fol. 45a. This tradition appears in B. Levi, *Sefer Toledot Rav Yitzhak Lampronti* (Lyck, 1877). See also A.N.Z. Roth, "Memento Moris in the Customs of the Khevra Kadisha," *Yeda-'Am* 3,1 (16) (1955), p. 17; A. Scheiber, *Essays on Jewish Folklore and Comparative Literature* (Budapest, 1985), Hebrew section, pp. 36–37 (= *Folklore Research Center Studies* 12 [Jerusalem, 1972], pp. 206–207); my edition of *Masechet Derech Eretz Zutta and Perek ha-Shalom*, on *Derekh Eretz Zuta* 9:13, p. 151; H.J. Zimmels, *Ashkenazim and Sephardim* (London, 1958), pp. 183, 267, with a reference to Rabbi Isaac Caro, *Toledot Yitzhak* (Amsterdam, 1708), 71b; Greenwald, *Kol Bo al Avelut*, Vol. 1, p. 182 (who cites this custom in the name of [Zevi Hirsch Koidonover,] *Kav ha-Yashar*, chap. 46).
4 M. Ha-Cohen, *Higgid Mordecai: Histoire de la Libye et de ses Juifs, lieux d'habitation et coutumes*, ed. H. Goldberg (Jerusalem, 1982), para. 70, p. 204 (Hebrew).

The custom: If a person dies childless, when he is buried, his coffin is covered with the board of his table (and Rabbi Abraham Halfon gave the reason for this in his book *Hayyei Avraham*).[5]

This practice obviously expresses the familiar motif of using something that will be an "advocate," but it also incorporates the conception that an object that was used to fulfill a commandment should be used for the fulfillment of an additional precept, based on Shabbat 117b: "Since one commandment has been performed with it, let another commandment be performed with it." In other words, every object with which a commandment has been performed is to be afforded special respect, and if possible, it should be used to perform an additional commandment.

S. Ashkenazy provides a wealth of sources for this,[6] from Rabbi Eliezer of Worms to Rabbi Meir Simhah of Dvinsk, a few of which we will cite.

* Rabbi Simeon ben Israel Ashkenazi (d. 1588), a rabbi in Cairo and one of the leading pupils of *Radbaz* (Rabbi David ben Zimra), ordered that his tomb be sealed with the board on which he would engage in study day and night.[7]

* A lament written on the death of Rabbi Solomon (d. 1591), the head of the rabbinical court in Lublin, includes the lines:

From a table set for Torah and testimony
A bier and coffin was made for the grave.[8]

* Rabbi Solomon ha-Levi of Salonika (1581–1634) ordered before his death that "a coffin be made from the bench on which he would place books when he was studying, for him to be buried in."[9]

The wealth of material supplied by Ashkenazy is supplemented by what

---

5   This book was published in Leghorn 1826; Calcutta 1844; and again in Leghorn 1857, 1861.

6   S. Ashkenazy, *Ages in Judaism: Each Age and Its Sages*[2] (Tel Aviv, 1987), pp. 309–310 (Hebrew).

7   See Rabbi Raphael Aharon Ibn Shim'on, *Sefer Tuv Mitzrayim* (Jerusalem, 1908), p. 31.

8   Based on S. B. Nissenbaum, *Le-Korot ha-Yehudim be-Lublin* (*On the History of the Jews in Lublin*) (Lublin, 1900).

9   I.S. Emmanuel, *Matzevot Saloniki* (*Precious Stones of the Jews of Salonica*) (Jerusalem, 1968), pp. 267–99.

appears in *Or ha-Ganuz* by Martin Buber on Rabbi Abraham Joshua Heschel of Apta:[10]

> On *Rosh Hodesh* [the beginning of the month] in which he would die, the rabbi of Apta spoke at his table about the death of the righteous. After Grace after Meals, he arose from his chair and began to walk to and fro with a glowing expression on his face. After this he stood before the table and said: "You, pure table, attest of me that I ate upon you properly, and I gave instruction upon you properly." After that, he ordered that his coffin be made from the table.

Rabbi Issachar Baer Bloch (d. 1798) wrote in his will that his coffin was to be fashioned from the table upon which he studied, and that a copy of the book that he wrote, Benei *Yissakhar*,[11] be buried with him.

Prof. Jacob Spiegal drew my attention to the following passage in *Nimukei Yosef*:[12]

> The author [R. Joseph Habiba] said in Barcelona, I saw that they were breaking apart the bier on which they brought the dead rabbi, and they buried the pieces in his grave. It would seem that great care must be taken in this matter. For this is associated with [the prohibition of] unnecessary destruction, and such instances are found in the Talmud only in reference to a king or prince and the vessels that are his; however, for the honor of the Torah, the public may [do so] with what is theirs, and especially since he is regarded as a prince.

Spiegal comments that it is difficult to propose that the reason for this is "Since one commandment ...," but perhaps because no one else would be allowed to use these objects once used by these exalted personages. We should examine why we do not act in such a manner for every person, possibly because this would constitute unnecessary destruction if done for ordinary individuals.

Note should be taken at this point of the passage in BT Sanhedrin 48b:

> Rabbi Simeon ben Gamaliel said: When is this so? When they [the

---

10 M. Buber, *Or ha-Ganuz* (*The Hidden Light*), sixth printing (Jerusalem and Tel Aviv, 1969), p. 320, based on Rabbi Eleazar ben Zev Wolf ha-Kohen of Sochaczew, *Hiddushei Ma-ha-Rakh* (Warsaw, 1913).

11 Prague, 1785.

12 *Nimmukei Yosef* on Avodah Zarah 10b, ed. M.Y. Blau (New York, 1969), p. 183.

garments] have not touched the bier. But if they touched the bier, they are forbidden [for use]. Ulla understood this as: **A bier that is buried with him**, [the garments then being forbidden] because they might be confused with the shrouds.

Rashi writes (s.v. "*Ba-Mitah ha-Nikveret Imo*") that this is the bier "on which he is borne to burial, that was usually buried with him." Within this context, albeit not directly related, mention should be made of a passage in *Sefer Hasidim*:[13]

Souls have books arranged on the table; just as they were accustomed to study in their lifetimes, so, too, do they study when dead. It once happened that non-Jews passed through a cemetery on a Sabbath eve, and saw a Jew reading in a book on his table.[14]

Interestingly, the motif of books, in a bookcase, or lying (and at times standing) on a table, is very common on tombstones in Eastern Europe, in Poland, and in other countries.[15] All these are graphic expressions of the concept to which the *piyyut* for Yom Kippur, *Enosh Mah Yizkeh*, alludes:[16] "If one has acted righteously, this shall accompany him to his eternal repose." Goldschmidt adds (n. to l. 17) that this is based on the rabbinic teaching[17] that when a person dies, he is accompanied neither by silver or gold, nor precious stones and pearls, but only by Torah and good deeds, as it is said (Prov. 6:22): "When you walk it will lead you" — in this world; "when you lie down it will watch over you" — in the grave; "And when you awake it will talk with you" — in the World to Come.

13 *Sefer Hasidim*, ed. Wistinetzki-Freimann, para. 1546, p. 379.
14 Cf. ed. Margaliot, p. 314, para. 456.
15 See, e.g., A. Schwartzman, *Graven Images: Graphic Motifs of the Jewish Gravestone* (New York, 1993), p. 108, Fig. 1: tombstones from Szydlowice (upper right, left; lower right) and Gesia Cemetery (Warsaw) (bottom left) in Poland; Fig. 2, from M. Krajewska, *Le Temps des Pierres* (Warsaw, 1983), p. 111, Fig. 3, from the Jewish cemetery in Warsaw (Poland); A. Multanowski (ed.), *Cmentarz Zydowski w Warszawie* (Warsaw, 1999), pp. 52–53; see the extensive and diverse material (albeit not all relating to the same topic) in E.Y. Guraryeh, *Chikrai Minhagim: Sources, Reasons, and Studies in Habad Practice* (Kfar Habad, 1999), pp. 256–64, "The Making of a Coffin for the Deceased from Objects Used by Him during His Lifetime for a Religious Purpose" (Hebrew).
16 D. Goldschmidt, *Mahzor le-Yamim ha-Nora'im* (Jerusalem, 1970), p. 118.
17 M Avot 6:9.

1. Gravestones, Poland, 19th century

**2. Gravestone
Warsaw 1914**

**3. Gravestone
Warsaw, 20th century**

10

THE ROLLING AND OVERTURNING OF THE COFFIN

And now, we turn to customs regarding the treatment of the coffin at the time of burial. M. Aslan and R. Nissim[1] write:

> After the removal of the body from the coffin at the time of the burial, the Jews of Iraq would roll the empty coffin seven times on the ground next to the open grave. This was a symbolic act that was meant to keep instances of death away from the mourning family.

Abraham Ben-Yaacob[2] similarly reports: "When the corpse is removed from the coffin, the coffin is turned over," albeit with no mention of "rollings" (seven, according to Aslan and Nissim). David Sassoon[3] (on whom Ben-Yaacob bases his description) also speaks of the overturning of the coffin, without specifying the number of times it is rolled over.

A somewhat similar custom was observed by the Jews of nearby Kurdistan. After portraying their funeral and burial rites,[4] and asserting that "coffins are unknown in Kurdistan," but rather a bier consisting of two poles that are tied to one another with ropes,[5] or, among the Jews of Seneh, an open basket with four handles, Erich Brauer writes:[6]

1 M. Aslan, R. Nissim, *From the Customs and Way of Life of Iraqi Jewry* (Tel Aviv, n.d.), p. 67 (Hebrew).

2 Ben-Yaacob, *Babylonian Jewish Customs*, Vol. 2, p. 313, para. 14. The number seven, in the seven rollings in Iraq, was apparently transferred from the seven sittings and standings of the burial practices (see below, chap. 14).

3 D.S. Sassoon, *Masa Bavel* (*Journey to Babylonia*), ed. M. Benayahu (Jerusalem, 1955), p. 206.

4 E. Brauer, *The Jews of Kurdistan*, ed. R. Patai (Jerusalem, 1947), pp. 164–66 (Hebrew).

5 Ibid., p. 165.

6 Ibid., p. 167.

The bier must be removed before anyone leaves the cemetery. It, however, is not carried outside, it rather is overturned, and pushed again and again until it is outside the cemetery, where it is immediately dismantled.

Once again, there is no mention of the number of "overturnings," but rather that is it "pushed again and again," until it is removed from the cemetery.

This seemingly quite strange custom has parallels, to a degree, in other cultures. Thus, for example, in Morocco:[7]

Before the hoes [...] with which the grave was dug are carried back from the cemetery, the heads may have to be removed from the handles, **turned upside down**, and then put back in this position [...]. In the Hiaina this is said to be done in order that the *bas* may not return to the house and cause another death. Among the At Ubahti the heads must remain reversed until the following morning, lest some person in the tent to which the hoe belongs should die. [...] In Andjra the bier is taken back to the mosque **upside down** so that it may not be needed soon again. In the Hiaina it is left on the grave till the third day,[8] when it is brought back by the women who then visit the grave;

---

7   Westermarck, *Ritual and Belief in Morocco*, Vol. 2, pp. 462–63 (emphasis added).

8   The motif of the first three days of mourning is also prevalent in the Islamic world. See, e.g., Westermarck, op. cit., pp. 469–71, 475–78, 507–508. Cf. Legey, *The Folklore of Morocco*, pp. 227, 231, 235. The first seven days also have a special status in these mourning practices. See ibid., pp. 470, 478. Muslims do not observe the thirty-day "*sheloshim*" of Judaism, but in its place they have the concept of "forty days"; ibid., pp. 471–72, 478–79, 485, 506, 509, 512; similar to Judaism, there is also the year of mourning (ibid., p. 479). For the mourning practices during the first three days according to Jewish law, see S. Glick, *A Light unto the Mourner: The Development of Major Customs of Mourning in the Jewish Tradition from after the Burial until the End of Shiva* (Efrat, Israel, 1991), pp. 59 ff. (Hebrew), and for the seven-day "*shivah*" period, ibid., pp. 73 ff. For the "*sheloshim*," see ibid., Index, s.v. "*Sheloshim*."

This is the place to indicate a number of additional parallels between Jewish and Islamic burial practices. Westermarck, p. 497: "It is the general Muhammadan custom that the corpse is laid in the tomb on its right side with the face towards Mecca" (cf. ibid., p. 458). For the direction of Jewish burial, see below, chap. 13, pp. 518–23. As regards interment on one's side, cf. PT Ketubot 12:3: "bury me on the side," which is the basis for the halakhah that permits lying the corpse on its side. See *Shulhan Arukh, Yoreh Deah* 362:2; also see below, chap. 11.

and among the Benei Aros it is left there until it is required for another funeral.

Thus, the reason here for overturning the coffin, or for leaving it in the cemetery, as well as the reversing of the hoe handles, is that these are symbolic acts performed with the aim that these implements will not be soon needed, or, as Westermarck summarizes:[9]

> If any one of these rules were not observed there would soon be another death in the family or the village.

The Jews of Morocco also acted in similar fashion, as is recorded by Raphael Bensimon:[10]

> When the deceased was removed from the coffin, it was the custom to immediately overturn the coffin. Leaving the coffin open was like requesting an additional death.

This should be compared with what Bensimon writes elsewhere (p. 448):

Westermarck further writes (p. 497): "It is also considered a meritorious act to assist in carrying a bier, hence the bearers are continually relieved." See BT Berakhot 17b: "The bearers of the bier, those who relieve them, and those who relieve the latter," on which Rashi comments: "It is the practice for those bearing to replace one another, for all desire the merit of this [act]." See Tykocinski, *Gesher ha-Hayyim*, Vol. 1, p. 114. And further in Westermarck (loc. cit.): "A person who is sitting should rise if he sees a funeral procession coming, and should remain standing until it has passed; and this he should do even if the dead one was a Jew[!]." See *Gesher ha-Hayyim*, p. 128, following PT Bikkurim 3:3 and *Shulhan Arukh, Yoreh Deah* 343.

Westermarck adds (p. 453): "a very small child [...] is carried to the grave in the arms of a man." Cf. *Shulhan Arukh, Yoreh Deah* 353:4; *Gesher ha-Hayyim*, p. 266: "If [a child] dies within thirty days, even if he reached his full [term of pregnancy], he is carried out in one's arms, that is to say, the beadle or one of those occupied with the dead bears him in his arms."

Westermarck (p. 458): "In Andjra myrtle sprigs are put at the bottom of the grave [...] the myrtle has the scent of Paradise, which is liked by the angels." For the use of myrtle, see Alfayah, *Kunteres ha-Yehieli*, 46b, para. 19.

As regards the garments of the corpse, see Westermarck, p. 447; cf. *Kunteres ha-Yehieli* 10a; the parallels are striking.

9 Westermarck, op. cit., p. 545.

10 R.J. Bensimon, *Le Judaism Marocain: Folklore: Du Berceau à la Tombe* (Lod, 1994), p. 514 (Hebrew).

In Meknes it was not customary to prepare graves in advance, for fear of the danger: "An empty grave invites a corpse" [with a reference to *Ma'avar Yabbok*, *"Sefat Emet,"* chap. 1].[11]

Although the significance of the Iraqi and Kurdish practice has not been determined, it was clearly meant to prevent a calamity, such as an additional death, and the overturnings and rollings are intended to confuse the destructive agents. Interestingly, a similar custom presents itself in England:[12]

> As soon as even the [funeral] procession moves off, the chairs, or whatsoever else the coffin has been laid on, are carefully upset, as otherwise there will be another death in the house within a week.[13]

There are testimonies to this in Scotland, as recently as the late 1950s (ibid.):

> There have been fairly recent instances of the chairs and tables supporting the coffin before it was borne away, being turned over in case the dead should return.

Needless to say, in these localities the coffin is buried in the ground as part of the funeral, and therefore could not be upset, but rather the stand on which it had rested. Thus this resembles what we have seen among the Moroccan tribes, who overturn the heads of the hoes, that is, they render unusable, as it were, the tools with which the grave had been prepared.

11 Cf. above, chap. 8, n. 3.
12 Opie and Tatem, *A Dictionary of Superstitions*, p. 92.
13 From the Orkney and Shetland Islands (northern Scotland), in 1878. See Gaster, *The Holy and the Profane*, pp. 171–72, and his references on p. 245, esp. to P. Sartori, *Sitte und Brauch*, Vol. 1 (Leipzig, 1910), p. 137 n. 20. For a similar phenomenon, but with a totally different purpose, see Puckle, *Funeral Customs: Their Origin and Development*, p. 43.

11

HOW THE DECEASED IS LAID IN HIS GRAVE

Rabbi Jeremiah ordered in his testament (PT Ketubot 12:3) that when he died,

> Wrap me in white shrouds, dress me in my stockings [*danarsai*, variant reading: *dagarsai*(?)], put my sandals on my feet and my staff in my hand, and bury me on the side. If the Messiah comes, I shall be ready.

The *poskim* derived from the words "bury me on the side" that it is permitted to bury the deceased when he is lying on his side. The *Shulhan Arukh*[1] establishes the law: "The corpse is placed on his back, with his face upwards, like a person when sleeping," to which *Be'ur ha-Gra* adds:[2]

> "Is placed" — see *Be'er ha-Golah*, and similarly, on his side, based on what is written in the Palestinian Talmud, that Rabbi Jeremiah ordered thusly; see *Beit Yosef*, in the name of *Torat ha-Adam*, and similarly in the [Babylonian] Talmud, Nazir (65a), "lying."

This is supported by Nahmanides, who reiterates in *Torat Adam*:[3]

> He is positioned with his face up [...] or, alternately, on the side, as the Palestinian Talmud states.

---

1 *Shulhan Arukh, Yoreh Deah* 362:2. Note the Muslim practice of laying the body on its right side. See Lane, *Arabian Society in the Middle Ages*, p. 262.
2 *Be'ur ha-Gra* on *Shulhan Arukh*, loc. cit., subpara. 4.
3 Nahmanides, *Torat ha-Adam*, in *Kitvei Rabbeinu Moshe ben Nahman* (*Writings of Nahmanides*), ed. C.B. Chavel (Jerusalem, 1965), Vol. 2, p. 115. See Chavel's note, pp. 115–16.

And, similarly, in the *Ahronim* (later authorities), as in *Kunteres ha-Yehieli*:[4]

> He is laid down on his back, with his face up [...] (or alternately, on the side, as the Palestinian Talmud states: and he is lain on his side, neither standing nor sitting, nor with his head placed between his knees, but only as one who is sleeping).[5]

S.H. Kook, however, cites S. Lieberman, as follows:[6]

> As regards the versions of the Palestinian Talmud, "and bury me on the side," the version of Rav Nissim Gaon is clearly correct. See *Or Zarua, Hil. Pesahim*, Vol. 2, para. 234, 55:3;[7] *Manhig*, ed. Berlin, *Hil. Pesahim*, para. 2,[8] in the name of *Megillat Setarim* by Rav Nissim,[9] both of whom have the reading: "*astrita*" (*Or Zarua*) or "*istrata*" (*Manhig*). Accordingly, the explanation is that R. Jeremiah ordered that he be placed along the king's highway, as this is understood in Genesis Rabbah, *Vayehi* 100:2:[10] "Bury me by the side of the road [*al orha*]," which is suitable for *istrata*.

According to Lieberman, therefore, the version of the PT maintained by Nahmanides, the version according to which the halakhah is established in the *Shulhan Arukh*, is fundamentally erroneous.

The original version was most probably "*a'asarta* [= *al istrata*]," since

4 Vol. 2, "*Beit Olamim*" (Cemetery), chap. 9, fol. 20a.
5 This, despite what is written in *Siftei Kohanim, Yoreh Deah* 362:2, on the statement in the *Shulhan Arukh* (above) that "the corpse is placed on his back, with his face upwards, like a person when sleeping": "For in any instance in which he is positioned in any other manner, whether standing or sitting, this is a reproachful manner." The *Shakh* is also cited in Danzig, *Hokhmat Adam*, 158:2 (see below).
6 S.H. Kook, *Studies and Researches* (Jerusalem, 1967), p. 100 (Hebrew).
7 "Collections from *Megillat Setarim* by S. A. Poznanski," *Ha-Zofeh le-Hokhmat Yisrael* 7 (1923), p. 36, para. 45. See also S. Asaf, "Index to *Megillat Setarim*," *Tarbiz* 11 (1940), p. 253 (Hebrew); Rabbi Eleazar ben Judah, *Ma'aseh Rokeah* (Sanuk, 1912) = B.M. Lewin, *Otzar ha-Gaonim*, Vol. 3 (Jerusalem, 1930), Pesahim, Responsa, para. 303, p. 112.
8 R. Abraham ben Nathan of Lunel, *Sefer Hamanhig*, ed. Y. Raphael (Jerusalem, 1978), Vol. 2, p. 424.
9 See S. Abramson, *R. Nissim Gaon: Libelli Quinque* (Jerusalem, 1965), p. 278 and n. 217 (Hebrew).
10 Ed. Theodor-Albeck, pp. 1285–86.

the regular spelling in the PT is "*israta*."[11] The copyists "corrected" this to *al sitra*, that is, on the side. The interim stage was undoubtedly *asrata*, with the striking of one *alef*.[12] In the next phase, *asrata* became *asarta*, with a slight interposition of the letters.[13] If these corruptions seem significant, what could we say about what appears in *Ha-Minhag* (ibid., l. 19): "Bury me *al asrata, istrata*: hit me *al i sirta*"!

This testament in PT also specifies "and my staff in my hand," which is most likely the source for the practice of placing thin rods in the hand of the deceased. Danzig[14] ridiculed this custom. Rabbi Moses Sofer[15] also wrote critically of it, and they apparently disregarded this passage in the PT. J. Schor[16] also relates to this:

> My precious son David, may he live long, has already drawn my attention to what is taught in *Kitzur Shulhan Arukh* 197:5: "Care should be taken not to allow the fingers of the dead to remain closed. The custom prevailing in some communities to shut his fingers should be abolished. The belief of some people that by this, they symbolize some Holy Names, is a mere fabrication. It is also a foolish custom to place in his hands some twigs, generally called forks; if they insist on putting this, it should be put alongside the corpse."[17]

The source for this is in *Rokeah*:[18] "We must check that the fingers of the corpse are not clenched," and in *Sefer Hasidim*:[19]

> When there is plague in the city, those corpses are searched, for

---

11 S. Krauss, *Griechische und lateinische Lehnwoerter im Talmud, Midrasch und Targum*, Vol. 2 (Berlin, 1899), p. 97; cf. pp. 82–83.

12 The likes of which we find in the Geonic tradition. See my article: "Philology and Daily Life in the Study of Rabbinic Literature," *Sidra* 1 (1985), p. 137 (Hebrew), for אאסקריא that became אסקריא; and my book, *Material Culture in Eretz-Israel during the Talmudic Period* (Jerusalem, 1993), p. 170 n. 4 (Hebrew).

13 See Krause, *Lehnwoerter*, Vol. 1 (Berlin, 1898), pp. 113–14. Some of this was already noted by H. Albeck in his *Minhat Yehudah* on Genesis Rabbah (ed. Theodor-Albeck), p. 1286, l. 1.

14 Danzig, *Hokhmat Adam*, end of "*Matzevet Moshe*."

15 *She'eilot u-Teshuvot Hatam Sofer, Yoreh Deah* 327.

16 In his edition of *Sepher ha-Ittim* by R. Jehuda ben Barsilai (Cracow, 1903), p. 233.

17 English: *Code of Jewish Law*, trans. H.E. Goldin (New York, 1961), Vol. 4, p. 99.

18 End of para. 316, p. 195.

19 Para. 451, ed. Margaliot, p. 310.

perhaps in some instances the corpse swallowed the shroud, which is dangerous,[20] or his hands are not extended, as it is said, "Everyone follows behind him" (Job 21:33) — anything that entails the saving of life may be done to the deceased.

And in the testament of R. Judah he-Hasid:[21]

It must be seen [when the corpse is placed in the grave] that the fingers of the corpse's hands are not clenched.[22]

The custom of the clenching of the fingers may have originated in the placing of a "rod" in the corpse's hand, in recollection of the testament of R. Jeremiah, and then closing the hand around it. When the practice of rods fell into disuse, some people still closed the fist of the corpse, because they no longer knew the reason for such an action. This, however, remains within the realm of conjecture.

R. Jeremiah also ordered in his testament to "put my sandals on my feet." Greenwald writes in *Kol Bo al Avelut*:[23]

In [the journal] *Pardes*, year 6, no. 5, Rabbi Eliezer Michel commented on the statement by Rashi in Yevamot 104[a] that it was the practice to bury the deceased with his shoes [...] perhaps he referred to special footwear for the corpse, like his shrouds; further study is required.

Greenwald further writes:[24]

See PT Kelaim 9:4, that it was a Jewish custom to place footwear on the dead, and R. Jeremiah ordered that he be buried in his sandals. See Rashi, Yevamot 104[end of a]: "For the death garments; since it is not intended for walking, it is not a shoe." This practice might possibly be the source for the custom not to receive the shoes of a dead person,

---

20 See above, chap. 7, n. 22.
21 Para. 7, p. 12.
22 See the note by Margaliot (no. 12), citing R. Jeroham, *Toledot Adam ve-Havvah*, para. 28, who cites this in the name of R. Eliezer ben Yakar; this rule is derived from *Sifrei*, end of *Haazinu*: "Moses said to Aaron: 'Stretch out your arms,' and he stretched out." And in Ecclesiastes Rabbah, chap. 5: "It is taught in the name of Rabbi Meir: And when he departed from the world, his hands were stretched out." See Tykocinski, *Gesher ha-Hayyim*, Vol. 1, pp. 138–39 and n. 4; Greenwald, *Kol Bo al Avelut*, Vol. 1, p. 218 n. 3.
23 P. 58 n. 51.
24 Op. cit., p. 91 n. 20.

since the shoes were earmarked for the death garments, and therefore no benefit could be derived from them. This requires further study, that possibly since then the Israelites were enjoined regarding this, and even though this is not the practice in our time, it nevertheless is a very ancient custom.

Greenwald's intent in "the source for the custom not to receive the shoes of a dead person"[25] apparently is to what is written in *Sefer Hasidim*:[26]

One who owes others should not engage extensively in charity until he repays. Neither should a person engage in charity with something that entails danger. A person was given the shoes of a dead person, and he wished to give them to a poor person. He was told "Love your fellow as yourself" (Lev. 19:18), rather, sell them to a non-Jew, so that no Jew would be endangered, and give the money to the poor person.[27]

A query was directed to Rabbi Wolf Leiter[28] "concerning a practice that was observed in the world of not wearing the shoes of a dead person, if this [custom] is to be found [i.e. recorded] anywhere," with a reference to the above passage in *Sefer Hasidim*. Leiter then continues: "perhaps this is

---

25 As regards a related topic: it would be proper to add here what was written by Rabbi Joseph Yuspa Hahn, *Yosif Ometz* (Frankfurt a.M., 1928 [photocopy edn.: Jerusalem, 1965]), p. 330: "I received from my teacher, the *Gaon*, our teacher and master, *Mahari Segal* [Rabbi Jacob ben Moses Moellin] that the practice of taking nothing from the house of mourning during the seven [days of mourning] is totally unfounded; he says that this error comes from what the *poskim* wrote, that if a person loans a cloak to his fellow in order to go to the house of mourning, he may not take it back from him until the mourning period has passed." This was quoted by Jousep Juspa Kaschmann, *Noheg ka-Tzon Yosef* (Frankfurt a.M., 1718 [Tel Aviv, 1969]), p. 50. See Rabbi Baruch Goldberg, *Penei Barukh* (Jerusalem, 1986), p. 100 n. 13 (Hebrew). It would seem, however, that the source of this custom lies elsewhere; as some *poskim* have suggested, this is because of the evil spirit that resides there (see the sources cited in *Penei Barukh*, p. 100 n. 14). Cf. the ancient (non-Jewish) Polish practice not to borrow anything from a house in which someone has died; mentioned in G.A. Murray, *Ancient Rites and Ceremonies* (London, 1929 [photocopy: London, 1966]), p. 181; nothing further need be added.

26 Ed. Margaliot, p. 312, para. 454 (= ed. J. Wistinetzki and J. Freimann, para. 1544, p. 379).

27 See ed. Margaliot, pp. 312–13 n. 2, for a lengthy discussion of this passage.

28 Rabbi Wolf Leiter, *She'eilot u-Teshuvot Beit David* (Jerusalem, 2000), p. 34, para. 31.

connected with illness, that is contagious, and therefore this poses a danger to those wearing them," following this with a discussion of the nature of the danger. He adds, however: "I heard that a copyist's mistake may have been introduced in *Sefer Hasidim*, and it should read *metah* [a dead (animal)], with the intent to what [is written] in Hullin 95 [it should read: 94a]: 'A person should not sell shoes from a *metah* because of the danger.' Rashi interprets this (s.v. "*Ha-Sakanah*"): 'Lest it died because of a snakebite, and the venom was absorbed in the hide.'"[29] Rabbi Judah Leib Zirelson[30] was of a similar mind, that there was a typographical mistake in *Sefer Hasidim*, and that the discarding of the shoes of a dead person constitutes wanton (and therefore forbidden) destruction.[31]

We have therefore seen two ways to resolve the question of the source for the custom not to wear the shoes of a dead person: either these were special footwear for the corpse, with a status similar to that of shrouds; or this practice can be traced to a copyist's mistake in the above passage in *Sefer Hasidim*.

It is noteworthy that the tradition of burying the dead in shoes appears in many diverse cultures, for example:[32]

> Where shoes are worn, the deceased is shod, for he had a long journey to take. Such, for example, is the custom in many parts of Europe: it extends in Great Britain as far back as the Late Celtic period.

In Morocco, as well, the corpse is generally interred wearing shoes, which are among the seven types of clothing suitable for burial.[33]

---

29 This belief, that illnesses may be transmitted by wearing an infected shoe, is shared by various peoples. See, e.g., Radford, *Encyclopaedia of Superstitions*, p. 218: "To burn an old shoe prevents infection. Nottingham"; Opie and Tatem, *A Dictionary of Superstitions*, p. 151. See also *Shulhan Arukh, Hoshen Mishpat* 228:8; *Semag*, op. cit., subpara. 112, and more.

30 *Atzei Levanon* (Klausenberg [= Clug], 1927), para. 46.

31 This topic is discussed by S.B. Freehof, *Reform Responsa* (Cincinnati, 1960), pp. 174–76. See also Lerner, *Shmiras Haguf Vihanefesh*, Vol. 1, pp. 236–37, para. 71:1, who cites additional sources, such as Rabbi Moses Feinstein, *Iggerot Moshe, Yoreh Deah* 133, and more.

32 Hastings, *Encyclopaedia of Religion and Ethics*, Vol. 4, p. 417b.

33 Westermarck, *Ritual and Belief in Morocco*, Vol. 2, p. 448. For how many types of clothing in which the deceased is to be garbed, see *Kunteres ha-Yehieli*, chap. 2, fol. 9b–11b.

Accordingly, "all the details of the testament of Rabbi Jeremiah are directed to one end, that he be ready to receive the Messiah. He therefore ordered that he be dressed in fine garments, that shoes be placed on his feet, and that his staff be placed in his hand."[34] In this light Kook explained the strange tradition connected with one of the tombs near Hammath-Tiberias, which relates that the person buried in that tomb (presumably R. Jeremiah) was interred upright, since he vowed during his lifetime that he would not sit until the advent of the Messiah. This is quite puzzling, since upright burial, according to R. Johanan[35] is considered to be "the burial of asses"; according to the PT,[36] it is not fit even for dogs; Rabbeinu Tam[37] characterizes it as "not a respectable manner"; and as we have seen above, both *Shakh* and *Hokhmat Adam* assert that "this is a reproachful manner." How, then, could someone have been buried in such a disgraceful fashion? S.H. Kook[38] explains that this aggadah was related regarding Rabbi Jeremiah, and not Rabbi Meir, as it appears in some of the traditions.[39] Since he ordered that he be buried in such a manner that he would be ready to receive the Messiah, and he said "*yahavuni* [place me]," and not "*hashkivuni* [lay me down]," by the side of the road, his intent was to be buried standing up. As time passed, his order was transformed into a vow, "and it was related that he vowed not to sit until the advent of *Shiloh* [= the Messiah]."[40] We should possibly add to this hypothesis an additional element that we found in two English sources. W.R. Wilson:[41] "At Copenhagen I found Jews were buried as standing upright";

---

34 Kook, *Studies and Researches*, p. 99.

35 BT Bava Batra 101a–b.

36 PT Bava Batra, end of chap. 6.

37 BT Menahot 33a.

38 *Studies and Researches*, pp. 97–101.

39 See the recent work: Z. Ilan, *Tombs of the Righteous in the Land of Israel* (Jerusalem, 1997), p. 229 (Hebrew). See also what S. Abramson wrote regarding upright burial: "Clarifications," *Sinai* 89 (1981), pp. 231–33 (Hebrew).

40 Perhaps we should engage in a precise reading of Genesis Rabbah, loc. cit. (100:2): "so that when I am summoned I may stand *otmos* [ετοιηος — ready]." See Krauss, *Lehnwoerter*, Vol. 1, p. 29, s.v. "*Etimos*." As regards "*denirsai*" in PT Ketubot 12:3, see the comment by I. Loew, *Lehnwoerter*, Vol. 1, p. 217, col. a, s.v. "*dardesin*," meaning stockings.

41 W.R. Wilson, *Travels in the Holy Land, Egypt, etc.* (first edn.: London, 1823; fourth edn. [in two volumes]: London, 1847), p. 331.

and O.B. Elliot:[42] "The Jews have here, as always, a separate burying ground. Their corpses are interred in a standing position, with the face turned towards Jerusalem." I have yet to determine if there is any basis for these reports; the subject deserves further study.

---

42 G.B. Elliot, *Letters from the North of Europe* (London, 1830 and 1832), p. 62 (cited in Cohen, *An Anglo-Jewish Scrapbook, 1600–1840*).

12

A SEPARATE ROW OF GRAVES FOR WOMEN WHO DIED DURING CHILDBIRTH

Incidental to our discussion of matters relating to cemeteries, Rabbi Wolf Leiter was asked in his collection of responsa[1] for the reason why women who died during childbirth are buried in a special row of graves. Leiter wrote that he did not know the source or the reason for this custom, and suggested several possibilities based on his own reasoning. In a drawing from the book *Judische Geschichte in der Schweiz* by Ulrich[2] (Fig. 1), we see a cemetery with rows of tombstones, with the rows marked by letters. Rows C-E are the graves of, respectively, men, women, and children. In the upper right-hand corner, close to the northern wall, is a lone grave (F), of a woman who died during childbirth ("einer Kindbetherin").

In Worms,[3] the practice was that

> if a person's family was buried there, he is buried with them, and if not, he is buried elsewhere, as the grave diggers see fit.

Schammes adds:[4]

---

1   *She'eilot u-Teshuvot Beit David*, Vol. 1, para. 196. His responsum was later cited by Rabbi Malkiel Zevi Tenenbaum of Lomza, *Divrei Malkiel*, Vol. 2 (New York, 1960), para. 94, and in Greenwald, *Kol Bo al Avelut*, Vol. 1, pp. 172–73. This practice was also noted by Elzet, *Reshumot*, Vol. 1, p. 370, para. 84; cf. ibid., p. 373.

2   Reproduced in *The Jewish Encyclopedia* (New York, 1902), p. 639. The full name of the author and his book: Johann Kaspar Ulrich, *Sammlung judischer Geschichten, welche schmit diesem Volk in dem XII und fogenden Jahrhunderten bis auf MDCCLX in der Schweiz von Zeit zu Zeit zugetragen ...* (Basle, 1768 [Berlin, 1922]).

3   Schammes, *Wormser Minhagbuch*, Vol. 2, p. 98.

4   Schammes, ad loc., gloss.

Except for women who died during childbirth. They are interred close to the wall, not in the midst of the other graves, with the purified dead who lie in the graves.

The editor adds (n. 5) that the register of the Frankfurt am Main burial society[5] contains the entry: "Hindle, the wife of Elias Remilt, died and was buried on Wednesday, 20 Sivan [1668], in the upper part of the cemetery, **close to the northern wall**" — exactly as in the drawing by Ulrich. The editor continues with a reference to a comment on this practice by Rabbi Solomon Lipmann Walder,[6] the head of the Schonlanke rabbinical court and a disciple of *Ketav Sofer* (Rabbi Abraham Samuel Benjamin Wolf Sofer):

> This is observed in all our land here, and as I learned, this is the practice in other lands as well: that the first row in the cemetery is reserved for the burial of women who died [within] a few days after giving birth [...] and I did not find this practice in the *Shulhan Arukh*, nor in the other books of the *Ahronim*.

Walder then continues by discussing the reasons for this custom.[7]

It seems that the rationale for this custom is implied in the above gloss by Schammes, in which he writes that a woman who died during childbirth "is interred close to the wall, not in the midst of the other graves, **with the purified dead** who lie in the graves," because "if a woman dies during childbirth and blood issues from her, **she is not to undergo purification**, but rather is to be buried in her garments,"[8] a ruling that is based on *Shulhan Arukh* (*Yoreh Deah* 364:4): "If an Israelite is found killed, he is buried as he was found, without shrouds, and without removing even his shoes." Rabbi Moses Isserles writes on this: "And likewise, this is done for a woman who died in childbirth." In other words, she is not among the "purified dead," and seemingly for this reason it was not desirable that she be buried with the other dead.[9]

---

5   *Gedenkbuch der Frankfurter Juden* (Frankfurt a.M., 1914), p. 424, no. 26.
6   In the journal *Yagdil Torah*, published by Rabbi Israel C. Ackermann (Berlin, 1881), para. 151.
7   See the discussion by Welder in the editor's note, along with relevant passages from Rabbi Jacob Ettlinger (the author of *Arukh la-Ner*), *Teshuvot Binyan Zion ha-Shalem* (Jerusalem, 1989), para. 70.
8   *Be'er Hetev on Yoreh Deah* 364:7.
9   See Rabbi Isaac Lampronti, *Pahad Yitzhak*, s.v. "*Yoldot* [Women Giving Birth]"

The cemetery depicted in this drawing is that in Endingen-Landau. It was established in 1750, shortly before the drawing was executed. The small number of graves appearing in the drawing is explained by the diminutive Jewish population in the vicinity.[10] Nonetheless, even here, it was customary to bury the women who had died during childbirth in a separate row, next to the northern wall.[11]

(Vol. 4, 11b–12a); Rabbi Samuel ha-Levi, *She'eilot u-Teshuvot Nahalat Shiv'ah* (= *Nahalat Shiv'ah*, Vol. 2) (Furth, 1724), para. 59; Klein, *Zikhron Shai* 14a, para. 16, and more. Cf. Bodenschatz, *Kirchliche Verfassung der heutigen Juden*, p. 171. It is noteworthy at this juncture that the customs of Germanic Christians also relate especially to the woman who dies while giving birth. See Grimm, *Teutonic Mythology*, Vol. 4, p. 1815, no. 900; p. 1823, no. 1049. Cf. also Hastings, *Encyclopaedia of Religion and Ethics*, Vol. 4, p. 420b, that in eastern and western Africa, women who die during childbirth "are buried apart." See also R.C. Thompson, *Semitic Magic: Its Origins and Development* (London, 1908), pp. 19–22.

10 The cemetery, which was between Endingen and Lengnau, was called "Waldfriedhof," and it was given to the local Jews in 1750. The Jewish community at the time was quite small, and in 1761 numbered 94 households (see *Encyclopaedia Judaica* [Jerusalem, 1971], "Endingen and Lengnau," Vol. 6, cols. 738–39). For a drawing of two tombstones "from the women's row" from 1752 (two years after the cemetery's establishment), see Fig. 2, from A. Weldler-Steinberg, *Geschichte der Juden in der Schweiz vom 16 Jahrhundert bis nach der Emanzipation*, ed. F. Guggenheim-Grunberg (Zurich, 1982), Vol. 1, no. VI. For Ulrich and his artistic activity, see ibid., pp. 80–83; the article by L. Rothschild in *Schweizer Studien zur Gesichtswissenschaft* 17,2 (1933); H. Guggenheim, "Johann Kaspar Ulrich — Documente," *Israelitisches Wochenblatt fur die Schweiz*, no. 5 (January 29), 1926, p. 5. A second edition of Ulrich's book already appeared in 1770 in Zurich. The drawing is by J.R. Holzhalb, with a bronze etching by J.B. Bullinger. For a depiction of the present-day cemetery, see W. Guggenheim et al., *Juden in der Schweitz: Glaube-Geschichte-Gegenwart* (Zurich, 1982), p. 29.

11 See *Medieval Folklore: A Dictionary of Myths, Legends, Tales, Beliefs, and Customs*, ed. C. Lindahl, J. McNamara, and J. Lindow (Santa Barbara, Denver, and Oxford, 2000), Vol. 1, p. 395; R. Mills, s.v. "Funeral Customs and Burial Rites": "Women who died in childbirth and suicides were also technically condemned to burial outside the perimeter of the churchyard for most of the Middle Ages, although in practice it seems that the regulations were rarely adhered to." (The reference is to R.C. Finucane, "Sacred Corpse, Profane Carrion: Social Ideals and Death Rituals in the Later Middle Ages," in *Mirrors of Mortality: Studies in the Social History of Death*, ed. J.W. Waley [New York, 1981], pp. 40–60.) Could this be the source of our (European) Jewish custom?

1. Graveyard in Endingen, Ulrich 1768

2. Gravestones in Endingen — Lengnau

13

THE DIRECTION OF GRAVES

An additional matter that may be learned from the drawing by Ulrich[1] relates to the orientation of the rows in the cemetery and the direction in which the corpse was laid in the grave. As Greenwald[2] states, "it is the practice throughout the Jewish world to bury in rows."[3] Opinions varied, however, as regards the direction in which the deceased was to be placed in his grave. According to one custom, the corpse's head was placed to the west and his feet to the east,[4] while another tradition called for a north to south

1   See above, chap. 12.
2   *Kol Bo al Avelut*, Vol. 1, p. 177.
3   On the other hand, it does not seem from the pictures of Buxtorf, Kirchner, and Bodenschatz reproduced above that there were orderly rows of graves. These drawings, however, are not precise. Thus, e.g., Buxtorf does not allow for sufficient space between the graves, and has other errors. Cf. the drawing by Bonar, above.
4   Thus was the practice in Worms, as is attested by Rabbi Moses Sofer, *She'eilot u-Teshuvot Hatam Sofer*, para. 332, as well as in Goppingen, as we learn from the map at the beginning of the book by N. Bar-Giora Bamberger, *Die judischen Friedhofe Jebenhausen und Goppingen* (Goppingen, 1990). The cemetery dates from ca. 1843. This was also the custom in Pressburg; see Klein, *Zikhron Shai* 14a, para. 15. (The *"Sefer Hayyim"* mentioned in the responsum of Sofer is apparently *Sefer ha-Hayyim: Ve-Hu Kollel Kol ha-Tefilot ha-Shayakhin le-Hevra Kadisha Gemilut Hasadim v-Khol Minhagei Hesed ve-Emet ... kefi Minhagei Sefardim* [*The Book of Life: That Includes all the Prayers of the Gemilut Hasadim Burial Society and all the Burial Practices ... according to the Customs of the Sephardim*] [Amsterdam, 1763], and not to the book of the same name by Rabbi Simon Frankfurter [Amsterdam, 1703]; I have not yet fully clarified this matter.) A discussion of the directions of interment in the different Jewish communities would exceed the scope of the present work. Let it suffice to mention that in Kurdistan, e.g., the deceased is placed on his

orientation.[5] *Maharil* (Rabbi Jacob ben Moses Moellin) in Worms ordered that the arrangement be changed to a north to south orientation.[6] *Hatam Sofer* provides an intriguing explanation for the differing practices:[7]

back, with his feet pointing towards Jerusalem (Brauer, *The Jews of Kurdistan*, p. 166), and in all the lands of the Maghreb the head of the deceased is regularly placed toward the west and his feet towards the east; or with the head towards the north and the feet towards the south (Ben Naim, *Noheg be-Hokhmah*, pp. 170–71, para. 6); or with his head to the east and his feet to the west (Rabbi Juda Ayache, *Recueil des Lois et Coutumes de la Communauté Juive d'Alger*, ed. I. Srour [Jerusalem, 1985], 12:9, p. 56 [Hebrew]). In Persia, the direction of burial was towards Mecca (Masse, *Persian Beliefs and Customs*, p. 88; cf. p. 81).

5 Thus in Eybeschuetz. See *She'eilot u-Teshuvot Hatam Sofer*, loc. cit.; Rabbi Abraham Isaac Glueck, *Yad Yitzhak*, Vol. 3 (Satmar, 1909), para. 193; and recently, J.M. Lilley et al., *The Jewish Burial Ground at Jewbury* (York, 1994), pp. 370, 372, that the direction of the graves in the ancient cemetery in York, England, between the years 1230–90, was north(east)-south(west). In contrast, the eight Jewish graves that are known from Winchester are of an east to west orientation (ibid., p. 308); and similarly in Cripplegate (ibid., p. 370, based on W.F. Grimes, *The Excavations of Roman and Mediaeval London* [London, 1968], p. 181); and also in Barcelona (ibid., based on A. Duran Sanpere and J.M. Millas Vallicrosa, "Una necropolis judaica en el Montjuich de Barcelona," *Sefarad* 7 [1947], p. 238). See Lilley et al., pp. 382–84 for coffins with metal nails; for the burial rows, see ibid., p. 521.

6 See Greenwald, *Kol Bo al Avelut*, Vol. 1, p. 177, with a reference to L. Lewysohn, *Nefashot Tzadikkim* (= *Sechzig Epitaphien von Grabsteinen des israelitischen zu Worms ... Friedhofes* [Frankfurt a.M., 1855]), p. 48; L.[Y.Y.] Greenwald, *Mahril and His Time* (New York, 1944), p. 78, n. 26 (Hebrew), with a reference to D. Kaufmann, "Der Grabstein des R. Jacob b. Mose ha-Levi (מהרי״ל) in Worms," *MGWJ* 42 (1898), p. 223; see also P. Arnsberg, *Die juedischen Gemeinden in Hessen*, Vol. 2 (Frankfurt a.M., 1971), p. 18, with a reference to S. Rothschild, "Zum 500 Todstag ...," *Gemeindeblatt der Israelitischen Gemeinde Frankfurt/Main* 5, 11 (July 1927). The tombstone of *Maharil* in Worms was restored in September 1927, on the occasion of the five hundredth anniversary of his death; see Arnsberg, loc. cit.; see also the summational article by M. Grunwald, "La Cimetière de Worms," *REJ*, New Series 4 (1938), pp. 71–112. And, here, Grimm, *Teutonic Mythology*, Vol. 4, p. 1799, no. 545 records: "The dead shall be laid with their face to the **east**, lest they be scared by the winseln[?] that swarm from the west." This superstition comes from "Worms and its neighbourhood" (ibid., p. 1798), with a reference to Grimm's source: *Journal v.u.f. D.* (1790), pp. 142–44. This region apparently also gave birth to the practice recorded by Hyatt, *Folk-Lore from Adams County, Illinois*, no. 10328, p. 592: "A body should be buried so that it faces the east." We therefore find that the non-Jews in Worms, at least as early as the eighteenth century, were exacting regarding the direction of burial, in a manner close to that of the Jews of

It is commonly said that people are buried with the feet opposite the entrance of the entry and exit gate to allude to the belief in the resurrection of the dead, that [the corpse] will arise from his grave and go forth through the gate.[...] And now, when we desire to travel to the h[oly] l[and] from our land, for we are dispersed in Europe, we have two ways before us: either to travel from north to south, to the middle sea [= the Mediterranean], and from there to change direction

the city, with which the *Maharil* disagreed, although the non-Jews naturally gave a completely different reason for this. See Puckle, *Funeral Customs: Their Origin and Development*, pp. 148–49, that in England corpses were laid to rest with their heads facing the east and their feet pointed towards the west; see his explanation ad loc.; this is corroborated by C. Kightly, *The Customs and Ceremonies of Britain* (London, 1986), p. 120. See also P.J. Baldensperger, "Birth, Marriage, and Death among the Fellahin of Palestine," *PEFQS* 1894, p. 142. M.M. Honig drew my attention to the original and instructive criticism by Rabbi Abraham, the son of Maimonides, in his book *Sefer ha-Maspik le'Ovdey Hashem* (*Kitab Kifayat al-'Abidin*), Part Two, Volume Two, ed. N. Dana (Ramat Gan, 1989), p. 159:

> I am amazed that his blindness led him to forbid facing the "*mizrah*" [east] while one is sitting and engaged in the Lord's service [= prayer] because this resembles a non-Jewish practice, while he does not prevent, and even establishes as law and accepted procedure, that the dead be buried in the direction of the "*mizrah*," that specifically is a non-Jewish practice, and has no tradition among Jewish customs; the early tradition even opposed this, and the logical reason derived by analogy disagrees with this. As regards the opposition by the early tradition, behold, the ancient Jewish graves point in every direction; as is indicated by the language of the Mishnah of [Bava] Batra [6:8]: "If a person sold to his fellow a place in which to make a tomb ... he must make the inside of the vault four cubits by six, and open up within it eight niches, three on this side, three on that side, and two opposite [the doorway]." Furthermore, see the eminent tombs, the tombs of the prophets and of the sages of Israel, that can be seen to this day in Syria. As regards the disagreement by the logical argument derived by analogy: this is because facing the "*mizrah*" is the manner of serving the Lord [i.e. the direction of prayer], but for the dead, the serving of the Lord in the manner of the living has been canceled for them, because their corpses are buried in graves; the [Rabbis,] of blessed memory, said: "What is meant by the verse 'released among the dead' [Ps. 88:6] — [...] released from the commandments."

See N. Wieder, *Islamic Influences on the Jewish Worship* (Oxford, 1947), p. 73 (Hebrew; = idem, *The Formation of Jewish Liturgy in the East and the West* [Jerusalem, 1994], Vol. 2, p. 727). It is also noteworthy that Muslims bury with the face towards Mecca. See Lane, *Arabian Society in the Middle Ages*, p. 260.

7   *She'eilot u-Teshuvot Hatam Sofer, Yoreh Deah*, para. 332.

to the east, to the Land of Israel; or to travel from west to east and Constantinople, and from there to change direction to the south, and come to the Land of Israel.[...] Accordingly, it is proper to bury [the corpse] either with his head to the north and his feet to the south, so that they will roll [underground, at the resurrection of the dead] in a southerly direction [...] or with his head to the west and his feet to the east, so that they will roll in an easterly direction, as it seems in my humble opinion.[8]

The details of the burial, in this instance the direction of the grave, were influenced not only by geographical factors, but also by the climatic element. In this context, we will cite the following passage from a responsum by Rav Natronai Gaon (following the version in Ibn Ghayyat):[9]

The master, Rav Natronai, was asked whether to lay [the body of the deceased] in a niche, and place a board over the niche, so that earth and mud will not touch his face; or, should the common practice be followed, of putting earth over all? He replied: The dead and the *ani* [lit. poor; *anav* (humble)?], of what concern is this to him? Nonetheless, putting mud in his face is disgraceful, and it is not fitting to do so. **But not all the lands are the same.** [In] a place of great *barad*,[10] as in the Land of Israel, he is placed in the niche, and no earth is put on him, for we rely upon the *barad* [*sharab*] there that dries the corpse, and prevents its decay. In Babylonia, on the other hand, where there is no *barad* [*sharab*], he is buried in a coffin, and earth is placed on his face and on his eyes. If there is rain, dry earth is brought and put on his face, his face is covered with his garment, and earth is put

8 Cf. above, chap. 11. What the *Hatam Sofer* writes has its basis in the testament of R. Jeremiah in PT 12:3, whose dying command included: "and bury me on the side [*al sitra*]," and in the parallel in Genesis Rabbah 100:2: "Bury me *al orha*," that is, by the side of the road, with his sandals on his feet and his staff in his hand, so that "If the Messiah comes, I shall be ready" to follow him (to Jerusalem).

9 Cited by Rabbi Isaac ben Judah Ibn Ghayyat, *Sha'arei Simhah*, ed. I. Bamberger (Furth, 1861), *Hilkhot Avel* (*Laws of Mourning*), p. 44; Nahmanides, *Torat ha-Adam*, ed. Chavel, p. 116; *Tur, Yoreh Deah* 362.

10 Lit., hail; Nahmanides reads *sharab* (dry heat); *Bah* (Rabbi Joel Sirkes, *Yoreh Deah* 362) understands this to mean great cold that dries the flesh of the corpse, with a similar understanding in *Perishah, Yoreh Deah* 362; the editor of *Sha'arei Simhah* proposes: *gerid* (dry season, summer).

on his garments, in which he is totally enrobed. When they reach the height of a handbreadth, they place a board, that is the cover of the coffin, over the earth, and once again place a great quantity of earth until there is a mound in the height of a cubit or more.

The intent of Rav Natronai Gaon is that in a warm and dry land, where rain is not common, the body of the deceased is not degraded by a little water falling on the earth. In a very moist location, however, he is to be buried in a coffin, and then we are compelled to place earth on his face and on his eyes, so that the flesh will quickly decompose, and will not be infested by worms.[11] We learn from this that the differences between a hot and dry climate, on the one hand, and a cold and wet environment, on the other, resulted in varying methods of burying the dead.

We cannot ignore the connection between this and the law set forth in *Shulhan Arukh, Orah Hayyim* 3:6:

And likewise, a person may not sleep between east and west if his wife is with him, and it is proper to take heed of this, even when one's wife is not with him.

And similarly in *Orah Hayyim* (end of 240):

A bed in which one sleeps with one's wife must have its head and its foot, one to the north, and the other to the south.

This is in accordance with a *baraita* in Berakhot 5b:

I troubled myself concerning two things all my life [...] and that my bed should be placed between north and south.

The Talmud adds:

Rabbi Hama ben Rabbi Hanina said in the name of Rabbi Isaac: Whoever places his bed between north and south will have male children, as it is said: "And whose belly You fill with Your treasure [*u-tzefunkha*, that also has the meaning of north], who have sons in plenty" [Ps. 17:14].[12]

---

11 See *Bah*, loc. cit.; see Rabbi David ben Solomon Ibn Abi Zimra, *She'eilot u-Teshuvot ha-Radbaz*, Vol. 1, para. 484.

12 See Rashi: "its head and its foot, one to the north, and the other to the south."

The *Zohar*,[13] however, prescribes that if a person positions the right side of his bed to the south and its left side to the north, he will have male children, with a similar interpretation given by Rashi in *Sefer ha-Pardes*: its head to the east, and its foot to the west.[14] This view is shared by Rabbi Isaac ben Solomon Luria:[15]

> The matter of placing the bed between north and south follows the example of Adam when he was created, with his head to the east and his feet to the west,[16] his right hand to the south, and his left hand to the north.

Magen Avraham[17] comments that Rabbi Menahem Azariah da Fano[18] ruled in accordance with the *Zohar*, that the head (of the bed) is to be to the west, and its feet, to the east.[19]

---

13 *Zohar, Bamidbar* 118b.
14 Cited in Jonah ben Abraham Gerondi, *Sha'arei Teshuvah* (*Orah Hayyim* 3:3).
15 Rabbi Hayyim ben Joseph Vital, *Sha'ar ha-Mitzvot, Bereshit* 4a.
16 Based on Rashi, *Hagigah* 12b, that Adam extended from one end of the world to the other, and when he lay down, his head was to the east and his feet to the west.
17 *Magen Avraham, Orah Hayyim* 3:7.
18 Para. 3.
19 Interestingly, men and women were buried in separate rows, even though there apparently is no such halakhic requirement. See the thorough discussion by Greenwald, *Kol Bo al Avelut*, Vol. 1, p. 179. For the west-east orientation of the graves in Eppingen, Germany, see R. Bischoff and R. Hauke, *Die judische Friedhof im Eppingen* (Eppingen, 1996).

14

THE SEVEN EVIL SPIRITS AND THE
SEVEN FUNERAL STATIONS

A responsum written by Sar Shalom Gaon (active mid-ninth century CE) reads:

> When the Rabbis said[1] that one who follows the deceased must sit seven times, they said this only regarding one who goes to the cemetery and upon his return sits; and they said this only regarding [...] in a place where this is the practice. It is necessary to sit seven times where this is the practice, because of the spirits that accompany him, and for every hour that he sits, one of them flees.[2]

This passage was recently discussed in detail by M. Benayahu,[3] who rightly concludes that "in the view of the Geonim, this [the stations for standing]

---

1 See Bava Batra 100b; cf. Megillah 23b.
2 *Teshuvot ha-Geonim: Sha'arei Tzedek* (Jerusalem, 1966), p. 48. See Lewin, *Otzar ha-Gaonim*, Vol. 4 (Jerusalem, 1932), *Mashkin*, para. 124, p. 42; *Teshuvot Rav Sar Shalom Gaon*, ed. R.S.H. Weinberg (Jerusalem, 1976), para. 108, p. 123. Cited in *Or Zarua*, in the name of Rav Natronai Gaon, from the book *Basar al gabei Gehalim*, para. 42, fol. 86b; *Tur, Yoreh Deah* 376. See Rashbam (Rabbi Samuel ben Meir) on Bava Batra 100b, that this reason is "not clear" to him. (For the book *Basar al gabei Gehalim*, see M.M. Kasher and J.B. Mandelbaum, *Sarei ha-Elef* [new edition: Jerusalem, 1978], p. 369, para. 32.)
3 *Studies in Memory of the Rishon Le-Zion R. Yitzhak Nissim*, Vol. 6 (*Ma'amadot ve-Moshavot*), p. 27; see the earlier article by N. Rubin, "*Ma'amad ve-Moshav* [Standing and Sitting] — For the Clarification of a Mourning Custom in the Talmudic Literature," *Avraham Spiegelman Memorial Volume* (Tel Aviv, 1979), pp. 135–44 (Hebrew).

was enacted only in order to be rid of evil spirits. And there seemingly were **seven spirits**, one of whom fled at each sitting."[4]

Benayahu did not discuss the source of this conception, according to which a person returning from the cemetery is accompanied by seven evil spirits, of whom it is desirable to rid oneself, nor did he examine the nature of these spirits. These demons are well known to us already from the Early Assyrian period (seventh century BCE, and even earlier), when they first make their appearance and we are presented with a depiction of all their bad attributes.[5] They are harmful for the world as a whole, and especially for humans, as is shown by the following text:

> Seven are they! Seven are they! [...]
> Evil are they, evil are they! [...]
>
> Destructive storms (and) evil winds are they, [...]
> Seven evil gods,

---

4   And similarly in *Mahzor Vitri*, para. 280, p. 248; Ibn Ghayyat, *Sha'arei Simhah*, Vol. 2, p. 42, in the name of Rav Paltoi; Nahmanides, *Torat ha-Adam*, p. 152, in the name of an anonymous Gaon; these sources are cited by Benayahu, op. cit., pp. 27–28. For the practice in Persia, see H. Mizrahi, *The Jews of Persia* (Tel Aviv, 1959), p. 96 (Hebrew):

> On the way back from the cemetery, each person reads seven times the chapter of Psalms "O you who dwell in the shelter of the Most High" (Ps. 91). Each time that he comes to the verse "For He will order His angels to guard you wherever you go" (v. 11), he lifts up two pebbles and throws them behind him, toward the grave, to stop the evil spirits who follow him. This verse contains seven words. He throws the stones the first time when he recites [the word] "*Ki*," the second time, "*malakhav*," the third time, "*yetzaveh*," and so on, until the seventh time, as he recites "*derakhekha*."

For the reciting of a "Song of *Pega'im* [Harmful Spirits]," see Benayahu, op. cit., pp. 39–43; Index, "*Shir shel pega'im* (p. 416). It is also noteworthy that the verse customarily recited at the funeral service, "But He, being merciful, forgave iniquity ..." (Ps. 78:38) has 49 (7 X 7) letters.

5   See Thompson, *Semitic Magic*, pp. 47 ff.; 54 ff.; *idem, The Devils and Evil Spirits of Babylonia ... being Babylonian and Assyrian incantations against the demons, ghouls, vampires, hobgoblins, ghosts, and kindred evil spirits, which attack mankind* (London, 1903–04), Vol. 1, Table 5, col. 4, ll. 37 ff., pp. XLII–XLVII, 60–72. This practice is also mentioned by T.H. Gaster, *Myth, Legend, and Custom in the Old Testament* (Gloucester, Mass., 1981), Vol. 1, pp. 321, 426; for a general treatment, see Trachtenberg, *Jewish Magic and Superstition*, p. 178.

Seven evil demons,
Seven evil demons of oppression, [...]

They spill their blood like rain,
Devouring their flesh (and) sucking their veins.
[...]
They are demons full of violence, ceaselessly devouring blood. [...]

Through the gloomy street by night they roam, [...]

Rending above, bringing destruction below,
They are the children of the underworld, [...]
They are the bitter venom of the gods;
No door can shut them out, no bolt can turn them back.[6]

And this is not all: they have a special affinity for graves, as is stated explicitly by another Assyrian source: The gods which seize (upon man)

Have come forth from the grave;
The evil wind-gusts
Have come forth from the grave;
To demand the payment of rites and the pouring of libations
They have come forth from the grave;
All that is evil of those seven
Hath come like a whirlwind.[7]

This ancient tradition of the seven evil spirits has continued through the centuries, with an allusion to it in the *Testament of Reuben* 2:1 (second or first century BCE), as was noted by scholars.[8] And once again, this theme

---

6   Thompson, *Semitic Magic*, pp. 47–50. A depiction of these seven spirits appears in the "Labartu [or Lamashtu] Plaque," reproduced in E.A.W. Budge, *Amulets and Talismans* (New York, 1961²), Table XVI and description, p. 113 (Fig. 1).

7   Budge, op. cit., p. 7. For more regarding cemeteries, see ibid., pp. 39, 100, with a reference to F.C. Conybeare, "The Demonology of the New Testament," *JQR* 5 (1895), p. 588; see Conybeare, op. cit., p. 583.

8   Trans. H.C. Kee, in J.H. Charlesworth, *The Old Testament Pseudepigrapha*, Vol. 1 (Garden City, NY, 1983), p. 782, n. 2a; Conybeare, "The Demonology of the New Testament," p. 584. The seven evil ones are similarly mentioned in the Samaritan *Memar Marqah* (3:6), which is dated, fully or in part, to the fourth century CE: *Memar Marqah: The Teaching of Marqah*, ed. J. MacDonald (Berlin, 1963), pp. 73, 117; *Tibat Marqe: A Collection of Samaritan Midrashim*, ed. Z. Ben-Hayyim

appears in express fashion in a magical Christian-Syrian fragment published by H. Gollancz,[9] where we read:[10]

Eye of the seven evil and envious neighbours.

And, further:

"Seven accursed brothers, accursed sons! destructive ones, sons of men of destruction! Why do you creep along on your knees and move upon your hands?"
And they replied, "We go on our hands, so that we may eat flesh, and we crawl along upon our hands, so that we may drink blood."[11]

Here, again, we encounter the motif that we saw above, of the consuming of flesh and the sucking of blood. These formulas crossed over millennia, and passed from one land to another, from culture to culture and from religion to religion. Such an oral transmission of motifs and magic formulas over the course of millennia is not a singular phenomenon.[12]

(Jerusalem, 1988), sect. III, 155a [65], pp. 210–11: "And if anyone will tell you a blasphemous story, turn away from him, so as not to hear this. This is the person about whom I warned you, because he contains seven evil ones" (from the translation by Ben-Hayyim). See S.J. Isser, *The Dositheans: A Samaritan Sect in Late Antiquity* (Leiden, 1976), p. 14.

The seven evil spirits also appear in an apocryphal work from the third or fourth century CE(?) entitled *The Testament of Solomon* (34–41); and they were likewise mentioned by Origenes (d. 254 CE) 6:30. See F.C. Conybeare, "The Testament of Solomon," *JQR* Old Series 11 (1899), pp. 12–13, 24–25; the edition by D.C. Duling, in Charlesworth, *The Old Testament Pseudepigrapha*, Vol. 1, pp. 969–70 n. 8a; cf. F.C. Conybeare, "Christian Demonology," *JQR* Old Series 9 (1897), pp. 448–49.

9 *The Book of Protection* (London, 1912). See also Budge, *Amulets and Talismans*, p. 279.

10 Gollancz, p. LXXXII, para. 19; p. 87.

11 Gollancz, op. cit., para. 10, pp. 70–71; also cited by Thompson, *Semitic Magic*, pp. 50–51.

12 See, e.g., S. Daiches, *Babylonian Oil Magic in the Talmud and in the Later Jewish Literature* (London, 1913), pp. 39–40 and more. For an extremely instructive example, see Avishur, "*Darkei ha-Emori*," pp. 21–23. Based on Avishur, we should reject the brilliant proposal by Lieberman, *Tosefta ki-Fshutah*, Vol. 3, pp. 92–93 (my thanks to Prof. S. Friedman for drawing my attention to this article). Also see the revealing passage by A.A. Barb, "The Survival of Magic Arts," in *The Conflict between Paganism and Christianity in the Fourth Century*, ed. A. Momigliano (Oxford, 1963), pp. 100–125.

It would seem, therefore, that the Gaon's explanation of the seven sittings and standings conducted on the way back from the cemetery, that were

13 This should perhaps be connected with what appears in a Babylonian bowl: "*Shivah benei iguri(?) ve-kirye*" ("the seven sons of roofs and towns"); see C.D. Isbell, *Corpus of the Aramaic Incantation Bowls* (*SBL Dissertation Series*, No. 17) (Missoula, Mont., 1975), Text Fifty-Three, l. 2, pp. 120–21; see also Text Five, l. 4, p. 27: "*Asarna [le-khon b'i]sura [...] de-istaru bei shivah kokhavin*" ("I am binding [you with] the [sp]ell [...] by which are bound the seven stars"); cf. Text Seven, l. 15, pp. 31–32. The motif of the seven forces of evil also is present in ancient Egypt. The reverse side of the large amulet known as the Metternich Stele, which was fashioned between 378–360 BCE, contains a depiction of a polytheistic figure that stands over "figures of the incarnations of the seven Powers of Evil." See Budge, *Amulets and Talismans*, pp. 168–69, and the illustration on p. 167 (Fig. 2). See *idem*, *Egyptian Magic* (London, 1899), pp. 147–52. For the number seven in general, see ibid., pp. 433–34; see the note by F.L. Griffith and H. Thompson, *The Leyden Papyrus: An Egyptian Magical Book* (New York, 1974 = *idem*, *The Demotic Magical Papyrus of London and Leiden* [London, 1904]), pp. 78–79 on l. 26. For the sanctity and uniqueness of this number, both in Babylonia and in Egypt, see Budge, *Egyptian Magic*, pp. 165–67, 179–80. The seven spirits make their appearance in a very early chapter of the *Egyptian Book of the Dead*, chap. 17. See Budge, *Egyptian Magic*, pp. 164–65, who quotes the passage as follows: "Hail, ye seven beings who make decrees [...] who cut off heads, who hack necks in pieces, who take possession of hearts by violence and rend the places where hearts are fixed, who make slaughterings in the Lake of Fire."

It should be added that in medieval Christian writings we encounter the "seven deadly sins," that appear as seven cruel demons. See W.M. Voelge, "Morgan Manuscript M.1001: The Seven Deadly Sins and the Seven Evil Ones," in *Monsters and Demons in the Ancient and Mediaeval World: Papers Presented in Honour of Edith Porada*, ed. A. Farkas, P.O. Harper, and E.B. Harrison (Mainz o.R., 1987), pp. 101–14 (esp. p. 103, with an anonymous Lollard text from 1410).

Morgenstern already alluded to this in his book *Rites of Birth, Marriage, Death and Kindred Occasions among the Semites*, pp. 141, 251 and n. 92; see also pp. 139–42. This belief in the seven destructive agents continues to this day among the Arabs of the Land of Israel, to the extent that when counting sacks of flour, for instance, they skip the number seven. See P.J. Baldensperger, "The Immovable East," *PEFQS* 1912, p. 9: "While the measuring [of wheat] is going on the man calls out and repeats the number.[...] Seven is omitted, being the number of the seven devils, which may come and take away the wheat." (See Morgenstern, op. cit., p. 25; what Morgenstern writes on p. 201 n. 12 should be corrected.) For these seven harmful spirits in the belief of the Arabs of the Land of Israel in recent generations, see T. Canaan, *Aberglaube und Volksmedizin im Lande der Bibel* (Hamburg, 1914), pp. 7, 21 ff.; *idem*, *Daemonenglaube im Lande der Bibel* (Leipzig, 1929), p. 40.

intended to drive off the seven evil spirits, can be traced to a belief that had its origins in ancient Assyria.[13]

It is against this background that we are to understand the custom of the Jews of Aden, a practice that Rabbi Samuel ben Joseph Joshua, *Nahalat Yosef* (Jerusalem, 1988), Part Two: *Customs*, para. 25, fol. 22a, called an "erroneous custom." He writes:

> It is the practice of some in the house of the woman about to give birth to break eggs where she will give birth, to burn for smoke galbanum, and the like. Moreover, on the seventh night after her giving birth, to either a male or a female, seven eggs and seven spices are brought. The eggs are broken on **seven entrances**, each egg on a different entrance. Galbanum and garlic husks are burned for smoke, each spice on a single entrance, even at the entrances to bathing rooms and toilets. And resin also is placed on the seven entrances, seven lines on each entrance. When the women were asked: "Why are you doing so?" they replied: "**To cause the demons and the destructive agents to pass away**, so that they would not harm the mother and her child." We said, in all innocence: "One entrance is sufficient," to which they replied: "This is the custom." Until the old woman and the midwife spoke further, saying, "To placate the demons, mortal one." [...] I said to them: "Pay attention to this foolish practice, because it [entails] a serious prohibition, [this] breaking of the eggs and the incense," and I hinted to them [regarding] the speech of the old woman.[...] All this, however, was to no avail, because [my] companions were divided into four opinions.[...] I argued with many and good, I labored in vain, and I was unsuccessful. The day will come when, with the help of the Lord, may He be blessed, this erroneous custom, that has no foundation, will be abrogated. May the good Lord atone for all Israel.

The matter of eggs was discussed by R. Patai, "Folk Customs and Charms Relating to Birth," *Talpioth* 9, 1–2 (1964), pp. 240–41 (Hebrew) (who also cited Brauer as describing such a procedure). Patai explains this as symbolizing fertility. The breaking of the eggs, however, on the seven doors, corresponding to the seven demons, is undoubtedly reminiscent of our seven evil spirits.

This may provide the background for our understanding of the practice of the Jews of Salonika, as recorded by M. Molho, "Birth and Childhood among the Jews of Salonica," *Edoth* (*Communities*) 2, 3–4 (1947), p. 257: "If a woman miscarried her foetuses [...] a linen cord was wound seven times around the tomb of a rabbi who was renowned for his holiness. Afterwards, the cord was wound around the stomach of the pregnant woman, who had to wear the cord until the birth." Molho explains that this cord "that was infused with holiness, guarded the foetus until the time arrived for it to leave its mother's womb." On the other hand, the **sevenfold** winding may possibly have been directed against the seven malicious fiends, who also harm foetuses, but this remains within the realm of conjecture.

1. Assyrian Lamartu or Lamashtu plaque (obverse)

2. The colossal Cippus of Horus, commonly known as the "Metternich stele" (obverse)

15

CASTING SEVEN COINS NEXT TO THE DECEASED

A practice that was prevalent in the cities of Mogu and Kuba in the Caucasus region is described by J. Chorny:[1]

> It is also the practice in Mogu and in Kuba to cover the deceased on the bier with a costly silk sheet, and cushions and bolsters are placed under the corpse. A silver coin broken into several pieces is placed within the sheet, and when the *Hashkavot* [prayers for the dead] are recited in the cemetery, after each *Kaddish* each person among those present takes one piece of the coin that is within the sheet that is on the corpse, and they cast and throw it to a distance. I asked what were these pieces of silver coins on the deceased, within the sheet. They told me that while the deceased in lying on the bier, the *Sitra Ahra* [here, evil spirits] encircles the bier at a distance, and the coins are thrown to them [the evil spirits], so that they will take a present and leave.[2]

I recently received a small booklet by R. Patai,[3] where I found the following:

> After the washing, the rabbi of the community encircled the dead person seven times. Each round was accompanied by the smashing

---

1   J.J. Chorny, *Sefer ha-Massa'ot be-Eretz Kavkaz* (*Book of Travels in the Caucasus*) (St. Petersburg, 1884), pp. 117–18.
2   See Trachtenberg, *Jewish Magic and Superstition*, pp. 162, 183, for the motif of giving money to the destructive agents.
3   R. Patai, *Historical Traditions and Mortuary Customs of the Jews of Meshed* (Jerusalem, 1945), p. 16 (Hebrew) (with thanks to Prof. I. Ta-Shma).

of one of the small pottery jugs filled with water that stood for this purpose beside the deceased. During each encircling, one of those present would also throw a coin up, in such a manner that it would fall outside the *ohel* [purification chamber].

Patai further writes (p. 21) about the *Jadidim* (Jews forced to convert to Islam) in Meshed:

> Within the cemetery is a large building containing a table, on which the deceased is laid. Seven coins are placed on the side, and during the prayer service, these are thrown outside, one by one.

It is known that some of the customs of the Caucasus are directly related to those of Persia; Meshed is located in northeast Iran.

The use of coins is also described by Hanina Mizrahi:[4]

> Following the eulogy and *Kaddish*, three coins, of gold, silver, and copper, each of which has been cut into four equal pieces, are brought before the mullah. Four times the mullah throws three pieces, of silver, of gold, and of copper, each time to a different direction, as he places a ban upon the "destructive angels" who were born from the nocturnally emitted semen of the dead man during his lifetime, so that they may not merit to inherit from the legacy of the deceased, not even from his shrouds.

This, then, is clear testimony as to the custom in Persia. All these means are to cause the destructive agents to flee; these are not just any ordinary agents, but the special demons created by the nocturnal emission of semen during the lifetime of the deceased.

Patai further states[5] that, according to another testimony that he collected, "they did this is the courtyard of the house, in a tent." Patai additionally notes that this custom was still observed by immigrants from Meshed in Jerusalem.[6] Interestingly, a somewhat similar practice existed among the

---

4   Mizrahi, *The Jews of Persia*, p. 95.
5   Patai, op. cit., p. 21 n. 24.
6   Similar customs involving the use of coins appear among other ethnic communities in Jerusalem, as well. See J. Bergman, *Judaism: Its Soul and Life* (Jerusalem, 1935), p. 76 (Hebrew); and among the Jews of Basra: M. Grunwald, "Aus Hausapotheke und Hexenkuche," in *idem* (ed.), *Jahrbuch für judische Volkskunde* (Berlin and Vienna, 1923), p. 219.

Marranos in Portugal. Nathan Slouschz reports:[7] "A silver or gold coin is passed over the face [of the deceased], and afterwards is given as charity to the poor." Slouschz further notes that this practice was observed in several places in Africa.[8]

And among the Jews of Morocco:[9]

> When the corpse is about to be lowered [into the grave], it is customary to sprinkle gold dust, or to throw silver coins, about the grave. This gold or silver is meant for the demons, who, according to the belief, are occupied in its collection, and therefore are not free to wreak havoc.

Ben-Ami then provides several explanations for this practice, among which that this money is intended for those demons that are the spawn of wasted semen emitted by the deceased, who thereby receive their portion of the inheritance. It therefore is customary to recite the verse: "But to Abraham's sons by concubines Abraham gave gifts while he was still living; and he sent them away from his son Isaac eastward, to the land of the East" (Gen. 25:6).[10]

This practice was thoroughly researched by Prof. M. Benayahu, in the memorial volume for his father Rabbi Yitzhak Nissim,[11] where he collected and analyzed the majority of material on this subject, and showed (p. 183) that this custom was first published in the *Hukat Olam* prayerbook[12] that was ordered by Solomon Mussayoff, a wealthy Bukharan Jew with a strong Kabbalistic bent. The passage from the prayerbook reads:

> This is the order of the circuits that were customarily conducted for someone who died in the holy city of Jerusalem, may it speedily be rebuilt:

---

7 N. Slouschz, *The Marranos in Portugal* (Tel Aviv, 1932), p. 131 (Hebrew).

8 N. 1; see also p. 132.

9 I. Ben-Ami, *Le Judaisme Marocain: Etudes Ethno-Culturelles* (Jerusalem, 1975), p. 167 (Hebrew). Cf. Legey, *The Folklore of Morocco*, p. 241: "Four particles of gold are supposed to be thrown into the four corners of the grave before lowering the body into it. (Custom of Jews of Morocco.)"

10 See BT Sanhedrin 91a; see also what I wrote in *A Dictionary of Greek and Latin Legal Terms in Rabbinic Literature* (Ramat Gan, 1984), pp. 104–105.

11 *Studies in Memory of the Rishon Le-Zion R. Yitzhak Nissim*, Vol. 6 (*Ma'amadot ve-Moshavot*).

12 Part 3 (Jerusalem, 1894).

When they arrive at the grave site, the coffin is placed on the ground, and ten men assemble [...] and encircle the corpse a single time. In their circling around they say:

"*Yoshev ba-seter* [Who dwells in secret]" [...] until "for you, O Lord, are my Shelter."

"*Ana ba-koah*," the first verse.

"But to Abraham's sons by concubines [...]," and with the word *matanot* [gifts], the greatest among them takes three small pieces, gold, silver, and copper, and he throws them. Following this, he recites: "Holy is he, holy is he, holy is he to his God. Please, atone, please, for this young man (so-and-so the son of [mother's name]), who is the son of Abraham, Isaac, Jacob, Reuben, and Simeon.[...]"

Benayahu (p. 184) also cites the Land of Israel practices as recorded by Abraham Luncz:[13]

On the corpse they place seven pieces of a silver coin, and, at the conclusion of each circuit, one of those encircling takes one of these pieces and casts it away, and recites the verse: "But to Abraham's sons by concubines...."[14]

A similar ritual was observed by the Jews of Salonika, as described by Joseph Molcho:[15]

13 A.M. Luncz, *Jerusalem, Yearbook for the Diffusion of an Accurate Knowledge of Ancient and Modern Palestine*, Vol. 1 (Vienna, 1882), p. 14 (in Hebrew edition); idem, *Lu'ah Eretz Yisrael* 4 (1898), p. 23.

14 This ritual is also mentioned by Tykocinski, *Gesher ha-Hayyim*, Vol. 1, chap. 15, p. 15 (Benayahu, op. cit., pp. 184–85): "Seven small pieces of silver metal from sectile silver coins are placed on the stomach of the deceased (and if there are no silver coins, a piece of silver is cut into seven parts), and if there is no silver, a copper coin is cut up. If there is no copper, pieces of some other metal are taken. [...] (And at present, the public, whether among the Sephardim or whether among the Ashkenazim, have begun taking seven small stones.)" This is followed by a description of the throwing of the pieces and the recitation of "But to Abraham's sons by concubines...."

The throwing of small stones at the grave site is extremely widespread among various cultures throughout the world. See Frazer, *The Golden Bough*, Part 6: *The Scapegoat*, pp. 15–30; on p. 23 Frazer explains the reason for these castings: that at times they are a means of expelling evil spirits.

15 J. Molcho, *Shulhan Gavo'ah, Yoreh Deah*, Vol. 3 (Salonika, 1784), para. 358:5, fol. 186a.

they would recite "But to Abraham's sons by concubines," and every time they would cast a single copper coin to the four corners of the world, **in order to give the inheritance of the deceased to the children that the evil spirits begat from the nocturnal emission**, so that they would not harm the dead. All this was performed for a man, but not for a woman or for an infant.[16]

Benayahu (p. 188) further cites a eulogy written by Rabbi Elijah ha-Kohen ha-Itamari (the author of *Midrash Talpiyyot*) for Rabbi Jacob Hagiz of Jerusalem (d. 1634):[17]

> When a person dies, all the *kelipot* ["shells," i.e. the forces of evil] that he made during his lifetime with the impurity of the drop of nocturnal emission gather by his side, therefore the encirclings were instituted. It is the practice to cast to each side in every circuit all types of metals,[18] to remove them from the person. Consequently, they must be buried immediately following their circuit, and not remain there for a moment.

The recital of the verse "But to Abraham's sons by concubines" apparently had not yet been instituted at this juncture. Benayahu writes (p. 188) that "Rabbi Elijah ha-Kohen was seemingly the first to mention the practice of throwing coins. Furthermore, the [ceremony] of 'public proclamation' against the children of harlotry publicized [this concept of the children of harlotry], and led to its widespread dissemination throughout the Jewish communities."[19]

Benayahu (p. 225) explains that this custom is erroneous, and is based on *Sof ha-Hakafot* by Rabbi Joseph Dela Reinna(?), according to which charity must be given for every circuit after the recitation of the Thirteen Attributes, "and this is the charity **that it is incumbent upon the deceased to place**, and that he ordered be given."[20] The word "*al*" (on) was, however,

16 Benayahu, op. cit., p. 185.
17 Published by ha-Itamari in *Midrash Eliyahu* (Izmir, 1759), para. 3, fol. 14a.
18 His intent is clearly that it is the pieces of metal that cause the destructive agents to flee, since it is well-known that metal is an effective means of protection against such demons. See what I wrote, *Minhagei Yisrael*, Vol. 1, p. 16. Consequently, ha-Itamari makes no mention of the verse from Genesis, since this metal is not a **payment** to the evil spirits, but a way of causing them to withdraw from us.
19 See Benayahu, op. cit., p. 250, for "public proclamation."
20 Benayahu, op. cit., p. 114, from the book *Yikare de-Shakhbi*, attached to the book *Beit Almin* (Salonika, 1800), 19b.

mistakenly added,[21] thus resulting in the understanding that the coins (= the charity) were to be placed **on the body of the deceased**, above the shrouds: "on the right thigh seven silver coins, and on the left thigh seven copper coins, and in his center seven gold coins or seven stones."[22]

This error, however, may have been introduced in the text of the rite under external influence. During the funeral, North African Muslims have the "scribes" read the *Burdah*, or a portion of it, outside the entrance to the house where the dead person is present, after which they are paid their wages with the **money that was placed on the body of the deceased**.[23] It would therefore appear that this Muslim practice led to this error, with the addition of the word "*al*," to the final formation of the version that speaks of the placing of coins "on the deceased," as Benayahu mentions.

Rabbi Aaron Berechiah ben Moses of Modena specified explicitly in his book *Ma'avar Yabbok* the giving, in each circuit, of "at least a *perutah* [a small coin] to charity on the deceased, or it is to be set aside in his pocket, to atone for his soul."[24] Benayahu further writes (pp. 225–26) that

> in the Land of Israel it was customary to cut a single gold coin into thin pieces and to mingle them with silver and copper coins. The pieces were placed on the body of the deceased. The source of this is undoubtedly the corrupted version. [...] This corruption led to a further corruption: the money was no longer earmarked for charity and good deeds,[25] but became part of the inheritance for the children of harlotry. [...] This is explicit in the order of "*Hanakhot*" ["Interments," i.e. burial procedures] of the Ghardaia community: in each circuit, after the verse "But to Abraham's sons," along with the poem in which it is said: "For your father will be consumed by his rebellion, because of his nocturnal emissions, he will be burnt in the flame," they recited: "All the drops that issued from so-and-so, behold, this is their portion."[26]

---

21 In MS. Jerusalem — Benayahu, op. cit., p. 114 n. 38.
22 Benayahu, op. cit., p. 116.
23 Westermarck, *Ritual and Belief in Morocco*, Vol. 2, p. 455: "Who are remunerated **with money laid on the corpse**." In other places, a coin was placed within the coffin. See Radford, *Encyclopaedia of Superstitions*, pp. 87–88.
24 Benayahu, op. cit., p. 129.
25 For the giving of charity during the funeral, see Westermarck, op. cit., pp. 462, 481, 483–84.
26 Cf. Benayahu, op. cit., p. 226.

By collecting testimonies from many remote communities in his comprehensive study, Prof. Benayahu has revealed to us the secret of these coins, their origins, and the evolution of this practice.[27]

27 We should also add what was written on the Jews of Algiers by T. Campbell, *Letters from the South* [1834–35] (London, 1837), Vol. 1, pp. 291 ff. (quoted by Cohen, *An Anglo-Jewish Scrapbook, 1600–1840*, p. 295):

when the body is [...] near the opened grave [...] a Rabbi [...] throws some gold pieces as far as he can in different directions. The devil, who is by this time either in the grave or near it is tempted by his avarice to pick up the money; and while he is thus employed, the corpse is hurried back to the tomb, and earth thrown over it. One day I talked about this custom to a Moor, who has a bigoted hatred of the poor Israelites. I asked him if it was not unlike a Jew to throw away his money? "Ah, yes," he said, "but it is very like a Jew to cheat the devil."

16

THE PLUCKING OF GRASS WHEN LEAVING
THE CEMETERY

In the picture from Bodenschatz,[1] on the bottom right, we see people plucking grass after the funeral, before they leave the cemetery.[2] This ritual is prescribed by the *Shulhan Arukh*:[3] "Earth is picked up, and grass is plucked," the intent being upon leaving the cemetery. This is based on *Tur* (376:4):

> And in these places it is customary for people to cleanse [the hands] with earth, to uproot grass from the ground after *Kaddish*, and to wash their hands with water. It is said that they [the earth and the water] allude to the departure of the soul [...] and the grass alludes to the resurrection of the dead, as it is said, "and let men sprout up in the city like country grass" [Ps. 72:16].[4]

1 Bodenschatz, *Kirchliche Verfassung der heutigen Juden*, Section 4, opposite p. 179 (above chap. 6, Figs. 1, 3).

2 See Greenwald, *Kol Bo al Avelut*, Vol. 1, p. 216, para. 23. Incidentally, in the upper part of the drawing we can distinguish several pebbles lying on the gravestones, in accordance with the custom of placing small stones on the tombstone. See Sperling, *Sefer Ta'amei ha-Minhagim u-Mekorei ha-Dinim*, para. 1069; this is specified in *Be'er Hetev*, *Orah Hayyim* 226, end of §8, in the name of *Derashot me-ha-Rash* (by Rabbi Shalom ben Isaac of Neustadt). This subject is worthy of a separate discussion. In the meantime, cf. Frazer, *The Golden Bough*, Part 6: *The Scapegoat*, pp. 15 ff., esp. p. 21.

3 *Shulhan Arukh, Yoreh Deah* 376:4.

4 This topic appears in Buxtorf, *Synagoga Judaica*, pp. 702–703; Medici, *Riti e Costume degli Ebrei Confutati*, p. 208. Cf. BT Ketubot 111b: "Rabbi Hiyya bar Joseph said: The righteous will in the future break through [the earth] and rise up in Jerusalem, as it is said, 'and let men sprout up in the city like country grass,' and

This practice is first mentioned by the *Rishonim*, such as Rabbi Eliezer ben Joel ha-Levi of Bonn:[5]

> It was the practice to pluck grass and throw it behind them, to separate themselves from death, in accordance with [the verse] "and let men sprout up in the city like country grass," and as a reminder of the resurrection of the dead.

R. Jousep Schammes records:[6]

there is no 'city' other than Jerusalem, as it is said, 'I will protect and save this city' [II Kings 19:34]." See also Sanhedrin 90b; *Kunteres ha-Yehieli*, para. 44, fol. 63b.

5   *Ravyah*, Vol. 3, p. 568. This also appears in Rabbi Eliezer ben Nathan of Mainz, *Raban, Even ha-Ezer* 11, and other *Rishonim*. *Raban*, ed. Albeck, p. 10, with a reference to *Or Zarua*, Vol. 2, end of para. 422, and additional sources. Aptowitzer (*Ravyah*, loc. cit., n. 1) provides additional sources, such as *Mahzor Vitri*, p. 247; *Ha-Pardes*, para. 290; *Ma'aseh ha-Geonim* (ed. A. Epstein and J. Freimann [Berlin, 1909]), p. 51; *Rokeah*, para. 314; *Shibbolei ha-Leket, Hil. Semahot* (*Laws of Mourning*), para. 145; *Orhot Hayyim*, Vol. 2, p. 575, and more. We should also add further sources, such as *Tashbetz*, para. 447; and *Etz Hayyim*, Vol. 1, p. 394, with mention only of the taking of earth (and not grasses), and the specification: "And each one takes earth or a pebble, and recites: 'Remember that we are earth,' and casts it behind him; this is done three times." And similarly in Pedahzur, *The Book of Religion, Ceremonies, and Prayers of the Jews*, p. 15: "When the Grave is filled up, and the Congregation going away, every Man as he marches, stoops three Times to the Ground, and pulls up a handful of Grass of the Burying-Ground, flinging the Grass each Time over his Head," and the mourner proceeds to his home, with the congregation following. The detail of three times is also mentioned by Kirchheim, *The Customs of Worms Jewry*, p. 19. The threefold performance strengthens the impression that this offers protection against the malevolent spirits (see above, chap. 7, n. 22). For the evolution of this custom, see what is written regarding this by Guedemann, *Ha-Torah ve-ha-Hayyim*, Vol. 1, p. 169 n. 5, who also refers to Wuttke, *Der deutsche Volksaberglaube der Gegenwart*, pp. 93, 145: "Hat Jemand ein Pferd gekauft [...] so muss man Erde nehmen und ruckwarts uber die Grenze werfen, so kann es nichbehext werden." Based on this and additional sources, Gudemanen concludes that this is "an old custom among the early Ashkenazim, to drive away the evil spirits." See also Trachtenberg, *Jewish Magic and Superstition*, pp. 178–79, 301 n. 53. This issue was recently discussed by Eidelberg, "Holy Earth: The Development of Two Customs," *PAAJR* LIX, 1993 [Heb.], pp. 7–14, who provides a comprehensive treatment of the sources, but whose conclusions are not plausible, especially concerning his attempt to link this with the practice of making the coffin from the table on which the deceased studied; see above, chap. 9.

6   *Wormser Minhagbuch*, Vol. 2, p. 95.

After the burial, when returning, the mourner recites the *Kaddish* after "The Rock! His deeds are perfect" [*Ha-Tzur Tamim* — Deut. 32:4]. [Those present] when returning, wash their hands, prior to that *Kaddish*, they [then] uproot grass and throw it over their heads, and recite: "and let men sprout up [in the city like country grass]."[7]

Thus, the verse brought by *Tur* as the reason for the act of the plucking of grass became a passage to recite on leaving the cemetery. After the funeral company leave the cemetery, the gates of the *beit ha-taharah* are closed, as we see in this illustration (Fig. 1).

7   And similarly in Kirchheim, *The Customs of Worms Jewry*, p. 311 (albeit with the reading: "and let men sprout up and blossom in the city like country grass"); Helma, *Avel ha-Shittim*, p. 41; *Levush, Yoreh Deah* 372 (with the version in Kirchheim). See *Kunteres Avel ha-Shittim*, loc. cit. In other cultures, in contrast, we find Death, or the Angel of Death, as the reaper. See the extensive discussion in Grimm, *Teutonic Mythology*, Vol. 2, p. 848, who writes:

> Holy Scripture having already likened our fleeting life to grass, it was not difficult to see in Death a *mower* or *reaper*, who cut men down like flowers and corn-stalks. *Knife, sickle,* or *scythe* is found in this connexion: "There's a reaper they call Death, Power from God most high he hath, He whets his knife to-day, Keener it cuts the hay; Look to thyself, O flowret fair!" Pop. Hymn. The older poets never give him these implements, but the figure of "Death carried out" is sometimes furnished with a *scythe* (p. 772). In later times the *harpe'* (sickle) of the Greek Kronos (O. Muller's Archaol. p. 599) may have had an influence too, conf. *falcitenens* in Radevicus 2, 11. To "match men with flowers, make them bite the grass," Lohengr. 138, is said equally of other conquerors beside Death. But he weeds out the plants: "in lebens garten der Tot nu *jat*" Turl. Wh. 23[b]. Conversely Death, like the Devil, is called a *sower*, who disseminates weeds among men: "do der Tot sinen *samen* under si gesaete," Wh. 361, 16. "er *ier* durch in *des Todes furch*," he eared through him D.'s furrow, Ulr. Trist. 3270, simply means: he planted in him a mortal wound.

And in the "Supplement," Vol. 4, p. 1558, he adds: "Death *mows,* Lett. nahwe plavj, Bergm. 69; des Todes *sichel,* Wolkenst. 278. He is a *sitheman,* Shah-nameh, v. Gorres 1, 105–6; conf. the 3 maidens that mow the people down with their *sithes,* Kulda in D'Elv. 110."

1. Exiting the graveyard, Bodenschatz, 1748

17

THE CANDLES, SPICES, AND FLUTES OF THE DECEASED

We now turn to a survey of some of the accouterments employed in funeral services. We read in PT Berakhot 8:6:

> Rav Abbahu [said] in the name of Rav Johanan [d. 279 CE]: A blessing is not recited, neither over the candle nor over the spices of the deceased. Rabbi Hezekiah and Rabbi Jacob bar Aha [stated] in the name of Rabbi Jose ben Hanina: What has been stated refers to those that are located above the bier of the corpse. If, however, they were before [i.e. on the same level as] the bier of the deceased, a blessing is recited [over them]. I say, that in honor of the living they do so.

The (partial) parallel in the BT[1] reads:

> What is the reason [for the prohibition against use]? The candle is kindled in honor [Rashi: of the dead], the spices are used to remove the odor [Rashi: they are used for the stench of the corpse, and are not used merely to smell their fragrance].[2]

The topic of the candle of the dead and the *ner neshamah* (memorial candle; the "*Yahrzeit* candle") will discussed extensively below, in Chapter 21.[3] We will limit ourselves here to the simple meaning of this issue in the Talmud, that if the candle is above the bier of the deceased, it is not meant to provide light for the living, it is, rather, **in honor of the dead**. Consequently, no

---

1   Berakhot 53a.
2   These are the sources for the practice of placing a candle by the head of the deceased.
3   Chap. 21, pp. 567–87.

blessing is to be recited over it, for a blessing is so recited over a candle only when people enjoy its light,[4] that is, only if the light is intended for the benefit of the living. This follows the interpretation of this passage by Rashi that the candle of the dead is "in honor of the dead," and not in order to illuminate for the living. The spices serve a similar function, to overcome the bad odor of the corpse, and they are not intended to be sniffed by the living. Therefore, no blessing is recited over such candles or spices.

Even when the candle is below, before the bier of the deceased, its halakhic standing is dependent to some degree on the intent of the person who kindles it. The Tosefta[5] states categorically:

> These matters constitute the ways of the Amorites: [...] "Put a light on the ground, so that the dead will suffer"; "Do not put a light on the ground, so that the dead will not suffer." [...] These are the ways of the Amorites.

If a person meant to cause the dead to suffer (by demons and destructive agents),[6] no blessing is recited over the light or candle used for such a purpose, and this constitutes an idolatrous practice.

There are extant descriptions, both literary and artistic, of mourning customs from the Roman period contemporary with the Sages (the first centuries CE). Thus, for example, in a Roman relief most probably dating from the first or second century CE,[7] we see, within the atrium of the house,[8] the funeral bier (*lectus funebris*) upon which lies the body of a woman, fully dressed.[9] Behind her and to the left are two standing women, obviously mourning,[10] with their hands on their breasts in a position of anguish and grief.

---

4 PT Berakhot loc. cit.

5 T Shabbat 6:1.

6 See below, chap. 21, pp. 576–77.

7 From the tomb of the Haterii, close to Rome, which was discovered in 1848; presently in the Lateran Museum in Rome (see Fig. 1).

8 Also visible are the roof tiles of the house. The atrium was the place where the bier of the deceased was placed. See W.A. Becker, *Gallus: or Roman Scenes of the Time of Augustus*, trans. F. Metcalfe (London, 1907), p. 508.

9 For the type of garments and their costliness, see E. Guhl and W. Koner, *Everyday Life in Greek and Roman Times* (New York, 1989), p. 592.

10 Possibly wailing women (the Roman *praeficae*). See M Ketubot 4:4: "Rabbi Judah says: Even the poorest in Israel [should hire] not less than two flutes and one wailing woman" (see below).

Next to them, to the right, a man is placing a tiara on the head of the deceased woman (the Roman custom);[11] two large burning torches flank the bier **above** it. Below, the members of the deceased's family beat their breasts in anguish, as they stand between two braziers of spices. Our identification of these braziers is based on a passage by the Roman author Festus (mid-second century CE), in which he relates that an *accera*, a sort of box for spices burnt over coals, was placed next to the bier of the dead.[12]

At the bottom left we see a woman playing a flute, another motif that is also known from the Jewish sources. As M Ketubot 4:4 teaches: "Rabbi Judah says: Even the poorest in Israel [should hire] not less than two flutes" (Albeck: as part of the burial service). This motif is also expressed in M Shabbat 23:4: "If a non-Jew brought the flutes on the Sabbath, an Israelite may not play dirges on them [after the Sabbath], unless they had been brought from near by [that is, from within the Sabbath bounds]." PT Berakhot 3:1 elaborates on this theme: "As we have stated [in M Shabbat 23:4]: One may wait at the Sabbath limit to see to the business of [the reception of] a bride or that of [the burial] of a corpse, to fetch its coffin, shrouds, flutes, and women mourners"; the mishnah in Berakhot, however, omits the last two words: "flutes and women mourners." In any event, flutes appear in both the Jewish sources and in Roman custom.[13]

The above discussion teaches that when the Sages related to Roman funerary customs, they regarded some as tainted by idolatry, and these were totally prohibited. Others were understood by the Sages as being in honor of the dead (or of the living), and these were permitted, and were practiced by Jews in that period.

---

11 Guhl and Koner, *Everyday Life in Greek and Roman Times*, loc. cit.; see also J.C. Lawson, *Modern Greek Folklore and Ancient Greek Religion* (New York, 1964), pp. 507–14, for oil-lamps in the funeral of the deceased; next to the tomb for three or forty days (p. 508); and in the room in which the death occurred (p. 509).

12 Cf. Masse, *Persian Beliefs and Customs*, p. 90: "Camphor and aromatics are burned, on the tomb. If they burn well and are consumed completely, the deceased has gone to paradise. If they burn poorly and smoke, his soul has gone to perdition."

13 Both the flutes and the brazier appear in a Roman relief depicting the *conclamatio*, the ululation for the dead. See Smith, Wayte, and Marindin, *Dictionary of Greek and Roman Antiquities*, Vol. 1, p. 889.

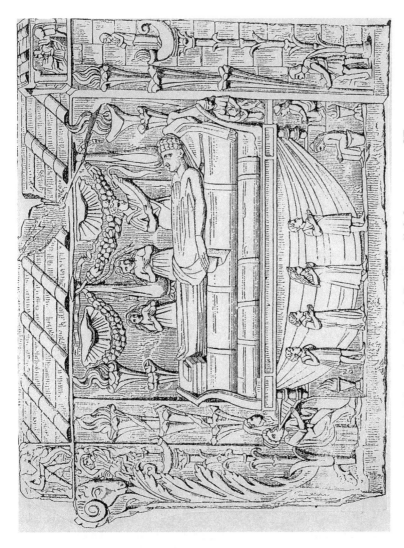

1. Mourning the dead, Roman relief, first century CE

18

KOHANIM WALKING ON THE GRAVES OF THE RIGHTEOUS

There are many examples of the survival of Jewish customs over the course of centuries, even when literary sources maintain almost total silence regarding their existence,[1] and, at times, even when they run counter to the prevalent halakhah and the rulings by a majority of *poskim*. I would first like to mention the comment made by my son David, regarding the testimony of *Kitzur Shulhan Arukh*, based on *Pithei Teshuvah*:[2]

> Some unlearned *kohanim* are accustomed to walk on the graves of the righteous, asserting that the graves of the righteous do not impart impurity. **They are in error in this**, and we must protest against it.

Pithei Teshuvah cites this in the name of *She'eilot u-Teshuvot Batei Kehunah*,[3] who wrote:

> Regarding the practice of some *kohanim* to prostrate themselves on the

---

1 An additional example appears in Scheiber, *Essays on Jewish Folklore and Comparative Literature*, Hebrew section, pp. 8–17, regarding the "*Shofar* in the Burial Ceremony," in which he demonstrates that the practice of blowing a *shofar* (ram's horn) during the burial, that was followed in several communities, originated in the apocryphal work *Life of Adam and Eve*. See further in Benayahu, *Studies in Memory of the Rishon Le-Zion R. Yitzhak Nissim*, Vol. 6, Subject Index, "*Tekiat shofar* [the blowing of the ram's horn]" (p. 409); see also S. Spiegel, *The Last Trial* (New York, 1969), pp. 118–20.

2 The full references: *Kitzur Shulhan Arukh* 24:14; *Pithei Teshuvah, Yoreh Deah* 372:2.

3 R. Isaac ben Judah ha-Kohen Rappaport, *She'eilot u-Teshuvot Batei Kehunah*, Vol. 1 ("*Beit Din* [Court]") (Izmir, 1736), para. 23.

graves of the righteous: they have no basis for this. If they were to rely upon what is taught in the midrash,[4] that it is cited in *Yalkut Mishlei*, para. 9, that Elijah said that impurity does not apply to Torah scholars, this is not so, since *Tosafot* already wrote in the chapter *"Ha-Mekabel,"* fol. 111,[5] and in the chapter *"Ha-B[a] a[l] Y[evamto],"* fol. 61,[6] that this proof is to be rejected, primarily for the reason that this refers to a *met mitzvah* [a corpse of unknown identity, whose burial is incumbent upon all]. He explained at length what compelled *Tosafot* to interpret this in such a manner. If they were to rely upon what is taught in the chapter *"Mi she-Met"*:[7] "we were skipping over coffins [...]," then here, too, since most coffins have an empty space of a handbreadth, then here [should read: there is no] Torah impurity, and a prohibition against prostrating oneself on the graves of the righteous was not enacted, this is an incorrect [argument], for [their jumping over the tombs, as a shortcut] was to fulfill some commandment or [for some other purpose that was] out of respect for other people. We have not found that prostrating oneself on the graves of the righteous is a known obligation or [relates to] the respect [to be afforded] sages. Furthermore, perhaps [the righteous one] was not buried in a coffin, or the [corpses] decomposed, in which case this would be as a "sealed grave" [i.e. with no space over the corpse], that is impure, by Torah law. Consequently, those who behave in this manner are acting improperly; see there at length.[8]

4   *Midrash Proverbs*, chap. 9, p. 62.
5   Bava Metzia, chap. 9; the reference should read: fol. 114b.
6   Yevamot, chap. 6.
7   Bava Batra, chap. 9.
8   See also *Rabad, Sefer Eshkol*, Vol. 2, para. 174: "Laws in the midrashim are not to be relied upon, unless they were accepted by the sages of the Talmud" (a view also held by *Ritba* [Rabbi Yom Tov Ishbili], Megillah 3b; Rabbi Menahem Meiri, Yevamot 61). And even according to the view that maintains that the law may be derived from this midrash, this applies only at the time of the burial, but does not sanction visiting the resting places of the righteous and prostrating oneself on their graves (see Rabbi Abraham Abele ben Hayyim Gombiner, *Zayit Ra'anan* [Dessau, 1704], Vol. 2, *Yoreh Deah*, para. 26; Rabbi Israel ben Samuel of Shklov [a pupil of the Vilna Gaon], *Pe'at ha-Shulhan* [Safed, 1836], 2:16; *Kitzur Shulhan Arukh* 24:14). Rabbi Hayyim Kohen (*Tosafot*, Ketubot 103b, s.v. *"Oto ha-Yom"*), however, permits this; cf. *Beit Yosef, Yoreh Deah* 374; *Daat ha-Haredim*, on PT Berakhot, beginning of chap. 3; the ruling by Nahmanides on Yevamot 61a, and in his commentary on Num. 19:2, that the righteous do not impart impurity; and

This practice has its origin in the *Zohar*:[9]

> For this reason the bodies of the righteous, who have labored in the Torah, remain undefiled after death (rather, they are pure, like Elijah in the cemetery, whom the rabbis met. They asked him: "Is not our master a *kohen*?" He replied to them, "The righteous do not become impure after their death [...].")

Sedei Hemed,[10] however, quotes the

> precious book of Ben Yohai [...] that in the continuation of chapter eight cited the wording of the holy *Zohar* and wrote that whatever was in parentheses [beginning with the word "rather"] is not from the text of the *Zohar*, but is an addition by a certain rabbi who wrote on the text and inserted it in [the page]; this is the statement by Rabbi Hayyim Kohen in *Tosafot*, Ketubot fol. 103b, and *Tosafot* disagree with him.[11]

similarly, *Sefer ha-Hinukh*, Commandment 263; *Hiddushei ha-Ritba*, Yevamot 61a. See Rabbi Hayyim Joseph David Azulai (*Hida*), *Penei David*, on *Shelah*; see the view held by *Rabad, Hasagot* on Maimonides, *Hil. Nezirut* (*Laws of the Nazarene Vow*) 3:17, that at the present time (i.e. after the destruction of the Temple), *kohanim* bear corpse impurity, and they are not obligated to be in a state of purity, a view shared by *Sefer Mitzvot Gadol*, Positive Commandment 231; *Mishneh le-Melekh*, Laws of Mourning, end of chap. 2; *Shei'ilot u-Teshuvot Rabbi Akiva Eiger*, second series, para. 18 (all of which are cited in Rabbi Ovadiah Yosef, *She'eilot u-Teshuvot Yehaveh Da'at*, Vol. 4, para. 58; see there). See also Medini, *Sedei Hemed* 24:93, Vol. 3, p. 272, who also raises the question whether a *kohen* at the present time (when everyone bears corpse impurity) who incurs impurity transgresses a Torah prohibition, or a rabbinic ordinance; see Medini, op. cit., 19:44 (pp. 128 ff.); see also ibid., 20:92 (pp. 267 ff.), the discussion of the question of whether, at the present time, *kohanim* are regarded as definite *kohanim*, or merely as doubtful possessors of this status, since they lack documents attesting to their lineage. Medini discusses the views of *Ribash* (Rabbi Isaac ben Sheshet Perfet; para. 92), *Maharashdam* (Rabbi Samuel ben Moses de Medina), *Mabit* (Rabbi Isaiah di Trani), Rabbi Jacob ben Joseph Reischer (in *Shevut Yaakov*), and others, each of whom maintains, based on his own reasoning, that *kohanim* at the present time are not definite *kohanim*; see also Medini, op. cit., Vol. 6, pp. 388–89 ("*Eretz Yisrael*," para. 3); and his lengthy exposition regarding the prohibited nature of this practice, Vol. 9, pp. 56–62 ("*Rosh ha-Shanah*," para. 1).

9   *Va-Yishlah*, 168a.

10   62a.

11   See *She'eilot u-Teshuvot Maharil*, para. 150 (161), p. 247 (para. 6):

> The graves of the righteous impart "tent" impurity [that is acquired from

It would appear, therefore, that most of the later halakhic authorities rule that this practice is forbidden. Nonetheless, it prevailed for many generations, despite its rejection as an erroneous custom that resulted in the violation of a categorical prohibition.[12]

being within the same structure as a corpse], as is learned in *Tosafot*, chap. "*Ha-Mekabel*" [Bava Metzia 114b]; who do we have who is greater than Joseph, and the bearers of his coffin were postponed [from observing the Paschal lamb sacrifice] until *Pesah Sheni* [Sukkah 25b], and, likewise, Mishael and Elzaphan [ibid.]. Possibly they [who thought that the graves of the righteous do not impart impurity] acted in this manner because their tombs had an opening of a handbreadth, and they had forgotten the reason and the custom from their forefathers. But we cannot rely upon [the argument that] coffins with a space of a handbreadth over the corpse [that confine the impurity, and do not impart it, as least not by Torah law], as is learned from *Tosafot* [Berakhot 19b, s.v. "*Rov*"; Bava Batra 100b, s.v. "*Ve-Roman*"], that it [the coffin] must be open on one side. See also *Pe'at ha-Shulhan*, Vol. 5, *Eretz Yisrael*, 2:18: "The practice of some people, *kohanim*, who walk on the graves of the righteous, the Tannaim, the Amoraim, and the Geonim, asserting that the graves of the righteous do not impart impurity, is to be prevented. **They are in error**"; and *Beit Yisrael* (on *Pe'at ha-Shulhan*, loc. cit.), para. 25, discusses this issue at length, including the passage from the *Zohar*, and writes: "It is clear to anyone who studies this that this [the statement in the *Zohar*] is a copyist's mistake [...] and a corruption. It should read: 'Their death is not caused by the Evil Urge, for no spirit of uncleanness rests upon them [in their lifetime]. [...]' The entire page was [written] by some pupil, and so I have found in the book *Zoharei Hammah* [Rabbi Abraham Azulai (Venice, 1655 and other editions)]."

12 See also Tykocinski, *Gesher ha-Hayyim*, Vol. 2, chap. 26, pp. 207–13. For a discussion regarding prostrating oneself on the graves of the righteous, as to the permissibility of asking for aid and succor from the dead, see also H. Pollack, *Jewish Folkways in Germanic Lands* (Cambridge, Mass., 1971), p. 49: "The validity of the custom of visiting graves had already been questioned by R. Meir of Rothenburg (d. 1293) when he urged that 'the people pray directly to God as did Abraham...'. Apparently the folk practice was not shaken by the critical viewpoint of this renowned scholar, but continued through the centuries." An additional lengthy discussion was devoted to this question by Rabbi A.M. Horovitz, *The History of Prostration on Holy Places and the Graves of the Righteous* (Jerusalem, 1971), pp. 17–43 (Hebrew) (my thanks to Prof. S.Z. Leiman, who drew my attention to this interesting book); A. Maged, *Beth Aharon: Encyclopedia of Talmudic Principles and Personalities*, Vol. 2 (New York, 1964), pp. 42 ff. (Hebrew); Greenwald, *Kol Bo al Avelut*, Vol. 2, pp. 65–66 (with a reference to Rabbi Ezekiel Shraga Halberstam [the son of Rabbi Hayyim of Zanz], *Divrei Yehezkel* [Podgorza, 1901], responsum 1, who ruled that this practice is prohibited). A student of mine, Rabbi Dr. Yehezkel Lichtenstein, recently completed an excellent doctoral dissertation that surveyed this whole issue comprehensively.

19

A KERCHIEF AROUND THE NECK OF
THE MOURNER, AND THE PRACTICE OF
COVERING THE HEAD

It is related of Iraqi Jews[1] that "a son in mourning for parents ties a kerchief around his neck." I initially thought to connect this practice with the verse in Proverbs (1:9): "a necklace about your throat." However, I then discovered in the small booklet by Raphael Patai[2] that in Meshed, "in place of the mourning gown that was customary in Kazvin [in Persia, from where the Jews of Meshed originated],[3] they now made use of a kerchief, that each one receives from those accompanying the deceased on the day of the funeral."[4] Similar mourning garb was worn by the Jews of Calcutta, India, during the entire mourning week, as is recorded by Jacob Saphir: "During the period of their mourning they bear a white kerchief on their neck, to the chest."[5] (As is well known, most of the Jews of Calcutta came from Baghdad in the first half of the nineteenth century; the connection is obvious.) And again, in Herat, Afghanistan, it was the practice that during "the entire mourning period, the members of the family wrap around their shoulders a white scarf, resembling a *talit* [prayer shawl]."[6]

1   Sassoon, *Masa Bavel*, p. 12.
2   Patai, *Historical Traditions and Mortuary Customs of the Jews of Meshed*, p. 13.
3   Patai, op. cit., p. 8; for the mourning gown, see ibid., p. 12.
4   In n. 12, Patai adds: "Cf. *Radbaz*, Vol. 2, para. 94[?]."
5   See J. Saphir, *Even Sappir*, Vol. 2 (Mainz, 1874), p. 101.
6   Z. Kurt, "Some Burial and Mourning Customs of Harat Jews (Afghanistan)," *Yeda-'Am* 18 (43–44, 1976), pp. 117–18 (Hebrew).

It would appear, however, that this is merely a variation of the ancient Talmudic practice of the mourner's "head covering," which is derived from the verse in Ezekiel (24:17): "do not cover your upper lip," from which the rabbis learned that a mourner is obligated to cover his head.[7] The manner of this head covering is stated by Samuel:[8] "Any covering [of the face] not after the Ishmaelites' manner of covering is not a proper covering [for a mourner]," and the "Ishmaelites' manner of covering" is described by Rabban Hananel (ad loc.): "Covering his moustache and beard, concealed by his turban or his cloak, which is *almanah*[9] in Arabic." This tradition was also adopted in Spain, and is mentioned by Alfasi, Maimonides, *Ritba* (Rabbi Yom Tov Ishbili), *Ran* (R. Nissim ben Reuben Gerondi), and *Tur*, followed by R. Joseph Caro in the *Shulhan Arukh*, who rules that the head covering is obligatory during the seven days of mourning.[10] *Ritba* takes note of the special practice of several communities in Spain in which "they place a piece of cloth on their moustache and beard, **and they do not cover their head**."[11] This strange practice also made its way to the Ottoman empire, as is attested by Caro:[12]

> And truly I personally experienced that I saw someone who was wrapped up.[13] I thought that he suffered from a pain in his mouth, until I later learned that he was a mourner.

Caro (ad loc.) also reveals the source of the "erroneous" custom, in the Palestinian Talmud,[14] which states:

> "Do not cover your upper lip" [Ezek. 24:17] — [we learn] from this that he must cover his mouth. **Does he cover it from below?** Rav Hisda said: So that people would not say: He suffers from a pain in his mouth.[15]

7 Moed Katan 15a.
8 Moed Katan 24a.
9 The Hebrew word for "widow."
10 *Yoreh Deah* 366.
11 On Moed Katan 24a.
12 *Beit Yosef* on *Tur*, *Yoreh Deah* 386.
13 That is, he wore under his beard a kerchief, that came up a bit to cover his moustache — a practice that he writes (above) that those doing so "are in error."
14 Moed Katan 3:5.
15 Rabbi Moses ben Simeon Margoliot, *Penei Moshe*, Moed Katan 3:5: "And covers it because of the pain, and it is not noticeable that he does so as a sign of mourning."

Based on this, Caro wrote in *Beit Yosef* (ad loc.):

> It seems from this [passage in] the Palestinian Talmud that those who
> are accustomed to wrap a kerchief **under their beard**, even though its
> end rises over their moustache, are in error, since this is not obvious
> that this is [on account of] mourning, people rather say: His mouth is
> hurting him.

Rabbi Issachar Tamar writes about this in his monumental work on the
Palestinian Talmud, *Alei Tamar*:[16]

> The person who covered himself did not act in this manner on his
> own, rather, there were those from an early time in the Land of Israel
> who would enwrap themselves in such a fashion, and it is to them that
> the Palestinian Talmud directed its question, "Does he cover it from
> below?" That is to say, such as those who behave in this manner. Rav
> Hisda stated, in this context, that this manner of enwrapping oneself
> is incorrect, lest people say: His mouth is hurting him. And here, we
> have the decision of the Palestinian Talmud, that the meaning of the
> verse "Do not cover your upper lip" is: over the head, downwards, to
> cover his face. This is also the view of the Babylonian Talmud, [Moed
> Katan] fol. 15, that calls this a head covering, which was interpreted
> by the *Rishonim* to mean that it covers the head to the height of the
> beard. There was, however, a second method in this, that the head was
> not covered, rather, a kerchief was wrapped under their beard, and they
> raised it upwards, to cover their moustache, thus interpreting the verse
> "do not cover your upper lip." It is to the latter that the Palestinian
> Talmud directs its question: "Does he cover it from below?", [relating
> to] the opinion of those who do so, and Rav Hisda rejects their view:
> "So that people would not say [...]."

As we have seen, this practice persisted for hundreds of years among Spanish
Jews.

In Ashkenaz, however, this custom ceased, for the most part, and the
Tosafists attest:[17]

> It is not the practice now to engage in covering the head [...] which

16 Tamar, *Alei Tamar*, *Moed*, Vol. 3 (Alon Shevut, 1992), p. 339.
17 *Tosafot*, Moed Katan 21a, s.v. "*Eilu.*"

would only result in derision addressed to the matter of the Ishmaelites' manner of covering.

Rabbi Moses of Coucy writes:[18]

18 *Sefer Mitzvot Gadol, Positive Rabbinical Commandments*; cf. *Haggahot Maimuniyyot, Hil. Avel (Laws of Mourning)* 5:70, who cites *Semag; Mahzor Vitri*, p. 243; *Orhot Hayyim*, Vol. 2, p. 588, and more; see *Minhagei Yisrael*, Vol. 3, pp. 79 ff.

Nonetheless, some German communities continued to observe this practice, as is warranted by Joseph Yuspa Hahn (*Yosif Ometz*, p. 331): "It accordingly is the practice in Worms, every holiday of theirs [the Christians], in which the Jews do not go outside to the street, they go about in mourning the entire day, wearing a *mitron* (*Kappe* in the German language). Consequently, a person should not change in this, either, from the practice of his forefathers, and they are to enwrap themselves in the synagogue courtyard in accordance with the custom, for the reason mentioned above" (cf. *Minhagei Yisrael*, Vol. 3, p. 95).

See also Schammes, *Wormser Minhagbuch*, Vol. 2, para. 248, p. 96, who wrote that "the mourner sits with the *mitron* around his neck, on his head, and he sits and is silent." For the *mitron*, see Schammes, loc. cit., editor's gloss 69. In Schammes, gloss 70, the editor explained that "the cloth that extended from the *mitron* (the *zipfel*) is wound around the neck," with a reference to the Yiddish *Minhagbuch*, "Laws of the *Seder* Night": "the mourner has a cap [i.e. scarf] wrapped around his head [and neck]." Also quoted is Rabbi Jedidiah ben Israel of Nuremberg, the pupil of Rabbi Meir ben Baruch of Rothenburg and Rabbi Jehiel of Paris, who wrote of the custom in his time: "A mourner is required to cover his moustache, thus leading to the practice that the mourner wears his hood, and places it somewhat on his chin" (*Shitah on Moed Katan, by a Pupil of Rabbeinu Jehiel of Paris*, ed. S. Eliesri and A. Jacobovitz, in: *Harry Fischel Institute Publications, Section III. Rishonim*, Vol. 1 [Jerusalem, 1937], p. 19 [Hebrew]). The editor comments on this:

In the following generations, as well, Ashkenazim may possibly have insisted that the winding of the *mitron* around the neck would also cover the chin. One of the Ashkenazim who resided in Turkey in the period in which the exiles from Spain arrived there might have seen our master Joseph Caro(?). [...] And now, even though *Maran*, [the author of] the *Beit Yosef* [i.e. Caro] rejects the practice of covering only the chin, we have seen that the sages of Ashkenaz consented to the practice. This might be so because in Ashkenaz the covering of the chin was a clear proof that [this person] is a mourner, and among them the person whose mouth hurt would cover it with another sort of cloth, and not with a *mitron*. In actuality, this matter is dependent upon custom, as in the words of *Maharil, Hil. Semahot* [Laws of "Celebrations" (= mourning)]: "The *Maharil* said that in the Rhineland the mourner covers himself around his neck with his *mitron*; he is so enwrapped all his seven days of mourning, and he would wear his cloak, because it is forbidden to walk about bareheaded. And if he would not enwrap

I have seen that this is practiced in Spain. In these kingdoms (Provence), however, it is not customary, since this results in the non-Jews greatly mocking us, as well as the maidservants in the home, and the servants and the youth.[19]

Communities of Eastern Jews and those in the Islamic lands continued to cover their heads while mourning, since in those localities apparently no shame was attached to the Ishmaelites' manner of covering. In some of these communities, however, those that had migrated east from Spain, the custom was modified, and the kerchief was worn under the chin, somewhat covering the moustache, as was shown above. This practice seemingly also was adopted in Baghdad, where it was expressed in the tying of the kerchief around the neck, and continued from that city to Persia (Meshed), and on to Calcutta in eastern India.[20]

himself as is the custom there, this constitutes being bareheaded" (*The Book of Maharil*, ed. Spitzer, p. 602, para. 13).

19 For the enwrapping of the head in general, see the concise presentation by Glick, *A Light unto the Mourner*, pp. 79–83; the excellent article by E. Zimmer, "The Covering of the Head during Mourning," *Sinai* 96, 3–4 (1984), pp. 148–68 (Hebrew) (to which we should add the gloss in Palache, *She'eilot u-Teshuvot Yafeh la-Lev*, Vol. 3, *Yoreh Deah* 386:1, fol. 105b, that "this enwrapping is not practiced in those cities, Izmir and its environs, nor is the head covered in the entire land of Turkey"). Possibly, this entire topic should be linked with that of the shapes of the Jewish turban in different times and places. See the comments in the instructive article: R. Mellinkoff, "Cain and the Jews," *Journal of Jewish Art* (1979), pp. 16–38, esp. 28–35. In some locations, a head covering in a certain style held extremely negative connotations, for both Christians and Jews. The practice of some Spanish communities mentioned above, of placing a garment over their moustache and beard, while not covering the head, may possibly have been dependent on the local style regarding head coverings. Thus, e.g., Mellinkoff attests (op. cit., p. 32 n. 45) that at times Jews in Spain were required to cover their heads with a special hood; see Rubens, *A History of Jewish Costume*, p. 89, and more.

It seems to me that this has no connection with what we found in the "Customs of Mattersdorf," at the end of *Beit Yisrael ha-Shalem*, Vol. 8 (Jerusalem, 1981), p. 307, para. 211: "The throat of the deceased was wrapped in scarves, and they would recite: 'For they are a graceful wreath upon your head, a necklace about your throat' (Prov. 1:9)." The custom of the mourner covering his face should rather be compared with similar Muslim practice. See Lane, *Arabian Society in the Middle Ages*, p. 261.

20 See above notes 4, 5.

20

THE MEANING OF THE *KADDISH*:
"MAY HIS GREAT NAME"

Much has been written about many diverse aspects of the *Kaddish*, for it is among the most frequently recited parts of the liturgy, and the most widely known element of the mourning rite. The history and sources of this prayer recited by mourners, developments in the customs regarding its recitation, and the types and versions of the *Kaddish* have all been the subject of various studies.[1] Here we will concentrate on only a single aspect, that of the recitation of "*Yehei shemei rabbah* ... [May His great name ...]."

There is a well-known comment by *Tosafot*,[2] on the wording in the Talmud text, "May His great name be blessed [*Yehei shemei ha-gadol mevorakh*]":

> This contradicts the interpretation given in *Mahzor Vitri* on "*Yehei shemei rabbah*," that this is a prayer we recite so that His name will be

---

1 See D. de Sola Pool, *The Kaddish* (New York, 1964), with bibliography on pp. VIII–X; D. Assaf, *Sefer ha-Kaddish: Its Source, Meaning, and Laws* (Haifa, 1966) (Hebrew; a popular halakhic work totally lacking critical examination); I. Elbogen, *Jewish Liturgy: A Comprehensive History* (Philadelphia, Jerusalem, 1993), pp. 80–84, 407–408; Z. Karl, "The 'Kaddish,'" *Ha-Shiloah* 35 (1915), pp. 36–49, 426–30 (reprinted as a separate booklet by the Snonit publishing house, Lvov 1935); J. Heinemann, "Prayers of Beth Midrash Origin," *JSS* 5 (1960), pp. 264–80; A.N.Z. Roth, "Yahrzeit and Orphan's Kaddish," *Talpioth* 7, 2–4 (1960), pp. 369–81 (Hebrew); I.M. Ta-Shema, "Some Notes on the Origins of the '*Kaddish Yathom*' (Orphan's Kaddish)," *Tarbiz* 53 (1984), pp. 559–68 (Hebrew); and recently, M.B. Lerner, "The Episode of the Tanna and the Dead Person — Its Literary and Halakhic Evolutions," *Asufot* 2 (1998), pp. 29–70 (Hebrew).

2 Berakhot 3a, s.v. "*Ve-Onim.*"

completed, as it is written, "Hand upon the throne of the Lord" [Exod. 17:16], that His name will not be complete nor His throne complete until the offspring of Amalek will be blotted out, understanding this as שם יה, יהא שמי"ה, *rabbah*, that is, we pray that His name will be great and whole; "*u-mevorakh le-olam* [and blessed forever]" — this is another prayer. [...] This is not plausible, for as it says here, "*Yehei shemei ha-gadol mevorakh*," meaning, this is [all] a single prayer.

This interpretation by the Tosafists is also adopted by *Tosafot Rabbi Judah Sir Leon* on this passage in Berakhot,[3] with minor changes.[4] Sir Leon raises an objection "against there being in **mahzorim**, in the interpretation of the *Kaddish*, '*Yehei shemei rabbah mevorah*' — שם יה," apparently in an additional reference to *Mahzor Vitri*. Sachs, the editor of *Tosafot Rabbi Judah Sir Leon*, already noted[5] that this does not appear in *Mahzor Vitri*'s explanation of the *Kaddish* in para. 84; to the contrary, at the end of this paragraph is an addition worded as follows:

> The interpretation of "*Yehei shemei rabbah*" is "May His great name." Accordingly, *shemei* is spelled deficiently (שמה), as they [the instances of this word in Daniel] all are in the *Targum* on Daniel.[6] Isaac son of Hayyim.[7]

The aim of this addition is to reject the view of *Mahzor Vitri* that has the plene reading, with the letter *yod* (שמיה), in order to understand this as שם יה. It is from this discussion in *Tosafot*, however, that we learn that something most likely was written in accordance with the version of *Mahzor Vitri*, as reported by *Tosafot*, but was deleted, following the view of *Tosafot*, who reject this interpretation. Thus, we are left only with the addition in accordance with the view of Tosafot.[8]

3 *Tosafot Rabbi Judah Sir Leon*, ed. N. Sachs (Jerusalem, 1969), pp. 13–14.
4 See also "The Completion of *Tosafot R[abbi] J[udah]* on the Tractate of Berakhot by R. Zebulon Sachs," *Sinai* 37 (1955), p. 91 (Hebrew); see also Rabbeinu Asher ben Saul of Lunel, *Sefer ha-Minhagot*, pub. by S. Assaf, *Sifran shel Rishonim: Responsa, Decisiones atque Minhagoth* (Jerusalem, 1935), p. 140, "*Yehei shemei rabbah ha-gadol....*" *Sefer ha-Minhagot* was written in the early twelfth century.
5 Sachs, ad loc., n. 142.
6 See Dan. 2:20: "Daniel spoke up and said: 'Let the name [שמה] of God be blessed forever and ever, for wisdom and power are his.'"
7 Ed. Horowitz, p. 56.
8 See the gloss by Sachs, ad loc. The interpretation by *Tosafot* also appears in *Tosafot*

This version of *Mahzor Vitri* (as written by *Tosafot*), which understands the name ‏י״ה‎ in "‏יהא שם י״ה רבא‎" as "may it be great and whole," separates the words "*Yehei shemei rabbah*" from the following words, that is, "*mevorakh le-olam*...." This version was rejected by the Tosafists and those sharing their view. This opinion is not unsupported; as we read in BT Sukkah (39a): "Rabba ruled: One should not say: "*Yehei shemei rabbah*" and then [pause and] say: "*mevorakh*,"[9] but rather "*Yehei shemei rabbah mevorakh*," all together."[10] Rabbi Moses Isserles establishes this view as the law:[11] "A person should not interrupt between '*Yehei shemei rabba*' and '*mevorakh*.'"[12]

Rosh on Berakhot 3a (see *Berakhah Meshuleshet* [Warsaw, 1863; photocopy edn.: Jerusalem, 1968]; Rabbi Jacob Landau, *Ha-Agur* [Naples, 1487], para. 93).

9 See Rabbi Abraham Landau, *Tzelota de-Avraham* prayerbook, ed. J. Werdiger (n.d., Tel Aviv), Vol. 1, p. 342.

10 See *Dikdukei Soferim*, Sukkot 39a, p. 120, para. 3, which omits the wording "all together," and has the version "‏רבה‎" in place of "‏רבא‎."

11 *Hagahot, Shulhan Arukh, Orah Hayyim* 56:1.

12 This interpretive disagreement between *Mahzor Vitri* and the Tosafists has a number of halakhic consequences. First, as was mentioned, is a pause to be inserted between the words "*Yehei shemei rabbah*" and "*mevorakh*," or are they to be recited together, without interruption? Second, Isserles, in *Darkei Moshe, Orah Hayyim* 56:1, cites Alexander Susslein ha-Kohen, *Sefer ha-Agudah* on Berakhot, para. 3 (Jerusalem, 1969), p. 14, that, according to the interpretation of *Tosafot*, we are to recite "*sheme*," without the vocalizing *mappik* in the letter *heh*, so this would not sound like the name of God. This view was copied by *Magen Avraham, Orah Hayyim* 56:2 (possibly the text of *Ha-Agudah* should read: "without the *mappik* in [the letter] *yod*"; see *Tzelota de-Avraham*, loc. cit.). Third, the question of plene spelling, with the letter *yod*, or deficient spelling, has an additional consequence. There is a tradition that the formulation "‏יהא שמה (?) רבא‎ ..." has 28 letters (see below), and if the plene spelling is used, the *yod* brings the total to 29 (see *Beit Yosef, Orah Hayyim* 56, s.v. "*Katav Ha-R[av] Abudarham*"). Following upon this, some *Rishonim* have the version "*ve-olmei olmaya* [‏ועלמי עלמיא‎]," without the letter *lamed*, in order to preserve the count of 28 letters, while for the other version of "‏שמה‎," without the letter *yod*, the reading is then "*ule-olmei* [‏ולעלמי‎]," with the addition of the letter *lamed*. See also *Ha-Pardes*, p. 92; *Beit Yosef, Orah Hayyim* 56, s.v. "*Katav Ha-R[av] Abudarham*," presents the view: "Our great master, Rabbi Israel Isserlein(?) [...] to recite '*le-olam le-olmei*.' The formulation established by the sages is seemingly not to be changed for any exposition, and since our predecessors accepted upon themselves to recite '*ule-olmei olmaya*,' anyone who changes is in an inferior position."

Despite the interpretation by *Tosafot*, the view of *Mahzor Vitri* is not to be totally discounted. Rabbi David ben Joseph Abudarham writes:[13]

> *"Yitgadal ve-yitkadash shemei rabbah"* — there are some who interpret this: שם יה רבה, that we pray for the name of God [שם י״ה], that is not whole, that it will be magnified and return to wholeness.[14] This is

13 *Sefer Abudarham*, ed. H.J. Ehrenreich (Deva, 1927), p. 245; and similarly in *Siddur Raschi*, ed. S. Buber (Berlin, 1911), p. 8; and in *Sefer ha-Pardes*, ed. H.J. Ehrenreich (Budapest, 1924), p. 323 (that only has the verse "O Lord, be mindful ...").

14 And similarly in many *Rishonim*. As this was formulated by Rabbi Abraham ben Azriel, *Arugat ha-Bosem*, ed. E.E. Urbach, Vol. 2 (Jerusalem, 1947), p. 198: "Consequently, they instituted '*Yehei shemei rabba mevorakh*,' which means: May the great name of God [י״ה] be blessed. That is, even though this is half the [Divine] name, it is great." See also R. Margaliot, *Sha'arei Zohar* (Jerusalem, 1978) on Berakhot 3a, p. 7, with a reference to *Zohar, Terumah* 165b: "It is His 'great name.' There is also another name less great [that is in] '*Amen. Yehei shemei rabbah mevorakh.*'" He writes, in the name of *Nitzotzei Orot*, by Rabbi Hayyim Joseph David Azulai (*Hida*), in the name of *Ramaz* (Rabbi Moses Zacuto), that this offers some support for the interpretation of *Mahzor Vitri*; see there.

See also R. Abraham ben Nathan of Lunel, *Sefer Ha-Manhig*, ed. Raphael (Jerusalem, 1978), para. 25, pp. 56–57 (and the references provided by the editor, p. 56, on l. 70, and esp. to Rabbeinu Asher ben Saul, *Sefer ha-Minhagot, Assaf, Sifran shel Rishonim*, p. 140: "Every *Amen. yehei shemei rabba ha-gadol* is a [Divine] name of four letters, which is a name that fills the whole world, for in the Exile it is not complete"); based on *Ha-Manhig* (with corruptions), in al-Nakawa, *Menorat ha-Ma'or*, ed. Enelow, Vol. 2, p. 89; and in Rabbi Isaac Aboab, *Menorat ha-Ma'or*, ed. Y. Paris-Horev and M.H. Katzenellenbogen (Jerusalem, 1961), para. 95, p. 214. This passage in *Ha-Manhig* does not originate in *Megillat Seterim* by Nissim Gaon; see the extensive discussion by Raphael, *Ha-Manhig*, p. 54, on l. 49 (according to which Enelow [n. to l. 1] should be corrected; and the editor's gloss on Aboab, *Menorat ha-Ma'or*, p. 214 n. 4).

It should also be noted, following this interpretation, that neither His name nor His throne are whole; the fourth of the following laudatory wordings: *ve-nehemata* (literally, and consolations) is no longer puzzling. For the Holy One, blessed be He, "needs consolation for the suffering He endures [...] as it is said in the first chapter of Berakhot [3a]: 'I heard a divine voice, cooing like a dove, and saying ["Woe to the children ..."].' And only in the End of Days, after the war of Gog and Magog, when the memory of Amalek shall be blotted out, will He be avenged and consoled" (*Siddur of R. Solomon ben Samson of Garmaise*, ed. M. Hershler [Jerusalem, 1971], p. 76 [Hebrew]; see the glosses by the editor; cf. *Ha-Manhig*, p. 57).

See also *Likkutei ha-Pardes* (from the school of Rashi) (Munkacs, 1896), 13b, who writes at length on this question:

for the time of the Redemption, when He shall be avenged of Amalek, who is from the seed of Esau, for He swore that He would not be whole until He shall be avenged of him, as it is said, "Hand upon the throne of the Lord" [Exod. 17:16] — the [full] Tetragrammaton was not used, but rather [the name of God, that is half of the Tetragrammaton:] י"ה; nor was כסא [the plene spelling for "chair"] used, but rather כס [the deficient spelling]. The Lord swore by His right hand and by His

How can a human being greaten the name of the Holy One? Perhaps, Heaven forbid, it is lacking, as it were? Yes, it certainly is lacking. As it is written, "Hand upon the throne of the Lord" — the Holy One, blessed be He, swore that the throne would not be whole until the memory of Amalek shall be blotted out. We have also found His name י-ה-ו-ה, and when it says כס יה, this is only half of the letters of the [Divine] name; similarly, the throne is called כס; we see that [the two words] are lacking letters. We therefore pray, "May it be magnified and sanctified," that is to say, may it be the will of the One who spoke and the world came into being, that they [the Jews] be redeemed from among the nations, and may the memory of Amalek be blotted out, [so that] His name will be sanctified, to be whole.

See also N. Weider, "The Shouting of '*Hu*' on the *Yamim Nora'im* [Days of Awe]," *Sinai* 89 (1981), pp. 21 ff. (Hebrew). The Kabbalistic interpretation of the *Kaddish*, from the school of Rabbi Isaac Sagi Nahor (the Blind), and the different trends in this interpretation in the literature of the school of Rashi, was recently the subject of an extensive and thorough discussion by H. Pedaya, "'Flaw' and 'Correction' in the Concept of the Godhead in the Teachings of Rabbi Isaac the Blind," *Jerusalem Studies in Jewish Thought* 6, 3–4 (1987), chap. 4, pp. 251–71 (Hebrew) (my thanks to Dr. Pedaya for drawing my attention to her instructive article). See also *Zeror ha-Hayyim*, by Rabbi Hayyim ben Samuel ben David of Tudela (the outstanding pupil of Rabbeinu Perez and R. Solomon ben Abraham Adret [*Rashba*]), ed. S.H. Yerushalmi (Jerusalem, 1966), p. 5 (para. 7):

There are people, who when the Reader begins to recite *Kaddish*, say: "Therefore, I pray, may the Lord's power be great ..." [Num. 14:17]. But I heard from my teacher the *Rashba*, who heard from [Nahmanides, of blessed memory,] that this is nothing; rather, he was accustomed to say: "O Lord, be mindful of Your compassion and Your faithfulness" [Ps. 25:6], because it was said in the first chapter of Berakhot [3a] that whenever [Israelites] recite in the synagogues "*Amen. Yehei shemei rabba mevorakh,*" [the Holy One, blessed be He,] shakes His head and says: "I destroyed My house and burnt My Temple ...."

The editor comments (p. 181): "This is found in many early prayerbooks in manuscripts, and especially in the customs of France." This passage is cited by Rabbi Hayyim Joseph David Azulai, *Birkei Yosef* (Leghorn, 1774) 56:4.

throne that they will not be whole until the name of Amalek is blotted out (*Tanhuma, Va-Yetze* 10).[15]

The opinion of *Mahzor Vitri* finds its full expression in the custom we find in *Sefer Haredim*:[16]

> I found in *T[urei] Z[ahav]*[17] that when the Reader recites the Kaddish, the congregation says: "Hand upon the throne of the Lord! The Lord will be at war with Amalek [throughout the ages]" [Exod. 17:16], and afterwards they respond "אמן יהא שמיה רבא." The elders also attested that this was the practice in Castille in the time of the great rabbis, the great rabbi R. Isaac Aboab[18] and the great rabbi R. Isaac De Leon, may the memory of the righteous be for a blessing. This is also the custom at present in many places.[19]

15 But he then adds: "*Amen. Yehei shemei rabbah mevorakh.*" Here, as well, "שמיה רבא" is interpreted as the divine name that will be restored to wholeness. He later adds, following the opinion of *Tosafot*: "But in all the books the version is 'Whoever responds "איש"ר [this should read: אמן יהא שמיה, without the letter *resh* = רבא]" [Berakhot 3a].'" This is a proof for the view of the Tosafist *Ri* (Rabbeinu Isaac ben Samuel), that this is merely a translation of "His great name" (as is cited by Moses of Przemysl in *Matteh Moshe*; *Levush, Orah Hayyim* 56). As this is formulated by *Beit Yosef* in *Tosafot Rosh* (*Berakhah Meshuleshet* on Berakhot 3a): "Thus it is to be found in all the old books." But see Rabbinovicz, *Dikdukei Soferim*, Berakhot 3a, p. 4, para. 20: "The version of MS. Munich: יהא שמיה רבא מברך." Rabbinovicz adds there: "And so it is in all the old editions that I possess. The *Maharshal* [Rabbi Solomon ben Jehiel Luria] corrected this in accordance with the version of *Tosafot*"; see there. And, similarly, further on, on Berakhot 21b: "In the printed versions it is: ליהא שמו הגדול מבורך, while in MS. Munich: שמיה רבא מברך"; see *Dikdukei Soferim*, op. cit., p. 102, para. *samekh*. Landau noted in *Tzelota de-Avraham*, p. 242, that the version of *Mahzor Vitri* may possibly have corresponded with MS. Munich. But see the gloss by Sachs, *Tosafot Rabbi Judah Sir Leon*, n. 140. See also *Ha-Manhig*, p. 57, ll. 80–81: "According to what is said at the beginning of Berakhot, that when Israel respond אמן יהא שמיה רב."

16 Rabbi Eleazar ben Moses Azikri, *Sefer Haredim*, ed. L. Deutsch (Kunszentmiklos, 1935), p. 19.

17 *Tikkunei Zohar*(?); I did not find this quotation (see Introduction, 13a).

18 I did not find this in Aboab's *Menorat ha-Me'or*, para. 95, pp. 214–15 (to the contrary, on p. 215, Aboab writes: "One should be careful not to interrupt there, and possibly the recitation by the congregation does not constitute an interruption for the Reader").

19 This was also the practice in Fez in the time of Rabbi Jacob Ibn Zur; see

This detailed description of the practice shows that the memory of Amalek is to be blotted out so that the Divine name will be whole, and that His throne will be whole.

The above discussion enables us to understand another practice described by *Mahzor Vitri*:[20]

> When the Reader begins [the *Kaddish* with] "*Yitgadal*," the congregation recites this verse: "Therefore, I pray, may the Lord's power be great, as You have declared, saying" [Num. 14:17], "O Lord, be mindful of Your compassion and Your faithfulness; they are as old as time" [Ps. 25:6].[21]

The first verse ("Therefore, I pray, may the Lord's power be great, as You have declared, saying") seems to strengthen and increase, as it were, the Lord's power, so that He will be able to gird Himself with strength and make His name and His throne whole. This accords with what is taught in BT Shabbat, that when Moses ascended on high and found the Holy One, blessed be He, tying crowns on the letters of the Torah, but did not extend a greeting to Him, the Holy One, blessed be He, said to him: "But you should have assisted Me"; Moses immediately responded: "Therefore, I pray, may the Lord's power be great, as You have declared...."[22] This means

---

D. Ovadia, *The Community of Sefrou* (Jerusalem, 1985), Vol. 4, "Popular Practices," p. 7 (Hebrew).

20 P. 64, "*Kaddish*."

21 A precise reading of the *Mahzor Vitri* is necessary, since its language contains two strata. In the first stratum: "the congregation recites this **verse**," that is, a single verse, namely, "Therefore, I pray" (a practice that is mentioned by al-Nakawa, *Menorat ha-Ma'or*, but, for some reason, is omitted from *Menorat ha-Ma'or* by Aboab). And afterwards, in the second stratum, an additional verse was added: "O Lord, be mindful," following another custom. See *Kol Bo*, para. 7, "The Law of the Interpretation of the *Kaddish*": "The public customarily recites in an undertone when the Reader begins '*Yitgadal*': 'Therefore, I pray, may the Lord's power be great,' 'be mindful of Your compassion,' 'The Lord desires.' After this, they respond '*A[men]. Y[ehei] Sh[emei] r[abba]*' with all their might." Here we have a third verse, "The Lord desires His [servant's] vindication, that he may magnify and glorify [*yagdil*] [His] teaching" (Isa. 42:21), which also contains the verb *gdl*, that connects with "*Yitgadal*." As regards the recitation of the verse "be mindful," see below, n. 22.

22 BT Shabbat 89a. See *Dikdukei Soferim* ad loc., p. 190, para. *shin*, that "'as You have declared' is absent from MS. Munich and from other manuscripts." Indeed, there is no need to complete the verse in this context.

that the recitation of this verse presumably aids the Holy One, blessed be He, by augmenting His power.

It would seem that the thematic-contentual connection was not the only reason for the selection of this verse to be recited during the *Kaddish*. The early Jewish sages engaged in counts[23] of the letters in verses, and they discovered that the verse "יהא שמה רבה מברך לעלם ולעלמי עלמיא" is composed of 28 letters,[24] which is the numerical value of the word "כח" (power). These correspond to the 28 letters of the verse from Numbers,[25] which also centers around the word *ko'ah*.[26] This numerical play[27] joins

23 See *Minhagei Yisrael*, Vol. 2, pp. 157–92, for an extensive discussion of this phenomenon of rabbinic numerology.

24 This is the proper spelling (with a defective "שמה," as it appears in the Book of Daniel). See *Tzelota de-Avraham*, p. 242; see also *Beit Yosef, Tur, Orah Hayyim* 56; and similarly in *Kol Bo*, para. 7.

25 See above, n. 17.

26 See *Mahzor Vitri*, end of para. 87, p. 55: "Thus said Rabbi Hashmonai(?), who saw in *Aggadat Otiot*(?) יהא שמיה רבא, as the number of letters in בראשית ברא ["When God began to create" — Gen. 1:1], which is 28 letters. This is to be recited until '*le-olam u-le-olmei almaya* [forever and to all eternity]'" (see below, n. 25). We should also comment regarding what appears in *Kol Bo*, loc. cit.: "I found in the *Kaddish* 7 words and 28 letters, as in the first verse of *Bereshit* [Gen. 1:1], and in the verse preceding the Ten Commandments [the reference is to Exod. 20:1: וידבר אלהים את כל הדברים האלה לאמר — "God spoke all these words, saying"]. This provides a basis for the exposition: Whoever responds '*Amen. Yehei shemei rabba*' becomes, as it were, a partner with the Holy One, blessed be He, in the act of Creation" (cited in *Matteh Moshe*, para. 73; cf. al-Nakawa, *Menorat ha-Ma'or*, Vol. 2, p. 89). See also *Ha-Pardes*, ed. Ehrenreich, p. 93, who concludes: "To tell you that if Israel had not accepted the Torah, the world would not exist." See also the interpretation of the *Kaddish* by Rabbeinu Meir of Narbonne, *Sefer Ham'oroth* (New York, 1964) on Berakhot 3a, p. 39. This, obviously, is related to what is stated in the *Kaddish*: "in the world that He created according to His will [*khiruteh*]. May He give reign [*Va-yamlikh*] to His kingdom," which speaks of the Creation, and which contains 28 letters (see S.I. Baer, *Avodat Yisrael* prayerbook [Roedelheim, 1868], p. 129, who mandates a pause between "*khiruteh*" and "*Va-yamlikh*"). *Shibbolei ha-Leket* and the *Tanya* comment that the ten wordings of praise in the *Kaddish*: "May [His name] be magnified, sanctified, blessed, praised, glorified, exalted, extolled, mighty, elevated, and lauded" correspond to the ten Sayings by which the world was created. This, once again, is connected to "in the world that He created according to His will" (see Baer, loc. cit.). See also the interpretation by Rabbi Judah ben Yakar in his commentary on the prayerbook, *Perush ha-Tefilot ve-ha-Berakhot* (ed. S. Yerushalmi, Vol. 1 [Jerusalem, 1968], p. 16), that שם יה is mentioned there,

together with the contentual link, and led to the creation of the custom of saying this verse during the recitation of the *Kaddish*.

and not the Tetragrammaton [...] because with יה He created two worlds, as it is written, 'For the Lord God is an everlasting Rock [*tzur olamim*, literally, the Rock (or, Creator) of worlds]' (Isa. 26:4)." Cf. Gen. Rabbah 12:10, ed. Theodor-Albeck, pp. 108–109 on this verse. *Kol Bo*, para. 17, adds: "With יי, which is the meaning of 'the wise shall obtain honor [כבוד]' (Prov. 3:35): the numerical value of כבוד is 32 [...] corresponding to the 32 ways in which the world was created" (see *Sefer Yetzirah* 1:1). The verse from Isaiah has 32 letters, as does "יהא שמיה"

This also provides the reason for the inclusion of the verse "O Lord, be mindful of Your compassion and Your faithfulness; they are old as time" (Ps. 25:6; see above, n. 20): for it, too, consists of 7 words and 28 letters.

Ateret Zekenim, by Rabbi Menahem Mendel Auerbach (a rabbinical judge in Cracow; 1620–80), *Orah Hayyim* 56, lists additional customs regarding the recitation of other biblical verses in the *Kaddish*, such as Ps. 111:6: "He revealed to His people His powerful works, in giving them the heritage of nations" (which contains 29 letters in the Hebrew and refers to the act of creation; see Rashi, Gen. 1:1) and Prov. 3:19: "The Lord founded the earth by wisdom; He established the heavens by understanding" (which consists of 7 words and, again, 29 letters), which relates to the Creation of heaven and earth (see *Targum Onkelos* on Gen. 1:1; *Tanhuma*, Gen. 1; *Tikkunei Zohar*, Introduction, 13; R. Margaliot, *Nitzotzei Zohar* 11 on *Tikkunei Zohar*, loc. cit.). As is known, *Mahzor Vitri* has the plene spelling שמיה, with the letter *yod* (cf. above, n. 22), with the verse "May His great name ..." then containing 29 letters. See *Tzelota de-Avraham*, p. 243 (see also *Seder Rav Amram Gaon*, ed. D. Goldschmidt [Jerusalem, 1971], p. 12).

27 This number 28 corresponds to the number of words from "יהא שמיה רבא" to "דאמירן בעלמא." Consequently, it is the custom of some to recite all this (through *de-amrinan be-alma*), and not only the seven words "יהא שמיה ... עלמיא," while others include "*yitborakh* [may be blessed]." See Margaliot, *Nitzotzei Zohar*, Berakhot 3a, p. 4, who cited the responsum on this issue attributed to Rabbi Isaac Gikatilla. For more regarding the recital of *yitborakh*, see A. Gaimani, "The Penetration of Rabbi Yosef Karo's Literary-Halakhic Work to Yemen," *Pe'amim* 49 (1991), pp. 12–34 (Hebrew), section 2: "The Practice regarding the Response of Amen in the *Kaddish*," in which he writes:

In the versions of the *Kaddish*, as well, we find differences between the law of Maimonides and that of [R. Joseph] Karo. One of the differences relates to the response by the congregation of "May His great name be blessed forever and ever." Some conclude their response with the word "*almaya*," while others add the following concluding word, "*yitborakh*." According to Maimonides, the word "*almaya*" is to be separated from "*yitborakh*": "When he [the Reader] first says '*ve-imru Amen* [and say: Amen],' all the people respond: "אמן יהא שמיה רבא מברך לעלם ולעלמי עלמיא." [...] And when he says: "*yitborakh*," all the

As was noted, the customs regarding this recitation are based on the version of *Mahzor Vitri*, a reading that was not accepted as the halakhah by the *poskim*. Nonetheless, this practice was followed for several centuries before falling by the wayside as time passed (along with other recitations; see nn. 20, 24), especially under the influence of the circles associated with the pupils of Rabbi Isaac Luria. A fine summation of this process is provided by Rabbi Jacob Hayyim Sofer:[28]

> people respond: "Amen"' (*Mishneh Torah*, Order of Prayers of the Whole Year, the Text of the *Kaddish*). R.J. Karo, on the other hand, maintains: "Those who respond only to '*almaya*' are in error, for it is forbidden to separate between '*almaya*' and '*yitborakh*'" (*Shulhan Arukh, Orah Hayyim* 56:3).
>
> In the work [by Rabbi David Mashriki] *Shetilei Zeitim* [Jerusalem, 1886[1]–1896[2]; Jerusalem, 1964–66, on *Shulhan Arukh*, loc. cit.], Mashriki quotes [Rabbi Joseph] Karo's wording on this law in *Beit Yosef*, according to which no separation is to be made: "Whoever separates, it is as if he separated and severed where there is no severance."
>
> This disagreement resulted in a third, intermediary, custom, which appears neither in Maimonides nor in the *Shulhan Arukh*, and may possibly **be intended to constitute correct practice according to all of them**: not to separate between the word "*almaya*" and "*yitborakh*," but **the word "*yitborakh*" is to be recited silently** [emphasis added — D. S.].

In his commentary on the *Kaddish* in *Etz Hayyim* (Vol. 1, 30a), *Maharitz* (Rabbi Yahya ben Joseph Salih) writes: "The early practice is to respond only to '*almaya*.' And it is now the practice of many to respond, close to '*almaya*,' '*yitborakh*' **silently**." Salih also explains how the new practice came into being:

> Regarding the matter of it being the custom to respond "*yitborakh*" silently, it seems, in my humble opinion, [correct] to provide this reason, namely, that it is explained for you that it is the view of Maimonides to respond only to "*almaya*," and it is known that since Maimonides is the leading authority in our place [i.e. for the Yemenite community], therefore **they did not want to act publicly** in accordance with the *Shulhan Arukh*. Accordingly, **they were accustomed to recite it silently, so as not to become embroiled in the disagreement**.

Salih draws an analogy from this practice to the Ashkenazic practice of wearing *tefillin* on *Hol ha-Moed* (the intermediary days of the Festivals of Passover and Sukkot), while reciting the blessing silently. See Palache, *Kaf ha-Hayyim*, para. 29; see also *Mahzor Vitri*, p. 21, editor's gloss, no. 30; *Shulhan Arukh, Orah Hayyim*, end of para. 87, p. 55. See the comment by N. Wieder, "'*Barukh Hu (u)Barukh Shemo*' — Its Source, Time, and Text," in *Studies in Rabbinic Literature Bible and Jewish History*, ed. Y.D. Gilat, C. Levine, and Z.M. Rabinowitz (Ramat Gan, 1982), p. 278 n. 5 (Hebrew).

28 *Kaf ha-Hayyim* 336, *Orah Hayyim* 56:1, para. 28(!).

When one begins *Yitgadal* [i.e. the *Kaddish*], one must recite "Therefore, I pray, may the Lord's power be great [...]." And so it is in the introduction to the *Tikkunim*.[29] R. Hayyim Vital, of blessed memory, wrote in *Sha'ar ha-Kavvanot*, at the end of the exposition "*Ha-Kaddish*," end of fol. 16d, in this wording: "Regarding the practice of the people to recite the verse 'Therefore, I pray, may the Lord's power be great' when the Reader says *Kaddish*, and as is mentioned in *S[efer] ha-Tikkunim* — now, my teacher [the intent is to the holy *Ari* — Rabbi Isaac Luria] prevented me from reciting it, but did not reveal to me the reason for this, possibly also because it does not appear in the *Tikkunim* [= *Tikkunei Zohar*]." And similarly, in *P[ri] E[tz ha-]H[ayyim]*, the Gate of *Kaddisim*, end of chap. 6. And also, in *Sefer Nagid u-Mitzvah* (by Rabbi Jacob Hayyim Zemah), *M[agen]A[vraham]*, 4, was cited. And similarly, *E[liah] R[abbah]* [by Rabbi Eliah Schapira], para. 4, in the name of *Maharil*, that it is not to be recited. And similarly, *Bir[kei] Y[osef]*, para. 4, in the name of his grandfather, Rabbi Abraham Azulai, who wrote, in the name of the Rashba and Nahmanides, that it is not to be said, see further there. They cited *Sh[almei] Tz[ibbur]*, fol. 88d and *Sh[a'arei] T[eshuvah]*, para. 5. And likewise, in *K[esher] G[udal]* 8:19, *B[eit] O[ved]*, 56:1:30:4. And similarly, this is how people conduct themselves, that it is not recited, not even in a place where it is permitted to interrupt, as is indicated by the plain meaning of the words of Rabbi Hayyim Vital, and not like the opposing opinion.[30]

---

29 *Tikkunei Zohar* 13a.

30 He continues: "And similarly, it was the practice not to recite the verse '[O Lord,] be mindful of Your compassion' [Ps. 25:6], and likewise, *Peri Megadim*, *Eshel Avraham* 6, [who states] that now the custom is canceled, and it is not recited at all, not even in a place where it is permitted to interrupt" (cf. Barsilai, *Sepher ha-Ittim*, p. 250; *Tur*, *Orah Hayyim* 57, and other sources cited by Wieder, p. 284 n. 39). See the observation by Ta-Shema, "Some Notes on the Origins of the '*Kaddish Yathom*,'" p. 561. See also *Hanhagat Adam*, attributed to R. Judah Leib ben Isaac: "The rabbi [...], of blessed memory, wrote not to recite 'Therefore, I pray, may the Lord's power be great' [in the *Kaddish*] even on the Sabbath. One should say only 'Amen,' but he did not desire to reveal the reason" (see also H. Liberman, *Ohel Rahel* [New York, 1980], Vol. 1, p. 225). For the book *Hanhagat Adam*, see Z. Gries, *Conduct Literature (Regimen Vitae)* (Jerusalem, 1989), p. 11, and more (Hebrew).

R. Isaac Luria did not reveal the reason for the cancellation of this phrase. Its omission, however, corresponds to the view of the Tosafists in the interpretation of the *Kaddish*, the opinion that was accepted as the halakhah in the literature of the *poskim*.

21

THE MEMORIAL CANDLE

In most instances, symbolic artifacts accompany symbolic acts and utterances, although at times we find these objects accompanying either a recitation or an act, but not both. In this chapter, we will limit our examination to a single group of practices in which symbolism is central, namely, the candle (or lamp), which appears in an extremely diverse range of Jewish customs. Itzchak Ganuz wrote a fine and comprehensive article[1] on this motif, beginning his discussion as follows:

> The candle accompanies the Jew from birth to death, and even after his decease the flame of the candle flickers to commemorate[2] the departed. Numerous customs, symbols, and motifs, which are deeply enrooted within Jewish culture throughout its history and dispersions, have been associated with the candle. The candle combines within it both the material and the spiritual realms. The expression *"ner neshamah* [literally, 'candle of the soul']"[3] defines that wonderful and diverse essence that Jewish culture has imparted to this concept. The multifaceted motif of the candle represents the joyful and the miraculous in the life of the individual and of the nation as one; the commandment; memory and identification; and expresses the honor afforded both the living and the dead. According to the sources, the candle is used for light; to fulfill the commandment,[4] without deriving

---

1   I. Ganuz, "The Candle in Jewish Folklore and Literature," *Yeda-'Am* 19 (1979), pp. 28–44 (Hebrew).
2   *Le-iluy zikhro*, literally, to (spiritually) elevate his memory.
3   Memorial candle; literally, the "candle of the soul."
4   Of Hanukkah.

any benefit from its use; and to give honor or for rejoicing. These three principles are the foundation stones from which these customs spread forth.

This subject is as broad as the sea, and a single survey is capable of drawing forth only a minuscule fraction of the plethora of material that exists on this subject. For each custom, symbol, or motif has its own background from which it evolves, the sources from which it is nourished, grows, and develops, and the diverse colorations it assumes in the different Jewish communities.

Ganuz then examines the candle as a symbol of life, a motif that has its basis in the verse "The lifebreath of man is the lamp of the Lord" (Prov. 20:27). And in the words of Rabbi Eleazer ben Judah of Worms (the author of *Rokeah*), in his book *Hokhmat ha-Nefesh*:[5] "The soul is the lamp of its Creator, as it is said, 'The lifebreath of man is the lamp of the Lord.'" "A certain Galilean" expounded on this before Rav Hisda:

> The Holy One, blessed be He, said: [...] The soul that I have planted in you is called a lamp, thus, I have enjoined you concerning matters of the candle. If you observe them, it is well; but if not, I will take your soul.[6]

The candle accompanies man from before his birth: while he is still in his mother's womb, "A light burns above its head and it looks and sees from one end of the world to the other,"[7] and at the end of his life, his dying is compared to the fading of the candle. Tractate *Semahot*[8] teaches:

> We may not close the eyes [of a dying man]. Whoever touches him and moves him is a murderer. Rabbi Meir **would compare him to a dripping candle, which if someone were to touch it, he would immediately extinguish it**. Similarly, anyone who closes the eyes of a dying person is regarded as if he releases his soul.

Ganuz further relates (p. 30):

Among Moroccan Jews, it was customary to light two candles on the

---

5 *Hokhmat ha-Nefesh*, ed. Z.E. (Shapira) Dynow (Safed, 1913), fol. 4a.
6 BT Shabbat 31b-32a (the "matters of the candle" refers to the Sabbath lights).
7 Niddah 30b.
8 *Semahot* 1:4 (*Treatise Semahot*, ed. Higger, p. 30).

wedding night, one for the groom and the other for the bride. It was said that the one whose candle was extinguished first would be the first to die.[9]

This belief has its origin in the Talmud,[10] where we read:

> One who wishes to learn whether he will live through the year or not should, during the ten days between Rosh Hashanah and Yom Kippur, kindle a lamp in a house in which there is no draft. If the lamp continues to burn, he shall know that he will live through the year.

This concept was later expressed in a practice in Eastern European cities and towns: during the day on which the "Thirteen Attributes" penitential prayers were recited, during the Ten Days of Repentance, women would engage in the making of candles for Yom Kippur. They would make two candles for the family: one, a *ner neshamah* in memory of the deceased, and the other, a "*ner hayyim*" ("candle of life"), or "*ner ha-bari*," on behalf of the living. If the *ner hayyim* continued to burn until totally consumed, this was an accepted omen that the owner of the candle would complete his year; and if, Heaven forbid, the candle were to be extinguished, this was a sign that the candle's owner would not see the end of the year. To prevent the owner of a candle that was extinguished from becoming alarmed, the practice evolved of each person entrusting the synagogue beadle with his *ner hayyim*, "who will put it among other candles so that the person will not know the identity of his candle."[11] Based on this belief, Rabbi Moses Isserles rules:[12]

> If a person's candle is extinguished on Yom Kippur, he rekindles it in the evening after the departure of Yom Kippur, and he does not extinguish it again, but rather lets it burn its full course. He should take

---

9 See also Legey, *The Folklore of Morocco*, p. 175, who states that among the Jews, at a circumcision ceremony (which is conducted seven days after birth), "two large candles, symbolizing the life of the child, are stood on each side [of the tray on which the bloodstained cloths are placed]. These candles should burn till they are quite finished. If they were to be blown out by mistake, or if they were to stop burning, it would augur a very short life for the babe."

10 Horayot 12a; Keritot 5b.

11 Rabbi Solomon Ganzfried, *Code of Jewish Law* 131:7 (trans. H.E. Goldin [New York, 1961], Vol. 3, p. 84).

12 Gloss on *Orah Hayyim* 610:4.

upon himself that, during his entire lifetime, he will not extinguish his candle in the evening after the departure of Yom Kippur, neither he nor anyone else.[13]

13 See Ashkenazy, *Ages in Judaism: Each Age and Its Sages*, pp. 322–27, for an extensive discussion. Interestingly, it is the belief in Wales that "If the wind blows out a candle on the altar of a church, the minister will soon die." See Radford, *Encyclopaedia of Superstitions*, p. 98.

I also found in Grimm, *Teutonic Mythology*, Vol. 4, p. 1822, no. 1038 (from his collection of Germanic superstitions): "If an altar-candle goes out of itself, the minister dies within a year." Cf. Grimm, p. 1843, no. 17 (from Estonia): "At the marriage-feast they set two candles before bride and bridegroom; the one whose light goes out first of itself, is sure to die first"; cf. p. 1644. See also L.J. Ivanits, *Russian Folk Belief* (New York and London, 1992), p. 55: "Many accounts tell how the *domovoi* [= spirit protector of the house, from Russian *dom* = house] foretold the master's death through [...] the extinguishing of a candle."

Also of interest is the following passage from the book *Hemdat Yamim* (attributed to Nathan of Gaza; Constantinople, 1635 [photocopy: Jerusalem, 1970]), "*Yamim Noraim* [Days of Awe]," 62a-b:

> This I have seen: it is the practice of many of the God-fearing to send oil on the eve of Yom Kippur to every synagogue, in order to fulfill their vows, for people visit one another in their celebrations and freely offer oil for lights, and I was pleased by their practice, and the intent is payment of their vows before Yom Kippur, for the above reason. And additionally, that they light from it on Yom Kippur itself, for the kindling of lights on this day is a very great matter, and it was stated in the *Zohar, Pinhas*, as follows: "Regarding the *benei heikhala*, on the ninth of the month [9 Tishrei — the eve of Yom Kippur], to be joyful [...], just as Israel fast for their sins, that atones for them, the celestial mother makes her countenance radiant to the *Matrona* [i.e. the *Shekhinah* looks favorably upon the people of Israel]." It therefore is customary to have many lights in the synagogue, to teach of the upper lights that join together to the *Shekhinah* [the source of] our strength, that is called *nun-resh* [i.e. *ner* = candle]. It is good for a person to have the intent when he kindles his lamp, to illuminate the upper lights above, for the lower [i.e. earthly] awakening [i.e. spiritual improvement] results in the upper [i.e. celestial] awakening. And it was said in the *Zohar, Bamidbar* 4b, that the lights are like the *shofar* on Rosh Hashanah, to cancel the accusers and to arouse compassion; see there. It was also said, regarding the intent of the lights, that *nun-resh* [= lamp, candle] has the numerical value of 248, corresponding to the limbs in the human body, with the remaining 2 [*ner* = 250] being the [two elements of] *nafsho ruho* [literally, "his soul, his spirit"]. The intent is that if a person is liable to [death by] burning, that light, that burns with a flame, will be as if his body and soul have been burnt; and this means: the wax that drips from it, is as if his fat and blood are dripping on the altar, and all 248 of his limbs are

After the departure of the soul from the body, the *ner neshamah* candle is lit, in accordance with the dictum of Rabbi (Judah ha-Nasi):[14]

completely consumed as burnt-offerings. It therefore was said that if these lights are extinguished, it is a bad omen for a person, Heaven forbid, that indicates the extinguishing of his soul and his spirit, and his candle will not serve as his proxy, exchange [from the pre-Yom Kippur *kaparot* ceremony], and remembrance.

The early ones already wrote that if this happened to someone, he should rekindle them in the evening after the departure of Yom Kippur, that they not be extinguished again, he rather leaves them before the sanctuary of the Lord [to burn] their full course. It once happened that a rabbi and pious one's light was extinguished on the night of Yom Kippur, and his heart died within him, for he said: "So I have died, I am lost." Within his great anguish, he entreated with prayer and great weeping all Yom Kippur regarding this. Nor was his mind at rest the night after the departure of Yom Kippur. He wore sackcloth and ashes, and, bemoaning, he greatly repented. He implored: "Please, O Lord, do not cause me to ascend in the midst of my life." He lit his light that had gone out in the synagogue, before the Ark of the Lord, in the evening after the departure of Yom Kippur. People estimated that lamp was sufficient to burn for a night and a day. A miracle occurred, and it continued to burn until the night of Hoshana Rabbah [i.e. for ten days]. This was a sign that his prayer had been accepted; the Lord responded to his entreaty, and no evil befell him. It accordingly seems that all these practices have a profound root and source, to which the verse "The lifebreath of man is the lamp of the Lord" [Prov. 20:27] alludes. Consequently, it is proper and correct that every person kindle some light or lamp in the synagogue, and it is good that he thereby intends to fulfill his obligation, if he vowed some [undefined] oil for light, without specification. And thus was the practice of many.

Much has been written about this book and its attribution. See A. Yaari, *Ta'alumat Sefer* (The Mystery of a Book: The Book *Hemdat Yamim*, Who Composed It, and What Was the Degree of Its Influence) (Jerusalem, 1954) (Hebrew). See the bibliography regarding this book in R. Margaliot, "Bibliographical Notes," *Aresheth* 1 (1958), p. 433 no. 854 (Hebrew); *idem*, "Bibliographical Notes III," *Aresheth* 4 (1966), p. 497 no. 854 (Hebrew).

Obviously, the extinguishing of candles in excommunication ceremonies is a symbolic act possessing the same meaning. It is for this reason that full leather bottles are brought and deflated, a bier is placed before the person being placed under the ban, and the like (see *Enziklopedia Talmudit*, Vol. 17, s.v. "*Herem* [Ban]," col. 325; for a description of the ban, see *Teshuvat Rav Paltoi Gaon*, cited in *Teshuvot ha-Geonim* (Lyck, 1864), para. 10; S. Assaf (ed.), *Teshuvot ha-Geonim* (Jerusalem, 1927; added title page in 1942 edn.: *Responsa Geonica*), p. 96 (Hebrew); see H. Tykocinski, *The Gaonic Ordinances* (Jerusalem, 1959), pp. 59 ff.; and the recent comprehensive work: I. Schepansky, *The Takkanot of Israel* (Jerusalem and New York, 1993), pp. 723–34 (Hebrew).

When Rabbi was about to expire, he said: "I require my sons." His sons came in to him, and he instructed them: "Take care regarding the proper respect of your mother. **The light shall continue to burn in its [usual] place**, the table shall be set in its [usual] place, the bed shall be made in its [usual] place. [...]"

Rashi explains:[15] "[The light shall continue to burn in its place] on the table, as during my lifetime, for on the eve of every Sabbath he would come to his home after he had died, as below." The reference is to the continuation of the passage in Ketubot:

"The light shall continue to burn in its place." [...] What is the reason? He used to return home at twilight every Sabbath eve. On a certain Sabbath eve a neighbor came to the door, speaking aloud, when his handmaiden said: "Be quiet, for Rabbi is sitting [there]." As soon as he heard this he came no more, so that no disrespect would come to the earlier righteous ones.[16]

This, apparently, was the reason for the practice in many Jewish communities to light candles in cemeteries every Sabbath and festival eve at the tombs of the righteous.[17]

We shall now devote our attention to the *ner neshamah* and "the sources from which it is nourished, grows, and develops."[18]

---

14 Ketubot 103a. For the sources of the custom of lighting a memorial candle, see S. Oppenheimer, "The Yahrzeit Light," *Journal of Halacha and Contemporary Society* 37 (1999), pp. 101–16, with citations of the relevant halakhic literature. See also the responsum of Rabbi Ovadiah Yosef, *She'eilot u-Teshuvot Yehaveh Da'at*, Vol. 5 (Jerusalem, 1983), para. 60, pp. 276–88, for a discussion on the permissibility of using an electric light as a memorial candle.

15 Rashi, Ketubot 103a, s.v. *"Ner Yehe Daluk bi-Mkomo."*

16 That is, they were not truly righteous, because they were not granted permission to return to their homes like Rabbi — Rashi, ad loc.

17 Ganuz, "The Candle in Jewish Folklore and Literature," p. 38.

18 See Zimmels, *Ashkenazim and Sephardim*, p. 187 n. 4, who quotes M. Guedemann, *Geschichte des Erzeihungswesens und der Cultur der Juden in Deutschland*, Vol. 3 (Vienna, 1888), p. 132, who is of the opinion that its source lies in Christianity, just as the term *Jahrzeit* (the anniversary of the death day — *Yahrzeit* in Yiddish) originated in the Church. On the other hand, I. Abrahams, *Jewish Life in the Middle Ages* (London, 1932), p. 156 n. 2, questions this proposal, and rightly comments that the connection between "a flame" and "the soul" predates the Christian period.

Rabbi Joseph ben Moses writes in *Leket Yosher:*[19]

> And he said: The practice is to stand [*la-amod* = *le-ha-'amid*, set up]
> each of the seven nights after they went to the cemetery a wax candle,
> water,[20] and salt (in a small container), in the place where the head of
> the deceased rested when his soul departed; and on Sabbath eve, this is
> done before going to the synagogue. I recall that I read[21] this practice
> before him [before Rabbi Israel Isserlein]; he shrugged his shoulder,
> but, at any rate, he did not tell me to erase it.[22]

The subject of the lighting of candles already appears in *Shibbolei ha-Leket:*[23]

> And in our place it was the practice to light a candle each night, all of
> the seven [days of the mourning week], where the corpse was washed,
> on the ground, **to please the soul, that returns** and mourns for [the
> body] all the seven, as it was said.[...][24]

By "as it was said," the author of *Shibbolei ha-Leket* refers to what he cited
beforehand, from *Pirkei de-Rabbi Eliezer*, namely:

> [During] the seven days of mourning, the soul goes back and forth
> from his home to his burial chamber, and from his burial chamber
> to his home, and after the seven days of mourning, the body begins

---

19 Rabbi Joseph (Joselein) ben Moses, *Leket Yosher*, ed. J. Freimann (Berlin, 1903),
    Vol. 2, pp. 96–97.
20 For the usage of a candle and a glass of water, cf. Grimm, *Teutonic Mythology*,
    Vol. 2, p. 586, regarding the γαστρομαντεία. See Westermarck, *Ritual and Belief
    in Morocco*, Vol. 2, p. 451.
21 Apparently in the notebook of Rabbi Judah Obernik.
22 See the editor's gloss, p. 97 (n. 312), with a reference to the book *Lehem ha-Panim*
    (Rabbi Moses Jekutiel [Jekubiel] Kaufmann [Furth, 1738]), para. 76, in the name of
    the author of *Ma'aneh Lashon* (Rabbi Jacob ben Abraham Solomon Shinena [Prague,
    1610, and additional editions]), which challenged this practice. This custom was
    similarly protested by Rabbi Zevi Hirsch ben Azriel of Vilna, *Bet Lehem Yehudah,
    Yoreh Deah* 376: end of 3.
23 *Hil. Semakhot*, end of para. 21, p. 350.
24 And so it is in *Tanya Rabbati, Hil. Avel* (*Laws of Mourning*), end of para. 67. It is
    instructive to compare this with the belief described by Frazer, *The Golden Bough*,
    Part 6: *The Scapegoat*, p. 16: "The Roumanians of Transylvania think that a dying
    man should have a burning candle in his hand, and that anyone who dies without a
    light has no right to the ordinary funeral ceremonies" (based on E. Geard, *The Land
    beyond the Forest* [Edinburgh and London, 1888], Vol. 1, pp. 311, 318).

to split[25] and decompose and return to the dust as it was, as it is said, "And the dust returns to the ground as it was, and the lifebreath returns to God who bestowed it" [Eccl. 12:7].[26]

25 *Le-hitbake'a* (variant: *le-tlo'a*, to be consumed by worms).

26 This is based on *Pirkei de-Rabbi Eliezer*, chap. 34 (ed. Luria, fol. 80b), but there the text is apparently abbreviated. See the gloss by Luria (52). Cf. *Rokeah*, end of para. 316; see the translation: G. Friedlander, *Pirke de Rabbi Eliezer* (London, 1916 [= New York, 1965]), p. 257, for the full text. And similarly in the MSS.; see the edition of M. Higger, "*Pirkei Rabbi Eliezer*," *Horeb* 10 (19, 20) (1948), p. 266 n. 98 (according to Codex Casanatense 1, XI, 1). Cf. PT Moed Katan 3:5, 82b, that "for three days the soul hovers over the body, it thinks it might return" (see Rabbi David Luria ad loc.); and the comment by I. Tamar, *Alei Tamar*, Moed Katan, p. 333; and similarly, in Gen. Rabbah 100:7 (ed. Theodor-Albeck, p. 1290): "Bar Kappara said: Mourning is at its most intense on the third day; until three days [after death] the soul keeps returning to the grave, thinking that it will return [to the body]. When it sees that the facial features have become disfigured, it departs and abandons [the body]. This is as it is said: 'He feels only the pain of his flesh [, and his spirit mourns in him]' [Job 14:22]" (see the editors' gloss on l. 4). See also *Zohar, Vayakhel* 199b; cf. Lev. Rabbah 18:1 (ed. Margulies, p. 398) (and Eccl. Rabbah 12:6). See *Midrash ha-Ne'elam, Hayyei Sarah* (*Zohar* 1:122b): "For it is taught: All the seven days, a person's soul visits his body and mourns for him, as it is written, 'He feels only the pain of his flesh, and his spirit mourns in him' [Job, loc. cit.]." Margulies, in his notes on the *Zohar* (loc. cit.), *Nitzotzei Zohar*, correctly refers to BT Shabbat 152a, but there the text reads: "Rav Hisda said: A person's soul mourns for him all seven [...]," without stating that it "visits his body"; the *Zohar* apparently had a different version of this passage in the Talmud (see *Dikdukei Soferim*, Shabbat 152a, p. 371, para. 30, that does not comment on this; nor did Margulies note this, not even regarding the version in *Pirkei de-Rabbi Eliezer*). Cf. also *Zohar, Vayehi* 218b: "Rabbi Judah said: All seven days, the soul goes from the house to the grave, and from the grave to the house, and mourns for the body"; and similarly in *Zohar*, op. cit. 226a. Cf. also *Zohar, Hayyei Sarah* 122b (mentioned in *Ma'avar Yabbok, Siftei Emet* 15). See: *Hokhmat ha-Nefesh* 6b: "The soul mourns for the body." See also *Maharsha* (Samuel Eliezer ben Judah ha-Levi Edels), *Hiddushei Aggadot*, Berakhot 18a, s.v. "*Ma'aseh be-Hasid Ehad*"; for "The journeys of the *neshamah* and the *nefesh* [both translated as "soul"], apart from the body," see Tykocinski, *Gesher ha-Hayyim*, Vol. 2, chap. 27, pp. 214 ff. (with thanks to my son David). For Muslim beliefs as to where the soul resides after death, see Lane, *Arabian Society in the Middle Ages*, pp. 263–64.

For this Persian belief, see S. Lieberman, "Some Aspects of After Life in Early Rabbinic Literature," in S. Lieberman et al. (Editorial Committee), *Harry Austryn Wolfson Jubilee Volume* (Jerusalem, 1965), p. 506 nn. 3–4; J. Bergman, *Jewish Folklore*[2] (Jerusalem, 1961), p. 37 (Hebrew).

The passage from *Shibbolei ha-Leket* implies that the candle provides light for the returning soul, thus "pleasing it."

And similarly, Rabbeinu Bahya writes,[27] albeit in a different style:

> It is known that the soul enjoys the lighting of candles, and it goes about with the delights of majesty and joy. It spreads and expands out of the enjoyment of the light, because it is a piece of light quarried from the light of the intellect. For this reason, it is attracted to the light, that is of a like kind, even though this is a physical light and the soul is a spiritual light, pure and simple. Accordingly, Solomon, may he rest in peace, compared it [the soul] to a lamp, for he said: "The lifebreath of man is the lamp of the Lord" [Prov. 20:27].[28]

Cohen, *An Anglo-Jewish Scrapbook, 1600–1840*, pp. 293–94, cites a passage from *Memoires of the Life and Labours of R. Morrison*, by his widow (1939), pp. 491 ff.: "... and for seven nights to leave a lamp lighted at home upon a foolish opinion that the soul doth so long return to the house to seek the body. [...]"

This belief is usually used to explain the widespread practice of covering mirrors in the house of mourning, or of turning them towards the wall. This custom apparently ensued from people's fear of the soul of the deceased, which remains in the house a number of days after the burial. See Trachtenberg, *Jewish Magic and Superstition*, p. 702 n. 56; Frazer, *The Golden Bough*, Part 1: *The Magic Art*, p. 253. This may also have been the reason for some communities in Provence not to recite the "*Nishmat Kol Hai* [The soul of every living being]" prayer during prayer services in the home of the mourner. See *Orhot Hayyim, Hil. Avel* (*The Laws of Mourning*), Vol. 2, paras. 3–4, p. 580, that this is the practice of Narbonne; cf. *Kol Bo*, Laws of Mourning (fol. 88a). It is difficult, however, to connect the reason given by *Orhot Hayyim* (see there) with the recitation of "*Nishmat*." On the other hand, the recitation of "*Nishmat* [The soul of every **living** being will bless Your name ...]" would likely be an affront to the bereft soul that wanders about by its body but cannot "bless His name." This proposal, however, is nothing more than conjecture.

For the soul in the rabbinic conception in general, see E.E. Urbach, *The Sages: Their Concepts and Beliefs* (trans. I. Abrahams [Jerusalem, 1975]), Vol. 1, chap. 10 (pp. 214–54).

27 *Commentary on the Torah*, Ex. 25:31, ed. Chavel, Vol. 2, p. 282.

28 This reason is also cited by Halfon, *Hayyei Avraham*, 56a, para. 386, in the name of Rabbi Samuel Feibush ben Joseph Katz, *Leket Shmuel* (Venice, 1694), in the name of Rabbeinu Bahya. Rabbi Yossef Ben Naim, *Noheg be Hokhmah*, ed. M. Amar (Israel, 1986), p. 154, cites, in the name of *Zohar, Hayyei Sarah*: "For by it [the candle that is lit for the dead in their place, for seven days], it is certainly satisfactory for the soul."

Orhot Hayyim[29] also mentions this practice and its reason, although in a different formulation:

> And why is the candle placed on the floor, on the very earth, in the house of the mourner? So as not to learn from the ways of the Amorite, for it is said in the Tosefta, Shabbat, that they [the Amorites] would say: "If a person places the candle on the ground, the dead suffer." That is to say, it is for this reason that they would place it, by the door, on the ground, so that the soul would see where to go when it returns to its house.[30]

The reference is to T Shabbat 6(7):2: "These are the ways of the Amorites [...] 'Put a light on the ground, so that the dead may suffer,' 'Do not put a light on the ground, so that the dead will not suffer.'"[31] This indicates that the light frightens, saddens, and drives away souls, and definitely does not

---

29 Vol. 2, *Hil. Avel*, p. 576.

30 This is understandable on the basis of what we have seen in *Pirkei de-Rabbi Eliezer* (above).

31 See Lieberman, *Tosefta ki-Fshutah*, Vol. 3, p. 83, with a reference to Rabbi Solomon Ibn Verga, *Shevet Yehudah* (ed. M. Weiner [Hanover, 1855], p. 82) (= ed. Y. Baer and A. Shochat [Jerusalem, 1947], p. 113), as follows

> The response of the important emissary: that the priest first said that it is written in the Talmud that a light is to be placed on the ground in the house of the deceased — he may possibly have dreamed a dream, and this is merely an ancient practice, that was meant to reject a belief of sorcerers, who said that the foe who desires to cause distress to the deceased should place a candle on the floor in his house, and therefore they would not place a light on the floor of the house of the deceased. But we, in opposition to that belief, that is held by the Amorite people, do place a light on the floor [of the house] of the dead person.

There is a further reference by Lieberman to the article by H. Lewy, *Zeitschrift des Vereins fur Volkskunde* 3 (1893), p. 28, who cites Canon 34 of the Elvira Synod, from 306: "Cereos per diem placuit in coemeterio non incendi, in quietandi enim sanctorum spiritus non sunt" (see the additional bibliography listed by Lewy). Lieberman writes, in summation: "and there is no precise parallel to our Tosefta." Here we should add the interesting, but somewhat puzzling, custom recorded by S. Lieberman, *Greek and Hellenism in Jewish Palestine* (Jerusalem, 1962), pp. 78–79 (Hebrew), namely, that upon a person's death, the lamps were "overturned," i.e. snuffed out. He refers us to *4 Ezra* 10:1, "*euertimus omnes lumina*." See *Piyyutei Yannai: Liturgical Poems of Yannai*, ed. M. Zulay (Berlin, 1938), p. 189, and *Midrash Echa Zuta*, ed. S. Buber (Berlin, 1894), p. 66, which also describe such a practice.

cause them "pleasure," and seemingly contradicts the thought expressed in *Pirkei de-Rabbi Eliezer*.[32] A distinction, however, should be drawn between two different terms: the "dead" in the Tosefta are demons and other undesirable destructive agents, who should be kept away from humans, and who, according to those who follow the ways of the idolaters,[33] do indeed fear the light of a candle. The "dead" of whom *Pirkei de-Rabbi Eliezer* speaks, in contrast, is the soul of the deceased, within a week of his demise, who causes no harm, but rather mourns for himself, and returns to commune with his body. Proof for this distinction is to be found in M Berakhot (8:6): "No blessing may be recited [...] over the lamp or spices used for the dead." The Talmud explains:[34] "What is the reason? The light is kindled only in honor [Rashi: of the dead]." It could not be said that this is a light connected with "the ways of the Amorites," because it plainly is forbidden to recite a blessing over a light used for idolatry.[35] In other words, the Mishnah speaks of a lamp that is in honor of the dead (in the wording of the Talmud), and that "pleases" the soul (based on the thought in *Pirkei de-Rabbi Eliezer*). The "hundreds of oil-lamps, many with charred mouths, indicating that they were lit once" that have been found attest to this practice.[36] It is inconceivable that all these were instances of pagan practices.

In many cultures a light is to be kindled in the place of mourning, as a means of causing the flight of demons (the *jnun* in the Islamic world). In order to strengthen their deterrent force against such entities, salt would be

32 A contradiction between the (early) Tosefta and the (relatively late) *Pirkei de-Rabbi Eliezer* should not unduly disturb us. As, however, we shall see below, this contradiction can be resolved, and there is no discrepancy here.

33 For this concept, see Avishur, *"Darkei ha-Emori."*

34 Berakhot 53a.

35 This is also the case for spices used for idolatrous purposes; see the continuation of the discussion in BT Berakhot loc. cit.

36 Y. Brand, *Klei Haheres Besifrut Hatalmud* (*Ceramics in Talmudic Literature*) (Jerusalem, 1953), p. 65 and n. 260 (Hebrew), cites additional literary sources for this custom (with a reference to Lieberman). Additionally, Bergman, *Jewish Folklore*, p. 37, notes that a wax candle as long as a sick person's thumb is taken and is buried in the cemetery, as if to say: "So-and-so has already been buried," or "May this candle take the place of so-and-so" (a sort of replacement for the Yom Kippur atonement *kaparah*). See Grunwald, "Aus Hausapotheke und Hexenkuche" (above, chap. 15, n. 7), p. 217; A. Ben-Yaakob, "Id el-Ziarah in Baghdad," *Edoth* 1,1 (1945–46), p. 39 (Hebrew) (Avishur, *"Darkei ha-Emori,"* does not discuss this subject).

added to the lights, since it is a known means of protection against such fiends.[37] The reason is given in a booklet from the island of Djerba[38] for the lighting of a candle to elevate the soul of the deceased:

> For the light shuts the mouth of Satan, [preventing him] from accusing, and drives away the destructive agents, even at night, that is the time of their dominion, as it is said: "A torch is as good as two [people]."[39]

For this reason, a candle is to be lit during the entire twelve-month mourning period.[40] Rabbi Isaac Lampronti describes the custom in Mantua:[41]

> It is the practice in Mantua, even in the daytime, to make for the dying person a wax candle in the shape of the *menorah* with seven

37 See *Minhagei Yisrael*, Vol. 1, p. 224. See Westermarck, *Ritual and Belief in Morocco*, Vol. 2, pp. 436, 451, 515–16, 526; P. Sartori, "Feur und Licht im Teutengebrauche," *Zeitschrift des Vereins fur Volkskunde* 17 (1907), pp. 363 ff. According to one explanation, the light is meant to illuminate the way of the soul to the heavenly world. See Radford, *Encyclopaedia of Superstitions*, pp. 52, 86; or, the light keeps the destructive agents away from the deceased, so that they will be unable to seize his soul; see Radford, op. cit., p. 57.

  Also see Lerner, *Shmiras Haguf Vihanefesh*, Vol. 2, p. 440 (para. 150:11), who writes that it is the practice of some people to light candles next to the new mother of a male son, and especially from the night preceding the circumcision until after this ceremony (Rabbi David Zacuto, *Zekher David* [Leghorn, 1737]). In n. 15 Lerner quotes Rabbi Issachar Dov Band, *Otzar Yad Hayyim* (Lvov, 1834?), para. 40:
  > As regards the lighting of candles next to new mothers of male sons, and especially on the night preceding the circumcision until after the circumcision; some place a rooster that night under the bed, see *Zekher David* 1:22, that this is for protection against the destructive agents that desire to harm the infant prior to the circumcision. [...] And it is written in the book *Zokher ha-Berit* [by Rabbi Solomon Zalman, London, Amsterdam 1613?] 3:15, that it is a highly efficacious charm to have many candles on the night of watching (*Wachtnacht*).
  For *Wachtnacht* (the night preceding the circumcision), see: Trachtenberg, *Jewish Magic and Superstition*, pp. 106, 157, 170–72, and more. See *Leket Yosher*, above.

38 Rabbi J. Guedj, *Hesed ve-Emet* (Djerba, 1895 [1938]), p. 47.

39 Berakhot 43b, where the full text reads: "Rav Zutra ben Tobiah said in the name of Rav: A torch is as good as two, and moon[light] as three." Rashi explains: "'A torch' — as two people, concerning the one who goes forth at night, for the Master said: A single person should not go forth at night."

40 Cited by Rabbi Y. Avida, "Chapters in the History of Yahrzeit," *Sinai* 14 (1951), p. 68 (Hebrew).

41 *Pahad Yitzhak*, s.v. "*Goses* [A Dying Person]" 7, Vol. 2, 22a.

lamps,[42] perhaps in an allusion to "The lifebreath of man is the lamp of the Lord" [Prov. 20:27], **and to drive away demons and [evil] spirits**, as it is said in the Talmud, "A torch is as good as two."[43]

The conception at the base of this practice, according to the above sources, is that the primary task of the candle is to distance the destructive agents from the house of mourning, and perhaps the seven lamps are to drive away the seven evil spirits referred to above (chap. 15). In line with this idea, salt was also added, to reinforce the means of defense against the *Sitra Ahra*.

The Jewish sources, however, also offer an additional explanation, namely, that the candle provides "pleasure to the returning soul" (in the wording of *Shibbolei ha-Leket*, cited above). The author of *Hemdat Yamim*[44] wrote, in a similar vein:

> A person should also take care to kindle a light in honor of the soul of his father and his mother throughout his [mourning] year, **and the deceased will derive pleasure**. For on Sabbath eve they come to visit their house.[45] [...] For all these reasons, the sages of antiquity saw fit to enact that every person shall burn in his house a special light for the soul of the dead. And so, today as well, Ashkenazim[46] maintain this practice, and take great care regarding it. *Rashal* [Rabbi Solomon

42 We have found the practice of lighting seven candles for the Sabbath. See *Magen Avraham, Orah Hayyim* 263:1; Rabbi Isaiah Horowitz, *Shenei Luhot ha-Berit; Be'er Hetev*, in the name of Rabbi Isaac Luria; *Kaf ha-Hayyim*, and more. See Rabbi J. Lewy, *Minhag Yisrael Torah* (North Bergen, NJ, 1990), p. 298. See also *Hemdat Yamim*, Vol. 1, *Shabbat*, 32a. See *Minhagei Yisrael*, Vol. 5, p. 163.

43 Zlotnik, n. 6. See *Minhagei Yisrael*, Vol. 4, p. 256, the practice of Habad (Lubavich) Hasidism to light five candles during the *shivah* mourning week, and on the anniversary of the death — is this not a sort of *hamsah* (the amuletic "hand of Fatimah" with five fingers] that protects against the destructive agents?

44 Vol. 1, "*Shabbat*," 33b.

45 As did Rabbi Judah ha-Nasi (Ketubot 103a), cited above. For the seven candles, see above, n. 41.

46 Which is not the practice of Sephardic Jews. See Zlotnik, op. cit., p. 68, who also quotes a letter by Rabbi Meir Ouziel (the late Rishon le-Zion [Sephardic Chief Rabbi] 1945–58) that concludes: "And know that in the Sephardic communities, this practice of lighting candles on the anniversary of parents' deaths was neither accepted nor observed. Rather, this is their custom: to provide all the oil required for lighting the synagogue on the Sabbath preceding the anniversary of the death [...] (when a person was called up to the Torah, he was called "the kindler of the lights")." See also Zimmels, *Ashkenazim and Sephardim*, p. 187.

Luria] permitted a non-Jew to kindle a light for the soul of a father or a mother *bein ha-shemashot* [at twilight — an hour that might already be the Sabbath].[47]

In many communities, it was also customary to place a cup of water next to the candle.[48] Brauer reports that this was the practice of the Jews in Amadia, in Kurdistan.[49] Libyan Jews also "were accustomed all the seven days of mourning to put in the place of the deceased two glass vessels, one full of water and the other burning."[50] A variant of this procedure is to be found in Morocco. Rabbi Yossef Ben Naim records:[51]

47 Zlotnik, loc. cit. This ruling by Luria is from his responsa, para. 46, in which he writes (at the end):

> And I similarly heard from an old man who ordered that a non-Jew be told on Sabbath eve, at twilight, to light in the synagogue, for they had forgotten to light during the day, that was the day on which his father had died, as it is customary to kindle a light on [this day] in all the land of Ashkenaz. The reason: since the world [i.e. everyone] is careful regarding [the kindling of] this light, it is regarded as a great need, and therefore it was permitted, for there is no difference [regarding the granting of permission] between a great need and an excessive loss, especially as regards this matter (cited by Goldberg, *Penei Barukh* 39:15, p. 425 n. 33, with additional sources).

See also Rabbi Ephraim Zalman Margolioth, *Mateh Efrayim* (Piotrkow, 1908), *Sha'ar* 3, in his supplementary *Elef ha-Magen*, p. 288:

> Concerning the lighting of the *Yahrzeit* candle [...] it is known that the soul derives pleasure from the lighting of candles, and it goes about with the delights of majesty and joy. It spreads and expands out of the enjoyment of the light, because it is a piece of light quarried from the light of the intellect. For this reason, it is attracted to the light, that is of a like kind [cf. Rabbeinu Bahya, above]. [...] Accordingly, King Solomon, may he rest in peace, compared the soul to a lamp, as it is said, "The lifebreath of man is the lamp of the Lord." Consequently, every year after the death of his father or mother, or other relatives, a person kindles a light in the synagogue, that is called "*Yahr zeit likht*" [death day anniversary light], for on this day the soul is permitted to wander, after having departed from this world.

See also *Ma'avar Yabbok, Siftei Emet* 15 (ed. Vilna 1927, pp. 173–74), for different reasons for the lighting of a memorial candle.

48 As was mentioned in *Leket Yosher*, above. See Greenwald, *Kol Bo al Avelut*, Vol. 1, p. 261; Vol. 2, p. 96, and more.

49 Brauer, *The Jews of Kurdistan*, p. 167.

50 See Ha-Cohen, *Higgid Mordecai: Histoire de la Libye...*, p. 219.

51 *Noheg be-Hokhmah*, s.v. "*Ashashit* [Lamp]," p. 156.

I found in a page in an old manuscript, as follows: The practice of our fathers is [i.e. has the authority of] Torah, that they were accustomed to kindle glass lamps in the synagogue; their inside has a bottom layer of fresh water, above which pure olive oil floats. They did not follow the practice as is conducted in houses and in courtyards, of lighting in metal lamps, that contain only oil, and no water.[52]

This may possibly be the source from which the practice in Aden evolved:[53]

It was the custom in our city [Aden] to turn the bed of the deceased mortal to the wall, to spread a sheet over it, and to place under it a burning lamp **on a pottery vessel** all three days.[54] And on the third day, the lamp together with the vessel are smashed on the grave of the deceased. There is a support for this in the Midrash and in the *Zohar*.[55]

---

52 He then provides an exegetical reason for this (that it corresponds to the four types of court-imposed death penalties), and an esoteric reason.

53 Rabbi Samuel ben Joseph Joshua, *Nahalat Yosef*, Part Two, fol. 21b.

54 See above, n. 25, the quotation from Gen. Rabbah 100:7, p. 1290, that "mourning is at its most intense on the third day," and the passage from PT Moed Katan cited there. Albeck, Gen. Rabbah, l. 4, prefers the version of the PT, that the mourning is most intense for all of the first three days, and not only on the third day, bringing further sources in support of his view. "And after three days the cup breaks by itself" (PT Moed Katan, loc. cit.), and then the soul departs. This apparently is the time to smash the lamp with its vessel, as if to release the soul. It should be noted that according to the Iranian religion, the "*urwan*," the parallel of the Jewish soul, passes over to the place of judgment, after having tarried in the vicinity of the body for three days. See W.W. Malandra, *An Introduction to Ancient Iranian Religion* (Minneapolis, 1983), p. 104.

55 See above, the reference to *Zohar, Hayyei Sarah*. See Bergman, *Jewish Folklore*, p. 18. The breaking of the vessel is reminiscent of the burial custom of Meshed Jewry, that after the washing of the corpse the rabbi of the congregation encircled the body seven times, with each circuit accompanied by the breaking of one of the small, water-filled clay vessels that were placed for this purpose on the table near the corpse (see above, beginning of chap. 15). Benayahu, *Studies in Memory of the Rishon Le-Zion R. Yitzhak Nissim*, pp. 179–80, quotes Abraham Moses Luncz, "Religiose und soziale Gebrauche der Israeliten im Heiligen Lande," *Jerusalem* (Vienna, 1882) (Hebrew); *Lu'ah Eretz Yisrael* 4, p. 21: "When the members of the [burial] society leave with the deceased from the entrance to his house, the beadle of the society breaks a pottery vessel on the threshold of the house, and proclaims: "By the ban of Joshua son of Nun, that all his offspring shall not follow his bier to accompany him until the members of the society have returned from

In a location, however, where prayers are held, the lamp burns all seven [mourning days], both by day and by night.

Apparently, the clay vessel on which the lamp was placed was (originally) filled with water, as is the practice of North African Jews.[56]

Y.H. Zlotnik thoroughly examined the "prohibition against drinking water at twilight,"[57] and provided copious sources that teach of the importance of water for the dead, from which we learn that anyone who drinks water at twilight any day of the year steals from his dead; there are dead in the Garden of Eden who stand over springs, with their tongue above the water, wanting to drink, but the water does not reach them. It would seem, in accordance with this tradition, that the cup is intended to give water to the dead, to cause them additional "pleasure."

It was such a "popular" reason, an actual "superstition," that probably aroused the ire and opposition of some of the later *poskim*. Rabbi Abraham Danzig writes in *Hokhmat Adam*:[58]

> [The custom] of placing a flask of water and a tablecloth (in the house of the deceased all the seven days) constitutes Amorite practices, and this custom must be halted.

the cemetery." And following Luncz, Rabbi Isaac Alfayah also writes (*Kunteres ha-Yehieli*, "Cemetery," 8b): "A pottery vessel or shards of a pottery vessel are broken at the entrance to the house, on the outside, and the ban of Joshua son of Nun is issued and decreed for all his offspring, that they are not permitted to follow his bier." It would seem, therefore, that this breaking of the pottery vessel is a part of the "ban" ceremony, possibly similar to "the inflated skin-bottles that are broken" during the ban ceremony (*Arukh ha-Shalem*, s.v. "*Heset*," Vol. 5, p. 229a).

Similar customs are also to be found among non-Jews, albeit for different reasons. See, e.g., Westermarck, *Ritual and Belief in Morocco*, Vol. 2, p. 481, that in Mequinez in North Africa, the Muslims place jugs filled with water on the grave, so that the deceased will be able to slake their thirst at the time of their resurrection.

56 In Yemen, "A candle is left burning all the seven days of mourning in the place where the corpse was washed, and a perforated clay vessel is inverted over it so that it will not be extinguished" (Y.L. Nahum, *Mi-Tzefunot Yehudei Teiman* [*From the Secrets of Yemenite Jewry*] [Tel Aviv, 1962], p. 173).

57 "Some Sabbath Aggadot and Customs," pp. 17–23. See C.M. Horowitz, *Uralte Tosefta's* (*Tosfata Atikata*), Vol. 5 (Frankfurt a.M., 1889), pp. 66 ff.

58 *Hokhmat Adam*, "*Matzevet Moshe*," Hil. *Avelut*, "*Hanhagat Hevra Kadisha* [*Burial Society Practices*]," para. 13.

Abraham Berliner writes:[59]

> Whenever the opportunity arose I attempted to fight against a worthless practice, that is frequently to be found. It resembles the practice that is very common among the Christians[60] in their homes, to place a flask of water, a sheet, and a burning lamp for the soul of the person who is departed, so that **it will bathe before approaching the throne of the eternal Judge**.

The author of *Sefer Toledot Menahem*,[61] on the other hand, complains against Danzig, and seeks to defend the practice of placing a full cup of water and a tablecloth next to the memorial lamp, since the soul descends every day of the thirty-day *sheloshim* mourning period. It is also written in *Va-Yelakket Yosef*:[62]

> That is, the reason why it is customary to place a glass cup filled with water in the house of mourning and to light an oil-lamp[63] is that the lamp of the oil for lighting alludes to the soul [...] and the water alludes to the material [...] and the glass vessel alludes to the resurrection [...] — if it breaks, it can be repaired.[64]

This explanation, therefore, is entirely allegorical and symbolical. Interestingly,

59 *Hayyei ha-Yehudim be-Ashkenaz be-Yemei ha-Beinayim*, pp. 57–58.

60 For the German belief that the dead are in need of bathing, see Wuttke, *Der deutsche Volksaberglaube der Gegenwart*, p. 472, para. 753; see Zlotnik, op. cit., pp. 22–23.

61 Rabbi Salamon Schuck, *Sefer Toledot Menahem*, "*Szidur Haminhagim*" (Munkacs, 1888), paras. 18, 19.

62 Rabbi Joseph Finzi, *Va-Yelakket Yosef* (Belgrade, 1842), 19b.

63 The intent is specifically to an oil lamp. See Rabbi Baruch Pinhas Goldberg, *Penei Barukh* (Jerusalem, 1986), 10:1, p. 108; Tykocinski, *Gesher ha-Hayyim*, Vol. 1, p. 98, based on *Tikkunei ha-Zohar* (*Tikkun* 19:281).

64 Based on Boskowitz, *Ma'amar Esther, Derush* 6, *Ma'amar* 2. See Zlotnik, "Some Sabbath Aggadot and Customs," p. 21, who provides additional sources in defense of the practice. The fact that glass vessels (in contrast to clay ones) can be repaired is mentioned in several places in the rabbinic sources. For example: "If glass vessels, although made by the breath of flesh-and-blood beings, can be repaired when broken, then how much more so flesh and blood [= man], who is created by the breath of the Holy One, blessed be He" (Sanhedrin 91a); "Just as gold vessels and glass vessels, though they be broken, can be repaired, so, too, a Torah scholar, even though he has sinned, has a remedy" (Hagigah 15a), and more. See A. Shenhar, "Glass Implements in Jewish Folk-Belief and Folk-Literature," *Yeda-'Am* 19 (45–46) (1979), pp. 45–50 (Hebrew).

in *Kol Bo al Avelut*,[65] the place of the glass cup is moved from the floor, where it (and the lamp) are situated in all the sources we have seen so far, to the windowsill. Consequently, Rabbi Greenwald could explain the custom in a more rational manner, stating[66] that the reason was "so that passersby would know that mourning was being observed there." Is there no other way, however, to inform those passing by that this is a house of mourning?[67]

As we have seen above, the command by Rabbi Judah ha-Nasi that "the light shall continue to burn in its [usual] place"[68] could hardly have been intended to drive away demons. Rather, this practice has seen the convergence and intermingling of a number of reasons from different worlds: the mundane with the holy, the impure with the pure, idolatrous practices with rabbinic dicta. This is an extremely common phenomenon in the realm of custom, and, as this is expressed by Judah Bergman:[69]

> The breaking of the cup on the wedding day is not meant to exorcise the demons, but rather to decrease joy and recall the destruction of Jerusalem. The tossing of wheat on the bride and groom has come to symbolize blessing, "that they shall be as fertile and numerous as wheat";

65 Vol. 1, p. 261; Vol. 2, p. 96.

66 Vol. 2, p. 96.

67 Greenwald also offers additional reasons, such as: to allude to the fact that only two elements — fire and water — remain, for the spirit returns to God, and the dirt returns to its place (Rabbi Joseph Schwartz, *Hadrat Kodesh* [Oradea, 1930], 47b), and the like. Rabbi A.L. Hirshovitz, *Otzar Kol Minhagei Yeshurun*[2] (Israel, 1970), 72:6, pp. 305–306, offers a logical reason for the source of the custom:

> In my humble opinion, this is because it was instituted to pray in the house of the deceased, and prior to prayer the hands must be washed, as is explained in *Orah Hayyim* 92. Now, in the synagogue, the basin is ready in the synagogue courtyard, and the hands are washed there. It therefore was instituted to prepare a cup of water in the house of mourning for the washing of the hands. The cup was placed in a special and prominent place, near the burning light, so that it would be ready for those entering. Over the course of time, however, the reason was forgotten, and it was thought that this, too, is a matter relating to the deceased.

In a similar manner we may also explain the role of the cloth, which joins together with the water, namely, to wipe the hands. See also the proposal by Trachtenberg, *Jewish Magic and Superstition*, p. 177, who thinks that the most reasonable explanation for the water and the cloth is so that the Angel of Death will be able to rinse and then wipe his sword(!).

68 Ketubot 103a.

69 Bergman, *Judaism: Its Soul and Life*, p. 83.

and the casting of salt on the bride and groom, which was considered to be a charm against the destructive agents, has become a propitious sign: and why is salt cast — as it is written, "an everlasting covenant of salt" [Num. 18:19]. It was the custom among the [non-Jewish] peoples for a bride to cast a coin to the earth upon leaving the house of worship, as a charm against sorcery; among the Jews of Ashkenaz, in contrast, the coins that were thrown at the bride and groom would be given to the poor. Among the non-Jews, coins would be placed before the bier of the dead as an offering to the demons, while at Jewish funerals charity is customarily given to the indigent, and a charm against the destructive agents was transformed by Judaism into a charitable act [see above, chap. 15]. **The light that is kindled for the deceased after the departure of his soul is not intended to drive away the spirits, it rather alludes to the soul that departs from the body**, recalls the life of the World to Come, or is because of the honor of the Divine Presence, that comes to receive the soul.

The "mother's milk" of the practice may be in the world of superstition, but as it "matured" and developed, it assumed a purely symbolic religious character. Bergman continues:

Superstition defiled what was pure in religion, desecrated and debased the sacred, until it became an act of sorcery and witchcraft.[70] The Jewish

70 As one of the innumerable examples of this, see H. Schwarzbaum, "Some Hebrew and Aramaic Formulae, Spells and Practices Designed to Allay and Calm a Tempestuous Sea," *Yeda-'Am* 20 (47–48) (1980), p. 58:

Tremendous power is also concealed within the piece of *matzah* of the "*afikoman* [eaten at the conclusion of the Passover *Seder*]," by means of which the raging storm is appeased. We read in the midrash Gen. Rabbah 5:4 [35]: "R. Johanan said: The Holy One, blessed be He, stipulated with the sea that it would split before Israel; thus it is written, 'the sea returned to its normal state [*le-eitano*]' (Ex. 14:27)," [i.e.] in accordance with its condition [*li-tena'o*, meaning, to the conditions stipulated with it by the Holy One, blessed be He]. At the time of the Exodus from Egypt, the sea remembered its promise, rent itself asunder, and formed a path for the Israelites. On the *Seder* night, *Yahatz* (that is, the breaking of the middle *matzah* into two) symbolizing the splitting [*hatzayah*] of the Red Sea, and the *afikoman* is simply the better half of the [*matzah* of] *Yahatz*. When the piece of *afikoman* is cast into the sea, the sea recalls the promise that it made to the Holy One, blessed be He, and it saves those who sail the sea from danger. And so the *afikoman* is transformed into *materia magica*.

Sages, on the other hand, sought to purify and refine the religious ideas and practices prevalent among the people of Israel, and to liberate the spirit of our people from the belief in spirits and demons.[71]

We see, therefore, that over the course of time the light and the cup in the house of mourning assumed clearly symbolic significance, and came to represent life and death. As was shown above, throughout the generations, and within a wide range of customs, the light symbolizes the soul.[72] As regards the cup of water, it perhaps should be linked with the following passage that is recited by Yemenite Jews on leaving the cemetery:

> O God, You proclaimed and acted, and You decreed death for all the living. In truth, You cause to decay, but do not perish, You bring down to the netherworld and bring up, **and in Your wisdom You have made death as the cup that is poured for all**. The end of the beast is to be slaughtered, and the end of man is to turn to death. Who is the man who shall live and not see death, may his soul escape the clutches of the netherworld, *Selah*. [...][73]

71 Cf. Shenhar, "Glass Implements," p. 46. Saul Lieberman expands on this (*Greek and Hellenism in Jewish Palestine*, p. 80): "The Babylonian Amoraim did not declare war against this superstition; to the contrary, they confirmed it and infused it with Jewish religious content. [...] The same is true for many other ceremonies [...]; their source may be enrooted in popular superstitions, but the Rabbis reinterpreted them to the extent that they became rites of truly religious content." The leading work written in this realm is Trachtenberg, *Jewish Magic and Superstition*.

72 Lewy, *Minhag Yisrael Torah*, Vol. 1, p. 207, cites Palache, *She'eilot u-Teshuvot Yafeh la-Lev* (on *Orah Hayyim* 154), who wrote that by the merit of our kindling lights in the synagogue, the Holy One, blessed be He, guards our souls, which are compared to a light.

73 See J. Kafih, *Halikhot Teiman (Jewish Life in Sana)*[3] (Jerusalem, 1968), p. 253; Nahum, *Mi-Tzefunot Yehudei Teiman*, p. 173, and more.

74 In the *piyyut* of Rabbi Samuel ha-Nagid, *Ha-Nirpah ha-Zeman mi-Mahalato*, we read: "Then he drank from the cup of death and played, as a cup of water, when you were thirsty, you drank of it." (See: *Divan Shmuel ha-Nagid: The Collected Poetry of Samuel the Prince, 993–1056*), ed. D. Jarden [Jerusalem, 1966], p. 159, l. 8 [Hebrew]). And, naturally, mention is made of the "cup of poison." See Shenhar, "Glass Implements," p. 49 n. 8. Additionally, there might be some connection to the non-Jewish practice of placing in the grave a bottle filled with tears (cf. Ps. 56:9: "put my tears into Your flask"), that was observed in Germany until recently; in Russia a handkerchief wet from tears was thrown into the grave. See J.A.E. Kohler, *Volksbrauch ... vis Voigtlande* (1867), p. 492; W. von Schulenburg, *Wendisches*

In other words, "the cup that is poured for all"[74] symbolizes death, and it belongs in the house of mourning, next to the *ner neshamah*.

Volksthum in Sage, Brauch und Sitte (Berlin, 1882), p. 280; F. Stahlin, *Die Schweiz in romisch Zeit* (1927), p. 361; idem, *Niederdeutsche Zeitschrift fur Volkskunde* 7 (1932), p. 47. According to one opinion, the purpose of these flasks of tears is to keep the corpse moist, and prevent it from drying out, thereby replacing the bodily fluids that have left the corpse, and prolonging the vitality of the body. See Gaster, *Myth, Legend, and Custom in the Old Testament*, Vol. 2, p. 759, para. 265. Could this common practice be the source for the custom under discussion? For the "flask of tears," see the *piyyut* by Amittai: "May it be Your will, O Keeper of the sound of weeping,/ that You place our tears in Your flask, to be [...]" (D. Goldschmidt, *Mahzor la-Yamim ha-Nora'im*, Vol. 2: *Yom Kippur* [Jerusalem, 1970], p. 664, l. 9); and the *piyyut* by Rabbi Abraham Ibn Ezra ("*Be-Shem El* [By the Name of God]"): "And he shall place in his flask his weeping, and He will pardon the multitudes of his sins." Incidental to our mention of the "cup of poison," note should be taken of the unique practice of *Hatam Sofer*. Rabbi Hayyim Hamburger relates, in the name of Rabbi Moses of Nove Mesto (nad Vahom), that it was the practice of the *Hatam Sofer* on the eve of every Ninth of Av fast, during the *seudah mafseket* (the last meal eaten before the fast), to take a cup in the measure of a *revi'it* (a measure of volume) and cry into the cup until it was filled with tears. He would then drink the tears in the cup, to fulfill the verse "and mixed my drink with tears" (Ps. 102:10). Rabbi Moses also yearned to do so, and on another Ninth of Av eve he wept copiously and filled the cup with tears. He could not drink even a quarter of the cup, however, before he vomited and was sick for many days. Amazed by this, he said: "The *Hatam Sofer* is capable of doing all, but not another person who is not like him" (H. Hamburger, *Sheloshah Olamot* [*Three Worlds*] [Jerusalem, 1939–46], Vol. 1, p. 27, quoted by Ashkenazy, *Ages in Judaism*, p. 242). Although the verse cited here is from Psalms, it seemingly refers to the verse in Isa. 51:17: "you who have drained to the dregs the bowl [*kuba'at*], the cup of reeling [or, poison — *kos ha-tareilah*]" (cf. v. 22). *Reshit Hokhmah, Sha'ar ha-Yir'ah*, chap. 13 ("*Masekhet Gehinom*") (ed. Jerusalem 1972, fol. 33a, *Heikhal* 2): "And in this chamber is one official, whose name is *Kos ha-Tareilah*, and all those who were executed by the court who drank the cup of poison in this world were saved from the cup of poison in the World to Come. And what is the cup of poison? When the soul leaves the body, this official, who is called *Kos ha-Tareilah*, seizes him and gives him to drink the cup of poison, that contains three drops: one is '*heletz*,' the second is 'more bitter than death,' and the third is '*kuba'at* [the bowl — see Isa. 51:17]." The drinking by the *Hatam Sofer* might have been a sort of symbolic act in this world of the drinking of the cup of poison, of the tears for the destruction of the Temple, that is efficacious for the life of the World to Come, but this remains in the realm of conjecture.

22

THE EASTERN MOURNING PRACTICES

We read in the book by Aslan and Jacob:[1]

> The defective [*he-haser*] month, that the Jews of Iraq call "*sha'i-(el) na'kitz*," begins on the twenty-second day, that is, three weeks after the death. The family of the deceased observes this day by visiting the grave of their beloved one, the [conducting of the] *Shaharit*, *Minhah*, and *Maariv* prayers in the house, the offering of [specific foods for] "blessings," and a *seudat mitzvah* [a meal connected with a religious event] in the evening, for the elevation of the soul of the deceased.

Ben-Yaacob[2] also mentions this practice; the concept of three weeks, however, is foreign to the Jewish Halakhah.

A similar custom, on the other hand, is to be found in Islamic communities:[3]

> Wailing is resumed by the women on Thursday of the first three weeks after the burial, and the men receive friends of the deceased in the house and hire *fiqis* to perform a *hatma* of the Quran; and on the Friday following these three Thursdays the women visit the tomb and go through various rites, including the placing of a broken palm branch[4] on the tomb and giving food to the poor.[5]

1   Nissim Aslan, *From the Customs and Way of Life of Iraqi Jewry*, p. 70.
2   Ben-Yaacob, *Babylonian Jewish Customs*, Vol. 2, p. 319, para. 2a.
3   Hastings, *Encyclopaedia of Religion and Ethics*, Vol. 3, p. 502.
4   Interestingly, a cut-off tree or branch is engraved on many Jewish tombstones, and in some instances the tombstone itself is fashioned as if it were growing out of a cut-off tree trunk; the symbolism is obvious. Similarly, other tombstones contain a

The Jewish Iraqi custom, therefore, appears to have come into being under the influence of the local Muslim practice.

An additional example of the mutual relations between Jewish and Muslim practices is to be found in an observance of Moroccan Jewry. Rabbi Yossef Ben Naim, from the city of Fez, records:[6]

> The practice regarding a woman whose husband died: during the first year she does not enter any house, not to visit a sick relative of hers, not even her father's house or her children's house. It is said that it is not an auspicious sign to enter the house of others during the year, for she would cause them harm. People fear this, especially the women. I have not found the reason for this practice. In truth, "there is no augury in Jacob" [Num. 23:23], "the Lord protects the simple" [Ps. 116:6].

depiction of a broken lamp. For the symbolism of the lamp in Jewish custom, see above, chap. 21.

Examples of the cut-off tree: Fig. 1, from Schwartzman, *Graven Images: Graphic Motifs of the Jewish Gravestone*, p. 47: from Ouderkerk, Holland (eighteenth century — a Sephardic tombstone); p. 50; Fig. 2, from Krajewska, *Le Temps des Pierres*, p. 123, Fig. 3; p. 124. See also Krajewska, pp. 73, 87, 111, all from Poland. For the broken lamp, see Fig. 4, Krajewska, p. 41, all from the eighteenth and nineteenth centuries. This should be compared with the depiction of the practice in Cairo and Fez of visits to the grave by relatives on the first three Fridays after the funeral (Westermarck, *Ritual and Belief in Morocco*, Vol. 2, pp. 511–12): "and a palm branch is generally taken to be broken up and placed on the tomb." Westermarck's explanation of this custom is based on a tradition described by al-Buhari, *Sahih* 23:82 (chap. 1, p. 439; cf. Westermarck, op. cit., p. 492 n. 3), according to which this commemorates an action taken by Muhammad: "Once when he passed two graves he heard the crying of two dead persons who were tortured there for minor offences. He then took a green palm branch, broke it into pieces, and planted one piece on each grave. When he was asked why he did so he answered, 'In the hope that they will feel some relief as long as these branches remain unwithered.'"

5 Cf. the portrayal by Lane, *The Manners and Customs of the Modern Egyptians*, p. 533. See also Westermarck, op. cit., pp. 480, 507, 511 (following Lane). The practices of the *fellahin* in the Land of Israel are somewhat different. See Baldensperger, "Birth, Marriage, and Death among the Fellahin of Palestine," pp. 143–44; P. Kahle, "Die Tokenlage im heutigen Aegyptien," in *Festschrift fur Herman Gunkel* (Gottingen, 1923), p. 2. For the significance of Friday in this context, see Legey, *The Folklore of Morocco*, p. 227, that every Friday the soul "comes back to earth, and pays a visit to the grave where the body it used to inhabit is buried."

6 Ben Naim, *Noheg be-Hokhmah*, s.v. "*Evel* [Mourning]," p. 19.

Westermarck reports of an analogous belief among the Muslim tribes in Morocco:[7]

> A woman's mourning (*l-'adda*) lasts, according to the Mohammadan law, four months and ten days. [...] Besides being prohibited from re-marrying, a widow is subject to various other rules during her period of mourning. [...] At Fez she cannot go to a hot bath nor leave her house except on Fridays to visit the grave of her husband; and should she go to one of her friends she would probably not be received, because her visit would be considered a cause of evil. At Tangier she can only leave her house on the third day after the funeral to go to her husband's grave together with the other women, and she must not see the face of any man belonging to her family.

And a related stricture derived from this Moroccan belief:[8]

> The people of Fez maintain that if a widow who is in mourning should enter the house of a lying-in woman (*nfisa*) while she is still behind the curtain, either the mother or the child would die.

Since Ben Naim was from Fez,[9] it is not surprising that echoes of the local Jewish practices in this city (that were influenced by local Muslim customs) are to be found in his writings.

---

7 Westermarck, op. cit., p. 473.
8 Westermarck, op. cit., p. 386.
9 See his biography by M. Amar at the beginning of *Noheg be-Hokhmah*.

23

MOURNING FOR THE FIRSTBORN

Rabbi Moses Isserles writes in his gloss:[1]

> According to one opinion, a person should not mourn over the death of his first son or his firstborn son. [...] This is an erroneous practice. Rather, mourning must be observed for them. Nonetheless, the practice has come down to our city [Cracow], that a father and mother do not follow their first son to the cemetery.

Rabbi Joseph Caro similarly rules:[2]

> The *Kol Bo*[3] writes that the "custom that has spread of not mourning for a first son who died, even if he was not the firstborn, is an erroneous practice.[4] Moreover, this practice is found [in the sources] only limited to firstborn, who, as it were, are not from their parents, because they are sacred to the Lord, may He be blessed." His writing not to mourn for firstborn is puzzling, and there is no basis for this.

Rabbi Isaac ben Sheshet Perfet (*Ribash*), as well,[5] challenged this practice, and found it to be

---

1 On *Shulhan Arukh, Orah Hayyim*, end of para. 374; based on *Darkhei Teshuvah* on *Tur, Orah Hayyim*, end of para. 374. See *Ma'avar Yabbok, Minhat Aharon*, beginning of chap. 11; see also *Ma'avar Yabbok, Sefat Emet*, beginning of chap. 11 (Vilna 1927 ed., p. 173).

2 *Beit Yosef* on *Tur, Yoreh Deah* 374, s.v. "*Katav*."

3 *Hil. Avel* (*Laws of Mourning*). Cf. Rabbi Aaron of Lunel, *Orhot Hayyim* 3:4, p. 562.

4 For the concept of "erroneous practice," see *Minhagei Yisrael*, Vol. 2, pp. 51–52, 76–128.

5 *She'eilot u-Teshuvot ha-Ribash*, para. 95. He writes as follows:

   As regards the custom that we find that a person whose first son dies mourns groundless, and it has no root or basis, [even though] it was advocated by some. We have no knowledge regarding any [community] that observed this practice.

This strange tradition also is mentioned by Meiri, as follows:[6]

Regarding the measure of twenty [years] that we wrote, according to one opinion, this is the current practice, that has its roots **in antiquity**, that one is not to mourn over the death of the first of his sons, and this practice has already spread. **The foolishness of this custom** has already been written, for it is not from the halakhah, nor does it originate in a fine point of exegesis, but rather is based on an early custom, for which we have not heard a satisfactory reason. Rather, weak reasons, that are not worth being written, are advanced for it.

only the day of the burial — **I say that this is a senseless practice**, and that, because he is the first, he is not his son, and his heart will not grieve for him? And would he [this son] not stand in the place of the father for the purpose of designation [i.e. the betrothal of a Hebrew handmaid to her master], for a field from his hereditary property, and for inheritance? And if he is not his son, then [if the father were to die without leaving any other offspring] his mother would require levirate marriage. And [if so], then he [the father] should not mourn, not even on the day of burial! **Rather, this is totally unfounded.** Those who claim so [have no basis for their view].

I found the following in the book *Orhot Hayyim* [above, n. 3]: "Rabbi Asher of Lunel, of blessed memory, wrote: 'It is the custom not to mourn for the firstborn. It seems to me that this is because the firstborn is for the Lord that they acted in this manner.' The *Ahronim* wrote: 'The practice that spread in many communities not to mourn for a first son who dies, even if he came to full term, even if he is not the firstborn, **is erroneous**, for the custom was originally to be found only applying to firstborn, for they are as ones who are not from their parents, since they are sacred to the Lord. And in all the districts of Catalonia, people mourn for him, even for the firstborn, provided that he was over thirty days old, when he has left the category of *nefel* [nonviable fetus, which died within thirty days after birth], and *tzidduk ha-din* [the justification of the Divine judgment] is recited over him; this is the law in practice.' This is the end of the quotation from that book." (This responsum is undated, but it may be assumed that it was written ca. 1440. Rabbi Isaac ben Sheshet Perfet was born in Barcelona in 1326 and died in Algiers in 1408.)

For what *Orhot Hayyim* quoted from *Sefer ha-Minhagot*, see Assaf, *Sifran shel Rishonim*, p. 180, para. 23, and the gloss by Assaf ad loc.

6 Rabbi Menahem Meiri, *Hibbur Teshuvah* (ed. A. Sofer [New York, 1950]), *Shever Gaon*, chap. 2, pp. 613–14.

They themselves taught that this is the practice only if he died before twenty. If, however, he was [at least] twenty [years] old, then he certainly is to be mourned. According to another opinion, this practice [of not mourning] was observed only if he died a minor, but if he died from the age of thirteen [years], then he is to be mourned. According to yet another view, this refers only to the first day,[7] that is by Torah law, but not to the Rabbinically mandated days [of mourning]. According to yet an additional opinion, mourning is not observed, not even on the first day. In Narbonne, on the other hand, the first day [of mourning] is observed, but not the other days. Although this is a tenuous custom, this practice was maintained by the great authorities from early times, and we do not possess the authority to abrogate it.

Sofer adds:[8] "I did not find this view, either, in the *Rishonim* who preceded our master."[9] It has been noted,[10] however, that this practice was already mentioned by *Rabad* (Rabbi Abraham ben David of Posquières, Provence, 1125–98) in his responsa:[11]

Regarding mourning for the first of his son[s], a person does not observe mourning at all, not even by the rending [of one's garment]. If [the dead son] was a minor, he should remain in his house for three days, and if [the son] was an adult, he should remain in his house all the seven [days of the usual mourning period].

We therefore have before us a strange custom that spread throughout the communities of France and Provence from the twelfth century on, and that still was discernible in Cracow, the city of Rabbi Moses Isserles, in the middle of the sixteenth century.[12] Rabbi Baruch ha-Levi Epstein, the author of *Torah Temimah*, sought to find the source for this baffling practice in *Targum Jonathan* on Gen. 38:4: "'and named him Onan' — because

7 Of mourning; see above, n. 4, the responsa by *Ribash*.
8 P. 613 n. 10.
9 Meiri lived in Perpignan, in Provence, 1249–1306.
10 See the comment by I. Ta-Shma in M. Margoliouth [Margulies], *Hilkhot Eretz Yisrael min ha-Genizah* (*Land of Israel Halakhot from the Genizah*) (Jerusalem, 1972), p. 36 n. 6.
11 Rabbeinu Abraham ben David (*Rabad*), *Yeshuvot u-Pesakim* (*Responsa and Rulings*), ed. J. Kafih (Jerusalem, 1964), para. 212, p. 263.
12 Isserles (*Rema*), 1525–72.

his father was indeed destined to grieve on account of him." Epstein writes:[13]

> Behold, there is no explanation for this interpretation, except in accordance with that practice mentioned by *Rema* in the name of the *Rishonim*, that is, upon the death of Er, his father did not mourn for him, since he was the firstborn, consequently, the second [son] was named Onan, to allude to the fact that they would be obligated to mourn for him.[14]

S. Assaf offers the explanation:[15]

> Incidentally, we learn the basis for the puzzling custom that is cited in *Orhot Hayyim* [...] that the firstborn is not to be mourned, "because the firstborn is for the Lord they acted in this manner." From this, the practice spread "in many communities not to mourn for a first son who dies [...], even if he is not the firstborn." [...] Its source, however, lies in the following: according to *Hukei ha-Torah*,[16] "the *perushim*

---

13 *Torah Temimah* on Gen. 38:10, p. 171, para. 7. Prof. S.Z. Leiman remarked that this proposal by Epstein already appears in the writ of approval given by Rabbi Hayyim Berlin to the book *Yenahenu* on *Targum Jonathan*, by Rabbi Yohanan Har Barzel (Eisenberg) (Warsaw, 1902), and in an explanation in a similar vein by Rabbi Benjamin Schmerler, *Ahavat Yonatan* (*Ahawas Jehonuson*) (Bilgoraj, 1932), on Gen. loc. cit.

14 *Onen* = a bereaved person prior to the funeral. This proposal, however, was totally rejected by Kasher, *Torah Shelemah, Va-Yeshev*, pp. 1447–48, para. 24. See Kasher's reference to Moed Katan 27b, which certainly does not constitute the source for this practice. See Rabbi Eliezer Judah Waldenberg, *Even Yaakov* (Jerusalem, 1962), para. 38, who sought to provide several reasons for this custom (with a reference to Waldenberg by Kafih in *Rabad, Yeshuvot u-Pesakim*, para. 212, p. 263, end of n. 2).

15 S. Assaf (ed.), *Rabbinic Texts and Documents 1, Gaonica* (*Mi-Sifrut ha-Geonim*) (Jerusalem, 1933), p. 4 n. 10, with a reference to this interpretation in *Sifran shel Rishonim*, p. 180 n. 7.

16 This is a thirteenth-century French(?) composition on educational methods; published by Guedemann in *Ha-Torah ve-ha-Hayyim*, Vol. 1, pp. 73–80. This passage is from version B, para. 5 (Guedemann, p. 77); see also what Guedemann wrote in *Tziyun* II at the end of his book (pp. 217–19). This work is brought by Assaf in *Mekorot le-Toledot ha-Hinukh ha-Yehudi* (*Sources for the History of Jewish Education*), Vol. 1 (Tel Aviv, 1954), pp. 6–16, with this passage on p. 13. It was also printed by M. Friedmann, *Beit ha-Talmud*, Vol. 1 (Vienna, 1881), pp. 61–62, 91–94.

[literally, those who are separated, in this context, the firstborn] are scholars who devote themselves exclusively to Torah study," and "the early ones, of blessed memory, instituted the dedication of the firstborn son while still in his mother's womb." Consequently, we see that this custom of not mourning for the firstborn was prevalent only in the French communities.

Due to its special relevance to our discussion, the entire passage from *Hukei ha-Torah* follows:[17]

The early ones, of blessed memory, instituted the dedication of the firstborn son while still in his mother's womb, with textual support for the custom [from the verse]: "Before I created you in the womb, I selected you; before you were born, I consecrated you" [Jer. 1:5]. This is the meaning of "who sanctified the beloved one from the womb" [from the circumcision blessings]. This refers to Abraham, which is derived from the wording of *yedi'ah* [here, with the meaning of designation]: it is written, regarding Jeremiah: "Before I created you in the womb, I selected [*yeda'tikha*] you," and regarding Abraham it is written: "For I have singled him out [*yeda'tiv*]" [Gen. 18:19], that is, already. Just as there [in Jeremiah], it was designated while in the womb, here, too [regarding the firstborn], it is designated while in the womb. The [husband whose wife is pregnant with their first child] accepts this upon himself and declares: "If my wife will give birth to a male, he shall be consecrated to the Lord, and shall recite His Torah day and night." On the eighth day, after he has undergone circumcision, the child is placed on a couch, with the *humash* [Pentateuch] of the Torah over his head,[18] and the congregation or the heads of the *yeshivah*

17 *Hukei ha-Torah* 2:3; see above, the preceding note.
18 A French custom. See *Mahzor Vitri*, p. 628 (Guedemann, p. 218; Assaf, *Mekorot le-Toledot ha-Hinukh ha-Yehudi*, p. 6). Cf. *Sefer Hasidim*, ed. Margaliot, para. 1140, p. 568.
See Patai, "Folk Customs and Charms Relating to Birth," pp. 257–58; see also *Shulhan Arukh, Yoreh Deah* 179:9, that a Torah scroll is not held over an infant who was injured (as a curative measure).
    Cf. the Libyan practice, *Yahadut Lub*, p. 391: "When an infant is sleeping in its crib and the mother must go out for a while and leave him alone, she places next to its head a *humash*, prayerbook, or *talit* and *tefillin* bag, to protect it, and she goes out, with complete trust that no harm will befall the child." See also Trachtenberg,

[Talmudic academy] bless him. They also recite over him the blessing: "May God give you of the dew of heaven" [...] to "Blessed be they who bless you" [Gen. 27: 28–29]. The head of the *yeshivah* places his hands on him and on the *humash*, and he recites: "May this one learn what is written in this. [...] May this one observe what is written in this."[19] Three times, "in order that the teachings of the Lord may be in your mouth" [Ex. 13:9], "Let not this book of the Torah cease from your lips [...]" [Josh. 1:8]. The father conducts a festive banquet for the circumcision and for the separation [of the infant, from regular worldly status], as it is written there, regarding Hannah: "he must remain there for ever" [I Sam. 1:22].

Assaf apparently meant that this practice of the "*perushim*"[20] led to the faulty understanding that the firstborn is consecrated to the Lord while still in the womb; he does not belong to his parents, and therefore is not to be mourned by them. This erroneous practice was later expanded to encompass every firstborn son, even if not from the "*perushim*," and not dedicated to the Lord. And, finally, it was further broadened, to include every first son, even if not the firstborn, among those not mourned by their parents.

The question of the source of this practice, however, has not been definitively answered. Assaf himself questioned the place of origin of this composition, and cited opinions that it is from Ashkenaz (= Germany), or even from Algiers.[21] According to our sources, however, this custom was limited to Provence. Additionally, there is no proof whatsoever that the original practice was observed exclusively by the "*perushim*," and the majority of the Jewish people undoubtedly did not dedicate their firstborn to Torah study. The origin of this practice must therefore be sought in some other reason, one that would also explain the expansion of its application to first sons who are not firstborn.

Jewish Magic and Superstition, pp. 105–106; *Sefer Hasidim*, ed. Wistinetzki and Freimann, para. 818, p. 207. Cf. Patai, op. cit., p. 250.

19 Based on Bava Kamma 17a.

20 For the "*perushim*," see Guedemann, *Ha-Torah ve-ha-Hayyim*, p. 219. See also G. Scholem, *Origins of the Kabbalah* (ed. R.J.Z. Werblowsky, trans. A. Arkush [Philadelphia, 1987]), pp. 229–33.

21 Assaf, *Mekorot le-Toledot ha-Hinukh ha-Yehudi*, p. 9. See also *Ha-Zofeh le-Hokhmat Yisrael* 8 (1924), pp. 119–21 (which is almost identical with what Assaf later wrote in *Mekorot*).

The following biblical verses constitute the source of the obligation to redeem the firstborn of humans (and of beasts): Ex. 13:2 specifies: "Consecrate to Me every firstborn; man and beast, the first issue of every womb among the Israelites is Mine"; Deut. 15:19 mandates: "You shall consecrate to the Lord your God all male firstlings that are born in your herd and in your flock"; and Num. 18:15 sets forth: "The first issue of the womb of every being, man or beast, that is offered to the Lord, shall be yours; but you shall have the firstborn of man redeemed, and you shall also have the firstling of unclean animals redeemed." The *Mekhilta* expounds this:[22]

> "Is Mine" [Ex. 13:2] — why was this stated? Because when it says, "You shall consecrate to the Lord your God all male firstlings" [Deut. 15:19], [it means:] consecrate it in order to receive reward. Or [perhaps it means]: [only] if you consecrate it, does is become consecrated, and if you do not consecrate it, it does not become consecrated? Scripture teaches, "[it] is Mine" — in any event. What, then, does "you shall consecrate" teach? Consecrate it in order to receive reward.

And likewise, in Arakhin 29a (on "You shall consecrate [to the Lord your God] all male firstlings"):

> If he did not consecrate it, would it not be sacred? Its sanctity is from the womb! Since, therefore, it is sacred even if it were not [specifically] consecrated, there is no need to consecrate it.[23]

The rabbis understood from these verses that the (animal) firstling is sacred from the womb, even if no act of consecration is performed; rather, the Torah commanded us to consecrate it in order thereby to receive reward for the performance of the commandment. This conception

22 *Mechilta d'Rabbi Ismael*, ed. H.S. Horovitz and I.A. Rabin (Jerusalem, 1998), p. 58. See Kasher, *Torah Shelemah*, Vol. 12, *Bo*, p. 93, and the glosses by Kasher, para. 25. See J. Gellis, *Tosafot Hashalem: Commentary on the Bible*, Vol. 7 (Jerusalem, 1987), p. 148 (Hebrew): "'Consecrate to Me every firstborn' [קדש לי כל בכור] — this has the numerical value of 'זהו לקבל בשכרך [this is to receive your reward]'."

23 Cf. Nedarim 13a: "For it was taught, on the authority of Rabbi [Judah ha-Nasi]: From where do we know that it is obligatory to consecrate the firstling that is born in one's house? As it is said, 'You shall consecrate [to the Lord your God] all male firstlings.' But the one who permits this [would argue]: If he did not consecrate it, would it not be sacred?"

undoubtedly was transferred to the human firstborn, as well. As we find in Cant. Rabbah:

> The Holy One, blessed be He, said to Israel: My son, I require nothing of you, except when a firstborn son is born to any one of you, let him consecrate him to My name, for it is written, "Consecrate to Me every firstborn."[24]

As we saw above, according to *Hukei ha-Torah*, the "*perushim*" acted in accordance with this practice but, of course, dedicated the firstborn to Torah study. Even without this act of dedication, however, the firstborn would still be consecrated. As this is formulated by *Seforno* on Ex. 13:2:

> "Consecrate to Me every firstborn" — that all would require redemption, as any other consecrated thing, so that they would be permitted [to engage in] mundane labors. For without this redemption, **they would be forbidden to engage in any mundane labor**. [...] [The amount of] this redemption for them is the value specified in the section [Lev. 27] of *arakhin* [valuations for something that is dedicated to the Sanctuary] for a month-old child, that being the time of his redemption, as it says, "[his] redemption, from one month old" [Num. 18:16].

Seforno also writes on v. 15 in this chapter:

> The Israelite firstborn should have been struck down together with them [the Egyptian firstborn]. [...] He saved them by His consecrating them to Him, in such a manner that the human firstborn in Israel shall be as Nazirites or especially dedicated, set apart for the service of God, may He be blessed, and are forbidden to engage in common labors. And "but redeem every firstborn among my sons" [in this verse] — so that they will be permitted to engage in mundane labor.[25]

It therefore was quite plausible that people would erroneously think that the sanctity of the firstborn to the Lord begins while he is still in the womb. This faulty understanding is strengthened and confirmed by the text of the Land of Israel redemption of the son ceremony discovered in a Genizah fragment, which reads as follows:[26]

---

24 Cant. Rabbah 7:2; cf. Eccl. Rabbah 3:9.
25 See what Kasher writes in *Torah Shelemah*, op. cit., p. 94, para. 28.
26 Margoliouth, *Hilkhot Eretz Yisrael min ha-Genizah*, p. 16, Genizah fragment T-S J 3/23.

This son is a firstborn, and the holy Torah said to redeem him, as it is said, "The Lord spoke further to Moses, saying: 'Consecrate to Me every firstborn [...].'"

This is followed by the declaration by the *kohen*:

> **When you were in your mother's innards, you belonged to your Father in Heaven, and now that you have come forth from your mother's innards, behold you belong to your Father in Heaven and to me**, for I am a *kohen*, **and [you also belong] to my brother kohanim**. Your father and your mother seek to redeem you from me for five silver *sela* [= 5 sacred *shekalim*].

The main text published by Margaliot there[27] states: "And they say to the father: This [your son] is sacred to God and [His *kohanim*], redeem him." These sources plainly teach of the singular conception that the firstborn belongs to Heaven, even while still in his mother's womb,[28] and upon his birth he comes into the possession of the *kohanim*, from whom the father

---

27 "*Afrukta de-Bakhor[a] de-bar Nasha [Redemption of the Human Firstborn]*," p. 30.

28 According to this conception, the firstborn is therefore sacred while still in his mother's womb. This is also inherent in the blessing recited by the father when he redeems his son, as is cited in the responsum by Rav Hai Gaon, cited in Jonah ben Abraham Gerondi, *Sha'arei Teshuvah*, para. 47: "Blessed are You, O Lord our God, King of the universe, who sanctified the fetus **in his mother's stomach**" (Nahmanides, *Hilkhot Bekhorot [Laws of the Firstborn]*, in the name of *Shimusha Atika de-Geonim*). Nahmanides writes on this: "I do not understand 'who sanctified the fetus in his mother's stomach'; if the reference is to the sanctity of the firstborn, the Torah placed this upon the first issue of the womb." Nahmanides further writes (*Hilkhot Bekhorot*, chap. 20): "It was not customary to recite this blessing in France and in Ashkenaz." See what Ta-Shma writes on this in *Hilkhot Eretz Yisrael min ha-Genizah*, pp. 33f., that despite the opposition by Nahmanides and the doubts expressed by Rosh (Rabbeinu Asher ben Jehiel) concerning the wording of this redemption formula (with many minor variants), it was accepted in Spain, as is evident from the statement by Nahmanides himself, and from Rabbi Menahem ben Aaron ben Zerah, *Tzeidah la-Derekh*; Abudarham, and others. See the extremely instructive continuation of Nahmanides. See Rabbi Moses ha-Kohen, *Berit Kehunah ha-Shalem*[4] (Bnei Brak, 1990), end of Section 1, n. 27, on the practices on the island of Djerba, who expressed his surprise at the formula "who sanctified [*kadesh*] the fetus in his mother's innards." After discussing this question, he cited a suggestion by a Torah scholar with the reading: "who congealed [*karesh*, substituting the letter *resh* for *dalet*]," based on Job 10:10, but rejects this suggestion.

must redeem his son. This (popular) understanding found expression in a query that was addressed to Rabbi Moses Isserlein that appears in *Terumat ha-Deshen*:[29]

> Regarding what you wrote, that if he were to give the son to the *kohen* he would thereby fulfill his obligation [...] this is a mistake. [...] At any rate, redemption is required [...]. For the one who addressed him thought that it would be possible for him, the father of the firstborn, to give to the *kohen* what belongs to him, and he would not need to redeem him at all.

Isserlein rejects this line of reasoning, and continues:

> And even if this were effective there [for the redemption of the firstling ass], this is because the body of the firstling ass is consecrated, even regarding the deriving of benefit [from it], before its redemption, that is not the case regarding a [human] firstborn son, for we clearly learn that **it is totally nonsacred**. Why does the *kohen* require him? Not as a slave: a free person does not become a slave. Not as a son, for he [the firstborn] is not his [the *kohen*'s] offspring!

Portions of the ancient redemption ceremony continued to exist here and there. The Italian *Tanya Rabbati* specifies:

> [The *kohen*] recites: "This son is a firstborn. [...] When you were in your mother's womb, you belonged to your Father in Heaven and to your father and mother, now you belong to me, and your father and mother desire to redeem you, **for you are a sacred firstborn**."[30]

This also appears in the Italian *mahzorim* (prayerbooks),[31] but not among the Jews of France or of Ashkenaz.[32] Nonetheless, it would not require a great leap of the imagination to assume that this understanding (which is expressed

---

29 *Terumat ha-Deshen, Pesakim (Rulings)*, para. 235.
30 *Tanya Rabbati*, para. 98, end of the "Order of Redemption of the Firstborn"; quoted by Ta-Shma, *Hilkhot Eretz Yisrael min ha-Genizah*, p. 36.
31 Margoliouth, *Hilkhot Eretz Yisrael min ha-Genizah*, p. 17. And in al-Nakawa, *Menorat ha-Ma'or*, ed. Enelow, Vol. 3, p. 488: "who sanctified the fetus in the womb." See the gloss by Enelow on l. 6.
32 Ta-Shma, loc. cit. See S. Pick, "Provencal Customs," Ph.D. diss., Bar-Ilan University, 1975, pp. 90–93 (Hebrew).

in, or ensues from, this formulation of the redemption of the son ceremony), formed the basis for this strange practice, that since the firstborn son does not belong to his parents, he therefore is not to be mourned by them if he dies. (Possibly, this practice initially related only to the instance of a firstborn who died before the redemption ceremony; in the words of Meiri [above], "if he died a minor.")[33]

The question of how this practice expanded to also include the first son who is not the firstborn can be thoroughly understood on the basis of the rabbinic sources and the *Rishonim*. *Midrash ha-Gadol*[34] expounds on the verse: "for there was no house where there was not someone dead" (Ex. 12:30):

> Rabbi Jacob says: And was there a house in which there was no firstborn? Rather, this was the custom of the early ones, **whoever did not have a firstborn son would call the oldest of his sons the firstborn**, similar to what is written, "[Hosah] of the Merarites had sons: Shimri the chief (he was not the firstborn, but his father designated him chief)" [I Chr. 26:10].[35]

33 Although the intent of "*katan*" in Meiri is to a minor, i.e. one less than 13 years of age. Or, possibly, the term "*katan*" is to be understood here literally, as "small." See *Ha-Hillukim she-bein Anshei ha-Mizrah u-Benei Eretz Israel* (*The Differences between the People of the East and Those of the Land of Israel*), ed. M. Margoliouth (Margulies), (Jerusalem, 1938), pp. 94–95, for the question of mourning for an infant that died before thirty days of age; see also above, n. 4.

34 *Midrash Haggadol on the Pentateuch*, ed. M. Margulies (Jerusalem, 1956), p. 209, based on *Mishnat Rabbi Eliezer* (*The Mishnah of Rabbi Eliezer*, ed. H.G. Enelow [New York, 1934]) 19, pp. 358–59; omitted by J.N. Epstein and E.Z. Melamed in *Mekhilta d'Rabbi Sim'on b. Jochai* (Jerusalem, 1955), p. 29. See the parallels listed in *Midrash Haggadol* and in *Mishnat Rabbi Eliezer*.

35 Cf. Rashi on the verse in Exodus; Kasher, *Torah Shelemah* on this verse, p. 35, para. 535. See Gellis, *Tosafot Hashalem*, Vol. 7, p. 121: "For in a place where there was no firstborn, the eldest died, as I explained." See Ravyah on Pesahim, end of para. 525, p. 174, on the issue of who fasts on the fastday of the firstborn: "even the firstborn from the mother [and not from the father], like the event of the plague of the firstborn in Egypt; however [unlike as in Egypt], the senior son in the house does not [fast], because we are not so strict"; see *Tosafot Hashalem*. See M.M. Kasher, *Divrei Menahem: Clarifications of Various Halakhot in Shulhan Arukh, Orah Hayyim, with Added Responsa*, Vol. 3 (Jerusalem, 1981), p. 142, para. 15, for the question of whether a female firstborn is obligated to observe the fast of the firstborn. See Rabbi Yitzhak Nissim, "The Glosses on the *Shulhan Arukh*," in

This interpretation of the word *"bekhor"* is not far removed from "firstling of the flock."[36] If indeed it was "the custom of the early ones" to define the first son as the "firstborn," we can easily understand the expansion of the practice not to mourn for the firstborn to also include the first son, even though he was not the firstborn.

Lastly, even if this practice was called "weak," "erroneous," and "foolish" by the leading *Rishonim*, since it (as they put it) "spread" and continued to be observed for several centuries, it behooves us to examine its source and the reasoning behind it, and, in general, how this "error" came into being.

Rabbi Yosef Caro: Studies in the Teachings of the Author of the Shulhan Arukh, ed. Y. Raphael (Jerusalem, 1969), p. 71 (Hebrew):

> The authors of *Siftei Kohen* and *Knesset ha-Gedolah* has already observed that in many places the references are sparce. The [author of] *Knesset haGedolah* thought that all the glosses were by R. Moses Isserles himself, and took pains to understand and resolve what he wrote. *Maran* [R. Joseph Caro] wrote in *Shulhan Arukh, Orah Hayyim* 470: "According to one view, even the female firstborn is required to fast." R. Moses Isserles accordingly added: "This is not the practice. *Maharil*." R. Hayyim Benveniste noted in his work *Pesah Me'ubin* on the *Haggadah* (para. 41) that *Maharil* was of the opinion that the female firstborn does fast, and he therefore shifted the reference, writing that the reference to *Maharil* refers to the statement by *Maran*. *Hida* [R. Hayyim Joseph David Azulai] comments on this, in *Birkei Yosef*: "What the *Knesset ha-Gedolah* wrote, to *** the version, is not clear, for the one who added the references [in the *Shulhan Arukh*] does not usually add a source as a reference to what is written in the *Shulhan Arukh*, for it is already known that the person who added these references is not our master, R. Moses [Isserles], and did not originate from R. Isserles; rather, they were written after the rabbi [Isserles' death], when the *Shulhan Arukh* and the glosses [by R. Isserles] were reprinted; they were derived from the book *Darkei Moshe*, and they were only intended to be references to R. Moses Isserles, as is well-known" (*Birkei Yosef, Orah Hayyim* 470:3). See there, that *Hida* shows that the *Maharil* maintains that it is not customary for the female to fast. Regarding, however, what he wrote above, that the one adding the sources does not usually add a source as a reference to what is written by *Maran*, we have already shown above that this is not so.

36 See *Minhagei Yisrael*, Vol. 1, pp. 151–52 n. 8.

24

"THE DEATH OF A *NASI*" AND THE MOURNING
FOR MOSES

In 1967 Israel Weinstock published an important article[1] in which he examined the evolution of the custom mentioned at the beginning of chap. 16 of Berakhot, which asks:

> Why do we not read [all of Scripture]? Because of the recess of the study hall.

The Talmud on this mishnah (116b) explains that this refers to "*Minhah* on the Sabbath," with the custom explained by Rav Sar Shalom Gaon:[2]

> Between one prayer and the next [i.e. between *Minhah* and *Maariv*] one sits and keeps silent. [...] He does not engage [in Torah study], not because this is prohibited, but out of respect for our teacher Moses, who died at that hour.

1   I. Weinstock, "The Neglect of the Study Hall at the Time of *Minhah* on the Sabbath," *Torah she-be-al Peh* 9 (1967), pp. 119–27 (Hebrew; = *idem, Studies in Jewish Philosophy and Mysticism*, pp. 271–84 [Hebrew]; all the following references are from the book).
2   Lewin, *Otzar ha-Gaonim*, Vol. 2 (Haifa, 1930), Shabbath, on *Shabbat* 116b, para. 315, p. 103, based on *Seder Rav Amram Gaon*, ed. Goldschmidt, Vol. 2, para. 35, p. 80. See *Sefer ha-Orah* (ed. S. Buber, Lemberg, 1905), p. 52; *Ha-Pardes* of Rashi, ed. Ehrenreich, p. 313; *Shibbolei ha-Leket*, para. 126, p. 98; *Or Zaru'a*, Vol. 2, para. 89, fol. 47a; *Sefer ha-Yashar* by Rabbeinu Tam, Responsa, 45:6 (ed. S. P. Rosenthal [Berlin, 1898], pp. 84–85), in different wording; *Sefer Hamanhig*, para. 63 (ed. Raphael, p. 187); *Mahzor Vitri*, p. 111; cited in *Tur, Orah Hayyim* 292. See *Teshuvot Rav Sar Shalom Gaon*, ed. Weinberg, para. 26, p. 69.

This Gaon further elaborates:

> It was enacted to recite [on the Sabbath, during the *Minhah* service]
> *tzidduk ha-din* because our teacher Moses, may he rest in piece, died
> at that hour.[3]

Weinstock[4] describes this in detail:

> This was the original form of the practice: "Between one prayer and

3   *Otzar ha-Gaonim*, para. 317; *Teshuvot Rav Sar Shalom Gaon*, ed. Weinberg, para. 26, p. 70 (based on Jonah ben Abraham Gerondi, *Sha'arei Teshuvah*, para. 30). See *Sefer Hamanhig*, pp. 186–87, and editor's gloss on l. 76; see Weinstock, *Studies in Jewish Philosophy and Mysticism*, p. 281.

    For the death of Moses on the Sabbath, see Weinstock, pp. 276–77; see the comment by J. Schor in *Sepher ha-Ittim* by R. Jehuda ben Barsilai, p. 290 n. 195; B. Ratner, *Midrash Seder Olam* (Vilna, 1894–97 [New York, 1966]), chap. 10, n. 11. According to one opinion, Moses did not die on a Sabbath, and therefore it cannot be said that "*Tzidkatkha* ['Your righteousness,' i.e. *tzidduk ha-Din*]," that is recited in the Sabbath *Minhah* service, is said in his memory. See Rabbi Nathan ben Judah, *Sefer ha-Mahkim*, ed. J. Freimann (Cracow, 1903), pp. 138–39 (and Freimann's glosses): "We recite *tzidduk ha-din* for the souls that return to their punishment upon the departure of the Sabbath" (see Freimann's glosses, p. 140, para. 367); see also Rabbi Gedaliah Felder, *Siddur Yesodei Yeshurun*, Sabbath, pp. 506–507; ibid., pp. 496–97, that water is not to be drunk between *Minhah* and *Maariv* on the Sabbath, for then the souls return to Gehinnom (Rabbi Moses Isserles, *Orah Hayyim* 292:2) — if so, what more need be added. See also Baer, *Avodat Yisrael* prayerbook, p. 265; see Trachtenberg, *Jewish Magic and Superstition*, pp. 68, 285 n. 11. Avida [Zlotnik], "Some Sabbath Aggadot and Customs," pp. 276–87, concerning the drinking of water at the time of *Minhah* on the Sabbath; I. Levi, "Le repos sabbatique des âmes damnées," *REJ* 25 (1892), pp. 1–13; *idem*, "Notes complémentaires sur le repos sabbatique des âmes damnées," *REJ* 26 (1893), pp. 131–37. See Rabbi Moshe Yehudah Katz, *Kunterest Va-Yaged Moshe*, in *Nahalei Binah* (Brooklyn, 1980), p. 225, who cites Rabbi Zevi Hirsch Boyarsky, *Tosefet Shabbat* (Warsaw, 1886) 290:1, who wrote: "I saw in *Knesset ha-Gedolah*, who wrote that it is customary on the Sabbath in the morning to eat eggs cooked in their shells that were placed in the oven. The reason is because of the mourning for our teacher Moses, who died on the Sabbath. It is written there in *Tosefet Shabbat* that for the same reason legumes are eaten on the Sabbath; Jewish custom is [as binding as if it were of] Biblical authority, and they [Israel] are not to be questioned." Katz then cites Rabbi David Lida, *Shomer Shabbat* (Zholkva, 1804) 6:6, who added that those who are exacting in their observance also eat them during the third Sabbath meal.

4   Weinstock, p. 275.

the next one sits and keeps silent." The wording of these descriptions attests that this is a mourning practice, from the identical wording in Lamentations (3:28): "Let him sit alone and keep silent" [...] one that is in the spirit of the early halakhah: "When a *Hakham* [the head of the academy] dies, his study hall is in recess. [...] When a *Nasi* dies, all the study halls are in recess."[5] [...] And now, [regarding] Moses, the teacher of all Israel, who died on the Sabbath, toward evening, the early generations already observed and accepted upon themselves to preserve the memory of his passing in this manner, for all time. [...] And in the wording of this law by Rabbi Joshua ben Korha,[6] all were "sitting in silence."

Weinstock continues:[7]

From the middle of the Geonic period [...] several responsa have come down to us, from the heads of the *yeshivot* in Sura and in Pumbeditha, the prominent Geonim: Rav Sar Shalom Gaon, Rav Natronai, and Rav Paltoi, that relate to the manner in which the custom was observed in their time. We learn from the writings by these Geonim that a change had occurred in the form of the practice: "Thus is the custom in the house of our masters in Babylonia: following the *Minhah* prayer on the Sabbath, [the tractate of] Avot and *kinyan Torah* [the last chapter added to M Avot] are studied."[8] [...] This means that in place of the original practice of total cessation from Torah study: "Between one prayer and the next one sits and keeps silent" — an enactment that many undoubtedly had difficulty in properly observing — a compromise was initiated: at that hour, people would study the tractate of Avot,[9] which begins with "Moses received the Torah from Sinai," an occupation that to some degree preserves the memory of Moses.[10]

---

5 Moed Katan 22b.

6 Moed Katan 23a. Cf. *4 Ezra* 10:1; Lieberman, *Greek and Hellenism in Jewish Palestine*, p. 78.

7 Weinstock, p. 278.

8 Lewin, *Otzar ha-Gaonim*, op. cit., para. 315.

9 See my edition of *Masechet Derech Eretz Zutta and Perek ha-Shalom*, pp. 172–75; Weinstock, p. 281.

10 The continuation of Weinstock's essay is equally instructive.

We wish to add an additional insight to the explanation of this singular phenomenon, as expressed by Weinstock:[11]

> Over the course of time, the early practice of "one sits and keeps silent" and the "study hall in recess" underwent a polar change, to its diametric opposite, that specifically at this hour, the time of the Sabbath *Minhah*, Jewish communities would assemble in the synagogues to listen to sages expound words of Torah.[12]

The recitation of the tractate of Avot, which begins with "Moses received the Torah from Sinai," certainly honored the deceased. Nonetheless, this practice would seem to contradict the law cited above: "When a *Nasi* dies, all the study halls are in recess."[13]

The *Rishonim* disagree concerning the basic meaning of the *baraita* in Moed Katan (22b–23a) that sets forth this early law:

> When a *Hakham* dies, his study hall is in recess; when the head of the rabbinical court dies, all the study halls in his city are in recess, and [the people of the synagogue] enter the synagogue and change their places. Those who [normally] sit in the north sit in the south, those who [normally] sit in the south sit in the north. When a *Nasi* dies, all the study halls are in recess, and the people of the synagogue enter the synagogue, seven read [in the Torah] and they go out. Rabbi Joshua ben Korha says: Not so that they will go forth and walk about in the marketplace, rather, they sit and keep silent.

The students of Rabbi Jehiel of Paris wrote on this:

> If a *Hakham* dies, his study hall in which he was accustomed to study Torah, and his pupils who were accustomed to study before him, are in recess **that entire day**, even after he was buried. But not the entire seven [days of mourning], and we have not found in any place

11 Weinstock, p. 280.
12 Weinstock, loc. cit., demonstrates that there are locations in which something of the early practice is preserved. Thus, e.g., Rabbi Joseph Yuspa Hahn, *Yosif Ometz*, pp. 150–51 states: "Between the *Minhah* and *Maariv* [prayers] on the Sabbath no sermon is established, out of respect for our teacher Moses, may he rest in peace, who died at that hour; consequently, the practice has developed not to expound in public at this time, as is the practice on holidays."
13 Cf. *Ha-Manhig*, p. 187, which lists this law.

that they need be in mourning (meaning, observing the mourning week).[14]

The meaning of this passage is that the students of R. Jehiel regarded the recess of the study hall as a sign of formal mourning.

Most of the *Rishonim*, however, disagreed with this opinion, and maintain that "his study hall is in recess" "means **all the seven** [days of mourning], because they eulogize him, and they do not engage in Torah study in his study hall, so that they would not shirk [the obligation of] his eulogy."[15] *Rabad* concurs: "He is eulogized **all seven**";[16] as does Nahmanides in *Torat Adam*:[17]

> Even though all acquire [corpse] impurity for a *Nasi*, **they do not mourn for him**. For all the funeral practices he has the status of *met mitzvah*, but as regards [formal] mourning, we have not learned that this applies to him at all; and *Rabad* wrote similarly [...].[18]

The *Shulhan Arukh* establishes the law on this point as follows:[19]

> If a *Hakham* dies, his study hall is in recess, **for he is eulogized**

---

14 *Shitah on Moed Katan, by a Pupil of Rabbeinu Jehiel of Paris*, pp. 97–98, in *Harry Fischel Institute Publications* (Jerusalem, 1937); *Piskei Tosafot* on Moed Katan, para. 121: "If a Torah scholar dies, his study hall is in recess only on the day of the burial, and not seven days, because for [a student's] teacher, who taught him wisdom, [the student] sits [in mourning] for him only a single day, and for other dead, only at the time that [the corpse] is brought out." And similarly in *Sefer ha-Mahkim*, p. 139; *Shibbolei ha-Leket, Hil. Semahot* (*Laws of Mourning*), para. 26, p. 353; *Tanya Rabbati*, para. 65, p. 139.

15 *Nimukei Yosef* on Moed Katan 22b (fol. 14a in Alfasi); N. Sachs (ed.), *Peirush le-Ehad ha-Kadmonim* (*Commentary by One of the Early Ones*) on Alfasi on Moed Katan (Jerusalem, 1966), pp. 209–11; M.Y.L. Sachs (ed.), *Peirush la-Masekhet Mashkin* (*Commentary on Tractate Mashkin by One of Our Early Masters, of Blessed Memory*) (Jerusalem, 1939), pp. 71, 72 (see n. 245).

16 *Nimukei Yosef*, loc. cit. And similarly in Rabbi David ben Levi of Narbonne, *Sefer ha-Mikhtam* (*Sefer ha-Michtam*, ed. M.Y. Blau [New York, 1962], p. 221; *Ha-Mikhtam*, ed. A. Schreiber [Sofer] [New York, 1959], p. 329, and see the editor's glosses ad loc.).

17 *Torat Adam*, ed. C.B. Chavel (Jerusalem, 1964), pp. 144–45.

18 As is the opinion of Rabbeinu Asher, Moed Katan, para. 45, in the name of *Rabad*; and *Ritba*, ed. Z. Hirschman (Jerusalem, 1975), p. 204.

19 *Shulhan Arukh, Yoreh Deah* 344:18.

all seven [days of mourning]. [...] If a *Nasi* dies, the study halls **everywhere that he is eulogized** are in recess.

This legal requirement differs from that governing formal mourning, as we see in the law:

Although all acquire [corpse] impurity for a *Nasi*, **they do not engage in mourning for him.**[20]

We therefore see that, according to this conception, the study hall is in recess to enable the proper eulogizing of the *Hakham*. Meiri writes:[21]

If a *Nasi* dies, all the study halls that are in the vicinity of the city, that are sufficiently close to come every day to eulogize him and return to their city, all are in recess.

The editors add (n. 1):

Our master [Meiri] interprets "all the study halls are in recess" to mean all those that are in the city and in its environs [are in recess] in order to go and hear the eulogy. According to this, [this applies] only to those that are close enough to come to the city each day. We have not found any concurring opinion.

Meiri's view is, however, shared by *Rabad*, as cited by Rabbeinu Jeroham:[22]

Rabad wrote: All the study halls are in recess, from all the towns **that are capable of coming to that city and returning on the same day.**[23]

Since the eulogy was *Rabad*'s sole reason for permitting the recess of the study halls, we may reasonably conclude that only those capable of attending the eulogy would be permitted to cancel their study.

We therefore have before us a fundamental disagreement concerning the recess of the study hall: either due to formal mourning, in which case it

---

20 *Shulhan Arukh, Yoreh Deah*, end of 374 (and Nahmanides, above).
21 On Moed Katan 22b; "*Beith Habchirah*," ed. S. Strelitz and B.Z. Rabinovitz, in *Harry Fischel Institute Publications*, p. 131.
22 Rabbeinu Jeroham ben Meshullam, *Sefer Toledot Adam ve-Havah* (Venice, 1553), *Netiv* 2, para. 5 (p. 22).
23 This was noted by Schreiber (Sofer), *Ha-Mikhtam*, p. 329 n. 46.

would only be in effect the first day, which constitutes the mourning period by Torah law; or it is for the purpose of eulogy, in which case this recess extends all the seven days of the mourning period, for those capable of participating in the eulogizing.

Based on the above, we could possibly propose that the two different customs relating to the study hall recess on the Sabbath at the time of *Minhah* (that of "one sits and keeps silent," and that of studying the tractate of Avot) originate in these two opposite interpretations of the law: "If a *Hakham* dies...." The practice of sitting in silence, which, according to Weinstock, is of early origin, is based on the conception that the study hall recess is an expression of formal mourning, as Weinstock correctly noted in his article. Those authorities, on the other hand, who instituted the recitation of the chapters of Mishnah beginning with "Moses received the Torah from Sinai" felt that this was a fitting eulogy, and, in the words of Rabbi Zedekiah ha-Rofe:[24]

> It therefore was instituted to recite *Pirkei Avot* [...] that is to say, we tell of his honor and relate his praise, and thereby he shall have good repose.[25]

---

24 *Shibbolei ha-Leket*, end of para. 126.

25 See the intriguing responsum in *Sha'arei Teshuvah*, para. 220, which cites a nonextant passage from "*ha-Yerushalmi*" (the Palestinian Talmud), apparently from *Sefer Yerushalmi* (for *Sefer Yerushalmi*, see A. Aptowitzer, *Introduction to Sefer Ravya* [Jerusalem, 1938], pp. 275–77 [Hebrew]; *Minhagei Yisrael*, Vol. 1, p. 63 n. 9, p. 157 n. 20, and more); nothing more need be added.

For the customs relating to the reading of Tractate Avot on the Sabbath, see the bibliography in my edition of *Masechet Derech Eretz Zutta and Perek ha-Shalom*, pp. 174–75; Y. Gartner, "Why Did the *Geonim* Institute the Custom of Saying 'Avoth' on the Sabbath?", *Sidra* 4 (1988), pp. 17–32 (Hebrew), in which the author attempts to demonstrate that in the background of this recitation is the disagreement between the Karaites and the Rabbanites regarding the Oral Law, in the course of which Gartner discusses in detail the various traditions regarding the day of Moses' death. Even, however, if we accept Gartner's hypothesis, this is not pertinent to our proposal, since it seeks only to explain those views that explicitly state that Moses died on the Sabbath.

BIBLIOGRAPHY

Bibliography of Primary Sources

Aaron ben Elijah of Nicomedia, *Gan Eden* (Eupatoria, 1866).

Aaron ben Elijah of Nicomedia, *Keter Torah* (Ramleh, 1972).

Aaron Berechiah ben Moses of Modena, *Ma'avar Yabbok* (first edition: Mantua, 1526).

Aaron ha-Kohen of Lunel, *Orhot Hayyim* (Berlin, 1902).

Aboab, Isaac, *Menorat ha-Ma'or*, ed. Y. Paris-Horev and M.H. Katzenellenbogen (Jerusalem, 1961).

Abraham, the son of Maimonides, *Sefer ha-Maspik le'Ovdey Hashem* (*Kitab Kifayat al-'Abidin*), ed. N. Dana (Ramat Gan, 1989).

Abraham ben Azriel, *Arugat ha-Bosem*, ed. E.E. Urbach (Jerusalem, 1947).

Abraham ben Azriel, *Arugat ha-Bosem* (Jerusalem, 1963).

Abraham ben David (*Rabad*), *Yeshuvot u-Pesakim* (*Responsa and Rulings*), ed. J. Kafih (Jerusalem, 1964).

Abraham ben David of Posquières, *Baalei ha-Nefesh*, ed. J. Kafih (Jerusalem, 1965).

Abraham ben Nathan of Lunel, *Sefer Ha-Manhig*, ed. Y. Raphael (Jerusalem, 1978).

Abudarham David, *Abudarham ha-Shalem*, ed. S.A. Wertheimer (Jerusalem, 1963).

Avraham ben David of Posquières, *Sheloshah Sefarim Niftahim* (*Three Books Opening*), ed. S. Shonblum (Lemberg, 1877).

Alfayah, Isaac, *Kunteres ha-Yehieli* (Jerusalem, 1975 [first edition: Jerusalem, 1928]).

Alfasi, Yitzhak, *She'eilot u-Teshuvot Rabbenu Yitzhak Alfasi*, ed. W. (Z.) Leiter (Pittsburgh, 1954), ed. D. Ts. Rothstein (New York, 1975).

Alter, J.A.L., *Sefat Emet* (Vilna, 1927).

Amittay ben Shfatyah, *The Poems of Amittay*, ed. Y. David (Jerusalem, 1975) (Hebrew).

Amram, Gaon, *Seder Rav Amram Gaon*, ed. D. Goldschmidt (Jerusalem, 1971).

Amsterdam Haggadah of 1695.

Amsterdam Minhagim Book (1662).

Anan ben David, *Sefer ha-Mitzvot le-Anan*, ed. A. Harkavy (St. Petersburg: A. Harkavy, 1903).

Ardit, Joshua Solomon, *Hina ve-Hisda* (Izmir, 1864–77).

Asaf, S., "Index to *Megillat Setarim*," *Tarbiz* 11 (1940), p. 253 (Hebrew).

Asaf, S. (ed.), *Rabbinic Texts and Documents* 1, *Gaonica* (*Mi-Sifrut ha-Geonim*) (Jerusalem, 1933).

Ashlag, Y., *Ha-Sulam* (Jerusalem, 1950).

Assaf, S. (ed.), *Teshuvot ha-Geonim* (Jerusalem, 1927).

Ascamoth da Sta. Irmandade Hesed veEmeth (Amsterdam, 1748).

Asher ben Saul of Lunel, *Sefer ha-Minhagot*, pub. by S. Assaf, *Sifran shel Rishonim: Responsa, Decisiones atque Minhagoth* (Jerusalem, 1935).

Aszod, Judah, *She'eilot u-Teshuvot Yehudah Ya'aleh* (Lvov-St. Petersburg, 1873–80).

Avot de-Rabbi Nathan, version A, ed. S. Schechter (Vienna, 1887 [photocopy edn.: New York, 1945]).

Azulai, Abraham, *Zoharei Hammah* (Venice, 1655 and other editions).

Azulai, Abraham ben Mordechai (*Hesed le-Avraham* [Lvov, 1863]), ed. H.J. Ehrenreich (Deva, 1927).

Azulai, Hayyim Yosef David, *Birkei Yosef* (Leghorn, 1774).

Azulai, Hayyim Yosef David, *Le-David Emet* (Leghorn, 1786); *Kaf ha-Hayyim* 134:12.

Azulai, Hayyiim Yosef David, *Moreh ba-Etzba* (Leghorn, 1782) 3:4.

Azulai, Hayyim Yosef David, *Sefer Refuah ve-Hayyim* (*The Book of Healing and Life*) (Izmir, 1875; Jerusalem, 1908).

Azulai, Hayyim Yosef David, *She'eilot u-Teshuvot Hayyim Sho'al* (Leghorn, 1795).

Azulai, Hayyim Yosef David, *She'eilot u-Teshuvot Yosif Ometz* (Leghorn, 1798).

Baer, S.I., *Avodat Yisrael* prayerbook (Roedelheim, 1868).

Bashyazi, Elijah, *Aderet Eliyahu* (Israel, 1966).

Belmonte, Isaac Nunis, *Sha'ar ha-Melekh* (Salonika, 1771).

Ben-Hayyim, Z. (ed.), *Tibat Marqe: A Collection of Samaritan Midrashim* (Jerusalem, 1988).

Ben Mattityahu, B.Z., *She'eilot u-Teshuvot Binyamin Ze'ev* (Jerusalem, 1959).

Ben Naim, Yossef, *Noheg be-Hokhmah*, ed. M. Amar (Israel, 1986).

Benvenist[e], Hayyim, *Keneset ha-Gedolah* (Izmir, 1731).

Berlin, Naphtali Zevi, *Ha-Emek She'alah* (Jerusalem, 1967).

Berakhah Meshuleshet (Warsaw, 1863; photocopy edn.: Jerusalem, 1968).

Caro, Isaac, *Toledot Yitzhak* (Amsterdam, 1708).

Castro, Jacob, *She'eilot u-Teshuvot Ohalei Yaakov* (Leghorn, 1783).

Cordovero, Moses, *Pardes Rimmonim* (Salonika, 1584).

Coronel, N.N., "*She'eilot u-Teshuvot Even ha-Roshah le-R. Eliezer bar Natan, z.z.l.*," *Shomer Tziyyon ha-Ne'eman* 4, *Mikhtav* 193 (Altona, 1855 [photocopy edn.: New York, 1963]).

David ben Levi of Narbonne, *Sefer ha-Mikhtam* (*Sefer ha-Michtam*), ed. M.Y. Blau (New York, 1962).

David ben Zimra (*Radbaz*) *Migdal David* (Lvov, 1883).

De Vidas, E., *Huppat Eliyahu Rabbah*, by Ch.M. Horowitz: *Kavod Huppah* (Frankfurt am Main, 1888).

De Vidas, E., *Reshit Hokhmah* by (Jerusalem, 1972).

Dikdukei Soferim ha-Shalem, in *The Babylonian Talmud with Variant Readings* (Jerusalem,1985).

Dio Cassius (second-third centuries CE), *Romaika* (ed. *LCL*).

Dittenberger, W., *Sylloge Inscriptionum Graecarum*[3] (Leipzig, 1920).

Eleazar ben Judah, *Ma'aseh Rokeah* (Sanuk, 1912).

Eleazar ben Judah of Worms, *Roke'ah*, ed. B.S. Schneersohn (Jerusalem, 1967).

Eleazar ben Moses Azikri, *Sefer Haredim*, ed. L. Deutsch (Kunszentmiklos, 1935).

Eleazar ben Zev Wolf ha-Kohen of Sochaczew, *Hiddushei Ma-ha-Rakh* (Warsaw, 1913).

Eleazar of Worms, *Hokhmat ha-Nefesh* (Safed, 1913).

Eliezer ben Judah of Worms, *Sefer Rokeah: Hilkhot Teshuvah he-Shalem*, ed. E. Rosenfeld (Brooklyn, 2000).

Eliezer ben Samuel of Metz, *Sefer Yere'im* (Vilna, 1892).

Elfenbein, I. (ed.), *Sefer Minhagim de-ve Maharam ... me-Rotenberg* (*Sefer Minhagim of the School of Rabbi Meir ben Baruch of Rothenburg*) (New York, 1938).

Elizur, S. (ed.), *The Liturgical Poems of Rabbi Pinhas Ha-Kohen* (Jerusalem, 2004).

Elliot, G.B., *Letters from the North of Europe* (London, 1830 and 1832).

Elijah ben Benjamin Wolf Shapira, *Eliyahu Rabbah* (Prague, 1660–1712).

Elijah ben Moses Zevi Posek, *Koret ha-Berit* (Lvov, 1893).

Emden, Jacob, *Beit Yaakov* (Lemberg, 1904).

Ephraim of Luntshits, *Olelot Ephrayim* (Amsterdam, 1710).

Epstein, J.N., "New Fragments of Sefer ha-Mizwot of Anan," *Tarbiz* 7 3–4 (1936) (Hebrew).

Epstein, J.N. and Melamed, E.Z., *Mekhilta d'Rabbi Sim'on b. Jochai* (Jerusalem, 1955).

Ettlinger, Jacob, *Teshuvot Binyan Zion ha-Shalem* (Jerusalem, 1989).

Eustathius (twelfth century CE), a commentary on the *Iliad* and the *Odyssey*: ed. G. Stollbaum, 1825–1831.

Eybeschuetz, Jonathan, *Kreiti u-Peleiti* (Altona, 1763).

Eylenburg, Issachar Baer, *Be'er Sheva* (Frankfurt, 1709).

Frankfurt Minhagim Book (Frankfurt, 1708).

Friedman, I.H., *Likkutei Maharih* (Sighet-Satmar, 1911 [photocopy edn.: New York, 1965]).

Gaguine, Shemtob, *Keter Shem Tov* (Kaiden, 1934).

Gamaliel ben Pedahzur, *The Book of Religion, Ceremonies, and Prayers of the Jews* (London, 1738).

Gans, D., *Tzemach David* (Sedilkow, 1834).

Gaon, Achai, *She'iltot*, ed. S.K. Mirsky (Jerusalem, 1964, 1966).

Gedenkbuch der Frankfurter Juden (Frankfurt a.M., 1914).

Gellis, J., *Tosafot Hashalem: Commentary on the Bible* (Jerusalem, 1987) (Hebrew).

Genesis Rabbah, ed. Theodor-Albeck (Berlin 1912–36).

Gershom ben Jacob ha-Gozer, *Zikhron Berit le-Rishonim*, ed. Rabbi Jacob Glassberg (Cracow, 1892).

Ginzberg, L., *Genizah Studies in Memory of Doctor Solomon Schechter* (New York, 1929).

Ginzberg, L., *Geonica* (New York, 1909).

Ginzberg, L., *Yerushalmi Fragments from the Genizah* (New York, 1909).

Goldschmidt, D., *Mahzor le-Yamim ha-Nora'im* (Jerusalem, 1970).

Gombiner, Abraham Abele ben Hayyim, *Zayit Ra'anan* (Dessau, 1704; Vienna, 1743).

Grace after Meals, executed by Meshullam of Polna in 1751.

Griffith, F.L. and Thompson, H., *The Demotic Magical Papyrus of London and Leiden* (London, 1904).

Griffith, F.L. and Thompson, H., *The Leyden Papyrus: An Egyptian Magical Book* (New York, 1974).

Ha-Eshkol, ed. Auerbach et al. (Halberstadt, 1867).

Ha-Cohen, M., *Higgid Mordecai: Histoire de la Libye et de ses Juifs*, ed. H. Goldberg (Jerusalem, 1982) (Hebrew).

ha-Kohen, M., *Berit Kehunah ha-Shalem*[4] (Bnei Brak, 1990).

Ha-Pardes, ed. H.J. Ehrenreich (Budapest, 1924).

Habermann, A.M., *Gezerot Ashkenaz ve-Tzarefat (Persecutions in Germany and France)* (Jerusalem, 1971).

Hahn, Joseph Yuspa, *Yosif Ometz* (Frankfurt, 1723 [photocopy edn.: Jerusalem, 1965]).

Halberstam, E.S. (the son of Rabbi Hayyim of Zanz), *Divrei Yehezkel* (Podgorza, 1901).

Halberstam (of Zanz), H., *She'eilot u-Teshuvot Divrei Hayyim* (Lemberg, 1875).

Halberstam, Mordechai, *Ma'amar Mordechai* (Brno, 1789).

Harkavy, A., *Zikkaron le-Rishonim ve-gam le-Aharonim (=Studien und Mittheilungen aus der Kaiserlichen Oeffentlichen Bibliothek zu St. Petersburg)* (Berlin, 1887).

Herlingen, Aaron Wolf, *Berakhot le-Nashim* (Vienna, 1739).

Hirschberg, H.Z. (ed.), *Rabbenu Nissim b. R. Jacob of Kairouan: Hibbur Yafeh me-ha-Yeshu'ah* (Jerusalem, 1970).

Hirschler, M. (ed.), *Ketubot*, ed. Makhon ha-Talmud ha-Yisraeli he-Shalem (The Complete Israeli Talmud Institute) (Jerusalem, 1972).

Hovav, Moshe, *Bendicion Despues de Comer* (= *Birkat ha-Mazon*, Amsterdam, 1723) (Jerusalem, 1979).

Ibbur Shanim (*The Intercalation of Years*) (Venice, 1578).

Isaac ben Judah Ibn Ghayyat, *Sha'arei Simhah*, ed. I. Bamberger (Furth, 1861).

Isaac ben Meir of Dueren, *Minhagim Yeshanim mi-Dura*, ed. I. Elfenbein (New York, 1948 [photocopy edn.: Jerusalem, 1969]).

Isaac ben Sheshet Perfet, *She'eilot u-Teshuvot ha-Ribash* (Constantinople, 1546).

Isaac of Shedlitz (Siedlce), *Matamim* (Warsaw, 1889).

Isbell, C.D., *Corpus of the Aramaic Incantation Bowls* (*SBL Dissertation Series*, No. 17) (Missoula, Mont., 1975).

Ishbili, Yom-Tov ben Abraham, *Hiddushei ha-Ritba*, ed. M. Goldstein (Jerusalem, 1990).

Israel al-Nakawa, *Menorat ha-Ma'or*, ed. H.G. Enelow (New York, 1932).

Israel ben Chaim Bruna, *She'eilot u-Teshuvot R. Yisrael Bruna*, ed. M. Hershler (Jerusalem, 1973).

Israel ben Samuel of Shklov (a pupil of the Vilna Gaon), *Pe'at ha-Shulhan* (Safed, 1836).

Isserles, Moshe, *She'eilot u-Teshuvot Rema* (Jerusalem, 1971).

Jacob ben David Tam Ibn Yahya, *Tummat Yesharim* (*Oholei Tam*), ed. Rabbi Abraham Motal (Venice, 1620).

Jacob ben Jehuda Hazan of London, *The Etz Hayyim*, ed. I. Brodie (Jerusalem, 1962).

??Jacob ben Samuel Aboab, *She'eilot u-Teshuvot Devar Shemuel* (Venice, 1702 [photocopy edn.: Jerusalem, 1983]).

Jacob of Vienna, *Peshatim u-Perushim* (Mainz, 1888).

Jacob Tam, *Sefer ha-Yashar*, ed. S.F. Rosenthal (Berlin, 1898).

Jacob Tam, *Sefer ha-Yashar, Helek ha-Hiddushim* ["Novellae"], ed. S.S. Schlesinger (Jerusalem, 1959).

Jehuda ben Barsilai, *Sepher ha-Ittim* (Cracow, 1903).

Jeroham (ben Meshullam), *Toledot Adam ve-Havvah* (Constantinople, 1516).

Johnson, M.D., "The Life of Adam and Eve," in J.H. Charlesworth, *The Old Testament Pseudepigrapha*, Vol. 2 (Garden City, N.Y., 1983).

Joseph (Joselein) ben Moses (ca. 1460), *Leket Yosher*, ed. J. Freimann (Berlin, 1903 [photocopy edn.: Jerusalem, 1964]).

Judah ben Yakar, *Perush ha-Tefilot ve-ha-Berakhot*, ed. S. Yerushalmi (Jerusalem, 1968).

Kahana, A. (ed.), *Ha-Sefarim ha-Hitzonim* (*The Apocrypha*)² (Tel Aviv, 1956).

Kalonymus ben Kalonymus (1286–1328), *Even Bohen*, ed. A.M. Habermann (Tel Aviv, 1956).

Kaschmann, Jousep Juspa, *Noheg ka-Tzon Yosef* (Frankfurt a.M., 1718 [Tel Aviv, 1969]).

Katz, Reuben Hoeshke ben Hoeshke, *Yalkut Reuveni* (Wilmersdorf, 1681).

Keter Torah (Lublin, 1901, and other editions).

Kimha de-Avishuna (Bologna, 1540).

Kirchheim, J.L., *The Customs of Worms Jewry*, ed. I.M. Peles (Jerusalem, 1987) (Hebrew).

Kirchner, P.C., *Judisches Ceremoniel, das ist: Allerhand Judisch Gebrauche* (published in Frankfurt in 1720, together with J. Meelfuhrer, *Synopsis Institutionum Hebraicarum*).

Kirchner, P.C., *Judisches Ceremoniel* (Nuremberg, 1724).

Kitvei Rabbeinu Bahya (*Writings of Rabbeinu Bahya*), ed. C.B. Chavel (Jerusalem, 1969).

Kluger, Solomon, *She'eilot u-Teshuvot Tuv Ta'am ve-Da'at* (Podgorze, 1900).

Kol Bo (Naples, 1490).

Klar, B. (ed.), *Megillat Ahimaaz: The Chronicle of Ahimaaz, with a Collection of Poems* .... (Jerusalem, 1974) (Hebrew).

Klausner, A., *Sefer Minhagim le-R. Avraham Klausner*, ed. Y.Y. Dissen (Jerusalem, 1978).

Kluger, Solomon, *She'eilot u-Teshuvot Tuv Ta'am ve-Da'at* (Podgorze, 1900).

Kook, Abraham Isaac HaKohen, *She'eilot u-Teshuvot Ezrat Kohen* (Jerusalem, 1969).

Kook, A.I., *Olat Re'iyah Prayerbook* (Jerusalem, 1962).

Kupfer, E., *Teshuvot u-Pesakim me'et Hakhmei Ashkenaz ve-Tzorfat* (*Responsa et Decisiones*) (Jerusalem, 1973).

Landau, Abraham, *Tzelota de-Avraham* prayerbook, ed. J. Werdiger (Tel Aviv, n. d.).

Landau, Jacob (fifteenth century), *Ha-Agur*, ed. M. Hershler (Jerusalem, 1942).

Lida, D., *Shomer Shabbat* (Zholkva, 1804).

Lieberman, S., *Hilkhot ha-Yerushalmi* (*The Laws of the Palestinian Talmud) of Rabbi Moses ben Maimon*) (New York, 1948).

Lieberman, S., *Tosefta, The Order of Moed* (New York, 1962).

Lipschutz, S., *Segulot Yisrael* (Munkacs, 1905; with additions: 1944).

Leone (Judah Aryeh) da Modena, *The History of the Rites, Customs, and Manner of Life, of the Present Jews, throughout the World*, trans. E. Chilmead (London, 1650).

Leone (Judah Aryeh) da Modena, *Historia dei Riti Ebraici* (Paris, 1637).

Lewin, B.M., *Otzar ha-Gaonim* (Haifa, 1930–31).

Luria, Johanan, *Meshivat Nefesh*, MS. Oxford Opp. Add. 4091 Institute of Microfilmed Hebrew Manuscripts, Jewish National and University Library, no. 16726.

Ma'aseh ha-Geonim, ed. A. Epstein and J. Freimann (Berlin, 1909).

MacDonald, J. (ed.), *Memar Marqah: The Teaching of Marqah* (Berlin, 1963).

Mahzor Vitri, by *R. Simha of Vitri*, ed. S. Hurwitz (Nuremberg, 1923 [Jerusalem, 1988]).

Malkiel Zevi Tenenbaum of Lomza, *Divrei Malkiel* (New York, 1960).

Mantua Haggadah (1560 [1568!]) (Tel Aviv, 1970).

Margaliot, M., *Ha-Hillukim she-bein Anshei ha-Mizrah u-Benei Eretz Israel* (*The Differences between the People of the East and Those of the Land of Israel*), ed. M. Margoliouth (Margulies) (Jerusalem, 1938).

Margaliot (Margulies), R., *Sefer Hasidim* (Jerusalem, 1970).

Margoliouth (Margulies), M., *Hilkhot Eretz Yisrael min ha-Genizah* (*Land of Israel Halakhot from the Genizah*) (Jerusalem, 1972).

Margolis, Y., *Seder Haget* (*Laws of Divorce*), ed. Y. Satz (Jerusalem, 1983).

Masechet Soferim, ed. M. Higger (New York, 1937).

Masekhtot Kallah, ed. M. Higger (New York, 1936).

Mashriki, David, *Shetilei Zeitim* (Jerusalem, 1886[1]–96[2]).

Mechilta d'Rabbi Ismael, ed. H.S. Horovitz and I.A. Rabin (Jerusalem, 1998).

Medici, P., *Riti e Costume degli Ebrei Confutati*[5] (Venice, 1757).

Medini, Hayyim Hezekiah, *Sedeh Hemed ha-Shalem* (Bnei Brak, 1963).

Meir ben Baruch of Rothenburg, *She'eilot u-Teshuvot ma-ha-Ram mi-Rotenburg* (ed. R.N.N. Rabbinovicz [Lvov, 1860]).

Meir ben Baruch of Rothenburg, *Teshuvot Pesakim ve-Minhagim ... me'et Yitzhak Ze'ev Kahana* (Jerusalem, 1957).

Meir ben Baruch of Rothenburg, *Teshuvot Maharam me-Rotenberg*, ed. M.A. Bloch (Budapest, 1895 [photocopy edn.: Tel Aviv, 1969]).

Meir of Narbonne, *Sefer Ham'oroth* (New York, 1964).

Meiri, Menahem, *Beit HaBechirah on Kiddushin*, ed. A Sofer (Jerusalem, 1963).

Meiri, Menahem, *Hibbur Teshuvah*, ed. A. Sofer (New York, 1950).

Menahem Ziyyoni, *Ziyyoni*, and the Tosafist Rabbi Isaac ben Judah ha-Levi, *Pa'ne'ah Raza* (Warsaw, 1928).

Michael Jozefs of Cracow, *Seder ha-Get im Perush Birkat ha-Mayim*, ed. M. Hershler (Jerusalem, 1983).

Midrash Eliyahu (Izmir, 1759).

Midrash ha-Hefets, ed. M. Havatselet (Jerusalem, 1990).

Midrash Haggadol on the Pentateuch, ed. M. Margulies (Jerusalem, 1956).

Minhag K[ehilah] K[edoshah] Posnen u-Ketzat Agafe[ha] (Dyhernfurth, 1796).

Minhagei K[ehilah] K[edoshah] Fuerth (*Practices of the Fuerth Community*) (Fuerth, 1767).

Mintz, Judah, *She'eilot u-Teshuvot ma-ha-Ri Mintz* (Cracow, 1882).

Mintz, Moshe, *She'eilot u-Teshuvot Rabbeinu Moshe Mintz*, ed. Y.S. Domb (Jerusalem, 1991).

Mishnat Rabbi Eliezer (*The Mishnah of Rabbi Eliezer*), ed. H.G. Enelow (New York, 1934).

Modena, *Hayye Yehuda*, ed. A. Kahana (Kiev, 1911).

Moellin, Jacob, *Responsa of Rabbi Yaacov Molin — Maharil*, ed. Y. Satz (Jerusalem, 1979).

Moellin, Jacob, *Sefer Maharil* (*The Book of Maharil*), ed. S.J. Spitzer (Jerusalem, 1989).

Moellin, Jacob, *She'eilot u-Teshuvot ha-Maharil he-Hadashot* (*New Responsa of Rabbi Yaacov Molin-Maharil*), ed. Y. Sats (Jerusalem, 1977).

Molcho, J., *Shulhan Gavo'ah* (Salonika, 1784).

Morpurgo, Samson, *She'eilot u-Teshuvot Shemesh ve-Tzedakah* (Venice, 1742–43).

Moses ha-Kohen, *Berit Kehunah ha-Shalem*[4] (Bnei Brak, 1990).

Moses of Przemysl, *Matteh Moshe*, ed. M. Knoblowicz (London, 1958).

Moses Parnas of Rothenburg, *Sefer ha-Parnas* (Vilna, 1891).

Moshe ben Maimon, *Teshuvot ha-Rambam* (*Responsa of Maimonides*), ed. J. Blau (Jerusalem, 1960); Vol. 2 (= ed. A.H. Freimann [Jerusalem, 1934]).

Moshe ben Nachman, *Kitvei Rabbeinu Moshe ben Nahman* (*Writings of Nahmanides*), ed. C.B. Chavel (Jerusalem, 1965).

Moshe ben Yaakov of Coucy, *Sefer Mitzvot Gadol ha-Shalem* (Jerusalem, 1993).

Nahman of Bratslav, *Sefer ha-Middot, o Hanhagot Yisrael* (Jerusalem, 1986).

Nathan ben Judah, *Sefer ha-Mahkim*, ed. J. Freimann (Cracow, 1903).

Nimmukei Yosef on Avodah Zarah, ed. M.Y. Blau (New York, 1969).

Nissim ben Jacob of Kairouan, *Rabbenu Nissim b. R. Jacob of Kairouan: Hibbur Yafeh me-ha-Yeshu'ah* (Jerusalem, 1970).

Noam, V. (ed.), *Megillat Taanit: Versions, Interpretations, History* (Jerusalem, 2004) (Hebrew).

Nuremberg Miscellany from Germany (1590).

Onkeneira, Isaac, *Ayumah ke-Nidgalot* (Constantinople, 1577 [Berlin, 1601]).

Ophir, B.Z. (ed.), *Pinkas Hakehillot, Germany — Bavaria* (Jerusalem, 1973) (Hebrew).

Orah Hayyim, ed. Machon Yerushalayim (Jerusalem, 1994).

Ovadia Yosef, *She'eilot u-Teshuvot Yehaveh Da'at* (Jerusalem, 1981).

Ovadiah Yosef, *She'eilot u-Teshuvot Yabi'a Omer* (Jerusalem, 1956, 1986).

Palache, Hayyim, *Tokhahot Hayyim* (Furth, 1841).

Palache (Palaggi), Hayyim, *Moed le-Kol Hai* (Izmir, 1861).

Palache (Palaggi), Hayyim, *Sefer Refuah ve-Hayyim* (*The Book of Healing and Life*) (Izmir, 1875).

Palache (Palaggi), Hayyim, *Yimtza Hayyim* (Izmir, 1831).

Palache, Rahamim Nissim Isaac, *She'eilot u-Teshuvot Yafeh la-Lev* (Izmir, 1846).

Paton, W.R., *The Greek Anthology*, trans. W.R. Paton (London, 1918).

Pausanias, *Description of Greece* (trans. W.H.S. Jones, *LCL* [London-Cambridge, Mass., 1945]).

Pesikta de-Rav Kahana, ed. Buber (Vilna, 1925).

Petah Einayim (Leghorn, 1790).

Photius (ninth century CE), *Bibliotheca*, ed. Bekker (Berlin, 1924).

Pickering, F.P. (ed.), *The Anglo-Norman Text of the Holkham Bible Picture Book* (Oxford, 1971).

Pinkas Hekhsharim shel Kehilat Pozna (*Acta Electorum Communitatis Judaeorum*).

Pinkas Kehillot Shnaittakh (*Acta Communitatis Judaeorum Schnaittach*), ed. M. Hildesheimer (Jerusalem, 1992).

Pirkei de-Rabbi Eliezer, ed. D. Luria (Warsaw, 1852).

Pliny, *Natural History*, trans. W.H.S. Jones, *LCL* (London-Cambridge, Mass., 1963).

Plutarch, *Moralia*, "The E at Delphi" (ed. *LCL*: [1936] *Posnaniensium*), ed. D. Avron (Jerusalem, 1967).

Poppers, Jacob, *Shav Ya'akov* (Frankfurt am Main, 1742).

Practices ... According to the Customs of the Sefardim (Amsterdam, 1763).

Prague Haggadah (1526).

Provintzalo, Moshe, *She'eilot u-Teshuvot Rabbi Moshe Provintzalo*, ed. A.Y. Yanni (Cracow, 1882 [Jerusalem, 1989]).

Raphael Aaron ben Simeon, *Nahar Mitzrayim* (Thebes, 1908).

Rapoport, Abraham Menahem ben Jacob, *Minhah Belulah* (Vienna, 1594).

Rappaport Isaac ben Judah ha-Kohen, *She'eilot u-Teshuvot Batei Kehunah* (Izmir, 1736).

Rappaport, U., *The First Book of Maccabees: Introduction, Hebrew Translation, and Commentary* (Jerusalem, 2004).

Ratner, B., *Ahavat Tziyyon ve-Yerushalayim* (*Ahawath Zion we-Jeruscholaim*) (Vilna, 1912).

Ravyah, ed. V. Aptowitzer (Jerusalem, 1938 [Jerusalem, 1964]).

Reischer, Jacob, *She'eilot u-Teshuvot Shevut Yaakov* (Lvov, 1861).

Reischer, M., *Sha'arei Yerushalayim* (Warsaw, 1879).

Roth, E. (ed.), *Takanot Nikolsburg* (*Constitutiones Communitatis Judaeorum Nikolsburgiensis*) (Jerusalem and Tel Aviv, 1961), no. 65 (Hebrew).

Sa'adia ben Joseph, Gaon, *Siddur R. Saadia Gaon*, ed. I. Davidson, I. Joel, and S. Assaf (Jerusalem, 1941).

Sachs,, N. (ed.), *Peirush le-Ehad ha-Kadmonim* (*Commentary by One of the Early Ones*) on Alfasi on Moed Katan (Jerusalem, 1966).

Sachs M.Y.L. (ed.), *Peirush la-Masekhet Mashkin* (*Commentary on Tractate Mashkin by One of Our Early Masters, of Blessed Memory*) (Jerusalem, 1939).

Sachs, Z., "*Tosafot R[abbi] J[udah]* on the Tractate of Berakhot by," *Sinai* 37 (1955).

Safrin, I.J. of Komarno, *Zohar Hai* (Lemberg, 1875).

Samuel ben David ha-Levi (Poland, 1624–81), *Nahalat Shivah* (Amsterdam, 1667; Warsaw, 1887, and others).

Samuel ben Joseph Joshua, *Nahalat Yosef* (Jerusalem, 1988).

Samuel ha-Levi, *She'eilot u-Teshuvot Nahalat Shiv'ah* (= *Nahalat Shiv'ah*) (Furth, 1724).

Saphir, Jacob, *Even Sappir* (Mainz, 1874 [photocopy edn.: Jerusalem, 1970]).

Schammes, Jousep, *Wormser Minhagbuch*, ed. B.S. Hamburger and E. Zimmer (Jerusalem, 1992).

Schapira, H.E. of Munkacs, *Nimukei Orah Hayyim* (Tyrnau, 1930 [photocopy edn.: Jerusalem-Brooklyn, 1968]).

Schapira, S., *She'eilot u-Teshuvot Hemdat Shaul* (Odessa, 1903).

Schick, Moses, *She'eilot u-Teshuvot Maharam Shik* (Munkacs, 1881–1904).

Schlesinger, Naphtali Hertz, *She'eilat Hakham* (Frankfort on the Oder, 1797).

Schuck, Solomon, *Szidur Haminhagim* (Munkacs, 1888).

Seder Berakhot (Amsterdam, 1687).

Seder Eliyahu Rabbah (16), ed. M. Ish Shalom (M. Freidmann) (Vienna, 1901 [photocopy edn.: Jerusalem, 1960]).

Seder R. Saadiah Gaon (Jerusalem, 1941).

Seder Rav Amram Gaon, ed. D. Goldschmidt (Jerusalem, 1971).

Sefer ha-Hayyim: Ve-Hu Kollel Kol ha-Tefilot ha-Shayakhin le-Hevra Kadisha Gemilut Hasadim v-Khol Minhagei Hesed ve-Emet ... kefi Minhagei Sefardim (*The Book of Life: That Includes all the Prayers of the Gemilut Hasadim Burial Society and all the Burial Sefer ha-Mohalim* [The Book of *Mohalim*]) (Vienna, 1728).

Sefer ha-Pardes, ed. H.J. Ehrenreich (Budapest, 1924).

Sefer Hasidim, ed. R. Margaliot (Margulies) (Jerusalem, 1957).

Sefer Minhagim de-Kehillatenu be-Fiurde (*The Book of Customs of Our Community in Fuerth*) (Fuerth, 1767 [photocopy edn.: Williamsburg, 1991]).

Sefer Raziel ha-Malakh (Amsterdam, 1701).

Sefer Tefilot u-Minhagim from Germany (1590).

Sha'ar ha-Otiyot (Josefov, 1878).

Sha'arei Shamayim (by the Vilna Gaon) (Vilna, 1871).

Shaare Teshubah: Responsa of the Geonim, ed. W. Leiter (New York, 1946).

She'eilot u-Teshuvot ha-Rashba (*Responsa Attributed to Nahmanides*), ed. Machon Yerushalayim (Jerusalem, 2001).

Shitah on Moed Katan, by a Pupil of Rabbeinu Jehiel of Paris, in *Harry Fischel Institute Publications, Section III. Rishonim*, ed. S. Eliesri and A. Jacobovitz (Jerusalem, 1937) (Hebrew).

Shulhan Arukh with the glosses of *Rema* (Cracow, 1578–80).

Siddur of R. Solomon ben Samson of Garmaise, ed. M. Hershler (Jerusalem, 1971) (Hebrew).

Siddur Raschi, ed. S. Buber (Berlin, 1911).

Simeon ben Zemah Duran, *She'eilot u-Teshuvot ha-Tashbetz* (first edn.: Amsterdam, 1638).

Solomon ben Isaac, *Sefer ha-Pardes le-Rabbenu Shlomo Yitzhaki (Rashi), Zikhrono Li-Vrakhah*, ed. H.J. Ehrenreich (Budapest, 1924).

Sofer, Jacob Hayyim, *Kaf ha-Hayyim* (first edn.: Jerusalem, 1910–26).

Sperber, D., *Masechet Derech Eretz Zutta and Perek ha-Shalom* (Jerusalem, 1994).

Sperber, D., *She'eilot u-Teshuvot Afarcaste de-Ania* (Satu-Mare, 1940 [photocopy edn., with additions: Jerusalem, 1981]).

Susskind, Alexander, *Yesod ve-Shoresh ha-Avodah* (Jerusalem, 1968 [first edition: Novy Svor, 1782]).

Susslein ha-Kohen, Alexander, *Sefer ha-Agudah* on Berakhot (Jerusalem, 1969).

Takanot de-Hevrah Kadisha Gemilut Hasadim de-K[ehilah] K[edoshah] Ashkenazim be-Amsterdam (Regulations of the *Gemilut Hasadim* Burial Society of the Ashkenazic Community in Amsterdam), 1776.

Tanhuma, Genesis, ed. Buber (Lvov, 1885).

Tanya Rabbati (first edn.: Cremona, 1565).

Tenenbaum, Jacob, *Naharei Afarsemon* (Paksa, 1898).

Teitelbaum, Jekuthiel Judah, *Avnei Zedek* (Lemberg, 1885).

Teshuvot Geonim Hemdah Genuzah (Jerusalem, 1963).

Teshuvot ha-Geonim: Sha'arei Tzedek (Jerusalem, 1966).

Tobias ben Eliezer, *Pesikta Zutarta* (first edition: Vilna, 1880).

Torat Adam, ed. C.B. Chavel (Jerusalem, 1964).

Tosafot Rabbi Judah Sir Leon, ed. N. Sachs (Jerusalem, 1969).

The Tractate "Mourning," ed. D. Zlotnick (New Haven and London, 1966).

Trabotto, Josef Colon b. Solomon, *She'eilot u-Teshuvot ve-Piskei Ma-ha-Rik he-Hadashim* (*Responsae and Decisions of Rabbi Joseph Colon*), ed. E. Pines (Jerusalem, 1984).

Treatise Semahot, ed. M. Higger (New York, 1937).

Tykocinski, H., *The Gaonic Ordinances* (Jerusalem, 1959).

Tyrnau, I., *Sefer ha-Minhagim (Rulings and Customs)*, ed. S.J. Spitzer (Jerusalem, 1979).

Tzarfatti, A., *Perushim u-Pesakim le-Rabbi Avigdor* (Jerusalem, 1996) (as yet unpublished).

Venice Haggadah (1601).

Ventura, Shabbetai ben Abraham, *Nahar Shalom* (Amsterdam, 1774).

Vital, Hayyim, in Hayyim Zemah, *Nagid u-Metzaveh* (Constantinople, 1726).

Waldenberg, Eliezer Judah, *Even Yaakov* (Jerusalem, 1962).

Weinberg, Jehiel Jacob, *She'eilot u-Teshuvot Seridei Esh* (Jerusalem, 1961).

Wilhermsdorf Haggadah (1687), ed. M. Hovav, *Seder Birkat Hamazon (Bendicion Despues de Comer)* (Jerusalem, 1981).

Yagdil Torah, published by Rabbi Israel C. Ackermann (Berlin, 1881).

Yehudah Ben Shemuel heHasid, *Sefer Hasidim (Das Buch der Frommen)*, ed. J. Wistinetzki and J. Freimann (Frankfurt a.M., 1924 [photocopy edn.: Jerusalem, 1969]).

Yerushlimski, Moses Nahum, *Be'er Moshe* (Warsaw, 1901).

Yikare de-Shakhbi, attached to the book *Beit Almin* (Salonika, 1800).

Yitzchak ben Moshe of Vienna, *Or Zarua* (Zhitomer, 1862).

Yitzchak ben Yaakov miKorville, *Semak of Zurich*, ed. Y.Y. Har-Shoshanim-Rosenberg (Jerusalem, 1977).

General Bibliography

Abbink Van der Zwan, P.J., "Ornamentation on Eighteenth-Century Torah Binders," *The Israel Museum News* (1978).

Abbot, G.F., *Macedonian Folklore* (Cambridge, 1903).

Abela, E., "Beitrage zur Kenntniss aberglaubischer gebrauch in Syrien," *ZDPV* 3 (1884).

Abrahams, I., *Jewish Life in the Middle Ages*[2] (London, 1932).

Abrams, I. (ed.), *Hebrew Ethical Wills* (Philadelphia, 1926).

Abramson, S., *Inyanut be-Sifrut ha-Geonim (A Direct Examination of the Geonic Literature)* (Jerusalem, 1974).

Abramson, S., "On R. Baruch Ben Melekh," *Tarbiz* 19 (1948).

Abramson, S., *R. Nissim Gaon: Libelli Quinque* (Jerusalem, 1965) (Hebrew).

Adam, A., *Roman Antiquities* (Philadelphia, 1872).

Additamenta as librum Aruch Completum, ed. S. Krauss (Vienna, 1937 [reprint: New York, 1955]).

Adler, B., *Nisu'in ke-Hilkhatam* (*All the Laws and Customs of Proper Marriage*) (Jerusalem, 1985²), (Hebrew).

Adler, E.N., "The Persian Jews: Their Books and Their Ritual," *JQR* 10 (O.S.) (1898).

Aescoly, A.Z., *Sefer ha-Falashim* (*The Book of the Falashas: The Culture and Traditions of the Jews of Ethiopia*) (Jerusalem, 1943) (Hebrew).

Ahavat Tziyon ve-Yerushalayim (*Ahawath Zion we-Jeruscholaim; Varianten und Erganzungen des Textes des Jerusalemitschen Talmuds*) (Vilna, 1901–12).

Ahituv, Y. et al. (eds.), *A Good Eye: Dialogue and Polemic in Jewish Culture. A Jubilee Book in Honor of Tova Ilan* (Israel, 1999) (Hebrew).

Aigremont (S. von Schultze-Gallera), *Fuss- und Schuhsymbolik und -Erotik: folkloristische und sexualwissenschaftliche Untersuchungen* (Leipzig, 1909).

Allony, S., *Studies in Medieval Philology and Literature* (Jerusalem, 1989) (Hebrew).

Alpert, S., "Practices and Customs of His Honored Holiness, Our Master, the [author of] *Penei Menahem* of Gur, May the Memory of the Righteous and the Holy be for a Blessing, regarding Circumcision," *Ohr Torah* 3,3 (11) (*Nisan* 1998) (Hebrew).

Altshuler, D. (ed.), *The Precious Legacy: Judaic Treasures from Czechoslovak State Collections* (New York, 1983).

Amar, R., *Minhagei ha-Hida* (*Customs of the* Hida) (Jerusalem, 1990).

Amer, A., & Jacoby, R., *Ingathering of the Nations. Treasures of Jewish Art: Documenting an Endangered Legacy* (Jerusalem, 1998).

Ammar, M., "Wedding Orders and the *Ketubba* Text among Moroccan Jews since the XVIth Century," in Chetrit et al., *The Jewish Traditional Marriage: Interpretive and Documentary Chapters* (Hebrew).

Anthologia Graeca (*LCL* edition: *The Greek Anthology* [London, 1916]).

Aptowitzer, V., *Mavo le-Sefer Rabiyah* (*Introductio ad Sefer Rabiyah*) (Jerusalem, 1938).

Arbel, R., "Georgian Ketubbot," *Rimonim* (ed. S. Sabar) 6–7 (1999) (Hebrew).

Arnbserg, P., *Die judischen Gemeinden in Hessen* (Darmstadt, 1973).

Art del Bene Morire (Florence, ca. 1495).

Artom, M., "On the Letters of R. Obadiah of Bertinoro," *Yavneh* 3 (1960) (Hebrew).

Aruch Completum (*Arukh ha-Shalem*), ed. A. Kohut (Vienna, 1878–92 [reprint: New York, 1955]).

Ashkenazi, S., *Avnei Hen: Topics in Jewish Customs* (Tel Aviv, 1990).

Ashkenazy, S., *Ages in Judaism: Each Age and Its Sages*² (Tel Aviv, 1987) (Hebrew).

Aslan, M., & Nissim, R., *From the Customs and Way of Life of Iraqi Jewry* (Tel Aviv, n. d.) (Hebrew).

Assaf, D., *Sefer ha-Kaddish: Its Source, Meaning, and Laws* (Haifa, 1966) (Hebrew).

Assaf, S., *Mekorot le-Toledot ha-Hinukh ha-Yehudi* (*Sources for the History of Jewish Education*) (Tel Aviv, 1954).

Aubrey, J., *Remaines of Gentilisme and Judaisme* (1686–87), ed. J. Britten (London, 1881).

Avida, Y., "Strange Immersions," *Yeda-'Am* 3, 1 (1955) (Hebrew).

Avishur, Y., "*Darkei ha-Emori*," *Sefer Meir Wallenstein* (*Studies in the Bible and the Hebrew Language Offered to Meir Wallenstein* ...) (Jerusalem, 1979) (Hebrew).

Ayache, J., *Recueil des Lois et Coutumes de la Communaute Juive d'Alger*, ed. I. Srour (Jerusalem, 1985), 12:9 (Hebrew).

Bachtold-Staubli, H., *Handworterbuch des deutschen Aberglaubens* (Berlin-Leipzig, 1930–31).

Baer, J.F., "The Religious-Social Tendency of 'Sepher Hassidim,'" *Zion* 3, 1 (1938) (Hebrew).

Baerwald, H., *Der Alte Friedhof der israelitischen Gemeinde zu Frankfurt a.m.* (Frankfurt am Main, 1883).

Bagdanavicius, V.J., *Wellsprings of Folktales*, trans. from the Lithuanian by J. Zemkalnis (New York, 1970).

Bailey, J., "Balancing Act," at www.yogajournal.com/wisdom/927_1.cfm

Bainbridge, R.B., "The Saorias of the Rajmahal Hills," *Memoirs of the Asiatic Society of Bengal*, Vol. II: 1907–1910 (Calcutta, 1911).

Baldensperger, P.J., "Birth, Marriage and Death among the Fellahin of Palestine," *PEFQS* (1894).

Baldensperger, P.J., "Peasant Folklore of Palestine," *PEFQS* (1893).

Baldensperger, P.J., "Morals of the Fellahin," *PEFQS* (1897).

Baldensperger, P.J., "The Immovable East," *PEFQS* (1912).

Bamberger, M.L., "Aus meiner Minhagimsammelmappe," *JJV* 1 (1923).

Banks, M.M., *British Calendar Customs: Scotland*, Vol. 3 (London, 1941).

Bar-Giora Bamberger, N., *Die judischen Friedhofe Jebenhausen und Goppingen* (Goppingen, 1990).

Bar-Ilan, M., *Some Jewish Women in Antiquity* (Atlanta, 1998).

Bar-Levav, A., "Books for the Sick and the Dying in Jewish Conduct Literature," in *Joseph Baruch Sermoneta Memorial Volume, Jerusalem Studies in Jewish Thought* 14, ed. A. Ravitsky (Jerusalem, 1998) (Hebrew).

Baram-Ben-Yosef, N., *Bo'i Kallah: Betrothal and Wedding Customs of Afghanistan Jewry* (Jerusalem, 1997).

Barb, A.A., "The Survival of Magic Arts," in *The Conflict between Paganism and Christianity in the Fourth Century*, ed. A. Momigliano (Oxford, 1963).

Barnett, R.D., *Catalogue of the Permanent and Loan Collections of the Jewish Museum* (London, 1974).

Baron, S.W., *The Jewish Community: Its History and Structure to the American Revolution* (Philadelphia, 1942).

Baron, S.W., *A Social and Religious History of the Jews*, Vol. 9 (New York and London, 1965).

Bartels-Reitzenstein, P., *Das Weib* (1927).

Baruch, Y.L., *Sefer ha-Moadim* (Tel Aviv, 1956) (Hebrew).

Basanavicius, J., *Lieturiskos pasakos yvairios* [Shenandoah, PA, 1898].

Becker, W.A., *Charicles: or Illustrations of the Private Life of the Ancient Greeks* (London, 1866³).

Becker, W.A., *Charikles, Bilder altgriechischer Sitte*, ed. H. Goell (Berlin, 1877–78).

Becker, W.A., *Gallus; or Roman Scenes of the Time of Augustus*, trans. F. Metcalfe (London, 1907).

Beer, M., "On Penances of Penitents in the Literature of *Hazal*," *Zion* 46, 3 (1981) (Hebrew).

Ben Shim'on, R.A., *Sefer Tuv Mitzrayim* (Jerusalem, 1908).

Ben Yehuda, E., *A Complete Dictionary of Ancient and Modern Hebrew* (Jerusalem, 1951).

Ben-Ami, I., *Le Judaisme Marocain: Etudes Ethno-Culturelles* (Jerusalem, 1975) (Hebrew).

Ben-David, S., "The Prohibitions Relating to Keeping Apart during the *Niddah* Period," *Granot* 3 (2003) (Hebrew).

Ben-Jacob, A., *Minhagei Yehudei Bavel ba-Dorot ha-Ahronim* (*Customs of Iraqi Jewry in Recent Generations*) (Jerusalem, 1993).

Ben-Yaacob, A., *Babylonian Jewish Customs* (Jerusalem, 1993).

Benayahu, M., *Sefer Toledot ha-Ari* (*The Toledoth ha-Ari and Luria's "Manner of Life" [Hanhagoth]*) (Jerusalem, 1967) (Hebrew).

Benayahu, M., *Studies in Memory of the Rishon Le-Zion R. Yitzhak Nissim* (Jerusalem, 1985) (Hebrew).

Bender, A.P., "Death, Burial, Mourning," *JQR*, Old Series 7 (1895).

Benjamin, Ch., *The Stiglitz Collection* (Jerusalem, 1987).

Bensimon, R.J., *Le Judaisme marocain* (*Life and Tradition in the Life Cycle*) (Lod, 1994).

Berger, A., *Encyclopedic Dictionary of Roman Law* (*TAPS* NS 43/2) (Philadelphia, 1953).

Berger, N., *Jews and Medicine: Religion, Culture, Science* (Tel Aviv, 1995).

Berger, N., *"Therefore Choose Life..." Jews and Medicine: Religion, Culture, Science* (Tel Aviv, 1995).

Bergman, J., *Judaism: Its Soul and Life* (Jerusalem, 1935), p. 76 (Hebrew).

Berliner, A., *Hayyei ha-Yehudim be-Ashkenaz be-Yemei ha-Beinayim* (*The Life of the Jews in Ashkenaz in the Medieval Period* [= *Aus dem Leben der Juden Deutschlands im Mittelalter* (Berlin, 1937)] [Warsaw, 1900] [photocopy edn.: Israel, 1969]).

Bialer, L., & Fink, E., *Jewish Life in Art and Tradition: from the Collection of the Sir Isaac and Lady Edith Wolfson Museum, Hechal Shlomo, Jerusalem*[2] (Jerusalem, 1980).

Bilder aus dem Leben der Juden in Venedig ausgangs des XVIII Jahrhunderts (Berlin, 1927).

Biton, E., *Ir ha-Tzevi: the Customs of the Holy City of Safed, from Eretz ha-Hayyim by R. Haim Sitehon* (Safed, 1996) (Hebrew).

Blakeborough, R., *Wit, Character, Folklore & Customs of the North Riding of Yorkshire* (London, 1898).

Blau, L., *Das altjudische Zauberwesen* (Budapest, 1898).

Blay, A.R. (ed.), *Eshkolot: Essays in Memory of Rabbi Ronald Lubofsky* (Melbourne, 2002).

Boase, T.S.R., *Death in the Middle Ages: Mortality, Judgment and Remembrance* (New York, 1972).

Bodenschatz, J., *Kirchliche Verfassung der heutigen Juden, sonderlich derer in Deutschland* (Ellangen, 1748).

Boecler, J.W. and Kreutzwald, F.R., *Die Ehsten aberglaublische Gebrauche: Weisen und Gewohnheiten* (St. Petersburg, 1851).

Boid, I.R.M.M., *Principles of Samaritan Halachah* (Leiden and New York, 1989).

Bolte, J. and Polivka, G., *Ammerkungen zu den Kinder- und Hausmarchen der Bruder Grimm* (Leipzig, 1913–30).

Bonar, A.A. and MacCheyne, R.M., *Narrative of a Mission of Inquiry to the Jews from the Church of Scotland in 1839* (Philadelphia, 1844).

Bondeson, J., *A Cabinet of Medical Curiosities* (New York and London, 1991).

Bonfil, R., "Aspects of the Social and Spiritual Life of the Jews in the Venetian Territories at the Beginning of the 16th Century," *Zion* 41 (1976) (Hebrew).

Bonfil, R., *Jewish Life in Renaissance Italy* (Berkeley, Los Angeles, and London, 1994).

Bonfil, R., *The Rabbinate in Renaissance Italy* (Jerusalem, 1979) (Hebrew).

Bonfil, R., "Un Antico Uso Nuziale Ebraico," *Annuario di Studi Ebraici* (1964–65).

Bonner, C., *Studies in Magical Amulets, Chiefly Graeco-Egyptian* (Ann Arbor and London, 1950).

Bonnerjea, B., *A Dictionary of Superstition and Mythology* (London, 1927).

Boskowitz, B.Z. (Wolf), *Ma'amar Esther* (Ofen, 1822).

Boyarsky, Z.H., *Tosefet Shabbat* (Warsaw, 1886).

Brand, J., *Observation on Popular Antiquities, chiefly illustrating the origin of our vulgar ceremonies and superstitions* (first edition: London, 1771, new edition, with additions by Sir Henry Ellis [1813; London, 1900]).

Brandes, Y., "The Marriage Date: A Rejected Halakha and Its Significance," *Akdamot* 13 (2003), pp. 57–76 (Hebrew).

Brashear, W.M., *Magica Varia* (Brussels, 1991).

Brauer, E., "Birth Customs of the Jews of Kurdistan," *Edoth* 1 (1945–46).

Brauer, E., "Rites and Customs in Times of Drought among the Jews of Kurdistan," in *Magnes Anniversary Book*, ed. F.I. Baer et al. (Jerusalem, 1938) (Hebrew).

Brauer, E., *The Jews of Kurdistan*, ed. R. Patai (Jerusalem, 1947) (Hebrew).

Brauer, E., *The Jews of Kurdistan* (Detroit, 1993).

Bresciani, A., *Dei costumi dell' isola di Sardegna comparati cogli antichissimi populi italiano* (Naples, 1850).

Brilling, D., "Sheep and Cattle Firstborn in Frankfurt am Main," *Yeda-'Am*, 3, 1 (1955) (Hebrew).

Bruck, F., *Totenteil und Seelgerat im griechischen Recht*[2] (Munich, 1926).

Buber, M., *Or ha-Ganuz* (*The Hidden Light*), (Jerusalem and Tel Aviv, 1969).

Buckingham, J.S., *Travels in Palestine*[2] (London, 1822).

Budge, E.A.W., *Amulets and Talismans* (New York, 1961[2])

Budge, E.A., *Egyptian Magic* (London, 1899).

Burkert, W., *Homo Necans: The Anthropology of Ancient Greek Sacrificial Ritual and Myth*, trans. P. Bing (Berkeley, Los Angeles, London, 1972).

Buxtorf, J., *Synagoga Judaica*[3] (Basel, 1712; first edition in German, entitled *Juden Schul*, 1603).

Byvogzel tot het Algemeen Groot Historisch Oordeelkundig, Chronologisch, Geographisch, en Letterlyk Naam-en Woord-Boek van den Ganschen H. Bybel..., translated and edited by Jacob van Ostade and Arn. Henr. Westerhovius (Amsterdam: Weststeins en Smith, 1731).

Cahun, L., *La Vie Juive* (Paris, 1886).

Campbell, T., *Letters from the South* (1834–35) (London, 1837).

Canaan, T., *Aberglaube und Volksmedizin im Lande der Bibel* (Hamburg, 1914).

Canaan, T., *Daemonenglaube im Lande der Bibel* (Leipzig, 1929).

Canelo, D.A., *The Last Crypto-Jews of Portugal*[2] (1990, n.p.).

Cecchelli, C., *Mater Christi* (Rome, 1946–54).

Cempla, J., *Avnei Kodesh* (*Holy Stones: Synagogue Remains in Poland*) (Tel Aviv, 1959).

Chavel, C.B., *Lekh Lekha* (Jerusalem, 1966).

Chetrit, J. et al. (eds.), *The Jewish Traditional Marriage: Interpretative and Documentary Chapters* (Haifa, 2003) (Hebrew).

Chidvilasananda, Swami, *A Golden Mind, a Golden Life: A Book of Contemplations* (New York, 1999).

Chorny, J.J., *Sefer ha-Massa'ot be-Eretz Kavkaz* (*Book of Travels in the Caucasus*) (St. Petersburg, 1884).

Christiani, F.A., *Der Juden Glaube und Aberglaube* (Leipzig, 1705).

Chronicle of Jewish Traditions: A Sentimental Journey: Yeshivah University Museum, March 8, 1992 (New York, 1992).

Cohen, A., *An Anglo-Jewish Scrapbook, 1600–1840: The Jew through English Eyes* (London, 1943).

Cohen, E., "Moritz Daniel Oppenheim," *Bulletin des Leo Baeck Instituts* 16–17 (1977–78).

Cohen, M.R., "Leone da Modena's 'Riti'; A Seventeenth Century Plea for Social Toleration of Jews," *Jewish Social Studies* 34 (1992).

Cohen, R.I., "The Visual Image of the Jew and Judaism in Early Modern Europe: From Symbolism to Realism," *Zion* 57 (1992) (Hebrew).

Cohen, R.I., *Jewish Icons: Art and Society in Modern Europe* (Berkeley and Los Angeles, 1998).

Cohen Grossman, G., *Jewish Art* (Southport, 1995).

Conybeare, F.C., "The Demonology of the New Testament," *JQR* 5 (1895).

Conybeare, F.C., "The Testament of Solomon," *JQR* Old Series 11 (1899).

Cook, A.B., *Zeus: A Study in Ancient Religion*, Vol. 1 (Cambridge, 1914); Vol 2. Cambridge 1925.

Cox, M.R., *An Introduction to Folk-Lore* (London, 1897).

Crawley, A.E., *The Mystic Rose* (London, 1902).

Crooke, W., *The Popular Religion and Folk-Lore of Northern India* (Westminster, 1896).

Cross, F.L. and Livingstone, E.A. (eds.), *Oxford Dictionary of the Christian Church*[2] (Oxford, 1983).

Cumont, F., *After Life in Roman Paganism*[2] (New York, 1959).

Cusin, S.G. and Nahon, U., *Art in the Jewish Tradition* (Milan, 1963).

Daiches, S., *Babylonian Oil Magic in the Talmud and in the Later Jewish Literature* (London, 1913).

Dalven, R., *The Jews of Ioannina* (Philadelphia, 1990).

Dan, J., "On the Historical Personality of R. Judah Hasid," in *Culture and Society in Medieval Jewry: Studies Dedicated to the Memory of Haim Hillel Ben-Sasson*, ed. M. Ben-Sasson, R. Bonfil, and J.R. Hacker (Jerusalem, 1989).

Davidson, I., *Thesaurus of Mediaeval Hebrew Poetry* (New York, 1925–33).

de Sola Pool, D., *The Kaddish* (New York, 1964).

Deinard, E., *Massa Krim: The History of the Israelites in the Crimean Peninsula, and Especially the History of the Kuzars, the Karaites, and the Krimchaks* (Warsaw, 1878).

Deitsch, E., Liberman Mintz, S., Light, W.M. and Wachtel, D., *From This World to the Next: Jewish Approaches to Illness, Death* (New York, 1999).

Dembitzer, H.N., *Kelilat Yofi* (Cracow, 1881).

Deneke, B. (ed.), *Siehe der Stein schreit aus der Mauer: Geschichte und Kultur der Juden in Bayern* (Nuremberg, 1988).

Dergny, D., *Usages, Coutumes et Croyances ou Livre des Choses Curieuses* (Paris, 1882).

Deviri, Y., *The Light in Dicta and Adages of the Sages* (Holon, 1976) (Hebrew).

Dicker, H., *Die Geschichte der Juden in Ulm* (Rottweil, 1937).

Diemerbroeck, Y., *De Peste* (Amsterdam, 1665).

Digot, A., *Histoire de Lorraine* (Nancy, 1856).

Dinari, Y., "The Impurity Customs of the Menstruate Woman — Sources and Development," *Tarbiz* 49, 3–4 (1979–80) (Hebrew).

Dinari, Y.A., *The Rabbis of Germany and Austria at the Close of the Middle Ages: Their Conceptions and Halacha-Writings* (Jerusalem, 1984) (Hebrew).

Dobrinsky, H.C., *A Treasury of Sephardic Laws and Customs: The Ritual Practices of Syrian, Moroccan, Judeo-Spanish and Spanish and Portuguese Jews of North America* (New York, 1986).

Dodwell, C.R. (ed.), *Jewish Art Treasures from Prague* (London, 1980).

Donath, L., *Geschichte der Juden in Mecklenburg ...* (Leipzig, 1874 [reprint: Germany, 1974]).

Doolitle, J., *Social Life of the Chinese* (New York, 1867).

Dover, K.J., *Greek Homosexuality* (London, 1978).

Drose-Gisermann, R., Kingreen, M. and Merk, A., *Der Zyklus "Bilder aus dem altjudischen Familienleben" un sein Maker Moritz Daniel Oppenheim* (Hanau, 1996).

Dubois, J.A., *Hindu Manners, Customs and Ceremonies*[3], trans. H.K. Beauchamp (Delhi-New York-Oxford, 1906).

Duda, E., *Old Jewish Postcards from Marek Sosenko's Collection* (Cracow, 1998).

Duran Sanpere, A. and Millas Vallicrosa, J.M., "Una necropolis judaica en el Montjuich de Barcelona," *Sefarad* 7 (1947).

Durer, A., *Kleiner Passion* (Nuremberg, 1511).

Dvorkes, E., *Bi-Shevilei ha-Minhag: Sources and Explanations of Jewish Customs* (Jerusalem, 1994) (Hebrew).

Dvorkes, E., *Bi-Shvilei ha-Halakhah, Shabbat u-Mo'adim* (Jerusalem, 1996).

Ehl, P., Parik, A. and Fiedler, J., *Old Bohemian and Moravian Jewish Cemeteries*, trans. G.S. Matouskova and Z. Joachimova (Prague, 1991).

Eichinger Ferro-Luzzi, G., *Anthropos* 69 (1974).

Eidelberg, S., "Holy Earth: The Development of Two Customs," *PAAJR* 59 (1993) (Hebrew).

Eidelberg, S., *Jewish Life in Austria in the XVth Century as Reflected in the Legal Writings of Rabbi Israel Isserlein and His Contemporaries* (Philadelphia, 1962).

Eijub Abela, E., "Beitrage zur Kenntnisse aberglaubischer Gebrauche in Syrien," in *Zeitschrift des Deutschen Palastina-Vereins* (Leipzig 1884).

Eisler, R., "Der Fisch als Sexualsymbol," *Imago* 3 (1914).

Elbogen, I., *Jewish Liturgy: A Comprehensive History* (Philadelphia, Jerusalem, 1993).

Elfenbein, I., "Year Round Customs from Ashkenaz of Rabbenu Isaac of Dura [= Dueren]," *Horeb* 10 (1948) (Hebrew).

Eliashvili, N., *The Jews in Georgia and in the Land of Israel*, ed. G. Kressel (Tel Aviv, 1975) (Hebrew).

Ellis, A.B., *The Ewe-Speaking Peoples of the Slave Coast of West Africa* (1890 [photocopy edn.: Amsterdam, 1970]).

Elmaleh, A., "From the Life of the Jews in Tripolitania," *Mizrah Oumaarav* (*Orient et Occident*) 3, 7 (1929).

Elzet, Y. (Yehuda Leib Zlotnik-Avida), *Reshumot* (Odessa, 1918).

Emmanuel, I.S., *Matzevot Saloniki* (*Precious Stones of the Jews of Salonica*) (Jerusalem, 1968).

Encyclopaedia Judaica (Jerusalem, 1971).

Encyclopedia Americana

Enziklopedyah Mikra'it (*Encyclopaedia Biblica*) (Jerusalem, 1965).

Enziklopedia Talmudit (*Talmudic Encyclopedia*) (Jerusalem, 1956).

Epstein, A., *Kitvei Avraham Epstein* (*Collected Writings of Abraham Epstein*), ed. A.M. Habermann (Jerusalem, 1950) (Hebrew).

Euchel, I., *Is Delaying the Burial of the Dead Truly Forbidden by the Laws of Israel?* (1797).

Faggiani, G., "Feste ed usanze della Sardegna," in D. Provenzal, *Usanze e feste del populo italiano* (Bologna, 1912).

Falk, Z., *Jewish Matrimonial Law in the Middle Ages* (Oxford, 1966).

Falk, Z., "The Standing of Women in the Communities of Germany and France in the Medieval Period," *Sinai* 48 (1961).

Farnell, L.R., *The Cults of the Greek States*, Vol. 4^2 (New York, 1977).

Feilberg, H.F., *Bidrag til en ordbog over jyske almuesmal*, Vol. 3 (Copenhagen, 1912).

Feilberg, H.F., *Tellaeg og rettelser* (Copenhagen, 1911–12).

Felder, G., *She'eilat Yeshurun* (New York, 1988).

Felsenstein, F. and Liberman Mintz, S.L. (eds.), *The Jew as Other: A Century of English Caricature, 1730–1830* (New York, 1995).

Fenester, H., "*Shtetl* Types," in *Yizkor Baranow: A Memorial to the Jewish Community of Baranow*, ed. N. Blumenthal (Jerusalem, 1964).

Festgabe Prof. Georg Lenhart Ano Dom und Dioceze (Mainz, 1939).

Feuchtwanger, N., "The Coronation of the Virgin and of the Bride," *Jewish Art* 12–13 (1986–87).

Feuchtwanger (Sarig), N., "Interrelations between the Jewish and Christian Wedding in Medieval Ashkenaz," in *Proceedings of the Ninth World Congress of Jewish Studies*, D, Vol. 2 (Jerusalem, 1986).

Feuchtwanger (Sarig), N., "Der Traustein an der Urspringer Synagoge — Beispiel fur einen weitverbreiteten Brauch," in *Das Projekt Synagoge Urspringen: herausgegeben im Auftrag des Landkreises Main-Spessart und des Forderkreises Synagoge Urspringen*, ed. H. Bald and K. Bingemheimer (Wurzburg, 1993).

Finamore, G., *Tradizioni popolari abruzzesi* (Palermo, 1890).

Fiocco, G., "Una pittura di Pietro Longhi," *Arte Veneta* 10 (1956).

Fishof, I., "'Jerusalem Above My Chief Joy': Depictions of Jerusalem in Italian Ketubot," *Journal of Jewish Art* 9 (1982).

Flagg, W.J., *Yoga or Transformation: A Comparative Statement of the Various Religious Dogmas concerning the Soul and Its Destiny, and of Akkadian, Hindu, Taoist, Egyptian, Hebrew, Greek, Christian, Mohammedan, Japanese and Other Magic* (New York and London, 1898).

Fleischer, E., "Aspects in the Poetry of the Early Italian *Paytanim*," *Hasifrut* 30–31 (1981) (Hebrew).

Fram, E., *Ideals Face Reality: Jewish Law and Life in Poland, 1550–1655* (Cincinnati, 1997).

Frawley, D., *Tantric Yoga and the Wisdom Goddesses: Spiritual Secrets of Ayurveda* (Delhi, 1999).

Frazer, J.G., *Aftermath: A Supplement to the Golden Bough*[3] (London, 1936).

Frazer, J.G., *Folk-Lore in the Old Testament: Studies in Comparative Religion, Legend and Law* (London, 1918).

Frazer, J.G., *The Golden Bough, Taboo and the Perils of the Spirit*[3] (New York, 1935).

Frazer, J.G., *The New Golden Bough*, ed. T.H. Gaster (New York, 1959 [New York, 1972]).

Frazer, J.G., *Taboo and the Perils of the Spirit* (part of the third edition of *The Golden Bough* [London, 1911]; first edition: London, 1891).

Freehof, L.S. and King, B., *Embroideries and Fabrics for Synagogue and Home: 5000 Years of Ornamental Needlework* (New York, 1966).

Freehof, S.B., "The Chuppah," in *In the Time of Harvest: Essays in Honor of Abba Hillel Silver on the Occasion of His 70th Birthday*, ed. D.J. Silver (New York, 1963).

Freehof, S.B., *Recent Reform Responsa* (Cincinnati, 1963).

Freehof, S.B., *Reform Jewish Practice and Its Rabbinic Background* (Cincinnati, 1944).

Freehof, S.B., *Reform Responsa* (Cincinnati, 1960).

Freimann, A.H., *Seder Kiddushin ve-Nissu'in Aharei Hatimat ha-Talmud* (*Marriage Law after the Conclusion of the Talmud*) (Jerusalem, 1945).

Frere, W.H., *The Use of Sarum*, Vol. I: *The Sarum Customs* (Cambridge, 1898).

Friedhaber, Z., "Religious-Ceremony Dances, Their History, Forms, and Dancers," *Dukhan: Journal for Jewish Music and Liturgy* 15 (eds. I.S. and A. Recanati) (2000) (Hebrew).

Friedman, M., "Chagall's Weddings," *Rimonim* 6–7 (1999) (Hebrew).

Friedman, M., "Transplanted Illustrations in Jewish Printed Books," *Jewish Art* 14 (1988).

Friedman, M.A., *Jewish Marriage in Palestine: A Cairo Geniza Study* (Tel Aviv and New York, 1980).

Friedman, M.A., "Matchmaking and Betrothal Agreements in the Cairo Geniza," *Proceedings of the Seventh World Congress of Jewish Studies: Studies in the Talmud, Halacha and Midrash* (Jerusalem, 1981) (Hebrew).

Friedmann, D., *Piskei Halakhot* (Warsaw, 1898).

Friedmann, M., *Beit ha-Talmud* (Vienna, 1881).

Friedmann, Y., "*Huppah* and *Kiddushin* in the Betrothal Blessing, [in] the Printed Editions of *Sefer Abudarham*," *Sinai* 76 (1975) (Hebrew).

Fritz, J.M., *Goldschmiedekunst der Gotik im Mitteleuropa* (Munich, 1982).

Fuchs, E.M., *Uber der ersten Niederlassungen der Juden in Mittelfranken* (Berlin, 1909).

Gager, J.G., *Moses in Greco-Roman Paganism* (Nashville and New York, 1972).

Gaguine, S., *The Jews of Cochin* (Brighton, England, 1953).

Gaimani, A., "The Penetration of Rabbi Yosef Karo's Literary-Halakhic Work to Yemen," *Pe'amim* 49 (1991) (Hebrew).

Gallus: or Roman Scenes of the Time of Augustus, new edition (London, 1907).

Gamlieli, N.B., *Ahavat Teman: Arabic Poetry and Songs of the Yemenite Jewish Women*[2] (Tel Aviv, 1979).

Garland, R., *The Greek Way of Death*[2] (Ithaca, NY, 2001).

Gartner, Y., "Fasting on Rosh Hashanah," *Hadorom* 36 (1973) (Hebrew).

Gartner, Y., *The Evolution of Customs in the World of Halacha* (Jerusalem, 1995).

Gartner, Y., "The Jewish Precedent for the Islamic Fast of Ramadan," *Sinai* 103 (1989) (Hebrew).

Gartner, Y., "Why Did the *Geonim* Institute the Custom of Saying 'Avoth' on the Sabbath?," *Sidra* 4 (1988) (Hebrew).

Gaster, M.H., *Harba de-Moshe, The Sword of Moses: An Ancient Book of Magic* (London, 1896).

Gaster, M., "Two Thousand Years of a Charm against the Child-Stealing Witch," *Studies and Texts in Folklore, Magic, Mediaeval Romance, Hebrew Apocrypha, and Samaritan Archaeology* (London, 1925–28 [photocopy edn.: New York, 1971]).

Gaster, T.H., *The Holy and the Profane* (New York, 1955).

Gaster, T.H., *Myth, Legend, and Custom in the Old Testament* (Gloucester, MA, 1981).

Gavra, M., "18th Century Yemenite Halachic Sages," Ph.D. diss., Bar-Ilan University, 1992 (Hebrew).

Geiger, A., *Kevutzat Ma'amarim* (*Collected Articles*), ed. A.A. Poznanski (Warsaw, 1910).

Gelbard, S.P., *Otzar Ta'amei ha-Minhagim* (*Compendium of the Reasons behind Customs*) (Petah Tikvah, 1998).

Gelman, A.L., *The Noda bi-Yehudah and His Teachings*[2] (Jerusalem, 1972) (Hebrew).

Gerondi, M.S. and Nippi, H., *Toledot Gedolei Yisrael be-Italiah* (*Annals of Jewish Sages in Italy*), (Trieste, 1853 [photocopy edn.: Brooklyn, 1993]).

Gerondi, Nissim ben Reuben, *Hiddushei ha-Ran*, ed. Y. Zaks (Jerusalem, 2001).

Geschichte der Juden in Speyer, Beitrage der Speyer Stadgeschichte 6 (Speyer, 1981).

Gies, F. and Gies, J., *Life in a Medieval Village* (New York, 1991).

Gilat, Y.D., Levine, C. and Rabinowitz, Z.M. (eds.), *Studies in Rabbinic Literature Bible and Jewish History* (Ramat Gan, 1982), (Hebrew).

Gillingham, J., *Richard the Lionheart* (London, 1978).

Gilnodes, P. Ch., "Marriage et Condition de la Femme chez les Katchins (Birmanie)," *Anthropos* 7 (Vienna, 1913).

Ginsburg, E.K., *The Sabbath in the Classical Kabbalah* (Albany, 1989).

Gladstein-Kestenberg, R., "The Breaking of a Glass at a Wedding," in *Studies in the History of the Jewish People and the Land of Israel In Honour of Azriel Schochat on the Occasion of His Seventieth Birthday*, ed. U. Rappaport (Haifa, 1978).

Glueck, A.I., *Yad Yitzhak* (Satmar, 1909).

Goitein, S.D., *A Mediterranean Society*, Vol. 3: *The Family* (Berkeley, 1978).

Goldberg, B., *Penei Barukh* (Jerusalem, 1986).

Goldberg, H.E., "The Zohar in Southern Morocco: A Study in the Ethnography of Texts," *History of Religions* 29, 3 (1989–90).

Goldberg, H.E., "Torah and Children: Symbolic Aspects of the Reproduction of Jews and Judaism," in *Judaism Viewed from Within and Without: Anthropological Studies*, ed. H.E. Goldberg (Albany, 1987).

Goldmann, F., "La Figue en Palestine à l'époque de la Mischna," *REJ* 62 (1911).

Goldshmidt, D., *On Jewish Liturgy: Essays on Prayer and Religious Poetry* (Jerusalem, 1978) (Hebrew).

Goldziher, I., *Mythology among the Hebrews and Its Historical Development*, trans. R. Martineau (London, 1877 [photocopy edn.: New York, 1967]).

Goodenough, E.R., *Jewish Symbols in the Greco-Roman Period* (New York, 1953).

Goodspeed, E.J., *The Apocrypha: An American Translation* (New York, 1959).

Gottlieb, M., *Darkei Noam* (Hanover, 1896–98).

Grandgent, G.H., *An Introduction to Vulgar Latin* (New York, 1962).

Greenwald, L. (Y.Y.), *Mahril and His Time* (New York, 1944).

Greenwald, Y.Y., *Kol Bo al Avelut* (*Compendium on Mourning*) (Jerusalem and New York, n. d.).

Gregor, W., "Some Marriage Customs in Cairaibuly in Inverallochy," *Folk-Lore Journal* 1 (London, 1883).

Gries, Z., *Conduct Literature* (*Regimen Vitae*) (Jerusalem, 1989).

Grimes, W.F., *The Excavations of Roman and Mediaeval London* (London, 1968).

Grimm, J., *Teutonic Mythology*[4], ed. J.S. Stallybrass (Berlin, 1875–78 [New York, 1966]).

Grohmann, J., *Auberglauben und Gebrauche aus Bohmen und Mahren*, Vol. 1 (Prague, 1864).

Groner, T., *The Legal Methodology of Hai Gaon* (Chico, California, 1985).

Grossman, A., *Pious and Rebellious: Jewish Women in Europe in the Middle Ages* (Jerusalem, 2001) (Hebrew).

Grossman, C., "The Real Meaning of Eugene Delacroix's 'Noce Juive au Maroc,'" *Jewish Art* 14 (1988).

Grunberg-Guggenheim, F., "A Lock in Grave as Means to Stop a Pestilence," *Yeda-'Am* 5, 1–2 (1959).

Grunwald, M., "Aus Hausapotheke und Hexenkuche," in *Jahrbuch fur judische Volkskunde*, ed. M. Grunwald (Berlin and Vienna, 1923).

Grunwald, M., "La Cimetière de Worms," *REJ*, New Series 4 (1938).

Guedemann, M., *Ha-Torah ve-ha-Hayyim be-Artzot ha-Maarav bi-Yemei ha-Beinayim* (= *Geschichte des Erziehungswesens un der Cultur der abendlandischen Juden wahrend des Mittelaters*) (Warsaw, 1897 [photocopy edn.: Jerusalem, 1972]).

Guggenheim, H., "Johann Kaspar Ulrich — Documente," *Israelitisches Wochenblatt fur die Schweiz*, no. 5 (29 January 1926).

Guggenheim, W., et al., *Juden in der Schweitz: Glaube-Geschichte-Gegenwart* (Zurich, 1982).

Guhl, E. and Koner, W., *Everyday Life in Greek and Roman Times* (New York, 1989).

Guil. Durandus. *Rationale Divinor. Officior* (Lugdun, 1605).

Gupta, M.P., *Dictionary of Indian Religions, Saints, Gods, Goddesses, Rituals, Festivals and Yoga Systems* (Agra, India, 2000).

Guraryeh, E.Y., *Chikrai Minhagim: Sources, Reasons, and Studies in Habad Practice* (Kfar Habad, 1999) (Hebrew).

Gutman, J. (ed.), *For Every Thing a Season: Proceedings of the Symposium on Jewish Ritual Art* (Cleveland, 2002).

Gutmann, J., "Christian Influences on Jewish Customs Klenicki, in *Spirituality and Prayer: Jewish and Christian Understandings*, ed. L. Klenici and G. Huck (New York, 1983).

Gutmann, J., "Die Mappe Schuletragen — An Unusual Judeo-German Custom," *Rimonim* 5 (1997) (Hebrew) (and in English translation: "Die Mappe Schuletragen — An Unusual Judeo-German Custom," *Visible Religion* 2 [Leiden, 1983]).

Gutmann, J., *Beauty in Holiness: Studies in Jewish Customs and Ceremonial Art* (New York, 1970).

Gutmann, J., "Jewish Medieval Marriage Customs in Art: Creativity and Adaptation," in *The Jewish Family: Metaphor and Memory*, ed. D. Kraemer (Oxford, 1989).

Gutmann, J., *Wimpel-Cloth for a Torah Scroll, A Memento from the Bar Mitzvah of Yair Agamnon* (Jerusalem, 19 *Tammuz* 5760 [July 2000]).

Gutmann, J., *The Jewish Life Cycle* (*Iconography of Religions* 23 [Leiden, 1987]).

Guttman, S., *Tiglahat Mitzvah ve-Inyanei Lag be-Omer* (*The Religiously-Mandated Cutting of the Hair and Matters Relating to* Lag be-Omer) (Bnei Brak, 2002).

Guttmann, J., "Wedding Customs and Ceremonies in Art," in *Beauty in Holiness* (first appearing in P. and H. Goodman [eds.], *The Jewish Marriage Anthology* [Philadelphia, 1965]).

ha-Levi Langbank, A., "Concerning the Practice of Betrothing with a Ring," *Bikkurim* 1 (1864 [photocopy edn.: Jerusalem, 1978]).

Hackenbroch, Y., *Renaissance Jewellery* (Munich, 1979).

Hadas-Lebel, M., "Le paganisme à travers les sources rabbiniques des II et IIIe siecles. Contribution à l'étude du syncretisme dans l'empire romain," in *Aufstieg und Niedergang der Romischen Welt: Geschichte und Kultur Roms im Spiegel der neuren Forschung*, ed. H. Temporini and W. Haase (Berlin, 1972–98).

Haeckel (Heikel), E.H.P.A., *Sandalion: Beitrage zur antiken Zauberriten bei Geburt* (Helsinki, 1915).

Hall, E., *The Arnolfini Betrothal: Medieval Marriage and the Enigma of Van Eyck's Double Portrait* (Berkeley-Los Angeles-London, 1994).

Halliwell(-Phillipps), J.O., *A Dictionary of Archaic and Provincial Words ... from the XIV Century* (London and New York, 1924 [photocopy edn.: London, 1989]).

Hamburger, B.S., *Shorshei Minhag Ashkenaz* (Bnei Brak, 2004) (Hebrew).

Hamburger, B.S., *Shorshei Minhag Ashkenaz* (*The Roots of Ashkenazic Custom*) (Bnei Brak, 2000) (Hebrew).

Har Barzel (Eisenberg), Y., *Yenahenu* on *Targum Jonathan* (Warsaw, 1902).

Harki, H.S.D., *Sefer Shiv'im Temarim* (Warsaw, 1900).

Harrison, J.E., *Prolegomena to the Study of Greek Religion* (New York, 1955 [first edn.: Cambridge, 1903]).

Harrison, J.E., *Themis: A Study of the Social Origins of Greek Legislation* (Cleveland, 1962).

Harrison, E.B., Farkas, A.E. and Harper, P.O. (eds.), *Monsters and Demons in the Ancient and Mediaeval Worlds: Papers Presented in Honour of Edith Porada* (Mainz o.R., 1987).

Hartland, E., *The Legend of Perseus* (London, 1894).

Hartland, E.S., *Primitive Paternity: The Myth of Supernatural Birth in Relation to the History of the Family* (London, 1909).

Hassel, W.O., *The Holkham Bible Picture Book* (London, 1954).

Hastings, J., *Encyclopaedia of Religion and Ethics* (New York, 1928).

Hausler, W., *Judaica: Die Sammlung Berger: Kult und Kultur des Europaischen Judenthums* (Vienna and Munich, 1979).

Hazlitt, W.C., *Dictionary of Faiths & Folklore: Beliefs, Superstitions and Popular Customs* (London, 1905).

Heilbronn, B., *Jacob's Ladder and the Anatomy of Meditation* (Birmingham, n.d.).

Heine, H., *Ludwig Borne: Recollections of a Revolutionist*, abridged and trans. T.S. Egan (London, 1881).

Heinemann, J., "Prayers of Beth Midrash Origin," *JSS* 5 (1960).

Helma, S., *Avel ha-Shittim*, ed. I. Koenig (Jerusalem, 1980).

Henkin, Y.H., "Ika d'Amrei/Others Say: The Significant Role of Habituation in Halakha," *Tradition* 34, 3 (2000).

Hennecke, E., *New Testament Apocrypha*, ed. W. Schneelmelcher, trans. R.M. Wilson et al., Vol. 1 (Philadelphia, 1963).

Henry, A., *Biblia Pauperum: A Facsimile and Edition* (Ithaca, NY, 1987).

Herlingen, A.W., *Berakhot le-Nashim* (Vienna, 1739).

Herschberg, A.S., "Betrothal and Marriage Customs in the Talmudic Period," *He-Atid* 5 (Berlin-Vienna, 1923) (Hebrew).

Heuberger, G. & Merk, A. (eds.), *Moritz Daniel Oppenheim: die Entdeckung der Judischen Selbstbewusstsein in der Kunst* (= *Jewish Identity in 19th Century Art*), catalogue of an exhibition held at the Judisches Museum, Frankfurt am Main, 16 December 1999–2 April 2000) (Cologne, 1999).

Heyman, E., *Alphonse Levy: Peintre de la Vie Juive* (Strassburg and Geneva, 1976).

Hillman, D.Z., "Separating Challa from One Kind on Another; Foreign Words in Maharil's Works," *Tzfunot* 3, 1 (1990) (Hebrew).

Hind, A.M., *An Introduction to a History of Woodcut* (New York, 1963).

Hirschberg, (J.W.) H.Z., *A History of the Jews in North Africa* (Jerusalem, 1965) (Hebrew).

Historia de'riti Ebraice (Paris, 1637; translation based on the Hebrew translation by S. Reuven [Vienna, 1827]).

Historisches Museum Frankfurt am Main, *Synagoga: Judische Altertumer, Handschriften und Kulturgerate*, exhibition catalogue (1961).

Holbein, H. the Younger, *Icones Historiarum Veteris Testamenti* (Lyons, 1538).

Horovitz, A. M., *The History of Prostration on Holy Places and the Graves of the Righteous* (Jerusalem, 1971) (Hebrew).

Horowitz, E., "On Kissing the Dead in the Mediterranean World," *Tarbiz* 67 (1997).

Horowitz, E., "Religious Practices among the Jews in the Late Fifteenth Century — according to Letters of R. Obadia of Bertinoro," *Pe'amim* 37 (1988) (Hebrew).

Hozeh, S., *Sefer Toledot ha-Rav Shalom Shabazi u-Minhagei Yahadut Sharab be-Teiman* (*The History of R. Shalom Sharabi and the Customs of Yemenite Jewry*) (Jerusalem, 1973).

Hughes, C. (ed.), *Shakespeare's Europe: Unpublished Chapters of Fynes Moryson's Itinerary: Being a Survey of the Conditions of Europe at the End of the Sixteenth Century* (London, 1903).

Hyatt, M.M., *Folk-Lore from Adams County, Illinois* (New York, 1935).

Ilan, Z., *Tombs of the Righteous in the Land of Israel* (Jerusalem, 1997) (Hebrew).

International Silver and Jewelry Fair & Jewish Marriage Rings Seminar, 22–25 April 1989.

Isaac Lampronti, *Pahad Yitzhak* (Lyck, 1864).

Ish Shalom, B. & Rosenberg, S. (eds.), *Yuval Orot* (*A Jubilee of* Orot) (Jerusalem, 1988) (Hebrew).

Israeli, Y. & Mevorah, D., *Eres ha-Natzrut* (*The Cradle of Christianity*) (Jerusalem, 2000), p. 116 (Hebrew).

Isser, S.J., *The Dositheans: A Samaritan Sect in Late Antiquity* (Leiden, 1976).

Jackson, A.M.T., *Folklore Notes*, ed. R.E. Enthoven (Bombay, 1915).

Jacoby, R., "The Relation between the Elijah's Chair and Sandak's (Godfather's) Chair," *Rimonim* 5 (1997) (Hebrew).

Jacoby, R., "The Small Elijah Chair," *Jewish Art* 18 (1992).

Jakobovits, I., *Jewish Medical Ethics* (New York, 1959).

James, M.R., *The Apocryphal New Testament* (Oxford, 1966).

Javalgekar, R.R., *The Yoga-Science [for Everyone]* (Varanasi, India, 1990).

Jellinek, A., *Bet ha-Midrasch*, Vol. 2 (Jerusalem, 1938) (Hebrew).

Jewish Encyclopedia (New York, 1904–05).

Judaica (Warsaw, 1993).

Judische Centralblatt 8 (1889).

Judische Gotheshauser und Friedhofe in Wurttenberg (Stuttgart, 1932).

Kafih, J., *Jewish Life in Sana* (Jerusalem, 1969³).

Kahle, P., "Die Tokenlage im heutigen Aegyptien," in *Festschrift fur Herman Gunkel* (Gottingen, 1923).

Kalir, J., "The Jewish Service in the Eyes of Christian and Baptized Jews in the 17th and 18th Centuries," *JQR* 56 (1965–66).

Kaniel, M., "The Wimpel: Binding the Family to the Torah," *Jewish Action* 53 (1993).

Kanof, A., *Jewish Ceremonial Art and Religious Observance* (New York, n. d.).

Karl, Z., "The 'Kaddish,'" *Ha-Shiloah* 35 (1915).

Kasher, M.M., *Divrei Menahem: Clarifications of Various Halakhot in Shulhan Arukh, Orah Hayyim, with Added Responsa* (Jerusalem, 1981).

Kasher, M.M., "Regarding the Incision Made in the *Tefilin* to Insert the '*Yod*,'" *Noam* 7 (1964) (Hebrew).

Kasher, M.M., *Torah Shelemah* (Jerusalem and New York, 1974–75).

Kats, S., *Kedoshim Tihiyu* (*Laws and Conduct in Society and the Youth Movement Concerning the Laws of Modesty*) (Jerusalem, 1979) (Hebrew).

Katz, J., "'Alterations in the Time of the Evening Service': An Example of the Interrelationship between Religious Costum [sic], Halacha and Their Social Background," *Zion* 35 (1970) (Hebrew).

Katz, M.Y., *Kunteres Va-Yaged Moshe*, in *Nahalei Binah* (Brooklyn, 1980).

Katz, Naphtali ben Isaac, *Semikhat Hakhamim: Kedushah u-Berakhah* (Frankfurt a.M, n.d.).

Kaufmann, D., "Der Grabstein des R. Jacob b. Mose ha-Levi in Worms," *MGWJ* 42 (1898).

Kayser, S.S. & Schoenberger, G. (eds.), *Jewish Ceremonial Art: A Guide to the*

Appreciation of the Art Objects ... Principally from the Collections of the Jewish Museum ... (Philadelphia, 1955).

Kehimkar, H.S., *The History of the Bene Israel of India* (Tel Aviv, 1937).

Kightly, C., *The Customs and Ceremonies of Britain* (London, 1986).

Kimelman, R., "Rabbi Yohanan and Origen on the Song of Songs: A Third-Century Jewish-Christian Disputation," *HTR* 73 (1980).

Kirschner, B., "Jewish Usages in Folk Art," *Yeda-'Am* 2,2–3 (1954) (Hebrew).

Kirshenblatt-Gimblett, B., *Fabric of Jewish Life: Textiles from the Jewish Museum Collection* (New York, 1977).

Kister, M., "Studies in 4QMiqsat Ma'ase Ha-Torah and Related Texts: Law, Theology, Language and Calendar," *Tarbiz* 68 (1999) (Hebrew).

Klagsbald, V., *Catalogue raisonne de la collection juive du Musée de Cluny* (Paris, 1981).

Klausner, I., *Korot Beit ha-Almin ha-Yashan be-Vilna* (*History of the Old Cemetery in Vilna*) (Vilna, 1935 [photocopy edn.: Jerusalem, 1972]).

Klein, M., *A Time to Be Born: Customs and Folklore of Jewish Birth* (Philadelphia, 1998).

Klein, M., *Wedding Traditions of the Various Jewish Communities* (Tel Aviv, 1994) (Hebrew).

Klein, M., *Zikhron Shai* (Simluel-Silvaniei, 1923).

Kleinschmidt, B., *Die heilige Anna: ihre Verherung in Geschichte, Kunst und Volkstum* (Dusseldorf, 1930).

Klibansky, R., Panofsky, E. & Saxl, F., *Saturn and Melancholy: Studies in the History of Natural Philosophy, Religion and Art* (Cambridge, 1964).

Kluger, S., *Moda'ah le-Beit Yisrael* (Breslau, 1859 [Jerusalem, 1993]).

Knoller, Ch., *Davar Yom be-Yomo* (Przemysl, 1933).

Knowlson, T.S., *The Origins of Popular Superstitions and Customs* (London, 1995).

Kohut, A., *Geschichte der deutschen Juden* (Berlin, 1898).

Kook, S.H., *Studies and Researches* (Jerusalem, 1967) (Hebrew).

Koppel Bible (Strassburg, 1530).

Koppelhausen, H., "Die Doppelkopf: sein Bedeutung fur das Deutsche Brauchtum des 13 bis 17 Jahrhunderts," *Zeitschrift fur Kuntswissenschaft* 14, 1–2 (1960).

Korman, G., "On the Practice of Enrapping a Torah Scroll in a 'Wimpel,'" in *Jubilee Volume of the Ahavat Torah Congregation in Haifa* (Haifa, 1990) (Hebrew).

Kosman, A., "Kissing the Dead — Transformation of a Custom," *Tarbiz* 65 (1995–96).

Kovetz Torani Zekhor le-Avraham (1994–95) (Hebrew).

Krasney, A., *Badhan* (Ramat Gan, 1999) (Hebrew).

Krauss, F.S., *Sitte und Brauch der Sudslaven: Nach heimischen gedruckten und ungedruckten Quellen* (Vienna, 1885).

Krauss, S., *Griechische und lateinische Lehnwoerter im Talmud, Midrasch und Targum*, Vol. 1, Vol. 2 (Berlin, 1898).

Krautheimer, R., *Mittelalterliche Synagogen* (Berlin, 1927).

Krinsky, C.H., *Synagogues of Europe: Architecture, History, Meaning* (Cambridge, MA and London, 1985).

Kumarappa, Bharatan, *The Hindu Conception of the Deity* (London, 1934).

Kundalini Yoga (at sivanandadlshq.org/download/kundalini.pdf).

Kuntres Tiglahat Mitzvah (*Booklet of the Obligatory Haircut*) (New York, 2003).

Kurt, Z., "Some Burial and Mourning Customs of Harat Jews (Afghanistan)," *Yeda-'Am* 18 (43–44, 1976).

Kurth, W. (ed.), *The Complete Woodcuts of Albrecht Durer* (New York, 1963).

Lachower, F. and Tishbi, I., *The Wisdom of the Zohar*, trans. D. Goldstein (Oxford, 1989).

Lamy, R.P., *Introduction à l'Ecriture sainte* (Leon, 1699; translation from the Latin).

Landau, "The Education of Children by Means of the '*Halakah*' Haircut," *Zekhor le-Avraham: Kovetz Torani* (1993) (Hebrew).

Landsberger, F., "Jewish Artists before the Emancipation," *HUCA* 16 (1941).

Lane, E.W., *An Account of the Manners and Customs of the Modern Egyptians* (first published in England in 1836; London 1966 edition, based on the 1860 edition).

Lane, E.W., *Arabian Society in the Middle Ages: Studies from The Thousand and One Nights* (London, 1883).

Lane, E.W., *An Arabic-English Lexicon* (1863–93).

Lange, I.S., "R. Meir of Padua ed. *Seder Gittin ve-Halitzah by Mahari Mintz*," in *Miscellanea di Studi in Memoria di Dario Disegni*, ed. E.M. Artom, L. Caro, and S.J. Sierra (Torina and Jerusalem, 1969) (Hebrew).

Langewiesche, K.R., *Deutsche Baukunst der Mittelalters und der Renaissance ...* (Taunis and Leipzig, n.d.).

Lask, J.H., "This is the Story of 'He-Goat of the Community,'" *Yeda-'Am* 2 (1954) (Hebrew).

Lask, M., *Ecstasy: A Study of Some Secular and Religious Experiences* (London, 1961).

Lauterbach, J.Z., "The Ceremony of Breaking a Glass at Weddings," *HUCA* 2 (1925).

Lauterbach, J.Z., "The Origin and Development of Two Sabbath Ceremonies," *HUCA* 15 (1940).

Lavan, Y., "The Embroidered *Talitot* from the City of Tunis," *Mahut* 12 (1994) (Hebrew).

Lawson, J.C., *Modern Greek Folklore and Ancient Greek Religion* (Cambridge, 1910), second edition (New York, 1965).

Leach, M. (ed.), *Funk and Wagnalls Standard Dictionary of Folklore, Mythology and Legend* (New York, 1949).

Leben, Y., "Customs Pertaining to the Elijah's Chair in the Jewish Communities of Southern Tunisia," *Rimonim* 5 (1997), pp. 54–55 (Hebrew).

Legey, F., *The Folklore of Morocco*, trans. L. Hotz (London, 1935).

Legrand, E., *Bibliothèque grecque vulgaire* (Paris, 1881).

Lehner, E. & Lehner, J., *Picture Book of Devils, Demons and Witchcraft* (New York, 1971).

Leiter, W., *She'eilot u-Teshuvot Beit David* (Jerusalem, 2000).

Leone Allaci, L., *Leo Allatius De Templis Graecorium* (Cologne, 1645).

Leonis Mutinensis Opusculum, *De Ceremoniis et Consuetudinibus Hodie Jedeos inter receptis ...* (Frankfurt A.M., 1693).

Lerner, M.B., "The Episode of the Tanna and the Dead Person — Its Literary and Halakhic Evolutions," *Asufot* 2 (1998) (Hebrew).

Lerner, Y.Y., *Shmiras Haguf Vihanefesh* (*Guarding the Body and the Soul*) (Jerusalem, 1988).

Leusden, J., *Philologus Hebraeo-Mixtus*[2] (Utrecht, 1682).

Levarie, N., *The Art and History of Books* (New York, 1968).

Levi, B., *Sefer Toledot Rav Yitzhak Lampronti* (Lyck, 1877).

Levi, D.A., *Succinct Account of the Rites and Ceremonies of the Jews: as Observed by Them, in Their Different Dispersions ... at This Present Time ...* (London, 1781).

Levi, I., "Le repos sabbatique des âmes damnées," *REJ* 25 (1892).

Levi, I., "Notes complémentaires sur le repos sabbatique des âmes damnées," *REJ* 26 (1893).

Levin, B.M., "Sefer Ma'asim le-Benei Yisrael," *Tarbiz* 1, 1 (1930) (Hebrew).

Lévy, A., *Scènes familiales juives* (Paris, 1903).

Lewinski, Y.T., "The Riddle of the Shoe and the Hebrew Inscription on a Flag from 1540," *Yeda-'Am* 4 (1957) (Hebrew).

Lewy, H., "Morgenlandischer Aberglaube in der romischen Kaiserzeit," *Zeitschrift des Vereins fur Volkskunde* 3 (1893).

Lewy, J., *Minhag Yisrael Torah*[2] (Israel, 1988–94).

Lewysohn, L., *Nefashot Tzadikkim* (= *Sechzig Epitaphien von Grabsteinen des israelitischen zu Worms ... Friedhofes* [Frankfurt a.M., 1855]).

Liberman, H., *Ohel Rahel* (New York, 1980).

Lichtman, G., "Why Is Matza Square?," *In Jerusalem* (pre-Passover edition, 1998).

Lieberman, S., *Greek in Jewish Palestine* (New York, 1965).

Lieberman, S., *Hellenism in Jewish Palestine* (New York, 1962).

Lieberman, S., "Roman Legal Institutions in Early Rabbinics and in the Acta Martyrum," *JQR* 35 (1944).

Lieberman, S., *Tosefta ki-Fshutah* (New York, 1955–88).

Lilley, J.M., et al., *The Jewish Burial Ground at Jewbury* (York, 1994).

Lindahl, C., McNamara, J. & Lindow, J. (eds.), *Medieval Folklore: A Dictionary of Myths, Legends, Tales, Beliefs, and Customs* (Santa Barbara, Denver, and Oxford, 2000).

Link, L., *The Devil: The Archfiend in Art from the Sixth to the Sixteenth Century* (London, 1995; New York, 1996).

Lipshitz, A., *Studies on R. Bahya ben Asher ibn Halawa's Commentary on the Torah* (Jerusalem, 2000) (Hebrew).

Lobacheva, N.P., "Wedding Rites in the Uzbek SSR," *Central Asian Review* 15, 4 (1967).

Lobel, D.T., *Hochzeitsbrauche in der Turkei: Nach eigenen Beobachtungen und Forschungen und nach den verlausslichsten Quellen ...* (Amsterdam, 1897).

Lubecker Bible (Lubeck, 1494).

Lukomskii, G.K., *Jewish Art in European Synagogues (from the Middle Ages to the Eighteenth Century)* (London and New York, 1947).

Luncz, A.M., *Jerusalem, Yearbook for the Diffusion of an Accurate Knowledge of Ancient and Modern Palestine* (Vienna, 1882, 1898; Jerusalem, 1906).

Maged, A., *Beth Aharon: Encyclopedia of Talmudic Principles and Personalities* (New York, 1964) (Hebrew).

Malul, M., "The *Sosbin* in the Wedding Ceremony in Morocco: A Study of the Sources of an Ancient Social Institution," in *The Jewish Traditional Marriage* (Hebrew), Jerusalem 1991.

Mann, V. (ed.), *Gardens and Ghettos: The Art of Jewish Life in Italy* (Berkeley, Los Angeles, and London, 1989).

Mann, V.B. (ed.), *I TAL YA': Isola della rugiada divina, Duemila anni di arte e vita ebraica in Italia* (Milan, 1990).

Mann, V., *Artibus et Historiae, an Art Anthology ... in Honour of Rachel Wischnitzer, IRSA* 17 IX (Vienna, 1988).

Manumenta Judaica Katalog (Cologne, 1964).

Marcus, I.G., *Piety and Society: The Jewish Pietists of Medieval Germany* (Leiden, 1981).

Marcus, I.G., "The Recensions and Structure of *Sefer Hasidim*," *PAAJR* 45 (1978).

Marcus, I.G., *Rituals of Childhood: Jewish Acculturation in Medieval Europe* (New Haven and London, 1996).

Marcus, I.G. (ed.), *Religion and Society in the Teachings of the Hasidim of Ashkenaz* (Jerusalem, 1987) (Hebrew).

Marcus, J.R., "The Triesch *Hebre Kaddisha*, 1687–1828," *HUCA* 19 (1945–46).

Margaliot, R., *Malakhei Elyon: That Are Mentioned in the Babylonian and*

Palestinian Talmuds, in All the Midrashim, Zohar and Tikkunim, Targumim, and Yalkutim ... of the Holy Books of the Kabbalah (Jerusalem, 1945).

Margaliot, R., *Sha'arei Zohar* (Jerusalem, 1978).

Marquardt, J., *Das Privatleben der Romer* (Leipzig, 1866 [photocopy edn.: Darmstadt, 1964]) (= *Handbuch der romischen Alterthumer*).

Masse, H., *Persian Beliefs and Customs* (New Haven, 1954).

Matras, H., "Amulets for Childbirth and the Child in Jerusalem Today," *Rimonim* 5 (1997) (Hebrew).

Matthew of Westminster (Flores ed. [1601]).

Mazor, J., "The *Badhan* in Hasidic Society: Historical, Social, and Musical Aspects," in *Dukhan* 15 (2000).

Mazor, J., "The Place of Music in the Hasidic Wedding," *Dukhan* 11 (Hebrew).

McLennan, J.F., *Studies in Ancient History: Comprising a Reprint of Primitive Marriage: an Inquiry into the Origin of the Form of Capture in Marriage Ceremonies* (London, 1886).

Ha-Me'assef (*Adar* [February–March] 1785), reprinted in *Bikkurei ha-Ittim*, 1823.

Melamed E.Z. (ed.), *Benjamin De Vries Memorial Volume* (Jerusalem, 1968) (Hebrew).

Melamed, O. (ed.), *Annals of Iraqi Jewry* (= *Kehilot Yisrael, Iraq*), trans. E. Levin (Jerusalem, 1995).

Mellinkoff, R., "Cain and the Jews," *Journal of Jewish Art* (1979).

Mellinkoff, R., *The Devil at Isenheim: Reflections of Popular Belief in Gruenewald's Altarpiece* (Berkeley-Los Angeles-London, 1988).

Memorboek: plateratlas van het leven der joden in Nederland van der middeleeuwen tot 1940 door Mozes Heiman Gans (Baarn, 1971).

Metzger, T. & Metzger, M., *Jewish Life in the Middle Ages: Illuminated Manuscripts of the Thirteenth to the Sixteenth Centuries* (New York, 1982).

Metzger, Z., *Ha-Refuah le-Or ha-Halakhah* (*Medicine in Light of the Halakhah*) (Jerusalem, 1984).

Meyer, E.H., *Deutsche Volkskunde* (Strassburg, 1898).

Mikdash-Shamailov, L. (ed.), *Mountain Jews: Customs and Daily Life in the Caucasus* (Jerusalem, 2002).

Mizrahi, H., *The Jews of Persia* (Tel Aviv, 1959) (Hebrew).

Molho, M., "Birth and Childhood among the Jews of Salonica," *Edoth* 2, 3–4 (1947).

Monumenta Judaica: 2000 Jahre Geschichte und Kultur der Juden am Rhein (catalogue of the exhibition in the Cologne Stadtmuseum, 15 October 1963–15 March 1964).

Morad, E., *Childhood Scenes from Father's House: Poems* (Tel Aviv, 1985) (Hebrew).

Moresinus, T., *Papatus: seu, depravatae religionis origo et incrementum* (Edinburgh, 1594).

Morgenstern, J., *Rites of Birth, Marriage, Death and Kindred Occasions among the Semites* (Cincinnati, 1966 [photocopy edn.: New York, 1973]).

Moshavi, B., "Customs and Folklore of the Nineteenth Century Bukharian Jews in Central Asia: Birth, Engagement, Marriage, Mourning and Others," Ph.D. diss., Yale University (1974), pp. 163–66 (Hebrew).

Mrejen-O'hana, S., "Pratiques et comportements religieux dans les 'quatre saintes communautés' d'Avignon et du Comtat Venaissin au XVIIIe siècle," *Archives Juives* 28, 2 (1995).

Muller-Lancet, A., (ed.), *La Vie Juive au Maroc* (Jerusalem, 1986).

Multanowski, A. (ed.), *Cmentarz Zydowski w Warszawie* (Warsaw, 1999).

Munitz-Hammer, S., "People's Names — Practice and Law," Master's thesis, Bar-Ilan University (Ramat Gan, 1989) (Hebrew).

Murray, G.A., *Ancient Rites and Ceremonies* (London, 1929 [photocopy edn.: London, 1966]).

Musée Conde, Chantilly MS. Fr. 139 (ca. 1600).

Nahum, Y.L., *Mi-Tzefunot Yehudei Teiman (From the Secrets of Yemenite Jewry)* (Tel Aviv, 1962).

Naor, B., "The Practice of Cutting the Son's Hair ('*Opsherenish*')," *Ohr Yisroel* 5, 4 (20) (2000) (Hebrew).

Nardi, E., *Procurato Aborto nel mondo greco romano* (Milan, 1971).

Nelken, H., *Images of a Lost World: Jewish Motifs in Polish Painting, 1770–1945* (New York, 1991).

The New Encyclopaedia Brittanica (1992).

Newall, V., *An Egg at Easter: A Folklore Study* (London, 1971).

Nissenbaum, S.B., *Le-Korot ha-Yehudim be-Lublin (On the History of the Jews in Lublin)* (Lublin, 1900).

Nock, A.D., *Early Gentile Christianity and Its Hellenistic Background* (New York, 1964).

Nork, F., *Die Sitten und Gebrauch der Deutschen und ihrer Nachbarvolker ... Mythen und Volkssagen* (Stuttgart, 1849).

Offenberg, A.K., Schrijver, E.G.L. and Hoggewoud, F.J. (eds.), *Bibliotheca Rosenthaliana: Treasures of Jewish Booklore, Marking the 200th Anniversary of the Birth of Leeser Rosenthal* (Amsterdam, 1994).

Ohana, Rephael, *Marehha-Yeladim, in Which Are Collected Several Remedies, Cures, Charms, and Spells from Several Manuscripts from East and West ... and Also from Printed Books* (Jerusalem, 1908).

Ona, A., "Ashkenazic Customs," in *Yalkut Minhagim*, ed. A. Wasserteil (Jerusalem, 1980) (Hebrew).

Opie, I.A. and Tatem, M., *A Dictionary of Superstitions* (Oxford and New York, 1992).

Oppenheim, M.D., *Pictures of Traditional Jewish Life*, ed. A. Werner (New York, 1976).

Otto, R., *Mysticism East and West: A Comparative Analysis of the Nature of Mysticism*, trans. B.L. Bracey and R.C. Payne (New York, 1932).

Ovadia, D., *The Community of Sefrou* (Jerusalem, 1985), "Popular Practices" (Hebrew).

Oxford English Dictionary, Compact Edition (Oxford, 1971).

Oxford Latin Dictionary, ed. P.G.W. Glare (Oxford, 1976).

Pahah, I., *Ulei Ayin* (Jerusalem, 1990).

Palmer, A.S., *Folk-Etymology: A Dictionary of Verbal Corruptions or Words Perverted in Form or Meaning by False Derivation or Mistaken Analogy* (London, 1882 [photocopy edn.: New York, 1969]).

Pappenheim, S., *The Jewish Wedding* (New York, 1977).

Parker, R., *Miasma: Pollution and Purification in Early Greek Religion*[2] (Oxford, 1996).

Patai, R., "Folk Customs and Charms Relating to Birth," *Talpioth* (1953–64) (Hebrew).

Patai, R., *Historical Traditions and Mortuary Customs of the Jews of Meshhed* (Jerusalem, 1945) (Hebrew).

Patai, R., *Man and Earth in Hebrew Custom, Belief and Legend: A Study in Comparative Religion* (Jerusalem, 1942) (Hebrew).

Patai, R., "Masekhet Segulot (The Tractate of Charms)," *Sefer ha-Shanah li-Yehudei Amerika* (*Yearbook of American Jews*), pp. 10–11 (1949).

Paulys Realenzyclopaedie der classischen Altertumswissenschaft (Stuttgart, 1941).

Pedayah, H., "Sabbath, Saturn, and the Deficiency of the Moon — The Holy Connection: Letter and Depiction," in *Eshel Beer-Sheva 4: Myth in Judaism*, ed. H. Padayah (Beersheva, 1996) (Hebrew).

Perelman, C., *Justice* (New York, 1967).

Pick, S., "Provencal Customs," Ph.D. diss., Bar-Ilan University (1975) (Hebrew).

Piprek, J., *Slawische Brautwerbungs- und Hochzeitsgebrauche* (Stuttgart, 1914).

Pitre, G., *Usi e costumi credenze e pregiudizi del populo siciliano* (Palermo, 1889).

Pollack, H., *Jewish Folkways in Germanic Lands (1648–1806): Studies in Aspects of Daily Life* (Cambridge, MA: M.I.T. Press, 1971).

Porter, R. and Harel-Hoshen, S. (eds.), *Odyssey of the Exiles: The Sephardi Jews 1492–1992* (Tel Aviv, 1992).

Preller, L. (= Vol. 1 of his *Griechische Mythologie*) (Berlin, 1894).

Preuss, J., *Biblisch-talmudische Medizin* ... (Basel, 1923).

Puckle, S., *Funeral Customs: Their Origin and Development* (London, 1926).

Qafih, Y., "An Ancient Wedding Custom," *Tema* 4 (1994) (Hebrew).

Questel, C., *De pulvinari morientibus non subtrahendo* (Jena, 1698).

Rabbinic Registry 1965 (*Reshimat Hevrei Histadrut ha-Rabbanim de-America, 5725*).

Rabin, M.M., *Masa Meron*[3] (*Meron Journey*) (Jerusalem, 1983).

Racolto deiriti ... di tutti populi del mondo ... (Venice, 1789).

Radford, E., & Radford, M.A., *Encyclopaedia of Superstitions* (New York, 1949).

Rajacic, K., *Das Leben, die Sitten und Gebrauche, der in Kaiserthume Oesterreich lebenden Sydslaven* (Vienna, 1873).

Rajewska, M., *Le Temps des Pierres* (Warsaw, 1983).

Rammurti S. Mishra, M.D. (Shri Brahmananda Sarasvati), *The Textbook of Yoga Psychology: The Definitive Translation and Interpretation of Patanjali's Yoga Sutras for Meaningful Application in All Modern Psychologic Disciplines*, ed. A. Adman (New York, 1987).

Raphael, Y. (ed.), *Rabbi Yosef Caro: Studies in the Teachings of the Author of the Shulhan Arukh* (Jerusalem, 1969) (Hebrew).

Rappaport, A., *Schlussel und Schloss* (Vienna, 1937).

Rappoport, A.S., *The Folklore of the Jews* (London, 1937).

Ratner, B., *Midrash Seder Olam* (Vilna, 1894–97 [New York, 1966]).

Ratzaby, Y., *Bem'agloth Teman (Yemen Paths): Selected Studies in Yemenite Culture* (Tel Aviv, 1988).

Ratzhabi, J., "The 'Dardaim,'" *Edoth* 1 (1946) (Hebrew).

Regardie, I., *Foundations of Practical Magic* (Wellingborough, 1979).

Reifmann, J., *Ma'amar Arba'ah ha-Rashim* (Prague, 1860).

Reik, T., *Pagan Rites in Judaism: From Sex Initiation, Magic, Moon-Cult, Tattooing, Mutilation, and Other Primitive Rituals to Family Loyalty and Solidarity* (New York, 1964).

Revel, B., *The Karaite Halakah and Its Relation to Sadducean, Samaritan, and Philonean Halakah* (Philadelphia, 1913).

Revel, D., "The Renewal of Ordination Four Hundred Years Ago," *Horeb* 6 (1942) (Hebrew).

Ricciardi, M.L., "Lorenzo Lotto Il *Gentiluomo* della Galleria Borghese," *Artibus et Historiae* 19 (1989), pp. 98–106.

Richental, U., *Chronik des Konstanzer Konzils, 1414–1418* (Bad Godesberg 1968).

Riefmann, J., *Moadei Arev 1* (Vilna, 1863).

Ritzer, K., *Formen, Riten und religioses Brauchtum der Eheschliessung in den christlichen Kirchen des ersten Jahrtausends* (Munster, 1962).

Rivkind, I., "A Responsum of Leo da Modena on Uncovering of the Head," *Louis Ginzberg Jubilee Volume* (New York, 1949).

Rivlin, J.J., *Shirat Yehudei ha-Targum* (*The Poetry of the Jews of the Targum: Narratives and Heroic Episodes by the Jews of Kurdistan*) (Jerusalem, 1959).

Rix, D., "Literal and Exegetical Interpretation in Chagall's 'Song of Songs,'" *Journal of Jewish Art* 6 (1979).

Rodocanachi, E., *Le Saint-Siege et les Juifes: le ghetto à Rome* (Paris, 1891 [Bologna, 1972]).

Rohde, E., *Psyche: The Cult of Souls and Belief in Immortality among the Greeks* (London, 1925).

Roheim, G., *Spiegelzauber* (Leipzig and Vienna, 1919).

Romanoff, H.C., *Sketches of the Rites and Customs of the Greco-Russian Church* (London, Oxford, and Cambridge, 1869).

Roscher, W.H., "Die Tesserakontaden und Tesserakontadenlehre der Griechen und anderer Volker," *Ber. Sachs. Ges. Wiss.* 61.2 (1909).

Rosen, H.O., *Om dodsrike och dodsbruk i fornnordisk religion* (Lund, 1918; Westminster, 1896).

Roth, A.N.Z., "Memento Moris in the Customs of the Khevra Kadisha," *Yeda-'Am* 3,1 (16) (1955).

Roth, A.N.Z., "Yahrzeit and Orphan's Kaddish," *Talpioth* 7,2–4 (1960) (Hebrew).

Roth, C., *Personalities and Events in Jewish History* (Philadelphia, 1953).

Rothschild, S., "Zum 500 Todstag ...," *Gemeindeblatt der Israelitischen Gemeinde Frankfurt/Main* 5, 11 (July 1927).

Rouse, W.H.D., *Greek Votive Offerings* (Cambridge, 1902).

Rubens, A., *A History of Jewish Costume* (London, 1967).

Rubens, A., *A Jewish Iconography*, revised edition (London, 1981).

Rubens, A., *Jewish Iconography: Supplementary Volume* (London, 1982).

Rubin, N., "Ma'amad ve-Moshav [Standing and Sitting] — For the Clarification of a Mourning Custom in the Talmudic Literature," *Avraham Spiegelman Memorial Volume* (Tel Aviv, 1979).

Rubinstein, J.J., *Zikhron Yaakov Yosef* (Jerusalem, 1930?) (Hebrew).

Rukmani, T.S., *Yogavartikka of Vijnanabhiksu*, Vol. 1: *Samadhipada* (New Delhi, 1981).

Sabar, S., "A Jewish Wedding in 18th Century San'a: The Story of the *Ketubbot* of the Al-Eraqi and Al-Sheikh Families — Between Tradition and Innovation," *Rimonim* 6–7 (1999) (Hebrew).

Sabar, S., "The Beginnings of *Ketubbah* Decoration in Italy: Venice in the Late Sixteenth to the Early Seventeenth Centuries," *Journal of Jewish Art* 12–13 (1986–87).

Sabar, S., "Childbirth and Magic: Jewish Folklore and Material Culture," in *Cultures of the Jews: A New History*, ed. D. Biale (New York, 2002).

Sacro Busto, J., *Sphaera Mundi* (Venice, 1488).

Safrai, S., *Pilgrimage at the Time of the Second Temple* (Jerusalem, 1985) (Hebrew).

Samter, E., "Hochzeitsbrauche," *Neue Jahrbuche fur die klassische Altertum Geschichte fur deutsche Literatur und fur Paedagogik* (Leipzig, 1907).

Samter, E., *Familienfeste der Griechen und Romer* (Berlin, 1901).

Samter, E., *Geburt, Hochzeit und Tod: Beitrage zur vergleichenden Volkskunde* (Leipzig and Berlin, 1911).

Saphir, J., *Even Sappir* (Mainz, 1874).

Saphir, J., *Masa Teman (Yemen Journey)*, ed. A. Ya'ari (Jerusalem, 1945).

Sarfati, S., *Tunis "El Khadra" la Verte: Traditions ancestrales Legendes et Coutumes juives en Tunisie 1881–1948* (Lod, 1993).

Sarfatti, G., "Latin in Hebrew Script in the Plastic Arts," *Leshonenu la-Am*, 47,1 (1996) (Hebrew).

Sartori, A., "Die Schuh im Volksglauben," *Zeitschrift des Vereins fur Volkskunde* 4 (Berlin, 1894).

Sartori, A., *Sitte und Brauch* (Leipzig, 1910), p. 194.

Sassoon, D.S., *Masa Bavel (Journey to Babylonia)*, ed. M. Benayahu (Jerusalem, 1955).

Satyendra Prasad Mishra, *Yoga and Ayurveda: (Their Alliedness and Scope as Positive Health Sciences)* (Varnasi, India, 1989).

Sauer, J., *Symbolik des Kirchengebaudes und seiner Ausstattung in der Auffassung des Mittelalters* (Freiburg, 1924).

Sauerlandt, M., "Ein Schmuckfund aus Weissenfels vom Anfang des 14. Jahrhunderts," *Cicerone* 9 (1919).

Schapira, H., "Those by Lyre and Those by Trumpet," in *Sefer Koznitz* (Tel Aviv, 1970) (Hebrew).

Schapiro, I., *Die haggadischen Elemente im erzahlenden Teil des Korans* (Leipzig, 1907).

Schapiro, M., *Late Antique, Early Christian and Mediaeval Art* (New York, 1979).

Schauss (Shoys), H., *The Lifetime of a Jew throughout the Ages of Jewish History* (Cincinnati, 1950).

Scheftelowitz, I., "Das Fisch-Symbolik im Judentum und Christentum," *Archiv fuer Religionswissenschaft* 14,1 (1911).

Scheftelowitz, I., "Das Stellvertretende Huhnopfer. Mit besonderer Beruecksichtigung des judischen Volksglaubens," *Religionsgeschichtliche Versuche und Vorarbeiten* 14,3 (1914).

Scheiber, A., *Essays on Jewish Folklore and Comparative Literature* (Budapest, 1985).

Schepansky, I., *The Takkanot of Israel* (Jerusalem and New York, 1993) (Hebrew).

Schmerler, B., *Ahavat Yonatan (Ahawas Jehonuson)* (Bilgoraj, 1932).

Scholem, G., *Origins of the Kabbalah*, ed. R.J.Z. Werblowsky, trans. A. Arkush (Philadelphia, 1987).

Schudt, J.J., *Juedische Merckwuerdigkeiten* (Frankfurt and Leipzig, 1714).

Schwab, C.A., *Diplomatische Geschichte der Juden Mainz und dessen Unsgehang ...* (Weisbaden, 1969).

Schwabe, M. & Gutmann, J. (eds.), *Commentationes Iudaico-Hellenisticae im Memoriam Iohannes Lewy (Jonathan Levy Memorial Volume)* (Jerusalem, 1949) (Hebrew).

Schwartz, F.L.W., *Der Ursprung der Mythologie, dargelegt an griechischer und deutscher Sage* (Berlin, 1860).

Schwartzman, A., *Graven Images: Graphic Motifs of the Jewish Gravestone* (New York, 1993).

Schwarzbaum, H., *Biblical and Extra-Biblical Legends in Islamic Folk-Literature* (Waldorf-Hessen, 1982).

Sebillot, P., *Croyances, mythes et legendes des pays de France* (Paris, 2002).

Seidmann, G., "Marriage Rings Jewish Style," *Connoisseur* 206 (1981).

Selden, J., *John Selden on Jewish Marriage Law: The Uxor Hebraica*, trans. and commentary by J.R. Ziskind (Leiden, 1991).

Seligmann, S., *Der Bose Blick und Verwandtes: ein Beitrag zur Geschichte des Aberglaubens aller Zeiten und Volker* (Berlin, 1910).

Sepp, J., *Volkerbrauch bei Hochzeit, Geburt und Tod* (Munich, 1891).

Serebryanski, Y.Y., *Yalkut ha-Tisporet: Likkut Nifla ba-Inyanei ha-Tisporet ha-Rishonah (The Haircut Collection: A Marvelous Collection on Aspects of the First Haircut)* (Beverly, NJ, 1990).

Settbon, D., *Kunteres Alei Hadas: Collection of Halakhic Practices of the Jewish Community of Tunis* (Jerusalem, 2003).

Shabbetai ben Abraham Ventura, "Nachtalmudische Fasttage," *Jewish Studies in Memory of G.A. Kohut* (New York, 1935).

Shachar, I., *Jewish Tradition in Art: the Feuchtwanger Collection of Judaica*, trans. and ed. R. Grafman (Jerusalem, 1981).

Shahar, Y., "'For Drinking and for Rejoicing, for Drinking One's Fill of Love' — Burial Society Cups and Jugs from Bohemia and Moravia," *Hadshot Muzeon Yisrael (Israel Museum Bulletin)* 9 (1972) (Hebrew).

Shapira, H.E., *Darkei Hayyim ve-Shalom*, ed. Y.M. Gold (Jerusalem, 1970).

Shemesh, A., "4Q271.3: A Key to Sectarian Matrimonial Law," *JJS* 49 (1998).

Shereshevsky, E., *Rashi, the Man and His World* (New York, 1982).

Shilo, M. (ed.), *To Be a Jewish Woman* (Jerusalem, 2001) (Hebrew).

Shmeruk, Ch., *The Illustrations in Yiddish Books of the Sixteenth and Seventeenth Centuries* (Jerusalem, 1986) (Hebrew).

Shtmer, M.M., "Why Is This Matzah Round?" *Zanz Journal* (*Nisan* 5703 [2003]).

Sigonu, Carol, *Historiar. de regno Italiae.* Book 15 (Basel, 1575).

Silvain, G., *Images et traditions Juives: un Millier de Cartes Postales (1897–1917)* ... (Paris, 1980).

Simrock, K., *Handbuch der deutschen Mythologie mit Einschluss der nordischen* (Bonn, 1887).

Slouschz, N., *The Marranos in Portugal* (Tel Aviv, 1932) (Hebrew).

Smith, W. (ed.), *Dictionary of Greek and Roman Biography and Mythology* (London, 1848).

Smith, W.R., *Lectures on the Religion of the Semites: First Series: The Fundamental Institutions*, second, expanded edition (London, 1894).

Smith, W., Wayte, W. and Marindin, G.E., *Dictionary of Greek and Roman Antiquities*[3] (London, 1890).

Sofer, J.H., *Kaf ha-Hayyim* (first edn.: Jerusalem, 1910–26).

Sofer, Y.H., *Biur Moshe* (Jerusalem, 1990).

Sofer, Y.H., *Or Moshe* (Jerusalem, 1990).

Sofer, Y.H., *Zekhut Yitzhak* (Jerusalem, 1992).

Sokolov, Y.M., *Russian Folklore*, trans. C.R. Smith (Detroit, 1971).

Soloveitchik, H., "Piety, Pietism and German Pietism: 'Sefer Hasidim 1' and the Influence of 'Hasidei Ashkenaz,'" *JQR* 92,3–4 (2002).

Soloveitchik, H., "Three Themes in the *Sefer Hasidim*," *AJS Review* 1 (1976).

Sommer, L., *Das Haar in Religion und Aberglauben der Griechen* (Muenster, 1912).

Speculum humanae salvationis, first Latin edition, ca. 1468.

Speiser, E.A., "Of Shoes and Shekels," *BASOR* 77 (1940).

Sperber, D. (ed.), *A Commentary on Derech Erez Zuta, Chapters Five to Eight, also called Derech Erez Ze'ira* (Ramat Gan, 1990).

Sperber, D., *A Dictionary of Greek and Latin Legal Terms in Rabbinic Literature* (Ramat Gan, 1984).

Sperber, D., *Magic, Folklore and History in Rabbinic Literature* (Ramat Gan, 1994).

Sperber, D., *Material Culture in Eretz-Israel during the Talmudic Period* (Jerusalem, 1993) (Hebrew).

Sperber, D., *Resh Kallah u-Mai Huppah* (Jerusalem, 2002) (Hebrew).

Sperber, D., *Why Jews Do What They Do: The History of Jewish Customs throughout the Cycle of the Jewish Year*, trans. Y. Elman (Hoboken, NJ, 1999).

Sperber, S., *Ma'amarot* (*Essays*), ed. D. Sperber (Jerusalem, 1978).

Sperling, A.I., *Sefer Ta'amei ha-Minhagim u-Mekorei ha-Dinim* (*The Book of the Reasons for Customs and the Sources of Laws*) (Jerusalem, 1982).

Spiegal, J.S., "R. Jacob Castro [Maharikas] and His Works," *Alei Sefer* (1990).

Spiegel, S., *The Last Trial* (New York, 1969).

Spiegel, Y.S., "Woman as Ritual Circumciser — the *Halakhah* and Its Development," *Sidra* 5 (1989) (Hebrew).

Spitzer, S., "The Practice of Austrian Jewry: Its Source and Development in the Medieval Period," *Sinai* 87 (1980) (Hebrew).

Spitzer, S.J. (ed.), *Hilkhot u-Minhagei Rabbeinu Shalom me-Neustadt* (*Decisions and Customs of R. Shalom of Neustadt*) (Jerusalem, 1977²).

Stauben, D. (1825–75), *Scènes de la vie juive en Alsace*, trans. R. Choron: *Scenes of Jewish Life in Alsace* (Malibu, 1994).

Steiman, S., *Custom and Survival: A Study of the Life and Work of Rabbi Jacob Molin (Moelln) Known as the Maharil ...* (New York, 1963).

Steinberg, A., "The Determination of the Time of Death " in *Sefer Assia*, ed. A. Steinberg (Jerusalem, 1982) (Hebrew).

Steinberg, A., *Encyclopedia of Jewish Medical Ethics* (Jerusalem, 1991) (Hebrew).

Stengel, P., *Opferbrauche der Griechen* (Teubner, 1910).

Stern, S.E., "The Order of the Redemption of the Firstborn Ceremony according to Our Masters the Geonim and the *Rishonim*," *Kovetz Torani Zekhor le-Avraham*, *Heshvan* 1992, pp. 13–20, 18 (Hebrew).

Stone, M.A., "Discoveries Relating to the Armenian Adam Books," *Journal for the Study of Pseudoepigrapha* 5 (1989).

Stow, K.R., "Marriages Are Made in Heaven: Marriage and the Individual in the Roman Jewish Ghetto," *Renaissance Quarterly* 48 (1955).

Strackerjan, L., *Aberglaube und Sagen aus dem Herzogthum Oldenburg* (Oldenburg, 1867).

Strauss, W.L., *The German Single-Leaf Woodcut, 1500–1550* (New York, 1975).

Sumner, W.G., *Folkways* (New Haven, 1906 [New York, 1959]) (reprint).

Synagoga (Cologne, 1961).

Ta-Shma, I.M., "The Attitude to *Aliya* to Eretz Israel (Palestine) in Medieval German Jewry," *Shalem* 6 (1992) (Hebrew).

Ta-Shma, I.M., "Law, Custom and Tradition in Early Jewish Germany — Tentative Reflections," *Sidra* 3 (1987) (Hebrew).

Ta-Shma, I.M., *Ritual, Custom and Reality in Franco-Germany, 1000–1350* (Jerusalem, 1996) (Hebrew).

Ta-Shema, I.M., "Some Notes on the Origins of the '*Kaddish Yathom*' [Orphan's Kaddish]," *Tarbiz* 53 (1984).

Tabak, I., *Judaic Lore in Heine: The Heritage of a Poet* (Baltimore, 1948).

Tamar, I., *Alei Tamar* (Tel Aviv, 1982), *Zeraim I* (Givatayim 1979), *Moed* (Alon Shevut, 1995), *Yerushalmi —Seder Nashim* (Jerusalem 1982).

Tambyah, T.I., *Psalms of a Saiva Saint ... from the Writings of Tayumanaswamy ...* (London, 1925).

Tausig, Y., *Beit Yisrael ha-Shalem* (Jerusalem, 1981).

Taylor, E.B., *Religion in Primitive Culture* (New York, 1959; first published as *Primitive Culture* in 1871).

The Grihya-sutras: Rules of Vedic Domestic Ceremonies, trans. H. Oldenberg (Oxford, 1886).

The Jewish Encyclopedia (New York, 1902).

The Jewish Lights Spirituality Handbook: A Guide to Understanding, Exploring Living a Spiritual Life, ed. S.M. Matlins (Woodstock, VT, 2001).

The Original Yoga: as Expounded in Siva-Samhita, Gheranda-Samhita and Patanjala Yoga-sutra, trans. and ed. Shyam Ghosh (New Delhi, 1980).

The Zohar, ed. M. Berg (New York, 2003).

Thesaurus Linguae Latinae (Leipzig, 1904–09).

Thompson, R.C., *The Devils and Evil Spirits of Babylonia ... being Babylonian and Assyrian incantations against the demons, ghouls, vampires, hobgoblins, ghosts, and kindred evil spirits, which attack mankind* (London, 1903–04).

Thompson, R.C., *Semitic Magic: Its Origins and Development* (London, 1908).

Thompson, S., *Motif-Index of Folk Literature* (Bloomington, Indiana, 1933).

Tigay, J.H., "Examination of the Accused Bride in 4Q159: Forensic Medicine at Qumran," *JANES* 22 (1994).

Tilly, R., *A History of Playing Cards* (New York, 1973).

Torczyner (Tur-Sinai), N.H., "*Regel Redufin* and From the Age of Twenty *Li-Rdof,*" in *The Language and the Book*[2] (Jerusalem, 1955) (Hebrew).

Trachtenberg, J., *Jewish Magic and Superstition: A Study in Folk Religion* (Philadelphia, 1961).

Trevelyan, M., *Folk-Lore and Folk-Stories of Wales* (London, 1909).

Twersky, I., *Introduction to the Code of Maimonides (Mishneh Torah)* (New Haven, 1980).

Tykocinski, J.M., *Gesher ha-Hayyim*[2] (Jerusalem, 1960).

Ulrich, J.K., *Sammlung judischer Geschichten, welche schmit diesem Volk in dem XII und fogenden Jahrhunderten bis auf MDCCLX in der Schweiz von Zeit zu Zeit zugetragen ...* (Basle, 1768 [Berlin, 1922]).

Ungerleider-Mayerson, J., *Jewish Folk Art: From Biblical Days to Modern Times* (New York, 1986).

Urbach, E.E., *The Tosafists* (Jerusalem, 1980[4]).

Urbini (Polydorus Vergilius Urbinatus) *De Rerum Inventoribus* (Amsterdam, 1671).

van der Horst, P.W., *Ancient Jewish Epitaphs: An Introductory Survey of a Millennium of Jewish Funerary Epigraphy (300 BCE–700 CE)* (Kampen, The Netherlands, 1996²).

Van Marle, R., *Iconographie de l'Art profane au Moyen Age et à la Renaissance, et la Decoration des Demeures²* (New York, 1971).

Verman, M., *The History and Varieties of Jewish Meditation* (Northvale, NJ, 1996).

Vernaleken, Th., *Mythen und Brauche des Volkes in Osterreich* (Vienna, 1859).

Vivekananda, Swami, *Vedanta Philosophy: Raja Yoga* (New York, 1920).

von Boehn, M., *Modes and Manners (= Die Mode)*, trans. J. Joshua (1932 [photocopy edn.: New York, 1971]).

von Erffa, H.M. and Rittmeyer, D.F., "Doppelbecher," *Reallexicon zur Deutschen Kunstgeschichte* 4 (Stuttgart, 1958).

von Reinsberg-Duringsfeld, F., *Das festliche Jahr* (Leipzig, 1863).

von Schoenwerth, F.X., *Aus der Oberpfalz, Sitten und Sagen*, Vol. 1 (Augsburg, 1957).

von Wlislocki, H., *Vom wandernden Zigeunervolke: Bilder aus den Leben der Siebenburger Zigeuner; geschichtliches, ethnologisches, Sprache und Poesie* (Hamburg, 1890).

Wahrig, G., *Deutches Worterbuch* (Munchen: Mosaik, 1982).

Waley, J.W. (ed.), *Mirrors of Mortality: Studies in the Social History of Death* (New York, 1981).

Wallich, H., *Die Mayerische Synagoga in Greiffswalde* (Greiffswalde, 1690).

Warringer, W., *Die altdeutsche Buchillustration* (Munich, 1921).

Wassan, *Secrets of the Himalaya Mountain Masters and Ladder to Cosmic Consciousness* (Punjab, 1927).

Wayman, A., *Yoga of the Guhyasamajatantra: The Arcane Lore of Forty Verses, A Buddhist Tantra Commentary* (Delhi, 1980).

Weich-Shahak, S., "Wedding Songs of the Sephardic Jews from Bulgaria," *Dukhan* 12 (1989) (Hebrew).

Weinberg, M., *Geschichte der Juden in der Oberplatz*, Vol. 3: *Der Bezirk Rothenberg* (Salzburg, 1909).

Weinstein, J., *A Collector's Guide to Judaica* (London, 1985).

Weinstock, I., "Gazing upon Shadows on Hoshana Rabbah Night," in his book, *Studies in Jewish Philosophy and Mysticism* (Jerusalem, 1969) (Hebrew).

Weinstock, I., "The Neglect of the Study Hall at the Time of *Minhah* on the Sabbath," *Torah she-be-al Peh* 9 (1967).

Weisberg, Y.D., *Otzar Habrith: Encyclopedia of Brith Milah* (Jerusalem, 1986) (Hebrew).

Weldler-Steinberg, A., *Geschichte der Juden in der Schweiz vom 16 Jahrhundert bis nach der Emanzipation*, ed. F. Guggenheim-Grunberg (Zurich, 1982).

Werdiger, J., *Avodat Yisrael* (Bnei Brak, 1965).

Werdiger, J., *Edut le-Yisrael*[2] (Bnei Brak, 1965).

Westermarck, E., *Marriage Ceremonies in Morocco* (London, 1914 [photocopy edn.: London and Dublin, 1972]).

Westermarck, E., *Ritual and Belief in Morocco* (London, 1926).

Westermarck, E., *The History of Human Marriage*[5] (New York, 1922).

Weston, J.L., *From Ritual to Romance* (New York, 1957).

Wieder, N., *Islamic Influences on the Jewish Worship* (Oxford, 1947).

Wieder, N., *The Formation of Jewish Liturgy in the East and the West* (Jerusalem, 1994).

Wilhelm, K., "The Orders of Tikkunim," in *Alei Ayin: The Salman Schocken Jubilee Volume* (Jerusalem, 1948–52).

Wilson, A. and Wilson, J.L., *A Medieval Mirror: Speculum humanae salvationis, 1324–1500* (Berkeley-Los Angeles-London, 1984).

Wilson, W.R., *Travels in the Holy Land, Egypt, etc.* (first edition: London, 1823; fourth edition: [in two volumes]: London, 1847).

Winsted, E.O., "Forms and Ceremonies," *Journal of the Gypsy Lore Society* 2 (Edinburgh, July 1908–April 1909).

Wischnitzer, R., *The Architecture of the European Synagogue* (Philadelphia, 1964).

Wischnitzer-Bernstein, R., *Symbole und Gestalten der Juedischen Kunst* (Berlin, 1935).

Wolff, L., *Universal-Agende fur judische Kultursbeamts: Handbuch fur den Gebrauch in Synagoge, Schule und Haus* (Berlin, 1891[2]).

Wood, E., *Yoga* (Harmondsworth, Middlesex, 1962).

Wordsworth, C., *Ceremonies and Processions of the Cathedral Church of Salisbury, ...* (Cambridge, 1901).

Worringer, W., *Die altdeutsche Buchillustration* (Munich, 1921).

Wuttke, A., *Der deutsche Volksaberglaube der Gegenwart* (Hamburg, 1860; third edition: Berlin, 1969), ed. E.H. Meyer (Berlin, 1900).

www.berotbatayin.org/yoga.htm.

www.shalach.org/Torah Yoga/Yoga Warning.htm.

Yaari, A., "History of the Pilgrimage to Meron," *Tarbiz* 31 (1962).

Yaron, Z., *The Philosophy of Rabbi Kook* (Jerusalem, 1974).

Yavetz, Z., *Augustus* (Tel Aviv, 1994).

Yehoshua, B.Z., *From the Lost Tribes in Afghanistan to the Mashhad Jewish Converts of Iran* (Jerusalem, 1992).

Yerushalmi, Y.H., *Haggadah and History* (Philadelphia, 1975).

Yesudian, S. and Haich, E., *Yoga and Health*, trans. J.P. Robertson (New York, 1953).

Yona, M., *Kurdish Jewish Encyclopaedia* (Jerusalem, 2003) (Hebrew).

Yosefov, M., *Ha-Yehudim ha-Harariyim ba-Kavkaz uve-Yisrael* (*The Mountain Jews in the Caucasus and in Israel*) (Jerusalem, 1991).

Yuval, I.J., *Scholars in Their Time* (Jerusalem, 1989) (Hebrew).

Zachariae, T., "Zum altindischen Hochzeitsritual," *Vienna Oriental Journal* 17 (1903).

Zell, M., *Reframing Rembrandt: Jews and the Christian Image in Seventeenth-Century Amsterdam* (Berkeley, Los Angeles, and London, 2002).

Ziegler, I., *Die Konigsgleichnisse der Midrasch, beleuchtet durch die romische Kaiserzeit* (Breslau, 1903).

Zimmels, H.J., *Ashkenazim and Sephardim: Their Relations, Differences, and Problems as Reflected in Rabbinical Responsa* (London, 1958).

Zimmer, E., "The Covering of the Head during Mourning," *Sinai* 96, 3–4 (1984) (Hebrew).

Zimmer, E., "The Kehillah: The Communal Life and Organization of Ashkenazi Jewry," in G. Hirschler, *Ashkenaz: The German Jewish Heritage* (New York, 1988).

Zimmer, E., "The Overturning of the Bed during Mourning and the Evolution of the Halakhah and Its Practice," *Sinai* 115 (1994/5) (Hebrew).

Zimmer, E., *Society and Its Customs: Studies in the History and Metamorphosis of Jewish Customs* (Jerusalem, 1996).

Zimmer, H., *The Art of Indian Asia: Its Mythology and Transformations*, completed and ed. J. Campbell (New York, 1955).

Zimmer, H., *Artistic Form and Yoga in the Sacred Images of India*, trans. and ed. G. Chapple and J.B. Lawson (Princeton, NJ, 1984).

Zimmer, H., *Philosophies of India*, ed. J. Campbell (New York, 1953).

Zinner, *Nitei Gavriel Marriage Law* (Jerusalem, 1998).

Zlotnik, Y.H., "Some Sabbath Aggadot and Customs," *Sinai* 25 (1949).

Zolar's Encyclopedia of Omens, Signs, and Supersititions (New York, 1995).

Zoldan, H.M., *Motza Tov: Marriage Laws and Customs* (Jerusalem, 1999).

Zunz, L., *Zur Geschichte und Literatur*[2] (Berlin, 1919).

GENERAL INDEX

A

Abudraham, David 52, 205, 277 n.24, 558, 599

Afghanistan. *See* Illness, Satan, arrow in the eye of, Mourning

A'fssai n'ihf [Jewish, Muslim]. *See* Wedding, preparations for

Alsace. *See* Wedding ceremony, chalk drawn circle

Amalek, blotting the name of 556, 558–560

Amorites, ways of 360–366, 387, 434 n.4, 472 n.22, 480, 543, 576–577, 582

Anatin. *See* Wedding ceremony, Coin in a cup of wine

Aravot, use of after Sukkot 143

Ashes 460

Ashkenaz. *See* Burial, Candles, Mourning, Pregnancy and childbirth, iron, *Tena'im*, Wedding day, fasting, Wedding days and dates, Wedding ceremony, Wimple

Ashkenaz Land of Israel customs, following of 178 n.18. *See also* Wedding days and dates, Wedding, preparations for, Wedding day fasting

Asia 384

Assuta 384, 389

Austria. *See* Wedding days and dates

Av HaRahamim 188. *See also* Fasting

Avodah Zarah 401 n.111

B

Babylonia. *See* Burial, Circumcision over earth, Wedding days and dates

Baal-beri. *See* Circumcision, drinking of the wine, *sandak*.

Baalat-berit 92. *See also* Circumcision, drinking of the wine, *sandak*

Badge, yellow 203 n.18

Bas [evil] 282, 317–318, 359, 503

Baldaquin 256–257 (Italy). *See also* Wedding ceremony

Beard, first shaving of 135 n.19. *See also* First haircut

Bekhor. *See* Firstborn

Betrothal. *See* Kiddushin

Binding of Isaac. *See* Akeda

Black cord around a condemned man's neck 99

Bohemia and Moravia. *See* Wedding days and dates

Board when taking an oath 334

Bread given to the bride 330

Breathing. *See also* Yoga
 Breath of life 395–397, 398
 Control of breath 399, 402 n.111

Inhaling and exhaling 399
Through one nostril 391 n.111,
393–394, 399 n.111
Bride's entry into the bridal suite
Breaking eggs 315–317
Breaking vessels 317–318
Egg enveloped in kerchief 315
Throwing eggs (Libya, Morocco,
Persia) 315–316
Painting with henna 316
Placing a mug upside-down with
an egg on top 316
Bride, kidnapping of 283
Bride's virginity 323
Making herself known 323
Proof of 324–325
Signing of the *ketubah* 324–325
Simlah (stained garment)
325–326
Bukhara. *See* Wedding ceremony
Bulgaria. *See* Wedding ceremony
Burial
Asking for forgiveness 471. *See
also* Death, moment of
Averting the face from the women
469 n.13
Behind the perimeter (Christian)
516 n.11
Beit Zur Tamim 465
Bier overturned (Kurdistan,
Morocco) 503
Black shroud (Ashkenaz, also
Christian) 476–477
Board for washing the deceased
333
Board not overturned 495 n.3
Board covered with earth 522
Bottle full of tears next to the grave
586 n.74–587

Breaking clay or pottery vessels
(Meshed, Iran) 581 n.55
Burial in loculi 473, 480 n.7
Burial in upright position 512
Burying the lock of the coffin 467
n.7
Burying the coffin unlocked
(England) 468 n.7
Burying without a coffin 476
n.25
By the side of the road 507, 521
n.8
Coffin covered with a board of a
table 498–499
Charity 535–536
Coin passed over the face of the
deceased (Portugal, Morocco)
533
Coins to ward off evil spirits
(Caucasus, Salonika, Greece,
Iran, Land of Israel) 531–532,
534–535, 585
Covered with his garment 521
Covered with silk sheet (Caucasus)
531
Deceased lies on the side 506
Deceased lies face up 506–507
Delaying the burial (Germany)
471–472, 478–480
Encircling the dead once 534
Encircling the dead seven times
531, 581
Eulogy 469
Examining the coffin on the
thirtieth day 477, 480
Fingers of the deceased not
clenched 508–509
Gold thrown in the grave
(Morocco) 533

Hashkavot [prayers for the dead] 531

In a niche with a board (Land of Israel) 521

In a coffin with earth over the face (Babylonia) 521–522

In a sheaf (Lithuania) 440 n.22

In sandals 506, 509

In shoes (also Morocco] 509–512

Jugs filled with water on the grave (Muslim) 582 n.55

Kaddish 532, 540, 555, 559–566. *See also* Prayer, May His

Kelipot 535

Key of the coffin 467–468 n.7

Kissing the deceased 472 n.22

Knife held by the blade 465 n.4–466

Men and women in separate rows 523 n.19

Met mitzvah [a corpse of unknown identity] (also Teutonic and Roman) 144 n.2, 474 n.22, 547, 607

Myrtle 504 n.8

Near sources of water 434 n.4

Ohel [purification chamber] 532

Opening the coffin before burial (also Russia) 465–466, 468–469, 472

Opening the grave on the third day 473 n.22

Overturning the coffin (also England) 502–503, 505

Overturning the coffin seven times (Iraq) 502

Overturning chairs 505

Overturning the hoes 503, 505

Padlocking the coffin 467 n.7

Placing earth from the Land of Israel 466–467 n.7

Placing earth on the eyes of the deceased 468 n.9, 469

Placing money on the body of the deceased 534 n.14, 536

Placing seven pieces of silver coins (Salonika, Greece, Land of Israel)

Placing the head on earth from the grave (Christian) 467 n.7, 473 n.22

Preparing graves ahead of time (Meknes, Morocco) 505

Preparing a grave next to relatives 469

Reciting "but to Abraham's sons" 533–535

Rending the clothes 465–467

Sack of earth placed under the head 473

Sitra Ahra [evil spirit] 401, 531, 579

Sprinking gold dust over the face (Morocco) 506

Staff in hand of the deceased 506

Swallowing the shroud (also Teutonic) 473 n.22, 509

Throat of the deceased covered with scarves 554 n.19

Throwing coins 531–532

Throwing handkerchief wet with tears into the grave 586 n.74

Throwing silver coins 533–534

Throwing earth on the grave 473–474 n.22

Throwing small stones at the grave and tomb 534 n.14, 538 n.2

Uncovering the face of the dead

471. *See also* Death, moment, covering the head of the deceased

Tzidduk ha-din 469

Upright position 512–513

White shroud 506

Burial of women who died during childbirth

Not purified 515

Special row of graves 514–516

Byelorussia. *See* Vessel, smashing of

C

Candles. *See also* Mourning

As an omen 359, 569–570 (also Teutonic)

As a symbol of life 568

At death 433, 436, 542, 577. *See also* Death, moment of, Funeral

Deceased derives pleasure from light 579–580

Extinguished during Yom Kippur 569–570

Extinguished after Yom Kippur 570

Five candles during the seven days (Habad) 579 n.43

For idolatry 577

Glass lamps in synagogue 581

In a dying man's hand (Romanian) 573 n.24

In excommunication ceremonies 571 n.13

In honor of the dead 569–570, 577–579, 585

In honor of deceased parents 579–580

In other life events 110 n.14

In the shape of the *menorah* 578

In the womb 568

Lighting after the wedding 319–322

Lighting by a non-Jew (Ashkenaz) 579–580

Lighting in cemeteries every Sabbath eve 572

Lighting next to a new mother 578 n.37

Lighting candles during a wedding 319

Making candles for Yom Kippur 569–570

Ner hayyim 569

Nner neshamah [memorial candle] 542, 567, 569, 571–572, 587

On the floor 576

One and Twelve candles at circumcision (Syrian Jews in Mexico) 108–109

Providing oil to the synagogue (Sephardic Jews) 579 n.46

Related to Circumcision (Eastern Jews, Germany, Sephardic Jews in the Land of Israel, Morocco) 107–109, 117, 569 n.9

Symbol of the soul 570, 575, 579, 586 n.72

Three days after circumcision 115

Wedding 198 n.14, 569 (Morocco). *See also* Wedding torches

Care cloth. *See* Wedding, *huppah*

Caucasus. *See* Burial, Candles related to Circumcision, *Regel Radufin*, Vessels smashing of, Wedding ring in a cup of wine

Cemetery, guarded by non-Jew 545 n.7

Chairs related to Circumcision 107
n.3, 108, 110 n.14, 114–116
Charm 19, 21, 25, 124, 452
Christian and local custom or belief,
similarity to or influence of 74
n.11, 128–129, 138, 145 n.5, 175,
200, 208, 210 n.32, 216 n.47,
251–252, 255–256, 281, 285, 300
n.31, 317, 323 n.2, 360, 380,
388–391, 405, 427, 435 n.4, 436
n.8, 440, 448, 467 n.7, 471–472,
477 n.26, 505, 512, 516 n.9, 527,
570 n.13, 583, 585–586
Circumcision and wimpel 144–147
Circumcision as a sacrifice
Akedah (Greece) 79–81
As a Paschal lamb 73–75, 78
Circumcision, drinking of the wine
Beadle 85, 93
Children 85, 93
Infant gets a taste of 84–90,
92–93
Infant's mother 85–90, 92–93.
See also Women, place in the
society
Niddah drinking at variance with
the Halakhah 90 n.30
One who recites the blessing
85–87 n.16, 92
Prayer for healing 87–90, 115 n.9
Sandak 59, 85, 90–93, 110 n.14,
144, 367–368
Circumcision on the seventh day (Beta
Israel) 97
Circumcision over earth or over water
Foreskin buried in sand 76–77
Karaite custom 74–75, 176 n.15,
272 n.24, 609 n.25
Over earth (Land of Israel) 71, 75

Over water (Babylon) 71, 77
Salt mixed with the earth 81
Circumcision, standing
Congregation required to stand
51–53, 55
Father of the baby 54–56
Mohel kneeling 58
Mohel required to stand 50–52,
54–59
Mohel sitting 57–58 (Yemen)
59, 81
While reciting the blessing of
circumcision 54–57, 59
Circumcision, third day after. *See also*
Chairs related to circumcision
Infant, washing of 116–118
Candle 107–109, 117. *See also*
Candles related to circumcision
Seuda shel mitzvah [meal related to
religious observance] 116
Cochin. *See* Wedding, Wedding ring
in the cup of wine
Coffin
Construction in the cemetery 494,
496
Made from table 497, 499
Coins 532 n.6. *See* Burial,
Kiddushin, Wedding ceremony
Custom and *Halakhah* 127, 369,
371–372. *See also* Omens
Cutting women's hair 135 n.19, n.20
(Greece), 137
Offering of 133–137

D
Dancing, Mixed (Italy) 294–297.
See also Wedding, dancing before
the bride
Darkei ha-Emori. See Amorite Ways

Death, Angel of
  At the head of the sick person
    423–428
  At the foot of the sick person
    423–426
Death, moment of
  Announcing death by placing straw
    in the street 440 n.22
  Bathing the body 441
  Binding of the chin 433
  Burning bed straw in the field 436
    n.10
  Candles. See Candles, at death
  Carrying the corpse feet first 437
    n.11
  Closing of the eyes 433
  Coating the head with eggs 441
    n.23, 442
  Covering the head of the deceased
    435 n.7, 436, 468 n.9
  Covering the corpse with his cloak
    437–438
  Covering mirrors 435 n.4, 575
    n.26
  Feet of the deceased facing the
    entrance 437, 447
  Hen's feather 495 n.3
  Imposing the four forms of capital
    punishment 438–439
  Kissing the deceased 449 n.17
  Kissing the feet of the deceased
    449 (Venice, Italy)
  Kissing the hand of the deceased
    449 n.17 (Salonika, Greece)
  Laying the corpse on straw [seven
    straws] (also Christian German)
    436–440
  Laying the corpse on the floor
    (Land of Israel) 439

  Mourners 434
  Opening the windows 437
  Pillow of feathers delaying death
    495 n.3
  Pouring water 435 n.4
  Salt 426 n.10
  Seizing the deceased's big toe to
    ask forgiveness 446–447, 449
  Straw placed opposite the entrance
    to the house 436
  Washing the head of the deceased
    with water 441 n.23
  Wine 441 n.23, 442
  Wrapping of the sheet 433, 440
Devil. See also Evil spirit
  At the sick bed 428–429
  Picks, money off the coffin 537
    n.27
  Encircling the bier 531
  Evil spirits, created by nocturnal
    emissions 532 n.6, 533, 535,
    537
  In the house of a woman giving
    birth 529
  Leaving the body through sneezing
    390–391
  Plucking grass at the cemetery
    539 n.7
  Reside in a house of mourning
    510 n.25
  Results from a divorce 356
  Seven evil spirits (Arabs of
    the Land of Israel, Egypt)
    526–528 n.13, 579
  Suffer from light on the ground
    577
  Wedding arousing their anger 192
    n.48 (Germany)
Divorce 353–355

Immersion in ritual bath after   355

Writ of divorce held in the husband's left hand   354

Dog as symbol of loyalty   202 n.18. *See also Ketubah*, dog

Didli. See Bride entering the bridal chamber

Doppelkopf. See Wedding, double cup

Dopplescheur. See Wedding, double cup

Drash fingerlein [groom's gift]   164 n.29

Drer (Morocco, Muslim)   169. *See also* Knots and binding

Drinking water at twilight   582

Drought   460

Cinders spread over the *Sefer Torah* 460

Kippat Sefer Torah   460 n.16

E

Eggs. *See* Bride's entry into the bridal chamber, Death, moment of, Mourning, Pregnancy and childbirth

Eggs, eating. *See* Fertility, Mourning, Pesah, Sabbath

Egypt. *See* Fertility, First haircut of, Evil spirits

England. *See* Burial, Graves, direction of, Pregnancy and childbirth, iron, Sneezing

Elijah, chair of   110 n.14. *See also* Chairs in circumcision

Engagement rings. *See* Rings

Erusin. See Kiddushin

Ethiopia. *See* Women *Mohalot* and Circumcision on the seventh day, Women, Circumcised

F

Fasting   186. *See also* Wedding day, fasting

Day of the Giving of the Torah 188

First Crusade massacres   187–188

Fertility

Barren women bathe under a hanged man   452

Barren women drinking water with which the corpse was washed (Tripoli)   452

Barren women passed under the stone where criminal's dead bodies were washed   452

Barren women wash their faces in bloody water (Egypt)   453

Barren women stand under a hanged man (Syria)   452

Cord wound around the stomach of a pregnant woman (Salonika) 529 n.13

Cord wound seven times around a tomb of a rabbi (Salonika, Greece)   529 n.13

Eating chicken   301

Eating eggs   300

Eating fish   303 n.33. *See also.* Wedding ceremony

Eating rooster   300

Entering under the stomach of a pregnant mare   452 n.9

Foreskin, swallowing of (North Africa)   14–17

Keys, use of   21–23

Moon, influence of (North Africa) 17–18

Rabbi holding an olive branch under the *huppah*   206 n.24

Shoes tied to the bridal carriage
282

Tossing wheat   584

Vessel, placing under the chair of
Elijah (Yemen, Land of Israel)
16

Roosters 299–300   *See also*
Wedding, roosters

First   haircut   130–140   (Egypt,
Germany, India)   146

Firstborn animal

Ass, redemption of   122

Care of   454 -455

Consecrated from the womb   120

In the cemetery   453–459, 461
(Germany)

Outside the Land of Israel   453

Firstborn

Consecration   120–121,   595
597–599

Dedication to Torah study   596,
598

Female firstborn   601–602 n.35

Forbidden   to   perform   labor
120–121

Humash   placed   next   to
after circumcision (Provence)
595–596. *See also* Protective
measures

Reciting a blessing   596

Mourning for a child over thirteen
593–594

Not   mourning   for   591–592,
601–602

Parents following to the grave
591

Firstborn, redemption of

Ceremony (Land of Israel)   121,
(Italy, Provence)   600

Belonging to the *kohen*   122–123,
599

Mitzvah of   119–121, 599

Mother begging the *kohen*   122

Mother   dressing   in   bridal
clothes   (Persia,   Sephardic
Communities, Syria)   122

Fish mahl. See Wedding, eating fish

Foreskin. *See also* Fertility

cast into earth   76–77, 102

Frazer, James G.   27 n.23, 99 n.26,
137, n.23, 180 n.33, 181, 285 n.20,
467 n.7, 534 n.14, 573 n.24, 575
n.26

Freya (Nordic goddess)   175

Funeral

Blessing over the candle or over
the   spices   of   the   deceased
542–543, 577

Carrying a dead baby in arms   504
n.8

Carrying the dead on the shoulders
474, 475 n.22–476

Carrying   the   dead   by   pallbearer
476 n.23

Carrying the dead on a board   476
n.25

Men   and   women   mixing   at   the
funeral   470 n.13

Men head the funeral procession
475 n.22

Playing the flute   544

Seven Sittings   524, 528. *See also*
Evil spirits

Sons following the bier   582 n.55

Tiara (Roman custom)   544

G

Gentile   custom,   similarity   of   and

influence on 128–129, 171, 173, 178

Germany. *See* Burial, delaying, Child, first haircut of, Death, Moment of, Evil Spirits, Firstborn animal in the cemetery, Omens, Pregnancy and childbirth, Newborn and child, Impurity, Protective measures, Wedding, Wedding ceremony, Wine drunk before the *Metztizah*. *See also* Ashkenaz

Goodenough, Erwin R. 27–28 n.26, 300 n.31, 303

Grave
    Digging on the day of the burial 495 n.3
    Open 192 n.48, 495 n.3

Graves, direction of
    Burial in rows 518
    Corpse head to the west 518–519 (Maghreb, North Africa)
    Corpse facing Mecca (Muslim custom) 503 n.8, 520 n.6
    Face to the east (England) 519 n.6
    Feet opposite the entrance 520
    Feet pointing toward Jerusalem 519 n.4
    North to south 518–519, 521

Greece. *See* Burial, Circumcision as a sacrifice, Cutting women's hair, Death, moment of, kissing the hand, Fertility

H

Halitzah. See also Wedding, shoe removing or throwing
    Back to the board 335
    Halitzh 126, 284 n.16, 332–33

Halutz (one who undergoes *halitzah*) 341
    Leaning against the board 334
    Need for a quorum 335–336, 342–343
    Shoe removed with left hand
    Shoe removed with right hand 337, 339–340
    Untying the straps 340–341
    Washing of the foot of the brother-in-law 337, 339
    Yabam 333
    Yevamah 333
    knots 139, 340–341, 345

Hametz 140 n.29, 143
    Laying ten morsels of 152 n.10
    Searching for [*bedikat hametz*] done with a broken plate 152 n.10

Hatan Bereshit 302

Hatan Torah 302

Husband, mastery over wife 128–129. *See also* Wedding ceremony

I

Illness
    Hesht (Afghanistan) 27–28 n.26

Impurity. *See also* New Mother,
    Impurity 38–40
    Bathing after seven days of menstruation (Germany, Austria) 37–38, 41
    Immersion after the 7 clean days 38–40, 42
    Karaite view 40–41
    Woman entering the synagogue 91
    White garments 38–40

India. *See* First haircut, *Kiddushin,*

Mourning, Sneezing, Wedding ceremony

Iran. *See* Burial, Mourning. *See also* Persia

Iraq. *See* Burial, overturning the coffin

Italy. *See* Baldaquin, Dancing, mixed (Padua), Death, moment of, Firstborn, redemption of, Newborn and child, Protective measures

J

Jacob ben Moses Moellin [Maharil] 43 n.11, 52, 88 n.24, 90–91, 102, 108 n.7, 109–110, 123 n.17, 129 n.7, 144–146, 160, 164 n.28, 175 n.15, 185 n.14, 186, 198–199 n.14, 211 n.32, 215, 217, 272, 288–289, 300 n.31, 322, 341, 360, 362, 367–368, 375, 468, 494, 510, 519–520, 553–554 n.18, 565, 602 n.35

Jadidim [Jews forced to convert to Islam] 532

Jnun [devil] 282, 577

Judische kerze. See Candles related to circumcision

Jus primae noctis [right of the first night] 198 n.14.

K

Kaparot 301 n.31, 571 n.13, 577 n.36

On *Hoshana Rabba* 377 n.62

Karaite customs. *See* Circumcision, standing, Circumcision over earth or over water, Impurity

Ketubah

[marriage contract] 196–197, 271–272, 323

Dog as a symbol of loyalty 202 n.18

Signed after cohabitation 324 n.8

Keys. *See* Burial, Fertility, Pregnancy and childbirth, Protective Measures

Kiddush Levana. See Moon

Kiddushin

and *nisu'in* 195

Blessing over a cup 278 n.28

Betrothal 195, 275

Betrothal money in a cup 278

Bride and groom enwrap themselves 206 n.24 (Izmir, Jerusalem, Sephardic)

Cup 213, 265, 270, 276–278. *See also* Wedding cup

Effected with groom's right hand 212

Effected with money (Cochin, India, Caucasus, Persia, Yemen) 274–275, 268–269, 275, 279

Huppah precedes *Kiddushin* 201

Kusan and Hutan. See Wedding, eating fish

Ring on the middle finger of the groom (Land of Israel) 211

Ring on the finger next to the thumb of the bride 212

Ten participants 199 n., 14, 330

Two cups 214 n.40, 265 n.3, 266

With a coin in a cup of wine 270–271, 272–274, 277

With golden belt 209 n.32

With a (gold) ring 275 279 n.30

With ring in a cup of wine 269, 272, 280. *See also* Wedding ring in a cup of wine

With a *shora* [embroidered belt] 209 n.32

Kittel 375 n.54. *See also* Wedding, groom attired in white

Kissing feet 448–449 (also Alsace). *See also* Death, moment of, Seizing the big toe of the deceased

Kissing hands 449

Knots and binding
Girdle tied to groom's stomach 168–169
Halitzah 284, 340–341
In bride's hair. *See* Wedding, preparations for
In shroud 168, 440 n.17
Magic 168

Knas mahl. See Tena'im

Kohanim
Walking on the graves of the righteous 546–549

Kos ha-tareilah. See Cup of Poison

Kurdistan. *See* Candles, Illness, Newborn and child, Pregnancy and childbirth, Tombstone, bier overturned, Wedding ring in a cup of Wine, Wedding, shoe removing or throwing

Kynoss. See Tena'im

L

Land of Israel. *See* Burial, Candles, related to Circumcision, Circumcision over earth, Death, moment of Fertility, *Kiddushin* Protective measures

Leaven. *See Hametz*

Leaving the Cemetery
Plucking grass 538–540
Washing the hands 538

Leilay Ukhta. See Wedding, preparations for

Lelat al-Qiddush [Wednesday night the evening of the betrothal] 167

Libya. *See* Candles, Firstborn, redemption of, New Mother, Impurity, Protective measures, Wedding *shushvinut*, Bride's entry into the bridal suite

Lilith (chief female devil) 26–27

Lithuania. *See* Burial, in a sheaf

M

Macedonia. *See* Omens

Maharil. *See* Jacob ben Moses Moellin

Mahzor Vitri 555–558, 560–561

Mapah shel betulim. See Bride, virginity of, *simlah*

Marriage contract. *See Ketubah*

Marriage of the youngest son [*mezhinik*] 282 n.2

Matron 434

Matzot
Baking of with *aravot* 143
Machine made 140–141
Power of *afikoman* 585 n.70
Round 140–142

Mazal Tov 155, 158, 163, 272 n.24

Mazikim [destructive agents] 467 n.7

Meir ben Baruch of Rothenburg (Maharam). *See* Wedding, days and dates, Women, place in society

Mezuzah 74 n.11

Mingling men and women 471 n.13. *See also* Burial

Mishnah, study of Shabbat afternoon 603–605

Mitron 305 n.37

Moon 180–181, 382–384. *See also* Wedding days and dates

Morocco. *See Assuta*, Bride's entry

into the bridal chamber, Burial, Candles, Newborn and child, Pregnancy and childbirth, iron Wedding, preparations for, Omens

Muslim custom similarity to and influence of 14–16, 166–167 169–170, 255 n.22, 315, 317, 433, 451–452, 503 n.8, 536, 551, 554 n.19, 582 n.55, 588–590

Mourning. *See also* Wedding Ceremony

Breaking eggs 317

Breaking vessels at the entrance to the house 582

Candle left burning (Yemen) 582 n.56

Covering the chin (Ashkenaz) 553 n.18

Covering the head (Herat, Afganistan, Ashkenaz, Calcutta, India, Meshed, Iran, also Muslim) 550–554

Cup of water next to the candle (Amadia, Kurdistan, Libya) 580, 582, 584 n.67, 586–587

Cup of poison 586–587

Drinking a vessel full of tears on *seudah mafseket* 587 n.74. *See also* Burial

Eating eggs and lentils 141, 305, 435, 441 n.23, 604 n.3. *See also Sabbath*

Eating chicken 305

Giving food to the poor 588

Kerchief (Meshed, Persia, Calcutta, India) 550, 552–553

Lighting oil lamp 581, 583

Most intense 574 n.26, 581 n.54

Onen 594 n.14

Overturning the bed 442

Placing burning lamp on a pottery vessel (Aden) 581, 583–584, 586

Placing a bowl of water with a piece of white tablecloth (also Christian) 434 n.4, 582–584, 586

Placing palm branch on the grave (Muslim) 588–589

Recess in the study hall on the death of a nasi 603–609

Reciting *Nishmat* 575 n.26

Seudat Mitzvah 588

Shai-(el). See Three weeks after death

Sheet or tablecloth on the bed turned to the wall 581–582

Sitting and keeping silent 604–606

Smashing the lamp and vessel on the grave (North Africa) 581

Soul mourns the body 574 n.26, 575, 577, 586

Three days 403 n.8, 581

Three weeks after death 588

Turning the bed of the deceased to the wall (Aden) 581

Widow not visiting 589–590

N

Names, identical 367, 371

Newborn and child. *See also* Protective measures

Brought to the synagogue for the first time. *See* Wimpel

Letter *heh* 124. *See also* Protective Measures

Lulav 27 n.26, 185, 373

Sword (Germany) 26, 30–31 (Afghanistan) 27; (Morocco) 30–31; (Kurdistan) 29, 282

Tefillin 29

New Mother, Impurity. *See also* Circumcision, drinking of the wine "Celebration of the forty days" (Bedouin, Libya, Greek, Non-Jewish) 43–46

Drinking wine at son's circumcision

Erroneous customs 37

Eighty days 42

Forty days 39–43

Greek custom 43

Maimonides opposition 40, 42, n.21

North Africa. *See* Fertility, Graves, direction of, Mourning, Pregnancy and childbirth

Numerology 76

O

Old shoes tied to the bridal carriage for luck (Great Britain, Transylvania) 282

Omens

Candles go out by themselves 359, 569 571. *See also* Candles

Fal [magic, influence, omen] 359

Groom having the same name as Father-in-law 371

Hen crowed like a rooster 138, 359, 363–364

Rooster crowed at midnight 360, 364

R. Judah he-Hasid's testament 361–366, 368–371

Shadow on the night of *Hoshana Rabba* 373–378, 379 n.68, 383

Shadow on Christmas eve or on St. Sylvester 380 n.72

Sneezing as a happy omen 405, 406

Sneezing from noon to night 403

Sneezing through left nostril 391 n.111

Sneezing twice a night for three nights 403

Tree bearing fruit twice a year 369–370

P

Pagan and Roman custom, similarity to or Influence of 27, 136–138, 199, 199 n.11, n.14, 203, 290 n.26, 329–331, 379–380, 387–388, 391–393, 395, 397, 402–405, 433, 473–474 n.22, 526 n.8, 544, 570 n.13, 573 n.20, 581 n.54

Pagei shevi't. See Unripe figs

Persia. *See* Bride's entry into the bridal chamber, Firstborn, redemption of, *Kiddushin*, Mourning Sneezing, Wedding, *shushvinut. See also* Iran

Pidyon ha-ben 80–81. *See also* Circumcision as a sacrifice

Pesah. *See also* Hametz, Matzot

Eating bitter herbs 141

Eating eggs 141

Poland. *See* Wedding days and dates, Wedding day, fasting, Wedding ceremony

Portugal. *See* Burial, coin

Prayer

May his great name be

blessed ["*Yehei shemei rabbah*"]
555–556, 560–563. *See also*
Burial, *Kaddish*
Our Father, Our King 375 n.54
Remember Your Mercies 375
n.54
Therefore I pray 565–566
Pregnant widow passing under the bier
(also Morocco) 451
Presence Divine 423–425
Pregnancy and childbirth
Amulets 28, 300 n.31
Breaking eggs 529 n.13
Giving birth on straw (Russia,
Bessarabia) 438
Iron (Ashkenaz, England, Morocco
Russia, Syria) 361
Kaparah 25 (Kurdistan)
Keys, use of (North Africa) 21–25;
(Serbia and Bosnia) 24 n.15
Metal object, use of (Germany and
Italy) 26 n.21
Opening of the Ark (North Africa)
19–20
Seven eggs 529 n.13
Seven spices 529 n.13
Smoking galbanum 529 n.13
Torah scroll, use of 20 n.3, 147
Tying a chicken 300 n.31
Protective measures. *See also* Burial,
Evil spirits, Fingers not clenched,
overturning the bier, overturning
the coffin, Funeral, Pregnancy and
childbirth
Amulets 74 n.11, 528 n.13. *See
also* Pregnancy and Childbirth
Blood, dashing to the doorpost
73, 75 (Land of Israel) 74
Breaking vessels at a wedding

(Muslim) 317
Candles 578 n.37
Drinking water between *Minhah*
and *Maariv* 604 n.3
Egypt (when Israel went forth from)
73–74
Even numbers 46 n.16, 474 n.22
Fish painted blue 302
Garlic 74 n.11
Hamsah painted blue 302
Letter *heh* 124. *See also* Newborn
and child
Making candles for a dying man
(Mantua, Italy) 578–579
Lighting in a place of mourning
577–578
Needle as protection against a *jnun*
282
Parting from the woman when she
returns from the dead 469 n.13
Placing religious artifacts next to
a child 595 n.17. *See also*
Firstborn
Preventing death at a wedding
192 n.48 (Germany)
Reading Psalms seven times 525
n.4
Resin placed on seven entrances
529 n.12
Rooster under the bed 578 n.37
Seven keys 23
Seven springs 23

R
Regel Redufin 327–328
ha-regel redufin 328
Relations, Sexual
Forbidden on the Sabbath 176
n.15. *See also* Karaite Customs

Romaniot Jewry. *See* Prayer, remember us for life

Rosh Hodesh. See Moon

Ring

betrothal 158, 163–165, 200, 211–212 n.35, 274

Embellished with Temple-synagogue 158, 161–164 n.29, 165

Wedding 159–163, 198, 211

For the groom. *See drash fingerlein*

Russia. *See* Burial, opening the coffin Pregnancy and Childbirth, giving birth on straw, iron

Ruth 205

S

Sabbath

Eating beets 303 n.33

Eating eggs 604 n.3

Eating fish 303 n.33

Eating garlic 303. n.33

Eating legumes 604 n.3

Moses, death of 603–605

Playing dirges on flutes 544

Reading tractate *Avot* 605

Sacrifice. *See* Circumcision as a Sacrifice, First haircut, Hair, offering of

Satan, arrow in the eye of Islamic legend 27 n.26

Lulav, to ward off the evil eye 27–28. *See also* Newborn and child

Schammes, Jousep (Juspa), *Wormser Minhagbuch* 72–73, 107, 110, 114, 152 n.9, 154 n.15, 174, 210 n.32, 215, 220, 222, 258 n.29, 288 n-290, 303 n.33, 305, 321, 322 n.11

436 n.9, 437, 459, 465, 473 n.22, 476, n24, 477, 494 n.3, 514 n.3, n.4, 539 n.6, 553 n.18

Serbia and Bosnia, *See* Pregnancy and childbirth

Seven 528 n.13. *See also* Burial, Encircling the dead seven times, Overturning the coffin seven times Circumcision on the seventh day, Death, moment of (seven straws) Fertility, Cord wound seven times around the tomb of a rabbi, Funeral, seven sittings, Impurity, bathing after seven days of menstruation, Pregnancy and childbirth, Seven eggs, Seven Spices, Protective measures, Reading psalms seven times, Seven keys, Seven Springs Seven blessings, Seven evil spirits, Wedding ceremony, Bride and groom sitting seven days

Segulah (charm) p.14

Shofar 28 n.26

Shalmonit 115 n.9

Shamash 470 n.13

Sheva Berakhot. See Seven blessings

Shelish ha-milah. See Circumcision, third day after

Shivah. See Mourning

Shoshvinim 324 n.3, 325 n.9

Sitting while visiting the sick 423–426

Sivlonot. See Wedding gifts

Slavs. *See* Omens, Wedding ceremony, breaking the glass, Wedding, roosters

Sleeping between east and west 522–523

Sleeping north to south 522–523

Sneezing 384–407
As an omen 389–390, 403. *See also* Omens
Praying (Persia) 391
Soul departing 390–391
Through one nostril 391 n.111. *See also* Breathing
Sotah 166–167
Spain. *See* Wedding, days and dates
Standing. *See also* Circumcision
Circumcision 50–59
Prayer 53 n.20
Targum reciting 54 20
Torah Reading 53 54 n.21
Sudar. See Wedding, cloth spread over poles
Syria. *See* Fertility, Firstborn, redemption of, Omens, Pregnancy and childbirth

T

Tahanun
On the day of Circumcision 112–113
Tefillin 29–30
Tena'im
Breaking of a plate or vessel (Ashkenaz) 151–155
Knas mahl [Kynoss=banquet] 155, 255
Signing 153
Tetragrammaton [God's name] 139, 399, 559, 563
Throwing wheat kernels. *See* Wedding, Confetti
Tombstone
Books on a table on tombstones 500

Branch engraved on tombstone 588 n.4
Erect (Ashkenaz, Kurdistan) 459 n.16, 460
Flat [Sephardic] 459 n.16
Tombstone as if growing from a tree trunk 588 n.4
Tree engraved on the tomb 588 n.4
Torah oath 273 n.24
Torah Scroll (Afghanistan) 147 n.11. *See also* Wimpel
In the cemetery 460
Torah ark curtain made from old clothes 145 n.9
Tunis. *See* Wedding ceremony
Tyrnau, Isaac *Sefer Haminhagim* 113 n.3
Tzintzenet. See Wedding, narrow-mouthed jar

U

Unripe figs around a condemned woman's neck 95, 98–100. *See also* Women *Mohalot*
Allusion to unripe fruit of the Sabbatical year 98, 100s
Uzbekistan. *See* Wedding

V

Vessel, breaking of. *See* Bride's entry into the bridal chamber, Burial, Mourning, Protective measures, *Tena'im*, Wedding ceremony

W

Water. *See* Burial, jugs filled with water, Near sources of water, Candles, cup of water next to a candle, Circumcision over earth and over water, Death, moment of, Pouring water, Washing the head of the deceased, Drinking water at twilight, Fertility, Barren woman drinking water, with which the corpse had been washed, Mourning, Placing a bowl of water, Sabbath, drinking water between *Minhah* and *Maariv*

Wearing the shoes of the deceased 509–510

Wedding canopy. *See Wedding, Huppah*

Wedding Ceremony
  Art 195–196
  Ashes on groom's head 159–160, 305 n.33. *See also* Mourning
  Badhan and violinist 210 n.32 (also a Roman custom), 298–299
  Breaking of a cup, glass or vessel (Bulgaria, Slavic countries, Worms) 127, n.6, 150 n.1, 160, 186, 216, 218, 266, 305 (Cochin, India) 584. *See also Tena'im*
  Bridal girdle 209 n.32
  Bridal procession 290 n.25
  Bride and Groom sitting for seven days 220 n.57
  Bride and groom sitting under the *huppah* 223–224, 257
  Bride brought to the ceremony under the *huppah* (Germany, Poland) 257
  Bride cast a coin to the earth (non-Jewish) 585
  Bride circling the groom 128–129 n.6, n.7
  Bride's coronet 193 n.2

Bride covering the face of 127, 166

Bride covered with a *Talit* [prayer shawl] 206 n.24

Bride extending her index finger to the groom 210

Bride's head covered with kerchief 201

Bride places her leg on the groom 128–129 n.7

Bride and Groom cutting fish 303

Buckets of water 299–300

Casting salt on the bride and groom 585

Children supporting the *huppah* 199 n.14

Chalk drawn circle 272 n.24 (Alsace)

Coin in a cup of wine or under 267, 270 n.21. *See also Kiddushin*

Coins next to the bride (Muslim Jewish) 170 n.12, 304

Coins thrown at the bride given to *Tzedakah* (Ashkenaz) 585

Cloth spread over poles 208, 250–252, 255 (also a Christian Custom)

Curtain before the bride (Baghdad, Iraq)

Conducted in the synagogue courtyard 210 n.32

Conducted in front of the Church 210 n.32

Confetti 287–291 (Worms) 299 n.31, 584

Couple led to the bridal suite accompanied by music 299 n.31

Cup of wine from *terumah* passed before a virgin bride   215

Cup dashed against a star   217

Cup thrown against a wall   217

Dancing before the bride   294–300

Dancing before the bride with myrtle twigs   206 n.24 (Central Europe)

Dancing with a broom   282 n.2

Deal del zevah [second day after the wedding]   301 n.33

Drinking wine   210 n.32, 213, 277

Double cup   215, 216 n.47

Eating Fish   301–303

Full cup smashed by the groom   218–219

Giving the groom a *revi'it*   210 32

Gold wedding belt   210 n.32

Groom attired in white   224 n.67

Groom bringing the bride home as *huppah*   202

Groom entering before the bride   129 n.7

Groom grabs the *tzitzit* (Cochin, India)   272 n.74

Groom places his leg on the bride   128 n.7 (Afghanistan, Germany, Tunis)

Groom raises the bride   267

Groom receives his bride on Friday (Egypt, Muslim)

Groom wears a kittel   224 n.67

Groom's mother sends the bride white hen   304

Hiaina (Morocco)   282, 389

Hallah dance (Koznitz, Neishtatel)   297–298

Handkerchief as a *huppah*   250

Huppah   194–195, 198, 201, 205–206, 219–220, 250–257

Huppah Clothes unfurled spread over a pole   206   n.24, 250–251, 256–257

Huppah under open sky   224

Huppah supported on two poles   205 n.25

Holding hands (Roman)   203, 331

Kabaluli dance   298. *See also Hallah* dance

Kippah as *huppah*   258 n.29

Kleizmerim   210 n.32, 298–299

Lad holding two small bottles or cups   213–215

Lighting candles   319, 331

Mitzvah tanz   305

Narrow-mouthed jar (virgin's wedding)   216

Nuts and grain scattered   331

One Cup   213–215, 276

Parting of mother and bride daughter   301–302, 304

Peru-u-revu [be fruitful and multiply]   288

Placing fowl before the new couple   304

Positioning of the bride and groom   212–213

Rabbi conducting the ceremony   321

Rabbi holding a branch   206 n.24

Rabbi reads the *ketubah*   210 n.32

Reciting: "If I forget you, O Jerusalem..."   160–161

Redemption of cooked hen (Rome, Italy)   301 n.31

Ring. *See* Ring

Roosters 299–300 (also a Slav custom)

Separation of the sexes 296–297

Sheet as a *huppah* 205

Sheet enwrapping the groom 204–205

Sheet enwrapping the bride and groom 208

Shoe, putting back (Kurdistan) 285

Shoe, removing or throwing 281–286. *See also Halitzah*

Spilling wine 219

Spinholz 255

Staff, breaking of (Germany)

Talit as *huppah* 205–206 n.24, 255, 257

Ten participants (also Roman pagan) 199 n.14

Throwing Seeds (non-Jewish) 290 n.26

Throwing a hen and a rooster 301

Torches candles 198–199 n.14 331 (Also Roman pagan). *See also* Candles

Two cups 214 n.40, 216 n.47

Veil [*hinumah*] 197–199, 201, 250, 252 (also Anglo-Saxon, Roman)

Veil as *huppah* 201 n.15, 209, 252

Warding off the threat of death 192 n.48

Without *Huppah* 197 (Venice, Tunisia) 201, 203

Wedding ring in a cup of wine (Cochin, India, Caucasus) 265–270, 280, 321

Wedding days and dates

Beginning of the month (Iberian Peninsula) 179

Everyday 171–172

Friday (Ashkenaz, Austria, Bohemia and Moravia, Germany, Christian, Poland, Spain) 174–176 n.15, 177, 321

Full Moon 179–180

Israel of Krems (Haggahot Asheri) view 178

Maharam's view 174, 178 n.18

Middle of the week (Ashkenaz, Poland) 177 n.16, 321

Sabbath eve. *See* Friday

Sefirat HaOmer 330

Three weeks 330

Thursday 171, 173, 178 (Babylonia, Teutonic)

Tuesday, 178 (Teutonic peoples)

Virgin 171–173, 177 n.16

Wednesday 171–172, 177 n.16, 178, 322

Widow 173

Wedding gifts

Ein worf [throwing of the presents] lists 221–223

Reciprocal gifts 223, 330

Shabash [gold coins gift] 222

Shushvinut [gift money for the wedding] (Libya, Persia) 221–223

Wedding gifts 164 n.27.

Wedding, preparations for

Bride's virginity 323–326

Bride's hair [*a'fssai n'ihf*] 167 [*leilay ukhta*] (Morocco, Yemen) 166–167, 282, 330

Wedding day, fasting

Bride and Groom 183–184, 187, 189–192 (Ashkenaz)

Groom 185 n.14, 188, 190

Eve of Sukkot 185 n.14

Relatives of the couple 187

Visiting the graves of relatives 192 n.48

Widower marrying a widow 187 n.20

Wedding, shoe removing or throwing 281–284

Westermarck E. 14, 15, 18, 21 n.1, 23 n.7, 127 n.3, n.6, 128–129 n.7, 133 n.18, 138 n.24, 169–170 n.12, 177–178 n.16 n.20, 191–192, 198 n.14, 208 n.28, 217 281–282, 290, 297 n.16, 303, n.33, 315–317 356 n.11, 359, 361, 389, 435 n.4, 451, 474 n.22, 503–504, 510 n.33, 536 n.23, 578 n.37, 582, 589–590

Wimpel [Torah binders] 143–146, 148–149, 196 n.10

And circumcision (Ashkenaz) 147

And Bar Mitzvah 147

Covering Torah Scrolls 147–148

Wedding canopy engraved on 217 n.51

Wine drunk before the *Metzitzah*

Poured out before the Torah Ark 102

Spitting into a cup (Germany) 102

Spitting on the earth 102

Women, circumcised 97

Women, place in society

Maharam's view 91–92

Mingling of boys and girls 92 n.39

Permission to kill unfaithful wives 93 n.39

Place in commercial life 93 n.39

Women *Mohalot* 94–96

Beta-Israel [Falasha] practice 96–97

Fit to circumcise in the absence of a male 97

Not fit to circumcise 94, 97–98

Punishment, unripe figs 95–96

Zipporah 95

Y

Yahr zeit likht [death day anniversary light, memorial candle] 580

Yahveh. See Tetragrammaton

Yihud 202, 250, 267 n.7

Yemen. *See* Circumcision, standing, Fertility, *Kiddushin*, Mourning, Wedding, Wedding, preparations for, Wedding ring in a cup of wine

Yoga 391–401

And idolatry 400

And Jewish mystical traditions 395–396

And The *Zohar* 396–397

And *Kabbalah* 397–401